MOON HANDBOOKS®

FLORIDA GULF COAST

FIRST EDITION

LAURA REILEY

AVALON TRAVEL

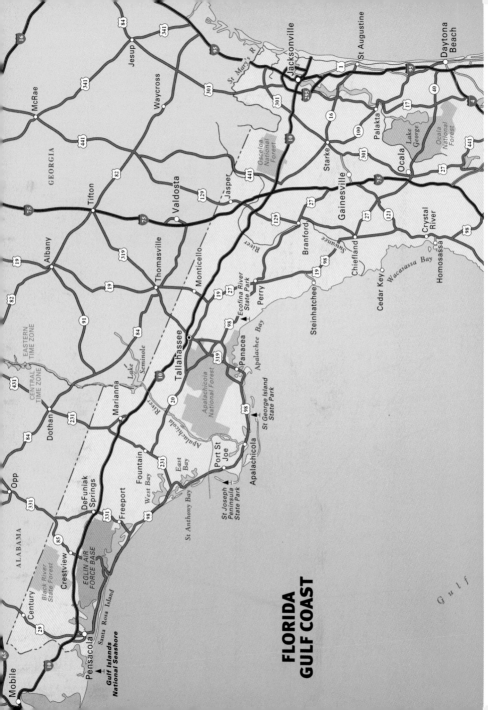

FLORIDA
GULF COAST

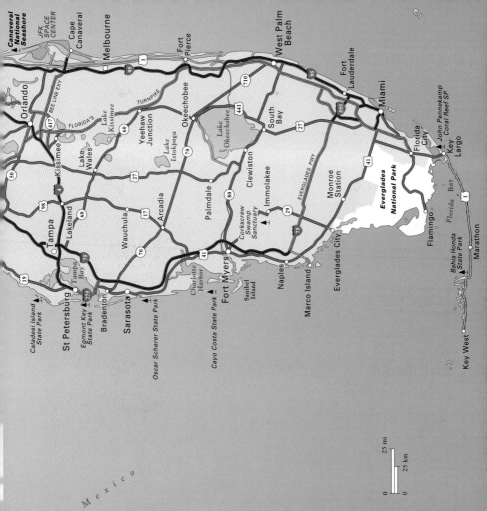

BAIT HOUS

FROZEN SHRIMP   BALLYHOO

CIGAR MINNOWS

LIVE SHRIMP

CONTENTS

Discover the Florida Gulf Coast

Explore the Florida Gulf Coast

The Paradise Coast 26

Know the Florida Gulf Coast

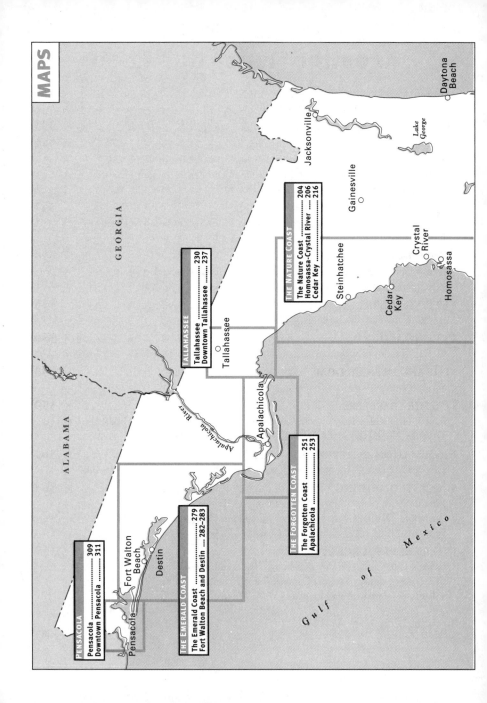

MAPS

GEORGIA

ALABAMA

Apalachicola River

Pensacola

Fort Walton
Beach

Destin

Apalachicola

Tallahassee

Steinhatchee

Cedar
Key

Homosassa

Crystal
River

Gainesville

Jacksonville

Lake
George

Daytona
Beach

Gulf of Mexico

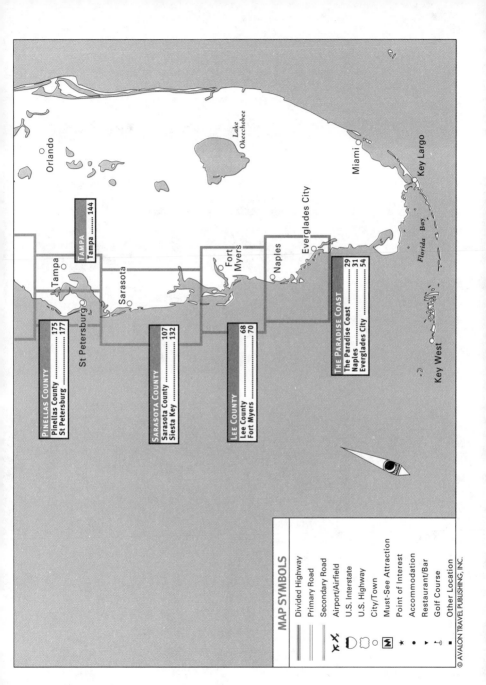

PINELLAS COUNTY
Pinellas County 175
St Petersburg 177

SARASOTA COUNTY
Sarasota County 107
Siesta Key 132

LEE COUNTY
Lee County 68
Fort Myers 70

TAMPA
Tampa 144

THE PARADISE COAST
The Paradise Coast 29
Naples 31
Everglades City 54

Orlando

Tampa

St Petersburg

Sarasota

Fort Myers

Naples

Everglades City

Miami

Key Largo

Key West

Florida Bay

Lake Okeechobee

MAP SYMBOLS

Divided Highway
Primary Road
Secondary Road
Airport/Airfield
U.S. Interstate
U.S. Highway
City/Town
Must-See Attraction
Point of Interest
Accommodation
Restaurant/Bar
Golf Course
Other Location

© AVALON TRAVEL PUBLISHING, INC.

Discover the Florida Gulf Coast

We drove through the last murk of dawn, only just remembering to flick off our headlights as we crunched over gravel into the parking lot. The marina looked bare without all the pelicans shifting their weight back and forth hopefully. (Where do pelicans sleep, anyway?)

We looked around for anyone who seemed to be looking around for us, and he was there. He was beyond ruddy, into something like plain old red-faced, a little portly, not old but not young. He was our captain, and our guide.

The problem was, if he was our Ahab, the *Pequod* was missing. In the shop. He'd had to borrow a boat from his neighbor, a real beauty, and the fishing was going to be so good, darned if the neighbor and his wife didn't decide to come.

There weren't too many pleasantries as we headed out on the *Miss Wanda,* its deck glinting white in the first strong light. Our would-be captain, displaced by the boat owner's seniority, felt content to nurse whatever chemical ills had befallen him the previous evening. And us, we were just nervous. It was our first time offshore trolling for gag grouper or whatever else we might find.

With a navigation system that was part science, part mysticism, the boat owner, Jimmy, and his wife, named Miss Wanda like the boat, took us to where the fish were going to be. They were there. Through a haze of big-fish stories and cigarette smoke, Jimmy set us up with rods, attaching huge lures that all looked like Mimi from the *Drew Carey Show,* or maybe Divine in *Pink Flamingos*—surely nothing like the mullet or mackerel they were supposed to resemble.

My hip bruised from where I anchored my rod, a little woozy from the smoke, the lite beer, and a superabundance of pork rinds, my mood could not be dampened. Every time we hooked one it was a delicious stew of fear, joy, hopefulness, and determination. The grouper were plentiful, the kingfish terrifying and fierce, the Spanish mackerel like luminous green jewels as they flopped into the boat.

As the sun sank lower in the sky and we headed for home, a companionable silence crept over us. Achy and sunburned, we unpacked the ice chests of fish, divided our treasures, and headed for home. I was going to like the Gulf Coast.

Since that time, countless trips later, I still feel that way. Susan Orlean, in her excellent book *The Orchid Thief,* wrote: "Florida was to Americans what America had always been to the rest of the world—a fresh, free, unspoiled start." That fresh start is still possible along the Gulf Coast. Except for Alaska, Florida has the longest coastline of any state—1,350 miles, a number that creeps up precipitously when you include islands, inlets, and estuaries. The majority of that length is on the Gulf side, the west coast of Florida, a maze of barrier islands, intracoastal waterways, and deep bays. And so much of life here centers on all that sustaining water.

The length of the Gulf Coast—from the mysterious Ever-glades in the south, up through the beachy beauty of west-central Florida, around the "Big Bend" and on to the antebellum grace of the Panhandle—offers the kind of rough-edged, front-row view into the natural world that is hard to come by these days. There are also posh and culturally rich urban centers (Naples and Sarasota), enduring historical sites (Apalachicola and Tallahassee), and family-friendly destinations to rival Disney (Tampa and St. Pete). But much of the Gulf Coast is decidedly rural, with vast swaths set aside as parkland, preserves, reserves, and animal refuges. Visitors come with rods and reels, with binoculars and dog-eared birding books, with arms ready to paddle and eyes ready to see.

And there's so much to see: Mullet jump clean out of the water in the mangrove maze of the Ten Thousand Islands. In the Homosassa River, a playful manatee calf tips over on his back so snorkelers can rub his itchy belly. The wind-swept beach of St. George Island State Park bears silent witness as a hundred baby loggerhead turtles flop their way back out to sea. The Gulf Coast embodies what Floridians refer to wistfully as "Old Florida" or "Real Florida," its unaffected beauty a siren's call to come and dive in headlong, or just sit quietly at the Gulf's edge and marvel.

WHEN TO GO

Florida is a year-round destination—24/7, 365, and all that. But each broad geographical area along the Gulf Coast has its own peak season, off season, and in-the-know in-between times.

Southwest Florida, with its unspoiled alabaster beaches, exotic wildlife, and lush subtropical foliage, sees a huge influx of "snowbirds" in the winter months. These northerners come after Thanksgiving and stay just through Easter, generally speaking, bumping up the populations in Naples and Fort Myers up through Sarasota and Bradenton. The timing isn't arbitrary—March and April along much of the Gulf Coast are magical: temperatures in the high 70s, a little breeze, low humidity, little rain, and Gulf water just warm enough for swimming.

That said, if you visit just after the snowbirds fly home and before summer sets in you'll find plenty of accommodations, unoccupied tables in restaurants, and room to roam unhindered on the beaches. (Be aware, though, that summer near the Everglades borders on intolerable, and lots of attractions even close up shop.) You may also find that it's a little cheaper after Easter. The same can be said of the fall, before the huge winter influx of visitors. September and October are lovely in southwest Florida, but it's also hurricane season, with reliable afternoon thunderstorms.

The Central West region encompasses the southern portion of Florida's Nature Coast, as well as the popular vacation destinations of Tampa, St. Petersburg, and Clearwater. Again, Thanksgiving to Easter is the peak visitor time, but it's less clear-cut here. A huge family draw, partly because of its proximity to Orlando and Walt Disney World, the area is at its busiest during school vacations. This also includes summer vacation—but I won't lie to you, it's like hot breath on your neck all summer, no remittance, and gloomy, stormy skies many afternoons. This area attracts crowds for Grapefruit League spring training fans, so the month of March sees many high-energy, Copenhagen-chewing ball fans cheering on their beloved teams.

On the Panhandle, which has colder winters and more moderate summers than elsewhere on the Gulf Coast, it's busiest during the summer. Many of the summer-season tourists here are, in fact, Florida residents from elsewhere hoping to improve upon the high temperatures and humidity of their hometowns. From Destin in the west to St. George Island off of Apalachicola in the east, the beaches are most crowded June to August. Still, they're not that crowded.

For college kids, the time to visit the Gulf Coast, and specifically Panama City Beach, is spring break, which falls during the months of March and April.

WHAT TO TAKE

Florida is casual, with all the good and bad that that entails. There are very few women on the Gulf Coast who could spot a knock-off Hermès Birkin bag at 20 paces. That's not all bad. In the absence of high fashion, what to pack is largely a function of comfort.

If you're spending time in Naples, Sarasota, or Tampa's Hyde Park, bring something festive to wear in the evening. Elsewhere, the name of the game all year is layering. For women a twin set and slacks when dressed up, for men a breezy collar knit and chinos. You need several pairs of shoes: something for dinner, sneakers for hiking (ones that can get wet repeatedly), and swim shoes or Teva sandals.

Even if you're visiting the Gulf Coast in the summer, bring a sweater. Everything is over-air-conditioned. Floridians tend to be large (as of two years ago, 57 percent of Floridian adults were overweight or obese), and maybe as a consequence they like interior temperatures brisk. In the winter, a long-sleeved pullover with light slacks is usually fine.

Bring sunscreen, binoculars, polarized sunglasses (for seeing depth when you fish), a bird book, snorkel, swim flippers, a juicy novel, more bathing suits than you can use, bug spray, flip-flops, a digital camera, and your cell phone (it won't work along rural parts of the Nature Coast, but everywhere else is fine, especially with Verizon service).

What you can rent: bikes, scooters, skates, strollers, beach chairs, boogie and surfboards, fishing equipment, motorboats, personal watercraft, kayaks, canoes, and sailboats.

WHAT IT WILL COST

This is the section that confuses me in every guidebook. What it costs depends largely upon what you're willing to spend. If I throw all the restaurants of the Gulf Coast into a hat, add them up, divide by the number of restaurants, I'd say that an average restaurant dinner for one person costs $22. If I were to do the same thing for accommodations, I'd find that an average hotel room costs $120. But who am I helping? It's a range, from fairly low to fairly high, on both counts.

Things are at their most expensive during peak season, which for the Florida peninsula is December–April; for the Panhandle it's June–August. What's helpful to know is—and it's actually kind of eerie—the Gulf Coast is less expensive the farther north and west you go. Top-dollar honors go to Naples, where an average dinner for one is about $30 and an average room night is about $140 mid-season. Then it gets cheaper and cheaper as you drive up I-75 and west along U.S. 98. Cheapest place on the Gulf Coast? Panama City Beach, where lots of bargain hotel rooms on the beach bottom out at $30. Pensacola, a very affordable town; Sarasota, not so affordable.

Beaches on the Gulf Coast are free, maybe a little extra for parking and sunblock. What you do at them may cost more—a half-day offshore fishing trip will run at least $300, an ecotour canoe trip $80, a brief Wave Runner rental $60. Of the attractions, everything pales financially by comparison to a day at Walt Disney World. Still, Busch Gardens in Tampa, Asolo theater tickets in Sarasota, snorkel-with-the-manatees charters in Homosassa—they're all going to cost you big.

If you can stay for a week, which I recommend, you can cut costs: A totally luxurious multibedroom beach house rental on St. George Island or even North Captiva Island will cost you less per night than a swanky single room in Naples. That way you can be even more fiscally prudent by preparing your own breakfasts and picnic lunches. Splurge on dinners.

With attractions, check their websites for their free or reduced-rate days or nights. Museums tend to admit people for free on Thursday nights or Sunday mornings, primarily to lure locals, but you can benefit. It's worth it to visit the local chambers of commerce or convention and visitors bureaus, not only for the information, but also for the coupons.

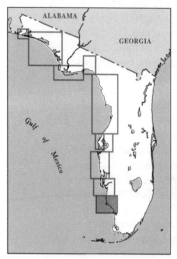

THE PARADISE COAST

What marketers call the "Paradise Coast" (really Naples, Marco Island, and Everglades City) is located at the southwestern tip of Florida's Gulf Coast. It's an area that remained virtually uninhabited until after the Civil War, and even then it was a handful of farmers, Seminoles trying to keep a low profile, squatters, and ne'er-do-wells evading jail or conscription.

But then, by dint of sheer beauty and fine weather, it started attracting the wealthy in the early 1900s. Barron Collier, a Memphis businessman who made his fortune off streetcar advertisements, traveled to the area to fish for tarpon and ended up so smitten he bought about 2,000 miles of what is now Collier County. There's been a lot of smiting in more recent times, too—Naples through the 1980s was one of the fastest-growing areas in the country. Affluent Midwesterners, with an eye toward retirement, bought up much of the area. To service their needs, the area soon swarmed with lavish resort hotels, high-end restaurants, and cultural amenities. Oh, and golf. Naples is said to have more golf courses per capita than anywhere else.

Naples is the most sophisticated spot on the Gulf Coast, with a gorgeous downtown. Marco Island, just to the south, the northernmost island in the string of what is called the Ten Thousand Islands, is in a similar vein, with tall resort hotels and condos rising up on a long crescent of white-sand beach.

Everglades City is the redheaded stepchild of the county. Until Hurricane Donna in the early 1960s, Everglades City was the county seat. Since then it's been known by nature lovers as the gateway to the Ten Thousand Islands, Big Cypress National Preserve, and Everglades National Park. Formally dedicated in 1947, Everglades National Park is the third-largest park in the United States, and an absolute must if you find yourself in the area. It's a paddler's paradise and one end of the Wilderness Waterway, the famous Everglades backcountry route linking Everglades City to Flamingo.

LEE COUNTY

Lee County comprises Fort Myers, Sanibel Island, and Captiva Island. Fort Myers is the largest and oldest city in southwest Florida, developed in the

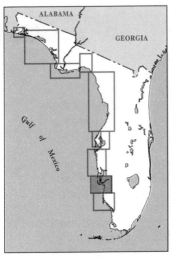

1860s by cattlemen and retired soldiers from the Seminole Wars. It sits on the banks of the Caloosahatchee River, not quite on the Gulf, and was once the winter retreat of Thomas Edison and Henry Ford. Their stately homes are now among the area's most popular attractions, located on a grand thoroughfare lined with 1,800 majestic royal palm trees, many of which Edison gave to the city as a token of his esteem.

Fort Myers's biggest draw is its neighbors, the many barrier islands that flank the city to the west. Some are accessible by causeway, others just by private boat or ferry. All are fringed by stunning, white-sand beaches. Perhaps the most famous of the bunch is Sanibel, anomalous as far as barrier islands go because of its east–west orientation. Sanibel is known as the best shelling beach in the country, where you'll find whelks, periwinkles, cones, coquina, fighting conch, lion's paws, and sunray venus dotting the 14 miles of fine white sand. It's a casual, low-rise beach town, with just enough to do (visit the J.N. "Ding" Darling National Wildlife Refuge and the Bailey-Matthews Shell Museum) to keep the whole family entertained.

There's less to do on neighboring Captiva, and that's just the way residents and visitors like it. The superlatives heaped upon it include "exclusive," "romantic," and "tranquil"—all accurate. Much of the little island, which used to be one island with Sanibel to the south, is taken up with single-family beach retreats for the rich and famous. Captiva has a small laid-back "downtown" area dotted with restaurants, shops, and galleries, with a heavy preponderance of beachside bars situated for maximal sunset viewing.

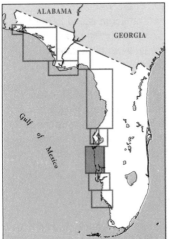

SARASOTA COUNTY

Elephants built Sarasota. Well, maybe not entirely, but it sure sounds good. Though it was officially founded in the 1840s, it wasn't until wealthy northerners like circus impresario John Ringling arrived that this backwater village 60 miles south of Tampa started really jumping. Chicago socialite Bertha Palmer built a mansion here on Sarasota Bay in 1910, inviting her friends to enjoy the area's many virtues. During the Roaring '20s, Ringling followed suit, constructing a huge winter residence, Cà d'Zan, and bringing his Ringling Bros. circus to winter here. That's where the elephants come in. In building the swishy dining/shopping area called St. Armands Key, the mighty circus pachyderms did some of the heavy lifting.

Ringling's legacy persists. In recent decades Sarasota has been recognized as Florida's cultural capital, home to a professional symphony, ballet, and opera. There are 10 theaters, 30 art galleries, the John and Mable Ringling Museum of Art, and the Van Wezel Performing Arts Hall, known for its kooky architecture and great acoustics.

A chain of narrow barrier islands sits offshore to the west. Lido and St. Armands Keys are fairly urban extensions of downtown Sarasota, connected by a causeway. Longboat Key to the north and Siesta Key to the south are more destinations in their own right, the former lined with posh resort hotels and condominiums, the latter a funkier, low-rise beach getaway.

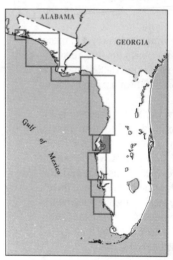

TAMPA

Busch Gardens, Ybor City, the Florida Aquarium, Tampa Bay Buccaneers, Tampa Bay Devil Rays, and Tampa Bay Lightning. But notice I didn't mention the beach. Tampa fronts Tampa Bay, not the Gulf of Mexico. A huge port city—the largest pleasure and industrial port in the southeast—it doesn't have any beaches to speak of. Before you despair, though, it's an excellent vacation destination, especially for families. There's a magical confluence of warm weather, affordable accommodations, professional sports, kids' attractions, and strangely posh shopping that seems to suit every taste.

Containing the biggest and best airport on Florida's west coast, Tampa is a natural embarkation point for a Gulf Coast vacation. It's adjacent to Pinellas County and, when combined with St. Petersburg, is the largest metropolitan area in the state. There is huge suburban sprawl in the north, where Busch Gardens and University of South Florida are, but farther to the south it's cheek to jowl: There's the elegant historic residential and commercial neighborhood of Hyde Park, the Cuban center of town in Ybor City (once famous for cigars, now more famous for bars), and MacDill Air Force Base, which takes up the entire southern third of the Tampa peninsula and is home to the U.S. Central Command. The Hillsborough River runs through the city, providing a peaceful natural counterpoint to all the more frantic, citified pleasures.

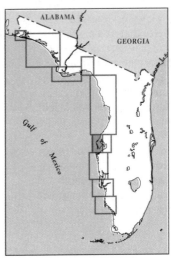

PINELLAS COUNTY

St. Petersburg, the last you heard, was a retirement community. It's different now—an influx of high-tech firms, mostly employing youngish people, has prompted a shift in the demographics. The median age of residents went from a high of 48.1 in 1970 to 39.3 in 2000. Pinellas County as a whole has seen enormous growth and fiscal health recently, a notable destination for family vacations. St. Petersburg itself faces Tampa to the east, with seven miles of inviting parkland touching placid Old Tampa Bay. On the west side of the peninsula, Clearwater Beach, protected by Honeymoon Island to the north, is a wide, welcoming swath of Gulf water lapping at white sand, backed by restaurants, souvenir shops, boogie-board-and-bikini boutiques, etc.

The city of St. Petersburg exerts its pull with a vibrant downtown of pastel art deco buildings and cultural attractions like the Salvador Dalí Museum, Florida International Museum, the symphony at Ruth Eckerd Hall, or theater at American Stage. St. Petersburg is also home to some of the most sophisticated restaurants in the greater Tampa Bay area.

Along the Gulf side of Pinellas County, Clearwater is not necessarily the most famous community. St. Pete Beach to the south, which is a distinct community from the larger, more urban St. Petersburg to its east, draws beach lovers from around the world. It's a classic Florida beach town, with late-night waterside clubs, deep-water fishing, and low-slung motels with views of the ocean. And there's a lot of beach, many local strands ranking high in international beach polls. Caladesi Island, Honeymoon Island, and Fort de Soto Park are all noteworthy Pinellas beaches.

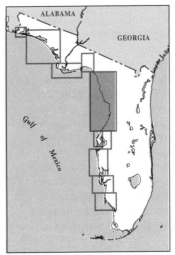

THE NATURE COAST

If the alligator is Florida's most famous reptile, surely the West Indian manatee is its favorite mammal. From the Anclote River in Pasco County to the Sopchoppy River in Wakulla, Florida's Nature Coast is chockfull of creatures, some of them manatees and gators, but you'll also see ospreys, eagles, herons, egrets, wood storks, ibises, deer, black bears, raccoons, armadillos, otters, and more fish than you could shake a rod at.

Observing, communing, and sometimes going *mano a mano* with nature is this area's most compelling activity. Marked by vast salt marshes, winding rivers, lakes ringed with cypress trees, and the mighty Gulf of Mexico to the west of it all, this is serious fishing, birding, and hunting territory.

Accessed along U.S. 19 (which isn't exactly a pretty road), the Nature Coast includes Homosassa and Crystal River in the south, both famous for their tarpon fishing and their manatee habitat. South of that, and worth a day's excursion, is Weeki Wachee Springs with its historic mermaid show. To the north, the small fishing communities of Cedar Key and Steinhatchee require a little extra effort to get to, but there's big payoff. Each is like a look back into Florida's Wild West past, populated by Orvis hat-wearing anglers telling fish stories, some great bars, relaxed motels, and myriad guides eager to take you out on their boats or in kayaks to initiate you into the lush, unmanicured beauty of the Nature Coast.

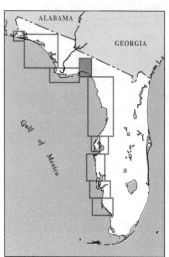

TALLAHASSEE

Its inclusion in this book may seem quirky, as Tallahassee doesn't really lie on the Gulf Coast, but sits inland a bit. Still, the city of Tallahassee is the gateway to the Panhandle and the seat of state government, and as such, it stays in the picture. The city was established in 1825, following a decision by the legislature to locate the capital of the new Florida Territory midway between the population centers of St. Augustine and Pensacola. Government offices share the largest sector of the labor force, but local universities Florida State University and Florida A&M each lend their influence to the rich cultural fabric of the city.

It's unapologetically Southern, this town, more so than anywhere else on the Gulf Coast, with the country's largest concentration of original plantations (300,000 acres, 71 plantations) between here and Thomasville, Georgia, 28 miles away. Genteel, rooted in history, the top attractions are the two capitol buildings, new and old. At the former you'll get a glimpse of government in action and a panoramic view of the city from the 22nd floor observatory. The latter sits in the shadow of giant live oaks, restored to its 1902 appearance with candy-striped awnings and a stained-glass dome.

Tallahassee even looks different than other palm-bedecked beach spots on the Gulf Coast. Its red-clay hills host dogwood and magnolia in majestic blossom each spring, and the major arteries into the city, like spokes on a wheel, enjoy the deep shade of ancient live oak canopies.

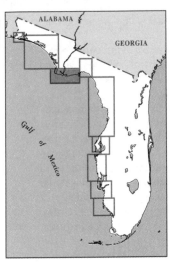

THE FORGOTTEN COAST

Toward the end of the 20th century, the area between Panama City and St. Marks was a marketing nightmare. Then someone came up with the catchy phrase, "The Forgotten Coast."

Apalachicola was once the third-largest port on the Gulf of Mexico, and its rich history and deep maritime roots are indelibly etched along the wide, tree-lined streets. With 200 historic homes and buildings on the National Register, and a downtown of repurposed 1850s brick cotton warehouses, it's got antebellum grace and charm to burn. The Apalachicola National Estuarine Research Reserve, historic Grady Market, and the sweet John Gorrie State Museum, which celebrates the inventor of modern refrigeration—there's enough here to occupy visitors for at least a couple of days, but then top it off with superlative nearby beaches such as St. Joseph Peninsula State Park in Port St. Joe and St. George Island State Park on St. George Island.

In fact, St. George Island is a worthy destination in its own right. Fairly recently settled, the long barrier island is dotted with hundreds of beach house rentals, all connected by a long bike path. Outdoor enthusiasts can explore the Gulf side or the bay side, its endless estuaries and waterways accessible by kayak, canoe, or flats boat.

Aside from tourism, the local big business here is oystering, with Franklin County harvesting 90 percent of Florida's eastern oysters. They're delicious. In

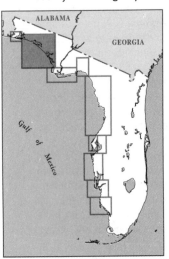

addition, you'll see the fleet hauling in shrimp, blue crab, and finfish of all sorts—marine treats that can be sampled that very night at dinner. Apalachicola seafood restaurants are among the best along the Gulf Coast.

THE EMERALD COAST

The Emerald Coast—Fort Walton Beach and Destin, Beaches of South Walton, Panama City Beach—got its name from the deep green color of its water, a striking counterpoint to its glinting white-sand beaches. But this is nearly all that the communities along this stretch of coast share. Its easternmost section, Panama City Beach, is a densely populated beachside playground, especially savored by college kids on spring break. At the city's eastern end, St. Andrews State Park is a lush, uninhabited beachside wilderness that stands in marked contrast to the more urban pleasures of downtown.

Farther west, the beaches of South Walton feature quieter, more contemplative beachside enjoyments. Personal-watercraft riding and beach volleyball aren't as zesty here, but the 13 beach communities the area comprises are beloved nonetheless. Largely residential, the area has a meticulous and deeply eco-friendly approach to growth, its stewards carefully husbanding along planned communities such as Seaside (featured in the movie *The Truman Show*) and Caribbean-inspired Rosemary Beach. This is a fine place to curl up and get away from it all for the week in a luxurious rental beach house.

The twin cities of Destin and Fort Walton Beach farther to the west are more historic and better known than the beaches of South Walton. Fishing is what put Destin on the map, continuing today with sportfishers arriving from all over the planet to get a crack at the local marlins, sailfish, and spearfish. Don't get the impression that this is a fishing backwater filled with possum-eating rednecks—it's fairly posh, with swanky beachside restaurants and lovely accommodations.

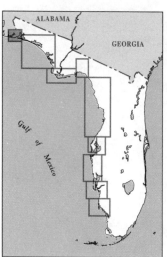

PENSACOLA

Pensacola, a city of 412,000, still thinks like a pokey southern town, in a good way. The local wisdom is that there are four seasons: almost summer, summer, still summer, and Christmas. People in Pensacola hunt, fish, and eat those leaden briquettes called hushpuppies. It's tried to shake off its "Redneck Riviera" nickname, with mixed success, focusing instead on monikers like "Cradle of Naval Aviation" (it's home to the Naval Air Station Pensacola and the Blue Angels) or even "America's first European settlement."

The latter is true, in a way, since the Spanish tried to colonize Pensacola in 1559, before they famously set up shop in St. Augustine on the other coast. Hurricanes caused the settlement to disperse, so St. Augustine gets the nod. Since that first ill-fated outpost, five different flags have flown over the city, each lending an architectural fillip and exotic-sounding street names.

The old historic part of town is lovely and walkable, the free National Museum of Naval Aviation is worthy of a day's exploration and Gulf Islands National Seashore and Santa Rosa Island contain miles of undeveloped beaches—a sophisticated mélange of allures. If they really want to ditch the redneck rep, though, the locals need to stop competing to see who can fling a dead mullet farthest into the state of Alabama.

"Real Florida"

In the late 1800s Harriet Beecher Stowe described her home state of Florida as "a tumble-down, wild, panicky kind of life—this general happy-go-luckiness which (is) Florida." I don't know about the panicky, but the rest of it nails why so many Americans have made regular pilgrimages to the Sunshine State since before Stowe was born. It's more than nice weather and fine beaches—Florida represents freedom and possibility, the final American frontier. But even along the Gulf Coast, much of that frontier has been prettified, codified, condo-fied. Where's Stowe's Florida?

You can still find it traveling from the Nature Coast to up around the Big Bend all the way to Apalachicola. Nature seems more natural, historic sites less mediated and sanitized for tourists.

DAY 1

Start your "Real Florida" tour in the capital city of Tallahassee, spending a day at the Old and New Capitols, driving the city's fabled canopied roads, maybe eating a little barbecue or fried fish and sweet iced tea. After you're fortified, drive due south of the city for 15 miles on Highway 363 to Wakulla Springs State Park. The untouched jungle hosted the location shooting for *Creature from the Black Lagoon* and a couple of Tarzan movies. Take the glass-bottomed boat tour of what is said to be the world's largest and deepest freshwater springs. Then settle in for the night at the historic Wakulla Lodge.

DAY 2

Continue south on Highway 363 a few miles and take a right onto U.S. 98, heading west for 60 miles. You'll drive through the fishing town of Carrabelle and the oystering town of Eastpoint. Continue west to Apalachicola and you can try a dozen of these briny bivalves before you walk among the fading antebellum Federal, Greek Revival, and Victorian homes set on wide, tree-lined streets. You could stay at one of Apalach's historic inns, but better to get back in the car and head over the new St. George Bridge to St. George Island. Unlike J. Lo, nothing about this barrier is-

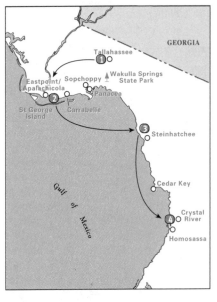

land is overexposed. Word of its first-class fishing and fabulous beaches just hasn't been disseminated widely, which much of the year means that you'll be walking alone in the 1,900-acre beachfront St. George Island State Park. The island has hundreds of beach house rentals, many of the homes large enough for family reunions or large group gatherings.

COURTESY OF VISIT FLORIDA

Apalachicola National Forest occupies over half a million acres to the south and west of Tallahassee.

DAY 3

Feeling rested and mellow, cross back over onto the mainland and head back east the way you came on U.S. 98, maybe taking a quick jog out of your way to see the sweet towns of Sopchoppy and Panacea. You'll drive about 95 miles along U.S. 98 as it skirts the Big Bend and joins with U.S. 19 at the town of Perry. Now head south along the Florida peninsula for 28 miles and drive eight miles west to the coast along Highway 51. The town of Steinhatchee has long been renowned in fishing circles for its trout and redfish—while the rest of the world says, "Stein who? How do you spell that?" (It's pronounced "STEEN-hachee," by the way.) Splurge a little and stay at the nicest place in town, the Steinhatchee Landing Resort, then figure out if you're going to go offshore fishing for black grouper or amberjack or closer in for redfish in the grass flats. If you visit between July 1 and September 10 you can try your hand at scalloping. It's also nice to just drift in a canoe along the Steinhatchee River.

DAY 4

Next stop, Cedar Key. It's not far as the crow flies, but you have to head back inland on Highway 51 for eight miles, go south on U.S. 19 for 45 miles, then cut back out west to the coast on Highway 24 for 21 miles. The town is actually a constellation of tiny islands that juts three miles out into the Gulf of Mexico, its downtown a collection of weathered wooden buildings up on stilts. What to do: fish, kayak, hike, sit. Cedar Key's lack of fancy attractions is part of its attraction.

And finish up your trip by communing with the West Indian manatees in Homosassa or Crystal River, both towns about 40 miles south along U.S. 19. Snorkel or just splash around in the warm waters of Kings Bay in Crystal River or the Blue Waters area of the Homosassa River, observing these endangered marine mammals that also seem so inexorably drawn to "Real Florida."

You see your first castle in Europe. "Fabulous, awe-inspiring." You see 10 such castles and it's a case of "seen one, you seen 'em all." You get castle callous; it's unavoidable. So it is with beaches—blue water lapping, the horizon a long line in the distance, gulls wheeling. The first day it's paradise; the fifth day it's sandy. Gulf Coast beaches are the answer, as they provide a diverse array of natural settings and an equally wide range of waterside activity.

DAY 1

Start in Naples at Naples Municipal Beach & Fishing Pier, an urban downtown beach that fronts Naples's famous Millionaires' Row. At the center of the gorgeous strand a 1,000-foot structure juts into the Gulf, a pier that has been knocked down and built again, in 1910, 1926, and again in 1960. It's really the heart of downtown Naples, a short walk from restaurants, shopping, and entertainment.

DAY 2

The next day, head north on U.S. 41 (the Tamiami Trail) for 10 miles, then take County Road 865 northwest for 14 miles into Lee County and try two of the best beaches on the same day. At

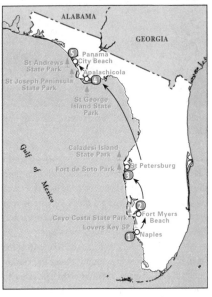

COURTESY OF VISIT FLORIDA

Have a front-row seat on St. George Island.

Lover's Key State Park in Fort Myers Beach on Estero Island, walk or take a tram through a bird-filled forest of mangroves to a gorgeous, unspoiled beach occupying four little barrier islands. The park offers 90-minute sunset ecotours most days, on which you'll see roseate spoonbills and snowy egrets. Lover's Key is a serious shelling beach for those in the know.

The same can be said of Cayo Costa State Park, known for its lack of people and abundance of starfish, conchs, and sand dollars. Accessible only by passenger ferry or private boat, Cayo Costa in Lee County is the least-visited state park in Florida.

It may be you all by yourself on this 2,132-acre barrier strip of sand, pine forest, oak hammock, mangrove swamp, and grasslands.

DAY 3

And then get up early the next day and do it all over again, only this time farther north in the St. Petersburg/Clearwater area. You'll drive 100 miles north on fast, easy, but scenery-free I-75, then cut over to I-275 in Tampa and head north to reach Pinellas County. Caledesi Island State Park in Clearwater Beach and Fort de Soto Park in St. Petersburg often make people's lists of top beaches in the world. The former is only accessible by ferry from Honeymoon Island State Recreation Area off Alternate U.S. 19 in Dunedin. It's a 3.5-mile-long island with a marina and swim beach right near where the ferry lets you off, but the rest of the island remains undeveloped. The bay side of the island is worth exploring, with a mangrove shoreline and seagrass flats (rent canoes and paddle the 3.5-mile canoe trail that meanders through the bay side). Then take U.S. 19 south 14 miles, merge onto I-275 south for seven miles, and take Pinellas Bayway (Hwy. 679) south 6.5 miles to Fort De Soto Park, a beach and history lesson in one. The fort was built in 1898 to protect Tampa Bay during the Spanish-American War. Explore the old fort and its history museum before you head on to one of the two swim beaches, the better of which is the North Beach Swim Center (it has concessions). Fort de Soto Park also has some of the most coveted beachside camping spots along the Gulf Coast.

DAY 4

After that it's another road trip to the north, this one nearly five hours as you traverse the Nature Coast and around Florida's Big Bend to the Panhandle, which itself is essentially a long, uninterrupted stretch of perfect beach. You'll take I-275 north for 20 miles, Highway 589 north for 54 miles, then U.S. 19/98 for about 300 miles. With Apalachicola as your home base, you can visit St. Joseph Peninsula State Park and St. George Island

State Park on the same day, the former a trip over a causeway west off Highway 30 in Port St. Joe, the latter over a bridge in Eastpoint on U.S. 98 onto St. George Island. St. Joe has tall dunes, pure quartz sand, and a huge expanse of heavy pine forest that is home to bobcats, deer, bald eagles, ospreys, and endangered peregrine falcons. In the fall you'll see monarch butterflies perch for a while on the beach during their migration to Mexico. Then rent bikes on St. George Island and pedal your way to the park, the longest beach of any state park in Florida—nine miles of white sand. The underpopulated 1,900 acres of windswept, sea oat–fringed dunes are the spot from which to plan your fishing campaign against the resident flounder, redfish, pompano, and sea trout.

DAY 5

Drive another 40 miles west on U.S. 98 and finish your tour of Gulf Coast beaches in Panama City Beach at the beloved St. Andrews State Park, with its preserved wilderness at the east edge of a built-up beach town. The park's allures include a lagoon swimming area, fishing jetties, hiking trails, 2.5 miles of beach, and two campgrounds.

Beachcombing on the barrier island of Cayo Costa yields serious shell treasures.

A caveat about Florida's 800-pound rodent: The word "Disney" appears 18 times in this book, not including these three paragraphs. It comes up—it's unavoidable. Just about everyone on the Gulf Coast has a strong opinion about Walt Disney World; most are not exuberantly positive. Tourism is the state's lifeblood, Walt Disney World is the biggest tourist attraction in the world, ergo Mickey gave Florida a life-saving transfusion. But most residents of the Gulf Coast think of their home as the un-Disney, the rebuttal to Disney, the real Florida before Walt perpetrated his theme park on an unsuspecting subtropical paradise.

This is not an anti-Disney book. Your relationship with the mouse is a function of your own personal morals and values. My husband: not a Disney person. Me: I enjoy a few days of rides, fried snacks, and large, mugging-yet-mute cartoon characters.

Whether you do it or eschew it, Orlando's not the only family-friendly game on the Gulf Coast. In fact, even without Orlando, the kids' "what-I-did-on-my-summer-vacation" essay could be a real page-turner this September. A family vacation on the Gulf Coast should start in Tampa—first, because it boasts a big, easy airport with lots of flights; second, because it's only an hour away from Walt Disney World and all the other hoo-ha in Orlando; and third, it's where Busch Gardens is.

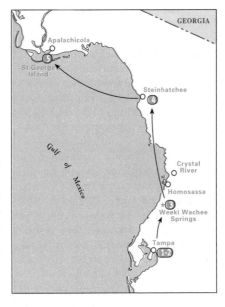

Day 1

Tampa really has family fun dialed. First stop, as I said, a day at the Gardens for a ride on the Montu, the Kumba, the Python, the Scorpion, and the tooth-rattling Gwazi, in descending order of priority. It's a park for all ages, with a mix of big, scary coasters and sweet animal attractions.

Day 2

Right across the street from Busch Gardens is Tampa's Museum of Science & Industry (MOSI), probably the best science museum on the Gulf Coast. It's nearly impossible to combine this in a day with Busch Gardens, so visit MOSI on your second day, with the other half of the day spent wandering at either the Florida Aquarium (with a stop-off for lunch across the street at the portside dining/entertainment complex of Channelside) or the Lowry Park Zoo. Both of these attractions are midsize, thus very walkable and requiring

COURTESY OF LEE COUNTY VISITOR AND CONVENTION BUREAU

Family vacations on the Gulf Coast may start and end at the water's edge, but there's also a lot of fun to be had on dry land.

under four hours to fully explore. Before you get out of Tampa, take one of the aquarium's Dolphin Quest Eco-Tours out into the bay to eagle-eye dolphins, manatees, and migratory birds.

DAY 3

Start heading north along the coast on U.S. 19. Hype seeing the manatees (submerged mammalian burritos with flippers), but before that, stop off and visit the mermaids (about an hour north of Tampa on 19). Some people insist that Weeki Wachee Springs is pure camp and nostalgia, but I think those mermaids put on a good show. It dates back to 1947, with powerful swimmers showing their underwater chops in a choreographed lip-synching performance (the audience sits outside the fishbowl). The show is brief, and afterwards the family can cool off at the attached Buccaneer Bay water park fed by a natural spring. This is warmup for the manatees, about another 30 miles north on U.S. 19.

DAY 4

You may need to stay overnight in Homosassa or Crystal River to get a jump on the day. You're going to commune with the West Indian manatee, still listed as an endangered species. From October 15 to March 31 you'll find hundreds of these gentle giants swimming in the warm waters of Kings Bay in Crystal River and the Blue Waters area of the Homosassa River. They are huge herbivores, and playful. Manatee Tour & Dive or Bird's Underwater will take whole families out for snorkel trips with the manatees. You're not supposed to touch, but sometimes they like you to rub their bellies.

If you find yourself and your family along the Nature Coast when manatees aren't in season, there are still good reasons to get wet. From July 1 to September 10, scalloping in Steinhatchee is a hoot (despite the fact that most children wouldn't eat a scallop on a double-dog dare). You wallow in the grassy shallows wearing a snorkel and swim shoes, scooping up the sweet bay bivalves. It's a good excuse to splash around and observe the wading birds and other animal life. Steinhatchee is about 80 miles north of Weeki Wachee Springs on U.S. 19, then seven miles west on County Road 358.

DAY 5 AND BEYOND

So far this family vacation has been action packed. You need a couple extra days to cool down—keep driving north up and around the Big Bend for 300 miles on U.S. 19/98. Apalachicola is a historic town filled with more adult allures (antebellum homes, fine dining), so head instead over the St. George Island Bridge for a couple days of fishing, beachcombing, and relaxing on St. George Island. It's very family focused, with comfortable beach houses (many with bunk-bed rooms and private pools), biking paths the length of the island, and a tremendous 1,900-acre state park that takes up the whole eastern end of the island.

It's an exciting time for birders in Florida. The Great Florida Birding Trail (GFBT) is a 2,000-mile trail through the state, its numerous sites selected for their excellent bird-watching or bird-education opportunities. The trail is split into three sections, the east, the west, and the Panhandle, and trail maps can be downloaded from the GFBT website (floridabirdingtrail.com). Even if you focus your energies on the western or the Panhandle sections of the trail, there's too much area to cover in a single trip. Pick a smaller section of either one (the western part is grouped into 17 smaller clusters, the Panhandle in 13), or play it fast and loose and hit a few spots in each, like this:

DAY 1

Start at the Lower Suwannee National Wildlife Refuge, which extends north and south along the Gulf Coast from the Nature Coast town of Suwannee and is one of the largest undeveloped river delta-estuarine systems in the United States. The refuge headquarters is on Highway 347, 16 miles west of U.S. 19, with a nearby river trail and boardwalk from which to see migratory songbirds. Citrus

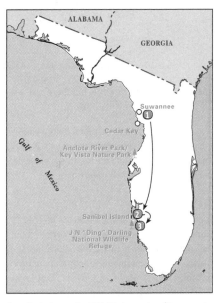

Hawks migrate through Florida, meaning that seasonally you're likely to see thousands of hawks of many species.

COURTESY OF VISIT FLORIDA

County is home to 250 bird species (the county has its own birding website at www.citrusbird-ingtrail.com), with red-cockaded woodpeckers, Bachman's sparrows, American white pelicans, and Florida scrub jays among the more rare.

Hightail it south about 30 miles on U.S. 19, then west on Highway 24 for 21 miles until you reach Cedar Key, where you can see a more dense concentration of Florida scrub jays at Cedar Key Scrub State Reserve, one of the fastest-disappearing habitats in Florida. The park has 12 miles of

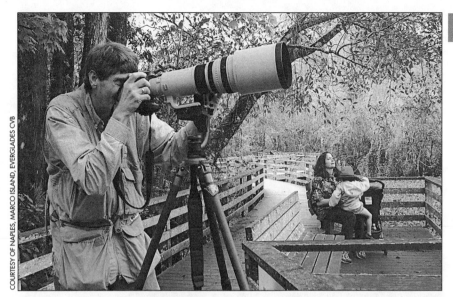

COURTESY OF NAPLES, MARCO ISLAND, EVERGLADES CVB

Nature photographers flock to Corkscrew Swamp Sanctuary along the Great Florida Birding Trail to see wood storks and other rare birds.

marked walking trails. Also in Cedar Key, the No. 4 Bridge and Fishing Pier affords great views of the tidal flats in the channels between the islands, flats in which you're likely to see snowy egrets, great blue herons, white ibis, terns, gulls, shorebirds, black skimmers, and brown and white pelicans.

No time to linger, though; you have a long drive south. You can stop along the way at Anclote River Park along U.S. 19 to look for reddish egrets, black-bellied plovers, and huge osprey nests, or maybe pause to observe the sandpipers, oystercatchers, terns, and plovers on the mudflats of nearby Key Vista Nature Park on Highway 595A. But you're heading 200 miles south to Sanibel Island, where you can stop for the night. You may choose to drive south along the coast on U.S. 19, cutting over in Tampa to the Tamiami Trail (U.S. 41), which takes you directly to Sanibel.

Day 2

Once on this island in Lee County, you can do a little birding warmup, looking for some of the many resident bird species. You'll find rare white pelicans hanging out in Pine Island Sound and ospreys and eagles nesting on telephone poles above the bike paths and along Sanibel-Captiva Road. The light-house area of Sanibel is a good place to see birds, as are the mangrove islands off Pine Island Sound, as is Tarpon Bay on Sanibel.

Day 3

But then you're going to hit paydirt at J.N. "Ding" Darling National Wildlife Refuge, which takes up half of Sanibel Island. It's serious birder territory; everyone is equipped with high-powered binoculars and huge camera lenses. There's a natural-ist-led tram ride on which you're bound to see rare species, colorful species, important life-list species. There are more than 238 species in the refuge, among them tricolored and little blue herons, black-crowned night herons, ibis, wood storks, peregrine falcons, roseate spoonbills, and anhin-gas. The best time to go is early morning, about an hour before or after low tide.

Those with a keen interest in Florida's Native American history could plan a whole vacation around visiting important Native American sites.

DAY 1

Some of the most compelling sites are centered in Lee County, so fly into the Southwest Florida International Airport in Fort Myers, or drive to the area via I-75 or U.S. 41. The Southwest Florida Museum of History in Fort Myers is a good place to start, with exhibits devoted to the history of the local Calusa and Seminole people. Kids may find the Seminole village replica at the Calusa Nature Center & Planetarium more diverting, a short drive away in Fort Myers. Once you've gotten your bearings, head to Pineland on Pine Island, 20 miles west of Cape Coral over a causeway, which has some of the most extensive Calusa mound and midden sites and cross-island Calusa canal works.

Boca Grande, an island at the southern tip of Cape Haze peninsula, is home to the tall, shellwork Big Mound Key.

These mounds, noticeable on such a flat island, are along its western side. Not far from there, Big Mound Key, accessed from Boca Grande at the southern tip of Cape Haze peninsula in Charlotte County, is a mound midden shellwork complex 23 feet high. Historians have proposed that this was a giant effigy, in an unusual spider-like shape with skinny ridges coming out like spokes from a central core. Other people say these ridges or dikes signal where Calusas directed fish and shellfish along canoe trails. Much of Big Mound Key has been vandalized, especially since the pirate Gasparilla is said to have buried gold and treasure there.

DAY 2

About 40 minutes north of Big Mound Key, in the small town of Englewood (north of Cape Haze, off

Hwy. 775A), is Paulson Point, a county park containing what is known as the Sarasota County mound. The park has walkways that go over and around the mound with interpretive signs along the trail.

From here, head north another 40 minutes into Sarasota County along the Tamiami Trail (U.S. 41) to the town of Osprey and Historic Spanish Point. Once the home of Chicago socialite Mrs. Potter Palmer, the complex contains several mounds and shell middens and a sweeping historical tour of a thousand years of human activity at the site. Interpretive markers and an "Indian village" show how early Floridian natives fished and hunted here, and an archaeology exhibit in the main hall gives you more background. The Hill Midden north of Webb's Cove is the most intact site.

Take U.S. 41 to I-75 and drive 20 miles north into Manatee County to Emerson Point Preserve, where you'll find a tall hill on Snead Island (take Exit 224 off I-75 and go west on U.S. 301 until it becomes Snead Island Rd.). Settlers in the 1800s liked the hill so much they built a plantation on it, overlooking the bay. The hill, in fact, is composed of millions of discarded oyster shells—one of the oldest known temple mounds in Florida, known as the Portavant Temple Mound. It's huge, with several rounded subsidiary mounds and middens scattered throughout the forest.

DAY 3

Just to the north, the greater Tampa Bay area is home to several notable sites. Off Highway 590 at Safety Harbor on Old Tampa Bay, Philippe Park Temple Mound is a massive structure, with a top 49 feet square and a base 146 feet by 162 feet. There are also burial mounds here. And in south St. Petersburg, on Pinellas Point Drive near 20th Street, Pinellas Point Temple Mound rises 15 feet, facing Tampa Bay.

There's not a lot to do at either site but observe, so if you feel yourself in need of action, you've got to get back in the car and drive nearly another two hours north on U.S. 19 to Crystal River State Archaeological Site in Crystal River. It's been estimated that from 300 B.C. to A.D. 1400 roughly 7,500 Native Americans visited here every year. There are six mounds, built by what are now referred to as the pre-Columbian mound builders, with a 40-foot truncated cone temple mound rising above the others. The small museum's exhibit chronicles the archaeological excavations begun in 1903. The park has a new dugout canoe exhibit and a "Sifting for Technology" interactive exhibit. With the latter, there are biweekly programs for the general public in which participants use sifting screens and other archaeological tools to recover artifacts from the spoil of a dredged boat slip.

COURTESY OF ST. PETE/CLEARWATER AREA CVB

Philippe Park, a historical site that overlooks Old Tampa Bay, is named for Count Odet Philippe.

Explore the Florida Gulf Coast

The Paradise Coast

Many people describe this part of Florida as the "Paradise Coast." Unhelpful, it seems to me, as one person's paradise is another's episode of *Survivor*. And really, the three cities that make up the paradise in question couldn't be more different. Like three wildly disparate siblings stifling under the umbrella of a common surname, **Naples** is all glamorous sophistication and effete charm; **Marco Island** is the uncomplicated, sunny, outdoors "jock" of the family; and **Everglades City** is the sinister, infinitely more interesting ne'er-do-well of the kids, the one Mama worries about.

Take a luxury boat tour through the canals that make up the backyards of the multimillion-dollar homes of Naples's Port Royal, then pilot your own kayak quietly through the mangrove jungle of the Ten Thousand Islands and you'll see: Paradise is in the eye of the beholder.

The Calusa people were the first to recognize paradise, settling in southwest Florida centuries before Spanish explorers found their way here. But even after the Spanish had evicted and killed off these first residents, the land lay virtually empty until the late 1800s. Survey teams brought back news of the beauty of the wilds of southwest Florida, sparking the imagination of General John S. Williams, a senator from Louisville, and Walter N. Haldeman, owner of the *Louisville Courier-Journal*. The men chartered a boat and came to look, mesmerized by the miles of white-sand beaches. Not long after, in 1886, the Naples Town Improvement Company was formed, purchasing

Must-Sees

M Naples Municipal Beach & Fishing Pier: Some of the area's top beaches here are a little more urban than in other parts of the Gulf Coast. Naples Municipal Beach features a 1,000-foot fishing pier considered the heart of the city, flanked on either side by a wide swath of beach the long length of fancy houses known as "Millionaires' Row" (page 33).

M Corkscrew Swamp Sanctuary: Head north out of Naples to this wildlife sanctuary. You'll see wood storks with faces only a mother could love and a strange wizened plant called a Resurrection Fern that comes back from the botanically deceased (page 33).

M Naples Museum of Art: A recent addition to the Philharmonic Center for the Arts complex, the museum packs quite a bit into its 15 galleries. From Dale Chihuly glasswork to Modern Mexican Masters to a tiny exhibit of antique walking sticks, exhibits are mesmerizing and expertly curated (page 38).

M Caribbean Gardens: Families visiting Naples usually find their way here, with good reason. Little ones enjoy the gator-feeding show, the Panther Glade, the big cats show, and the boat ride out to see the antic monkeys on their little islands. Parents, on the other hand, will appreciate the park's incredible native and exotic plants, as well as the adult humor of the animal handlers (page 39).

M 3rd Street South: Some of Florida's most sophisticated boutiques, antiques shops, and galleries line both sides of Naples's main drag. There's even a street concierge to help get you oriented (page 46).

M Tigertail Beach: Against the backdrop of Marco Island's tall skyline of resort hotels, Tigertail Beach draws a fun-seeking crowd. For some, fun is Jet Ski rentals and water sports, for others a cutthroat game of beach volleyball, and still others linger equipped only with a pail and shovel (page 48).

M Calusa Shell Mounds: Take a boat tour through the deep backwater with Florida Saltwater Adventures. You'll motor out through the tiny mangrove islands near Marco Island, stopping to gingerly walk around, peering to find remnants of this extinct Native American culture (page 50).

M Everglades Rentals & Eco Adventures: Paddle through the Ten Thousand Islands and part of Everglades National Park with this ecotour company out of Everglades City. A guide glides with you through mangrove tunnels, drifting by wading birds, rare orchids, and gators of all sizes (page 58).

M Totch's Island Tours: There are other ways to get out and explore the area's exotic "walking trees." Don a pair of protective headphones and hop aboard a backcountry or open-water airboat tour at mangrove islands with Totch's Island Tours (page 58).

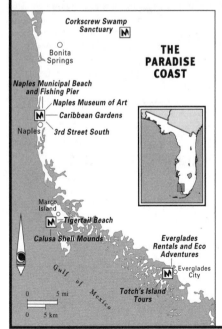

Corkscrew Swamp Sanctuary **M**

Bonita Springs

THE PARADISE COAST

Naples Municipal Beach and Fishing Pier

Naples Museum of Art **M**

Caribbean Gardens

Naples **M** 3rd Street South

Marco Island

M Tigertail Beach

Calusa Shell Mounds

Everglades Rentals and Eco Adventures

Everglades City **M**

Totch's Island Tours

Gulf of Mexico

0   5 mi

0   5 km

3,712 acres between the Gulf of Mexico and what is now known as Naples Bay.

They had big plans. The name alone says quite a bit: These founders were modeling the new Naples on the cultured and thriving Italian seaport city (heck, if you squint, the Florida peninsula looks a little like the Italian peninsula, right?). They built a pier, blocked out plans for a city, built their own homes on the beach—and then the Naples Town Improvement Company ran out of money. It was sold at a public auction in 1890 to the only bidder, Walter Haldeman, who now owned 8,600 acres of land, the swanky Naples Hotel, the pier, and a steamship that brought guests to and from Naples. Instead of making him rich beyond his wildest dreams, Naples was more of an avocational interest, a financially draining hobby for Haldeman. In fact, in the early 1900s, the area that is now Collier County was mostly populated by feisty herds of scrub cattle that grazed the open prairies.

The city chugged on with minimal growth until rail service came to Naples in 1927 and Memphis-born millionaire Barron Collier's Tamiami Trail was completed the next year. Poised at the verge of vigorous expansion, the city's growth was quashed by the Great Depression followed swiftly by World War II. A direct hit by Hurricane Donna in 1960 devastated Everglades City but served to bolster growth in Naples—not long after the storm, the county seat was transferred from Everglades City to East Naples.

Since then, Naples has experienced an enormous population boom, mostly amongst Midwestern retirees (it's funny, but every other person you meet here used to live in Chicago, Milwaukee, and so forth), such that it was deemed the fastest-growing community in the country in the 1980s. It's got the look of many monied, sunny American cities (Santa Barbara, Palm Springs): lawns that seem maintained round the clock with tweezers and nail scissors, women of a certain age in Lilly Pulitzer pink-and-green cardigans, and everywhere fancy new Mercedes badly parked, their gleaming bumpers shellacked with "I'd rather be golfing" stickers. (People here are Republican, but

not way to the right; often county and state offices are filled with pro-choice, anti-school-voucher candidates.)

As for Marco Island and Everglades City, differences go deeper than a lack of Lilly Pulitzers and a dearth of Mercedes. It's not a story of the haves (Naples) and the have-nots (Marco and E.C.). Much of Marco Island is a real place to live—year-rounders' houses are modest, ranch-style homes built a couple of decades ago before the Deltona Corporation began building and the island heated up as a vacation destination. The heat is focused on the beach, where tall resort hotels and condos stretch for two miles along the strand on Collier Boulevard. Vacationers (often families) may never see much of the island, their eyes focused assiduously on the gorgeous warm water of the Gulf, the maze of mangrove islands just to the south, and whether their tans are even.

Everglades City and the little town to the south called Chokoloskee (that's pronounced "chuck-uh-LUSK-ee," not "chock-oh-losk-ee") are the end of civilization before you run into Everglades National Park. Some of the mystery and wildness of that park has rubbed off on these little towns, or maybe it's just that the residents, over generations, have self-selected an iconoclastic, entrepreneurial-unto-illegality, free-spirited bunch. Hang out at the Rod and Gun Club, or paddle a kayak through the quiet tunnels of mangroves, and you'll feel like you've entered the Wild West, only with gators.

PLANNING YOUR TIME

How much you do during a visit here depends on the size of your luggage. You need three utterly distinct sets of duds to blend in in Naples, Marco Island, and Everglades City. For urban, sophisticated Naples, you need clothing that could be described as millennial-preppy (Lacoste shirts, navy blue blazers sans brass buttons, maybe a pair of those weird red golfing pants); on Marco you need beachwear (no thong, please), and lots of it, and maybe a Hawaiian shirt; in Everglades City you need your oldest sneakers (what my dad calls "manure

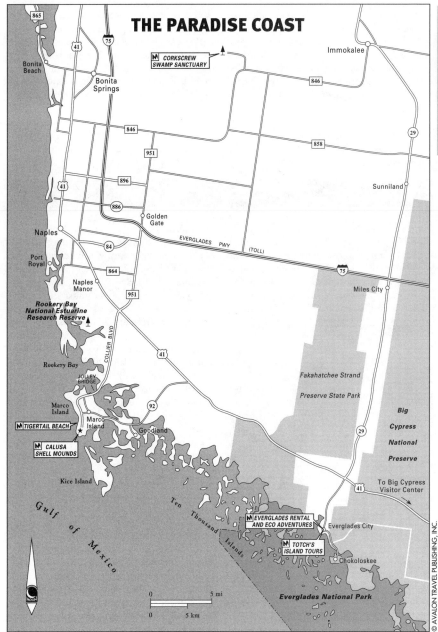

THE PARADISE COAST

The Paradise Coast

spreaders"), comfy T-shirts, and a constant sheen of bug spray.

Obviously, where you stay depends on what your primary objectives are. Naples's accommodations are generally fairly expensive, as are those on Marco Island. Everglades City is more budget-minded and a little lean on luxury. For romantic travel *a deux*—dinner at a fine restaurant, then a moonlit walk on the beach—you'll find plenty in Naples. A couple of fishing poles, a double kayak, and your sweetie paddling in sync with you—this is Everglades City. Family travelers are courted

most diligently on Marco Island, with most of the large hotels offering programs for kids.

Peak season in and around Naples is roughly December 23 to April 16. Rates for hotels reflect this, and you may save a bundle visiting instead in the late spring or early fall (when the weather in Naples and on Marco Island is divine). Everglades City, on the other hand, can be a little trickier as things heat up. The thick heat, the wet blanket of humidity, and dense fog of mosquitoes act as a real enthusiasm damper as you tramp around outdoors in the Everglades.

Naples

Naples has been dubbed "the Palm Beach" of Florida's Gulf Coast. With more than 50 golf courses, Naples has the highest ratio of greens to golfers in the United States. Beyond the links, Naples is known for world-class shopping, dining, and a preponderance of beautiful people. Although a stroll of trendy 5th Avenue is certainly

COURTESY OF NAPLES, MARCO ISLAND, EVERGLADES CVB

This great white egret exhibits breeding plumage. These birds were once hunted in this area just for their feathers.

reminiscent of the posh Atlantic Coast resort, the analogy breaks down as soon as one sees Naples's tranquil beauty, which begins just five miles out of town: the Rookery Bay National Estuarine Research Reserve (with sprawling mangroves and a rainbow of rare birds), Big Cypress National Preserve to the east, and the untamed mystery of Everglades National Park.

And then there are the nine miles of sun-soaked, white-sand beaches. A locus of sun-worshipping these days, the Naples shorefront was once populated by the Calusa people. In the late 1860s, Roger Gordon and Joe Wiggins were the area's first white settlers, drawn to the abundant fish and mild climate—a climate that was often compared to the bay in Naples, Italy. (Thus the name.) In 1887, a group of wealthy Kentuckians, led by Walter N. Haldeman, owner of the *Louisville Courier-Journal,* purchased enormous parcels of land in the town of Naples. Quickly gaining a reputation as a winter resort, Naples boasted a glamorous social life that revolved around the exclusive Naples Hotel, a magnet for celebrities at the turn of the 20th century.

As their first civic act, Haldeman and the Naples Town Improvement Company set to work building a 600-foot-long wooden pier in a T shape to allow large ships to dock easily. Completed in 1888, the pier was destroyed and rebuilt three times (most recently demolished by Hurricane Donna in 1960) and remains the center of the town's fishing activity.

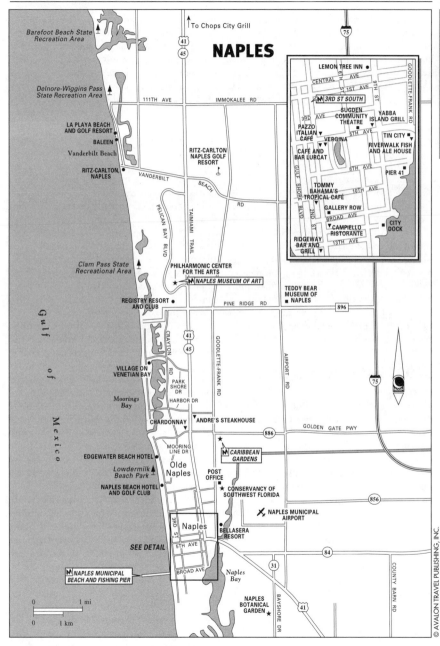

NAPLES

To Chops City Grill

Barefoot Beach State
Recreation Area

Delnore-Wiggins Pass
State Recreation Area

LA PLAYA BEACH
AND GOLF RESORT
BALEEN
Vanderbilt Beach
RITZ-CARLTON,
NAPLES

Clam Pass State
Recreational Area

Gulf

of

Mexico

REGISTRY RESORT
AND CLUB

111TH AVE   IMMOKALEE RD

VANDERBILT   BEACH   RD

RITZ-CARLTON
NAPLES GOLF
RESORT

PELICAN BAY BLVD
TAMIAMI TRAIL

PHILHARMONIC CENTER
FOR THE ARTS
NAPLES MUSEUM OF ART

PINE RIDGE RD

TEDDY BEAR
MUSEUM OF
NAPLES

896

LEMON TREE INN
CENTRAL   AVE
3RD ST SOUTH
SUGDEN
COMMUNITY
THEATRE
PAZZO
ITALIAN
CAFE
VERGINA
CAFE AND
BAR LURCAT
YABBA
ISLAND GRILL
TIN CITY
RIVERWALK FISH
AND ALE HOUSE
PIER 41
TOMMY
BAHAMA'S
TROPICAL CAFE
GALLERY ROW
CAMPIELLO
RISTORANTE
CITY
DOCK
RIDGEWAY
BAR AND
GRILL

GOODLETTE-FRANK RD
1ST AVE
9TH ST
3RD AVE
5TH AVE
GULF SHORE BLVD
2ND ST
8TH AVE
10TH AVE
BROAD AVE
13TH AVE

CRAYTON RD

41
45

GOODLETTE-FRANK RD

AIRPORT RD

75

MOON

Village on
Venetian Bay

Moorings
Bay

CHARDONNAY

PARK
SHORE
DR

HARBOR DR

ANDRE'S STEAKHOUSE

GOLDEN GATE PWY

886

EDGEWATER BEACH HOTEL
Lowdermilk
Beach Park
NAPLES BEACH HOTEL
AND GOLF CLUB

MOORING
LINE DR

Olde
Naples

POST
OFFICE

CARIBBEAN
GARDENS

CONSERVANCY OF
SOUTHWEST FLORIDA

NAPLES MUNICIPAL
AIRPORT

856

3RD ST
5TH AVE
BROAD AVE

Naples

SEE DETAIL

NAPLES MUNICIPAL
BEACH AND FISHING PIER

BELLASERA
RESORT

Naples
Bay

31

84

41

NAPLES
BOTANICAL
GARDEN

BAYSHORE DR

COUNTY BARN RD

0   1 mi
0   1 km

© AVALON TRAVEL PUBLISHING, INC.

At the western end of 12th Avenue South, locals and visitors alike congregate at the pier, but the city has a number of draws that are broadly distributed around town. The shopping district nearest the pier is called Old Marine Market Place or, alternately, Tin City. For more upscale commerce, walk along 5th Avenue, between 3rd and 9th Streets South, chockablock with stylish shops, restaurants, and cafés. Not far from there, in the center of town, the 13 acres of the Conservancy of Southwest Florida provide opportunities for canoe tours and nature hikes, as well as aviaries and a serpentarium (that's a snake house).

Boosters often describe Naples as the crown jewel of southwest Florida. The jewel that sparkles brightest may just be the downtown beach, arguably the finest city beach in Florida. Accessed at the Gulf end of each avenue—the downtown is a grid, streets run north and south, avenues run east and west—the beach has ample metered parking (bring quarters). There you may find a loggerhead sea turtle nest, a swirl of prehistoric-looking pelicans, or any of the other allures that have made Naples a vacation spot among the cognoscenti for the past 150 years.

SPORTS AND RECREATION

Beaches

Stop someone on the street in Naples and put them on the spot: Quick, what's the greatest thing about this town? Some of them will immediately point to the cultural amenities (museums, theater, cosmopolitan restaurants, incredible shopping), others will unswervingly steer you to the beaches. Who's right depends on your own predilections. There are 11 miles of stunning beach and nature preserve bordering the Gulf of Mexico in Naples that exert their magnetic pull on millions of would-be beach bums from around the globe.

The two most notable beaches are at either end of Naples—to the south, **Clam Pass State Recreational Area** (at the end of Seagate Dr., 239/353-0404, $3 parking, 8 A.M.–sunset) and to the north, **Delnor-Wiggins Pass State Recreation Area** (11100 Gulfshore Dr., five miles west of I-75, Exit 17, 239/597-6196, $4 parking, five

parking areas, 8 A.M.–sunset). Clam Pass consists of 35 acres of mangrove forest, rolling dunes, and 3,200 feet of white-sand beach. There's a three-quarter-mile boardwalk from a high-rise development through the mangroves and out to the beach. It's easily walkable (and you're likely to see eagles, ospreys, and waddling, pillbug-like armadillos along the way), but you can also take a fun, free tram that runs continuously throughout the day. Once at the beach, there are kayak, canoe, sailboard, and catamaran rentals. The water is shallow and the surf mild, a perfect combination for a family day at the beach. Clam Pass also contains a concession area and picnic pavilions.

Delnor-Wiggins regularly makes Dr. Beach's (a.k.a. Dr. Stephen Leatherman of the University of Maryland) top 20 list of America's best beaches, the white sand swath framed by picturesque sea oats, sea grapes (Seminoles and early settlers ate their ripe berries, but it's a seriously acquired taste), and cabbage palms. Delnor-Wiggins is on a narrow barrier island separated by a maze of mangrove swamp and tidal creek, and boasts a nature trail and observation tower from which to spy on the abundant wildlife. It's a superior shelling beach, and Wiggins Pass generates much enthusiasm amongst anglers. Again, the water is shallow, with a gentle slope and calm surf suitable for swimming. There are picnic facilities, a lifeguard on duty, and a boat ramp. (Caution: Stay out of the dunes and don't pick the sea grass, which is protected due to its important role as a sand stabilizer.)

Other beaches in the area would be star attractions anywhere but here, but the wealth of possibilities make **Lowdermilk Beach Park** (Gulf Shore Blvd. S, 239/263-6078), **Vanderbilt Beach** (near the Ritz-Carlton at the end of Vanderbilt Dr., 239/353-0404), and **Barefoot Beach State Recreation Area,** also known as **Lely Barefoot Beach** (take U.S. 41 to Bonita Beach Road and head west, 239/353-0404) "also rans" here in Naples. All of them have restrooms and picnic facilities, are open sunrise to sunset, and charge $3 for parking. In addition, Lowdermilk has lively sand volleyball courts (all the guidebooks say the play is "world class," but I certainly didn't see any Olympic hopefuls, or even particularly impressive play); Vanderbilt offers exceptional bird-watching; and Barefoot boasts a learning center with exhibits on sea turtles and shorebirds as well as a nature trail.

Naples Municipal Beach & Fishing Pier

For a more urban beach experience, stroll along **Naples Municipal Beach & Fishing Pier** (access the pier at 12th St. and Gulf Shore Blvd., just south of downtown, 239/434-4696, open 24 hours, no fee, metered parking near entrance). Known locally as "The Pier," the 1,000-foot structure that juts into the Gulf attracts anglers, new and old (best fishing months: May–July and Sept.–Oct.). There's a bait house, fish cleaning tables, chickee shelter, restrooms, and concessions on the pier, which was originally built in 1888 as a freight and passenger dock. The pier is a symbol of the locals' tenacity and civic pride, having been damaged by fire and hurricanes and rebuilt repeatedly in 1910, 1926, and 1960. It's perhaps

Fishing opportunities abound from area shorelines, piers, and bridges.

COURTESY OF NAPLES, MARCO ISLAND, EVERGLADES CVB

the most photographed spot in Naples, the emerald green Gulf water and wide swath of beach flanking it on either side. The beach's proximity to downtown (and the stretch of fancy houses known as "Millionaires' Row") makes it ideal for a moonlit stroll after dinner or even a bit of sandy respite from an afternoon of serious shopping.

Nature

For all of Naples's effete indoor cultural enticements, nature exerts its own draw on visitors. The greater Naples area offers several outstanding—and easily accessible to those with disabilities, seniors, or the stroller-bound—opportunities to commune with nature.

Corkscrew Swamp Sanctuary

In Collier County, huge swaths of bald cypress forest stood until right around World War II. Logging quickly decimated most of it, with just one virgin stand of cypress left in southwest Florida—the Corkscrew Swamp near Immokalee, now Corkscrew Swamp Sanctuary (take I-75 to Exit 111, go approximately 15 miles, turn left on Sanctuary Rd., 375 Sanctuary Rd. W, Naples, 239/348-9151, 7 A.M.–7:30 P.M. daily April 12–September 30, 7 A.M.–5:30 P.M. October 1–April 11, $10 adults, $6 college students, $5 Audubon Society members, $4 children 6–18, children under 6 free). It offers visitors a 2.25-mile raised boardwalk—also a 1-mile trail if the longer one sounds daunting, and benches and rain shelters along the way—through four distinct local environments: a pine upland, a wet prairie, a cypress forest, and a marsh. Interpretive signs along the boardwalk give you the basics, but the docent-led tours are tremendous (some of the docents seem a little crotchety and dictatorial, but stick with it), and there's a field guide and a kids' activity book that you can pick up at the admissions desk. There's a birders' checklist and a white board for birders to jot down what they've seen for the benefit of those who've just arrived—make no mistake, birders here can be dead serious, and don't get them talking about wood stork nesting. (Wood storks are these magnificent endangered wading birds that often nest here—up close, the ugliest birds ever with nubby, featherless heads,

TEE TIME

Naples isn't called the golf capital of the world for nothing. Here are the courses available to visitors, plus the driving ranges and pro shops. All of the greens fees quoted fluctuate seasonally and according to the time of day. Call ahead.

The Courses:
Arrowhead Golf Course 2205 Heritage Greens Dr., 239/596-1000
semiprivate, 18 holes, 6,832 yards, par 72, course rating 73.4, slope 132
Greens fees: $35 before 10 A.M., $27 10 A.M.–2:30 P.M., $23 after 2:30 P.M.

Boyne South Golf Course 18100 Royal Tree Pkwy., 239/732-0034
public, 18 holes, 6,476 yards, par 72, course rating 71.1, slope 122
Greens fees: $70 for 18 holes, $35 for 9 holes

Cedar Hammock Golf & Country Club 8660 Cedar Hammock Blvd., 239/793-1134
public May–October, 18 holes, 6,834 yards, par 72, course rating 71.2, slope 128
Greens fees: $36, cart included

Cypress Woods Golf and Country Club 3525 Northbrook Dr., 239/592-7860
semiprivate, 18 holes, 6,330 yards, par 72, course rating 71.7, slope 136
Greens fees: $55 before noon, $50 after noon, $25 after 3:30 P.M., cart included

Eagle Creek Country Club 11 Cypress View Dr., 239/793-0500
public, 18 holes, 6,909 yards, par 72, course rating 73.8, slope 138
Greens fees: $50–79

Hibiscus Golf Club 175 Doral Cir., 239/774-3559
semiprivate, 18 holes, 6,540 yards, par 72, course rating 70.5, slope 125
Greens fees: $75 before noon, $60 afternoon, cart included

Lely Flamingo Island Club 8004 Lely Resort Blvd., 239/793-2223
Classics Course: private, 18 holes, 6,805 yards, par 72, course rating 72.4, slope 128
Flamingo Course: resort, 18 holes, 7,171 yards, par 72, course rating 73.9, slope 135
Mustang Course: resort, 18 holes, 7,217 yards, par 72, course rating 75.3, slope 141
Greens fees: $45–149 depending on the month for both Flamingo and Mustang courses, cart included

Marriott Marco Island Resort and Golf Club 400 Collier Blvd. S, Marco Island, 239/793-6060
resort, 18 holes, 6,898 yards, par 72, course rating 73.4, slope 137
Greens fees: $149 before noon, $105 after noon, $60 after 3 P.M.

Naples Beach Hotel and Golf Club 851 Gulf Shore Blvd. N, 239/261-2222
resort, 18 holes, 6,488 yards, par 72, course rating 71.2, slope 129
Greens fees: $120 before noon, $95 after noon, $55 after 3 P.M.

Naples Grande Golf Club 7760 Golden Gate Pkwy., 239/659-3700
resort, 18 holes, 7,102 yards, par 72, course rating 75.1, slope 143
Greens fees: $185, $160 after 1:30 P.M.

Quality Inn and Suites Golf Resort 4100 Golden Gate Pkwy., 239/455-9498
resort, 18 holes, 6,564 yards, par 72, course rating 70.8, slope 125
Greens fees: $70 until 2 P.M., $55 after 2 P.M., $25 after 4 P.M., cart included

Riviera Golf Club of Naples 48 Marseille Dr., 239/774-1081
public, 18 holes, 4,090 yards, par 62, course rating 60.4, slope 95
Greens fees: $45, $38 after 2 P.M., cart included

Tiburon Golf Club 2620 Tiburon Dr., 239/594-2040
North Course: resort, 9 holes, 3,693 yards, par 36, course rating N/A, slope N/A
South Course: resort, 9 holes, 3,477 yards, par 36, course rating N/A, slope N/A
West Course: resort, 9 holes, 3,500 yards, par 36, course rating N/A, slope N/A
Greens fees: $250 before noon, $200 after noon, $140 after 3 P.M.

Valencia Golf Course 1725 Double Eagle Trail, 239/352-0777
public, 18 holes, 7,145 yards, par 72, course rating 74.3, slope 130
Greens fees: $78 before noon, $68 after noon, cart included

Driving Ranges:
Briarwood Golf & Practice Center 5051 Radio Rd., 239/262-4955
Ferguson Golf Center 9100 Immokalee Rd., 239/353-3699
Naples Golf Center 7700 Davis Blvd., 239/775-3337
North Naples Golf Range 16979 Old 41, 239/566-1303

Pro Shops:
Coral Isle Golf Center 4748 Championship Dr., 239/732-6900
Different Strokes Golf & Tennis Outlet 6308 Trail Blvd., 239/514-0065
Edwin Watts Golf 3980 Tamiami Trail N, 239/403-0615
Fix Up Stix 1101 Sun Century Rd., 239/591-3743
For the Love of Golf 9765 Tamiami Trail N, 239/566-3395
Golf Balls Galore & More 2181 J&C Blvd., 239/597-6528
Naples Golf Center 7700 Davis Blvd., 239/775-3337
Naples Golf Co. 1029 Industrial Blvd., 239/643-5577
Pro-Am Discount Golf & Tennis
13000 Tamiami Trail N, 239/597-1222
Pro Line Golf And Sportswear 680
Tamiami Trail N, 239/643-1599

COURTESY OF NAPLES, MARCO ISLAND, EVERGLADES CVB

Greater Naples is world-renowned as a golf destination.

but they have gorgeous white-plumed bodies trimmed elegantly with black.) It's also a great place to see gators and rare orchids.

Rookery Bay National Estuarine Research Reserve

Another worthwhile day trip is to be had at Rookery Bay National Estuarine Research Reserve (about 13 miles south of Naples, 300 Tower Rd., 239/417-6310, 9 A.M.–4 P.M. daily, adults $5, children 6–12 $3, children under 6 free). Rookery Bay and Ten Thousand Islands estuarine ecosystem is one of the few pristine mangrove estuaries in North America, with 110,000 acres of forest, islands, bays, interconnected tidal embayments, lagoons, and tidal streams that are home to bald eagles, cotton-candy-pink roseate spoonbills, and lots of other birdlife. You can explore the estuary on your own by kayak or volunteer to assist scientists with environmental research. They opened a new 16,500-square-foot Environmental Learning Center in 2004, with 5,000 square feet of interactive exhibits and a visitors center, four marine research laboratories, a coastal training center, and five aquaria. (The big fish at the entrance, by the way, is a polka-dot batfish.) The coolest part of the center is the climb-in "bubble" that allows visitors to observe the many creatures that live among the roots of a 14-foot mangrove in the center aquarium.

The **Briggs Nature Center** (401 Shell Island Rd., Naples, 239/775-8569) is within the reserve, fairly close to Marco Island, and offers a lovely half-mile boardwalk through a hammock to a coastal pond and a fairly new butterfly garden worth an hour in itself for quiet contemplation of all the fluttering bits of color. There's an interpretive center where you can get maps of the wonderful trails in the area, as well as boat tours and canoe and kayak rentals.

Big Cypress National Preserve

This part of Florida also boasts the first national preserve in the national park system, the Big Cypress National Preserve (Oasis Visitors Center, midway between Naples and Miami on U.S. 41, 239/695-4111, 9 A.M.–4:30 P.M. daily,

WALKING TREES

This area owes much of its landmass to the mangrove tree. They are often called walking trees because they hover above the water, their arching prop roots resembling so many spindly legs. The mangrove is one of only a handful of tree species on planet Earth that can withstand having its roots sitting in ocean water, immersed daily by rising tides, and that thrives in little soil and high levels of sulfides. The mangrove's hardiness is just one among many of its idiosyncrasies, however.

Mangroves are natural land builders. Seed tubules about the heft and length of an excellent Cuban cigar sprout on the parent tree, drop off, and bob in the brackish water until they lodge on an oyster bar or a snag in the shallows. There, the seed begins to grow into a tree, its leaves dropping and getting trapped along with seaweed and other plant debris. This organic slurry is the bottom of the food chain, supplying food, breeding area, and sanctuary to countless tiny marine creatures. In addition, it is the foundation upon which a little island or "key" begins to take shape, this buildup of sediment and debris creating a thick layer of organic peat upon which other plant species begin to grow. This first tree drops more seed tubules, which get stuck in the soft mud around the base of the parent tree and begin to grow. Soon, it's an impenetrable tangle of trees and roots extravagant enough to support birdlife and other animals.

Three types predominate in the Everglades and Ten Thousand Islands: The red mangrove forms a wide band of trees on the outermost part of each island, facing the open sea. The red mangrove encircles the black mangrove, which in turn encircles the white mangrove at the highest, driest part of each mangrove island (they are the least tolerant of having their roots sitting in saltwater). The mangroves' leathery evergreen leaves fall and stain the water a tobacco-colored tannic brown, but in fact the mangroves and all of the species dependent upon them do much to keep the waters clean and pure.

For all these reasons, mangrove trees are protected by federal, state, and local laws. Do not injure, spindle, mutilate, or even taunt a mangrove or face steep penalties.

free admission), contiguous with Everglades National Park and just about as big. The preserve encompasses 720,000 acres of the Big Cypress Swamp of southwest Florida—terrain is varied, with swamp, freshwater marshes, forests of slash pine and palmetto, and wet prairies containing abundant wildlife. But how best to investigate this vast area?

Hike it. The **Florida Trail** stretches across the state from Gulf Islands National Seashore through the Big Cypress National Preserve. It's wonderful hiking, which the park rangers divide into three logical sections. Part 1, **Loop Road to U.S. 41** (6.5 miles one-way) begins at Loop Road about 13 miles from its east end on U.S. 41. The other end is across from the **Big Cypress Visitors Center** (53 miles east of Naples on U.S. 41). The easy path meanders through dwarf cypress and prairies and crosses through Robert's Lake Strand (can be very wet during rainy months). Part 2, more for the seasoned backpacker, **U.S. 41 to I-75** (28 miles one-way) has trailheads on U.S. 41 near Big Cypress Visitors Center and on I-75 at the rest area at mile marker 63. A harder hike (for which you'll need to pack in all your own water), it takes you through hardwood hammocks, pinelands, prairies, and cypress. There is high-ground camping at the 13-mile mark. Part 3, **I-75 to Preserve North Boundary** (8 miles one-way) follows an old oil road through hardwood, prairie, and pine forest. (Part of this trail is restricted to members of the Florida Trail Association.)

Canoe it. The park's main canoe trail begins at U.S. 41 and follows the **Turner River** until it ends in Chokoloskee Bay (about a five-hour paddle). You can also put in at the Everglades National Park Gulf Coast Visitors Center. There's another trail called the **Halfway Creek Canoe Trail,** for which you can put in at Seagrape Drive and paddle south past Plantation Island.

Big Cypress also accommodates camping, hunting, biking, and sightseeing by car. You'll need to go to the visitors center (or visit the National Park Service website at www.nps.gov/bicy) to see an informative 15-minute movie about the preserve, view a small wildlife exhibit, and pick up literature and books about the preserve.

If all this sounds like too much driving followed by too much walking, the **Naples Botanical Garden** (4820 Bayshore Dr., Naples, 239/643-7275) won't tax you too much. It's still in the midst of gearing up, but it will be a living botanical museum within minutes of downtown, featuring exotic plant collections, history exhibitions, and lecture series.

Boat Tours

So many ways to get out on the calm Gulf waters and Naples Bay, wind through the Ten Thousand Islands, and idle along the Gordon, Barron, Marco, or one of the area's many other rivers. Here's just a sampling of the tours to be had. The *Sweet Liberty* (City Dock, 880 12th Ave. S, 239/793-3525) is a 53-foot sailing catamaran available for public tours and private charters. Departing from Boat Haven, the boat offers shelling tours (9:30 A.M.–12:30 P.M., $38 adults, $15 children), sightseeing tours (1:30–3:30 P.M., $25 adults, $15 children), and sunset tours (2 hours, $25 adults, $15 children). On all of the cruises, the boat is trailed by a playful bevy of dolphins and you'll have an opportunity to see the lovely homes of Port Royal.

The *Lady Brett* (departing from Tin City, 1200 5th Ave. S, 239/263-4949, 10 A.M., noon, 2 P.M., 4 P.M., and one hour before sunset, $25 adults, children under 12 half price) offers five one-hour narrated cruises daily out on the lovely waters of Naples Bay, and the double-decker *Double Sunshine* (departing from Tin City, 1200 5th Ave. S, 239/263-4949, 7:45 A.M. and 1 P.M., $55 adults, $50 children under 12) takes folks out on half-day deep-sea fishing trips aboard a 45-foot USCG-inspected vessel equipped with bathrooms. Rod, reel, bait, and fishing license are included, but bring your own drinks and lunch. If you want to wet a line in the Ten Thousand Islands, **Captain Paul** (departing from Tin City, 1200 5th Ave. S, 239/263-4949, $50 adults, $45 children under 12) takes people on half-day bay fishing trips on a comfortable pontoon boat.

A fancier experience, the *Naples Princess* (departing from Port-O-Call Marina, 550 Port-O-Call Way, 239/649-2275, $23.95–43.95) has narrated breakfast, lunch, and sunset buffet dinner cruises on a 93-foot air-conditioned luxury yacht that can accommodate 149 passengers.

And **Sail Kahuna** (13635 Vanderbilt Rd., 239/642-7704) has a range of nice boat trips in and around the Ten Thousand Islands, the most fun of which is the Big Kahuna Luau (10 A.M.–4 P.M. Tues. and Thurs., $85 adults, $50 children 12 and under), in which a 44-foot sailing catamaran takes people out for a day of sun among the mangrove islands near Marco Island, where there's kayaking, playing bocce, shelling, etc., all culminating in a beach buffet provided by Moran's Barge Marina. Sail Kahuna also has a smaller catamaran for shelling, dolphin-watching, and sightseeing tours.

SIGHTS

Trolley Tours

A good place to start and orient yourself in Naples is with a long ride aboard a **Naples Trolley Tour** (1010 6th Ave. S, 239/262-1914, hourly 8:30 A.M.–5 P.M., adults $18, children $8). The open-air trolley has a narrated tour of more than 100 local places of note, including historic Naples Pier and Tin City. The tour itself lasts about two hours, but you can embark and disembark to explore, catching the next trolley when it suits you. Tickets are available at all boarding stops, but to get oriented you might want to begin at the Smith General Store, the trolley depot and welcome center.

Galleries

Naples has 94 commercial art galleries at last count, wedged in among the shops of downtown, largely congregated along the length of **3rd Street South,** on what is called "Gallery Row" on Broad Avenue off 3rd Street South, and along **5th Avenue** (many between the 600 and 800 blocks). *American Style Magazine* named Naples in the top 25 arts destinations in the U.S., with good reason. Whether you're looking for carved African masks, Limoges boxes, or contemporary photography, window-shopping downtown is the way to go. To see the work of many local artists, stop in at the **von Liebig Art Center** (585 Park St., next to Cambier Park, 239/262-6517, 10 A.M.–4 P.M.

Broad Avenue at 3rd Street South in Naples has so many art galleries, it's known as Gallery Row.

COURTESY OF NAPLES, MARCO ISLAND, EVERGLADES CVB

Mon.–Sat., free admission). It houses the Naples Art Association and features changing exhibitions in five galleries.

Ⓜ Naples Museum of Art

The Naples Museum of Art is the crown jewel of Naples's cultural attractions, located at the drop-dead-gorgeous $19.5 million Philharmonic Center for the Arts (5833 Pelican Bay Blvd., Naples, 239/597-1900, www.thephil.org, 10 A.M.–4 P.M. Tues.–Sat., noon–4 P.M. Sun. May 2–Oct. 31; closed Aug.–Labor Day; open until 5 P.M. Nov. 2–May 1; general admission $8 adults, $4 students, but some exhibits require an additional admission ticket). The visual arts center, opened in 2000, is a three-story, 30,000-square-foot museum with 15 galleries. Exhibits are varied and expertly curated, from a small antique walking stick show to the underwater-phantasmagorical blown glasswork of Dale Chihuly, from an Andy Warhol print show to Modern Mexican Masters. Beyond the permanent collection and visiting shows, the space itself is a work of art with a huge glass-domed conservatory, stunning entrance gates by metal artist Albert Paley, and a spectacular Chihuly chandelier.

In my experience, docents here are about as crackerjack as at any museum, able to inform, guide, and cajole you into learning a great deal. There are also film series and lectures held at the museum—many of them sell out, but you can peruse upcoming events and buy tickets via the website.

Collier County Museums

Five minutes east of downtown Naples, history enthusiasts flock to the Naples site of the Collier County Museums (3301 Tamiami Trail E, Naples, 239/774-8476, 9 A.M.–5 P.M. Mon.–Fri., until 4 P.M. Sat., free admission). There are two other locations of the museum, the Museum of the Everglades in Everglades City and the Immokalee Pioneer Museum at the home of the Robert Roberts family, but it's the Naples part that's worth the most time. Established in 1978, the museum offers interpretive exhibits that illuminate the history, archaeology, and development of this part of Florida, as well as a five-acre botanical park with a native plant garden, orchid house, two early Naples cottages, a logging locomotive, swamp buggies and, somewhat strangely, a World War II Sherman tank. The museum holds the **Old Florida Festival** every year on the first weekend in November—a hoot for people who like reenactments and historical pageantry.

Palm Cottage

Another walk through Naples history can be had at Palm Cottage (137 12th Ave. S, Naples, 239/261-8164, $5 donation suggested). On the National Register of Historic Places, it's the second oldest house in Collier County, built for Henry Watterson, the editor of the *Louisville Courier-Journal*. It reopened recently after a significant facelift that includes new woodwork, a new roof, and improved landscaping. The house is one of the few remaining "tabbie mortar" structures in the area—a mortar goo made from burned seashells mixed with lime and seawater. The Palm Cottage is now home to the Naples Historical Society. Tours of the house are offered 1–3:30 P.M. Monday–Friday. (You may get a broader historical picture by picking up a copy of the pictorial history titled *Naples,* published in early 2005 and compiled by the former Naples Historical Society executive director, Lynne Howard Frazer. It contains fascinating pictures and oral histories and is available at most local bookstores.)

Southwest Florida Holocaust Museum

Growing out of an exhibit created by Golden Gate Middle School students in Naples, the Southwest Florida Holocaust Museum (4760 Tamiami Trail N, 239/263-9200, www.swflhm.org, 1–4 P.M. Tues.–Fri. and Sun., $5 suggested donation) is another small history museum. The students collected more than 300 death camp and Holocaust artifacts, which constitute the bulk of the exhibit. Docents lead tours for individuals as well as local school groups. The museum has also embarked on an oral history project with local survivors, liberators, and others, and it installs traveling Holocaust exhibits in local schools as well.

◪ Caribbean Gardens

Adults will be able to while away days in Naples with the sophisticated pleasures of dining, shopping, the arts, and so forth. But as every parent knows, the kids must be entertained with regularity, or mutiny is assured. The single most mutually agreeable family attraction in Naples is Caribbean Gardens (1590 Goodlette-Frank Rd., 239/262-5409, www.napleszoo.com, 9:30 A.M.–5:30 P.M. daily, adults $15.95, children 4–15 $9.95, children 3 and under free), an "Old Florida" attraction in the best sense. By that I mean that it's slow, sweet, pokey, without any whiff of glitz or Disney slickness.

It began as a botanical garden, founded by botanist Henry Nehrling in 1919. The original garden was expanded in the 1950s by Julius Fleischmann, and the Tetzlaff family introduced the rare animals in 1969. In much of the 52-acre garden, the animals are an afterthought, the incredible native and exotic plants taking center stage. There's a cypress hammock, a cactus garden, a dense wall of mondo-huge bamboo, banyan, and other trees ensnared in all directions by strangler fig (in this part of Florida, nights aren't warm enough for the strangler fig to create a tall canopy and kill its host tree, so they live in a certain kind of dramatic symbiosis, the strangler resembling a scary vegetable octopus).

Kids will prefer the baby alligator feeding shows, and be sure to catch the Planet Predator and Meet the Keeper live animal shows. Seeing these animals up close inspires a certain amount of awe, but it's the keepers' wry over-the-heads-of-babes banter that makes the shows so entertaining. There's also a wonderful short boat ride (also with an archly ironic narration) that takes you past a bunch of tiny islands from which various species of primate will grimace at you and sometimes throw unspeakable things.

The zoo has a few new additions worth noting: The Panther Glade separates you from the big cats by a thrillingly thin sheet of glass; there are two new rare and beautiful Indochinese tigers; and the zoo has launched a new multimedia show called *Serpents: Fangs & Fiction* to shed some light on these slithery stars.

Other Attractions for Kids

Head out of town on I-75, and you'll find the **Teddy Bear Museum of Naples** (2511 Pine Ridge Rd., Naples, 239/598-2711, www.teddy-museum.com, 10 A.M.–5 P.M. Tues.–Sat., adults $8, children $3), which is worth an hour or so of your time. The place has more than 5,000 teddy bears arranged into diorama-like scenes (there's a wedding, a teddy bear picnic, a parade—you get the picture). There are handmade artisanal bears and manufactured bears, Pooh bears and Paddington bears, bear bronzes and crystal bears. In the spring the museum even offers weekend bear-making classes ($35 per student). It's all good until you get to the gift shop. Brace for impact.

If the weather is nice during your visit, which it doubtless will be, kids enjoy a round of mini golf at **Coral Cay Adventure Golf** (2205 Tamiami Trail E, one mile east of Tin City, 239/793-4999, 10 A.M.–11 P.M. daily, adults $7, children 5–11 $6, children 4 and under $3), with its exotic tropical setting with caves, reefs, and a waterfall. There's a snack bar with semi-real food, slushies, and ice cream, and a game room as well.

King Richards Family Fun Park (6780 N.

Airport Rd., 239/598-2042, 11 A.M.–9 P.M. Sun.–Thurs., until 10 P.M. Fri. and Sat., admission to all amusements $24.95, seniors $15.50) is another family crowd pleaser, with go-carts, bumper boats, batting cages, a pee-wee roller coaster, and a dozen other training-wheels-type amusement rides.

For a real cheap family date, head out to see the **Gulf Coast Skimmers Water Ski Show** (Sugden Regional Park at Lake Avalon, one mile east of the Collier County Courthouse, turn right on Avalon Dr. and follow the signs, 239/269-7625, 6:30 P.M. Sat. May–Nov., 3 P.M. Sun. Oct.–Apr., admission free). A bunch of wholesome local teens get out there on water skis to form pyramids and do ballet, barefooting, jumping, and a little physical comedy (complete with costumes). The organization is a Christian nonprofit that enables some disadvantaged kids to try out their skiing chops and take part in a sport that's notoriously the purview of the affluent.

ARTS AND ENTERTAINMENT
Music and Theater

The **Philharmonic Center for the Arts** (5833 Pelican Bay Blvd., 239/597-1900, www.the-phil.org, ticket prices and times vary, box office hours 10 A.M.–4 P.M. Mon.–Fri.) is an outstanding venue hosting more than 400 events a year including world-class dance, opera, classical, and popular music, and traveling Broadway musicals. The center contains a 1,221-seat main hall and a 200-seat black box theater. The **Naples Philharmonic Orchestra** (239/597-0606) performs here with more than 120 concerts per year including classics, pops, chamber orchestras, and numerous educational performances. The **Miami City Ballet** is in residence performing four programs with the orchestra during the season.

There isn't any resident professional theater company in Naples, although the **Sugden Community Theatre** (701 5th Ave. S, 239/263-7990) is home to the 40-year-old **Naples Players**, a fairly amateurish community theater troupe that stages somewhere around 14 musicals, comedies, dramas, and children's productions (they also host a program called KidzAct with musical theater workshops for kids) annually. The Sugden also screens a "Films on Fifth" series, mostly independent and art house films. And the **Naples Dinner Theater** (1025 Piper Blvd., 239/514-7827) may help you scratch a theater itch with a dinner buffet and a musical or comedy (something like *Victor, Victoria* or *Cabaret*).

And for mainstream movies, head to the 20-plex **Regal Hollywood 20** (6006 Hollywood Dr., 239/597-4252), the **Towne Centre 6 Theater** (3855 Tamiami Trail E, 239/774-4800), **Pavilion Cinemas** (833 Vanderbilt Beach Rd., 239/596-0008), or even the **Naples Drive-In** (7700 E. Davis Blvd., 239/774-4661) for usually family-oriented comedies.

ACCOMMODATIONS

$50–150

My favorite midpriced hotel in Naples is the **Lemon Tree Inn** (250 9th St. S, 239/262-1414, www.lemontreeinn.com, $80–160). The owner recently remodeled the 35 rooms, adding new carpeting, linens, and bedroom furniture. Some rooms have mahogany four-poster beds. There's a sweet little gazebo and swimming pool, where breakfast is served each morning. But the real draw is the people—the owner is incredibly warm, as are all the people he employs. It has an Old Florida charm married with a sophisticated Naples aesthetic. Oh, and there's free lemonade in the office, very quenching after a long day of beach bumming.

In terms of other decent midpriced chains, **The Holiday Inn Naples** (1100 9th St. N, $79–139) is in a good location with pleasant rooms, a nice pool, and easy access to the beach and shopping; **Comfort Inn on the Bay** (1221 5th Ave. S, 239/649-5800, $50–180) has spacious rooms, a very central location, and a full-service marina; and **Hampton Inn** (2630 Northbrooke Plaza Dr., 239/596-1299, $120–150) is off Exit 111, closer to I-75 and Corkscrew Sanctuary Swamp.

Over $150

Where to even begin? Naples is awash in luxury hotels—so much so, in fact, that the Ritz-Carlton boasts not one property, but two in town. Once you enter the luxury accommodation price point, where to stay depends largely on your priorities. If you want an urban experience, so you can roll out of bed and be wandering the downtown shops within minutes, consider **The Inn on Fifth** (699 5th Ave. S, 239/403-8777, www .naplesinn.com, $270–400), a boutique hotel filled with Mediterranean charm. The 87 rooms are truly elegant, with sliding French doors to a balcony or terrace. The common space features burbling fountains, courtyards, and lavish gardens—all at the center of downtown. The inn opened the Asian-influenced **Spa on Fifth** in 2004, purportedly adhering to feng shui principles.

Not far away is the **Hotel Escalante** (290 5th Ave. S, 239/659-3466, www.hotelescalante.com, $205–725), with 71 rooms and suites housed in eight buildings named after flowers (Azalea, Begonia, yada, yada). The garden estate is a great place to stay for the budding botanist, as the hotel's grounds are spectacular, all species labeled and attended to by a staff horticulturist. Inside, there's a wood-paneled library, a gorgeous reception area, and a wide courtyard that just begs for a few hours of sun worship. The rooms are subtly elegant, with Frette linens, mahogany plantation-style furniture, and the kind of bath amenities that make anyone feel like royalty. While the hotel isn't beachfront, it's really just steps away from the beach. It also has a small spa that is open to the public for luxurious (and not crazy expensive) massages, scrubs, and wraps.

On a slightly more residential street downtown, the **Trianon Old Naples** (955 7th Ave. S, 239/435-9600, www.trianon.com, $120–500) is another small luxury hotel with a pool, a lounge, off-street parking, and complimentary continental breakfast served in the lobby (although there's no on-site restaurant, so you can't order room service or just go downstairs for dinner). The 55 roomy guest rooms and three large one-bedroom suites have all the usual fine amenities with balconies, multiline phones, computer data ports, and easy access to Tin City and 5th Avenue South.

Relatively new in Naples, **Bellasera Resort** (221 9th St. S, 239/649-7333, $240–475) opened in 2003 and features 100 luxurious studios, one-, two-, and three-bedroom suites with kitchens and spacious living and dining areas, all with bold Tuscan-style architecture and decor. It's a AAA Four Diamond award-winner just far enough removed from the hubbub of 5th Avenue to seem restful. A heated outdoor pool, fitness center, Zizi Restaurant & Lounge, meeting space, and business center round out the amenities.

If your favorite time is tee time, there are several golfy wonderlands. The **Naples Beach Hotel & Golf Club** (851 Gulf Shore Blvd. N, 239/261-2222, www.naplesbeachhotel.com, $199–420) is a 125-acre beachfront resort with 318 guest rooms and suites, on-site championship golf, an award-winning tennis center, large beachside swimming pool, fitness center and spa, complimentary kids' program, four restaurants and an open-air beach bar from which to choose, and a handful of lovely boutiques. Opened in 1946, the hotel was renovated in 2002, with a new $5 million lobby with luxurious tropical decor and furnishings.

LaPlaya Beach & Golf Resort (9891 Gulf Shore Blvd. N, 239/597-3123, $300–1,400) was already a stunning property, but then it had its multimillion-dollar makeover in 2002, so it's *da bomb*. The 189 spacious guest rooms and suites are stunningly appointed (I could live here), with goose-down pillows and Frette linens to satisfy even the most persnickety sleeper. There are those cushy waffle-weave bathrobes, marble bathrooms with jetted tubs, a tremendous spa, twice-daily maid service. Oh, and there's golf. You have to drive a little over three miles from the hotel, but enthusiasts say the new Bob Cupp–designed course is worth it. It's an 18-hole, par 72, 6,907-yard championship layout with a driving range, practice area, and 12,000-square-foot clubhouse.

Not to be outdone, the **Ritz-Carlton Naples Golf Resort** (2600 Tiburon Dr., 239/593-2000, $419–900) has received kudos from *Golf Digest* as one of the best golf resorts in North America. And in fact all of the 295 guest rooms manage to look out on the sweeping vistas of the Greg Norman–designed Tiburon Golf Club. Guests can also enjoy the amenities at the sister Ritz-Carlton in town.

And if your aim is to have sand in your bed, or at least the beach within walking distance, there are several wonderful luxury hotels that fit the bill. The **Edgewater Beach Hotel** (1901 Gulf Shore Blvd. N, 239/262-6511, $200–900) is an intimate, 126-suite boutique hotel right on the beach. Many of the suites had a fairly hip redecoration in 2003. It's another AAA Four Diamond property, with a nice sixth-floor restaurant called The Club Dining Room. Guests also have dining and recreational privileges at the Registry Resort, its sister property.

Speaking of the **Registry Resort & Club** (475 Seagate Dr., 239/597-3232, $164–869), it's one of the area's most beloved landmarks, surrounded by 200 acres of tropical mangrove preserve, with beach access and five swimming pools. All tower rooms and suites have private balconies with great views. If you don't want to spend the dough to stay here, stop in one night at Luna, the resort's stylish nightclub.

The other **Ritz-Carlton, Naples** (280 Vanderbilt Beach Rd., 239/598-3300, $229–489) is a Mobil Five-Star, AAA Five-Diamond resort, all 463 rooms with stunning views of the Gulf of Mexico. There are seven on-site restaurants, tennis courts, a 33-treatment-room spa with fitness center, two pools, championship golf nearby at Tiburon, and white sand as far as the eye can see.

If you want to totally and completely get away from it all, there's **Key Island Estate** (800/770-SAND, www.keyislandestate.com, $2,000/day for up to 14 people). You get your own private island. Located on the eight-mile-long barrier Keewaydin Island between Naples and Marco Island, it's accessible only by boat and overlooks the Rookery Bay Reserve on one side and the Gulf of Mexico on the other. There's a master suite and two separate wings for additional guests, wraparound porches, huge open kitchen, and lovely detailing throughout. It's something to think about for weddings, corporate retreats, or big family getaways.

FOOD

In Tanzania they say "Jambo." In Papua New Guinea it's "Moning tru." In Australia, "G'day." But in Naples, the greeting goes like, "Have you been to [insert name of red-hot new restaurant here] yet?" It's one of those cities where everyone jostles in line to taste the doings of the latest macaroni maestro, the newest sushi shaman. Dining at the latest big hot spot is a form of social currency, made more delicious in the retelling. Of course, once the cat is out of the bag, he's free to claw your furniture. In high season, this means you need to make a reservation at most of the hip spots.

Festivals

At the beginning of May, there's the annual **Taste of Collier** in Naples. All the froufrou Naples restaurants showcase their wares in a one-day family-friendly festival.

5th Avenue South

There are a few dense concentrations of wonderful restaurants in downtown Naples; 5th has the greatest embarrassment of riches, assembled between 9th Street and 3rd Street. The gamut is impressive, from trendy to fancy "continental," covering a range of prices and ethnicities. The best ones are listed here from east at 9th (the beginning of downtown) to the west as it reaches the Gulf.

St. George & The Dragon (936 5th Ave. S, 239/262-6546, 11 A.M.–4 P.M. and 4–10 P.M. Mon.–Sat., $14–50) isn't trying to keep up with any of the trendy places nearby. It does what it's been doing best for more than 30 years, with moody lighting, a reason to get dressed up, and nostalgic continental fare like fat escargots redolent of garlic and dripping butter, or creamy Delmonico potatoes. Nearby **Pazzo Italian Café** (853 5th Ave. S, 239/434-8494, 5–10 P.M. weekdays, until 11 P.M. weekends, $15–28) presents diners with an instant conundrum—sit in the lovely modern dining room with its open bar and kitchen, or settle into one of the sidewalk tables through open French doors and watch the world stroll by? Pazzo makes a mean Bellini, those champagne and peach nectar cocktails that are the height of festivity, and lots of elegant spins on familiar Italian dishes. Worth trying are the grouper saltimbocca and the "Vincenzo," a molten chocolate cake oozing its way into soft

vanilla ice cream and raspberry coulis. Practically right next door is one of downtown's most happening places, **Chops City Grill** (837 5th Ave. S, 239/262-4677, 5–10 P.M. weekdays, until 11 P.M. weekends, $15–34). If I start enumerating the menu possibilities it just sounds schizophrenic, but it all works. I ate the following one night: tuna three ways (citrus seared tuna tataki, shrimp and tuna sushi roll, and tuna summer roll), an order of Mongolian beef satay with an addictive peanut sauce and five-spice apple slices, and a stacked tomato-napoleon salad with a precarious avalanche of Roquefort crumbles. Singles: Dine at the long food bar and you won't be alone long. Everyone's friendly, the dining room has palpable buzz, decor is hip.

A block down you'll find the other hippest, waitlist-for-miles place, **Yabba Island Grill** (711 5th Ave. S, 239/262-5787, 5–10 P.M. weekdays, until 11 P.M. weekends, $17–27). It's no coincidence, really, as Pazzo, Chops, and Yabba are all owned and operated by the same folks. Again, a drama, an excitement that only a very popular restaurant can generate, but in this case the food is a little goofier. It may speak only to my tastes, but it's an island-themed menu in which there's one too many ingredients in everything and a piled-up architectural approach that makes eating hazardous to your outfit. Still, I can recommend the sugarcane-skewered grilled chicken with sweet and spicy barbecue sauce, and the sautéed plantain and

COURTESY OF NAPLES, MARCO ISLAND, EVERGLADES CVB

5th Avenue South encompasses 12 blocks and 50 buildings, split between chic restaurants and upscale boutiques.

macadamia-encrusted black grouper with rum butter sauce and a bunch of other fruity stuff.

From here, take it down a frenzy notch and step into the elegant, breezy world of **Vergina** (700 5th Ave. S, 239/659-7008, 11:30 A.M.– 4 P.M. Mon.–Sat., 5–10 P.M. daily, $15–25). I'm sure the word means something beautiful in Italian, but its unfortunate genital sound means that all the ladies-who-lunch in Naples whisper, "Meet me at Vagina" into their cell phones and then cackle. Again, there's wonderful outdoor seating in a sheltered plaza and a soaring indoor space with a long, inviting bar. The food is all familiar Italian, with a punchy Caesar salad and robust seafood pastas. The Italian waiters are simultaneously solicitous and able to poke good-hearted fun at you, an endearing Italian skill.

A fun and rollicking Irish hangout lies just across the street. **McCabe's Irish Pub & Grill** (699 5th Ave. S, 239/403-8777) is in the lobby of the Inn on Fifth, and while the atmosphere is all jovial Irish pub (live, brogue-dripping singers, heavy on the Guinness), the food is fairly sophisticated, from a grilled swordfish napped with a capery lime beurre blanc to an applecranberry cobbler with slowly melting vanilla bean ice cream.

A recent addition to the strip, **Ⓜ Café and Bar Lurcat** (494 5th Ave. S, 239/213-3357, 11:30 A.M.–1 P.M. daily, $11–32) has been knocking people's socks off with its New American cuisine and uber-stylish atmosphere. It's owned and managed by D'Amico & Partners, which also owns Campiello (see *3rd Street*). The first floor is the bar, with live music and a wonderful small plate approach (the tiny sirloin burgers make a bold case for a carnivorous diet), and the upstairs is the more formal dining room. The wine program is quirky and thoughtful, with keen energy brought to bear on food and wine pairings. And what food it is: pot roast slowly braised in cabernet sauvignon with roasted root veggies; velvety foie gras outfitted with roasted pears; buckwheat crepes with smoked Kentucky ham and figs.

There are plenty of other fine choices along 5th—walk and peer in, reading menus as you go. For a casual sandwich, coffee, or ice cream, try **Cheeburger Cheeburger** (505 5th Ave. S, 239/435-9796), **PJ's Coffee & Tea** (599 5th Ave. S, 239/261-5757), and **Regina's Ice Cream Pavilion** (824 5th Ave. S, 239/434-8181).

3rd Street

3rd Street South was once the central business district of Old Naples, and these days it's fairly overrun with galleries and high-end boutiques and antiques shops. The restaurant choices aren't as myriad as on 5th, but in fact a few of Naples's absolute best restaurants line up along 3rd.

Ⓜ Campiello Ristorante (1177 3rd St. S, 239/435-1166, 11:30 A.M.–2:30 P.M. Mon.–Sat., noon–2:30 P.M. Sun., 5:30 P.M.10 P.M. Sun.– Thurs., until 10:30 P.M. Fri. and Sat., $17–38) may be my favorite restaurant around (and a lot of other people's, too, judging from the crowds). It's got a spare, understated elegance achievable only at the best Cal-Ital bistros. Lunch here is an experience that harkens back to the boom-boom '80s power-lunching phenomenon. Biting into a spit-roasted pork sandwich with red onion and smoked mozzarella, or nibbling the point of a housemade chicken sausage and gorgonzola pizza slice, everyone looks like a high-powered executive in the midst of clinching a big deal—wealthy, healthy, and self-satisfied. But maybe it's just because the food is good. At lunch and dinner, presentations are simple and flavors are clean and steady, with a gutsy reliance on great produce and slow-roasted meats.

A totally different vibe, but equally popular is **Tommy Bahama's Tropical Café** (1300 3rd St. S, 239/643-6889, 11 A.M.–2:30 P.M. Mon.–Sat., 5–10 P.M. daily, $11–29). It's the same company as the clothing line or, as they like to say, "purveyor of island lifestyles" (what *does* that mean, exactly?—I'd like to buy me a couple of them there lifestyles), and as one might expect this means an upscale interpretation of island cuisine—smoldering jerk chicken, incredible fruity cocktails—served in a tasteful Polynesian setting with bamboo-blade fans and thatched-roof tikis. Tommy Bahama's also has live music most evenings, making it a wonderful place for a cocktail (Tommy's Bungalow Brew) and some lively conversation.

A longtime Naples institution, **Ridgway Bar & Grill** (1300 3rd St. S, 239/262-5500, 8 A.M.–10:30 P.M. Mon.–Sat., 11:30 A.M.–10:30 P.M. Sun., $16–30) actually closed up a while back and then was reborn. Owner Tony Ridgway is something of a legend in Naples, having brought one of the first gourmet aesthetics (and wine knowledge) to Naples 30 years ago, when most Americans were woefully in the pre–Julia Child dark ages. He owns a small cooking school as well as **Tony's Off Third** (1300 3rd St. S, 239/262-7999) gourmet deli and wine shop next door, and the restaurant's wine offerings reflect this close proximity, with more than 600 bottlings on the far-reaching list. The food is pretty squarely American, but with a sophisticated French fillip here and there. Live entertainment is provided Thursday through Sunday nights by pianist and comedian Jim Badger.

Tin City

Tin City Waterfront Marketplace is a fairly well done waterside indoor shopping center with about 40 mostly nautical-theme boutiques and a couple of good restaurants. The complex is on U.S. 41 at Goodlette Road. The most casual of the restaurants is **Cafe Europa** (239/262-5911), where you'll find sandwiches, hamburgers, and subs at decent prices. A little more upscale is the lively **Riverwalk Fish & Ale House** (239/263-2734). Stay with the simple here, as the kitchen has a tendency to add just a couple of rogue ingredients to their more "gourmet" items. And then there's the newer **Pier 41** (239/649-5858), a lively seafood house with big windows that face out on the water and pier. Shrimp scampi, Diablo mussels, fried grouper—it's all straightforward. Right across from Tin City is a casual joint called **Kelly's** (1302 5th Ave. S, 239/774-0494, 4:30–10 P.M. daily, $15–25) where you'll find the city's best stone crabs. Nothing fancy, but it's one of the oldest restaurants around here.

Elsewhere

The rest of the area's top restaurants are fairly spread out, although there's a dense concentration of fine eats north of downtown on the Tamiami Trail (U.S. 41) between about Golden Gate Parkway and Pine Ridge Road. **Andre's Steakhouse** (2800 Tamiami Trail N, 239/263-5851, 5–9 P.M. daily, $24–35) falls squarely in the luxury American steakhouse idiom. Try the porterhouse for four people, like something from the *Flintstones,* paired with an important California cab or first-growth Bordeaux (the list contains 4,000 bottlings) and surrounded by baked potato, creamed spinach, maybe a vat of gilding-the-lily béarnaise sauce.

Another wine list to reckon with comes at **Chardonnay** (2331 Tamiami Trail N, 239/261-1744, 5:30–10 P.M. Mon.–Sat., open Sun. too in high season, $24–32.50). They have the *Wine Spectator* awards of excellence and others to show for their tireless efforts, but you'll get a sense when you sample the duck pâté with pistachios, the veal sweetbreads braised with Madeira and cream, or the poufy Grand Marnier soufflé. It's mostly classic French and super rich.

Chef Claudio Scaduto has serious francophilic followers at his **Cote D'Azur** (11224 Tamiami Trail N, 239/597-8867, 5–9 P.M. daily, $18–28). The menu at the warm, intimate restaurant is pure Provence: *loup de mer Antibois* (Mediterranean sea bass), *noisettes d'agneau peillois* (roasted spring lamb loins), etc.

Back downtown, next to Sugden Theater, **Trulucks** (698 4th Ave. S, 239/530-3131, 4–10 P.M. daily, $15–34) is a fairly new addition to the dining scene, part of a small chain out of Texas, but the seafood is pretty darned good. Especially the crab, and there's lots of it: Northwest Dungeness crab, Florida stone crab, Alaskan Norton Sound Bairdi crab, red king crab.

Great Hotel Restaurants

These are all pretty fancy, pretty pricey, best for when you can expense it or that wealthy Floridian maiden great-aunt aims to shower you with her beneficence. All of them suggest reservations and slightly fancy dress. Starting at the top, maybe even the over-the-top, **The Dining Room** (The Ritz-Carlton, 280 Vanderbilt Beach Rd., 239/598-3300, 6–10 P.M. daily, Sun. brunch 10:30 A.M.–2 P.M., regular menu priced $58–74 per person with $10–15 surcharge on selected items; daily degustation menu $65–95 per person;

eight-course blind tasting menu $85–130 per person, jacket suggested) is the only AAA Five Diamond restaurant in southwest Florida. Super luxurious French- and Mediterranean-inflected cuisine, stellar wine list. People used to contend that Lafite at the Registry was the top dog, but it closed at the very end of 2004. Now if you want to eat at the Registry, you'll have to opt for the more casual, seafood-heavy **Brass Pelican** or the beachfront **Paradise Grill** (both at the Registry Hotel, 475 Seagate Dr., 239/597-3232, 6 A.M.–10:30 P.M. daily, $15–30). **Baleen** at LaPlaya Beach & Golf Resort (9891 Gulf Shore Dr., 239/597-3123, 7 A.M.–9:30 P.M. daily, $23–37) is also a favorite among visitors and locals livin' large. The dining room has wonderful indoor-outdoor seating that overlooks a perfect swath of beach and Gulf of Mexico. The menu contains some Asian-inspired fare as well as more continental dishes: seared sea scallops with a lo mein noodle cake and charred scallion-miso butter, alongside a Roquefort-crusted filet mignon with potato puree and red wine sauce.

SHOPPING

Of anyplace along the Gulf Coast of Florida, Naples is the reigning queen of retail, no contest. There are often comparisons made to Rodeo Drive and some of the U.S.'s other prime shopping spots, but really Naples may win for sheer diversity.

3rd Street South

3rd Street South is where to start, with exquisite clothing and giftware shops, chic restaurants, and dozens of galleries. Just a couple blocks from the beach and Naples Pier, the street was Naples's real core at the turn of the last century. Don't know where to begin? Consult the **street concierge** (239/434-6533, 10 A.M.–6 P.M. Mon.–Sat., noon–5 P.M. Sun.) located just opposite the Fleischmann Fountain at 1203 3rd Street South for help navigating the area's shops and restaurants.

5th Avenue South

Not far from there 5th Avenue South (239/435-3742) is another huge draw. Seminoles once sold

their crafts from a stand on 5th, and before that Calusas used this area as a canal connecting Naples Bay with the Gulf. The Ed Frank Garage was the first commercial building built erected in 1923, and growth puttered along organically for decades (maybe a hardware store, then a gas station). Then, as in so many cities around the country, the birth of the mall heralded the death of downtown.

In 1996, savvy civic planners had 5th Avenue South join the Florida Main Street Program, and a master plan was created with the help of Miami urban planner Andres Duany. The upshot was that dilapidated one-story storefronts were razed and replaced with sleek Mediterranean two- and three-story buildings (with room for people to live above). Today, 5th Avenue encompasses 12 blocks and 50 buildings (including the Bayfront and Tin City shopping and dining complexes), with such a crafty mix of shops, dining, and nightlife possibilities (as well as a strange preponderance of brokerages and realties) that the length of it is busy at most hours. There is free street entertainment the second Thursday of the month during "Evenings on Fifth," tucked at intervals along the banyan- and flowering-poinciana-bedecked avenue.

Other Shopping

Equally fancy-pants is the **Village on Venetian Bay** (4200 Gulf Shore Blvd., 239/261-6100), with a kind of Venetian canal-side vibe. You'll find lots of independent clothing boutiques (plus familiar faces like Sunglass Hut, the White House/Black Market, and Chico's), a couple of high-end shoe stores, a handful of restaurants (plus Ben & Jerry's), and some home interior shops.

More overtly touristy, but really fun, **Tin City** (at the eastern end of downtown, U.S. 41 E at Goodlette Rd., 239/434-4693, www.tin-city.com) was built in 1976 on the site of a 1920s clam- and oyster-processing plant. It incorporated the crusty waterfront buildings, with oodles of rustic maritime charm, into a shopping emporium (surf shop, bikini shop, Jimmy Buffet-themed gewgaws) with a few restaurants (Riverwalk Fish & Ale House, Pier 41) worthy of your money. The Naples Trolley drops you right here, and it's an easy walk from 5th Avenue South.

The **Waterside Shops** (5415 Tamiami Trail N, in Pelican Bay, 239/598-1605, www.watersideshops.com) are anchored by huge draws such as Saks Fifth Avenue, Polo Ralph Lauren, Max-Mara, Pottery Barn, Banana Republic, and stuff like that. It's a classic, high-end mall with covered walkways and restaurants like the California Pizza Kitchen.

Before you start getting fatigued by all this shopping, let me put in a word for the boutiques along the **Dockside Boardwalk** (corner of 11th St. and 6th Ave. S) and **Crayton Cove** (at the historic City Dock, off 10th St.), and if you need a good old-fashioned JCPenney or Sears to offset all this glitz, there's the **Coastland Center Mall** (1900 9th St. N, 239/262-2323), with Burdines, Dillard's, and a could-be-any-where-in-the-country food court.

Marco Island

The largest and northernmost of the Ten Thousand Islands, Marco is an example of poor civic planning and rapacious builders and developers allowed to run amok. Them's fighting words, I know, but Marco Island might have been the kind of tranquil beach paradise Jimmy Buffet is wont to sing about. Gorgeous sunsets, gentle Gulf breezes, a subtropical lushness—Marco Island has lots going for it, not to mention easy access to the more urbane and sophisticated Naples just to the north and the western gateway to the mysterious Everglades National Park just to the south.

What's my beef, then? It's tall resort hotels and condominiums along the beach that blot out the sun and obscure all beach vistas to those unlucky enough to be staying elsewhere. It's the fact that no overarching development plan established any kind of walking-friendly "downtown" area that makes use of the four miles of glinting quartz sand beaches and picturesque mangrove islands that dot the blue Gulf waters.

That's off my chest now, so I can afford to be less cranky. Marco Island really is a fairly dreamy family vacation spot. The average annual high temperature is 85 degrees, average low is 65, so most of the year it's a joy to be outside. Beyond the beaches, there are several fine private and semi-private golf courses; lots of good snook, redfish, and pompano fishing; and access to more tiny, wonderful islands than you can count. People really do live on Marco, many of them in modest, low-rise ranchers on the bridge end of the island, but as I said, the rest of the island is given over to

a luxury-resort paradigm, which works nicely when you're in an all-id-all-the-time vacation mode (Marco is one of the few places on the Gulf Coast where a Jet Ski doesn't look out of place).

The island used to be two separate land-masses—one part of it a shell mound raised by generations of shellfish-eating Calusas. Their

COURTESY OF NAPLES, MARCO ISLAND, EVERGLADES CVB

The Ten Thousand Islands' mangrove estuaries are populated by bald eagles, pink roseate spoonbills, and dozens of other birds.

detritus, along with some more recent swamp dredging and so forth, yielded the current-day 6,800-acre island with its rolling sand hills, beaches, and slash pine forests. It's accessed easily from Exit 101 off of I-75, heading south on Collier Boulevard for 20 miles until you cross Jolley Bridge.

The island was named La Isla de San Marco, the Island of St. Mark, by the Spaniards shortly after they landed on these shores in 1513 (around the time the Calusa disappeared). The island's history dates back much further, though—archaeology enthusiasts and history buffs flock to the island's historic markers and wealth of artifacts. A dozen markers around town chart Marco Island history, including one of the most significant excavations in North America—the priceless Key Marco Cat, the first known North American example of a half man-half animal figurine. The cat itself is now at the Smithsonian, but the small sculpture was unearthed here in 1896 and is thought to be more than 3,000 years old (there's a replica in the historical society museum).

Despite all that ancient history, W. T. Collier is credited with founding Marco Island in 1870—the northern end was called Key Marco, the southern end Caxambas. Not too long after that it was incorporated as Collier City. But it wasn't until the 1960s when the Deltona Corporation got big ideas about the island's potential as a resort and leisure destination that Marco became recognizable as the place it is today. A mad scramble of residential and commercial building turned the sleepy town of a few thousand into a beachy retreat for more than 14,000 people in high season.

SPORTS AND RECREATION
Ⓜ Tigertail Beach

Marco Island boasts a four-mile crescent of white sandy beach. Not too far from the long stand of tall condominiums and resort hotels, Tigertail Beach (entrance at Spinnaker Dr. and Hernando Dr., 8 A.M.–sunset daily, parking $3, showers and restrooms) is pretty much all things to all people. There's a rental stand for water sports and toys, umbrellas, and chairs; volleyball nets that see heavy action; a concession stand; and

Leave your mark along Marco Island's long stretch of beach.

children's play area. You'll see little Sand Dollar Island out in the lagoon, which was Tigertail's sandbar only 10 years ago, a perfect place for shelling and desultory sand sifting at low tide. The 32-acre beach park is also a birder's favorite for watching shorebirds (but the bird sanctuary nearby is off-limits to visitors).

Other Beaches

There are two other "residents" beaches—the main one that requires a permit for entry or parking, and **Residents Beach South** (walkway access from Collier Blvd. north of Cape Marco, 8 A.M.–sunset daily), which has public parking and access. This beach has no facilities, but is a good place to beachcomb for Florida sand dollars, whelks, fighting conchs, lion's paws, calico scallops, and others of the more than 400 types of seashells found on the island. Be sure to leave all live shells on the beach. Pets are prohibited on Marco Island beaches.

Fishing

Island visitors and locals surf cast for black drum and sheepshead; they take boats out in the back-country mangrove flats to fish for tarpon, snook, and redfish; or head into deeper water offshore for grouper, amberjack, snapper, and kingfish. A number of species in the area have "gamefish" status, and are thus the more exotic and often the most sought after. This means redfish, snook, tarpon, bonefish, and sailfish are illegal to buy or sell (that's why you don't ever see them on restaurant menus, although you wouldn't want to eat a

THE STINGRAY SHUFFLE

It's not a dance, exactly.

It's strictly anecdotal, but Marco Island seems to have more than its share of flat, seafloor-living stingrays. Visitors occasionally step on these creatures, their winglike fins hidden in the sandy shallows. When trod upon, a stingray flips up its tail in self-defense and delivers a nasty stinging puncture with its barb. To avoid this, drag your feet along the sandy bottom (as opposed to stepping up and down). The "shuffle" may not look too swift, but it alerts stingrays to your approach. They are just hanging around the shallows to catch shellfish and crustaceans and they'd rather not waste their time on stinging you.

If you are unlucky enough to be stung, it's important that you clean the wound with freshwater immediately (other bacteria in seawater can infect the area). As soon as you can, soak the wound in the hottest water you can stand for up to 90 minutes to neutralize the venom. The pain can be severe, often accompanied by weakness, vomiting, headache, fainting, shortness of breath, paralysis, and collapse in people who are allergic to the venom. You may want to see a doctor, who might add insult to injury with a tetanus shot.

Always report stingray injuries to the lifeguard on duty.

---

tarpon even if you were offered one with a delicate beurre blanc and fancy capers), and many of them have very persnickety catch limits and seasons. For instance, snook season is limited to December 15–January 31 and June, July, and August; in season you can keep two per day, and they must be under 34 inches and over 26 inches. Don't wet a line until you've studied up on what you can catch, how many, and when.

If you want to head out fishing with an expert, Marco Island, as with much of the Gulf Coast, has many specialists willing to show you the way. Specializing in light tackle and fly fishing, **Captain Brien Spina** (239/642-9779, www.marcoislandcharters.com, $375–750, depending on the boat and location) has a number of boats from which to choose, lots of experience in the area, and a fun website on which you and your trophy catch can be immortalized. He does individual private charters (no split charters) with six passengers at the most. (Captain Spina also owns the excellent Captain Brien's seafood restaurant on Collier Blvd. N.)

Captain Bill Walsh takes visitors out with his company **Dawn Patrol** (Marco River Marina, 951 Bald Eagle Dr., 239/394-0608, $200 for four people for a half day), known for fishing the nearshore artificial reefs and ledges. Dawn Patrol specializes in family trips and will tailor a fishing trip to include a mix of shelling, fishing, and sightseeing so even nonfishers in your group are entertained.

If you want to go it alone, **Marco River Marina** (951 Bald Eagle Dr., 239/394-2502) itself rents out the largest array of boats on the island, and boats at **Cedar Bay Marina** (705 E. Elkcam Circle, 239/642-6717; deck boat $285 for full day, $210 for half; pontoon boat $260 for full day, $195 for half, center console $260 for full, $195 for half) all come equipped with a bimini (sun top), plastic cooler stocked with ice and drinks, VHF radio, USCG equipment, and an easy-to-navigate color chart of the local waters. They're endlessly patient with beginners, too. The Marco River Marina is also the debarkation point for **Sea Key West Express** (239/394-9700), a three-hour cruise to Key West (a very affordable way to explore Key West without having to fly).

Golf

Guidebooks all bandy about the statistic that Naples has more golf courses per capita than anywhere else. Many of these are in East Naples, and many are private. On Marco Island there are several notable private courses—**Hideaway Beach Club** (250 Beach Dr. S, 239/642-6300), **Island Country Club** (500 Nassau Rd., 239/394-3151), and others—but only a couple of public possibilities. The Marco Island Marriott's **Rookery Golf Club** (400 Collier Blvd. S, 239/793-6060), designed by Joe Lee, is an 18-hole, par-72, Scottish links–style course built on 240 acres of rolling terrain and featuring several mounds coming into play around the greens.

The signature hole is No. 16, a 165-yard par 3, requiring a tee shot over water to a peninsula green. Beginners can learn at the Marriott's John Jacobs' School of Golf, recently rated a "Golf School of Choice" by *Golf Magazine*.

Despite its name, the **Marco Shores Country Club** (1450 Mainsail Dr., Naples, 239/394-2581) is in Naples, but very close by. The course has long, wide fairways and well-maintained greens blended seamlessly into the native mangroves and waterways of the Ten Thousand Islands. With four separate tees, Marco Shores accommodates all skill levels.

If you're a golf glutton and want to try out a handful of the legendary local courses, **Golf Vacation Web** (877/767-5445) puts together a five-night stay at the **Hilton Marco Island Beach Resort** with a round of golf at each of the Lely Flamingo Island Club, Lely Mustang Golf Club, Tiburon, Naples Lakes, and Cedar Hammock courses.

M Calusa Shell Mounds

The Calusa (kah-LOOS-ah) lived on the coast and along the inner waterways in this area. They were tall and fierce, with a marked inability to play nicely with others. They did not farm, but rather fished and hunted for their sustenance from the bountiful bays, rivers, and Gulf (these were so bountiful, in fact, that as many as 50,000 Calusas may have been living here at a time). They controlled much of the southwest coast of Florida, and many other tribes justifiably feared their aggression. This is all ancient history, though, as the Spanish settlers ran them off or killed them off, either actively or passively with the introduction of smallpox and other diseases, starting close to when the Spanish arrived in the 1500s. By the 1700s the tribe was wiped out, the remaining handful of Calusas purportedly lighting out for Cuba when the Spanish turned Florida over to the British in 1763.

The Calusas' impact on the area and their unique way of life are still apparent today, however. They built homes on stilts with palmetto leaf roofs and no walls and fashioned nets from palm tree fiber to catch mullet, catfish, and pinfish. But their most ingenious work was with shells.

Shellfish provided a staple in the Calusa diet—then once the succulent meat was removed, the shells were used to make jewelry, utensils, spearheads, other tools, and vast heaps upon which other things could be built. Little mangrove keys, uninhabitable on their own, became homes or sacred places with the addition of a few thousand carefully piled shells.

These shell mounds are literally the building blocks for Marco Island and many of the Ten Thousand Islands. If you want to spend a day exploring the remnants of Calusa mounds, **Florida Saltwater Adventures** (239/595-7495, $270 for a three-hour trip for up to six people, $350 for four hours, $425 for five, reservations necessary) offers wonderful eco-tours. Captain Alex Saputo takes small groups out on his 24-foot boat, weaving in and out of the Ten Thousand Islands while pointing out wildlife and spouting horticultural and local history. He's a Calusa and Seminole buff, big time, and his enthusiasm is infectious as you tramp around a shell mound, crouching to see a fat whelk shell once used as a hammerhead or other tool. And on the way back, watch for dolphins who leap in the wake of the boat—they're either playing or "drafting" off the boat's speed (even dolphin experts disagree about why they do it)—but it's about as close as you'll ever get to dolphins outside of Sea World.

SIGHTS

Museums

History enthusiasts have a couple of tiny yet illuminating museums on-island. Marco Island Historical Society operates the **Museum at Olde Marco** (168 Royal Palm Dr., 239/389-6447, 7 A.M.–7 P.M. daily, free admission) next to the oldest building on the island, the Olde Marco Island Inn. The focus is on archaeological finds of the area with an emphasis on Calusa culture. There's even a sweet life-sized diorama of a Calusa household. The second museum, the **Key Marco Museum** (in the lobby of the Board of Realtors office, Waterway Ct., 9 A.M.–4 P.M. Mon.–Fri., free admission) covers some of the same ground, with Calusa treasures displayed prominently. But it moves forward in time to capture moments of pioneer history, early island industries, and up into the 20th century. Both museums are really unstaffed, but a docent tour can be arranged by calling ahead. There are also maps at the museums for a self-guided tour of Marco Island's 13 historical markers, including that of the Cushing Archaeological Site from 1895, said to be one of the most historically significant excavations in North America (it unearthed the Key Marco Cat). It doesn't take long to zip through the tour, either by car or bike, and it's a good orientation to the island.

ACCOMMODATIONS

Under $50

There's not much on Marco Island for the budget traveler. However, satisfaction is just a couple minutes away. Goodland is a little town adjacent to Marco Island, plopped on an Indian shell mound. It's about a mile square and boasts a few hundred residents, mostly rough fisherfolk, and a bunch of down-home bars. Things are changing (a sign in town now advertises 52 new luxury townhouses, the asking price upwards of $600,000), but you can still get a taste of yesterday at the **Pink House Motel** (310 Pear Tree Ave., Goodland, 239/394-1313, $59) and the **Village Inn Motel** (212 Harbor Place, Goodland, 239/642-3338, $59–99). The former is a historic family-owned waterfront motel with boat docking, efficiency kitchens, laundry facilities, and the Marker 7 Marina and Tackle Shop. The latter is a clean, no-frills, one-story motel.

$50–150

In a similar vein on Marco Island, but a little pricier, the **Boat House Motel** (1180 Edington Pl., $68–290) is a little more glamorous, two stories with a gazebo and boat docks, but still really a straightforward low-rise motel, while **Moran's Barge Marina, Motel, and Restaurant** (3200 U.S. 92, Marco Island, 239/642-1920, $70–150) offers 12 rooms with kitchenettes in a fishing-friendly waterfront motel with a marina and boat ramp. Pets accepted.

There are also hundreds of vacation rental

homes and condominiums on Marco Island. Many of these rent only by the week, especially in high season. Several rental companies have nice websites from which you can peruse properties: **Coldwell Banker** (800/733-8121, www.marcoislandvacations.net) seems to rent largely in high-rise condos, **Holiday Homes of Marco Island** (239/389-9940, www.marco-island.com) represents a number of single-family homes, and **Prudential Florida Realty** (239/642-5400, marcobeachrentals.net) offers a wide range, from fancy high-rise condos to individual homes right on a golf course.

Over $150

Maybe it's an "if you can't beat 'em, join 'em" mentality, but if you're going to stay on Marco Island you might as well pony up the dough and stay at one of the "Big Four." Four beachfront resorts dominate the most coveted piece of shoreline. Each has lots of amenities, fairly good restaurants on-site, and a broad price range to accommodate different budgets.

Families are best served at the **Radisson Suite Beach Resort** (600 Collier Blvd. S, 800/992-0651, www.marcobeachresort.com, $99–520), which features large suites with kitchens, a compelling and varied children's program, nice pools, and great wooden beach chairs on a stunning swath of sand.

Having just experienced a vigorous renovation ($60 million), the **Marco Island Marriott**

COURTESY OF NAPLES, MARCO ISLAND, EVERGLADES CVB

Tall beachfront hotels dot the edge of the Gulf along Marco Island's four miles of white-sand beaches.

Resort, Golf Club, and Spa (400 Collier Blvd. S, 239/394-2511, www.marcoislandmarriott .com, $135–850) may be more suited to a romantic golf-and-pampering getaway, with more than 700 rooms and lavish resort activities and facilities, the 24,000-square-foot Balinese-themed spa, a new "tiki" pool, and the Rookery at Marco, the resort's newly upgraded golf course.

The **Marco Beach Ocean Resort** (480 Collier Blvd. S, 239/393-1400, www.marcoresort.com, $279–1000) opened in late 2001 with 103 one- and two-bedroom suites, a spa, fancy Italian restaurants (Sale e Pepe's chef is so exacting that he imports flour for pasta from his hometown in Italy), and a stunning rooftop swimming pool with a panoramic view of the Gulf.

And the 20-year-old **Hilton Marco Island Beach Resort** (560 Collier Blvd. S, 239/394-5000, www.marcoisland.hilton.com, $99–379) is a luxury resort that consistently wins four-diamond status and so forth for its large guest rooms with Gulf-view private balconies, lighted Har-Tru tennis courts, vast amoeba-shaped pool, and other amenities. A new spa is planned for 2006.

Right out the back door of all four hotels you can rent aqua trikes, banana rides, and Wave Runners with **Marco Island Ski & Watersports** (239/642-2359) and **Holiday Water Sports** (239/642-3467), both of which also offer parasailing and dolphin-watching tours on the Gulf.

For a more historic, small inn experience, try **Olde Marco Island Inn & Suites** (100 Palm St., 239/394-3131, $90–600), a 116-year-old Victorian in the historic district. It features one- and two-bedroom suites with roomy screened lanais. There are six luxurious penthouses and a much-lauded restaurant. It's a convenient location, near beaches, shopping, golf, etc., and guests enjoy complimentary use of the inn's 38-foot catamaran.

FOOD

All the times listed below reflect peak season hours. If you're dining here during the off-season, it's best to call for hours of operation.

Something Different

Dine one of several ways aboard the brand-new 74-foot *Marco Island Princess* (departs from the marina, 951 Bald Eagle Dr., 239/642-5415, $30–50), sister ship to the *Naples Princess*. There's the "Sea Breeze" lunch buffet cruise, a sunset hors d'oeuvres cruise, or a sunset dinner cruise. Head out on the luxury yacht as it glides along scenic Marco River into the Gulf of Mexico with leaping dolphins in hot pursuit. The ship itself is beautiful, as is the scenery, either by day or with a peachy sunset casting its warm glow. The food is unremarkable but pleasant (the cash bar will set you back a hefty pile if you're not careful), especially when nibbled on the open-air deck above. The ship gets busy for holidays (Valentine's, Mother's Day, New Year's Eve) and is often rented out for private parties, so reserve early if you can.

Marco boasts another unusual dining experience. An evening at **Marco Movies** (599 Collier Blvd. S, Ste. 103, 239/642-1111, $8–14) is the oldest date-night one-two punch in the books: dinner and a movie, but both at the same time. A small, family-owned four-screen theater, it shows first-run movies (there's always at least one family-appropriate pick) along with very respectable Greek salad, delicious sweet-potato fries, several robust tortilla-wrapped sandwiches, beer, wine, and fancy cocktails, oh, and popcorn.

Casual

Originally called the "Snook Hole" (that has kind of an unseemly ring to it, doesn't it?) for the wealth of snook you could catch right off the dock, the **Snook Inn** (1215 Bald Eagle Dr., 239/394-3313, 11 A.M.–10 P.M. daily, $13–20) was first a sprawling, casual restaurant that catered to the Deltona Corporation's construction workers who built up Marco Island in the 1960s. Right on the Marco River, the Snook Inn is a fun indoor-outdoor joint with live music and long lines. Locals and visitors seem to come for the grouper and the vast salad bar (more than a few locals harangued me about the glories of the old-fashioned pickle barrel, its bobbing dills crisp and monstrously big). The garden courtyard is a great locale for sipping creamy seafood chowder

CHICKEES

What is a **chickee**, you ask? You'll see the term a lot around here. It's a Seminole word for an open, handmade structure comprised of cypress poles and a roof of palm fronds. Historically, there was an art to erecting chickees, the cypress stripped in a process called "draw knife," the fronds nailed in a particular pattern to keep out the area's heavy rains. A chickee is now more broadly defined as any open-air structure, but usually ones in which there's boozing and general merriment.

or tackling a pile of peel 'n' eat shrimp (if you aren't wild about seafood, the jerk chicken quesadilla is commendable). There's docking available for more than 20 boats near the chickee.

Most of the island's other restaurants are lined up along Collier Boulevard. You'll see a lot of locals at **Bimini's** (near the Radisson, 657 Collier Blvd. S, 239/394-7111, 11:30 A.M.–10:30 P.M. daily, $10–20), who swear by the eatery's housemade bread and the Capt. Bimini's platter of broiled grouper, shrimp, and sea scallops, and you'll hobnob with locals while tucking into a thick-crust, heavy-on-the-cheese pie at **Joey's Pizzeria** (257 Collier Blvd. N, 239/389-2433, $10–15).

Or browse the range of possibilities at the Marco Island Town Center Mall: **Crazy Flamingo** (1047 1/2 Collier Blvd. N, 239/642-9600, 11 A.M.–2 P.M. daily, $10–20) is a lively raw bar with fairly good fish entrées, **Cheeburger Cheeburger** (1075 1/2 Collier Blvd. N, 239/642-6556, 11 A.M.–9 P.M. daily, $6–10) turns out a respectable burger and milkshake, while **Kahuna Restaurant** (1069 Collier Blvd. N, 239/394-4300, 8:30 A.M.–9 P.M. daily, $8–15) also serves a fine burger and crabcake in a Hawaiian-themed joint with nice outdoor seating.

Upscale

Marek's Collier House (1121 Bald Eagle Dr., 239/642-9948, 5:30–10 P.M. daily, $25–35) gets the nod from local publications nearly every year for fancy, romantic "continental" dining. It's

partly due to the setting—the restaurant is nestled in Captain Bill Collier's lovely historic home—and partly because of chef/owner Peter Marek's *luxe* take on classical (read: sinfully rich) seafood dishes. This guy is a triple gold medallist at the World Culinary Olympics—yes, there is such a thing—and his lamb chops, swordfish swaddled in green peppercorn sauce, and veal scaloppini with blue crabmeat all score a solid 9.8 (except with the Russian judges, who quibble with the dismount).

The restaurant at the **Olde Marco Island Inn** (100 Palm St., 239/394-3131, 4–10 P.M. daily, $25–35) is another favorite with foodies or those who just feel like dropping a bundle on a nice bottle of wine and a perfectly prepared steak. There are five individual dining rooms, each with a slightly different feel, so try to wander through each before settling on a table (there's also an upper dining deck that looks out over the inn's gardens).

And **Arturo's Italian Restaurant** (844 Bald Eagle Dr., 239/642-0550, 4:30–10 P.M. daily, $15–25) has been nurturing Italophiles since 1994 with its justifiably famous stuffed pork chop and a range of hearty pastas. The wine list is worth a lengthy study, but for an Italian restaurant the mixologists whip up a mean Cosmopolitan and green apple martini.

SHOPPING

Marco isn't as replete with fancy shops as Naples to the north, nor is it as retail-impoverished as Everglades City to the south. There are a few concentrated areas: The **Esplanade** (740–760 Collier Blvd. N, 239/394-7772) is a new development with clothing and home decor stores, a few restaurants, and a fancy day spa. It's also the only place on the island with a Starbucks (and a Cold Stone Creamery). Beyond that, there's a collection of shops at the ambitiously named **Marco Island Town Center Mall** (on Collier Blvd. N at Bald Eagle Dr.) and a number in **Mission Plaza** (on Collier Blvd. across from the Hilton). Adjacent to the Olde Marco Island Inn at the northern tip of the island, the **Shops at Olde Marco** (100 Palm St., 239/475-3466) complex has a couple boutiques, gourmet food shops, and the inn's spa and fitness center.

But for the big kahuna of shopping you have to drive back north off the island. The **Prime Outlets** (7222 Isle of Capri Rd., just north of Marco Island, 239/775-8083, 10 A.M.–8 P.M. Mon.–Sat., 11 A.M.–6 P.M. Sun.) has more than 40 stores, most of them big names, with designer clothes and shoes, books, and housewares at up to 70 percent off retail prices.

Everglades City

The way he told it, hardly anyone was innocent. He hunched low at the bar as he spoke—clamming up whenever the bartender came our way. But over the course of about an hour, he revealed

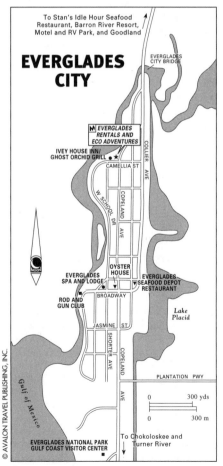

To Stan's Idle Hour Seafood
Restaurant, Barron River Resort,
Motel and RV Park, and Goodland

EVERGLADES CITY

EVERGLADES CITY BRIDGE

M EVERGLADES RENTALS AND ECO ADVENTURES

IVEY HOUSE INN/ GHOST ORCHID GRILL ● ★

CAMELLIA ST

COLLIER AVE

W. SCHOOL DR

COPELAND AVE

MOON

OYSTER HOUSE

EVERGLADES SPA AND LODGE ●

EVERGLADES SEAFOOD DEPOT RESTAURANT

ROD AND GUN CLUB

BROADWAY

Lake Placid

JASMINE ST

SHORTER AVE

COPELAND AVE

PLANTATION PWY

AVE

0   300 yds

0   300 m

Gulf of Mexico

EVERGLADES NATIONAL PARK GULF COAST VISITOR CENTER ■

To Chokoloskee and Turner River

© AVALON TRAVEL PUBLISHING, INC.

the story of "Operation Everglades." There were maybe 550 residents of the little town of Everglades City in the late 1970s—tough, independent-minded folks who mostly kept to themselves and made their living off the Gulf waters, shrimping, fishing, or whatnot. But, as the guy at the bar explained, there was more going on than met the eye—in those days you were likely to see a double-wide trailer or a Cracker shack with a Maserati out front and a shiny Cessna 206 parked out on the back 40.

Drug money, plain and simple. Law enforcement agents launched Operation Everglades in 1981, monitoring the sizable marijuana traffic through this sleepy town. And when the dust had settled, more than 125 residents were carted away in yellow school buses in one of the biggest stings the state had seen. Kids at the high school, carpool moms, busboys—everyone was somehow involved in the smuggling of pot up from Colombia and elsewhere through the maze of mangrove islands.

My friend at the bar—I promised I wouldn't give his name or that of the bar—paid his debt to society. But looking back through the mist of a couple of lite beers, it's clear it was a wild ride. Guns, bales of fragrant dope piled on shrimp boats slicking silently through the swamps, vindictive drug lords, and a whole lot of mullet, pompano, and stone crabs—it's cinematic (why hasn't anyone made a big-budget movie of this with Tommy Lee Jones in the role of Lieutenant Charles Sanders, who made the bust, and the whole cast of *Pirates of the Caribbean* as the denizens of Everglades City?), but true.

There's a hallowed and time-honored tradition of nefarious activity and seat-of-the-pants entrepreneurship in Everglades City. The first

COURTESY OF NAPLES,
MARCO ISLAND, EVERGLADES CVB

Everglades National Park is the only subtropical preserve in North America.

white settlers arrived just before the Civil War, many of them evading conscription, the law, or the expectations of nagging spouses. Lots squatted, not comfortably given the heat, humidity, mosquitoes, and awkward nature of mangrove islands (no dirt, lots of knotty roots dipping down into murky, tannin-tinged water). Farming was hard-won (tomatoes, cucumbers, peppers, Florida avocados, pineapple, and sugarcane grew okay thanks to hard labor and low expectations), but the fishing was good. Mullet jumped so the waters fairly churned, the oily fish caught by net then salted down and barreled for sale in Key West.

Seminoles and the new white settlers mostly kept to themselves, as did the descendants of the fabled Calusa in these parts. John Weeks and William Smith Allen are said to be the area's first permanent residents, settling sometime around 1870 along the Allen River (now the Barron River), the latter building himself a home on the site of the present-day Rod and Gun Club. George W. Storter Jr. opened the first general store and trading post in 1892, in which the locals traded alligator hides, furs, and plumes for ammo and such.

The area's biggest growth spurt came when wealthy businessman Barron G. Collier made it the headquarters for his Tamiami Trail road-building company in 1923. He purchased more than a million acres in southwestern Florida, promising the Florida legislature he'd complete the half-finished Tamiami Trail (linking Tampa with Miami through the swamp) in return for the

creation of Collier County. Collier got to work dredging to make land and then paving over it to make the first real roads in the area, but his efforts eventually petered out and the state stepped in to finish the job.

The trail was finished in 1928, and improved access made the area's cattle ranching, commercial fishing, and produce farming more viable. For a while it was the county seat, but storms, along with Collier's decision to move his headquarters up to Naples, sealed Everglades City's fate as the sleepy mile-long mangrove island at the highway's dead end. In the 1940s many locals made their living sponge diving; after that came shrimping, stone crabbing, gator skinning, and sport fishing when wealthy outdoorspeople came to the "wilderness" for a little R&R.

Today, Everglades City's year-round population is as teeny as it ever was, its residents as self-reliant and dubious about authority. It's a locus of eco-tourism, with canoe tours, airboat rides, fishing guides, and other nature-based businesses capitalizing on the mystery and majesty of the million acres of mangrove jungle just to the south. It's significantly more rustic than swanky Naples to the north, there are no Ritz-Carltons, tux-clad waiters, or turndown mints on the pillow anywhere near, but Everglades City is a must for adventure seekers. A couple days of paddling Everglades National Park, gliding past 12-foot gators giving you the hairy eyeball, delicate epiphytes (air plants) festooning the mangroves like some kind of alien Christmas trees, the birds engaged in a strenuous call-and-response—it's all enough to elicit a healthy sense of awe even in the most world weary.

EVERGLADES NATIONAL PARK

Everglades National Park (mailing address: 40001 Hwy. 9336, Homestead, FL 33034-6733, 305/242-7700; Gulf Coast Visitor Center in Everglades City, 815 S. Copeland Dr., 239/695-2591, 7:30 A.M.–5 P.M. Nov.–April, 9 A.M.–4:30 P.M. May–Nov., no entrance fee on this side of the park) is the third-largest park in the United States, outside Alaska, and has been designated a World Heritage Site, an International Biosphere

THE EVERGLADES

The Everglades proper is the mainland, about 4,000 square miles of flat prairie grass that slopes southward at one-fifth of a foot per mile. The rainfall averages fifty-five inches, June through October. In rainy season, the most southwest part near the mangroves gets anywhere from a few inches up to two or three feet under water. . . . The strip of mangrove mainland has many little rivers not much wider in the narrows than a rowboat, running all the way to the grasslands of the Glades. In rainy season these rivers slowly drain the rainwater off the Glades into the Islands. As the rainwater from the Glades mixes with the saltwater coming in from the Gulf, it becomes brackish. Most all the fish and a big portion of the wildlife, especially the saltwater birds, do most of their breeding and feeding in the brackish water here.

The fish and the wildlife all follow the brackish water line. In the driest of the season, April and May, the brackish line is at the very head of the rivers near the Glades, and so are the fish and game. As the rains come on, the brackish line slowly drifts down the rivers into the Islands and eventually to the coast.

—Totch, *A Life in the Everglades*
by Loren G. "Totch" Brown

He would know. He spent most of his life finding ways to eke out a life in this lush, junglelike wilderness at the bottom of the state of Florida.

Things That Can Kill You in the Everglades
Eastern diamondback rattlesnake, dusky pigmy rattlesnake, cottonmouth, and coral snake. Alligators very, very seldom attack people, even if you're thrashing about in the water. Dogs and small children are less safe from them. Keep both away from water's edge unattended. Do not, under any circumstances, feed the alligators, even if it's entertaining. It teaches them bad habits. You don't want to see a gator sit up and beg. Crocodiles, on the other hand (there are fewer of these in the Everglades, but there are some), are larger and more ferocious.

Things That Can Really Bother You in the Everglades
Mosquitoes. They are pretty fierce in the summer (always bring bug spray and long sleeves to thwart them as best you can). Information on mosquito levels during the summer is available at 305/242-7700. Also, there are a few poison plants: poison ivy, poisonwood, and manchineel tree. You might want to research these plants' leaf shape so you can avoid brushing up against them.

Where to See Good Stuff
The Anhinga Trail (at Royal Palm) and Eco Pond (a mile past the Flamingo Visitor Center) are good for birding. There's also a train tour at Shark Valley

Reserve, and a Wetland of International Importance. It's the only subtropical preserve in North America, containing both temperate and tropical plant communities. Really, it's the only everglade in the world.

Still, I don't think any of this conveys exactly what's so cool. The Seminoles called the park "grassy water," because it is essentially a wide, shallow river with no current, no falls or rapids, that flows very slowly southward along the subtle slope of the land, eventually meeting open water

in Florida Bay 100 miles away. This river flows along sawgrass prairies, mangrove and cypress swamps, pinelands, and hardwood hammocks. Everywhere there are wading birds, alligators, dense and exotic tropical plantlife. But the U.S. government looked on all this as a dud, a big goose egg. In 1850 the federal government passed the Swamp and Overflowed Lands Act, which essentially gave people the latitude to manhandle this delicate ecosystem in any way they saw fit (in an effort to make the land "useful").

that birders enjoy. Canoeists like paddling into Chokoloskee Bay (Gulf Coast) and Snake Bight (near Flamingo) to see the waterbirds feeding on mud flats. For freshwater canoeing, try Nine Mile Pond. Serious canoeists tackle the Wilderness Waterway, the backcountry route linking Everglades City to Flamingo. Check at the Gulf Coast Visitor Center for canoeing maps and directions, and rentals (there's no launch fee at the Gulf Coast Visitor Center). A quick and easy way to get a sense for the immensity and majesty of the Everglades is by taking one of the 90-minute boat tours (from the Gulf Coast Visitor Center, 239/695-2591, on the half hour 9 A.M.–4:30 P.M., no reservations necessary).

Camping
Even if you're planning on doing primitive camping, backcountry permits are required (they're free, they just help keep track of visitors). There's established beach camping in the Everglades, chickee (little cabin structures) camping along the rivers and bays; New Turkey Key camping, Plate Creek camping, and camping at South Lostmans. Go to the visitors center to get a map and detailed description of all of the established campsites and more primitive options.

Staying in the Park, But Not in a Tent
The Flamingo Lodge (239/695-3101) is the only lodging available in the park. It is open year-round, with 103 rooms, plus 24 cottages with kitchen facilities. A restaurant and café are open during the winter.

Everglades boosters Ernest F. Coe and Marjory Stoneman Douglas (author of *The Everglades: River of Grass*) prevailed, cajoling President Harry S. Truman to dedicate the vast swath as Everglades National Park in 1947. The park is still being rerouted, uprooted, and damaged in a variety of ways, requiring continued vigilance and stiffer environmental laws. But, in most ways, the wilderness is protected, and you have the privilege of visiting.

The Everglades region is mild and pleasant December–April, rarely reaching freezing temperatures, and mostly without a drop of rain. Summers are hot and humid, with temperatures hovering around 90°F and humidity at a fairly consistent steamy 90 percent. And, as with most places along the Gulf Coast, there are tremendous afternoon thunderstorms in the summer.

SPORTS AND RECREATION
Canoeing
Everglades National Park is America's only subtropical wilderness, a third of it given over to marine areas and shallow estuaries easily paddled by rookie or seasoned kayakers or canoers (in my experience, a kayak seems easier to navigate through these sometimes-tight quarters). The mangroves form canopied tunnels through the swamp, through which you pick in a peculiar way: Often the flat of your paddle is used to gently push off from the tangle of mangrove roots when it's too tight to actually dip into the water. In this way you "pole" through the tight spots, the nose of your craft sometimes hitching up in the roots, necessitating backward paddling to disengage.

Mosquitoes are surprisingly not a real problem until the summer, when you absolutely don't want to be paddling through the steamy swamp anyway (think 90 degrees with more than 90 percent humidity, no respite). Still, you'll need bug spray, water, sunglasses, a flotation device (required by law), shoes you don't mind getting wet or muddy, comfortable clothes, a hat—and a plan.

Check at the **Gulf Coast Visitor Center** (815 S. Copeland Dr., 239/695-3311, 8 A.M.–4:30 P.M. daily) for maps and directions, and you can rent canoes downstairs from the visitors center at **Everglades National Park Boat Tours** (239/695-2591, $24/day). It's fairly daunting to head off by yourself the first day, so the visitors center and Everglades National Park Boat Tours both offer guided tours on a first-come, first-served basis. For more advanced paddlers, there's a trip that departs at 9:30 A.M. on Saturday mornings that lasts seven hours; a Sunday morning trip more for beginners is only four hours.

After that, if you want to push off on your own, put in at the canoe ramp next to the visitors center or the NPS ramp next to Outdoor Resorts on Chokoloskee Island. As everyone will tell you: Don't overestimate your abilities, and time your trip with the tides (a falling tide flows toward the Gulf of Mexico; a rising tide flows toward the visitors center). If you want to pick up a nautical chart, No. 11430 covers the Chokoloskee Bay area. There are also detailed descriptions to be had at the visitors center and other local shops of how to traverse the **Wilderness Waterway,** a 99-mile canoe trail that winds from Everglades City over to the Flamingo Visitor Center at the southeast entrance to the national park. It's about an eight-day excursion, to be undertaken only after lots of diligent preparation.

Everglades Rentals & Eco Adventures

Everglades Rentals & Eco Adventures (Ivey House Inn, 107 Camellia St., 239/695-3299, $95–750) offers spectacular half-day, full-day, and overnight guided canoe, kayak, and boating adventures led by naturalist guides. I was the only customer on my five-hour kayak tour. My guide, Courtney, a lovely young woman with a clear passion for the abundant natural beauty of the area, led the way, stopping occasionally to point out an unusual orchid, a dozen striped baby alligators sunning, an eagle overhead. Paradise, really, with the dense lushness and lack of human marks that make one feel as if she's fallen somehow into a prehistoric jungle. Substitute pterodactyl babies for the osprey fledglings you see peering from that huge nest above, and the illusion's complete.

My guide and I entered the water off U.S. 41 at the old Turner River, quickly passing into narrow mangrove tunnels, then out into lagoons and past sawgrass prairies and into Turner Lake. The company runs its tours November 1 through the end of April and offers a range of specialty tours, from photography workshops to night paddles (I admit it, the swamp was too eerie by day for me to consider this one). It also rents out equipment sans guide to the bold.

Totch's Island Tours

Lots of airboat companies offer competent tours with nature-focused narration, but the most historically significant is **Totch's Island Tours** (929 Dupont St., just before the Everglades City Bridge, 239/695-2333, 30-minute, 1-hour, and 1.5-hour tours, $15–40). Loren "Totch" Brown, author of *Totch: A Life in the Everglades* (a must-read if you are interested in the crusty, taciturn folks who've eked a living out of the Everglades over the past 100 years), grew up on an island near Chokoloskee during the Depression.

As a young man he fought in World War II before going home to work variously as a pompano fisherman and stone crabber (legally) and an alligator poacher and marijuana smuggler (well, illegally). You can see a picture of the local legend in Smallwood's Store, a tiny museum on Chokoloskee Island (150 acres made entirely of shells by the Seminoles), or catch a glimpse of him in the 1955 film *Wind Across the Everglades* with Christopher Plummer.

Totch died a few years ago, but his tour company consists of his family members and a number of fourth- and fifth-generation Everglades residents. They'll take you out either in back country or open water to Totch's island to see his rustic family cottage on a tiny mangrove island. Along the way, you'll be trailed by pelicans, catch glimpses of manatees lumbering along the brackish shallows beneath

COURTESY OF NAPLES, MARCO ISLAND, EVERGLADES CVB

Rent a kayak or canoe and paddle out among the Ten Thousand Islands. There are tides and currents, so don't overestimate your own ability.

you, and see alligators (big ones), wild pigs, ospreys, and incredible plantlife. The guides know a lot about the local fauna but seem to fly by the seat of their pants on the flora (my guide spouted some botanical names that sounded suspiciously ad-libbed).

Other Airboat Rides

You've seen them. They're the embodiment of Newton's Third Law: Those tall boats propelled by air whooshing through their giant fans—with no outboard motor and rudder for propulsion and control, these boats can scoot through extreme shallows on their flat bottoms, perfect for swamp exploration. It's an Everglades cliché, and a loud one, but fun (although they're not allowed in Everglades National Park proper, they scoot around the edges in the Ten Thousand Islands).

Another successful airboat company is **Captain Doug's Florida Boat Tours** (102 Broadway, at the Captain's Table Resort, 800/282-9194, $29.95 adults, children half price, children 3 and under free). The airboat tour groups are small and the tour is one hour of meandering through the mangrove forest backcountry and a sawgrass wetland. Back at the headquarters, visitors are treated to a free alligator show and are welcome to walk around a replica of a Native American village.

Wooten's Airboat Tours, Swamp Buggy Rides and Animal Sanctuary (32330 Tamiami Trail E, Ochopee, five miles south of Everglades City, 239/695-2781, 9 A.M.–4:15 P.M. daily, adults $16 for either tour, $13 for kids, $8 for the farm) is a little farther afield. It's fairly famous in these parts, but to my mind the 30-minute airboat ride through the mangroves and marshlands is very similar to that of the others (and it's a less intimate group, taking up to 18 people at a time). Much neater are the 30-minute swamp tours on the swamp buggy. You'll travel through spooky cypress swamp and spot alligators (as well as North American crocodiles—the Everglades being the only area you'll find these guys in the U.S.), deer, snakes, and tons of birds. Wooten's also has a little "farm" with native Florida creatures brought in expressly for your excitement (Florida panthers, bobcats).

Airboats are an indigenous species, whooshing through the mangroves past gators and nonplussed wading birds.

More Boat Tours

A quieter ride, with a more overtly eco-tourism piety, the **Everglades National Park Boat Tour** (at the ranger station on the causeway between Everglades City and Chokoloskee Island, 239/695-2591, every 30 minutes after 9:30 A.M. until 4:30 P.M., $16 for adults, $8 for children) is a wonderful two-hour motorboat tour departing from the Gulf Coast Visitor Center. The cruise is slower, following a loop through a dizzying number of the Ten Thousand Islands. Along the way tour-goers are likely to see manatees, frisky bottle-nosed dolphins, bald eagles, and loads of smirking alligators.

If you want to do it up super fancy, you can explore the Everglades and Ten Thousand Islands aboard the *Iva W.* (www.ivawcruises.com, $1,200 per day for the crew and boat), a historic wooden boat with accommodations for up to six (three double cabins). It's a 60-foot wooden freighter from the Chesapeake Bay that has been converted to take charters through coastal waters. In 2005, the ship arrived at the northern edge of Everglades National Park, taking groups to sail, shell, fish, swim, and generally enjoy the backcountry of beautiful mangrove islands.

SIGHTS

Big Cypress Gallery

East of Everglades City, famous black-and-white landscape photographer Clyde Butcher has a photo gallery worth the drive. **Clyde Butcher's**

Big Cypress Gallery (52338 Tamiami Trail, Ochopee, 239/695-2428, 10 A.M.–5 P.M. Thurs.–Mon.) features Butcher's own work on local themes—he is to Big Cypress and the Everglades what Ansel Adams was to Yosemite—as well as the work of other nature-inspired photographers. If you happen to be in the area around Labor Day, the gallery sponsors a huge party with a naturalist-led swamp walk, music, and more.

Museums

The dire economic climate of Reconstruction after the Civil War prompted some robust families to move to the southwest Florida frontier, as "grass is always greener" hopefulness that didn't necessarily pan out as planned. They came, cleared the land on little islands (many of them now named after the original family inhabiting them), built rough-hewn cabins of pine and cypress, and hunted, fished, and farmed to keep the wolf from the door. Stoically, they made do in the wilderness, many of them visiting their neighbors by boat only infrequently. Then Ted Smallwood opened Chokoloskee Island's first general store in 1906. There, white settlers and the remaining Seminoles alike would bring in their hides, furs, and produce in exchange for sugar, coffee, ammunition, and other of life's essentials. You can read all about the Smallwood Store and its first customers in Peter Matthiessen's riveting book *Killing Mister Watson*. It tells the story of the legendary killer Edgar J. Watson, who is said to have killed the outlaw Belle Starr and then lived a mysterious life in the wild Florida Everglades. The book is arranged as a fictionalized oral history of the intertwined lives of 10 of the area's quirky and often trigger-happy residents.

Today, **Smallwood Store** (three miles south of Everglades City, 360 Mamie St., Chokoloskee, 239/695-2989, open daily, $2.50) is preserved as a 1920s-era general store with its original structure and its last stock of merchandise. The small museum provides stirring insight into the hard lives of the pioneers who settled at the edge of this vast wilderness, and the isolation born of living on tiny, remote mangrove islands. The store was placed on the National Register of Historic Places in 1974 and reopened as a museum by Ted Smallwood's granddaughter in 1989.

Just off the circle in the center of Everglades City, the little **Museum of the Everglades** (105 W. Broadway, 239/695-0008, 11 A.M.–4 P.M. Tues.–Sat., suggested donation $2) is in the town's Old Laundry, a building that dates to the 1920s, when Everglades City was Barron Collier's "company town," during the construction of the Tamiami Trail. The focus is more on the area's Seminoles and other tribes who inhabited the area before white settlers arrived. The building is of note for the history buff—listed on the National Register of Historic Places, it's the only unaltered original building in town—but the artifacts and period photographs don't quite manage to tell a rich or compelling story. You'd get a better sense of the area's unique history by chatting with the locals or gliding through the mangroves in a canoe. Still, on a rainy day it's probably worth an hour.

ACCOMMODATIONS
Under $50

Camping opportunities are abundant around here, but not recommended in the hot, wet season. Too many critters with which to compete. If you do want to camp in Everglades National Park, stop off at the Gulf Coast Visitor Center for an overnight pass, and always make sure someone has a fairly good idea of where you're camping.

The **Barron River Resort, Motel and RV Park** (803 Collier Ave., 239/695-3591, $28–48 for RV spots, $75 for motel) is an old-time favorite, right on the Barron River at the Everglades City Bridge. There are simple waterfront efficiencies, one- and two-bedroom apartments, and an RV park with full hookups, cable TV, and telephone. The motel also runs a full-service marina and a bait and tackle store, and offers boat rentals. It may be the quickest route from under the covers to steering through the magical Ten Thousand Islands. Pets welcome.

RV campers have another appealing option at **Outdoor Resorts of America** (at the entrance to Chokoloskee Island, 239/695-2881, $49–69).

Tent and van camping are prohibited, but the RV campsites are lovely and the campground offers cabin rentals along with kayak rentals (at the dock), showers, laundry, and a small convenience store.

$50–150

There are three wonderful places to stay in Everglades City—none is glamorous, but all are significant pieces of local history and legend. The white clapboard **Rod and Gun Club** (200 Broadway, 239/695-2101, $85–125, no credit cards) was built in 1850 on the site of the first homestead in Everglades City. It has hosted movie stars, U.S. presidents, and lots of other celebs needing to get away from it all. The Rod and Gun Club was for years where local and visiting sportspeople gathered to tell big fish stories or share hunting information. A long, low lodge, it contains 17 comfortable rooms, a waterfront restaurant, and dock space. The **Everglades Spa and Lodge** (201 W. Broadway, 239/695-3151, www.banksoftheeverglades.com, $100–125) is right next door to the Rod and Gun Club and is another piece of local history. It was built as the Bank of the Everglades, the first bank to serve Collier County in the 1920s, and has now been converted to a small bed-and-breakfast. The refurbished building has 12 rooms called things like the Mortgage Loan Department and the Dividends Department, and breakfast is served in the vault. And the **Ivey House Bed and Breakfast** (107 Camellia St., 239/695-3299, $70–155), my favorite, was first built as a recreation hall for workers on the Tamiami Trail. The building was subsequently moved and converted to a boarding house—it's not fancy, with cinderblock walls and simple room furnishings, but the restaurant is wonderful (a delicious à la carte breakfast is included). The inn's staff is a wealth of information on the area, there's a small Everglades library on-site, and the complimentary bikes make familiarizing yourself with the area a snap (take a bike and ride all the way to Chokoloskee Island for dinner at JT's). The Ivey House is also the headquarters for Everglades Rentals & Eco Adventures, with charter trips and canoe and kayak rentals.

FOOD

Dining in Everglades City is unilaterally casual, but with no fast food and very few ethnic restaurants. All the times listed below reflect peak season hours. If you're dining here during the off-season, it's best to call for hours of operation. Several spots are outstanding, both for the food and the convivial ambience. The **Ghost Orchid Grill** at the Ivey House (107 Camellia St., 239/695-3299, 6:30 A.M.–9 P.M. daily, $11–24) serves a crowd-pleasing menu of accessible American and Italian dishes. Grilled grouper, snapper piccata, chicken carciofi—Chef David has a deft hand and an unfussy aesthetic. **JT's Island Grill and Gallery** (238 Mamie St., Chokoloskee, 239/695-3633, 11 A.M.–3 P.M. Mon.–Wed., 11 A.M.–3 P.M. and 5–9 P.M. Thurs.–Sun., $10–15) is something else entirely. It has a bohemian vibe, not exactly hippie, but a free-spirited something like that. The food gives a truly sophisticated and contemporary spin to local seafood, drawing broadly from Latin America, the Caribbean, and Southeast Asia. The cute little restaurant and shop (great array of books on the Everglades and lovely local handicrafts) was established circa 1890 as C.G. McKinney Store and looks today like a sprawling, comfortable house with extra tables set up in the side yard under a papaya tree. The lunch menu is fancy sandwiches and salads, and at dinner there's a fish of the day sautéed in a house key-lime marinade topped with

COURTESY OF NAPLES, MARCO ISLAND, EVERGLADES CVB

Everglades City is the stone crab capital of the world. Crab companies provide fresh claws to the area's seafood restaurants during stone crab season from October through May.

zingy salsa and served with organic greens and black beans and rice; one evening's soup brought a spicy Thai curry broth cradling sweet local shrimp. There's no booze, but excellent iced tea and the archetypal key lime pie.

The **Oyster House** (901 S. Copeland Ave., 239/695-2073, 11 A.M.–9 P.M. daily, Fri. and Sat. until 10 P.M., $10–19) is fun, but don't be a stickler on the culinary details. A sprawling, goofy place with model boats, murals, mounted largemouth bass, swordfish, and assorted taxidermatological handiwork. The safest bet is a fried fish platter and a beer (if you order something fancy like a glass of chardonnay there's no telling when that bottle was opened). Stone crabs are also a house specialty—eat them like the locals, chilled (it's gauche to ask for them hot) with mustard sauce—as is fried gator tail. And here's a must after lunch or dinner: Take the walk up to the top of the Ernest Hamilton Observation tower right behind the restaurant. This is a 75-foot-tall structure built in 1985, with a panoramic view of Chokoloskee and the Ten Thousand Islands.

Beyond these three, a few other places will feed you satisfactorily (maybe not precisely with gourmet aplomb) and perhaps introduce you to something new. At the **Everglades Seafood Depot Restaurant** (in the old train depot opened in 1928, 102 Collier Ave., 239/695-0075) try the deep-water lobster or stone crabs (their season is Oct. 15–May 15); when visiting the **Oar House Restaurant** (305 Collier Ave. N, 239/695-3535) work up your nerve to order "cooter," a local specialty of fried freshwater turtle; and at the **Rod and Gun Club** restaurant (200 Broadway, 239/695-2101, $12–25, no credit cards) set your sights on the conch fritters, gator nuggets, hushpuppies, or blue crab claws.

Cocktails

Anyplace that's known for a dance called the Buzzard Lope and that throws the biggest annual party around in honor of the lowly mullet is worth some investigation. **N Stan's Idle Hour Seafood Restaurant** (221 Goodland Dr. W, Goodland, 239/394-3041, 11 A.M.–10 P.M. Tues.–Sun., $14–25) is on the tiny island of Goodland, in between Marco Island and Ever-

glades City, connected by causeways. Sunday afternoons are the time to go to Stan's—heck, anytime's a good time to go to Stan's—when a fair percentage of the island's 200 or so residents show up for some live music, pitchers of beer, peel-and-eat shrimp, and fried oysters. (For fisherfolk, Stan's also has a "you caught 'em, we cook 'em" policy.) Stan is a real guy, a hellion dubbed the Buzzard King and the author of the "Buzzard Lope Song," which goes something like this:

Going down the highway feeling fine

Doing 55 and right on time

Look up ahead and saw something in the highway, looks dead

A bunch of buzzards standing around

They all step back, with a lot of hope

Start doing the Buzzard Lope . . .

Flap your wings up and down

Take a few steps back

Go round and round . . .

Enough said? The weekend after the Super Bowl every January brings the Mullet Festival to Stan's, with lots of hilarity and hijinks.

Festivals

The annual **Everglades Seafood Festival** in Everglades City draws thousands the first weekend in February with the promise of stone crabs (they say Everglades City is the world's capital, with more than 400,000 pounds of crab claws harvested Oct. 15–May 15), fish chowder, gator nuggets, Indian fry bread, and mud buggy races—not to mention a cutthroat mullet-toss competition.

SHOPPING

There's a squat nondescript building in the middle of nothing near where the road ends in the Everglades. Maybe you can buy ice there, or bait, I'm not sure. It's called the Chokoloskee Mall. I'm sure it's a joke the locals play on tourists, but that about sums up the shopping options in this edge-of-the-wilderness area. Head back up into Naples if the retail bug bites.

Information and Services

AREA INFORMATION

Naples and environs are on eastern time. The telephone area code is 239, but it used to be 941 (unfortunately, some guides and brochures still list the old area code, and the automatic call-forwarding expired in 2003).

Tourist Information

The *Naples Daily News* (239/262-3161, www.naplesnews.com) may be the best way to find out about local events and entertainment (it also produces the *Bonita Daily News*, the *Marco Island Eagle*, and the *Bonita Banner*). Kiosks are pretty much everywhere, and it will run you 53 cents. For visitor information, visit the convenient **Chamber of Commerce Visitors & Information Center** (895 5th Ave. S, Naples, 239/262-6141) to pick up brochures, maps (there's a good city one that's worth the couple of bucks they ask for it), and lots of coupons. The **Convention and Visitor Bureau** (800/2-ES-CAPE) has recently launched a super visitor information website at www.paradisecoast.com.

Golfers have lots of local publications at their fingertips, such as the freebie *Golf Naples Times* (www.golfnaplestimes.com).

Marco Island events and information can be found easily in a copy of *Marco Island Sun Times* (239/394-4050), the widely distributed free community paper. And for Everglades City information, call the **Everglades Area Chamber of Commerce** (800/914-6355, www.florida-everglades.com), or visit it at the junction of U.S. 41 and County Road 29, where there's a nice little gift shop and lots of good books on the area.

Police and Emergencies

As always, if you find yourself in a real emergency, pick up a phone and dial 911. For a non-emergency police need, call or visit the **Naples Police Department** (355 Riverside Circle, 239/213-4844, www.naplespolice.com). The **Marco Island Police Department** can be reached at 239/389-5050, and the sheriff in **Everglades City** can be reached at 239/695-3341. In the event of a medical emergency, stop into the **Naples Community Hospital** (350 7th St. N, 239/436-5000) or **Marco Healthcare Center** (40 S. Heathwood Dr., Marco Island, 239/394-8234). To fill a prescription, try the **Naples Fifth Avenue Pharmacy** (800 5th Ave. S, 239/261-8556); **Island Drug** (1089 Collier Blvd. N, #409, Marco Island, 239/394-3111) has met Marco Island's pharmaceutical needs for 30 years.

Radio and Television

For when you feel like cranking a little music around here, turn to 98.9 FM for smooth jazz, the Storm 106 FM for dance and R&B, 99.3 FM for new music, and 1480 AM for some sports and talk radio.

And on the television, WBBH Channel 2 out of Fort Myers is the NBC affiliate, WEVU Channel 8 out of Naples is the UPN affiliate, WINK Channel 11 out of Fort Myers is the CBS affiliate, WZVN Channel 7 out of Fort Myers is the ABC affiliate, and WGCU Channel 30 out of Fort Myers is the PBS affiliate.

Laundry Services

If you're staying at one of the upscale hotels, condos, or inns on Marco Island or in Naples, most offer their own laundry services to guests. There's also a cool **24 Hour Laundromat** (4045 Golden Gate Pkwy., Naples, 239/352-2349) that doesn't use coins. You stick in bills and it issues you a card, which you then stick in the washer or dryer. In Everglades City it's a little trickier—the Ivey House and a few other accommodations have launderettes for their guests.

Getting There and Around

DRIVING

Main driving access to the area is via I-75, either from the north or straight west across the bottom of the state (this section of I-75 is known as Alligator Alley, with ample cause). From I-75, you may take Exit 101 to Highway 84, which leads to downtown Naples (best if your aim is to do a little shopping or dining along 5th Avenue South or 3rd Street South, or if you want to amble along the Naples Pier). Exit 107 (Pine Ridge Rd.) takes you directly to U.S. 41, otherwise known as the Tamiami Trail, the best exit for reaching Clam Pass and Vanderbilt Beach parks and beaches. National Audubon Society's Corkscrew Swamp Sanctuary is easiest accessed by Exit 111 (Immokalee Rd.), which also takes you to North Naples.

To get to Marco Island, take Exit 101, then follow Collier Boulevard (Hwy. 951) west to the island. And to reach Everglades City, continue south from Naples on U.S. 41.

If you're coming from Miami, take U.S. 41 the whole way. The Tamiami Trail is little slower than I-75, but it offers more sightseeing possibilities, as it has been designated a National Scenic Byway and Florida Scenic Highway. The route celebrated its 75th anniversary in 2003 and takes you right through the Everglades and Big Cypress National Preserve.

FLYING

By air, the closest large airport is **Southwest Florida International Airport** (239/768-1000, www.swfia.com), 40 minutes to the north in Fort Myers. Most major domestic airlines serve the airport, and there are international flights from Germany and Canada.

The airport has enjoyed enormous growth recently, finishing an expanded terminal and new runway opening in 2005. There is a little commuter airport in Naples, the **Naples Municipal Airport** (239/643-0733, www.flynaples.com), which offers nonstop jet service between Naples and Delta's Atlanta hub with three flights daily on Delta affiliate carrier Atlantic Southeast Airlines as well as regular flights to Miami and the Florida Keys. And private planes can fly into Marco Executive Airport, Immokalee Regional Airport, and Everglades Airpark in Everglades City.

Alamo (800/327-9633), **Avis** (800/831-2847), **Budget** (800/527-0700), **Dollar** (800/800-4000 domestic, 800/800-6000 international), and **National** (800/227-7368) provide rental cars from Southwest Florida International Airport. From the Naples Municipal Airport, there is a convenient **Naples Airport Shuttle** (888/569-2227).

PUBLIC TRANSPORTATION

Amtrak (800/USA-RAIL) offers train service as far south as the Fort Myers station, 40 miles or so north of Naples, but you'll have to drive from there. Also, Greyhound Bus Line (239/774-5660) provides regular service into Naples, and Collier Area Transit operates a reliable network of city buses ($3 for a day-long pass). One of the most pleasant sightseeing opportunities in Naples is the **Naples Trolley** (1010 6th Ave. S, 239/263-7400, day passes $18 for adults, $8 for children 4–12, free for children under 4, free reboarding). The narrated tour covers over 100 local points of interest and a nice historical overview of the area. You can disembark whenever something captures your interest, then hop the next trolley shuffling by.

Lee County

The area between Sarasota and Naples was inhabited for 2,000 years by the fierce, tall, and agriculturally impaired Calusas. No matter, because the fishing was good and the shell-fishing was better. For a while Lee County had a slick ad campaign that read: "Ancient cultures once used shells as currency. Guess this place must have been Fort Knox." They seem to have retired the campaign, but the fact remains: The long lengths of beaches in this area are spectacular for their sand, their birds, their sunsets, and, most strikingly, for their shells. You could stub a toe on a lightning whelk (an anomaly in the mollusk world, opening to the left and not the right) or strain your sciatic stooping for perfect Florida fighting conch along the water's edge.

Gold-seeking Spanish conquistadores all but wiped out the Calusa and then never really settled here with any impressive numbers. The nearly unpopulated barrier islands became a hideout for pirates, most famously Jose Gaspar, the "last of the buccaneers." Whether apocryphal or not, in 1783 Gasparilla, as he called himself, commandeered a Spanish ship, the *Floridablanca,* and roamed the Gulf Coast waters plundering treasure and capturing beautiful women (his "captives," it is said, were warehoused on "Captiva" Island).

The area, sometimes called Lee Island Coast (although there's no Lee Island, just Lee County, named after Confederate general Robert E. Lee), was the site of one of the southernmost land battles of the American Civil War. It was

Must-Sees

Look for **N** to find the sights and activities you can't miss and **N** for the best dining and lodging.

N Lovers Key State Park: Lee County beaches are ranked some of the best in the nation for shelling, with more varieties found here than anywhere else in North America. Of the 50 miles of white sand, Lighthouse Beach & Fishing Pier and Bowman's Beach, both on Sanibel, are each worth a day of lolling, but if you have time for only one in the area, Lovers Key State Park gives you the widest range of options, from the 2.5-mile stretch of beach to 5 miles of bike trails (page 72).

N Edison-Ford Winter Estates: Thomas Edison, who spent 46 winters in Fort Myers, is considered to be the most inventive man who ever lived, holding 1,097 patents for everything from

COURTESY OF VISIT FLORIDA

In 1925, Harvey Firestone gave Thomas Edison a banyan tree to add to his botanical garden. It's still growing.

light bulbs, cement, phonographs, and the natural rubber he made from goldenrod. His estate and that of his buddy Henry Ford are fascinating (page 73).

N J.N. "Ding" Darling National Wildlife Refuge: Occupying more than half of Sanibel Island, the park is home to a tremendous array of birdlife (page 85).

N Bailey-Matthews Shell Museum: It's a crash course in Neptune's treasures, a must if you want to know which species you're painstakingly unearthing along the shoreline (page 86).

N Palm Island: If you have the resources of time and money, a day or two on Palm Island is good for the soul, and most other parts, too. It's an unbridged barrier island paradise (page 96).

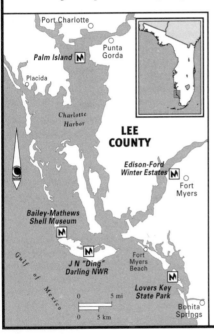

Port Charlotte

Punta Gorda

Palm Island **N**

Placida

Charlotte Harbor

LEE COUNTY

Edison-Ford Winter Estates **N**

Fort Myers

Bailey-Mathews Shell Museum

N

N

Gulf of Mexico

J N "Ding" Darling NWR

Fort Myers Beach

N

Lovers Key State Park

Bonita Springs

0   5 mi

0   5 km

fought in Fort Myers on February 20, 1865, with both sides claiming victory (the confusing event is celebrated annually in North Fort Myers with a battle reenactment during its Cracker Festival). The county was named after the war, when it separated from nearby Monroe County in 1887.

Lee County's draw for the visitor is sheer variety. The city of **Fort Myers,** in large measure due to its most famous residents, Thomas Edison and Henry Ford, is culturally rich, with attractions spread along the banks of the Caloosahatchee River. It is the oldest and largest city in southwest Florida, and as such, dense with history. Nearby, the barrier islands offer tropical island getaways.

The most well known of this group of islands are **Sanibel** and **Captiva.** Once connected to each other at what is now Blind Pass, the siblings bear a family resemblance but have vastly different personalities. Both cater to affluent winter visitors, but Sanibel is more accessible (financially, physically, etc.), with miles of bike paths, low-rise independently owned inns and teeny hotels. Living here is casual; a tremendous wildlife refuge takes up nearly half of the island, with white-sand beaches on the Gulf side and picturesque mangrove forests on the eastern side. Captiva, to the north and connected by a causeway, is the playground of the even more affluent. Many people own homes on Captiva (you won't see it, but artist Robert Rauschenberg has an unassuming white, beachfront mansion and studio on the island), most tucked down driveways shielded from prying eyes by lush foliage. There's less to do on Captiva, there are fewer places to stay, fewer tourist amenities. But that's how people on Captiva like it.

Then there are the other barrier islands, each with its own character. Fort Myers Beach is on the long strip of coast-hugging land known as Estero Island. It's the closest thing this area has to a "spring break" type beach, with cheap motels and crowded, family-friendly beaches. Gasparilla Island has made a name for itself as the tarpon capital and host to American presidents and a wide array of fish-seeking celebrities. Its town of Boca Grande is worth the quick boat ride or slightly longer car ride (you've got to go north and then out a causeway) to see. Cabbage Key, North Captiva, and Useppa are accessible only by boat but make a lovely day trip. And Pine Island is the largest of the barrier islands in this area, mostly residential, with the charming maritime towns of Matlacha, Bokeelia, Pineland, and St. James City. Anglers know it for its "Fishingest Bridge in the U.S."

PLANNING YOUR TIME

The area could entertain the troops for a week or more. The budget traveler will make his or her home base in Fort Myers or Fort Myers Beach, slinking over the very expensive causeway ($6) to Sanibel and Captiva for a day of rejuvenating beach therapy. The Edison and Ford estates in Fort Myers will occupy much of a day, as will the Ding Darling National Wildlife Refuge on Sanibel. The rest of the area's attractions are more fleetingly entertaining (although the beach never gets old). Families will spend a fair amount of time at the kids' water park and attractions to the north in Cape Coral; history buffs will likely occupy themselves at one of several Calusa museums; the outdoors enthusiast will choose fishing, canoeing, or sailing, or all of the above.

Summers are fairly tolerable in the area, but still soporific with heat and humidity. Fall is beautiful, but if your aim is winter, it's cheaper to visit in the first two weeks of December. Rates generally increase for high season during the third week of December, and the large crowds arrive in February and March. In early December, you'll find lots of accommodations and nominal traffic (which can be frustrating on Sanibel and Captiva in March).

HURRICANES

More than $14 billion in property damage, and counting. Hurricane Charley's legacy is still profoundly felt. And, often, heard. The hew and cry of construction crews, the plaintive

Lee County

LEE COUNTY

74

80

Babcock

Alva

Caloosahatchee River

82

31

Leigh Acres

Cleveland

Manatee Park

CALUSA NATURE CENTER AND PLANETARIUM

SOUTHWEST FLORIDA INTERNATIONAL AIRPORT

75

Bonita Springs

To Naples

North Fort Myers

Fort Myers

41

Estero

Estero Bay

Estero Island

MCGREGOR BLVD

SHELL FACTORY AND NATURE PARK

PINE ISLAND RD

DEL PRADO BLVD

LOVERS KEY STATE PARK

75

TAMIAMI TRAIL

765

BURNT STORE RD

78

Cape Coral

Fort Myers Beach

SANIBEL CAUSEWAY

SANIBEL LIGHTHOUSE

Punta Gorda

Cape Haze

PALM ISLAND

Matlacha

STRINGFELLOW RD

J N "DING" DARLING NWR

Port Charlotte

41

Charlotte Harbor

Bokeelia

Pineland

Pine Island

SANIBEL-CAPTIVA RD

Sanibel Island

Placida

Cabbage Key

Useppa Island

Pine Island Sound

Captiva Island

BAILEY-MATHEWS SHELL MUSEUM

Boca Grande

Gasparilla Island

Cayo Costa

North Captiva

Englewood

Manasata Key

Don Pedro Island

Gulf of Mexico

0   5 mi

0   5 km

© AVALON TRAVEL PUBLISHING, INC.

ping of one hammer driving home a roofing nail, the wheeze of a bulldozer as it's put in park—these are not the sounds you want to hear on your beach getaway. But it's getting better. The fury of Charley, a Category IV storm on August 13, was the most cataclysmic for this region of the 2004 hurricane season's four Florida-coast storms. By the beginning of November, Lee County's inns, resorts, condos, time-shares, bed-and-breakfasts, and motels had made it to the end of a vicious hurricane season. But they anticipated the approaching tourist season with trepidations.

Almost half a million winter visitors arrive in Fort Myers, Sanibel, Captiva, and the other barrier islands for some fun in the sun. And most of those visitors will find accommodations, restaurants, and attractions up and running. The parts that take time, however, are those parts left in the hands of Mother Nature. The hurricane denuded trees, pulling unlucky ones out of the ground, root ball and all. The

lush canopy that defined Sanibel and Captiva will take a while to return. Banyans, Australian pines, sea grape trees, and stately palms no longer line the streets and coyly obscure the gorgeous houses from view.

Still, reports of Lee County's death are greatly exaggerated. Tourists have been slow to come back, fearing the worst. Consequently, there are still good deals to be had and fairly low occupancy even during peak times. One caution, though: Charley was not an even-handed storm. It was small, violent, and fast, knocking flat what was in its path and leaving most everything else unscathed. North Captiva Island took a bashing, as did the Bokeelia part of Pine Island, then on up toward Charlotte Harbor and Punta Gorda. Call before you go, and ask questions about what kind of damage your hotel sustained. Even places that are operational are known to have a blue tarp-and-plywood decorating motif that is less than charming.

Fort Myers

A hurricane in the 1840s drove the soldiers out of Seminole War Fort Dulaney at the mouth of the Caloosahatchee. The evacuation had an upside. First Lt. John Harvie found a safer, more sheltered place for a fort, which he named Fort Myers in honor of that war's Colonel Abraham C. Myers. Retired soldiers came back to the area after the war, making use of the picturesque Caloosahatchee to ship cattle to Cuba. Fort Myers was a sleepy cowpoke town, not even on the beach, when Thomas Alva Edison visited and fell in love with it in 1885.

Fort Myers was incorporated that same year, and the banks of the Caloosahatchee Intercoastal Waterway started to be settled by intrepid northerners. Edison talked his buddy Henry Ford into exploring the area, and Ford promptly bought the house next door on McGregor Boulevard. Because of Edison's gift to the city of hundreds of royal palms, its nickname is "City of Palms," which I suppose has a catchier ring to it than

"Gladiolus Capital of the World" (some of the area's original settlers were zealous gladiola growers from Belgium, The Netherlands, and Luxembourg).

These days, Fort Myers is Lee County's working center, the biggest city in southwest Florida. There are attractions, restaurants, and hotels centered around the bustling downtown historic district and along the riverfront. Its easy access to nearby barrier islands (Sanibel, Captiva, Pine Island, Gasparilla, etc.), combined with its wealth of family-friendly attractions, makes it an obvious home base for the dynamic traveler. There are full-service marinas connected to several of the hotels along the river, so boaters can pull right up.

While the city of Fort Myers is beachless, head down to Fort Myers Beach on Estero Island for fun in the sun and sand—its gentle slope and lack of steep drop-offs make it a safe beach for young swimmers or waders. At the north end of the island a casual beach village offers a cluster of

Lee County

FORT MYERS

Caloosahatchee River

CALOOSAHATCHEE BRIDGE

To Manatee Park

BURROUGHS HOME ★

EDWARDS DR

FLORIDA REPERTORY THEATER ★

1ST ST

BAY ST

BARE BREAD BISTRO ▼

MONROE ST

MAIN ST

HENDY ST

BROADWAY

JACKSON ST

LEE ST

2ND ST

FOWLER ST

THOMPSON ST

VERANDA ▼

MARTIN LUTHER KING JR BLVD

SOUTHWEST FLORIDA MUSEUM OF HISTORY ★

HEITMAN ST

MONROE ST

HOLIDAY INN RIVERWALK ●

CLIFFORD ST

McGREGOR BLVD

UNION ST

LIBERTY ST

VICTORIA AVE

SKATIUM ■

HOOPLE ST

FOWLER ST

LAFAYETTE ST

EDISON-FORD WINTER ESTATES ★

Sanctuary State Park

City of Palms Park

BROADWAY

EDISON MALL ■

EDISON AVE

S CLEVELAND AVE

CENTRAL AVE

LLEWELLYN DR

LLEWELLYN   DR

GRAND AVE

41
45

CANAL ST

LEE MEMORIAL HOSPITAL ■

CORTEZ BLVD

LINHART AVE

| 0   200 yds |
| 0   200 m |

To Six Mile Cypress Parkway

HANSON ST

© AVALON TRAVEL PUBLISHING, INC.

restaurants and shops, and at Estero's southern end Lovers Key State Park is a huge draw, with a number of nearby resort hotels.

SPORTS AND RECREATION

Spring Training

The Red Sox and the Patriots made New England swell with pride in 2004–2005. If you're a fan and you want to do some extra gloating, take in a **Boston Red Sox Spring Training** (City of Palms Park, 2201 Edison Ave., Fort Myers, 239/334-4700, $10–44) game. It's a great little ballpark that Lee County has poured tons of money into in the past year—a good place to see a Grapefruit League home season game, and to get a preview of what the Sox are capable of this season.

Minnesota Twins Spring Training (Hammond Stadium, 14400 Six Mile Cypress Pkwy., Fort Myers, 239/768-4210, www.miraclebaseball.com, $16–18) also takes place locally at the Lee County Sports Complex. Games are at 12:05 P.M. all of the month of March, and after that, in April, fans can watch the Miracle League, a minor-league affiliate of the Minnesota Twins and member of the Florida State League.

Beaches

Fort Myers Beach is actually on the island of Estero, connected to Fort Myers by a causeway. There are several worthwhile beaches here. **Bowditch Point Regional Park** (50 Estero Blvd., 239/432-2004) is a 17-acre park that fronts both the Gulf and the bay at the northern tip of Estero Island, with a boardwalk over to a beach with beautiful views of nearby barrier islands. Parking is available behind the bathhouse (nice showers and changing rooms), and there's a 25-cent trolley from the Main Street parking lot. Just a bit to the south and on the Gulf side, **Lynn Hall Memorial Park** (950 Estero Blvd., 239/463-1116, parking $.75/hour) is a great family beach and a teen hangout. There's also a fishing pier here, heavily frequented by opportunistic pelicans. (If you happen to hook a pelican or other bird while

COURTESY OF LEE COUNTY VISITOR AND CONVENTION BUREAU

Lee County

Like its New York counterpart, Times Square on Fort Myers Beach is a hub of activity. It is a highly traveled pedestrian shopping, dining, and entertainment district where high heels and bare feet are both acceptable.

fishing, reel the bird in slowly; cover its head with a towel to calm it; cut the line close to the hook and remove all monofilament from wings and body; then call **Clinic for the Rehabilitation of Wildlife,** C.R.O.W., 239/472-3644, a local nonprofit bird rescue organization.)

Lovers Key State Park

Lovers Key State Park (8700 Estero Blvd., Fort Myers Beach, 239/463-4588, 8 A.M.–sundown, $5 per car up to eight people, single occupancy car $3, pedestrians and bicyclists $1) is the newest of Florida's state parks and actually occupies four small barrier islands (Black Island, Long Key, Inner Key, and Lovers Key) between Fort Myers Beach and Bonita Beach to the south. The park contains a 2.5-mile stretch of beautiful beach and 5 miles of bike trails (bike, canoe, and kayak rentals available on-site), including the Black Island Trail through a maritime hammock. There are brand-new picnic facilities at the New Lovers Key Bayside area on Estero Boulevard. Hurricane Charley did leave its mark here, though—the wooden pedestrian bridge leading from the main parking area to the mid-island beach is not currently open, but there's free tram service to the beach (9 A.M.–5 P.M. daily).

In addition to roseate spoonbills, snowy egrets, and American kestrels, birders will see active osprey nests and a couple of bald eagle nests. The park offers 90-minute sunset eco-tours (239/314-0110, $20 adults, $8 children) Tuesday, Thursday, Friday, and Saturday, and there is a dolphin cruise and shelling excursion every Sunday, 8:15–9:15 A.M.

See the Manatees

Spend a little time on the Orange and Caloosahatchee Rivers, and chances are you'll see a West Indian manatee. Take a 90-minute boat tour with **Manatee World** (5605 Palm Beach Blvd., Fort Myers, 239/693-1434, www.manateeworld.com; tours depart 10 A.M., noon, 2 P.M., and 4 P.M. daily, $15 adults, $7 children, 2 and under free) and the odds are better you'll see a few of these mammals, related biologically to the elephant and, unlikely though it may seem, the aardvark. The narrated ecotour provides insight

into the life of the area's most famous species, as well as information about their continued plight (outboard motors, habitat destruction, etc.). Manatees seem to congregate in the Orange River in the winter, basking in the waters warmed by the outflow of the nearby power plant. This is a good family adventure, and if you are smitten by these gentle sea cows, you can trudge over to **Manatee Park** (10901 Hwy. 80, 1.5 miles east of I-75, North Fort Myers, 239/694-3537, 8 A.M.–8 P.M. daily, until 5 P.M. in the winter, parking $.75/hour). There are three observation decks for viewing and hydrophones so you can listen in (I don't speak manatee, but the cool thing is, even scientists are unsure how they make these chirps, whistles, and squeaks). A cow and her calf are especially talkative, vocalizing back and forth. The park rents kayaks in winter and on summer weekends, with kayak clinics the second Saturday of the month and free guided walks through the native plants habitats at 9 A.M. every Saturday.

Golf

The greater Fort Myers area has around 100 public and semiprivate golf courses, the egalitarian nature of which makes the city duly proud. The city of Fort Myers itself maintains two professionally designed golf courses. **Fort Myers Country Club** (3591 McGregor Blvd., 239/936-3126, public, 18 holes, par 71, 6,414 yards, course rating 70.5, slope 118, greens fee $25–50, depending on season and time of day) was designed by the great Donald Ross in 1916 and opened in 1917—one of the oldest courses on the Gulf Coast. It hosts the pro-am Beck's Open every year in January and is only a mile from downtown. **Eastwood Golf Course** (4600 Bruce Herd Lane, 239/275-4848, public, 18 holes, par 72, 6,772 yards, course rating 73.3, slope 130, greens fee $25–60) was rated 32nd among "America's Top 75 Public Courses" not long ago by *Golf Digest*. A hilly course by Florida standards, with lots of wildlife in a tranquil setting, it features 84 reconstructed bunkers.

Tracker School

North and east of Fort Myers is a little town called Alva. Not much to do there amongst the dense

Florida live oak, slash pine, and palmetto, unless you want to learn to be a tracker. New Jersey-based **Tom Brown, Jr.'s Tracker School** (13300-56 S. Cleveland Ave., Ste. 221, Fort Myers, FL 33907, www.trackerschool.com, 908/479-4681, $950 for one-week class) recently relocated part of the year to this lush stretch of Florida wilderness. Students spend a week learning how to observe nature, track animals, and survive in the wilderness. Brown started his tracking school in 1978, on the heels of a number of successful books like his first, *The Tracker, Tom Brown's Field Guide to Wilderness Survival,* and *Grandfather.* The Florida school site has swimming holes, trails, and camping areas, all dense with local flora and fauna. If you need a hair dryer and a dry pair of socks, this may not be for you.

SIGHTS

 Edison–Ford Winter Estates

The 90-minute guided tour is a must at the Edison-Ford Winter Estates (2350 McGregor Blvd., Fort Myers, 239/334-3614, www.edison-ford-es-tate.com, combined tour of the estates 9 A.M.–5:30 P.M. Mon.–Sat., noon–5:30 P.M. Sun., with last tour leaving promptly at 4 P.M., botanical tours 9 A.M. Thurs. and Sat., $16 adults, $8.50 children 6–12, electric launch ride $5.50). This is obviously the biggest show in town, Fort Myers's Statue of Liberty or Eiffel Tower, the kind of attraction you owe it to yourself and others to see. It's great, it really is, and the tour gives it extra depth and drama. I learned that Henry Ford stuffed the seats of his first Model T imprudently with local Spanish moss, which prompted the first automotive recall when little chiggers started crawling out and biting early drivers on the rear ends. I learned that the huge banyan tree out front is the largest in the U.S., the aerial roots' circumference at more than 400 feet, and that it was a gift to Thomas Edison from his tire-making buddy Harvey Firestone. It's a wonderful tour.

The two estates encompass 14 acres of botanical landscaping, the two American titans' historic homes and guest cottages, Mr. Edison's laboratory, a museum containing his famous inventions

Lee County

COURTESY OF LEE COUNTY VISITOR AND CONVENTION BUREAU

Thomas Edison, Harvey Firestone (both pictured), Henry Ford, and John Burroughs went off on a series of motor camping caravans in 1914 and 1915, said to be the first link between the automobile and "road tripping."

COURTESY OF VISIT FLORIDA

Edison invented the modern incandescent lamp, sticky tape, the tinfoil phonograph, and the kinetophone (a dud). See all these inventions and others at the laboratory at the Edison estate.

and exhibits, a museum store, garden shop, an outdoor café, and three electric launches for cruising the picturesque Caloosahatchee River. It's worth at least a couple of hours of wandering through the gorgeous environs, but the real draw is peeking into the lives of these fascinating men.

Thomas Edison arrived in Fort Myers on March 20, 1885. Not one to be indecisive, evidently, he had purchased 13-plus acres along the river within 24 hours, with the aim of building his winter home. "Seminole Lodge" was duly built from his own designs in pieces in Maine and then sailed down to Florida and assembled. The home served as the winter retreat and workplace for the prolific inventor until his death in 1931. It's encircled with large overhanging porches, with grand French doors to encourage a cross breeze. There are electric chandeliers ("electroliers") designed by Edison. It's a fascinating house, donated to the city for $1 by Edison's widow.

Edison's close buddy Henry Ford was obviously smitten, too, upon his visit to Fort Myers in 1915. He bought the house next door, "The Mangoes" becoming another mecca for the country's elite—Harvey Firestone, naturalist John Burroughs, Nobel Laureate Alexis Carrel, and Charles Lindbergh all made their way to this little Florida paradise.

Poke your head into the laboratory and the museum of Edison's inventions and artifacts, spend a little time in Henry Ford's garage, then walk through the tropical botanical garden. Edison planted it as an experimental garden with more than 1,000 species, focusing on the byproducts of plants (rubber for his buddy Firestone's tires, for instance). Later, Mrs. Edison prettied it up by adding roses, orchids, and bromeliads. Unfortunately, Hurricane Charley damaged about 50 percent of the garden's vegetation—it is slowly on the mend, but many exotic and champion trees have needed to be replaced.

McGregor Boulevard

Fort Myers is sometimes called the City of Palms. Why? Edison and Ford's estates are poised just at the edge of McGregor Boulevard, which is lined on both sides by 60-foot-tall royal palms. The original 200 or so, from Cuba, were gifts from Thomas Edison to the city. The idea caught on, and now more than 2,000 palms flank the roadside of stately McGregor Boulevard. Drive the length of the 15-mile boulevard and the city's nickname seems fairly apt. (Palms around the city were knocked over by Hurricane Charley, so some are newly planted now.)

Museums

Southwest Florida Museum of History (2300 Peck St., 239/332-5955, www.cityftmyers .com/museum, 10 A.M.–5 P.M. Tues.–Sat., a fairly steep $9.50 adults, $8.50 seniors, $4 children 12 and under) is a quirky mix of stuff, but its wide net gathers a broad catch. The history of the Calusa and Seminole people, as well as that of this area's Spanish explorers, is a major focus of the museum, and more broadly the history of Fort Myers. Set in a restored Atlantic Coastline railroad depot built in 1924, the museum houses photographs and memorabilia; there's an 84-foot-long Pullman rail car built in 1929 and a replica of a late 1800s Cracker house. But then, get this: A current show is called the "Roswell Exhibit" and includes artifacts, documents, and dioramas about the mysterious 1947 crash of an unidentified "something" in the desert 30 miles north of Roswell, New Mexico. So it's Calusas, Spanish explorers, and alien abductions. The museum also runs 90-minute architectural and historic downtown walking tours in Fort Myers on Wednesday and Saturday ($5 adults, $3 children, reservation required).

If you like your history living, then stop in for an hour at the **Burroughs Home** (2505 1st St., 239/332-5955, www.cityftmyers.com, open to the public for guided tours on the hour 11 A.M.–3 P.M. Tues.–Fri. mid-Oct.–mid-May). By living history I mean people in period dress stubbornly insisting they are the original residents of a stately riverfront, turn-of-the-last-century Georgian Revival home. The house is largely used for special events, but it makes for a quick peek at the time in Fort Myers history when it went from being a sleepy cow town to a sophisticated winter retreat for the northern elite.

Koreshan State Historical Site

Hands-down winner of Weirdest Attraction in the Area prize is the Koreshan State Historical

GET OUT OF TOWN

Something to think about: If you have an extra day and nothing on the docket, why not pop off to Key West? Explore the country's southernmost city just for the day. There are high-speed shuttles from Fort Myers, a welcome alternative to driving (about seven hours) or flying (usually several hundred clams).

Key West Express (239/394-9700, $129 adults, $119 seniors, $109 children 6–12, children 5 and under $3) has a couple of boats that head out of Fort Myers. The 140-foot *Atlanticat* (Fisherman's Wharf under the Fort Myers Beach bridge) is a fast (40 mph) catamaran ferry that zips over to Key West in 3.5 hours. Most seating on the boat is contoured, airplane-like chairs, but there are also plush couches with tables. The floor-to-ceiling windows provide plenty of entertainment (and there's a full outdoor deck upstairs), but there are still six plasma screen TVs showing movies, sports, whatever. The 155-foot *Big Cat Express* (Salty Sam's Marina, 2500 Main St., Fort Myers) features two enclosed cabins, a sun deck, satellite TV, slot machines, and full galley and bar. The ships depart Fort Myers Beach 8 A.M., arrive Key West 11:30 A.M.; depart Key West 5 P.M., arrive Fort Myers Beach 8:30 P.M. That gives you five hours or so to noodle around town. Alternatively, you can find a hotel or inn, stay overnight, and come back on the next day's ferry for no additional ferry fee. This tiny 3- by 5-mile island, 100 miles from the coast, has the only living coral reef in the U.S. in addition to great restaurants and nightlife. And for 10 days in October, Fantasy Fest makes Key West the biggest party around.

Site (U.S. 41 at Corkscrew Rd., Estero, 239/992-0311, 8 A.M.–sundown, $4 per car, $1 for walkers or bicycles). It commemorates an eccentric religious sect begun by Dr. Cyrus Teed in 1894 after he had a spiritual "great illumination." It seems he and his followers believed the world is a hollow globe, with mankind residing on the inner surface, gazing into the universe below. Whoa. This Koresh, by the way, is no relation to the other wacky Waco Koresh of more recent vintage. The Koreshan followers (at its peak there were 250 of these) gave their commune to the state if it would be maintained as a historic site in perpetuity. Now the site is a compound of buildings and a theater, but visitors also avail themselves of the park's fishing, camping, nature study, and picnicking. There's a boat ramp and canoes for rent, and guided walks and campfire programs are offered seasonally.

ARTS AND ENTERTAINMENT

Wine-Tasting
About 10 miles east of Fort Myers you'll run across the southernmost bonded winery in the continental United States. **Eden Vineyards** (19709 Little Ln., at Exit 25 off I-75, Alva, 239/728-9463, www.edenwinery.com, 11 A.M.–4 P.M. daily, free) makes six wines (all around $11), none of them identified by varietal. They're made of hybrid grapes that have proven themselves capable of withstanding the Florida sun and heat. It's fun to do a little tasting in an area not known for its wine—and these fruity, low-alcohol wines somehow suit the climate.

Music and Theater
The **Barbara B. Mann Performing Arts Hall** (on the campus of Edison College, 8099 College Pkwy., 239/481-4849, www.bbmannpah .com) is the center of arts activity for Fort Myers. The full-sized and fully equipped stage hosts traveling Broadway musicals, popular music, and **Southwest Florida Symphony** (4560 Via Royale, 239/418-1500, www.swflso.org) concerts. The professional symphony orchestra offers classical and pops series annually (its chamber orchestra series takes place in Schein Hall at BIG Arts on Sanibel Island).

For theater, the **Florida Repertory Theatre** (Arcade Theatre, 2267 1st St., 239/332-4488) is a fairly new ensemble-based company with a year-round season. Split between musicals, comedies, and serious dramas, the professional repertory's season features nine productions, staged in a great restored 1908 Victorian movie house.

Broadway musicals and family-friendly comedies are the mainstay at **Broadway Palm Dinner Theatre** (1380 Colonial Blvd., 239/278-4422, www.broadwaypalm.com), which has a main stage as well as a more intimate black-box theater (in which "Off Broadway Palm" stages smaller-scale comedies and musical revues as well as children's theater). Some of the performers are local, and they occasionally bring in talent from farther afield. Performances are accompanied by cocktails, salad bar, and a buffet.

Visual Arts
Lee County isn't the visual arts smorgasbord of Naples to the south. Still, there are several nice galleries and the local arts center. The Lee County **Alliance for the Arts** (10091 McGregor Blvd., 239/939-2787, 9 A.M.–5 P.M. Mon.–Fri., 10 A.M.–3 P.M. Sat., free admission) is a multi-pronged arts organization founded in 1975. On a 10-acre campus, the organization contains the Frizzell Cultural Center of galleries, classrooms, a 175-seat indoor theater, and an outdoor amphitheater. The adjacent Edwards Building houses local artists and arts groups. Local, regional, and national art and crafts are displayed in the public galleries, and the theaters host live theatrical performances and festivals throughout the year. Locals use the facility for adult and youth art classes of all kinds, from glass fusing to acrylics.

A Laurel Art Gallery (2112 Crystal Dr., 239/278-0489) carries impressionistic landscapes and still-life paintings in vivid oils and acrylics by Charles Laurel Vavrina; **Gallery Naïve** (3334 Cleveland Ave., 239/939-1545, www.gallery-naive.com), located in a pretty frame shop, features bold, colorful naïf-style work; and if you're into the work of "America's most-collected living artist," the **Thomas Kinkade Gallery** (Bell Tower Gallery, 13499 S. Cleveland Ave., 239/415-7000) is for you.

FOR KIDS

Cape Coral, north of Fort Myers, isn't among the area's biggest draws for adults. As soon as children get a say, however, you may find yourself driving north with regularity. On a hot day, the kids will help navigate you to **Sun Splash Family Waterpark** (400 Santa Barbara Blvd.,

COURTESY OF LEE COUNTY VISITOR AND CONVENTION BUREAU

Cape Coral, to the north of Fort Myers, is home to a passel of family-friendly attractions such as Sun Splash.

239/574-0557, www.sunsplashwaterpark.com, open March 12–Sept. 25, mostly 10 A.M.–6 P.M., Thurs. and Sat. until 9 P.M. in the summer, $11.95 adults, $9.95 children under 48 inches tall, $2.95 age 2 and under), on the shore of Lake Kennedy. It's not huge, but there's a water flume ride, a big family pool, a tot playground, a "river" tube ride, a café, and a new super-fast ride called the Electric Slide, which is an enclosed tube in which you twist and turn at high speed. Not far away is **Mike Greenwell's Family Fun Park** (35 Pine Island Rd., Cape Coral, 239/574-4386, 10 A.M.–10 P.M. Sun.–Thurs., Fri. and Sat. until midnight, $2.50–5.50 for mini golf, 18 pitches/$1 in batting cages, plus equipment rental $1, $3–5.75 for go carts). It fills in the gaps, with miniature golf, batting cages, four go-cart tracks, a maze, an arcade, a sweet fish-feeding dock, and that abomination called paintball.

The **Children's Science Center** (2915 Northeast Pine Island Rd., 239/997-0012, 10 A.M.– 4 P.M. Mon.–Sat., $5 adults, $3 children 4–12, children under 3 free), also in Cape Coral, is a good rainy-day activity for younger kids. It's a hands-on science and technology center, with a bunch of live iguanas, a butterfly garden, optical illusions, computer activities, a little nature park

with "bug hunt" trails, and telescope viewing January–April. It's one of those friendly museums in which preschoolers enjoy pressing buttons, even if they never exactly figure out what the apparatus in question is supposed to do (watch them at the "It Does What?" tool display to see what I mean).

Located in downtown Fort Myers, another bad-weather delight for fairly little kids comes at the **Imaginarium Hands-On Museum** (2000 Cranford Ave., 239/337-3332, www.cityftmyers.com/Imaginarium, 10 A.M.–5 P.M. Mon.–Sat., noon–5 P.M. Sun., $8 adults, $7 seniors, $5 children 3–12, under 3 free). In January 2005, it launched a wonderful exhibit called Robo-Bugs: The World of Giant Insects exhibit, which contains lots of gigantic robotic replicas including a truly nightmare-inducing 20-foot preying mantis. It's a fairly calm hands-on museum in which kids can fly and be free. A hurricane simulator, fossil dig, a mini TV weatherman studio—it's hard not to get engrossed. There's also a fairly decent aquarium here, with scary moray eels and a lively coral reef tank.

Bigger kids have a couple of similar options in Fort Myers, science and nature centers more suited to school-age kids and adults. The **Calusa Nature Center & Planetarium** (3450 Ortiz Ave., Fort Myers, 239/275-3435, www.calusanature.com, museum and trail 9 A.M.–5 P.M. Mon.–Sat., 11 A.M.–5 P.M. Sun., $8 adults, $5 children 3–12) enables people to learn about southwest Florida's natural history in a number of ways. There are nature trails on boardwalks through pine flatwoods and cypress wetlands, on which you'll pass a Seminole village replica, a live bobcat, and a native birds-of-prey aviary for permanently injured birds. Inside the nature center, there are live animals and exhibits about their habitats. The best parts of the center are the regularly scheduled guided walks and animal lectures. The center also has a planetarium, in which you can learn about the Hubble telescope and the night sky or just chill out while watching a Pink Floyd laser light show.

The kind of Old Florida tourist draw people get nostalgic for, the **Shell Factory & Nature Park** (2787 Tamiami Trail N, North Fort Myers,

Lee County

239/995-2141, www.shellfactory.com, free admission) adopts a something-for-everyone approach (and has been doing so more or less successfully since the 1950s). There's a lot of kitschy shell-themed merchandise (inlaid shell toilet seats) to peruse while littler kids get wrapped up in the mini golf, bumper boats, pitching cages, and a video arcade. Supposedly it has the world's largest collection of rare shells and coral, but the glass-blowing artisans are more entertaining to watch (there's also a funny little History of Glass Museum on-site). Outdoors you'll have to visit the newly renovated nature park with a petting zoo (camels, llamas, donkeys, potbellied pigs, goats), trails, and a botanical garden. Sounds like a lot under one roof, huh? This is the kind of place where you simply have to give in and consume a batter-dipped hot dog followed by a pound of fudge.

After the fudge, you may need to get the blood flowing at Fort Myers's **Skatium** (2250 Broadway, Fort Myers, 239/461-3145, www.fmskatium.com, public skating 7:30–10 P.M. Fri., 1–3:15 P.M. and 7:30–10 P.M. Sat., 1–3:30 P.M. Sun.), a 72,000-square-foot facility with an ice-skating rink, an inline rink, laser tag arena, and video arcade. Most of the time, the rink is given over to local youth hockey and figure skating. If your kids are more into outdoor inline skating or skateboarding, Fort Myers has two skate parks, with ramps and half-pipes, etc.: **Slick's Sk8 Park** (17687 Summerlin Rd., near Fort Myers Beach, 239/267-2200) and **Sanctuary Skate Park** (2277 Grand Ave., downtown Fort Myers, 239/337-5297).

ACCOMMODATIONS
Around $50
For not a lot of money, you can get just about everything at **Rock Lake Resort** (2930 Palm Beach Blvd., 239/332-4080, www.bestlodgingswflorida.com, $40–89). The nine little cottages (18 units) encircling a little lake were built in 1946. Canoeing, lighted tennis courts, a nature trail, barbecue facilities, and comfortable porches overlooking the water—it all sits on Billy Creek, which allows direct access for small boats to the

Caloosahatchee River. Rock Lake isn't fancy, but it's just a short drive to the beach and half a mile from downtown. Rooms are handicapped accessible and they also have rooms for the hearing impaired. Pets welcome.

In a similar vein, the **TaKiki Riverfront Inn** (2631 1st St., 866/613-9330, $46–105) is an affordable efficiency motel opened in 1960 and renovated in 2001. No frills, but within walking distance of the downtown historic district, the City Yacht Basin, and Harborside Convention Center.

$50–150
The **Holiday Inn Riverwalk** (2220 W. 1st St., Fort Myers, 239/334-3434, www.hiriverwalk.com, $89–194) is right on the Caloosahatchee River a half mile from downtown Fort Myers and within walking distance of the Edison and Ford estates. The 146 rooms are simple but newly renovated, some with Jacuzzis. The on-site Toucan Charlie's outdoor tiki bar is fun for a drink.

On Fort Myers Beach, a natural family destination, there are lots of midprice hotels and motels that fit the bill. **Sandpiper Gulf Resort** (5550 Estero Blvd., 239/463-5721, $75–225) is a fairly big, fairly low-rise hotel set in a few buildings. Opened in 1969, the resort has 63 large guest suites, some of them recently remodeled. There's a big pool surrounded by tropical gardens and the beach just beyond. Significantly more money, but probably still a fairly good deal for what you get, **Gull Wing Beach Resort** (6620 Estero Blvd., 239/765-4300, $190–500) is a high-rise hotel on the quiet south end of Estero Island. There are 66 fairly upscale luxurious one-, two-, and three-bedroom family suites, with a lovely Gulf-side swimming pool, tennis courts, outdoor spa, barbecues, and gazebo area.

Over $150
Sanibel Harbour Resort & Spa (17260 Harbour Pointe Dr., Fort Myers, 239/597-4991, www.sanibel-resort.com, $150–600) had a huge renovation during 2004, reopening in February 2005 with swanky new guest rooms, lobby, meeting space, and restaurants (including a good Chicago-style steakhouse). This is a big place,

with 240 hotel rooms, 107 more elite and "I-vant-to-be-alone" private concierge-style accommodations at Grande Bay, and waterfront condominiums as well. This is the just about the most luxurious resort-style spot in Fort Myers, with two gorgeous pools, five restaurants and lounges, and a spa.

Bonita Springs is a growing residential area of Florida's Gulf Coast, and one of the allures for the visitor is **N Hyatt Regency Coconut Point Resort & Spa** (5001 Coconut Rd., Bonita Springs, 239/444-1234, $255–600), halfway between Fort Myers and Naples in Bonita Springs. It's a deluxe destination-style hotel with 454 elegantly appointed guest rooms and lots of stuff on-site, including a Raymond Floyd–designed championship golf course, a day spa, and views of pretty Estero Bay (beach not far away). Golf packages ($225–425 for a standard room) include accommodations, one round of golf at 18-hole Raptor Bay per night stay, a golf cart, unlimited range balls, a yardage book, and a golf club bag tag.

FOOD

Fort Myers is awash in chains, from Carrabba's to Olive Garden to T.G.I. Friday's. You have to look a little to find the quirky, independent gems.

Breakfast

Breton baker Jean Pierre Cadiou turns out a perfect French breakfast of flaky warm croissant accessorized by ham, butter, jam, and so forth, all at the little **Bara Bread Bistro** (1520 Broadway, 239/334-8216, 7 A.M.–3 P.M. Tues.–Fri., opens at 8 A.M. weekends, $6–8). Bara also produces ethereal omelets and lovely traditional European pastries.

For more rib-sticking Am-UR-ican breakfasts, **Mel's Diner** (4820 S. Cleveland Ave., 239/275-7850, 6:30 A.M.–9 P.M. Sun.–Thurs., until 10 P.M. Fri. and Sat., $4–6) gives you competent diner staples. Mel's biscuits and sausage gravy will give you the get-up-and-go for a day at the beach, and kids love it here. It's a regional chain.

Locals swear by the hangover special at **Oasis Restaurant** (2222 McGregor Blvd, 239/334-

1566, 7 A.M.–3 P.M. Mon.–Fri., 8 A.M.–2 P.M. Sat. and Sun., $5–9), not that I'd ever need to know about that kind of thing—three fluffy eggs enfolding cheese, sausage, and sautéed veggies, instrumental in the post-booze, saturated-fat-induced flushing, topped off by 26 ounces of Gatorade in the car on the way back to the hotel to take a nap. Anyway, it serves breakfast all day, very unfussy, near the Edison and Ford estates.

Casual

With live piano and jazz singers nightly, **Biddle's Restaurant & Piano Bar** (Sanibel Beach Plaza, 20351 Summerlin Rd., 239/433-4449, 11 A.M.–10 P.M. Sun.–Thurs., until 11 P.M. Fri. and Sat., $14–26) is a fairly chic hangout: faux-painted walls, richly upholstered booths, and a Pacific Rim fusion menu at dinner (macadamia-crusted grouper). The weekend brunch is lovely and à la carte, with excellent shrimp and grits and nice outdoor seating.

If you find yourself at the Bell Tower shopping center, you can't go too far wrong with a stop at **Blue Pointe Oyster Bar & Seafood Grill** (13499 S. Cleveland Ave., 239/433-0924, www.bluepointerestaurant.com, 11:30 A.M.–10 P.M. Mon.–Thurs., until 11 P.M. Fri. and Sat., noon–9 P.M. Sun., $18–31). It's a slick New England–style fish restaurant with exemplary broiled swordfish and Florida black grouper, a pleasant crabcake, and good but slightly pricey oysters on the halfshell. The same company owns **Carson's American Bistro** (18767 Tamiami Trail, 239/489-1027, 5–10 P.M. Mon.–Sat., 4–9 P.M. Sun., $18–28), which is a similarly slick enterprise with good service and American cuisine prepared with panache by an attentive kitchen (mushroom-dusted medallions of beef over rosemary mashed potatoes with grilled asparagus and a red wine demiglace).

Also at the Bell Tower, **Bistro 41** (13499 S. Cleveland Ave., 239/466-4141, 11:30 A.M.–10 P.M. Mon.–Thurs., until 10:30 P.M. Sat. and Sun., 4–10 P.M. Sun., $10–30) seems to be a local business favorite, sophisticated with an American seafood-and-steaks menu. Beware the daily specials' prices, which can run close to $40.

Otherwise, it's a pleasant, something-for-everyone kind of place with a nice outdoor patio.

On Fort Myers Beach on Estero Island, lots of casual beachfront restaurants make great use of the location and purvey mostly seafood-centric cuisine. **Matanzas Inn Restaurant** (416 Crescent St., 239/463-3838, 11 A.M.–10 P.M. daily, $17–20) has a great deck and a nice fried grouper plate. **Chloe's on the Beach** (2000 Estero Blvd., 239/765-0595, 11 A.M.–10 P.M. daily, $14–28) is in the Diamondhead Beach Resort, with more upscale continental cuisine and gorgeous water views. Watch for Bonnie Lancaster on piano and check out the daily frozen drink special. And **Beach Pierside Grill** (1000 Estero Blvd., next to the pier, 239/765-7800, 11 A.M.–11 P.M. daily, $12–19) is more family friendly, featuring ribs, fried seafood platters, and the fat beach burger.

Fine Dining

My favorite fancy restaurant in Fort Myers is **Ⓜ Veranda** (2122 2nd St., 239/332-2065, 11 A.M.–2:30 P.M. Mon.–Fri., 5:30–10 P.M. Mon.–Sat., $19–32), partly because it's set in two stately 100-year-old homes joined by publishing heir Peter Pulitzer in the 1970s for his buddy Fingers O'Bannon, who ran the restaurant then. So, it's the history, but the Veranda also seems like a happening place. The day I was there it was overrun by dozens of women in the Red Hat Society. (If you don't know about this, it's a huge international society of fun-loving older women who were galvanized by Jenny Joseph's poem "Warning," which reads: "When I am an old woman I shall wear purple/With a red hat which doesn't go and doesn't suit me./And I shall spend my pension on brandy and summer gloves/And satin sandals, and say we've no money for butter." It goes on, but what you need to know is: older women in purple dresses and crazy red hats with plumes, whooping it up.) The menu at Veranda is traditional but with contemporary touches, meaning parmesan-encrusted snapper, New York steak swathed in gorgonzola, and artichoke fritters stuffed with blue crab.

SHOPPING

Downtown Fort Myers is the city's entertainment district, but east of **Centennial Park** there is a strip of cute shops, galleries, and cafés perfect for exploring on a walk. Strictly a driving route, the **Tamiami Trail,** or U.S. 41, is lined with the basic businesses that cater to locals. You'll also find chain restaurants of all stripes along the busy road.

Serious shoppers will head to **Tanger Outlets** (20350 Summerlin Rd., 239/454-1974), which has more than 60 shops stocking deeply discounted clothing, housewares, and gifts. It's nothing you haven't seen before: Polo Ralph Lauren, Liz Claiborne, Mikasa, Jones New York, Fossil, GAP, Dana Buchman, Ellen Tracy, Casual Corner, Nine West, Easy Spirit, Greg Norman, Bass, Coach, Van Heusen, Izod, Koret, Swim Mart, Zales, etc.

A more pleasant shopping experience, capitalizing on the area's glorious weather, is the **Bell Tower Shops** (13499 U.S. 41 SE, 239/489-1221). It's an outdoor mall anchored by Saks Fifth Avenue with the usual upscale chains (Banana Republic, Ann Taylor, Williams-Sonoma) and a 20-screen movie theater.

Edison Mall (4125 Cleveland Ave., 239/939-5464) is more of a workhorse mall serving the local community, with Burdines, Dillard's, JCPenney, Sears, and lots of little mall stores. It's the biggest mall in southwest Florida.

Fleamaster's (4135 Dr. Martin Luther King Blvd., 239/334-7001, www.fleamall.com, 8 A.M.–4 P.M. Fri., Sat., and Sun.) is a serious hoot. It's a vast, 400,000-square-foot indoor flea market with something like 900 vendors—perfect for a rainy day exploration. From hardware to bath soap, this place sells some of everything.

Sanibel Island

There are more than 100 tiny, squiggly barrier islands that flank the coastline of the greater Fort Myers area. Of these, Sanibel stands out. Literally because it bucks the system and lies east–west in a gentle, shrimp-shaped curve, and figuratively because it is so well known and widely trafficked. The single biggest draw is nothing the chamber of commerce had any control over. The island's orientation, coupled with the fact that there are no offshore reefs, means that Sanibel is the recipient of the Gulf of Mexico's beneficence: more than 400 varieties of shells have been found along the 16 miles of white-sand beaches. The gently sloping sea floor, the patterns of tides and water circulation—it means that crown conch, lion's paw, angel wings, alphabet cones, and sand dollars wash up whole at your feet.

Birders would take issue with the smug shellers, though, on top draw. The birding on Sanibel is impressive for breadth as well as sheer numbers. Nearly half the island is taken up with a wildlife refuge, 6,354 acres of preserved subtropical barrier island habitat for Florida's native wetland, part of the largest undeveloped mangrove ecosystem in the country. Either on foot, biking, canoeing, or with a narrated tram ride—but invariably with reverence and binoculars—naturalists and sightseers observe wading birds, wetland birds, and the array of other Sanibel wildlife.

Connected to the mainland by a three-mile-long scenic drive across a causeway from the mainland, Sanibel is a comfortable island. It welcomes families and traveling couples with an affable, easy charm and fairly reasonable prices. It isn't the kind of island on which you'll find

Lee County

COURTESY OF VISIT FLORIDA

Sanibel is connected to the mainland by a three-mile-long causeway, with the Gulf of Mexico on the west side and tranquil Pine Island Sound on the east.

gigantic resort hotels. Most accommodations are low-rise; in fact, buildings on the island can be only as tall as the tallest palm. There are no traffic lights, no street lamps, no motorized water sports (Jet Skis, Ski-Doos).

Sanibel's main street is Periwinkle Way, a picturesque thoroughfare historically canopied by a tall stand of Australian pines and palms. Many of these trees were uprooted by Hurricane Charley, so the foliage these days is less dense, but the appeal has not been lost. Shops, small inns, and casual restaurants punctuate the road from the Sanibel Lighthouse to Tarpon Bay Road, the air along the way alternately scented with fragrant blooming joewood and buckthorn and then a whiff of fat shrimp tossed in the deep-fryer. Fort Myers is where to have your home base if you want museums, spectator sports, attractions; Captiva is where to go for blissful inaction. Sanibel is like the middle child who likes to mix it up a little—there are things to do beyond beach walking, with friendly restaurants and a great shell museum, but there's an inexorable pull toward sloth. It can't be a mortal sin if it's a vacation, right? Then it's just a venal one?

SPORTS AND RECREATION
Beaches
Sanibel is unusual among barrier islands due to its east–west orientation. Because of this, the surf is gentle and the shells arrive whole and pristine. The beaches along East, Middle, and West Gulf Drive slope gradually, making the shallows vast and safe for young waders and beachcombers. There are some beach rules to follow: pets must be on leashes and cleaned up after (no pets at all on Captiva beaches); no alcoholic beverages on the beaches November–May; no open fires; and no collecting live shells. All public beach accesses on the island have restrooms, some with concessions and picnic tables. Beach parking is $2/hour.

If you have to pick two beaches to visit from among the 14 miles of sand, start with **Lighthouse Beach & Fishing Pier** (turn left on Periwinkle Way, the first stop sign as you enter island, and follow Periwinkle Way, which terminates at the parking lot for the boardwalk) and **Bow-**

man's Beach (off Sanibel-Captiva Rd.; turn left on Bowman's Beach Rd.). The heart of the former is the **Sanibel Lighthouse Boardwalk** (1 Periwinkle Way, Sanibel, 239/472-6397, www.ci.sanibel.fl.us, parking $2 per hour), the most frequently photographed landmark on the island. It's been here since 1884 on the eastern tip of the island, near the bay side. The beach has a lovely T-dock fishing pier and a boardwalk nature trail through native wetlands. Bowman's Beach is more remote and quiet. Park in the lot and walk over a bridge to secluded white beach. It also offers showers and barbecue grills.

Beyond these, **Gulfside City Park** (mid-island on Algiers Ln. off Casa Ybel Rd.), **Tarpon Bay Beach** (also mid-island at the south end of Tarpon Bay Rd. at W. Gulf Dr.) and the **Causeway Beaches** (adjacent to the causeway on both sides) are inviting.

Shelling
With the reopening of **Bowman's Beach** in December 2004, all of the island's beaches and parks, including the public boat ramp, are back up and running after post-Hurricane Charley clearing and restoration. That's a good thing, because beaches are the most magnetic draw on Sanibel, with wide lengths of white sand beaches and some of the best shelling in the world. Some say

Sanibel Island and environs are hotbeds of avid shell collecting.

COURTESY OF VISIT FLORIDA

SEA TURTLES

From the beginning of May to the end of October, the beaches of Sanibel play host to a different kind of visitor. Loggerheads, the most common sea turtles in Florida, make their way out of the Gulf and up the beaches to lay their eggs. An estimated 14,000 females nest in the southeastern U.S. each year, many of them from the northern tip of Fort Myers Beach to the Lee-Collier border of Bonita Beach. Called loggerheads because of their big heads, they can reach 200–350 pounds and measure about three feet long.

Female loggerheads return to the beaches on which they were born to lay their own eggs. They painstakingly dig nest cavities with their rear flippers, deposit about 100 ping-pong-ball-sized eggs, cover them up, and head back out to sea. And two months later the two-inch hatchlings bust out and flap their way toward the moonlit sea. Sanibel has a lights-out policy on beaches so the little turtles aren't confused in their mission, stumbling toward a brightly lit condo instead.

Some experts say that roughly half of Florida's sea turtle nests were wiped out by 2004's summer hurricanes, but even before the storms it appeared that 2004 was going to be a below-average nesting year. Habitat is being eroded and turtles are succumbing to commercial fishing with shrimp nets or long-line fishing for grouper or shark.

What you can do to help:
- Pack up your beach trash, monofilament fishing line, and especially plastic bags and those plastic six-pack holders (they should have a name—I will henceforth refer to them as "flanisters"). Turtles mistake this stuff for tasty sea creatures undulating in the water, and they often get snarled in fishing line.
- Observe nesting turtles only from a distance. That goes for your curious pets, too. Dogs must be leashed on Sanibel, but do so even at night when no one's around to bug you. Last year a dog on one of the local beaches wiped out 67 hatchlings with one exuberant gambol.
- Stack up beach chairs or other items that might impede the baby loggerheads' progress toward the water.
- If you're staying in a beach house, close your drapes or blinds after dark and make sure if you use exterior lights that they are 25-watt yellow bug lights. Don't use flashlights, fishing lanterns, or flash photography on the beach.
- Leave nest identification markers in place. To report a wandering hatchling or a dead or injured turtle, call the Florida Fish & Wildlife Conservation Commission (800/DIAL-FMP) or the volunteer organization Turtle Time (239/481-5566).

Lee County

400 species of seashells dot the beaches here, from polka-dotted junonia to lacy apple murex and fat lightning whelks.

The most fruitful time to shell is early morning, at low tide, and after a storm, especially after the big-wave coastal storms in January and February. Other experts say the peak season for shelling is May through September. Walk slowly and look for seashells hidden just beneath the surface of the sand where the surf breaks, about where the water comes up to your knee. Wear polarized sunglasses so you can see into the water, bring a bag or fanny pack for your treasure, and don't take any shell that's inhabited.

The south side of Sanibel has a wide shallow beach that seems to attract shells without battering them—they stay whole and perfect. You're

more likely to find good ones where the competition isn't too fierce—the less populated stretch of beach, the better. (The beaches of North Captiva and Cayo Costa islands are known, among aficionados, for their lack of people and wealth of starfish, conchs, and sand dollars.) Generally, smaller shells are found closer to the **Lighthouse Beach** end, with larger shells the closer you get to Captiva. Common shells include: junonia, lightning whelk, cockle and scallop, murex, tulip, olive, little coquina, and conch.

If you're coming up empty-handed, turn it over to the professionals, with one of the local shelling charters. **Duke Sells** ('Tween Waters Marina, Captiva, 239/472-5462) customizes three- and four-hour trips to include nature tours and shelling. **Captain Mike Fuery's Shelling**

Charters (Captiva Island, 239/466-3649, private charter for up to four passengers is $180 for a three-hour trip) is another famous shelling outfit, its tours featured in *National Geographic, Southern Living, Martha Stewart,* and other magazines. Shelling trips for romantic couples seem to be a specialty.

But as Anne Morrow Lindbergh exhorted in *Gift from the Sea,* a book the aviator's wife penned in these parts:

> *The sea does not reward those who are too anxious, too greedy, or too impatient. To dig for treasures shows not only impatience and greed, but lack of faith. Patience, patience, patience, is what the sea teaches. Patience and faith. One should lie empty, open, choiceless as a beach—waiting for a gift from the sea.*

Kayaking

The water's always been here, but the trail is new. The **Great Calusa Blueway** (trail maps available at http://greatcalusablueway.com) has just opened the second segment of its paddling route. The first portion of the trail passes through Estero Bay to the south, while the second segment centers on Pine Island Sound. It's a gentle, sheltered area in which to paddle through the gorgeous bays, rivers, backwaters, and shorelines of southwest Florida. You'll see bald eagles, herons, egrets, ospreys, pelicans, roseate spoonbills, and wood storks; dolphins and manatees; and countless tiny mangrove islands.

The website gives details on the route, what you'll see along the way, where to launch or stop, maps, etc., but you still need to pick up a kayak or canoe somewhere. Outfitters offer guided trips (even some moonlight excursions), and there are numerous rentals and launch areas if you want to head out on your own.

It's one of the only ways to see sites like **Mound Key Archaeological State Park** (Boca Grande, 239/992-0311, daylight hours, free), a 32-foot shell midden that is thought to be one of the more elaborate Calusa ruins. The shell construction contains mounded platforms, ceremonial mounds, ridges, substantial carved-out canals, and open water courts—evidence of a fairly elaborate community some 2,000 years ago. There are not a lot of interpretive markers or signs here, but it's a nice place for a picnic.

Adventure Sea Kayak ('Tween Waters Inn Marina, 14000 Captiva Dr., Captiva, 239/437-5161, www.geocities.com/Adventureseakayak, $40/person) conducts kayak tours, its specialty being interactive trips that focus on the wildlife, ecology, and history of the barrier islands. Also based in Captiva, **Captiva Kayak Company & Wildside Adventures** (11401 Andy Rosse Ln. at bayside McCarthy's Marina, Captiva, 239/395-2925, www.captivakayak.com) offers rentals, instruction, and sunrise, sunset, and starlight tours. On Sanibel, **Tarpon Bay Explorers** (900 Tarpon Bay Rd., Sanibel, 239/472-8900, www.tarponbayexplorers.com, $15–40) has a range of services, from canoe, kayak, and bike rentals to guided tours. And if you just want to rent a kayak or canoe, try **Gulf Coast Kayak** (4530 Pine Island Rd., Matlacha, 239/283-1125, www.gulfcoastkayak.com, single kayak or canoe $30 half day, $40 full day) or farther south with **Estero River Canoe & Tackle Outfitters** (20991 S. Tamiami Trail, Estero, 239/992-4050, www.allflorida.com/swestero.htm), which offers 300 canoes and kayaks, all different kinds.

Biking

It's an island pastime partly because it's relatively safe (there are 25 miles of wide, paved biking path) and partly because you can cover serious ground on these pancake-flat islands. I biked blissfully from the eastern tip of Sanibel to the northern tip of Captiva, stopping occasionally to dip my toe in the Gulf. You can bike on the main drag, Sanibel-Captiva Road, or swing through a stretch of the Ding Darling Wildlife Refuge, or skirt the water's edge along Gulf Drive. The **Sanibel-Captiva Islands Chamber of Commerce** (1159 Causeway Rd., Sanibel, 239/472-1080) has a free bike path map.

Many inns on Sanibel and Captiva offer bikes complimentary to their guests—ask before you set up a rental elsewhere. The oldest bike shop on Sanibel is **Billy's Rentals** (1470 Periwinkle Way, 239/472-5248, www.billysrentals.com, two-hour bike rentals range $5–10, also daily and weekly rentals). Billy's offers regular hybrids, but a range of kooky stuff as well, from adult trikes to recumbent bikes and these multiperson surreys (that, given their width, seem more dangerous out sharing the roads with traffic). You can also rent jog strollers and cool motor scooters at Billy's. **Finnimores Bikes & Skates** (2353 Periwinkle Way, 239/472-5577, www.finnimores.com, 9 A.M.–5 P.M. daily, four-hour rentals $8–15) is another wonderful shop, with no charge for delivery and pickup for a multiday rental. It also has inline skates (they come with free helmet and pad rentals), tennis rackets, fishing equipment, boogie boards, and most other fun-in-the-sun paraphernalia.

Birding

Birds just like it here. Some live here year-round, other migrating species choose this island as a stopover or a convenient flyway terminus. J.N. "Ding" Darling National Wildlife Refuge is an embarrassment of avian splendor, but the rest of the island is a birder's paradise, too. Sanibel boasts so many habitats—freshwater wetlands, brackish mangrove estuaries, beaches, woodland—that 240 different species feel at home here.

The ornithologically inclined have websites and chat groups devoted entirely to bird trails and spots on Sanibel. One of the local papers even has a regular bird column, and traffic stops fairly regularly for the recalcitrant crossing heron or egret.

Part of the thrill is the chase, tramping around with your binoculars trained on the treetops or water's edge at low tide. Here's where to look for them: rare white pelicans hang out in Pine Island Sound; ospreys and eagles nest on telephone poles above the bike paths and along Sanibel-Captiva Road; wood storks troll for snacks in roadside ditches in the winter; burrowing owls dig tunnels in shopping center parking lots; sandhill cranes walk gracefully across expanses of lawn in groups of three. The list goes on. The lighthouse area of Sanibel is a good place to see birds, as are the mangrove islands off Pine Island Sound, as is Tarpon Bay on Sanibel. The little clumps of island off the causeway area attract lots of species as well. For an absolute sure thing, you'll hit pay dirt in Periwinkle Park, which has an aviary for lovebirds, toucans, flamingos, and talking birds.

J.N. "Ding" Darling National Wildlife Refuge

J.N. "Ding" Darling National Wildlife Refuge (1 Wildlife Dr., Sanibel, 239/472-1100, dingdarling.fws.gov/index.html, 7:30 A.M.–sunset, $5 per vehicle, $1 walker/biker, tram ride $10) takes up more than half of Sanibel Island. The refuge was named for Pulitzer Prize–winning cartoonist Jay Norwood Darling, the first environmentalist to hold a presidential cabinet post (during FDR's administration), and is an absolute marvel.

It suffered fairly serious damage during Hurricane Charley's ferocious Category IV storm on August 13, 2004, closing officially for cleanup and recovery until mid-October 2004. It's up and running again, with a visitors center, a five-mile driving tour route, hiking trails, tram service, canoe and kayak rentals, and guided interpretive programs.

The 6,354-acre refuge is made up of a variety of estuarine and freshwater habitats. You'll see mud flats and mangrove islands, wide swaths of seagrass and open water, West Indian hardwood hammocks and ridges, places poetically described as spartina swales, etc. But the real draw is birds.

Ordinarily I'd advise walking or biking through a refuge like this, 2,825 acres of it designated as wilderness area—you know, go at your own pace, get a close-up look at things. But then you'd miss out on the naturalist-narrated tram ride full of competitive birders. Equipped with binoculars, one yells out, "There's a tricolored heron." Someone else, dripping disdain, counters, "No, it's a little blue."

An up-close look at birders is half the fun of a day at Ding Darling. On the tram ride, listening to these birders, I learned to recognize black-crowned night herons and immature ibis, I saw wood storks, peregrine falcons, and a wealth of the 238 bird species that hang out in the refuge. The best birding time is early morning, about an hour before or after low tide, when you'll see birders equipped with cameras set up on tripods. Watch what they're watching, and ask questions. You'll see things rare and magnificent. The

COURTESY OF LEE COUNTY VISITOR AND CONVENTION BUREAU

Canoe & Kayak Magazine and *Paddler Magazine* both list Sanibel as a top paddling destination, its J. N. "Ding" Darling National Wildlife Refuge replete with amazing birds and wildlife.

wildlife observation tower is a glorious place to hang out any time of the day, and the education center (open 9 A.M.–5 P.M. daily Nov.–Apr., until 4 P.M. the rest of the year) provides a little guidance to the rookie.

Tarpon Bay Explorers (900 Tarpon Bay Rd., Sanibel, 239/472-8900), which runs the tram tour, also offers a 90-minute kayak trail tour ($30 adults, $15 kids) along the Commodore Creek water trail and a sunset paddle ($40 adults, $25 kids) out to the rookery islands in the refuge. You'll see hundreds upon hundreds of egrets, herons, anhingas, ibis, etc., all bedded down in the treetops for the night, the lush green dense with brilliant puffs of white feathers.

SIGHTS
Bailey–Matthews Shell Museum
Slippersnail. White baby ear. Ponderous ark. So poetic, these names for shells. The Bailey-Matthews Shell Museum (3075 Sanibel-Captiva Rd., Sanibel, 239/395-2233, www.shellmuseum.org, 10 A.M.–4 P.M. daily, $6 adults, $3 kids 5–16, kids 4 and under free) will make a

shell collector out of most people. It's not a vast museum, a pleasant 90 minutes or so, but it equips you to go out there and get yourself some of Neptune's treasures. Shells are arranged in thematic groupings from around the world, with an emphasis on the local offerings, and there are anthropological exhibits on humanity's relationships to shells (did you know that Native Americans' use of conch shells as weapons was the origin of the expression, "conk on the head"?). Children, upon entering the museum, are given a maddeningly difficult scavenger hunt sheet, in which they need to locate certain kinds of shells around the museum. I'm going to find them all next time.

Sanibel Historical Village
A work in progress, Sanibel Historical Village and Museum (950 Dunlop Rd., Sanibel, 239/472-4648, 10 A.M.–4 P.M. Tues.–Sat., until 1 P.M. in the summer, $3 suggested donation) is the kind of loving effort feasible only by a truly smitten group of local boosters. Longtime residents of Sanibel are zealots, and as such they celebrate the local history with a vengeance. This

little cluster of historic buildings dragged from all over the island includes pioneer Clarence Rutland's original island home from the early 1900s, the Burnap Cottage built in 1898, Miss Charlotta's Tea Room restored to its 1930s look, Bailey's General Store, the original Sanibel post office, an old schoolhouse, an antique Model T, a Sanibel Lighthouse display, archived newspaper, articles, and photos. The on-site town historian is a wealth of information and a wonderful storyteller.

Old Town

For more historical sightseeing, the East End village of Old Town was originally a fish camp built by Cuban fishermen in the 1860s, prior to construction of the lighthouse in 1884. The Sanibel Historical Society has a walking and biking tour map of 19 historic sites along a stretch of about 2.5 miles. You can pick up a copy of the map at the chamber of commerce (1159 Causeway Rd.) or at the Sanibel Historical Village and Museum.

ARTS AND ENTERTAINMENT

Theater

The **Schoolhouse Theatre** (2200 Periwinkle Way, Sanibel, 239/472-6862, www.theschoolhousetheater.com, 8 P.M. Mon.–Sat., $25), an institution in town, moved in October 2004 to a larger, 160-seat theater. The little community group puts on crowd-pleasing musical reviews. With a grand piano on stage, the theater does all-music performances (no acting). The restored 1896 one-room schoolhouse that used to house the theater has been hauled over to the **Sanibel Historical Village and Museum** to add another element to the little cluster of historic sites.

If you're just itching to be entertained, catch a flick at the **Island Cinema** (535 Tarpon Bay Rd., in Bailey's shopping center, 239/472-1701). It shows first-run mainstream films.

Festivals

The biggest festival in the area takes place peak season, in March, but it's still worth considering. Sanibel hosts an annual **Shell Fair,**

which draws serious shell collectors from around the world.

ACCOMMODATIONS

There's very little on Sanibel Island that's dirt cheap. On the other hand, nothing is particularly glamorous and uber-swanky. It's the kind of place where you get a sweet apartment, hotel, or motel rental a few steps from the beach, and you don't worry about whether there are luxurious Aveda products in the bathroom because you are lulled to sleep by the sound of gentle, rhythmic surf.

If you're thinking about staying for a whole week it makes sense to rent a condo or cottage. **Cottages to Castles of Sanibel & Captiva** (2427 Periwinkle Way, 239/472-6385, www.cottages-to-castles.com) has a number of intimate and affordable one-week rentals (Okay, they also offer this gigundo seven-bedroom pink house called Sandhurst that was featured as the 2004 MTV Summer Beach House). The rates on the condos are very reasonable off-season ($600–1,110 weekly).

$50–150

My two favorites on the island have a subtle patina of "Old Florida" nostalgia to them. Both are well-appointed and with contemporary touches (data ports, yada, yada), but they have a historic feel, the kinds of places you could imagine visiting unswervingly for decades until you're putting your teeth in a glass before you turn the bedside light off. The **N Island Inn on Sanibel Island** (3111 W. Gulf Dr., 239/472-1561, www.islandinnsanibel.com, $165–560) in fact opened in 1895. Look at the scrapbook of clippings to get a sense for who has roamed this compound of lovely little cottages and larger lodges on 10 acres with 550 feet of unobstructed beachfront. Allures include shuffleboard, ping-pong, and bike rentals, but it's the warmth of the staff and other guests that seems anachronistic. The same can be said of **N West Wind Inn** (3345 W. Gulf Dr., 239/472-1541, www.westwindinn.com, $154–303), a casual beachfront place in the quiet part of the island. Rooms have kitchenettes, but don't skip breakfast at its Normandie Seaside Restaurant, which seems to be a locals' morning hangout. West Wind's stretch of beach is a marvel for stargazing.

Shalimar Resort (2823 W. Gulf Dr., 239/472-1353, www.shalimar.com, $139–329) is another beloved getaway, with 33 one- and two-bedroom cottages and motel efficiencies spread around a huge property right on the Gulf. All units have full kitchens and the pool is lovely.

Over $150

Two of the island's most popular destinations fully reopened May 1, 2005, after Hurricane Charley damage repairs. **Sundial Beach Resort** (1451 Middle Gulf Dr., Sanibel, 239/472-4151, www.sundialresort.com, $179–749) has 270 one- and two-bedroom suites that all have a condo vibe, complete with full kitchens. It sits in 33 acres of tropical lushness right along the beach and has a tremendous weekday camp for children 4–11. **Sanibel Inn** (937 E. Gulf Dr., Sanibel, 239/481-6424, www.sanibelinn.com, $179–579) is smaller, with 68 hotel rooms and one-bedroom suites. Outside, the inn sits in the shade of more than 600 palms, with the gentle flutter of butterfly gardens all around. Inside, Zen-like bamboo flooring and a warm palette of grass green, sea blue, and golden wheat imbue rooms with a quiet grace. The Sanibel Inn also offers a wonderful children's educational/entertainment program. For adults, the nearby Dunes Golf & Tennis Club awaits.

FOOD

There's something funny about the restaurants of Sanibel. Mostly spread out across Periwinkle Way, there's a tremendous homogeneity to them: fun, a little raucous, lots of fried seafood, a stunning dearth of green vegetables. (Iceberg lettuce doesn't count as a green vegetable. It's a cellulose doorstop.) Prices are steep but not alarmingly so at most Sanibel restaurants. You're paying for the view, but you can defray the cost by doing the, gulp, early-bird special before 6 P.M. offered at many restaurants.

Breakfast

Lighthouse Cafe (362 Periwinkle Way, 239/472-0303, breakfast served 7 A.M.–3 P.M. daily, open until 10 P.M. nightly, $5–8 for breakfast) usually beats the early-morning competition, hands down, whether you're a fan of the seafood Benedict or the blueberry whole-wheat hotcakes.

Lunch

Novelist Randy Wayne White is about the biggest booster this area has. Although I know when he was young he was a light tackle fishing guide right in this neighborhood, I'm not totally sure what his connection is to this restaurant (Doc Ford is the main character running through many of his books set in these parts). Regardless, **Doc Ford's Sanibel Rum Bar & Grille** (975 Rabbit Rd., 239/472-8311, 11 A.M.–1 A.M. daily, $11–30) is a hoot, with lots of TVs blaring the game, good sandwiches, great drinks. The food—panko-crumb fried shrimp, Cuban sandwich, pulled pork—is better than it needs to be for such a laid-back setting.

Sanibel Cafe (2007 Periwinkle Way, 239/472-5323, 7 A.M.–9 P.M. daily, $8–15) seems like a locals' hangout, unpretentious and friendly. Go for the fat hamburgers peeking from under a mantle of molten blue cheese.

Dinner

The menus at the following three places seem cut from the same mold. At **McT's Shrimp House & Tavern** (1523 Periwinkle Way, 239/472-3161, 4–10 P.M. daily, $12–22) the draw is the Sanibel Steamer, a huge tray of steamed seafood, or the all-you-can-eat shrimp and crab platters. It's lively, it's casual. The same can be said of **Island Cow** (2163 Periwinkle Way, 239/472-0606, 7 A.M.–10 P.M. daily, $8–16), which occasionally has a mooing contest among the guests, the winner of which gets a T-shirt in addition to deep and abiding respect. There's also live music, a wonderful outdoor patio, and generous heart-stopping seafood baskets with fries. And **Jacaranda** (1223 Periwinkle Way, 239/472-1771, 5–10 P.M. daily, $16–32) has a funky bar and a screened patio (good for when the bugs are biting). The Jac has music nightly (reggae on the weekends), sweet briny treats from the patio raw bar, and a fairly extensive late-night menu.

For Italian cuisine, Sanibel has a couple of options. **Dolce Vita** (1244 Periwinkle Way, 239/472-5555, 5:30–10:30 P.M. nightly, $17–30), glamorous by island standards, is organized around a central bar with live music on a baby grand. The menu is really only nominally Italian (there's veal piccata), but other items, like rotisserie chicken with corn tortillas or Moroccan chicken tagine, are nicely done, so why be a stickler. **Matzaluna** (1200 Periwinkle Way, 239/472-1998, 4:30–9:30 P.M. daily, $11–17) is more traditional. The wood-fired pizzas get top honors, with sturdy baked pasta dishes (lasagna, stuffed shells) placing a close second. Like many island spots, it offers 2-for-1 drink specials during happy hour, and 99-cent pizza slices at the bar.

SHOPPING

Sanibel's shopping is as low-key as the island itself. **Periwinkle Place** (2075 Periwinkle Way, www.periwinkleplace.com) boasts 28 cute shops, a tropical bistro called Gully's, and the pleasant Sanibel Day Spa, all connected by covered walkways and shaded by banyan trees. Its clothing shops are mostly geared to beach- and sportswear; there are nice toy and swimsuit shops. **Olde Sanibel Shoppes** (630 Tarpon Bay Rd., 239/939-3900) is another cluster of gift shops, clothing, and jewelry, with a couple of casual restaurants thrown into the mix. The **Village Shops** (2340 Periwinkle Way) has roughly a similar lineup, and the 15 shops arrayed in the low pink buildings of **Tahitian Gardens** (1975–2019 Periwinkle Way) sell artisan candles, bright cotton clothing, jewelry, bathing suits, T-shirts, giftware, etc. This center also contains one of the island's best breakfast spots, the **Sanibel Café.**

None of this will rock your world—for a real one-of-a-kind island shopping experience, browse a while in **She Sells Sea Shells** (1157 Periwinkle Way, 239/472-8080). The funky shop contains shells from all over the place, but many are the same species you'll see stooped enthusiasts minding for (some even have lighted miner's hats in the early mornings) along Sanibel beaches.

And if you need a regular old grocery store, **Bailey's** (2477 Periwinkle Way, 239/472-1516, 7 A.M.–9 P.M. daily) is the biggest local market.

Galleries

Now, Sanibel has got some galleries worth investigating. It seems to attract residents of artistic temperament, many of them opening shops that feature their work. **Tower Gallery** (751 Tarpon Bay Rd., 239/472-4557, www.towergallery-sanibel.com) is a good place to start, and it's hard to miss in an electric blue and green building. It's a cooperative of 23 local artists. Representing all media and a real mix of styles, the work in the gallery is all juried. Right nearby you'll find another small cooperative called the **Hirdie Girdie Gallery** (2490 Library Way, 239/395-0027), and next door to it the **Tin Can Art Gallery** (2480 Library Way, 239/472-9002), with the whimsical work of artist Bryce McNamara.

Sanibel's **BIG Arts** (Barrier Island Group for the Arts, 900 Dunlop Rd., 239/395-0900) is a community cultural arts organization that has a center for island arts. It has two galleries open to the public (weekdays only, 1–4 P.M.), a sculpture garden, and performance space. Exhibits change monthly, and there are frequent workshops, lectures, films, and concerts.

Periwinkle Way is home to several small galleries. Ikki Matsumoto's work, delicate Japanese silkscreens and intricate paintings of Florida birds and fish, can be found at **Matsumoto Gallery** (2340 Periwinkle Way, Ste. B3, 239/472-2941, www.ikkimatsumoto.com). In the same building, **Aboriginals: Art of the First Person** (2340 Periwinkle Way, 239/395-2220, www.tribalworks.com) shows ethnographic and tribal art. **Sanibel Gallery** (1628 Periwinkle Way, 239/472-3307, www.sanibelgallery.com) displays fine American arts and crafts that draw their inspiration from the natural beauty of the barrier island. **Seaweed Gallery** (2055 Periwinkle Way, 239/472-2585) is an explosion of color, showing local artists' work from whimsical painted furniture to tropical paintings, jewelry, pottery, and mermaids.

Captiva Island

Sanibel's northern neighbor, Captiva Island, is tinier, only about a half-mile wide and five miles long. It is at once more laid-back and more exclusive, perfect for meditative solipsism or romantic cocooning. Captiva has less commerce, fewer hotels and inns, fewer people in general. A fair percentage of the island's houses, all recessed demurely behind dense pines and brambly foliage, are the beach retreats of affluent and often absentee owners.

It's quieter than Sanibel, Captiva Drive running its length. Captiva has a relaxed downtown area of beach bars, restaurants, and gift shops that draw their inspiration from the beaches of Key West and the winsome lyrics of Jimmy Buffet tunes. "Captiva Village" uses loud pastels with reckless abandon, the colors of orange sherbet and plastic pink flamingos, and some of the restaurants adopt a flotsam-and-kitschy-jetsam approach to decorating (see the Bubble Room), but there's still an underlying sophistication. Things are casual without being slipshod—which allows for much more upscale accommodations on Captiva without them seeming out of place. South Seas Resort dominates a whole section at the northern tip of Captiva, where it breaks before the island of North Captiva (once attached). It suffered during Hurricane Charley and was closed until mid-2005, but its sprawling grace and glorious beach set a tone for the island.

There are few attractions on the island, although much to do. Walk, run, fish, canoe, sit and read, or just sit. Anne Morrow Lindbergh was so inspired by Captiva's tranquility that it's where she wrote her best-selling book, *A Gift from the Sea*, parts of which serve as testament to this small island's salubrious effect on people's psyches:

> *I want first of all . . . to be at peace with myself. I want a singleness of eye, a purity of intention, a central core to my life that will enable me to carry out these obligations and activities as well as I can. I want, in fact—to borrow from the language of the saints—to live "in grace" as much of the time as possible.*

SPORTS AND RECREATION

Beaches

Captiva's beaches are less populated than those on Sanibel, for a couple of reasons. First, there are more private homes on Captiva, visited sporadically by their affluent owners. Thus, there are just fewer feet to churn the sand and rustle the packs of waterbirds. Second, the shelling is better on Sanibel. But Captiva's waters are clearer, the swimming slightly better. **Captiva Beach** (at the end of Captiva Dr., free but limited parking) is a case in point—beautiful sand, lovely clear water, and only a few people in sight. It's a great place from which to watch the sunset. Because of fairly swift currents, don't count on swimming at **Turner Beach** (Sanibel-Captiva Rd. at Blind Pass Bridge), but it's still a favorite among fisherfolk and shellers.

Gulf-side beach erosion has been a problem in recent years, exacerbated by recent storms. Private funds have been raised to restore beaches by pumping in sand from offshore.

Fishing

Usually at the beginning of July, anglers start convening in Boca Grande Pass for the annual **World's Richest Tarpon Fishing Tournament** (www .worldsrichesttarpon.com), which hands out $250,000 in prize money. And despite fairly hefty hurricane damage, South Seas Resort hosts its 16th annual **Caloosa Catch & Release Tournament** on Captiva in June 2005. This one is known as the largest single-site public flats tournament in Florida, with more than $28,000 in cash and prizes. People here are serious about fishing, and not just about the seasonal giant tarpon.

What are you likely to catch? Redfish is a pretty steady catch in these parts, some over 10 pounds. The species has rebounded since the New Orleans blackening craze made them a hot commodity. They can be fished on the flats. Snook is best in the springtime (season is closed Dec. 15–Jan. 31 and June, July, and Aug.), and you'll catch lots of speckled trout in the winter

COURTESY OF VISIT FLORIDA

The private island community of Boca Grande boasts the deepest natural port between Tampa and Miami.

when they're especially large. They tend to hang out in 3–5 feet of water near the edges of the grass flats and sand holes. Tarpon are the area's biggest draw, huge fish that range 100–150 pounds with lots of fight in them. (Some say the very first tarpon ever taken on rod and reel was in southwest Florida, near Punta Rassa across San Carlos Bay from Sanibel in 1885—but how would anyone know that?) Tarpon season runs from the latter part of April through August. Then there are cobia (here Feb.–July, but best in Apr. and May), tripletail, and jacks for much of the year on the flats, and black grouper far out in the Gulf. Commercial catches of grouper have been limited recently, so sportfishers might benefit from increased numbers.

Fishing charters start at around for $200 for a half-day trip, and the charter captain provides the boat, fishing license, fishing gear, equipment, and bait. Sometimes the client pays an additional fee for gas—ask about this. As a matter of etiquette, a tip of $20–50 is customary, as is buying your captain and crew a meal or drinks at the end of your fishing trip. Many guides will clean and fillet your edible catch—if you don't want all the fish, give it to whomever seems interested

dockside. As per mounting and taxidermy these days: Big fish are largely catch and release, so have a picture taken of yourself with your catch before you release it. Then, one of the new breed of taxidermists will create a lifelike plastic model of your prize.

Figure out whether you want to do deep-water fishing, cast in the flats, or maybe take a fly-fishing lesson, then visit the marinas to ask around about charter captains, prices, what people are catching, and where. **Capt. Jim's Charters** ('Tween Waters Marina, 15951 Captiva Dr., 239/472-1779, $175–300) does back-bay fishing; **Capt. Joe's Charters** (Castaways Marina, Sanibel-Captiva Rd., Sanibel, 239/472-8658, www.captjoescharters.com, $180–300) does back-bay and fly fishing; **Captain Van Hubbard/Let's Go Fishin'** (239/697-6944, www.captvan.com, $275–500) does sight casting for giant tarpon and snook seasonally; **Soulmate Charters** (17544 Lebanon Rd., Fort Myers, 239/851-1242, www.soulmatecharters.com, $275–375) offers backcountry fishing with light spin tackle and fly-fishing. The list goes on, with more than 50 charter captains willing to help you wet a line.

Sailing

I have a little book that looks like a passport. I keep it in a safe place and flip it open occasionally to impress people. It says I'm U.S. Sailing certified for basic keelboat, which means I am henceforth only to be addressed with, "Hey, sailor." I took the three-day certification program with **Offshore Sailing School** (16731 McGregor Blvd., Fort Myers, 800/221-4326, www.offshore-sailing.com, courses for beginners, racers, and cruisers, basic keelboating class tuition $895). It's a tremendous amount of fun, three days on the water with an instructor and three other students, plus hours of classroom time learning all the sailing jargon (who you calling a "jibe ho"?), parts of the boat, points of sail, etc. At the end of the class you take a fairly difficult 80-question test, and you get out and show your sailing chops to your teacher, complete with man-overboard demonstrations and doing a quick stop by "shooting" into the wind (I stank at that).

If you're a goal-oriented person, it's a great activity to build a vacation around. You learn on a midsize daysailer, a Colgate 26, designed specifically for training and chosen by the U.S. Naval Academy to replace their training fleet. From here, you can take any number of other courses designed for more advanced sailors—performance sailing, live-aboard cruising, a camp for racing sailors—or just occasionally wave your little blue U.S. Sailing book around like I do, and as a party trick tie nautical knots.

Historically, Offshore taught its classes out of South Seas Resort on Captiva Island, which has been closed due to Hurricane Charley damage. Until it reopens, classes are held at the Pink Shell Beach Resort & Spa in Fort Myers Beach. Call for information.

ACCOMMODATIONS

$50–150

If you want to be where the action is, **Ⓜ Captiva Island Inn** (11508 Andy Rosse Ln., 239/395-0882, www.captivaislandinn.com, $99–300) is a darling bed-and-breakfast right in the middle of teeny Captiva Village. There are traditional B&B rooms, one- and two-bedroom cottages, a loft,

and a suite. The owners also have a five-bedroom, five-and-one-half-bath for big gatherings.

Jensen's has two options, one more fishing-focused, the other beachier. **Jensen's on the Gulf** (15300 Captiva Dr., 239/472-5800, motel suites $150–300, apartments $175–400, houses $300–600) has nine units directly on the Gulf. **Jensen's Twin Palm Cottages** (15107 Captiva Dr., 239/472-5800, one-bedroom $110–180, two-bedroom $125–190), on the other hand, are spread out along the bayside marina and fishing action. You can rent a boat right here, grab some bait, and be out on the water before your pajamas have had time to miss you. The 14 cheerful tin-roofed cottages have kitchens and screened porches.

Over $150

The biggest game in recent years in town has been **Ⓜ South Seas Resort** (5400 Plantation Rd., Captiva, 239/472-5111, www.south-seas-resort.com, $229–1259) at the northern tip of the island. Unfortunately, because of Hurricane Charley, the resort is closed for reconstruction. It will be up and running in the middle of 2005. Set in 330 acres of lush mangroves, the resort (which has an ownership timeshare complex, too) is casual but stunning, with lovely rooms and added draws such as a much-lauded children's program, world-renowned sailing, pools, kayaking, a fishing pier, and Gulf-edged golf. Hope for a swift recovery.

'Tween Waters Inn Beach Resort (15951 Captiva Dr., Captiva, 239/472-5161, www.tween-waters.com, $155–650) is another heavy-hitter on the island, with a huge resort complex that stretches from the bayside to the Gulf side. The inn dates back to 1926, when the collection of cottages hosted Teddy Roosevelt, Charles and Anne Lindbergh, Roger Tory Peterson, and J.N. "Ding" Darling. There are 137 water-view rooms, suites, and cottages; Olympic-sized and children's pools; tennis courts (free to guests); day spa; four restaurants; and a full-service marina. The rooms are perfectly lovely, and there's a nice complimentary breakfast for guests, but it's all the cool amenities that make this a great experience. Rent a canoe or kayak and head out for the day.

FOOD

How to break this into categories? There are few discernible cuisines in restaurants here, and most all of them are casual and reasonably priced, set in pastel-colored cottages with sprawling outdoor seating. There's a pervasive beachy aesthetic and a funky charm.

A case in point is the ridiculous **N** **Bubble Room** (15001 Captiva Dr., 239/472-5558, 11:30 A.M.–2:30 P.M. and 5–10 P.M. daily, $13–20). First off, the waiters and bartenders are all in scouting uniforms, with patches of their own devising meticulously sewn on. They wear neckerchiefs, deep tans, weird hats, and mischievous grins. No explanation. Then there's the decor—like Santa's workshop, with toy trains and elves and hobbyhorses, but then add in 2,000 movie stills and glossies, lots of Betty Boop stuff, oh, and a list of other stuff too long to enumerate. It's a "more is more" motif. The food is fairly good, from fried shrimp to grilled fish brushed with a pineapple/ginger marinade, but beware the mammoth cakes in the dessert case—when taken

N Lee County

TROPICAL FRUIT

Jackfruit, carambola, mamey sapote, sapodilla, lychee, longans, pineapple, papaya. These are the kinds of fruits you imagine eating on a far-flung tropical island. Fling a little closer, and you've got Pine Island. Just west of Cape Coral, it is the largest island along the southwest coast of Florida and the producer of some of the state's most exotic fruits. Not the humdrum Florida orange, Pine Island's king of fruits is the mango. Its reign is so celebrated that there is an annual two-day festival, the **Pine Island Mango Mania Tropical Fruit Fair** (239/283-0888) in July with mango-inspired foods, entertainment, and lots of fragrant fruits and plants for sale.

From late May to about Labor Day, enthusiasts can also stop into the tent-covered **Pine Island Tropical Fruit Market** in Bokeelia (10 A.M.–4 P.M. Fri.–Sun.) for a wide array of tropical fruits. Even the **Beach Farmers' Market** (7307 Estero Blvd., in the unpaved area underneath the Matanzas Pass Bridge, between First St. and Estero Bay, Fort Myers Beach, 239/463-4293) offers a fair sampling of the local exotic fruits (7 A.M.–2 P.M. Fri. Dec.–Apr.).

Even the local **Eden Vineyards** applauds the local fruits with one of its wines, made from carambola.

But what is a carambola, exactly, you say? Maybe you need a few pointers:

Carambola is another word for starfruit, that light yellow, ribbed, ovoid fruit that, when sliced, has star-shaped cross-sections. The flesh is yellow, crisp, juicy, and not fibrous, ranging from very sour to mildly sweet.

Mamey sapote is a large, football-shaped fruit that grows on an ornamental evergreen. The brown skin has a rough texture like a kiwi, only rougher. The flesh is either creamy pink or salmon color, and it has a big avocado-like pit. The flavor is described as a combination of honey, avocado, and sweet potato. Closely related, the **sapodilla** has soft brown flesh that tastes a little like very sweet root beer. The sapodilla tree is also the source of chicle, a chewing gum component.

Lychee are those beautiful, nubby red fruits you see in Chinese painting. The inside is pearly white, the texture of a grape. The flesh is sweet but tart, and highly perfumed. Experienced lychee eaters bite lightly through the skin of the top and then squeeze the fruit out (if you bite off a chunk, the black seed with the white fruit around it looks disconcertingly like an eyeball). The **longan** is known as the little brother of the lychee. They look alike, only the longan is smaller. The flesh is whitish and translucent like the lychee, but less perfumey and a little muskier.

Jackfruit is the fruit for the intrepid. The largest tree-borne fruit in the world, up to 80 pounds, the unopened fruit has a strong, disagreeable smell. The exterior is spiky and green, and the inside has these large edible bulbs that taste like a cross between banana and papaya. Sound creepy? Fine, you don't need to know jack about jackfruit, but check out the rest of Lee County's tropical bounty.

internally, they are known to cause side effects such as bloating, night sweats, and, in very rare cases, total paralysis.

Andy Rosse Lane, the area often called Captiva Village, has a cluster of fun places. The **Keylime Bistro** (in the Captiva Island Inn, 11509 Andy Rosse Ln., 239/395-4000, 8 A.M.–10 P.M. daily, lounge until 1 A.M., live entertainment daily) has a robust purple and lime green color scheme, hard to miss, and a guy on the patio playing Jimmy Buffet covers or things that sound like Jimmy Buffet covers. The kitchen serves a great grouper sandwich as well as a delicious but dangerously drippy sausage sandwich with onions and peppers; at dinner, head for shrimp scampi or grouper piccata. Good margaritas, and they have a Bloody Mary bar for Sunday brunch.

RC Otter's Island Eats (11506 Andy Rosse Ln., 239/395-1142, 7:30 A.M.–10 P.M. daily, $8–12) is right across the street, with a vast menu of accessible American staples, with care put into vegetarian options. The wine list is fairly decent, and they have housemade beer. Depending on the weather, you can sit indoors, on the covered veranda, or out on the patio where there's usually live island music. **Mucky Duck** (11546 Andy Rosse Ln., 239/472-3434, 11:30 A.M.–2:30 P.M. and 5–9:30 P.M. daily, $13–20) is more of an English pub vibe, only set right on the beach. The only thing on the menu that might be construed as English is fish and chips, but no matter when the seafood platter and its accompanying creamy dill sauce are so good. Every night at sunset, revelers convene on the beachside patio to watch the colorful show.

The **'Tween Waters Inn** (15951 Captiva Rd., 239/472-5161) is something of an institution around here, going from the bay side to the Gulf side across the island, and with a couple of restaurants on-site. For my money, I'd skip the fine-dining **Old Captiva House** (7:30–11 A.M. and 5:30–10 P.M. daily, $18–34) and head for the **N Crow's Nest Island Pub** (5:30–10 P.M. daily, cocktails until late, $8–15). Not that the former isn't good—it often wins "Florida's Golden Spoon Award," with elegant swordfish saltimbocca,

jerked grouper, seafood jambalaya, and the archetypal key lime pie served in a intimate "special occasion" kind of space (sit in the Sunset Room). It's more because the latter is so fun. Good drink specials, fine bar staples, a band Tuesday–Sunday. But it's Monday you need to go. It's the NASCrab races, 6 P.M. for families, 9 P.M. for adults. Pick your hermit crab, the one who looks most like Dale Earnhardt Jr. or Jeff Gordon, and line him up. Who wins is ESPN-worthy drama. For lunch at 'Tween Waters, opt for the **Canoe and Kayak Waterfront Restaurant** (11 A.M.–6 P.M. daily, $7–10) on-site, where you can eat a fat deli sandwich while watching the marina's commotion.

For when you're looking for a cocktail and a place to watch the sun go down, the **Green Flash Bayside Bar & Grill** (15183 Captiva Dr., 239/472-3337, 11:30 A.M.–3:30 P.M. and 5:30–9:30 P.M. daily, $13–20) is the place. At the site of the longtime island favorite called The Nook, the two-story restaurant is situated on Roosevelt Channel and overlooks Buck Key and Pine Island. What you need to know about the menu is what is written at the top:

A green flash occurs because sunlight spreads out in air of increasing density, just like water vapor creates a rainbow. The atmosphere refracts the light into a spectrum with the longest (red-orange) wavelengths at one end and the shortest (violet-blue-green) at the other. The dispersion is greatest at sunset and sunrise because that's when sunlight takes a long, low path through the atmosphere. The blue-green light is bent toward the top of the sun, but usually it is scattered by air molecules. But sometimes only the blue is scattered, leaving the root of the bent light—the green part—visible once the sun sets. The chances of seeing the green flash are better in tropical or desert areas since an observer has more opportunities to view a horizon free from clouds and haze. Experts recommend watching a sunset from the beach on a calm day with a horizon free of clouds. A yellow sun, rather than a red one, will have the best potential for a green flash.

SHOPPING

Hand-painted gew-gaws and shell trinkets, you'll find this stuff along Sanibel-Captiva Road and in the Captiva Village area along Andy Rosse Lane, at the only four-way stop on Captiva. The most compelling of the shops here is **Jungle Drums** (11532 Andy Rosse Ln., 239/395-2266), a collection of wildlife, island, and environmental art in an array of media. **HO2 Island Outfitters** (Celebration Center, Andy Rosse Ln., 239/472-7507) nearby purveys funky sandals, sunglasses, and beach-appropriate attire.

Other Barrier Islands and Charlotte Harbor

From Charlotte County to Fort Myers, a stew of wonderful little islands thickens the waters of the Lee County coastline. A long line of curves, squiggles, and dots on the map between the Gulf waters and the Intracoastal Waterway, some of these islands are accessible by causeway, others just by boat. What unifies them is robust natural beauty, romantic, often pirate-related histories, and a recent walloping by Hurricane Charley. Sailboating outfits, fishing charters, regularly scheduled ferries, and water taxis head out to these barrier islands; if you'd like to stay on one, call ahead to get updated information on the post-hurricane state of things. Tourism has been affected drastically in this area, which might mean a good deal for the bargain hunter.

Babcock Wilderness Adventures in Punta Gorda offers a 90-minute swamp buggy tour.

COURTESY OF LEE COUNTY VISITOR AND CONVENTION BUREAU

One of the area's first tourists was Spanish explorer Ponce de Leon, who ended up taking a Calusa arrow and dying in these waters. The natives are friendlier now.

CHARLOTTE HARBOR

Most people hadn't heard of Florida's Charlotte Harbor and Punta Gorda until Hurricane Charley blew through and over them. Punta Gorda took one of the storm's worst beatings, with loads of people months later still trying to decide whether to renovate or rebuild. The thing about that storm on August 13, 2004, though, was that it raked hard against the southeastern section of Charlotte County, but it left the other side virtually intact. The beach towns of Englewood, Placida, Cape Haze, and Palm Island weathered the storm almost entirely unscathed.

Some parts of the greater Charlotte Harbor area were lucky, others were not. Still, the whole area is worth exploring, especially for the eco-traveler. Charlotte Harbor is the second-largest estuary in the state, encompassing 270 square miles. It has 365 miles of canals, 190 miles of them saltwater, 175 miles freshwater. Most of the area bordering the harbor is preserved land, with parks, 53 blueway trails, and the largest undisturbed pine flatwoods in southwest Florida.

Ignore the hurricane hype and don't skip **Punta Gorda.** It's worth the drive north from Fort Myers to visit **Babcock Wilderness Adventure** (8000 Hwy. 31, Punta Gorda, 800/500-5583; tours by reservation 9 A.M.–3 P.M.; adults $17.95, children 3–12 $10.95, also special group and seasonal prices) for a swamp buggy ride in which you are taken on a 90-minute tour

Lee County

through the Babcock Ranch, Telegraph Cypress Swamp, and the 90,000-acre Crescent B Ranch. Guides offer narration on birds, animals, plants, and the cattle and horses that are raised on the ranch. You'll see Florida panthers (okay, not wild exactly), big gators, white-tailed deer, wild turkeys, and ornery-looking Florida Cracker cattle. It's thrilling, but especially so for kids.

Out of Fisherman's Village in Punta Gorda, **King Fisher Fleet** (1200 W. Retta Esplanade, 941/639-0969, cruises roughly $21.95 adults, half price for kids 3–11, free under 3, back bay fishing $400/day, deep water $650/day) pays equal attention to sightseers and anglers. It offers sightseeing cruises to the out islands, ecotours, full- and half-day cruises, sunset cruises, and harbor tours. Dolphins chase the boat on the sightseeing tours, grouper and snapper practically jump into the boat on the deep-sea charters.

If you want to learn to sail or cruise in the sheltered waters of Charlotte Harbor, **Florida Sailing & Cruising School** (Burnt Store Marina on Charlotte Harbor, 800/262-7939, www.flsailandcruiseschool.com) offers live-aboard sailing beginning at $395 for a two-day basics class.

And the little town of Englewood, west of Charlotte Harbor and north of Cape Haze, is definitely worth the drive. I spent a whole evening hanging out with the hippies and perennially bronzed beach folk for an impromptu barbecue and sing-along in the covered pavilion of downtown beachfront **Chadwick Park.**

Englewood is on Lemon Bay, at the north end of Cape Haze peninsula, where evidence suggests early Floridians lived swimmingly from about 1000 B.C. to A.D. 1350. You can see their faint evidence at **Paulson's Point** (Orange St., 941/474-3065, dawn to dusk, free), also known as the Sarasota County mound. The tall shell mound park features helpful interpretive markers and a lovely gentle walkway around and through the Native American mound.

Food

The area has a number of worthwhile restaurants. The best is undoubtedly **The Perfect Caper** (320 Sullivan St., Punta Gorda, 941/505-9009, 11:30 A.M.–9 P.M. Tues.–Thurs., until

10 P.M. Fri. and Sat., $16–26). "Gourmet" is such a bankrupt word these days, but James and Jeanie Roland's approach to California-Asian fusion is cerebral and stunning. You can't help but hint at insulting questions like why such a sophisticated restaurant is located *here.* Lunch and dinner are a revelation, and not financially taxing if you head there early for the prix-fixe two courses with wine and coffee for $30.

Then there's **Amimoto Japanese Restaurant** (2705 Tamiami Trail, Punta Gorda, 941/505-1515, 11 A.M.–2:30 P.M. and 5:30–9:30 P.M. Mon.–Sat., $15–22), with clean, bright sushi flavors presented artistically. A great lunch spot. Also worthwhile in Punta Gorda are **Celtic Ray Irish Pub** (145 E. Marion Ave., 941/505-9219) for a casual Irish vibe and live music; **Mamma Nunzia Ristorante** (1975 Tamiami Trail, 941/575-7575) for solid Italian; **Riva's** (127 W. Marion Ave., 941/639-9080) for more contemporary Italian; and the restaurants of **Fisherman's Village** (1200 W. Retta Esplanade, www.fishville.com), including **Village Oyster Bar** (941/637-1212) and **Bella Luna** (941/575-4544).

Then in the sweet town of Englewood, sophisticated water-view dining can be had at **Gulfview Grill** (2095 N. Beach Rd., 941/475-3500). Get the stone crab claws if they're in season.

PALM ISLAND

Almost everything on Palm Island revolves around **Palm Island Resort** (7092 Placida Rd., Cape Haze, 941/697-4800, www.palmisland .com, $300–1,200), and it's practically my favorite place to stay on the entire Gulf Coast. You drive to Cape Haze, the directions are a little tricky. Take I-75 29 miles north from Sanibel. Take the CR-768 W exit (Exit 161) toward Punta Gorda. Almost immediately, turn right onto Taylor Road (CR-765A), which then runs into the Tamiami Trial (US-41 N). Follow this 9 miles, then turn left onto El Jobean Rd. (FL 776 W). Follow this 8 miles, turn left onto Gasparilla Rd. (CR 771) and drive another 8 miles. Turn right onto Placida Rd. (CR 775), go 2 miles and you're there. Then you wait in line in your car for the car ferry. It comes, you drive on, and about 60 seconds later the ferry lands on Palm Island (but not before the salty-seadog ferry captain has had a chance to be crabby with a few ferry passengers). Then you're in paradise. Nice young men in shorts greet you, take all your stuff, and tell you where to ditch your car; you get your own golf cart, and you motor over to your unit along gravel roads. (Careful: My 8-year-old drove the cart recklessly, fatally wounding a frog, first-degree frogslaughter.)

The island is really due north of Boca Grande, with about 200 private homes, plus 15 more private homes within the resort. Resort guests stay in 154 one-, two- or three-bedroom villas right on the Gulf. There are several pools, tennis courts, a comfy restaurant called the Rum Bay, kids' programs, kayak rentals (a good first-kayak experience in the protected inner-island waterways, with the mullet jumping enough to add some excitement). My only caveat is this: Bring your own groceries from the mainland, as the prices at the little on-island market are mercenary.

Luscious beaches, clear green-blue waters, gorgeous sunsets, gently undulating sea oats—it's all worth the price of admission, and makes a perfect multigenerational getaway that everyone will appreciate, except for that one frog.

GASPARILLA ISLAND

Named for the infamous pirate Jose Gaspar, who may or may not have hidden out (and buried his treasure, never to be found) on this island in the 1700s with his band of bloodthirsty men, **Gasparilla Island** has had a much more posh and refined recent history. Connected to the mainland by a short causeway near Punta Gorda, the island was founded as a vacation retreat and fishing spot by the DuPont family in the late 1800s. Its town of **Boca Grande,** at the mouth of Charlotte Harbor, is besieged May through mid-July by tarpon fishers; the opening between Cayo Costa and Gasparilla islands was once considered by some to be the "Tarpon Fishing Capital of the World." Tarpon are sparser in the pass and the estuarine waters of Pine Island Sound these

days, but during peak season the dense cluster of fishing boats makes a picturesque scene. There is driving access to the island via the Boca Grande Causeway, the causeway at County Road 775, and at Placida.

Boca Grande is on the southern tip of Gasparilla Island and retains its quaint fishing village aura, but with enough swanky shops and restaurants to lure affluent anglers (President Bush has been a regular guest). While there, walk around **Boca Grande Lighthouse Park** (Gasparilla Island State Park, 880 Belcher Rd., Boca Grande, 941/964-0375, 8 A.M.–sunset, $2/car). The wooden Boca Grande Lighthouse was built

Beautifully restored, the Boca Grande Lighthouse sits at the extreme southern end of Gasparilla Island.

Lee County

in 1890 and is a maritime landmark. The lighthouse is open to the public 10 A.M.–4 P.M. the last Saturday of the month, and there's a little lighthouse museum ($1), gift shop, and the Armory Chapel. The waters in these parts have strong currents, not great for swimming, but you'll see people sailboarding.

USEPPA ISLAND

Across from Cabbage Key is **Useppa Island,** which pirate Jose Gaspar supposedly named for one of his more favored captives, a Mexican princess named Joseffa. Calusas may have lived here as far back as 5000 B.C., discarding their oyster and clam shells so as to create a greater swath of dry land. Barron Collier, for whom Collier County is named, bought the 100-acre island in 1912 and built a resort there in his own name that lured wealthy and famous fishing enthusiasts from all over. The island is really a chichi private residential club called the Useppa Island Club, but the inn is still there. Due to Hurricane Charley, the **Collier Inn** (plans to reopen in May 2005, 239/283-1061) is currently closed to guests, but the **Useppa Marina** and **Tarpon Restaurant** are in full operation. In spring 2005, the Village Dock was just about finished being rebuilt, and the Useppa Island Historical Society had the little **Useppa Museum** (239/283-9600, noon–2 P.M. Tues.–Fri., 1–2 P.M. weekends, $2.50 suggested donation) up and running. It's a very worthwhile museum, full of an odd assortment of things. There are uniforms, from when Cuban leaders of the Bay of Pigs were chosen on Useppa in secrecy by the CIA as part of the preparations for the doomed Bay of Pigs invasion. And there's a forensic restoration of the "Useppa Man" taken from a skeleton unearthed during an archaeological dig in 1989. Other finds delve into the Paleo nomadic hunter-gatherer people who must have hung out here 10,000 years ago when the island was part of the mainland.

If you'd like to visit the island, **Captiva Cruises** (239/472-5300, 10 A.M.–3:30 P.M. Tues.–Sun., $27.50 adults, $15 kids) has a luncheon cruise to Useppa that includes a visit to the museum.

CABBAGE KEY

Charley did some damage on this little 102-acre island, too, but it's now fully operational. The **Cabbage Key Inn** (Intracoastal Waterway, Marker #60, Pineland, 239/283-2278, www.cabbagekey.com, $99 rooms at the inn, transient dockage available), built by writer Mary Roberts Rinehart and her son in 1938, has two very tempting allures for the visitor. Ostensibly it was here that Jimmy Buffet drew his inspiration for "Cheeseburger in Paradise." And indeed, the inn serves a fairly laudable burger, cheese optional. The second reason is the Dollar Bill Bar, located in the inn, which rides atop a 38-foot Calusa shell mound. The pub is lined with dollar bills, a custom that began in 1941 when a fisherman autographed and taped his last dollar to the wall for safekeeping (assuring a beer on his return). Since then, people sign and date a buck, and tack them up—more than

Enough George Washingtons to make Martha nervous—the bar at Cabbage Key Inn has a unique decorating motif.

30,000 $1 bills are taped to the walls, ceilings, and woodwork, providing a historical collage. (It's illegal to deface currency, but no one in this live-and-let-live bar will tell on you.)

Cabbage Key is accessible only by boat, helicopter, or seaplane, located directly across from mile marker 60 on the Intracoastal Waterway. It doesn't really have sandy beaches or many amenities, but it's a great day trip or overnight. **Captiva Cruises** (239/472-5300, 10 A.M.–3:30 P.M. Tues.–Sun., $27.50 adults, $15 kids) also offers a narrated cruise to Cabbage Key, and there are regularly scheduled water taxis every day from Pine Island, Captiva Island, and Punta Gorda.

CAYO COSTA

It's one of the quietest, unbridged barrier islands in the chain, but one of the largest. Immediately to the west of Cabbage Key, stretching from Boca Grande Pass to Captiva Pass, it offers eight miles of pristine beach and unspoiled beauty. **Cayo Costa State Park** (P.O. Box 1150, Boca Grande, 941/964-0375, 8 A.M.–sunset, $1 honor system) is the least-visited state park in Florida, but it's because there are no cars, no electricity, and no hot water, not because it's not worthy. It is where Hurricane Charley made landfall in October 2004, so its vegetation is still recuperating from the effects of high winds and high water. Mature trees that once cloaked the island will take decades to regrow.

Calusas occupied the island for hundreds of years, then in the early 1800s Cuban fishermen landed here, and in 1848 the U.S. government started managing the land. There are 20 private homes on the island, only a couple of them lived in year-round. Really, it's a place to tent camp ($18/night) or overnight in one of 12 rustic cabins ($30), all on the northern end of the island. There's a small pioneer cemetery and a fair number of wild pigs—other than that it's sea creatures, birds, and swaths of sun-warmed sand.

Cayo Costa is accessible only by passenger ferry or private boat. Call **Tropic Star of Pine Island** (239/283-0015) to make reservations.

NORTH CAPTIVA ISLAND

Once a part of Captiva Island, this island was severed during the hurricane of 1926. And darned if it didn't just happen again. The right eyewall of Hurricane Charley in October 2004 passed over North Captiva Island and severed it into two parts, resulting in a breach 450 meters wide along an uninhabited stretch of refuge land. The storm came ashore with 145 mph winds and 10-foot waves, leaving a handful of the island's roughly 300 houses and establishments in Safety Harbor (like The Mango Café and Barnacle Phil's) marooned on the new island. A fair number of the luxury homes on the island lost rooftops, but due to good construction, few lost walls (a more serious problem). Docks were demolished down to their pilings and large specimen trees were wrenched out of the ground.

The island in recent years has been a remote retreat for the super wealthy. There are four miles of state-owned beaches—the state bought 350 acres, almost half of the island, in 1975. At the turn of the 20th century the island contained a vast tomato plantation; after that it was the processing plant for the Punta Gorda Fish Company. In recent years there have been about 50 year-round residents on the island, most of them on the northern part in an enclave known as the Island Club, with the rest of the island given over to affluent vacationers driving golf carts and strolling the sparsely populated beaches. If you aim to visit, now is a strange time: It's still recovering from the storm's savagery, but it might be more affordable than ever since lots of luxury homes are offering great deals.

PINE ISLAND

Pine Island is one of the largest islands off the Gulf Coast of Florida and consists of **Matlacha** (mat-la-SHAY), **Pine Island Center, Bokeelia** (bo-KEEL-ya), **Pineland,** and **St. James City.** The north side of Pine Island fared pretty badly in Charley's fury, with lots of homes, two mobile home parks, and several marinas on the Bokeelia side of the island devastated. Still, rebuilding has moved apace, and most businesses are up and

Lee County

COURTESY OF LEE COUNTY VISITOR AND CONVENTION BUREAU

The sunset over Pine Island's town of Bokeelia slides ostentatiously through sherbert-hued pinks and oranges.

running again. It's a great fishing retreat (the tarpon fishing craze started here in the 1880s) and a lovely place from which to observe wildlife, such as the bald eagle nesting sites.

Matlacha is a funky fishing village, with a drawbridge over Matlacha Pass that has seen a lot of fishing action in its day. If you want to wet a line, there are plenty of bait and tackle shops and boat rentals at the **Olde Fish House Marina** and **Viking Marina.** Pine Island Center is the island's commercial district, where you'll go for shopping, with the school, fire station, ball fields, and community pool.

Bokeelia is the home port for many of the island's commercial fishing boats and the agricultural part of the island (you'll see mangoes and a whole bunch of only vaguely familiar-looking tropical fruits: carambola, longan, loquat). This part of the island contains a few historic buildings, including the **Museum of the Islands** (5728 Sesame Dr., Bokeelia, 239/283-1525, www.museumoftheislands.com, 11 A.M.–3 P.M. Tues.–Sat., 1–4 P.M. Sun., in

the winter only Tues.–Thurs., $2 adults, $1 children 12 and under), with exhibitions on Pine Island pioneers.

Pineland is home to the **Randall Research Center** (13810 Waterfront Dr., Pineland, 239/283-2062, www.flmnh.ufl.edu/RRC, $7 adults, $4 children), one of the main historical sites of Calusa mounds. It opened a new Calusa Heritage Trail at the end of 2004, with 13 artistic signs interpreting the Calusa way of life and religious beliefs. There are also guided tours Wednesday at 10 A.M. Also in Pineland you'll find one of the country's smallest **post offices** and boat rentals and fishing charters out of **Pineland Marina.** For dinner, stop into the **Tarpon Lodge** (13771 Waterfront Dr., Pineland, 239/283-3999) or its Sportsman's Lounge for a drink.

St. James City is Pine Island's residential community, with about two-thirds of the island's population living here. Most homes are located on canals with easy access to Pine Island Sound, San Carlos Bay, and the Gulf of Mexico.

Information and Services

AREA INFORMATION

Lee County is on eastern time. The telephone area code is 239, but it used to be 941, an area code now used farther north.

Tourist Information

For visitor information, the **Lee County Visitor & Convention Bureau** (12800 University Dr., Ste. 550, Fort Myers, 239/338-3500 or 800/237-6444, www.FortMyersSanibel.com and www.leeislandcoast.com) has an absolutely tremendous website, with well-written text, good graphics—an easy resource for planning a trip. Its office is less convenient for walk-ins. The **Sanibel & Captiva Islands Chamber of Commerce** (1159 Causeway Rd., Sanibel, 239/472-1080, www.sanibel-captiva.org) maintains a visitors center on Causeway Road as you drive onto Sanibel from Fort Myers. The chamber gives away an island guide and sells a detailed street map for $3.

This area has a fair number of small papers that serve Lee County, but no big metro paper. The *Fort Myers News-Press* (239/335-0233) is the daily in these parts. In Fort Myers Beach, look for the *Fort Myers Beach Observer* (239/765-0400), which is the weekly newspaper distributed every Wednesday. The *Island Reporter* (239/472-1587) is the newspaper of record for Sanibel and Captiva Islands, and there's also a magazine covering Sanibel called *Times of the Islands Magazine.* On Boca Grande, look for the weekly *Boca Beacon.*

Police and Emergencies

As always, if you find yourself in a real emergency, pick up a phone and dial **911** or the local **Emergency Management Office** (239/477-3600). For a nonemergency police need, call the **Sheriff's Office** (239/332-3456), **Florida Highway Patrol** (239/278-7100), **U.S. Coast Guard** (239/463-5754), or **Florida Poison Information Center** (800/222-1222).

Sanibel and Captiva medical facilities serve the local community during business hours. For emergency medical needs, **HealthPark Medical Center** (16131 Roserush Ct., Fort Myers, 239/433-4647) and **Lee Memorial Hospital** (2776 Cleveland Ave., Fort Myers, 239/332-1111) are full-service hospitals on the mainland with 24-hour emergency service. For your pharmacy needs on the islands, **Eckerd Drugs** (2331 Palm Ridge Rd., Sanibel, 239/472-0085) is convenient, and if your pet has a medical problem, there's **Coral Veterinary Clinic** (1530 Periwinkle Way, Sanibel, 239/472-8387).

Radio and Television

If you're looking for NPR radio, turn to **WGCU 90.1 FM**. For local music programming, **WARO 94.5 FM** is classic rock; **WCKT 107.1 FM** is country music; **WDRR 98.5 FM** has smooth jazz; **WINK 96.9 FM** offers adult contemporary programming; **WJBX 99.3 FM** is alt rock; **WOLZ 95.3 FM** is, of course, oldies; **WRXK 96.1 FM** gives you classic rock; and **WXKB 103.9 FM** is top 40 radio.

And on the television, **WBBH Channel 2** is the NBC affiliate, **WINK Channel 11** is the CBS affiliate, **WZVN Channel 7** is the ABC affiliate, **WGCU Channel 30** is the PBS affiliate, and **WFTX Channel 4** is the FOX affiliate out of Cape Coral.

Laundry Services

Large hotels and beach rentals often have laundry services of one sort or another. If you need to throw in a load of wash, launderettes are limited on the islands. Try an RV park along the route. In Fort Myers the laundry options are much broader. **60 Minute Cleaners** has three locations (12842 S. Cleveland Ave., 239/936-3616; Cypress Trace Shopping Center, 239/481-1900; and 16970 San Carlos Blvd., 239/466-5115). In Fort Myers Beach, there's **Beach & Bubbles Coin Laundry & Dry Cleaners** (7205 Estero Blvd., 239/765-1771), a garden-variety coin-op laundry.

Fishing Licenses

Fishing licenses are sold at all county tax collectors' offices and at many bait-and-tackle shops, or by phone (888/347-4356). On Sanibel, you can buy a license at the **Bait Box** on Periwinkle Way; at **Bailey's** at the corner of Tarpon Bay Road and Periwinkle Way; at **Tarpon Bay Recreation;** and at all the marinas. Also pick up the Florida Marine Fisheries Commission's publication about size and bag limits. You do not need a license if you are fishing from a boat that has a valid recreational vessel saltwater fishing license, if you are under 16, or if you are Florida resident fishing from a pier or bridge.

COURTESY OF LEE COUNTY VISITOR AND CONVENTION BUREAU

If you want to see what's biting, grab a fishing license sold at many bait-and-tackle shops (kids under 16 don't need a license).

Getting There and Around

DRIVING

Lee County is along southwest Florida's Gulf Coast between Naples and Sarasota. The biggest north–south driving routes are I-75 and U.S. 41. East–west major arteries include Alligator Alley (I-75) and U.S. 41 (where it jogs east at around Naples).

To get to Fort Myers, you can take either I-75 or U.S. 41. In town, McGregor Boulevard runs alongside the Caloosahatchee River and is also called Highway 867. Highway 865 (also known as Hickory Boulevard, Estero Boulevard, and San Carlos Boulevard, depending on where you are) is the route south to Fort Myers Beach on Estero Island.

To get to Sanibel from I-75, take New Exit 131 or Old Exit 21 (Daniels Parkway) west to Summerlin Road, approximately seven miles. Turn left on Summerlin Road and drive approximately fifteen miles to the Sanibel Causeway (a $6 toll). Drive across and onto Sanibel Island. At the four-way stop at Periwinkle Way, either a right or a left turn will lead you to beaches, shops, and accommodations. Sanibel Island has a couple of main roads that parallel each other: Periwinkle Way, the main business route, and Gulf Drive, segmented into East, Middle, and West Gulf Drive. Tarpon Bay Road

connects Sanibel-Captiva Road with Periwinkle Way at its west end. And Sanibel-Captiva Road—most folks call it San-Cap—goes by most of Sanibel's attractions before crossing over a short bridge at Blind Pass, where it becomes Captiva Drive on Captiva Island.

So, to reach Captiva, turn right on Periwinkle Way, drive two miles, turn right onto Tarpon Bay Road, and at the next left turn onto Sanibel-Captiva Road. Drive for approximately eight miles, cross Blind Pass Bridge, and you're there.

Driving into Florida from the north via Jacksonville, take I-95 south to I-4 to I-75, and then follow the directions above.

FLYING

By air, the area is served by **Southwest Florida International Airport** (16000 Chamberlin Parkway, Fort Myers, 239/768-1000, www.swfia.com or www.flylcpa.com). Most major domestic airlines serve the airport, and there are international flights from Germany and Canada. The airport, opened in 1983, has enjoyed enormous growth recently, finishing an expanded terminal and new runway opening in 2005. It currently serves: Air Canada, America West, American, Continental, Delta, Frontier, Jet Blue, Northwest, United, US

Airways, and many smaller carriers, as well as German airlines Condor and LTU International.

Alamo (800/327-9633), Avis (800/230-4898), Budget (800/227-5945), Dollar (800/800-3665), Enterprise (800/736-8222), Hertz (800/654-3131), National (800/227-7368), and Thrifty (800/847-4389) provide rental cars from Southwest Florida International Airport. Enterprise and Thrifty offices are off-site, a short shuttle away.

PUBLIC TRANSPORTATION

Reservations are not required for taxis and limousines from the airport. Go to the ground transportation booth in the median between the terminal and the parking lot (ground transportation information 239/768-4457). Lee Tran Airport Service (239/275-8726, www.rideleetran.com) has hourly service 6 A.M.–10 P.M. to a transfer point at Daniels Parkway and U.S. 41 with connections to other routes.

Amtrak (800/USA-RAIL) offers train service to the Fort Myers station, as does Greyhound Bus Line (239/774-5660), but from here you really need to rent a car. Public transportation to and between the islands is limited to taxis and limousines.

Lee County

Sarasota County

Want a stiff shot of culture? Sarasota's the place to go. Arts vie with more than 35 miles of dazzling Gulf Coast beaches for top draw. But Sarasota was a slow starter. It took its time becoming the sophisticated, culturally rich city it is today. Centuries after Ponce de Leon, Panfilo de Narvaez, and Hernando De Soto came through this part of the Gulf Coast, the area went mercifully unnoticed by white settlers. Even after Florida was acquired by the U.S. in 1821, the only white men to linger here were a handful of entrepreneurial fishermen who sup-

plied salted fish and live turtles from the area for export to Cuba. In 1842, William Whittaker homesteaded in the area, planting some orange trees. Not many followed suit, perhaps because the local Seminoles' reputation for fierceness was widely acknowledged.

In fact, it was the brutal seven-year Seminole War that brought Whittaker and a stalwart few to town as part of the Armed Occupation Act, which deeded 160 Florida acres and six months' provisions to any person who agreed to carry arms and protect the land for five years.

Must-Sees

Look for **M** to find the sights and activities you can't miss and **M** for the best dining and lodging.

M Siesta Key Beach: Beaches are a central draw of this area, with a couple of world-class contenders. Siesta Key Beach, with its pure-quartz white sand (it's more like powdered sugar than granulated sugar, so each time you stand up you look like a Greek wedding cookie in a bathing suit), usually gets top honors (page 108).

M Ed Smith Stadium: Take me out to the ballpark. Ed Smith Stadium is the spring-training home of the Cincinnati Reds, with all the Grapefruit League teams cycling through in preparation for the summer season. It's thrilling to see big-league teams in such a small-town setting. Tickets are cheap and the hot dogs are good (page 110).

M Marie Selby Botanical Gardens: You don't have to be a master gardener or panting horticulturalist to enjoy a day here. In 11 bay-front acres, the open-air and under-glass museum has more than 6,000 orchids and more than 20,000 other

the Ringling Estate, now famous for the John and Mable Ringling Museum of Art

plants, many of which have been collected in the wild by the gardens' research staff. Most impressive is the vast array of otherworldly epiphytes, or air plants (page 114).

M John and Mable Ringling Museum of Art: This museum is a must-see for fans of Flemish and Italian baroque art, with room after room of breathtaking canvasses, the most impressive of which is a series by Peter Paul Rubens known collectively as *The Triumph of the Eucharist* (page 115).

M Asolo Theatre Company: Sarasota has an embarrassment of riches when it comes to the arts. One of the flashiest jewels is this professional company, which stages productions year-round in both the Fred and Ethel Mertz, I mean the Harold E. and Esther M. Mertz Theatre, and the black-box Jane B. Cook Theatre. It's a testament to the theater's quality that many season ticket holders come from all over the country to see the dramas, musicals, and comedies each year (page 120).

M Film Festivals: Time a trip to Sarasota to catch one of the city's two film festivals, the Sarasota Film Festival and the Cine-World Film Festival. The former is in January, the latter in November—both are a citywide excuse for a party, in between two-hour popcorn-eating jags at all the city's many movie theaters (page 124).

Sarasota County

Forty years later, as a means for drumming up some new residents, the Florida Mortgage and Investment Company started talking up Sarasota, with a few egregious exaggerations, in Scotland. Sixty Scottish families took the bait, arriving in 1885 to find a water-logged Main Street and a decided lack of amenities. Being Scottish, they promptly built a golf course (possibly America's first) and then got to work making it a real town. Because there was no overland transportation, sailing ships and steamboats were the only connection to the outside world. In 1902 came the railroad, which connected Sarasota to Tampa; electricity and paved roads followed not too long after.

An influx of wealthy socialites settled the area starting around 1910, establishing Sarasota as a winter resort for affluent northerners. It was during this time that Sarasota's performing and visual arts institutions were established, to entertain those first hoity-toity tourists. Among the early tourists to be smitten by the town was circus magnate John Ringling. He scooped up property all around Sarasota, moving the circus's winter home here, building himself a winter residence, art museum, circus museum, and college.

The population doubled in the Florida land boom of 1924–1927—it was Roaring '20s indeed for Sarasota, with tourist hotels, tourist attractions, and a causeway over the bay sprouting up to accommodate the surge in interest.

Growth in neighboring towns (Bradenton, Venice, North Port), as well as along the chain of narrow barrier islands (from north to south: Anna Maria Island, Longboat Key, St. Armands Key, Lido Key, Siesta Key, Casey Key) was slower, largely due to limited access. Tourists gradually settled their sights on the keys, noticing the 35 miles of glistening white-sand beaches that fringe their Gulf side.

Because of this head start, the city of Sarasota is the undisputed cultural center of the area, with theater, opera, symphony, ballet, art museums, and restaurants to rival those in much bigger cities. Each of the keys maintains its own identity, with glorious beach access being the central unifying theme. Lido and St. Armands are really just extensions of downtown Sarasota, connected by a causeway, and fairly urban. Started as a quiet fishing village, Longboat Key is now strictly the purview of the posh, with tall resort hotels and condominiums and a glut of golf courses. Siesta Key is much more low-rise, with a personality to match. It's relaxed, laid-back, with a high funk-factor. It's the most youthful spot on this part of the Gulf Coast. Casey Key is less of a tourist draw, mostly dotted with single-family homes.

PLANNING YOUR TIME

Florida's calamitous hurricane season of 2004 barely affected the greater Sarasota area at all. In its aftermath, hotels, restaurants, and attractions are all business as usual, with a slight resultant slowdown in tourism (which means less competition for you). A typical vacation in this area is about a week. This is partly because there's a week's worth of things to do, and partly because many of the beach houses/condos/whatever rent only by the week, especially in high season. Staying downtown in Sarasota is a little cheaper than staying beachside somewhere. Downtown streets and roads run east–west; avenues and boulevards run north–south. The main street downtown is called, um, Main Street.

From downtown, go east across the John Ringling Causeway to access St. Armands Circle and Lido Key (St. Armands is a shopping and restaurant destination of note). Continue north to Longboat Key, where there's not a lot of draw beyond swanky hotels, golf courses, a few restaurants, and slightly inconvenient beach access and parking. To reach Siesta Key, head south on U.S. 41 (also called the Tamiami Trail), then take a right onto either Siesta Drive or Stickney Point Road—the former takes you to the northern, residential section of the key; Stickney takes you closer to the funky Siesta Village. The public beaches on Siesta Key are among the finest in the state.

The area's peak season begins in February and continues until Easter (average temperatures in

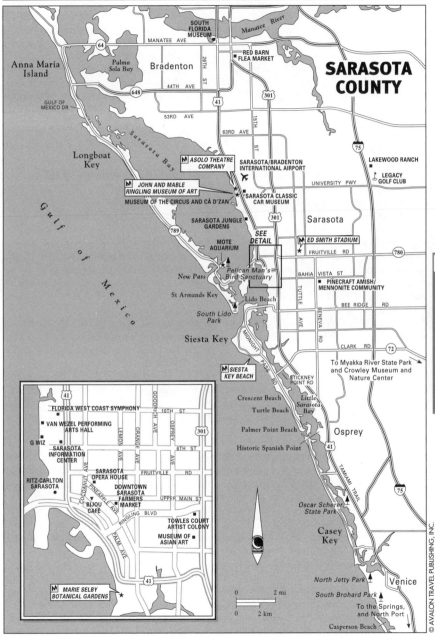

SOUTH FLORIDA MUSEUM
MANATEE AVE
Manatee River

SARASOTA COUNTY

Anna Maria Island

Palma Sola Bay

Bradenton

RED BARN FLEA MARKET

64

648

44TH AVE

53RD AVE

63RD AVE

28TH ST

41

301

15TH ST

75

GULF OF MEXICO DR

Sarasota Bay

Longboat Key

ASOLO THEATRE COMPANY

SARASOTA/BRADENTON INTERNATIONAL AIRPORT

LAKEWOOD RANCH

LEGACY GOLF CLUB

UNIVERSITY PWY

JOHN AND MABLE RINGLING MUSEUM OF ART
MUSEUM OF THE CIRCUS AND CÀ D'ZAN

SARASOTA CLASSIC CAR MUSEUM

789

SARASOTA JUNGLE GARDENS

MOTE AQUARIUM

SEE DETAIL

301

Sarasota

ED SMITH STADIUM

FRUITVILLE RD

780

G u l f

New Pass

Pelican Man's Bird Sanctuary

BAHIA VISTA ST

PINECRAFT AMISH/ MENNONITE COMMUNITY

St Armands Key

Lido Beach

TUTTLE AVE

BEE RIDGE RD

o f

South Lido Park

BENEVA RD

M e x i c o

Siesta Key

MIDNIGHT PASS RD

CLARK RD

72

SIESTA KEY BEACH

STICKNEY POINT RD

To Myakka River State Park and Crowley Museum and Nature Center

Crescent Beach

Turtle Beach

Little Sarasota Bay

Palmer Point Beach

Osprey

Historic Spanish Point

41

FLORIDA WEST COAST SYMPHONY

VAN WEZEL PERFORMING ARTS HALL

G WIZ

SARASOTA INFORMATION CENTER

RITZ-CARLTON SARASOTA

SARASOTA OPERA HOUSE

DOWNTOWN SARASOTA FARMERS MARKET

BIJOU CAFÉ

TOWLES COURT ARTIST COLONY

MUSEUM OF ASIAN ART

41

LEMON AVE

ORANGE AVE

GOODRICH AVE

OSPREY AVE

10TH ST

6TH ST

FRUITVILLE RD

UPPER MAIN ST

RINGLING BLVD

COCOANUT AVE

PINEAPPLE AVE

PALM AVE

301

MARIE SELBY BOTANICAL GARDENS

MOON

0   2 mi

0   2 km

Oscar Scherer State Park

Casey Key

TAMIAMI TRAIL

75

North Jetty Park

South Brohard Park

Venice

To the Springs, and North Port

Casperson Beach

© AVALON TRAVEL PUBLISHING, INC.

Sarasota County

the mid-70s F). During that time, prices are hiked and reservations are necessary for accommodations. What travel agents call "the value season" is pretty much all summer in Sarasota, June–September. The Gulf waters are bathwater temperature during much of the summer—and as gentle and safe to swim in as your bathtub, too. On a hot day (in the summer, this means about 90 degrees with a lot of humidity), the water temperatures aren't exactly refreshing, but that's the price to pay for a peaceful, sparsely populated day at the beach. Many of Sarasota's cultural institutions (symphony, ballet, opera, theaters) take a hiatus during the summer months, another drawback to visiting then.

Sarasota

The circus built Sarasota. Sure, a bit of what drew smart and affluent northerners here was the weather (something preposterous like 361 days of sun each year) and the exotic subtropical flora and fauna. But it was when circus impresario John Ringling snapped up real estate that other wealthy, worldly northerners started giving this Podunk orange grove and celery farm another look. And in the 1920s, as Ringling began amassing huge numbers of baroque paintings in his new mansion, Cà d'Zan, so too did Ringling's cohorts begin assembling in all their baroque and even rococo finery for a little winter rest and relaxation. The sunny clime was not enough to entertain for any duration, so cultural amenities like opera, and theater, and symphony orchestras blossomed.

Beyond Ringling's generous bequeathal of house, museums, etc., to the city, the Circus King gave Sarasota a tradition of patronage, a habit of high expectations and connoisseurship when it comes to the arts. Sarasota's population of 52,000, with a little help from twice that number of winter visitors, supports a vast number of arts events, with gusto, along with an equally robust restaurant and shopping scene.

The striking thing is that there's other stuff to do. It's not as if *Die Fledermaus,* or *Swan Lake,* or the comedies of Shakespeare are needed to while away an afternoon or evening in Sarasota. It is home to world-class beaches and all the attendant beach activities, with easy access to notable state parks and outdoor fun. A vacation in Sarasota does not boil down to a dilemma about what to do, just what to do *first.*

SPORTS AND RECREATION

M Siesta Key Beach

We have a winner of the international whose-beach-is-better smackdown. In 1987 scientists from the Woods Hole Oceanographic Institution in Woods Hole, Massachusetts, convened to judge the "Great International White Sand Beach Challenge," with more than 30 entries from beaches around the world. To this day, Siesta Key Beach remains the reigning world champ, with all other beaches too cowed, or too chicken, to demand a rematch. Its preeminence has long been known—supposedly in the 1950s a visitor from New York, Mr. Edward G. Curtis, sent a pickle jar of Siesta's sand to the Geology Department of Harvard University for analysis. The report came back: "The sand from Siesta Key is 99 percent pure quartz grains, the grains being somewhat angular in shape. The soft floury texture of the sand is due to its very fine grain size. It contains no fragments of coral and no shell. The fineness of the sand, which gives it its powdery softness, is emphasized by the fact that the quartz is a very hard substance, graded at 7 in the hardness scale of 10."

The real test can't be done with sand in a pickle jar. You need to lie on the sloping strand, run the warmed granules through your fingers, sniff the salt air, and listen to a plaintive gull overhead. That way, too, Siesta Key Beach wins—it's been named "America's Best Sand Beach" and ranked in "Florida's Top Ten Beaches" on the Travel Channel in 2002 and 2003. Dr. Beach named it in his top 10 beaches

COURTESY OF SARASOTA CVB

Siesta Key's sand is powdered-sugar fine and whiter than white—the building blocks of the perfect sand castle.

Sarasota County

in America in 2004; *National Geographic Traveler* also named Siesta "One of America's Best Beaches" in 2003. The list goes on.

Other Beaches

But this is hardly a one-beach town. The greater Sarasota area has lots of beaches to recommend. Moving from north to south:

Longboat Key has 10 miles of white, powdery beach, but most of it is accessible only to those who live there or are staying in a resort or condo. **Longboat Key Beach** is accessible at several points—at Longview Drive, Westfield Street, Mayfield Street, and Neptune Avenue. It's mostly underpopulated and often offers incredible sand dollar collecting. **Beer Can Island Beach,** at the very north end of Longboat Key and accessible by boat or from North Shore Road off Gulf of Mexico Drive, attracts a fair number of anglers and sun worshippers.

North Lido Beach is just northwest of St. Armands Circle, off of John Ringling Boulevard on Lido Key (which really itself is just a 2.5-mile spit of beach from Big Sarasota Pass to New Pass). It's a short walk from shops or restaurants, and fairly secluded. No lifeguards, swift currents, no real amenities. In the other direction from St. Armands Circle, southwest, you'll run into **Lido Beach,** which has parking for 400 cars, cabana beach rentals at the snack bar, playground equipment, and bathrooms. It's a good hang-out-all-afternoon family beach. It's more crowded that North Lido. The third beach on Lido Key is called **South Lido Park,** on Ben Franklin Drive at the southern tip of Lido Key. The park is bordered by four bodies of water: the Gulf, Big Pass, Sarasota Bay, and Brushy Bayou. It has a nature trail, and the beach offers a lovely view of the downtown Sarasota skyline. There's a nice picnic area with grills, as well as volleyball courts. Kayakers use this area to traverse the different waterways.

Then there's the aforementioned Siesta Key Beach, on the north side of Siesta Key (it is contiguous with another favorite beach called Crescent Beach—good snorkeling off this one), with white sand so reflective it feels cool on a hot day. Scientists estimate that the sand on this beach is millions of years old, starting in the Appalachians and eventually deposited on these shores. The water is shallow, the beach incline gradual, making it a perfect beach for young swimmers. There are 800 parking spots, which tend to fill up, and the lifeguard stands are painted different colors (as points of reference, so you don't lose your way). The Siesta Key beaches south of a rock outcropping called Point of Rocks are not as white and soft, the sand being shellier and grayer. Still, **Turtle Beach,** on Midnight Pass Road near the south end of Siesta Key, is another popular beach, prized for its more private feel, large picnic shelter, and good shelling opportunities.

There used to be a small inlet that separated Siesta Key from Casey Key, an inlet called Midnight Pass that, amongst great controversy, was filled in in 1983. There are unpleasant environmental consequences to this choice, but for the visitor it means you can walk all the way on **Palmer Point Beach** from Siesta Key to Casey Key. The northern part of the beach was the former home of Mote Marine Laboratory. These days it's a quiet dune-backed beach, populated mostly by people trudging with determination at the water's edge. No lifeguards, no facilities. Casey Key also has **Nokomis Beach** directly west of the Albee Road Bridge, a pleasant but unremarkable beach, and **North Jetty Park** at its southernmost tip. North Jetty Park is one of the few Gulf Coast spots that draws surfers, and fisherfolk seem to congregate here, too. Boats pass through the jetties from the Intracoastal Waterway to the Gulf.

South from here you enter into the beaches of Venice, rightfully known as the place to go when you're hunting shark's teeth. So, now you might be worried that there are loads of sharks lurking offshore waiting to gum you to death. The shark's teeth that wash up on the beach are fossilized, floating in from a shark burial ground a few miles offshore, a deep crevice where these cold-blooded predators once went to die. In addition to these gray/black teeth, fossilized bones of prehistoric animals like camels, bison, and tapirs sometimes wash up on this beach. In local shops you can rent or buy a shark-tooth scooper, a wire rake with a mesh box that sifts the sand and shell fragments at the water's edge, leaving the teeth behind in the basket. **Venice Beach** (so different from the beach of the same name in California)

is at the west end of Venice Avenue not that far from town. **Brohard Park,** at the southernmost part of Venice, is the beach of choice among anglers, with a 740-foot fishing pier on the property for public use. (Dogs are also allowed at South Brohard Park, with a fenced area, a beach, and dog showers.) Further south, near Venice's little airport (which houses Huffman Aviation, the flight school where, unfortunately, terrorists responsible for 9/11 were trained to fly), **Casperson Beach** is really the locus of shark's teeth mania. Truth is, it's harder to find teeth than it used to be, partly because city boosters have replenished the sand on the beach with sand from an offshore sandbar. It's a very pretty beach left in its natural state, with people surf casting and red-shouldered hawks swooping above the shorebirds.

Golf

Sarasota is Florida's self-described "Cradle of Golf," having been home to the state's first course built in 1905 by Sir John Hamilton Gillespie, a Scottish colonist. The nine-hole course was located right at the center of what is now Sarasota's downtown. That first course is long gone, but there are more than 1,000 holes to play at public, semiprivate, and private courses in Sarasota, at all levels of play and most budgets. Of the top 20 Southwest regional courses voted by the readers of *Florida Golf News,* nine are in the Sarasota area.

Now, I'm not one of those women with the bumper sticker that says, "I got a set of golf clubs for my husband, and I must say, it was a damn good trade!" See sidebar for a list of the public, semiprivate, and resort courses recommended to me by golfers, with their top picks indicated. Call for tee times and greens fees, as they vary wildly by time of day and time of year.

Ed Smith Stadium

Sarasota has been an exciting part of the Grapefruit League's spring training program for years. The New York Giants arrived back in 1924, followed by the Red Sox and then the White Sox. These days, Sarasota's Ed Smith Stadium (2700 12th St. at the corner of Tuttle Ave.; from I-75, take Exit 210, Fruitville Rd., 941/954-4101, box seats $14, reserved $12, general admission $7) is

SARASOTA'S GOLF COURSES

Bobby Jones Golf Complex 1000 Circus Blvd., Sarasota, 941/365-4653, 6,039 yards, par 71, course rating 68.4, slope 117

Heather Hills Golf Course 101 Cortez Rd. W, Bradenton, 941/755-8888, 3,521 yards, par 61, course rating 58.6, slope 96

Imperial Lakes Golf Course 6807 Buffalo Rd., Palmetto, 941/747-GOLF, 7,008 yards, par 72, course rating 68.7, slope 117

Legacy Golf Club at Lakewood Ranch 8255 Legacy Blvd., Bradenton, 941/907-7067, semiprivate, 7,123 yards, par 72, course rating 73.7, slope 143

◪ The Links at Green Field Plantation 10325 Greenfield Plantation Blvd., Bradenton, 941/747-9432, 6,720 yards, par 72, course rating 72, slope 128

◪ Manatee County Golf Course 6415 53rd Ave. W, Bradenton, 941/792-6773, 6,747 yards, par 72, course rating 71.6, slope 122

Palma Sola Golf Club 3807 75th St. W, Bradenton, 941/792-7476, 6,264 yards, par 72, course rating 68.4, slope 115

Palmetto Pines Golf Course 14355 Golf Course Dr., Parrish, 941/776-1375, 5,358 yards, par 72, course rating 68.4, slope 92

◪ Peridia Golf & Country Club 4950 Peridia Blvd., Bradenton, 941/758-2582, www.peridiagcc.net, 3,344 yards, par 60, course rating 55.0, slope 86

Pinebrook/Ironwood Golf Club 4260 Ironwood Circle, Bradenton, 941/792-3288, 3,706 yards, par 68, course rating 59.9, slope 101

River Club 6600 River Club Blvd., Bradenton, 941/751-4211, 7,026 yards, par 72, course rating 74.5, slope 135

River Run Golf Links 1801 27th St. E, Bradenton, 941/747-6331, 5,900 yards, par 70, course rating 67.9, slope 115

Rosedale Golf and Country Club 5100 87th St. E, Bradenton, 941/756-0004, 6,779 yards, par 72, course rating 72.9, slope 134

Sarasota Golf Club 7280 N. Lee Wynn Dr., Sarasota, 941/371-2431, 6,980 yards, par 72, course rating 72.9, slope 122

Terra Ceia 2802 Terra Ceia Bay Blvd., Palmetto, 941/729-7663, 4,001 yards, par 62, course rating 67.9, slope 99

Timber Creek Golf Course 4550 Timber Lane, Bradenton, 941/794-8381, 9 holes, 2,086 yards, par 3

◪ University Park Country Club 7671 Park Blvd., University Park, 941/359-9999, 27 holes, 4,914–7,247 yards, par 72, course rating 67.8–74.4, slope 113–138

Village Green Golf Course 1401 Village Green Pkwy., Bradenton, 941/792-7171, 2,735 yards, par 58

◪ Waterlefe Golf & River Club 1022 Fish Hook Cove, Bradenton, 941/744-9771, 6,908 yards, par 72

the spring training home of the Cincinnati Reds (as well as the minor-league Sarasota Red Sox of the Florida State League—the Boston Red Sox now train a bit to the south in Fort Myers, and the Pittsburgh Pirates play in nearby Bradenton).

The little 7,500-seat stadium provides intimate access to big-league play in a small-time venue. Cheap tickets and up-close seats—it's a perfect outing on a warm Sarasota spring evening even if baseball's not your sport. Day games start at 1:05 P.M. and night games at 7:05 P.M.; practices begin at 9 A.M. Many spring-training games

sell out, so you might want to buy tickets by mail or phone. Send an SASE to: Reds Tickets, Ed Smith Stadium, 1090 N. Euclid, Sarasota, FL 34237, or call 800/955-5566.

Polo

There are scads of spectator sporting opportunities in Sarasota, but polo trumps a fair number of them. Games are enormous fun, the horses racing around tearing up the lush sod of the polo grounds while their riders focus fiercely on that pesky little ball. For a sport with such an effete pedigree, it's amazingly physical and exciting to watch, whether you're in your fancy polo togs (what's with all the hats?) or your weekend jeans. **Sarasota Polo Club** (Lakewood Ranch, 8201 Polo Club Lane, 941/907-0000, 1 P.M. Sun. December 12–April 10, $8, children 12 and under free) is in its 15th year, with professional-level players coming from around the world to play on the nine pristine fields. Bring a picnic or buy sandwiches and drinks once you're there. Gates open at 11:30 A.M. and dogs on leashes are welcome. You can also take polo lessons at Lakewood Ranch. Call Stuart Campbell (941/907-1122).

Cricket

Polo's not the only game in town for the super fancy-pants Anglophile: Cricket, anyone? The **Sarasota International Cricket Club** (Lakewood Ranch, 7401 University Pkwy., just east of Lorraine Rd., 941/232-9956) was founded in 1983 and has 42 playing members who play about 35 matches a year with clubs from around the Southeast. The season runs weekends from late September through the end of May, and watching is free. Call for game schedule.

Lawn Bowling

Are you starting to see a theme? Lush expanses of perfect grass, a ridiculous number of beautiful sunny days—people in Sarasota clearly need elaborate excuses to spend their days outside. The **Sarasota Lawn Bowling Club** (809 N. Tamiami Trail at 10th St., 941/316-1123, beginning at 9:30 A.M. weekdays May–Oct., beginning at 1 P.M. Oct.–Apr., $3/day to play) is the oldest sporting club in Sarasota, with three greens, "boule" (ball) rentals, and free lessons. Wear flat shoes if you want to play. And if you just want to be a spectator for some serious play, schedule a trip for October 22–28, 2006, when the club hosts the 2006 United States Open.

Pétanque

Similar to lawn bowling but a little more obscure, pétanque is played at Lakeview Park (7150 Lago St., 941/861-9830, free to watch). Players toss and roll a number of steel balls as close as possible to a small wooden ball called the "cochonet," the piglet. Pronounced "pay-tonk," it's another great spectator sport, especially when accompanied by a wide blanket, a nice bottle of wine, and a tasty picnic. Lakeview Park, which is adjacent to Lake Sarasota, also contains a fabulous enclosed dog park—even if Rover stayed at home, visitors find it fun to just watch all that canine enthusiasm (over-exuberant dogs have to sit in the "time out" cage). It's open daily 6 A.M. until dark.

State Parks and Nature Preserves

If you want to spend a day out in nature but can't decide how best to engage with the great outdoors, the **Myakka River State Park** (nine miles east of Sarasota, 13207 Hwy. 72, 941/361-6511, 8 A.M.–sunset daily, $5 per vehicle up to eight people) presents pretty unbeatable one-stop shopping. The 28,875-acre park offers hiking, off-road biking, horseback riding, fishing, boating, canoeing, camping, and airboating. Both part of Florida Division of Forestry's Trailwalker Program, the North Loop (5.4 miles) and South Loop (7.4 miles) are fairly easy but scenic marked trails. Beyond these, there are 35 miles of unmarked trails open to hikers, mountain bikers (rentals $4 per hour, $18 full day), and equestrians (BYOH—that's bring your own horse, but with proof of current negative Coggins test). If you just want to breeze in for an few hours, a ride on Myakka Wildlife Tours' "Tram Safari" (runs Dec.–May only) takes visitors on a whirlwind tour of the park's backcountry, through shady hammocks, pine flatwoods, and lush marshes.

The 14-mile stretch of the scenic Myakka River has fairly easy-to-follow canoe trails (bring your own or rent at the Myakka Outpost; rentals $15 for two hours, $40 full day). Canoes and kayaks can be launched at the bridges, fishing area, other picnic areas, or at the boat ramp. During periods of low water (winter and spring), you'll have to portage around the weir at the south end of the Upper Lake. If you don't want to travel under your own paddle power, the park has a boat tour that runs every hour and a half or so ($8, $4 for kids, 941/365-0100) and a couple of the world's largest airboats, the *Gator Gal* and the *Myakka Maiden,* conduct guided one-hour

COURTESY OF SARASOTA CVB

Myakka River State Park protects a vast region of wetlands, lakes, prairies, and subtropical forest.

Sarasota County

tours on the one-mile-wide and 2.5-mile-long Upper Myakka Lake (serious gator territory).

The park's most unique feature is a fairly new addition. In conjunction with Marie Selby Botanical Gardens, the park recently opened a Canopy Walkway, the first of its kind in North America: the idea is that you amble along an 80-foot-long observation deck that hangs 100 feet in the air in the midst of a subtropical forest canopy. Perched in the tops of live oaks, laurel oaks, and cabbage palms, your perspective on bird and animal life is unparalleled, if a little vertiginous.

The park offers primitive camping and more equipped campsites ($22 per night including water and electric), but the neatest option might be one of the five palm log cabins built in the 1930s. They're pretty comfortable, with two double beds, linens, blankets, kitchen facilities, etc. The fee is $60 per night for up to four people (call 800/326-3521 to reserve far in advance).

Adjacent to the state park you'll find the **Crowley Museum and Nature Center** (16405 Myakka Rd., 941/322-1000, 10 A.M.–4 P.M. Thurs.–Sun. May–Dec., Tues.–Sun. Jan.–Apr., $5 adults, $3 children 5–12, children under 5 free), a 190-acre wildlife sanctuary and education center. A couple of hours here dovetails

nicely with time spent hiking or paddling in Myakka River State Park—there's a short nature trail, a boardwalk across Maple Branch Swamp, and an observation tower overlooking the Myakka River. To give more of a historical context to the area, the Crowley's real core is a pioneer museum tricked-out with a rustic one-room cabin, a restored 1892 Cracker house, a working blacksmith shop, and a little sugarcane mill. The museum sponsors Pioneer Days every December, an annual antiques fair, a folk music festival in October, and a yearly star-gazing night with high-powered telescopes.

It won't knock your socks off with stunning topography or habitats, but **Oscar Scherer State Park** (1843 S. Tamiami Trail, Osprey, 941/483-5956, 8 A.M.–sundown daily, entrance fee $4 per vehicle) is a local hangout for birders and families who want to spend an afternoon in nature without a lot of hassle. Much of it is a classic Florida flatwoods (scrub pine and saw-tooth palmetto, some endangered scrub jays, gopher tortoises, and an indigo snake or two). The park has several marked trails open to hikers and bikers (it's sandy terrain, most suitable for mountain bikes), and kayakers paddle around South Creek (bring your own canoe or

HOPE SPRINGS ETERNAL

Sometimes being the driver is good, because you don't need to argue with those in the backseat, you merely set your jaw and direct the car where *you* want it to go. We are going to the **Warm Mineral Springs** (12200 San Servando Ave., North Port, 941/426-1692, 9 A.M.–5 P.M. daily, weather permitting, $14 adults, $12 seniors, $9 students, $5 children 12 and under). And it's going to be fun, no matter what the detractors in the backseat are yelling.

Nine million gallons of warm mineral water flow here daily, with a higher mineral content than any other spring in the United States. Eighty-seven degrees year-round. It's thought to be Ponce de Leon's fabled "Fountain of Youth," for crying out loud. How could it be bad?

It wasn't bad exactly, just one of those parallel-universe experiences. First off, North Port isn't exactly a tourist destination. It's a fairly rural, unsexy town that looks like it needs a cash transfusion if the patient is to be saved. The big draw is this natural wonder, an hourglass-shaped sinkhole, 1.4 acres around and 230 feet deep, filled with heavily mineralized water.

We learned quickly upon exiting the car, some of us in a huff, that heavily mineralized water means stink. The sulfurous stink of a really rotten egg. Also, the water's mineral content makes it slimy and viscous-feeling. Also, it's not that warm.

But here's the thing: Russians come from across planet Earth to splash around in this particular sinkhole. Sturdy women in industrial-looking one-piece suits wade in reverently like it's the healing water of the Ganges. English was not a first language for any of the bathers or those relaxing in white plastic patio chairs strewn around the periphery, but lest you think we had merely stumbled upon a large Russian tour group, the snack bar is the proof. It's an all-Russian menu. Goulash, something called Russian ravioli—there were pictures of these things with descriptions beneath, written *in Russian.*

Because the spring contains no dissolved oxygen, organic matter that gets into the springs stays more or less intact. In 1973, a scientist named Wilburn A. Cockrell brought up a nearly complete skeleton of an adult Paleo-Indian male that was dated at 11,000 years old. Dated to nearly the same time period, part of a saber cat was also found. I like the idea that in a few thousand years, divers may pull up an order of Russian ravioli and just scratch their heads and wonder what it was doing here in a rural Florida backwater.

kayak or rent canoes from the ranger station, $5/hour, $25/day), launched from the South Creek Picnic Area. Birders may want to join the informal Thursday morning bird walks at 7:30 A.M., or the Friday and Sunday morning guided walks at 8:30 A.M. Check in at the park's nature center.

SIGHTS

☒ Marie Selby Botanical Gardens

Much has been written in recent years about the mystery of orchids, bromeliads, and other epiphytes. *The Orchid Thief, Orchid Fever* in the same vein, the more historical *The Orchid in Lore and Legend,* and then a whole bunch of books on monomaniacal plant hunters who scour the globe for their personal botanical holy grail—

still, if you're not an enthusiast, the mania may just elude you. Big whoop, you may say.

The word epiphyte comes from the Greek words "epi," meaning "upon," and "phyton," meaning "plant." Beginning their life in the canopy of trees, their seeds carried by birds or wind, epiphytes are air plants, growing stubbornly without the benefit of soil on the branches or trunks of trees. Orchids, cacti, bromeliads, aroids, lichens, mosses, and ferns can even grow on the same tree, a big interspecies jamboree. And if you want to see some heartbreakingly beautiful and alien epiphytes, spend a long afternoon at Marie Selby Botanical Gardens (811 S. Palm Ave., 941/366-5731, 10 A.M.–5 P.M. daily, $12 adults, $6 children 6–11, children under 5 free). The nine-acre gardens on the shores of Sarasota Bay are one of Sarasota's absolute

COURTESY OF SARASOTA CVB

The Sarasota skyline has been glamorized in recent years by an influx of cultural venues and visitor attractions.

jewels. Marie Selby donated her home and grounds "to provide enjoyment for all who visit the gardens." Meandering along the walking paths through the hibiscus garden, cycad garden, a banyan grove, a tropical fruit garden, and thousands of orchids—there's a lot of enjoyment to be had. The botanical gardens also host lectures and gardening classes, and have a lovely shop (beginners should opt for a training-wheels phalaenopsis—very hard to kill—or an easy-care bromeliad) with an exhaustive collection of gardening books (80 on orchids alone). Spend an hour gazing at epiphytes in the tropical greenhouse and you'll never say "big whoop" again. Caveat: Kids get fairly bored here, with a brief flurry of interest around the koi pond and butterfly garden. I would tend not to bring them unless they're very mature or stroller-bound.

◪ John and Mable Ringling Museum of Art

John Ringling's lasting influence on Sarasota is remarkable, but the John and Mable Ringling Museum of Art makes it simply incontrovertible (5401 Bay Shore Rd., 941/351-1660, 10 A.M.–5:30 P.M. daily, adults $15, seniors $12, children 12 and under, Florida teachers and stu-

dents free; Mon. free with admission to other attractions, $10). The whole museum complex is spectacular, but the art museum is definitely worth its fairly hefty admission price, having been built in 1927 to house Ringling's nearly pathological accretion of 600 paintings, sculptures, and decorative arts including more than 25 tapestries. The Mediterranean-style palazzo contains a collection that includes a set of five gargantuan paintings by Peter Paul Rubens, lots of wonderful Spanish work (soulful El Grecos, Velázquez's portrait of King Philip IV of Spain, etc.), and the music room and dining room of Mrs. William B. Astor (Ringling bought all this in 1926 when the Astor mansion in New York was scheduled to be demolished). The permanent collection is opulent, stunning, with Van Dycks, Poussins, and lots of other baroque masters, but there are shows such as a recent one on surrealism and another on the photos of Ansel Adams and Clyde Butcher that enter beautifully into at least the 20th century.

But wait, that's not all. (Do I sound like that old Ginsu Knife commercial?) The complex also houses the **Museum of the Circus,** a peek into circus history. It achieves a certain level of hyperbole in the interpretive signs when it parallels the ascendance of the circus with the growth of the country more generally. Still, the museum's newspaper clippings, circus equipment, parade wagons, and colossal bail rings make one nostalgic for a time and place one probably never knew.

Fully restored and reopened in 2002, John Ringling's home on the bay, **Cà d'Zan** (House of John) is also open to the public, an ornate structure evocative of Ringling's two favorite Venetian hotels, the Danieli and the Bauer-Grùnwald. Completed in 1926, the house is 200 feet long with 32 rooms and 15 baths (a comfort to those of us with small bladders). All kidding aside, there's something about the quality of light much of the year in Sarasota that seems utterly appropriate as host to such a magnificent Venetian Renaissance-style mansion.

Other Museums

A small museum opened in 2000 in downtown Sarasota, the **Museum of Asian Art** (640 S.

Washington Blvd., 941/954-7117, 11 A.M.–5 P.M. Wed.–Fri., $5 adults, free for students and children). It's a serene exhibit space featuring works from its permanent collection from Thailand, Cambodia, Nepal, Vietnam, and Myanmar. The works span 2,000 years of history and include pieces in bronze, stone, wood, iron, and, to my mind some of the most exquisite works, jade. Since its launch, the museum has hosted several exhibits focusing on Asian cultural traditions, and it presents an annual lecture series featuring guest speakers from museums and educational institutions throughout the United States.

What's your dream car? DeLorean? Ferrari? Mini Cooper? The **Sarasota Classic Car Museum** (5500 N. Tamiami Trail, 941/355-6228, 9 A.M.–6 P.M. daily, $8.50 adults, $7.65 seniors, $5.75 children 13–17, $4 children 6–12, children under 6 free) has got examples of everyone's favorite wheels. A recent facelift has added some pizzazz to the collection of more than 100 vehicles, from muscle to vintage to exotic cars. You'll see a rare Cadillac station wagon, one of only five ever made, and the gift shop has collectibles for most automotive preoccupations. The museum rents out some of its cars if you want to make a grand entrance somewhere, and the cars are also available for photo ops.

History buffs may want to visit **Historic Spanish Point** (337 N. Tamiami Trail, Osprey, 941/966-5214, 9 A.M.–5 P.M. Mon.–Sat., noon–5 P.M. Sun., $7 adults, $3 children 6–12), operated by Gulf Coast Heritage Association. Bordered on its western edge by Little Sarasota Bay and by pine flatlands to the east, the 30-acre site tells the story of life in the greater Sarasota area going back many generations. Interpretive markers and an "Indian village" show how early Floridian natives fished and hunted here, building middens, or shell mounds, and a burial mound (an archaeology exhibit in the main hall gives you the background on this). Then there's a pioneer home and chapel that have been restored, revealing the story of the early white settlers here, the Webb family. After that, you'll stroll the gardens of heiress Bertha Matilde Honore Palmer's winter estate on Osprey Point. In 2004, the site opened a butterfly garden to add to the mix, showing the larval and nectar plants for monarch, zebra longwing, swallowtails, and other butterflies native to the area. Slightly incoherent to the outsider, this National Register historic site has clear support from stalwart local boosters and zealous volunteers.

Tours

I went to Disney World and couldn't ride the best ride. It wasn't that the ride was sold out, or that I didn't meet the height requirements, it was that the ride wasn't open to the public. It was only for Disney employees (they're known by a euphemism—cast members? honorary rodents?). The people who directed your car to its final resting place in the Disney theme park parking lots were riding the coolest vehicles ever, called Segways. You can rent a Segway Human Transporter of your very own in Sarasota, however, with **Florida Ever-Glides** (200 S. Washington Blvd., Ste. 11, 941/363-9556, tours 9 A.M.–2 P.M., $56, no kids under 13) and take a 2.5-hour guided tour of downtown Sarasota along the bayfront and arts community. The two side-by-side wheels (as opposed to a bike or motorcycle, in which the two wheels are in a line) are self-balancing, and you stand above the wheels on a little platform and steer the electric-powered vehicle with the handlebars. With speeds of up to 12 mph, they can be used in pedestrian areas and are a perfect way to cover serious ground at a pace slow enough to really appreciate things. Plus, you look really cool.

COURTESY SARASOTA CVB

Glide through downtown Sarasota and around the bayfront on the new Segway tour.

If your passion is architecture, you won't need to be told that Sarasota is the birthplace of a certain strain of American modernism. (If this is news to you, pick up a copy of the excellent *The Sarasota School of Architecture, 1941–1966,* by John Howey.) The **Sarasota Architectural Foundation** (P.O. Box 3678, Sarasota, FL 34230-3678, 941/926-2821, ext. 723, www.saf-online.org) hosts architectural tours, educational events, film screenings, exhibits, and parties for architecture lovers who travel to Sarasota to see its architecture up close and personal. A list of tours is posted on their website.

After indulging in several of Sarasota's effete cultural attractions, you need to clear your head and take a **Walk on the Wild Side** (3434 N. Tamiami Trail, Ste. 817, 941/351-6500, $30–65). The very friendly tour providers tailor trips, taking small groups kayaking, canoeing, day hiking, backpacking, camping, auto touring, bird-watching, or wildlife-viewing, according to people's interests and mobility. You don't need prior canoeing or kayaking experience (they instruct you, but you still have to be fairly fit to work that paddle) for them to take you out on the area's bays, estuaries, and rivers, pointing out birds, dolphins, gators, and manatees along the way. You can choose where you go and for how long (half day, full day, or overnight), but the most romantic is the sunset canoe outing with wine and cheese.

Several companies offer boat tours on Sarasota Bay and into the Gulf of Mexico. **Enterprise Sailing Charters** (2 Marina Plaza, 941/951-1833, 8 A.M.–8 P.M. daily, $35 for two hours, $50 for three hours, $60 for four hours, group and child discounts) takes people out on a tall-masted three-sail ketch. **Key Sailing** (2 Marina Jack, Bayfront Plaza, 941/346-7245, two-, three-, and four-hour sails daily, $40–120) offers charters and sailing instruction aboard a pretty 41-foot Morgan Classic II (their website's cheesy and incessant rendition of Buffet's "Margaritaville" could kill a person, though). **LeBarge Tropical Cruises** (U.S. 41 at Marina Jack, 941/366-6116, 9 A.M.–6 P.M. daily, $18) offers two-hour cruises of Sarasota Bay, either a dolphin watch narrated by a marine biologist, a nar-

rated sightseeing cruise, or a tropical sunset cruise with live entertainment. And the 92-foot luxury yacht **Lady Sarasota** (941/953-5239) does large private charters only.

Farmers Market

Despite the fact that Florida is a huge agricultural state (citrus, sugarcane, tomatoes, strawberries, etc.), much of the Gulf Coast doesn't have a dense enough concentration of foodies and gourmandizers to support serious farmers markets. Sarasota is an exception. Every Saturday morning along Pineapple Avenue at Herald Square you'll find all the sights and smells that are unique to the breed-stacked produce; the cookie lady; an earnest band of musicians passing the hat; babies in strollers, smiling around a mouthful of gummed peach; wind chimes and handicrafts hawked by dreadlocked waifs; and bromeliads, orchids, and cut flowers festooning the bulging bags of nearly every shopper. The **Downtown Farmers Market** has been going on for 27 years, the tents and tables of 50 or so vendors erected Saturday mornings by 7 A.M. and broken down around noon. For now, you'll find the market at South Pineapple Avenue between Dolphin Street and Selby Lane in historic Burns Square, but soon it will move to Lemon Avenue, from 1st Street to State Street, upon the completion of the city's Lemon Avenue Streetscape project.

For Kids

My favorite family attraction in Sarasota is **Sarasota Jungle Gardens** (3701 Bay Shore Rd., 941/355-5305, 9 A.M.–5 P.M. daily, $11 adults, $10 seniors, $7 children 3–12, children under 3 free), but then I'm a sucker for quirky "Old Florida" attractions. Once part boggy banana grove, part universally agreed-upon "impenetrable swamp," the subtropical jungle was purchased in the 1930s by newspaperman David Lindsay. He brought in tropical plants, trees, and bird species. It opened in 1940 as a tourist attraction, and it puttered along through a couple of ownership changes until it ended up in the hands of the Allyn family. Every elementary student within 100 miles has made the trek by school bus to sit and watch the short birds of

Jane and David Allen Manatee Habitat

COURTESY OF VISIT FLORIDA

The Mote Marine Laboratory and Aquarium has a 135,000-gallon shark habitat, sea turtles, jellyfish, sea horses, and two touch pools.

prey show (there's also a show that features animals linked only, I think, by their universal repugnance to human beings—things like giant Madagascar hissing cockroaches, I kid you not), and then wander along the paths through the lush formal gardens, the farmyard exhibit, the tiki gardens, and the majorly stinky flamingo area. The zoological gardens are home to about 100 animals, many of them abandoned pets, so it's an odd assortment. (I spent about half an hour trying to get two former pet myna birds to say, "Put a sock in it" to the next person to speak to them.) The most peculiar part of the park, however, has nothing to do with plants or animals. In one back corner of the park there's something called the Gardens of Christ. It's a series of eight two-dimensional dioramas by Italian-born sculptor Vincent Maldarelli depicting the most important events in the life of Jesus Christ. So, to review, Sarasota Jungle Gardens: tropical plants, hissing cockroaches, large colorful birds, and the life of Jesus Christ.

The **Mote Aquarium** (1600 Ken Thompson Pkwy., City Island, 941/388-2451, 10 A.M.–

5 P.M. daily, $12, $8 children 4–12, children under 4 free) is a pleasant small aquarium that also serves as a working marine laboratory. For kids, the coolest parts are the 135,000-gallon shark tank, the "Sea Cinema" 12-minute big-screen movie presentation about life as a voracious shark, and the underwater microphone in its Marine Mammal Center, which allows visitors to hear the resident manatees chirping at each other and methodically munching the heads of romaine lettuce that bob at the top of their tank. There's a touch tank, where you'll see parents cajoling their small ones to feel up a sea urchin, starfish, horseshoe crab, or stingless stingray, as well as nicely interpreted exhibits of eels, puffer fish, sea horses, and extraterrestrial-looking jellies.

The more impressive part of the Mote is not really open to the public—the Mote Marine Laboratory is known internationally for its shark research and more locally for its research on "red tides" or algal blooms that occasionally adversely affect Sarasota's summer beach season with these yucky floating plants that wash ashore with all the fish they've killed.

Sarasota Bay Explorers (941/388-4200) works in conjunction with Mote Marine Laboratory and runs their science boat trips out of the facility. They offer several wonderful styles of eco-tours, all perfect for a fun, yet educational family outing. There are narrated **Sea Life Encounter Cruises** ($24 adults, for $30 you get aquarium admission, too; children $20, $24 including aquarium admission), backwater **guided kayak tours** ($50 adults, $40 kids), and private charters aboard the 40-foot pontoon *Miss Explorer* ($275 for a four-hour trip, $375 for a six-hour trip).

Right next to the Mote Marine Aquarium is the largest wildlife rescue and rehabilitation center in Florida. **Pelican Man's Bird Sanctuary** (1708 Ken Thompson Pkwy., 941/388-4444, 10 A.M.–4 P.M. daily, $6 adults, $4 children 12–17, $2 children 4–11) treats more than 5,000 sick, injured, and orphaned birds every year, as well as mammals and reptiles. As the name implies, the biggest patient group is brown pelicans, which often become entangled and are injured by monofilament fishing line. Dale Shields, that's Pelican Man to you, started the center in the early 1980s to care for the injured among the area's many avian species, and now his facility (he died in 2003) hosts something like 275 permanently disabled birds (lots of amputees, so be forewarned if you're squeamish), representing 70 species of Florida's native and migratory birds. A visit to the sanctuary takes you along a covered boardwalk that winds past cages containing all kinds of birds in natural-looking habitats. The center has educational "animal encounters" throughout the day.

The sanctuary also owns the 40-foot pontoon *Peli-Boat,* which offers avian-centric narrated eco-tours (departs from Holiday Inn Marina, 941/388-4444, 10 A.M.–noon Thurs. and Sat., $16 adults, $8 children). And here's an idea for your favorite bird lover's next birthday gift: Adopt one of the sanctuary's permanent residents ($300–600). Your money goes to feed the bird and cover any medical needs. In exchange, you get to name the bird and write the text for a plaque outside its house, and you receive a photo of your bird, information about the species, and visitation privileges.

If fate hands you a foul-weather day during your visit, a lovely family afternoon can be had at **G. WIZ** (1001 Boulevard of the Arts, 941/309-4949, 10 A.M.–5 P.M. Tues.–Sat., 1–5 P.M. Sun., $7 adult, $6 seniors, $5 children 2–18). It stands for the Gulf Coast Wonder & Imagination Zone, but it could best be summarized as a 33,000-square-foot facility of interactive science-focused exhibits. There are traveling shows (most recently one from the wonderful Exploratorium in San Francisco), and the permanent exhibits are compelling. Kids can fly, be free, as they zoom through the EcoZone (snakes, box turtles, and other native Florida creatures), the EnergyZone (with exhibits on electricity, sound, light, and neat building materials made out of magnets), the TechZone (where you can design a robot or create an animated video), and the BodyZone (exhibits on human anatomy, strength, endurance, and flexibility). Which is handy, as parents will need some strength and endurance of their own to keep up with their scampering progeny. The G. Wiz also offers programs for school groups and summer day camps.

Sarasota has a pleasant paint-your-own-pottery center, **S'Platters Pottery Painting Place** (2110 Gulf Gate Dr., 941/926-3070, 11 A.M.–6 P.M. Tues., Wed., and Sat., 11 A.M.–9 P.M. Thurs. and Fri., noon–5 P.M. Sun., prices start at $7, most pieces $14–26, which also includes paint, time, and firing), another satisfying bad-weather family activity. S'Platters has jumped on a couple of current trends in kids' entertainment, offering a build-your-own-teddy bear option, a bead-painting option so you can make your own beaded jewelry, and some neat mosaic-making kits. You can also take your favorite photo from your family vacation and have it fired onto a ceramic piece as a keepsake of your trip.

ARTS AND ENTERTAINMENT

Sarasota describes itself as the "cultural coast" of Florida. And as Mohammed Ali said back when he was Cassius Clay, it ain't braggin' if it's true. It starts getting monotonous when you enumerate all the professional arts options in Sarasota, but I suppose I'm getting paid to do so.

𝕸 Asolo Theatre Company

Celebrating more than 40 years of professional theater in Sarasota, the Asolo Theatre Company (5555 N. Tamiami Trail, 941/351-8000, www.asolo.org, curtain times generally 2 P.M. and 8 P.M., prices vary) is a professional company that performs primarily in the 500-seat Harold E. and Esther M. Mertz Theatre at the Florida State University Center for the Performing Arts, a theater originally built as an opera house in 1903 in Dunfermline, Scotland. There's a second, smaller 161-seat black-box Jane B. Cook Theatre on-site for performances of the conservatory season and smaller productions of the Asolo Theatre Company. The theater, adjacent to the Ringling Museum of Art, hosts the Asolo Theatre Festival, the only winter destination theater festival in the country (meaning more shows annually, thus more variety). This means that in a single season you might see J. M. Barrie's original *Peter Pan,* followed by Neil Simon's *Broadway Bound* Shakespeare's *A Midsummer Night's Dream,* and a musical comedy called *Menopause.*

Other Theater

Because the Florida State University Conservatory for Actor Training's graduate-level program yields so many newly minted thespians in Sarasota, the whole theatrical playing field has been elevated. Worthwhile community and professional theater troupe efforts include the contemporary dramas and comedies at **Florida Studio Theatre** (1241 N. Palm Ave., 941/366-9000), mostly Broadway musicals at **Golden Apple Dinner Theatre** (25 N. Pineapple Ave., 941/366-5454), six annual musical productions with **The Players of Sarasota** (838 N. Tamiami Trail, 941/365-2494), dramas in the summer with **Banyan Theater Company** (at the Asolo's Jane B. Cook Theatre, 941/358-5330), the all–African American **West Coast Black Theater Troupe** (at Florida Studio Theatre, 1241 N. Palm Ave., 941/954-4651), the more avant-garde readings of **Infinite Space** (different locations, 941/330-8250, www.infinite-space.org), and even the little community productions on two stages of the **Venice Little Theatre** (140 W. Tampa Ave., Venice, 941/488-1115).

COURTESY OF SARASOTA CVB

The Asolo's resident equity company performs in rotating repertory on the historic mainstage.

Music and Dance

The oldest continuously running orchestra in the state of Florida, **Florida West Coast Symphony** (Van Wezel Performing Arts Hall, 709 N. Tamiami, box office 941/953-3434, www.fwcs.org, prices and times vary) offers a wide array of more than 100 symphonic and chamber music concerts in a 37-week annual season and is host to the internationally recognized Sarasota Music Festival each June. Seven Masterworks programs are presented by the symphony throughout the season, as well as a four-concert Composer's Series and a set of six Great Escapes programs of light classics and pops on Thursday, Friday, and Saturday evenings and Friday mornings. The symphony also occasionally presents Symphonic Pops concerts with special guests. The orchestra, under the current direction of artistic director Leif Bjaland, has experienced a period of real growth and international accolades.

But even if you're not a huge symphonic music fan, it's a good excuse to check out Sarasota's most distinctive landmark, the **Van Wezel Performing Arts Hall** (777 N. Tamiami Trail, 941/953-3368, www.vanwezel.org, times and prices vary). Designed by William Wesley Peters of the Frank Lloyd Wright Foundation, the building riffs on a seashell found by Frank Lloyd Wright's widow, Olgivanna, near the Sea of Japan. It has an eye-popping lavender/purple color scheme, and it looks accordioned, like a scallop shell (supposedly to maximize the space's acoustical possibilities). Love it or hate it, the Van Wezel presents a wonderful range of Broadway productions, world-class dance, music, comedy, and popular acts, as well as being the home base for many of the local arts organizations.

For instance, the **Sarasota Ballet of Florida** (5555 N. Tamiami Trail, 941/351-8000, www.sarasotaballet.org, times and prices vary) splits its performances between the Van Wezel and the Asolo, offering a combination of treasured classical works and contemporary and modern dance. The ballet was founded as a presenting organization in 1987 by Jean Allenby-Weidner, former prima ballerina with the Stuttgart Ballet. Through community support,

it became a resident company in 1990. The ballet often works collaboratively with other local arts organizations on productions—in 2005 they staged a ballet with Circus Sarasota that tells the story of John Ringling's life, complete with aerialists, clowns, and such. (The Sarasota Ballet also runs the Sarasota Ballet Academy; The Next Generation, an award-winning scholarship program for youth at risk; and an international summer school.)

The **Sarasota Opera** (61 N. Pineapple Ave., 941/366-8450, ext. 1, www.sarasotaopera.org) has similar youth outreach, its Sarasota Youth Opera receiving all kinds of plaudits for its productions. The acorn doesn't fall far from the tree: The Sarasota opera presents concerts year-round, but its much-anticipated (often sold out) repertory season is every February and March, housed in the beautifully restored 1926 Mediterranean Revival–style Edwards Theatre. Productions range from the very familiar (Mozart's *Don Giovanni*) to the less so (Léo Delibes's *Lakmé*), and all are sung in their original language with real-time English translations projected above the stage. And while you're hanging around in the gorgeous art deco lobby during intermission, look up: the chandelier is from the movie *Gone with the Wind.*

Sarasota also has an annual chamber music festival each April, **La Musica International Chamber Music Festival** (rehearsals in Mildred Sainer Pavilion at New College of Florida, performances in the Edwards Theatre, 61 N. Pineapple Ave., 941/366-8450, ext. 3, www.lamusicafestival.org, 8 P.M., $35 single tickets). The public is welcome to watch rehearsals free of charge, to see the musicians work their way through complicated pieces by Tchaikovsky, Schubert, Mendelssohn, Prokofiev, Brahms, Mozart, and others. Before the actual evening performances there are short lectures about the pieces.

Circuses

Five of the seven sons of August and Marie Salomé Ringling of Baraboo, Wisconsin, ran away and joined the circus. Or, rather, they invented their own. In 1870, they premiered their show and charged a penny admission, building it

CLOWNING AROUND

"Snakes don't bond."

I'm getting a lesson in reptile psychology from T.M., The Gator Guy, one of the acts in the 132nd edition of Ringling Bros. and Barnum & Bailey Circus. The T.M. stands for Ted McRae, and while he talks to me by cell phone, McRae is on the world's largest privately owned train, the Ringling Train, stretching one mile and 53 cars long. Cellular service from this train stinks.

He keeps calling me back to say things like: "Reptiles are totally alien. Mammals do certain things that you are familiar with, but reptiles might as well be from another planet. An alligator might sit there for three days without moving. It is an ambush-type predator. It's waiting to kill something. And their eyes don't give anything away."

The Gator Guy is a crusader of sorts, a promoter of human-reptile relations who travels with his trusty pet python and his Savannah Monitor lizard, Jake. He's ridden the wave of interest prompted by Steve Erwin, the Crocodile Hunter.

"Thank you, Steve Erwin. Kids love alligators right now. I was in the right place at the right time—people are fascinated. And it's a good thing, because all animals are being pushed aside in their natural habitats, not just the cute, fuzzy ones. The ones that scare you and are dangerous, they're getting pushed aside as well."

The animal-rights activists that are a fixture outside the circus might not agree with his reasoning—that the circus gives visibility to endangered or ignored animals' plights—but McRae certainly seems like an enthusiast. He places his entire head into the open mouth of a 10-foot alligator, wraps himself with his beloved 200-pound python, and soothes his cold-blooded wards into stillness.

The Gator Guy is one of several acts to anchor the ever-changing circus. Ringling Bros., the oldest—in addition to being the greatest—show on earth, reinvents itself every two years, with two totally different traveling units. The Red Unit and the Blue Unit each tour North America 11 months out of the year for two years before going back to winter quarters (now in Tampa, but historically here in Sarasota) and preparing a new edition. The Red Unit presents the odd-numbered editions, the Blue Unit presents the even-numbered editions (so, for instance, if you saw the 134th edition Blue Unit last year, you'll see the 135th edition Red Unit this year).

So one year the show's centerpiece might be the Living Carousel, an assemblage of 105 people, 27 animals, and more gold lamé than a Liberace concert, with something like two million rhinestones and elephant blankets inset with 81,000 mirrors turning the whole arena into a disco-ball fantasy.

Or it's the Globe of Death, a 16-foot steel globe, into which rides a trio of motorcyclists. Erwin, Melvin, and Victor Urias ride a complicated routine of loops around the interior, reaching speeds of 60 mph, and then Erwin's wife, Jodie, gets in and stands there, daring one of them to flub up. Talk about extreme sports.

Or maybe Sara, no last names please, the "tiger whisperer," who gently coaxes four different types of Bengal tigers to romp around the center ring. Then there are always the high-wire acts, the elephant poop-scooping guys, the

year by year from a modest wagon show (its first "ring" a strip of cloth staked out to form a circle) to a major national show that traveled via rail from town to town. Meanwhile, circus titans P. T. Barnum and James A. Bailey teamed up in 1888 to create "The Greatest Show on Earth," blowing away all the competition with their glitz, animals, and death-defying acts. It was Bailey's untimely death in 1906 that led the "Greatest Show" to be bought out by the Ringling brothers. The two

circuses ran separately until 1919, when they were joined to form the mega-huge **Ringling Bros. and Barnum & Bailey Circus,** and the rest is history.

In the 1920s, John Ringling and his wife Mable built a stunning Venetian-style estate on Sarasota Bay, called Cà d'Zan ("House of John" in Venetian dialect). In order to house their bursting-at-the-seams collection of works by Peter Paul Rubens, 17th-century Italian paintings, and Flemish art, they built an art museum.

classic Clown Alley, and a live band performing the swelling circus music.

But in some ways, the movies are ruining the circus. Ringling Bros. and Barnum & Bailey Circus comes to town in the new millennium with its usual splash, pageantry, and death-defying acts, and audiences sit in stony, underwhelmed silence. Audience members are no longer able to mentally separate the wheat (high-wire acts without a net) from the chaff (computer-generated explosions and disembowelments).

The Gator Guy explains why we should have respect for the performers under the bigtop.

"Circus performers do things that are very difficult, almost impossible. We try it, and then we practice it, and then we present it to you. You have so much fun, and you think, 'There's gotta be a trick.' Well, there is no trick. It's real, and that's the magic of the circus."

To get a sense of how much the magic used to mean, you need only to visit the **Ringling Museum of the Circus** (5401 Bay Shore Rd., 941/359-5744, 10 A.M.–5:30 P.M. daily, $15 adults, children 12 and under free). It was John Ringling who brought the circus to Sarasota, moving the winter quarters of the Ringling Bros. and Barnum & Bailey Circus from Bridgeport, Connecticut, to Sarasota in 1927—thus changing this part of Florida forever. The museum documents, preserves, and exhibits the history of the circus with props, rare handbills, parade wagons, tent poles, and memorabilia.

As for me, I wanna join the circus. Maybe my act will be something modest like Svetlana

COURTESY OF SARASOTA CVB

Everyone's a clown at Ringling Museum of the Circus.

Shemsheeva's, an exotic woman who trains Persian cats to walk tightropes and cavort with doves. She even gets a bird to land on a cat's back, and neither one seems disgruntled. Sure, it's not a planet exploding or an alien birth, it's just a little piece of reality that makes up the greatest show on earth.

But it was in 1927 when Sarasota became an official circus town—the Ringling Bros. and Barnum & Bailey Circus's winter quarters were moved here, giving the sedate Florida town an indelible whiff of the oddity, eccentricity, and glamour that is the circus.

Many of the circus performers who acted in the *Wizard of Oz* and that ultimate un-p.c. film *Terror of Tiny Town* (a musical western starring all little people) called Sarasota home, with specially built homes in a section of town called, unsurprisingly, **Tiny Town** (you can tour this area on the Ever-Glide guided tours).

Today visitors get a sense of Sarasota's circus history at the **Museum of the Circus** on the Ringling grounds, but during February and March the circus comes alive with **Circus Sarasota** (8251 15th St. E, 941/355-9335, ringside $35, Section A $25, Section B $20, Section C $12). Founded in 1997 by Ringling Bros. alums, Pedro Reis and Dolly Jacobs (an aerialist, she's a second-generation circus performer—her father

Sarasota County

was the famous clown Lou Jacobs), it's a single-ring, European-style circus that changes every year. Reis and Jacobs often perform an aerial pas de deux, and there are tightrope acts, trained horses, aerial acrobats from China, clowns, tumbling, contortionists, and so forth, all performed in an intimate setting.

And Sarasota's training the next generation of circus performers. **PAL Sailor Circus** (2075 Bahia Vista St., 941/361-6350, 11:45 A.M. and 7 P.M., $10–14) has been thrilling audiences for more than 50 years, educating kids 8–18 in the circus arts and then letting them put on a show. About 90 students participate in the twice-annual training sessions, where they learn circus skills like clowning, tumbling, high-wire and flying trapeze, unicycling, juggling, rigging, and costuming. Then, in the beginning of April and the end of December, the students perform for the public in an exciting four-ring circus.

▌M▐ Film Festivals

Sarasota supports not one, but two film festivals. By far the more famous of the two is the **Sarasota Film Festival** every January (multiple venues, mailing address 635 S. Orange Ave., Ste. 10-B, Sarasota, FL 34236, 941/364-9514, www.sarasotafilmfestival.com). The fastest-growing film festival in the country, it showcases 150 independent features, documentary, narrative, and short films, throws lavish parties to which the celebrities and filmmakers actually come, and uses the opportunity to watch sedate Sarasota carouse with great diligence. The event usually includes a Shorts Fest, a couple of family-oriented events, and lots of panel discussions with industry leaders and symposiums with guest stars. And every November there's the Sarasota Film Society's 10-day **Cine-World Film Festival** (Burns Court Cinemas, 506 Burns Ln., 941/955-3456), which showcases Florida film artists in addition to presenting the best of the preceding Toronto, Cannes, New York, and Telluride film festivals.

Other Festivals

February's not a bad month to visit, because you can catch the month-long annual run of the European-style **Circus Sarasota**. Sarasota is the self-described "circus capital of the world," after all. Music lovers may want to come in February or March for the repertory season of the **Sarasota Opera,** although in April there's **La Musica International Chamber Music Festival** (and also in April you'll encounter the weeklong **Florida Wine Fest & Auction**).

If you're coming to the area strictly for the white, powdery sand, you might think of coming in May for the cutthroat pro-am **Sand Sculpting Contest** on Siesta Beach (also, the Fourth of July fireworks over the Gulf are wonderful from the vantage spot of Siesta Beach).

ACCOMMODATIONS

There are scads of condos and beachfront rentals in the greater Sarasota area, but most of these rent only by the week. If that's your time frame, the weeklong rentals often are a more financially prudent choice. Try giving **Argus Property Management** (941/346-3499) or **Florida Vacation Accommodations** (800/237-9505) a call. There are also golf resort condo communities such as **Heritage Oaks Golf and Country Club** (4800 Chase Oaks Dr., 941/927-0000) and **Timberwoods Vacation Villas & Resort** (7964 Timberwood Cir., 941/923-4966) that rent by the week. If you're only in for a few days, hotels and motels run the gamut from fairly inexpensive and no-frills to truly luxurious. Generally speaking, beachside places are pricier than mainland or downtown accommodations, and winter rates are highest, dropping down usually by a third to summer rates. Listed here are Sarasota and Lido Key accommodations—Longboat Key, Siesta Key, Venice, etc., are covered in a separate section.

Under $50

The **Cadillac Motel** (4021 N. Tamiami Trail, 941/355-7108, $40–58) is a no-frills, clean, single-story motel. It's a bit away from all the action of downtown (about a mile), but there's a sweet little pool and shuffleboard to entertain you. For a simple room, efficiency, or apartment, rented by the day or by the week, try **Southland Inn** (2229 N. Tamiami Trail, 941/954-5775, rooms starting at $45). Rooms have been recently remodeled, most with kitchens, and there's a large heated pool. Near the Ringling School of Art and Design.

$50–150

The three-story **Wellesley Inn Sarasota** (1803 Tamiami Trail N, 941/366-5128, $79–109) is not far from Ringling School of Art and Design, a few minutes' drive from downtown. Rooms are midsize, some with sofa beds, and those on interior hallways have desks. There's a serviceable outdoor pool, a pleasant complimentary breakfast, free parking, and pets under 30 pounds are accepted.

Business travelers enjoy **Springhill Suites by Marriott** (1020 University Pkwy., 941/358-3385, $89–149), a moderately priced all-suites approach fairly close to the airport. All rooms have a king or two double beds with separate sleeping, eating, and working areas. There's also a pullout sofa bed, a pantry area with mini-refrigerator, sink, and microwave, and a big desk with fancy chair and two-line telephones with data port. The free continental breakfast isn't an afterthought, with items like sausage, eggs, oatmeal, and make-your-own waffles.

Courtyard by Marriott (850 University Pkwy., 941/355-3337, $99–159) is a mostly business, recently renovated three-story hotel directly across from the airport. It's convenient to both Bradenton and Sarasota. Great hotel for business trips or family vacations. There's wireless high-speed Internet throughout the hotel, and a hot breakfast buffet.

Opened in 1975 but also recently remodeled, the 12-story **Hyatt Sarasota** (1000 Boulevard of the Arts, 941/953-1234, $119–299) is a big convention hotel right downtown with easy access to Van Wezel Performing Arts Hall, the Municipal Auditorium, and other attractions. It's right in the downtown business district, but waterside, with its own private marina, a new floating dock, and a beautiful lagoon-style pool. The 294 guest rooms all have a view of the bay or marina, most with little balconies.

Over $150

It was controversial when it opened a few years ago, but the **Ritz-Carlton Sarasota** (1111 Ritz-Carlton Dr., 941/309-2000, reservations 800/241-3333, www.ritzcarlton.com, $249–569), a 266-room, 18-story luxury hotel right downtown, has managed to blend in beautifully, as if it has always been here. Ritz-Carlton's signature service (warm, efficient, but seldom verging on obsequious), spacious rooms with balconies and marble baths, and great amenities make it the top choice among business and high-fallutin' travelers. The downtown location is convenient to restaurants (although there are two laudable ones on-site) and attractions; there's a lovely pool, and the wood-paneled Cà d'Zan Bar & Cigar Lounge is always hopping.

N Radisson Lido Beach Resort (700 Benjamin Franklin Dr., 941/388-2161, $202–481) is a favorite among families vacationing in the area. Newly remodeled and doubled in size—the north building being older, cheaper, and less elegant than the 12-story south tower of one- and two-bedroom suites with kitchens. The hotel has two gorgeous free-form pools and three hot tubs all right on the beach, and one of Sarasota's few beachside "tiki" bars. It's a brief walk out the door to Lido Beach and St. Armands Circle shopping/dining area, 10 minutes to downtown, and 15–20 minutes to the airport. The hotel offers an engaging children's program for kids ages 8–13, dry cleaning, laundry, business services, and meeting rooms.

Another classic beachfront motel choice on Lido Key is the art deco **Half Moon Beach Club** (2050 Benjamin Franklin Dr., Sarasota, 800/358-3245, www.halfmoon-lidokey.com, rooms with kitchenettes start at $155) built around a circular swimming pool. The 84 rooms are all decorated in a sunny Key West style, facing the beach and kitted out with patios or balconies. There's also an on-site restaurant and guest laundry.

If for you small is beautiful, you may want to take a gander at **The Cypress, a Bed & Breakfast Inn** (621 S. Gulfstream Ave., 941/955-4683, $150–240), with only four distinctly decorated rooms. Set in a 1940s tin-roofed cypress home, the four suites are kitted out with American and European antiques, paintings, and artifacts, and the house's common space is lovely (but not precious). Room rates include an extravagant breakfast and an afternoon social hour with hors d'oeuvres and refreshments. The inn is across the street from Bayfront Park and down the block from Marie Selby Botanical Gardens. No children, no pets.

FOOD

Strips of chain restaurants pop up on the Gulf Coast of Florida like so many noxious mushrooms after the wet season. In fact, many chains (Outback, Hooters, etc.) call the Gulf Coast home, and new chains are often market tested first in the urban areas along this part of Florida. Why, I ask myself? It's demographics. In an area that still has a fairly dense concentration of retirees, the newest growth segment is young families. And what do the elderly and young families have in common? They like to eat out, but they want things to be familiar. They want to go to Chili's and eat the same thing they ate last time. They don't want food that is spicy, weird looking, hard to eat, or intellectually or emotionally challenging. They want the sauce on the side, all vegetables recognizable, and to be able to count on the regular, soothing presence of ranch dressing.

Before you get insulted by my gross overgeneralization, you need to know I resemble that remark. I have a 9-year-old who is, as is common to the species, a creature of habit. Change is met with fear and loathing. Thus, chain restaurants provide her a modicum of control over her world. An auteur's mercurial whim, evidencing itself as a daily-changing menu or serendipitous food marriages—that stuff is lost on her.

Well, Sarasota restaurants are fighting the creeping encroachment of chains. Twenty-eight independent restaurants in town joined together not long ago to build public awareness about the importance of the community's unique cuisine. They formed the Sarasota Originals, the first Florida Chapter of the Council of Independent Restaurants of America (CIRA). For the visitor, this is good news. The city has a super-abundance of fairly stylish restaurants and the sophisticated diners who love them.

Downtown

I'll start with the heavy hitters. Sarasota's **M Bijou Cafe** (1287 1st St., 941/366-8111, 11:30 A.M.–2 P.M. Mon.–Fri., 5–9:30 P.M. Mon.–Thurs., until 10:30 P.M. Fri. and Sat., until 9 P.M. Sun., $17–29) has been a local sparkling jewel since 1986, making everyone's top 10 list and garnering lots of drippy adjectives from *Zagat, Bon Appetit* and *Gourmet*. It's what you'd call Continental-American fare, presided over by chef Jean-Pierre Knaggs and his wife, Shay. Located a couple blocks from Ritz-Carlton Sarasota in a 1920s gas station turned restaurant, the vibe is special-occasion or big-time-business dining. A fairly recent renovation (after a fire) has yielded a new bar, lounge, private room, and outdoor dining courtyards. The wine list is unusual, with a fair number of South African wines (Knaggs is South African), and the menu contains dishes like velvety shrimp and crab bisque, crispy roast duck napped with orange-cognac sauce, or luscious crabcakes with Louisiana rémoulade. All hail the crème brûlée.

A relative newcomer, opened in 2003, **Mattison's City Grill** (1 N. Lemon Ave., 941/330-0440, 11 A.M.–11 P.M. Mon.–Thurs., until midnight Fri. and Sat., until 10 P.M. Sun., $17–25) has added a little vim and vinegar to the downtown dining scene. It's casual, hopping, with Italian-ish small plates and pizzas and lots of pretty people. It feels more urban than many of the other downtown restaurants, with great outdoor seating, cool wine events and cigar dinners, and live jazz nightly.

Another longtime downtown favorite has nightly live music but a totally different feel. **Marina Jack's** (2 Marina Plaza, 941/365-4232, 11:30 A.M.–1 A.M. daily, main dining room closed 2–5 P.M., $8–36 depending on which dining room you choose) is all about waterside dining for the masses, with a few different ways to consume your comestibles with the water in view. Choose from the second-level Bayfront Restaurant, the Portside Patio, or a cocktail at the Deep Six Lounge and Piano Bar. If you still don't feel aquatic enough, there's the *Marina Jack II* yacht, which wines you and dines you in the bay (nothing cutting-edge about the food, but it's fairly decent prime rib, lemon sole, and such). Back on land, the menu leans to crowd pleasers like crab-stuffed mushrooms, conch fritters, steaks, and grilled grouper.

In a similar idiom (fun, casual, seafood-centric American cuisine), but with no water views, **Barnacle Bill's** has had a recent makeover in its downtown location (1526 Main St., 941/365-6800; other locations at 3634 Webber St., 941/923-5800; 5050 N. Tamiami Trail, 941/355-7700; and 8383 S. Tamiami Trail, 941/927-8884; 11:30 A.M.–9 P.M. daily, with a small-plate menu only 4–5:30 P.M., $12–24). It's still a little dumpy, but people don't notice as they decimate an order of crabcakes, fried popcorn shrimp, or snapper Grenoble.

It's not exactly downtown, but just slightly south. Still, any list of important downtown restaurants has to include **M** **Michaels On East** (1212 East Ave. S, 941/366-0007, 11:30 A.M.–2 P.M. Mon.–Fri., 5:30–10 P.M. daily, $18–31). It's won best-of-Florida accolades from nearly everyone since its opening at the beginning of the 1990s—and it's kept up with all the newcomers, consistently pushing the envelope and wowing diners with its "New American" take and opulent decor. During the day it's a power-lunching crowd enjoying Wendy's warm chicken salad with dried cranberries, goat cheese, and candied pecans in honey-lemon-basil vinaigrette and a big bottle of bubbly water; at night, romantic dinners *a deux* include a grilled duck breast paired with Bermuda onion and shiitake fondue, and fig and pecan risotto, all flavors elegantly showcased with a gorgeous big-ticket Burgundy or California pinot noir.

For when you're tired of fish, **M** **Patrick's** (1400 Main St., 941/952-1170, 11 A.M.–midnight daily, $9–18) gets top honors for Sarasota's best burger. It's another casual spot, with no reservations accepted, but with more of a patina of glamour. The crowd is a little hipper, the bar scene is fun.

Just want a quick, inexpensive bite, no fuss, no muss? Head to downtown's **Cafe Epicure** (1298 N. Palm Ave., 941/366-5648, 11 A.M.–10:30 P.M. Mon.–Fri., 9 A.M.–10:30 P.M. Sat. and Sun., $5–25). It's a cool bistro/deli/market, with a

tacked on gelato/coffee shop called **Jolly** (941/906-1551). It's an easy place to hang out on the terrace and write postcards while sipping a nice wine by the glass and enjoying an addictive *insalata di polpo con patate e fagiolini* (octopus salad with potatoes and string beans).

Best breakfast? It's a chain, but this location is without a doubt the best of the breed. **First Watch Restaurant** (1395 Main St., 941/954-1395, 7:30 A.M.–2:30 P.M. daily, $5–12) serves Sarasota's finest quick, no-fuss, inexpensive breakfasts with bottomless coffee and cheery service. Investigate the "Greek fetish" omelet (roasted red peppers, feta cheese and spinach, topped with black olives and red onions) or the cranberry nut pancakes. Lines can be long, but they move quickly. If you just can't wait, walk south along Central Avenue and stop into one of the sidewalk coffee houses.

St. Armands Circle and Lido Key

In 1893, a Frenchman named Charles St. Amand bought a little mangrove island off Sarasota, homesteading in the usual way with fishing, hunting, and growing a little produce. In the land deeds his name was misspelled, so it stuck when circus magnate John Ringling bought the property in 1917. He planned for St. Armands Key to be a residential and shopping development laid out in a circle, bringing people over first by steamer and then via the John Ringling Causeway completed in 1926 (the major lifting done by circus elephants). The area has had a fairly consistent commitment to all that is posh since Ringling wheeled it away from old Charles St. Amand. It's often compared to Rodeo Drive and other famous shopping districts.

Here's the thing: The shopping isn't so great these days. My rule of thumb is, if there are more than two shops that sell fudge and saltwater taffy, and if there are more than two boutiques in which you can buy T-shirts with cats and funny feline slogans on them, then you're in a tourist trap. St. Armands is such a place. However, some of the city's best restaurants line up around the circle. So, buy your fudge, smirk at the T-shirts, and go to dinner.

Two of the oldest on the stretch are **Café L'Europe** (431 St. Armands Circle, 941/388-4415, 11:30 A.M.–3 P.M. and 5–10 P.M. daily, Sun. brunch 11:30 A.M.–3 P.M., $23–40) and the **Columbia Restaurant** (411 St. Armands Circle, 941/388-3987, 11 A.M.–11 P.M. Mon.–Sat., noon–10 P.M. Sun., $8–28). Close together, both feature beautiful dining rooms and wonderful sidewalk dining, but the food's better at Café L'Europe. The Columbia opened in 1959, making it the oldest restaurant in Sarasota. (Its sister restaurant in Tampa goes one better, being the oldest restaurant in the state of Florida.) The Cuban food is pretty bland and dated, and even its "world-famous" dishes—the 1905 Salad with chopped cheese, olives, and a ho-hum vinaigrette; the sangria; the red snapper Alicante—don't thrill the way they used to. The black bean soup and pompano in parchment seldom disappoint, though. As per Café L'Europe, it's a sophisticated stew of culinary influences that's hard to pin down: the kitchen does an equally adept job with shrimp pad thai, veal cordon bleu with luxe chanterelle mushroom risotto, and a Mediterranean chicken Kavalla that pairs chicken breast with feta, spinach, and crab.

Newcomer **15 South Ristorante Enoteca** (15 S. Boulevard of Presidents, 941/388-1555, 4–11 P.M. nightly, open for lunch during high season, nightclub 7 P.M.–2 A.M. nightly, $14–34) seems to be the place to go in the area for sophisticated northern Italian, and the upstairs **Straight Up Night Club** features an excellent martini bar and equal-opportunity music nightly (Latin acts, belly dancing, Caribbean tunes, a big band, you name it). The ristorante's menu will be familiar, but the execution of dishes like classic carpaccio, grilled veal chop topped with gremolata, or a plate of zingy-with-garlic bruschetta is exceptional.

It's a chain of sorts, so I hesitate to praise it too vociferously, but **Tommy Bahama Tropical Café & Emporium** (300 John Ringling Blvd., 941/388-2888, 11 A.M.–10 P.M. weekdays, until 11 P.M. weekends, $20–33) is just plain fun, the food is excellent, and the drinks too good for common sense to kick in. The store downstairs carries its signature mix of tropical leisurewear and strangely hip housewares—you have to take a flight of stairs off to the side to reach the upstairs restaurant, which has huge windows that look out on all of the circle. Salads and cocktails are fairly pricey, but worth it. A key lime martini managed to marry so elegantly with a tropical chicken salad that it hovers in my taste memory like a beautiful mirage.

Oh, and **Cha Cha Coconuts** (417 St. Armands Circle, 941/388-0325) is a good place for a drink, as are **Margarita Mateo's** (328 John Ringling Blvd., 941/388-0325) and **Hemingway's Restaurant & Bar** (325 John Ringling Blvd., 941/388-3948, 11:30 A.M.–4 P.M. daily, 4–10 P.M. Sun.–Thurs., until 11 P.M. Fri. and Sat., $15–22). **Blue Dolphin Cafe** (470 John Ringling Blvd., 941/388-3566, 7 A.M.–3 P.M. daily) is where to go for cheap, diner-style breakfasts with a twist (lobster Benedict, raspberry pancakes), and, finally, when you're ready for that fudge, head to **Kilwin's** (312 John Ringling Blvd., 941/388-3200).

Southside Village

You may drive right through Southside Village and before you have time to ask, "Hey, why are there all these beautiful young professional types drinking glasses of red wine at sidewalk tables on the middle of a Tuesday afternoon," you've passed right through it on your way downtown. Visitors don't hit this little shopping/restaurant area with frequency, which is a shame. A few of Sarasota's most contemporary, most gastronomically forward-thinking restaurants are right here. Southside Village is centered on South Osprey Avenue between Hyde Park and Hillview Streets, about 15 blocks south of downtown.

The undisputed king of the hill here is ‍**M** **Fred's** (1917 S. Osprey Ave., 941/364-5811, 11 A.M.–10 P.M. Mon.–Thurs., until 11 P.M. Fri. and Sat., until 9 P.M. Sun., $18–45). Chef Mario Martinez is doing some exciting work (e.g., local jumbo stone crab claws with a crab-essence seafoam and a fresh mango-mustard sauce), a necessity when you have such a stompin' wine list (a

Wine Spectator "best of" award winner). The food is somewhat hard to characterize, but sumptuous spins on comfort foods sums up most of it: filet mignon au poivre with foie gras cognac butter, or a creamy chocolate tower of layered chocolate mousse crowned with dark-chocolate spirals and raspberries. Meat entrées seem a little overpriced, and it can be a bit of a scene on Friday nights. Outdoor tables are at a premium on a lovely day.

Perhaps the best place in Sarasota to pick up the ingredients for a picnic is in the same block. **Morton's Gourmet Market** (1924 S. Osprey Ave., 941/364-2283, 8 A.M.–8 P.M. Mon.–Sat., 10 A.M.–5 P.M. Sun.) has the kind of fresh salads, deli items, fancy specialty sandwiches, and cooked entrées that make you press your nose up against the glass case, leaving an embarrassing smudge. Most items are fairly cheap, and you can eat on the premises or take it all out.

Pacific Rim (1859 Hillview St., 941/330-8071, 11:30 A.M.–2 P.M. Mon.–Fri., 5–9 P.M. Mon.–Thurs., 5–10 P.M. Fri. and Sat., $7–15) takes you on a very pleasant pan-Asian romp, from Thai curries redolent of basil and galangal to expertly rolled tekka maki sushi and beyond. You can play chef here and select your combinations of meats and veggies to be grilled or wokked.

Nearby **Hillview Grill** (1920 Hillview St., 941/952-0045, 11 A.M.–10 P.M. Mon.–Sat., 5–9 P.M. Sun., $13–29) traffics in another melding of cuisines, this time Cajun and Creole with a dollop of several other ethnic influences. It's more of a neighborhood joint, with easier prices and a relaxed setting. Its more high-flying flights of fancy aren't always successful, but if you stick with dishes like roast chicken with red bliss potatoes or New Zealand lamb chops with apple-mint salsa, you'll be satisfied.

International District at Gulf Gate

So far I've focused on fairly high-end eats—but you're in luck. The **Gulf Gate neighborhood** is a tiny international district that spans a three-block area from Gulf Gate Avenue to Superior Avenue, Mall Drive around the block to Gateway Avenue. It's where to go to get a quick meal on the fly, takeout, or just something that won't break the bank. There are Philly cheesesteaks at **Walt's Tuscany Grill** (6584 Superior Ave., 941/927-1113), then big sandwiches at the **Italian Village Deli** (6606 Superior Ave., 941/927-2428). Around the corner on Gateway Avenue you'll come upon the little French bistro **Le Parigot** (6551 Gateway Ave., 941/922-9115), **Pontillo's Pizza** (6592 Superior Ave., 941/921-0990), and **Rico's Pizzeria** (6547 Gateway Ave., 941/922-9604). After all that pizza, and for something totally different, try the pirogues at **Lucy's Polish Delicatessen** (6542 Gateway Ave., 941/926-8980) or the fun Cajun fare at **Greer's Grill** (6566 Gateway Ave., 941/926-0606). Then you'll need a beer at **Paddy Wagon** (6586 Gateway Ave., 941/925-2344). And once you hit Gulf Gate Drive, there are a couple of Chinese and sushi takeout places, a Russian joint, and a British tearoom.

Amish Cuisine

If that looks like a typo sitting there, you'll need to adjust to the fact that Sarasota is a huge Amish and Mennonite winter resort. Both groups come down from Pennsylvania and the Midwest looking for sun and good Amish food, with luck on both counts. The locus of Amish activity here is in Pinecraft, where you'll see the bearded men in suspenders and wide straw hats, the women in long skirts and bonnets, all enjoying the Florida weather. What do they do while here? Go to **Yoder's** (3434 Bahia Vista, 941/955-7771, 8 A.M.–8 P.M. Mon.–Sat., $6–14) to find out. It's been a Sarasota institution since 1975, with wholesome, rib-sticking country ham and corn fritters, turkey and gravy, meatloaf and mashed potatoes, and pies, pies, pies. **Troyer's Dutch Heritage** (3713 Bahia Vista, 941/955-8007, 6 A.M.–8 P.M. Mon.–Sat., $5–12) is even more venerable, dating back to 1969, with sturdy, accessible buffet-style meals and a gift shop on the second floor. Another one people seem devoted to is **Sugar and Spice Family Restaurant** (4000 Cattleman Rd., 941/342-1649). All of them are closed on Sunday and serve no alcohol.

NIGHTLIFE

Bars

Downtown has a few of the kind of nightspots that feel like the epicenter of something big. **Zoria** (1991 Main St., 941/955-4457, 11 A.M.–2 P.M. Mon.–Fri., 5–10:30 P.M. Mon.–Sat., bar menu 10:30 P.M.–midnight, 5–9 P.M. Sun., $19–31) deserves a fairly lavish restaurant description, but its vital bar scene is its most notable quality, young professionals drawn by the globetrotting by-the-glass wine list. The French-Asian fusion small-plate menu at **Silver Cricket** (1923 Ringling Blvd., 941/955-9179, 5–10 P.M. daily, after-hours menu until 1 A.M., $6–32) is a draw for the same crowd, as is the sleek, clubby interior. For a more rarefied experience, head to the **Cà d'Zan Bar** at the Ritz-Carlton (1111 Ritz-Carlton Dr., 941/309-2000, 4 P.M.–midnight Sun.–Thurs., until 2 A.M. Fri. and Sat., $10–25). Overstuffed couches, clubby leather chairs, gleaming hickory wood walls, and a specialty martini menu that will shake *and* stir you.

Beyond these, there are refreshing drinks and engaging conversations to be had nearly everywhere here—the **Beach Club** in Siesta Key Village and **Fandango** on the south side of Siesta Key; **Sharky's** on the Pier in Venice; the **Sports Page** and **Findaddy's** in Sarasota for watching the big game, and **8 Ball Lounge** for when you feel like working on your own game.

Dance and Music Clubs

For when you're ready to rev the engine a little, the **Five O'Clock Club** (1930 Hillview St., 941/366-5555, happy hour noon–8 P.M. daily, small cover charges change nightly depending on band, www.5oclockclub.net for concert schedule) in Southside Village has what the mechanic ordered. There's live music seven nights a week, with national and local rock/blues/whatever bands taking the stage at 10 P.M. The 5-O draws a 30s and 40s crowd, and just a smattering of college kids. If you're looking for a more youthful crowd, your best bet is **Club Envy** (1927 Ringling Blvd., 941/951-0335), which has two rooms of sound (mostly hip-hop and house) and up to 1,000

sweaty bodies on some nights. The **Gator Club** (1490 Main St., 941/366-5969) is another longtime nightlife haunt for the fully adult (read: those who are secretly somewhat flattered when they still get carded). Again, there's live music every night, often of the Jimmy Buffet–cover variety, pool tables upstairs, and an impressive single-malt selection.

SHOPPING

The shops of **St. Armands Circle** on Lido Key have been a primary retail draw in Sarasota for a long time, historically known for high-end boutiques. These days the shops cover familiar ground—chains like **Chico's** (443 St. Armands Circle, 941/388-2926), **Tommy Bahama** (300 John Ringling Blvd., 941/388-2888), **Fresh Produce** (1 N. Boulevard of the Presidents, 941/388-1883), and **The White House/Black Market** (317 St. Armands Circle, 941/388-5033)—and a paltry handful of upscale, independently owned boutiques. You'll have better luck noodling in the circle's novelty and giftware shops: **The Alphabet Shop** (toy store, 386 St. Armands Circle, 941/388-1505), **Wet Noses** (pet stuff, 472 John Ringling Boulevard, 941/388-3647), or **Kilwin's** (ice cream and fudge, 312 John Ringling Blvd., 941/388-3200).

Towles Court Artist Colony (Adams Ln. or Morrill St., downtown Sarasota) is a collection of 16 quirky pastel-colored bungalows and cottages that contain artists working furiously and the art they've been working furiously on. You can buy their work and watch them in action most Tuesdays through Saturdays 11 A.M.–4 P.M., or visit Towles Court on the third Friday evening of each month for Art by the Light of the Moon.

Palm Avenue and **Main Street** downtown are lined with galleries, restaurants, and cute shops, and historic **Herald Square** in the SoMa (south of Main St.) part of downtown on Pineapple Avenue has a fairly dense concentration of antiques shops and upscale housewares stores. Also on Pineapple you'll find the **Artisan's World Marketplace** (128 S. Pineapple Ave., 941/365-5994), which promotes self-employment for low-income artisans in developing countries worldwide by selling their baskets, clothing, and handicrafts.

Westfield Shoppingtown Southgate (3501 S. Tamiami Trail, 941/955-0900) is a pretty standard mall, with several anchor stores (Saks Fifth Avenue, Dillard's, Burdines) and many of the usual suspects (Ann Taylor, Talbots, Pottery Barn, Banana Republic, Gap, Limited Too, The Disney Store). For when you need to make those credit cards sizzle, you have to head north on I-75 to the **Prime Outlets** in Ellenton (5461 Factory Shops Blvd., Ellenton, 941/723-1150). There are more than 100 stores (Ralph Lauren, Gap, Geoffrey Beane, Tommy Hilfiger, Nike, Off Fifth) with deep, deep discounts.

And if your mantra is "reduce, reuse, and recycle," you'll find lovingly used doodads of all stripes at the more than 400 covered booths of the **Red Barn Flea Market** (1707 1st St. E, Bradenton, in Manatee County to the north, 941/747-3794). Go on the weekend for the greatest number of vendors and the widest variety of things, from collectibles to antiques to out-and-out junk.

The Keys

The northernmost of Sarasota's stretch of keys, Longboat Key is a 12-mile barrier island for the wealthy who *vant to be alone*. What you can see of the posh residences is showy enough, but I have a sneaking suspicion that the really jaw-dropping manses are down all those long driveways and behind those tall hedgerows. There are only about 8,000 full-time residents, but in high season (Dec.–Mar.), Longboat Key is where the rich and/or famous come to play a little golf and get a little sun away from the prying eyes of the hoi polloi. If you are, like me, one of the hoi polloi with prying eyes, hang around at the **Longboat Key Club** or on the golf courses to catch a glimpse of Robert DeNiro or Tom Selleck or Bill Cosby or that guy in Aerosmith.

The island hasn't always been so swanky. It was the Arvida Company that laid the foundation in the late 1950s (literally, enabling construction to occur on previously loose, shifting soil) for the development of the island. Generally speaking, visitors stay in the imposing high-rises that line the impeccably groomed Gulf of Mexico Drive; residents live on the bayside in discreet, shielded estates.

Siesta Key is something else again. It's a similar eight-mile-long barrier island with even more gorgeous beaches, some insist. But Siesta is for the proletariat—it's family-owned accommodations, none outlandishly fancy, easy access to the beach from anywhere, fishing, boating, kayaking, snorkeling, scuba diving, and sail-boarding. And at night, unlike on Longboat, these people like to party. Siesta Village has the area's most lively nightlife.

Farther south, Casey Key is eight miles long, stretching from Siesta Key on the north to Venice at the southern tip. It is almost exclusively single-family homes (getting fancier and pricier by leaps and bounds), with just a few low-rise "Old Florida" beach motels. Two bridges provide access to the key, including a cool old "swing bridge" dating back to the 1920s. Parts of the key are only 300 yards wide.

The town of Venice is more like a real place than a tourist destination, in good and bad ways. The residents seem to be mostly retirees, very chummy, very active, with keen civic pride. The downtown is quaint—a handful of boutiques and galleries, a couple of restaurants, a place to get ice cream, a couple of coffee shops, and a good wine bar. There's a little community theater, of which the residents are inordinately proud. Really, the biggest draw in Venice is teeth.

Every August, the Venice Area Chamber of Commerce holds the **Shark's Tooth and Seafood Festival,** with arts, crafts, food stalls, and lots of little pointy black fossils. It seems that sharks of all species shed their teeth continually. They have 40 or so teeth in each jaw, with seven other rows of teeth behind that first one waiting in the wings, as it were, to mature. The average tiger shark produces 24,000 teeth in 10 years. In order to find them when they wash up on Venice beaches,

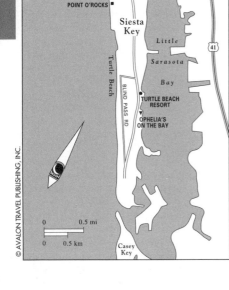

SIESTA KEY

Roberts Bay

THE OLD SALTY DOG
BROKEN EGG
OCEAN BLVD
TROPICAL BREEZE RESORT OF SIESTA KEY
BLASÉ CAFÉ
DAIQUIRI DECK
Siesta Key Village
SIESTA KEY OYSTER BAR

758

THE BEACH PLACE

To Sarasota

41

BEACH RD

SIESTA KEY BEACH

MIDNIGHT PASS RD

TAMIAMI TRAIL

Crescent Beach

STICKNEY POINT RD

72

SIESTA HOLIDAYS
SIESTA SOUTH SHOPPING DISTRICT

POINT O'ROCKS

Siesta Key

Little

41

Sarasota

Turtle Beach

Bay

BLIND PASS RD

TURTLE BEACH RESORT

OPHELIA'S ON THE BAY

0   0.5 mi
0   0.5 km

Casey Key

© AVALON TRAVEL PUBLISHING, INC.

stop by one of the gift shops downtown and ask for a shark tooth shovel. And once you've found a few, visit www.veniceflorida.com/shark.htm to identify the species.

SPORTS AND RECREATION

Beaches

Swimming, snorkeling, boogie boarding, beach-combing, and just wiggling your toes in the sand are the primary activity on the keys. Even if you're staying in Sarasota, you'll manage to try many of the key beaches—I've described them all in the *Sports and Recreation* section under *Sarasota*.

Golf

In the early 1920s, John Ringling purchased major acreage on the south end of the Longboat Key. He constructed a golf course and planted Australian pine trees along Gulf of Mexico Drive, along with the construction of a luxurious Ritz-Carlton, which he eventually abandoned. With this legacy, the **Longboat Key Golf Club** (301 Gulf of Mexico Dr., 941/383-9571, resort courses, greens fees $78–140) offers several remarkable golfing experiences to guests (and their guests' guests). Opened in 1960, the Bill Mitchell–designed Islandside Course (par 72, 6,792 yards, course rating 73.8, slope 138) features 18 holes of crisp, up-and-down shot-making through a 112-acre bird sanctuary filled with more than 5,000 palm trees and flowering plants. Water appears on 16 of its 18 fairways. With a more country-club feel (and where more of the private members play), the resort also has three 9-hole courses, played in three 18-hole combinations: blue/red (par 72, 6,709 yards, course rating 72.6, slope 130), red/white (par 72, 6,749 yards, course rating 72.7, slope 131), white/blue (par 72, 6,812 yards, course rating 73.1, slope 132).

Fishing

Venice is a fairly well-known fishing destination—you'll see people wetting a line at the Venice jetties, Sharky's Pier, or Caspersen Beach. If you try your hand, expect to catch snook, redfish, Spanish mackerel, sheepshead, sea trout, and flounder, depending on the time of year.

ANNA MARIA ISLAND

Stand at the northern end of Longboat Key and look north. You'll see another long, seven-mile strip of sandy barrier island that couldn't be much different from Longboat. Manatee County's Anna Maria Island is an island both literally and metaphorically—it is far enough south of Tampa to be removed from the city's urban hubbub, and it's far enough north of Sarasota to escape being just another feather in that city's cap. It's the northernmost of the string of barrier islands that extend down to the Florida Keys, with three distinct towns spread along its length. There's the town of Anna Maria at the northern end, Holmes Beach in the middle, and Bradenton Beach at the southern end—all of them linked by their sweet, laid-back atmosphere. Three drawbridges access the island, one from Longboat Key and two from the mainland (Hwy. 64 and Hwy. 684).

Really, the little island community owes it very existence to the Fig Newton. The inventor of the "oo-ee, gooey, rich and chewy" Newton, Charles Roser, sold the recipe to Nabisco, made a fortune, and then bought up Anna Maria land and started building. (Actually, to pick some nits, the island probably owes its existence to James Henry Mitchell, who invented the *apparatus,* a kind of funnel within a funnel, that supplies the necessary steady stream of fig jam while outside it there's a tube-like stream of dough. But, enough with the Newtons already.)

These days, there's an active year-round community as well as a robust tourist trade (for some reason you'll encounter more Danish, German, British, and Australian visitors than Americans). Tourists come for the outstanding boating, sailing, scuba, snorkeling, and fishing. Parking is the only hassle on the island, so park your car where you're staying and walk across to the beach—Holmes Beach, Anna Maria Beach, Coquina Beach, Cortez Beach, and Manatee Beach are all equally lovely stretches of white sand and blue-green water. (Manatee has the most parking and a nice picnic area.) None have lifeguards or restrooms.

It's the kind of island on which it's easy to do nothing—not because there's nothing to do, but because the pace is such that you feel entitled to stuporous, languorous, slack-jawed relaxation. If your puritan work ethic forces you to do *something,* I recommend a sunset sailing cruise with **Mabina La** (departures from Seafood Shack Restaurant at Cortez Beach, 941/761-4779, $35/person). Our captain, a man named Espen, had a wealth of information about Florida history, fishing, and the area's recent environmental challenges.

Accommodations

Palm Tree Villas (207 66th St., 888/778-7256, www.palmtreevillas.com, $115–170) is an inviting, warm, "boutique-style" haven, whether it's for honeymooning couples or families. The low-rise Old Florida-style motel has been lovingly refurbished, the nicely appointed units clustered around a central courtyard and swimming pool. There's a great packet of literature in each villa, and the warm owners, Peggy and Ashok Sawe, are serious boosters of the area.

Another favorite on the island is **Harrington House Beachfront Bed & Breakfast** (5626 Gulf Dr., Holmes Beach, 941/778-5444, www.harringtonhouse.com, $139–259), a converted 1925 coquina brick beachfront house. Most rooms feature French doors opening onto balconies that overlook the heated swimming pool, the beach beyond, and beyond that the Gulf. The breakfasts here are legendary (many recipes are featured in *From Muffins to Margaritas—Visit the Kitchens of Florida's Finest Inns*), there's a sweet little beach gazebo from which you watch the sunset, and the common living room is a surefire place to start lively conversation with total strangers. (The same people own and operate The Beach Inn, a more affordable, family-oriented beachfront motel.)

Food

Beach Bistro (6600 Gulf Dr., Holmes Beach, 941/778-6444, www.beachbistro.com, $15–40) beats much fancier restaurants in Sarasota, Tampa, and beyond for best restaurant on the Gulf Coast, according to *Zagat, Wine Spectator,* and numerous other publications. The place is quirky and cozy, with the kind of charm that comes of an independent (noncorporate) culinary vision. The food is largely excellent, but there are sometimes too many ingredients thrown in for good measure.

(continued on next page)

Sarasota County

ANNA MARIA ISLAND (cont'd)

The kitchen might benefit from just a bit of restraint—flavors end up getting muddy when there's too much going on in a dish. The dining room, its ceiling draped with luxurious raw silk, is stunning, with long single roses adorning the center of each table. Geared toward romantic dining, the Beach Bistro still extends real warmth and care to visiting children. For a restaurant of this caliber it isn't outlandishly pricey if you opt for the "small plates," which are certainly ample if you have an appetizer as well.

For other "splurge" restaurants, try **DaGiorgio Ristorante** (5702 Marina Dr., Holmes Beach, 941/779-0220, $15–25) for elegant northern Italian, mostly the usual suspects, and **Bistro at Island's End** (10101 Gulf Dr., 941/779-2444,

$12–25) for sophisticated Mediterranean cuisine served in a laid-back atmosphere with live music. For more everyday dining, it's hard to go wrong with the barbecue at **Mr. Bones** (3007 Gulf Dr., Holmes Beach, 941/778-6614, $6–14), and it also has fairly good Indian food; go figure. And you pick your beer from a coffin in the reception area. Then there's **Rotten Ralph's** for fish 'n' chips and an excellent blackened grouper sandwich. You can pull your boat up to the dock and place your order.

For more information about the island, contact **Anna Maria Island Chamber of Commerce** (5313 Gulf Dr. N, Holmes Beach, Florida 34217, 941/778-1541) and they'll send you a great packet of information and maps.

There are also lots of charter companies willing to take you deep-sea fishing out in the Gulf (grouper and snapper most of the year; kingfish, cobia, greater amberjack, and mahimahi seasonally). At the end of East Venice Avenue on the Myakka River, **Snook Haven Fish Camp** (941/485-7221) has a fun riverside restaurant, boat rides, and fishing. **Reel Fast Charters** (941/650-4938, $375 for four hours, $500 for six hours, $650 for eight hours) takes groups out fishing as well as on nonfishing sunset cruises ($25/person). And **Triple Trouble Charters** (941/484-3225, rates vary) takes small groups out from the Dona Bay Marina in Nokomis, just minutes from the Venice Inlet, on a 25-foot custom-rigged Parker for inshore and offshore fishing.

Waterway Park

The recently completed **Venetian Waterway Park** (daylight hours, admission free) in Venice is a 10-mile-long mixed-use linear park with trails through some of the area's least developed land along the east bank of the Intracoastal Waterway, ending on Caspersen Beach, one of the prettiest on the Gulf. It's a long, winding, wheel-friendly park, good for rollerbladers, bikers, even jog-strollers. Rent bikes at **Beach Bikes & Trikes** (127 Tampa Ave. #10, Venice, 941/412-3821, $10/day, $25/week).

While in Venice, visit the recently renovated **Venice Train Depot** (depot tours are free) downtown. The Mediterranean-style depot was constructed in 1927 and is listed on the National Register of Historic Places.

ACCOMMODATIONS

Longboat Key

Longboat Key is mostly dotted with swishy highrise condos and resort hotels that loom over the beaches. If you like a more modest scale, the **Wicker Inn** (5581 Gulf of Mexico Dr., 941/383-5562, www.wickerinn.com, cottages $980–2,700 per week) is on a more human scale. There are 11 breezy Key West–style cottages set around an inviting pool and festooned with purple hibiscus and oleander. There's a private beach just steps away and a 16-acre public park.

Colony Beach & Tennis Resort (1620 Gulf of Mexico Dr., 941/383-6464, www .colonybeachresort.com, from $275) has been patronized over the years by George W. Bush, Tom Brokaw, Dustin Hoffman, and countless other luminaries. It's the area's oldest beach resort, with 235 luxuriously large suites, a relaxed atmosphere, two popular restaurants, private beach access, and 21 tennis courts (with 10 pros on staff). It's considered by many to be the nation's top tennis resort, but there are plenty of other distractions such as a lovely beachfront pool and luxury spa.

The other big gun in town is **M The Resort at Longboat Key Club** (301 Gulf of Mexico Dr., 941/383-8821, www.longboatkeyclub.com, from $285). Serious golfers come for the 45 holes of the private Longboat Key Club, but there are lots of other reasons to settle into one of the 210 suites (with full kitchens) or one of 20 hotel rooms. There's a fine restaurant on-site, 38 tennis courts, bike and beach rentals, great pools, and a private stretch of white-sand beach with lovely cabana rentals and beachside service. Despite the fact that this is luxury with a capital L, the people who work here are friendly and personable, never lapsing into the kind of obsequiousness that gives me the heebie-jeebies. (Speaking of heebie-jeebies, this site was once owned by John Ringling, where in the 1930s he built a Ritz-Carlton. The hotel was never completed because of the Great Depression, and it sat abandoned until it was demolished in 1963. Locals called the hulking shell the "Ghost Hotel," spreading all the requisite apocryphal tales of horror, ghost sightings, and untimely death.)

Another big, but less expensive, favorite on Longboat is the **Hilton Longboat Key Beachfront Resort** (4711 Gulf of Mexico Dr., 941/383-2451, $100–430). The large, newly renovated rooms are decorated in jewel tones with contemporary furniture, all rooms with either two queen beds or one king. It sits adjacent to a private stretch of white-sand beach. The hotel provides free shuttle service to the shopping on St. Armands Circle.

Siesta Key

There are not too many chain hotels and no huge resorts on Siesta Key—which is fine, because you're more likely to have a memorable time in one of the modest mom-and-pop house rentals or small hotels. The warm, independent spirit of many of these hoteliers is apparent in the relaxed decor and their easy beachside pleasures. Many accommodations on Siesta Key adopt an efficiency approach, with little kitchens,

essential for keeping vacation costs down (snarf a bowl of cereal in the morning, then prepare yourself a great picnic lunch for the beach).

Rented by the week, the tropical garden beach cottages of **The Beach Place** (5605 Avenida Del Mare, 941/346-1745, www.siestakeybeachplace.com, $500–950/week) make a nice romantic or family beach getaway. There's a pool (but the beach is 30 seconds away), a tiki cabana with wet bar, beachside barbecue facilities, lounge chairs, beach cruiser bikes, and free laundry. The cottages themselves are modest but recently repainted and pleasant, whether it's the one-bedroom Coquina, the one-bedroom Seahorse, the two twin-bed Starfish, the large one-bedroom Sand Dollar, or the huge studio cottage called the Dolphin.

M Siesta Holidays (1017 Seaside Dr., 941/312-9882, www.siestaholidays.com, $675–1400/week, depending on the season and unit) is a similar place, with two options. It has the Siesta Sea Castle directly on Crescent Beach, consisting of a large two-bedroom, two-bath apartment, and four one-bedroom efficiency apartments. The ground-level units have patios directly on the beach. Then there's the Siesta Holiday House, a little farther from the beach, with two one-bedroom apartments on the ground floor (with a big private screened pool) and two two-bedroom, two-bath apartments on the second floor. Pets are allowed in the Holiday House.

The **Tropical Breeze Resort of Siesta Key** (5150 Ocean Blvd., 800/300-2492, www.tropicalbreezeinn.com, $149–466/night) also offers a range of choices, spreading across four blocks of a cute neighborhood between the village and the shoreline. There are one-, two-, and three-bedroom efficiencies and suites located directly on the beach as well as more privately located units in lush tropical gardens. Each building comes with its own pool, and the property has a centrally located yoga deck. Everything is within walking distance of Siesta Key Village.

On the south end of the island, **Turtle Beach Resort** (9049 Midnight Pass Rd., 941/349-4554, www.turtlebeachresort.com, doubles from $190) is one of the area's best-kept secrets, only now the secret's been blabbed by lots of travel magazines. Reservations are harder to come by, but the 10 clapboard cottages, each individually decorated with its own porch and hot tub, are worth waiting for. With views of Little Sarasota Bay, Turtle Beach is a short walk away, and guests have free use of bikes, hammocks, canoes, kayaks, paddleboats, and fishing poles. Eat at Ophelia's next door. Pets welcome.

Venice

If you've come to the Sarasota area with the express purpose of collecting shark's teeth, then it makes sense to stay in Venice. Otherwise, Venice lacks a lot of the amenities of Sarasota, Lido Key, Longboat Key, or Siesta Key, and the downtown pretty much closes up at night. There's a fairly inexpensive **Holiday Inn** (455 U.S. 41 Bypass N, 941/485-5411, $98–159) and a **Best Western** (400 Commercial Court, 800/611-7450, $99–189), both perfectly fine.

FOOD
Longboat Key

One of Sarasota's most long-term love affairs has been with **Euphemia Haye** (5540 Gulf of Mexico Dr., 941/383-3633, 5:30–10 P.M. Sun.–Thurs., 5–10:30 P.M. Fri. and Sat. in the restaurant., 6–10 P.M. daily in the dessert room, 5 P.M.–midnight in the HayeLoft, $22–43). Opened in 1975 on Longboat Key, the restaurant has marched to the beat of its own drum, serving wildly sophisticated and far-reaching food in a lush garden setting. It always wins top honors from local magazines and national food mags as well, and you need only to try the smoked salmon on buckwheat crepes, fried green tomatoes, or pistachio-crusted Key West snapper to see why. The wine list is broad, with good depth at every price point. As far as the food, prices are high and dishes are rich in the restaurant, so you can try the lighter/cheaper fare upstairs in the HayeLoft if you feel inclined. Chef/owner Raymond Arpke also offers cooking classes at the restaurant.

The other Goliath on Longboat Key is clearly the **Colony Restaurants** (1620 Gulf of Mexico Dr., 941/383-5558, 11:30 A.M.–9:30 P.M. daily

MAMA MIA

Quick, who said: "If the definition of poetry allowed that it could be composed with the products of the field as well as with words, pesto would be in every anthology"?

Longboat Key's one and only Marcella Hazen. She's the mother of Italian cooking in this country, the author of *The Classic Italian Cookbook, Marcella Says, Marcella Cucina, Marcella's Italian Kitchen,* and a few other Marcella books I can't remember. She introduced balsamic vinegar to this country (by way of Chuck Williams, of Williams-Sonoma), and just as Julia Child's *Mastering the Art of French Cooking* was a book that many Francophile cooks slept with under their pillows, so too was Hazen's first book in 1973 the kind of cookbook that serious students of Italian cuisine eventually had to replace with a fresh copy (too much sauce gumming up the pages).

Hazen's in her 80s now, but she still teaches recreational classes twice a year in New York. Look for her books in Sarasota's Main Street bookstores, such as **Sarasota News & Books** (new books, nice café, 1341 Main St., 941/365-6332), **Main Bookshop** (four stories of remainders, 1692 Main St., 941/366-7653), or **Book Bazaar** (used and out-of-print books, 1488 Main St., 941/366-1373). She also occasionally does book signings at these places.

All of her books lay out the principles of Italian cooking in no-nonsense, understandable prose, and the most recent, *Marcella Says* (2004), is filled with the wisdom—and the passion—she's shared at her culinary classes for more than three decades.

It's as she says: "Music and cooking are so much alike. There are people who, simply by working hard at it, become technically quite accomplished at either art. But it isn't until one connects technique to feeling, turning it into the outward thrust of that feeling, that one becomes a musician, or a cook."

and Sunday brunch in the dining room; breakfast and dinner in the Monkey Room, no lunch; 11:30 A.M.–1 A.M. in the bar, $8–38) at the 30-year-old Colony Resort, partly for the sheer range of choices, and partly because so many local chefs cut their chops here. There's the fancy continental Colony Dining Room (opt for the red snapper "Colony" with wild mushroom risotto and lump crabmeat), the more casual Monkey Room and Bar, or the outside Monkey Room Patio and Bar. The Monkey Room is a must for party animals, the drinks tall and goofy (screaming yellow monkey, anyone?), the views stunning, and the island-inflected cuisine pleasant (although I'd take the plain old burger before the jerk chicken or froufrou Caribbean lobster tails). Live entertainment nightly.

Located mid-key on the bay side of Longboat Key is a wonderful find, **Pattigeorge's** (4120 Gulf of Mexico Dr., 941/383-5111, 5–9:30 P.M. nightly, $16–28). Chef Tommy Klauber experiments with an East-West fusion style that somehow never seems precious or contrived (he came from a place in Aspen called "Giusseppi Wong," a purveyor of Italian/Chinese cuisine). Pattigeorge's has been around since 1998, making it another old-timer on the island. The dining room is comfortable but upscale and the views are nice—still, the main attraction is dishes like crackling five-spice calamari with orange blossom honey-mustard, or Thai green curry red snapper fillet, or maybe a hoisin grilled duck pizza.

Siesta Key

Like everything else on Siesta Key, restaurants are mostly more casual here than on Longboat Key. Ocean Boulevard runs through Siesta Village, which is lined with loads of fun, laid-back, beachy bars and restaurants. Most places have outdoor seating, and many have live music at night.

For when you need a little romance, though, only one place on Siesta Key will do. **N Ophelia's on the Bay** (9105 Midnight Pass Rd., 941/349-2212, 5–10 P.M. daily, $20–29), at the southern tip of the key, has a waterfront terrace that I swear the moon favors with an extra luminous show over Sarasota Bay and the mainland. The interior of the restaurant is elegant, but you just gotta sit outside. The chef seems smitten with sweet-and-salty combinations that marry meats with fruits (coconut-and-cashew-crusted grouper with papaya jam) and salty meats with fish (black sea bass and cockle clams pan roasted with applewood smoked bacon and leeks). It's a distinctive and memorable palette of flavors that is complemented by a quirky wine list. Try the macadamia nut torte for dessert. (Oh, and the oyster bar next door to Ophelia's is a wonderful place to kill a little time, and appetite, if you have to wait for a table at Ophelia's.)

Another of the longtime faves on the key closed amid much protest in May 2005—Summerhouse Restaurant was a perennial special-occasion choice for locals, but the space will now be used as a clubhouse for condos going up in that area.

The Siesta Key restaurant that thrills me the most is **Siesta Key Oyster Bar** (5238 Ocean Blvd., 941/346-5443, 11 A.M.–midnight daily, $6–15), but that's because the acronym on the sign out front is SKOB. It's the exact onomatopoetic word that would be elicited by an oyster going down the wrong way. But then, I'm immature that way. Their sandwiches are, in fact, called skobwiches, which is just gross. Still, the swordfish skobwich or the crabcake skobwich is mighty fine washed down with a house margarita while listening to a live rock band. Margaritas seem to find their foothold in Siesta Key, reaching their volatile tequila effulgence here in the white powdery sand under the hot sun. But if rum's more your poison (and, unfortunately, sometimes that feels literal), right down the way you'll enjoy the **Daiquiri Deck** (5250 Ocean Blvd., 941/349-8697, 11 A.M.–1 A.M. daily, $6–17). The most sophisticated drink is the Grateful Deck, a mélange of Bols raspberry liqueur, light rum, gin, vodka, raspberry juice, and sour mix. Tangy, yet sweet, yet boozy. Lots of other mad-scientist brews are powered by grain alcohol, something no one over 22 or so should wittingly consume.

Beer batter–dipped hot dogs. I kid you not. And they're pretty good. **The Old Salty Dog** (5023 Ocean Blvd., 941/349-0158, and another location at 1601 City Island Rd., 941/388-4311, 11 A.M.–midnight Mon.–Thurs., until 1 A.M. Fri. and Sat., noon–midnight Sun., $5–15) is an institution among locals, who come for that particular gastronomic challenge or a bowl of clam chowder and a beer. It's open-air, with great views, good burgers, saucy waitresses. The beer bar is fashioned from the hull of an old boat, which adds a little nautical tilt to every drinker's voice.

Best breakfast? That's the easiest call on Siesta Key. Anyone in town will promptly steer you to **M The Broken Egg** (210 Avenida Madera, 941/346-2750, 7:30 A.M.–2:30 P.M. daily, $5–9). The place is such a cheery mob scene most mornings that they're opening a second location in June 2005 at Lakewood Ranch. It's no accident that their website plays the theme song from *Cheers*—it is the kind of place "where everybody knows your name," even if you've only been there a couple of times to dispatch a "scram sam" (three eggs scrambled with smoked salmon and chives, served with tomatoes, onion, cream cheese, and a bagel) or banana-nut-bread french toast. The verdant patio is the place to sit, despite the crusty white molded plastic patio chairs.

Blasé Café (5263 Ocean Blvd., 941/349-9822, 9 A.M.–9:30 P.M. daily, $7–23) gives the Broken Egg a run for its money, with expertly prepared egg dishes and a fine burger at lunch. Be sure to ask for outside seating on the wooden deck with the big palm tree in the middle (but if you're just stopping in for a drink, the beautiful bar is the seat of choice).

Casey Key

On Casey Key, the place to go is **Casey Key Fish House** (801 Blackburn Point Rd., 941/966-1901, 11:30 A.M.–9 P.M. daily, $5–15). Despite a recent fire and Hurricane Charley's best efforts, this shambling restaurant-and-tiki bar still does a brisk business with people who navigate peel-'n'-eat shrimp while watching the sunset over picturesque Blackburn Point Marina. Casual seafood is the mainstay, but fancier white wine–steamed mussels and almond snapper are wonderful.

Venice

Along Nokomis Avenue (the main drag downtown) you'll find shops, diners, coffee houses, and lunch spots (the best of which is **Venice**

Venice is a "Florida MainStreet City," a designation awarded by the State of Florida for Historic Preservation.

COURTESY OF VISIT FLORIDA

Wine and Coffee Co., a coffee shop by day and wine bar at night). To find Venice's "Old Florida" dining possibilities, all fun, all casual, you'll have to go farther afield. The **Crow's Nest, Marina Restaurant and Tavern** (1968 Tarpon Center Dr., 941/484-9551, 11 A.M.–11 P.M. Mon.–Thurs., until midnight Fri. and Sat., happy hour in the tavern 4–6 P.M., marina hours 8 A.M.–7 P.M. daily, $13–32) has been feeding locals since 1976, with a fun tavern and pretty views of the marina, Venice Inlet, and the Intracoastal Waterway. The wine list is incongruously sophisticated for this fried oysters-fried shrimp-steamed clam, friendly kind of menu.

The **Snook Haven Restaurant and Fish Camp** (5000 Venice Ave. E, past River Rd., 941/485-7221, 11 A.M.–9 P.M. daily, $9–20) has a similar vibe, only more downhome and bayou-style, right on the Myakka River (rent a pontoon boat or kayak before you eat). The burgers are good and you can count on some entertaining fellow customers and occasional live entertainment.

Sharky's on the Pier (1600 S. Harbor Dr., 941/488-1456, 11 A.M.–11 P.M. Mon.–Thurs., until midnight Fri. and Sat., $12–24) is closer to civilization, with beach views and the day's catch offered broiled, blackened, grilled, or fried. Sit outside on the veranda and enjoy a "bait bucket" margarita that's finished off with triple sec and blue curaçao for that irresistible Windex look.

SHOPPING

Shopping on Longboat Key is fairly limited: On the lush, tropically landscaped Avenue of the Flowers there's a little shopping center (525 Bay Isle Pkwy.) where you'll find a larger Publix grocery and a drugstore; at the **Centre Shops** (5370

Gulf of Mexico Dr., 941/387-8298) about mid-island, you'll find a small collection of boutiques (tourists' T-shirts, resortwear, and such), galleries, and little restaurants.

On Siesta Key there are two main shopping areas, **Siesta Key Village** on the northwest side of the key about one block from the Gulf, and **Siesta South shopping area** beginning at the Stickney Point Bridge and going south along Midnight Pass Road. Both have the ubiquitous T-shirt-'n'-sunglasses shops, the shell-themed beachy giftware shops, and a few useful stores. Neither area boasts much in the way of high-end merchandise (fine-art galleries, antiques, clothing), but that's just fine.

Information and Services

AREA INFORMATION

Sarasota and environs are in the eastern time zone. The local telephone area code is 941.

Tourist Information

The **Sarasota Convention & Visitors Bureau** (655 N. Tamiami Trail, 941/957-1877, www.sarasotafl.org, 9 A.M.–5 P.M. Mon.–Sat., 11 A.M.–3 P.M. Sun.) and the **Sarasota Chamber of Commerce** (1945 Fruitville Rd., 941/955-8187, www.sarasotachamber.org, 8:30 A.M.–5 P.M. Mon.–Fri.) both offer heaping piles of reading material on the area. The former has more useful material and a more central location.

Sarasota has its own daily newspaper, the *Sarasota Herald-Tribune,* with multiple zoned editions serving the area, along with a 24-hour television news station, SNN. Local weekly publications include the *Longboat Observer,* Siesta Key's *Pelican Press,* and a business newspaper, the *Gulf Coast Business Review.* Nine magazines cover different aspects of Sarasota County, from business to the arts and the social scene.

Police and Emergencies

In any emergency, dial 911 for immediate assistance. If you need the police in a nonemergency, Sarasota's Police Department Headquarters Build-

ing is at 2050 Ringling Blvd. (941/954-7025). For medical emergencies, or problems that just won't wait until you get home, the nicest facilities are at the emergency care center at **Sarasota Memorial Hospital** (1700 S. Tamiami Trail, 941/917-8555).

Radio and Television

Ten radio stations are located within Sarasota County, with 40 more stations in neighboring counties, including all major affiliates. Tune to **WFLA 970 AM** for news and talk radio; **WDDV 92.1 FM** is a new-music ClearChannel affiliate. You'll find National Public Radio at 89.7 FM and 90.1 FM.

On television, **WFLA Channel 8** is the NBC affiliate, **WTVT Channel 13** is the FOX affiliate, and **WWSB Channel 7** is the ABC affiliate. There are additional public television and local news channels.

Laundry Services

One of the perks of renting a beach house is the reliable presence of non-coin-op laundry facilities on-site. Big resort hotels in Sarasota and on Longboat Key invariably offer laundry services. If you absolutely need a launderette, there are several in Sarasota, such as **All Star Laundry & Dry Cleaning** (2241 Bee Ridge Rd., 941/921-1258).

Getting There and Around

DRIVING

Sarasota is along I-75, the major transportation corridor for the southeastern United States. Sarasota County is south of Tampa and north of Fort Myers, 223 miles from Miami (about four hours drive time), 129 miles from Orlando (about two hours drive time), and about 5–6 hours from the Florida-Georgia line. If you prefer I-95, take it to Daytona Beach, then follow I-4 to I-75 before heading south.

U.S. 301 and U.S. 41/Tamiami Trail are the major north–south arteries on the mainland; the Gulf-to-Mexico Drive (County Road 789) is the main island road. The largest east–west thoroughfares in Sarasota are Highway 72 (Stickney Point Road); County Road 780, University Parkway; and (to the islands) Ringling Causeway, which takes you right to Lido Beach.

FLYING

Sarasota-Bradenton International Airport (SRQ) (6000 Airport Circle, at the intersection of U.S. 41 and University Pkwy., Sarasota, 941/359-2770) is certainly the closest, served by commuter flights and a half dozen major airlines or their partners, including Continental, Delta, Northwest, TWA, and US Airways. Another option is to fly into **Tampa International Airport** (813/870-8700), which offers more arrival and departure choices, and often better fares on flights and even rental cars. Tampa International Airport is just 53 miles north of Sarasota County via I-75 or I-275. Also check flights through **St. Petersburg-Clearwater International Airport** (although usually they aren't as often or as cheap as through the Tampa airport). Private planes can use the **Venice Municipal Airport** in the City of Venice, just down U.S. 41 from Sarasota.

Alamo (800/327-9633), **Avis** (800/831-2847), **Budget** (800/527-0700), **Dollar** (800/800-4000 domestic, 800/800-6000 international), **Enterprise** (800/736-8222), **Hertz** (800/654-3131), and **National** (800/227-7368) provide rental cars from Sarasota-Bradenton International Airport. **Diplomat Taxi** (941/355-5155) is the taxi provider at the airport.

PUBLIC TRANSPORTATION

Sarasota County Area Transit, or **SCAT** (941/316-1234), runs scheduled bus service 6 A.M.–7 P.M. Monday–Saturday. A 50-cent fare will take you to stops in the city and St. Armands, Longboat, and Lido Keys. **Greyhound** (575 N. Washington Blvd., Sarasota, 941/955-5735) offers regular bus service to Sarasota from Fort Myers and points north, and Miami to the southeast, and **Amtrak** (800/872-7245) provides shuttle buses between the Tampa station and Sarasota.

Tampa

How many times have you heard tourists in Manhattan lean conspiratorially toward a friend and say, "It's a great city to visit, but I wouldn't want to live here"? Tampa is a little bit of the inverse. It's had a huge renaissance in recent years, drawing businesses and workers in droves. They come for the lovely climate, for the inexpensive price of housing and generally low cost of living, for the lack of state income tax. It's a safe, family-friendly town with decent infrastructure, respectable schools (at least by Florida standards), and enough sophistication and culture to cover the law. The University of South Florida (USF), University of Tampa, and Hillsborough Community College—all large—lend a fillip of youth and vitality. And, perhaps most importantly for some, Tampa is home to a superabundance of professional sporting teams.

The city is fairly urban to the south, where it runs into MacDill Air Force Base, which takes up the entire southern third of the Tampa peninsula and is home to the United States Central Command (coordinating all U.S. military operations in Africa and the Middle East). North of downtown, Tampa gets suburban quickly, then rural up into Pasco County. The amount of construction and the speed with which huge developments have been added to the city's north is a testament to Tampa's recent boom.

What this means for the visitor is this: Tampa is centrally located, with a superlative airport, an ideal city in which to begin or end a trip to other parts of the Gulf Coast. It contains Busch Gardens; a great zoo and aquarium; professional football, baseball, hockey, whatever; and affordable accommodations and restaurants. The

Must-Sees

▣ **Spring Training:** Tampa has both the boys of summer and the boys of spring. You can see professional baseball much of the year, with Tampa's own Devil Rays during the regular season and the Grapefruit League's spring training at the end of February and in March (page 146).

▣ **A Walk Along Bayshore Boulevard:** The five miles of sidewalk are bordered on one side by the wide open bay and on the other side by the fanciest historic homes on this stretch of Florida's Gulf Coast. Runners, walkers, bikers, and skaters take advantage of the amazing views and long expanse of carefully maintained walkway (page 150).

▣ **Ybor City:** Once known as the "Cigar Capital of the World," with nearly 12,000 cigarmakers employed in 200 factories that produced 700 million cigars a year, Tampa's Latin Quarter is one of only three National Historic Landmark Districts in Florida. Today it has something of a Jekyll and

COURTESY OF VISIT FLORIDA

Kumba, Busch Gardens's first multi-loop coaster, opened in 1993.

Hyde personality that offers visitors historic shops by day and the city's most vital nightlife and dining when the sun goes down (page 152).

▣ **Tampa Theatre:** The theater, elaborately decorated to resemble an open Mediterranean courtyard, features 1,446 seats, 99 stars in the auditorium ceiling, and nearly 1,000 pipes in its Mighty Wurlitzer Theatre Organ (page 155).

▣ **Busch Gardens:** The park's inverted steel roller coaster called the Montu won ninth place in *Amusement Today* magazine's survey of top roller coasters worldwide; its Kumba took the 19th spot. The park is an unusual mix of thrill rides, animal attractions, and entertainment. It's a something-for-everyone approach that really works (page 156).

▣ **Florida Aquarium:** A marvelous Tampa attraction, this 152,000-square-foot aquarium focuses on Florida's relationship to the Gulf, estuaries, rivers, and other waterways, with a strong environmental message (page 158).

TAMPA

Clearwater

Tampa Theatre
Busch Gardens
Tampa
Spring Training ▣ ▣
Florida Aquarium ▣ ▣ Ybor City
▣
A Walk Along Bayshore Boulevard

St Petersburg

Tampa Bay

Gulfport

Gulf of Mexico

0   5 mi
0   5 km

Bradenton

perfect ingredients for a family vacation. For history buffs, Tampa is somewhat stymieing. Much of it is just not that old.

For centuries the sheltered Tampa Bay area was a quiet Native American fishing backwater. Even after Hernando de Soto sailed into the bay in 1539, the area went largely untouched by whites for another couple of hundred years. Dutch cartographer Bernard Romans named the Hillsborough River and the upper arm of Tampa Bay in 1772, in honor of Lord Hillsborough, British secretary of state for the colonies. The U.S. purchased Florida from Spain in 1821, with traders setting up shop along what is now downtown Tampa in 1855.

It wasn't until Henry B. Plant extended his railroad into Tampa in 1884 and started a steamship line from Tampa to Key West to Havana, Cuba, that the city really began to grow. In 1891, Plant built the Tampa Bay Hotel, which launched the city as a winter resort for the northern elite. Around the same time, O. H. Platt purchased 20 acres of land across the Hillsborough River creating Tampa's first residential suburb, Hyde Park (named after Platt's hometown in Illinois). Hyde Park was, and still is, the residential area of choice for many prominent citizens. Many of the 19th-century bungalows and Princess Anne-style cottages are still occupied today, and the Old Hyde Park Village collection of boutiques and restaurants is one of the city's biggest draws.

Don Vicente Martinez Ybor, an influential cigar manufacturer and Cuban exile, moved his cigar business from Key West to a scruffy stretch of land east of Tampa in 1885. His first cigar factory drew others, and the Spanish, Italian, German, and Cuban workers who settled here to work in the area's more than 200 cigar factories created a vivacious Latin community known as Ybor City. The area is now designated one of three National Historic Landmark Districts in Florida, with a mix of historic buildings, artisan shops, restaurants, and nightclubs.

When the U.S. declared war on Spain in 1898, Tampa was the port of embarkation for troops headed to Cuba. A vital colonel named Theodore Roosevelt organized his "Rough Riders" at the Tampa encampment. Not longer after

COURTESY OF VISIT FLORIDA

The Hillsborough River begins in the Green Swamp and threads 55 miles through Central Florida to empty in Hillsborough Bay.

that, another Tampa neighborhood, Davis Islands, developed during the Florida land boom. Two little islands off downtown Tampa, where the Hillsborough River empties into Hillsborough Bay, became booming real estate developments. Today, the islands are home to an airport, Tampa General Hospital, and more than 100 of the original homes.

Growth continued apace through the Roaring '20s, slowing, as it did everywhere, during the Great Depression. Since then, Tampa hasn't been buoyed by the tourist dollar to the degree other Gulf Coast cities have, and thus has been less susceptible to the vicissitudes of American travel since 9/11.

Unlike other urban centers along the Gulf, there are no beaches in Tampa to speak of. For beaches, you need to drive over the causeway to St. Pete or Clearwater (about 30 minutes from downtown Tampa). Still, Tampa offers visitors all of the amenities that have made it such a sought-after place to live.

PLANNING YOUR TIME

How long you spend vacationing in Tampa largely depends on whether you have kids in tow. Not a city known for its urbane cultural

Tampa

TAMPA

To Jay B Starkey Wilderness Park and New Port Richey

589 (TOLL)

41

275

Bruce B Downs Blvd

75

Hillsborough River

EHRLICH RD

BEARSS AVE

■ MALIBU GRAND PRIX

FLETCHER AVE

UNIVERSITY OF SOUTH FLORIDA

Lettuce Lake Park

CANOE ESCAPE ■

GUNN HWY

LYNN TURNER RD

597

UNIVERSITY OF SOUTH FLORIDA CONTEMPORARY ART MUSEUM

■ USF SUN DOME

FOWLER AVE

★ MUSEUM OF SCIENCE AND INDUSTRY

M BUSCH GARDENS

★ ADVENTURE ISLAND

WATERS AVE

DALE MABRY HWY

Lowry Park Zoo

■ TAMPA GREYHOUND TRACK

NEBRASKA AVE

583

301

580

HILLSBOROUGH AVE

LEGENDS FIELD ■

41 92

M SPRING TRAINING

589 (TOLL)

TAMPA INTERNATIONAL AIRPORT

■ RAYMOND JAMES STADIUM

BUFFALO AVE

4

75

M YBOR CITY

275

PORT OF TAMPA

60

M Tampa Theatre
Tampa Museum of Art ★★

■ ★ THE FLORIDA AQUARIUM

41

KENNEDY BLVD

HOWARD FRANKLAND BRIDGE

92

HENRY B PLANT MUSEUM

Davis Island

Harbour Island

CAUSEWAY BLVD

BAYSHORE BLVD

M A WALK ALONG BAYSHORE BOULEVARD

TAMIAMI TRAIL

GANDY BRIDGE

Hillsborough Bay

MACDILL AIR FORCE BASE

Alafia River

41

75

0   2 mi
0   2 km

Tampa Bay

Tampa

© AVALON TRAVEL PUBLISHING, INC.

amenities or even one-of-a-kind nature experiences, Tampa is a paradise for kids. Obviously, the big kahuna is Busch Gardens, but that's just Day One. There are at least four or five other attractions worthy of a day of family focus.

Many people choose to visit Orlando's Disney attractions and then tack on a day or two at Tampa's Busch Gardens. While this is a perfectly fine strategy (Orlando's only an hour away), it seems like too much of a good thing. After a few days of Disney, come to Tampa and rent a canoe, go to the zoo, visit the science museum, and then head over to Clearwater for a day of leisurely beach time.

As with much of the Gulf Coast, the fall and early spring are the most luscious weather-wise, with days in the low 80s and very dry. The summer is unremittingly hot and humid, right through each afternoon's huge thunderstorm.

Sports and Recreation

SPECTATOR SPORTS

DirectTV has something called the Sports Fan Passion Index. Tampa Bay sports fans are at the top of it, fanatical for their professional sporting franchises. Why shouldn't they be at a constant fevered-pitch of enthusiasm? There are the Tampa Bay Buccaneers for football, Tampa Bay Lightning for hockey, Tampa Bay Devil Rays for baseball (not to mention spring training for the New York Yankees, Philadelphia Phillies, Toronto Blue Jays, and their own Devil Rays spread around the Bay Area), Tampa Bay Storm pro arena football, and the gamut of University of South Florida Bulls athletics.

Tampa Bay Buccaneers

Locals are still basking in the triumph of Super Bowl XXXVII. The past couple of years have been anticlimactic, but **Raymond James Stadium** (4201 N. Dale Mabry Hwy.) is still a wonderful venue in which to see Tampa's beloved Buccaneers (813/879-2827, www.buccaneers.com) play (it also hosted the Super Bowl in 2001). Raymond James Stadium, completed in 1998, holds more than 66,000 fans—52,000 in general seating—but tickets sell out for the season opener and other big games. In 2005's regular season, the Bucs play host to Buffalo, Chicago, Detroit, Miami, and Washington, as well as NFC South opponents Atlanta, Carolina, and New Orleans, in addition to two pre-season games. Tickets for individual games are sold in person at TicketMaster outlets, via

813/287-8844, and by visiting www.ticketmaster.com, not at the stadium or the Bucs' ticket office. Tickets for the 16 regular-season games from September to December are $29 for general admission, one of the lowest ticket prices in the NFL; special seats range from $71 down to $35. The $168.5 million stadium features "Buccaneer Cove," a 20,000-square-foot replica of an early 1800s seaport village, complete with a 103-foot-long pirate ship that blasts its cannons every time the Bucs score.

Raymond James also plays host every New Year's Day to the **Outback Bowl** (Raymond James Stadium, 813/287-8844, 11 A.M. kickoff, $55), the first collegiate bowl game of the year. The game matches the third-pick team from the SEC and the third-pick team from the Big Ten Conference and is the culmination of a week-long festival in Tampa.

USF Bulls

The powers that be at University of South Florida have made a judgment call in the past few years. They want the university to be big league, no longer a workhorse state school with a preponderance of commuting students. They've thrown money into the effort, constructing state-of-the-art academic buildings and housing, hiring prestigious senior faculty and promising junior profs. But maybe the single biggest indicator is the **football team:** The USF Bulls (800/462-8557, game schedule varies, individual tickets $20–24) have gone from nonexistence to Division I-AA Independent, to I-A to Conference USA, and now into the Big East Conference in 2005. For the spectator, this means real college football is played during the fall, also at Raymond James Stadium (4201 N. Dale Mabry Hwy.).

Bulls' **basketball** has also been notched up in recent years, resulting in the team moving to the Big East conference in 2005. Home games are played at the **USF Sun Dome** (4202 E. Fowler Ave., 800/462-8557, tickets $15).

Tampa Bay Storm

The local Tampa Bay Storm arena football team, five-time ArenaBowl champs, plays at the **St. Pete Times Forum** (401 Channelside Dr., 813/301-6600, $12 general admission). Arena football is played on an indoor padded surface 85 feet wide and 50 yards long with eight-yard end zones. There are eight players on the field at a time, and everyone plays both offense and defense, with the exception of the kicker, quarterback, offensive specialist, and two defensive specialists. It's a dynamic game in a more intimate space, and the Storm provides a good introduction to the game, having made it to the playoffs for 14 consecutive seasons.

Tampa Bay Lightning

The 21,000-seat, $153 million **St. Pete Times Forum,** on Tampa's downtown waterfront, is also home to Tampa's professional hockey team, the Tampa Bay Lightning (813/301-6600, game times and prices vary). Stanley Cup champions in 2004, the team is a relative newcomer to the ice. Its season runs October–April.

Spring Training

Tampa is also home to Major League Baseball's **Tampa Bay Devil Rays.** Their first season was 1998. The Devil Rays play at Tropicana Field in St. Petersburg (1 Tropicana Dr., St. Petersburg, 888/326-7297, game days vary, times usually 2:15 or 7:15 P.M., tickets $5–32). As a concession to summer temperatures and humidity in these parts, the ballpark has a dome roof (which is lit orange when the Devil Rays win at home) and artificial turf.

The Devil Rays team is the first major league franchise to train in its home city since 1919, when the St. Louis Cardinals and Philadelphia Athletics trained at home. For spring training, though, the Devil Rays play at **Progress Energy**

Home of the NHL Lightning and arena football league Storm, the St. Pete Times Forum holds nearly 20,000 fans.

Park, Home of Al Lang Field (180 2nd Ave. SE, St. Petersburg, 888/326-7297, $7–19). Spring training games are all month in March, and tickets usually go on sale January 15.

The Grapefruit League's spring training is a serious draw for sports fans in March. Since 1988, the **New York Yankees** have based their minor league operation, spring training, and year-round headquarters for player development in Tampa. Modeled after the original Yankee Stadium in the Bronx, Legends Field (1 Steinbrenner Dr., off N. Dale Mabry, 813/287-8844, $13–19) has been the Yankees' home since 1996. The complex houses a 10,000-seat stadium, a community-use field, and a major league practice field.

Other spring training venues require only a short drive: the Philadelphia Phillies play at Bright House Networks Field in Clearwater; the Boston Red Sox play in City of Palms Park and the Minnesota Twins play at Hammond Stadium, both in Fort Myers; the Toronto Blue Jays play at Knology Park in Dunedin; the Cincinnati Reds play at Ed Smith Stadium in Sarasota; and the Pittsburgh Pirates play at McKechnie Field in Bradenton.

Other Spectator Sports

Spectator sports—this might be broadly interpreted to include **Tampa Greyhound Track** (8300 N. Nebraska Ave., 813/932-4313, www.tampadogs.com, grandstand admission $1

LIGHTNING

Almost nobody is killed by alligators in Tampa. Hardly anyone is even roughed up by them. Surely it's a comfort to find out that lightning is a much more deadly killer in Florida. About 50 people are struck by lightning each year in the state. Most of them are hospitalized and recover, but there are about 10 fatalities annually. And Tampa is the "Lightning Capital" of the U.S. (Rwanda is the lightning capital of the world), with around 25 cloud-to-ground lightning bolt blasts on each square mile annually. The temperature of a single bolt can reach 50,000 degrees Fahrenheit, about three times as hot as the sun's surface.

The problem is the tropical afternoon thunderstorms each summer, about 90 of them electrical storms. Short-lived but intense, the storms' clouds are charged like giant capacitors, the upper portion of the cloud positively charged and the lower portion negatively charged. Then, current flows between the negative cloud bottom and the top or, in the case of cloud-to-ground lightning, the positively charged earth's surface. This discharge of current substantiates the adage "opposites attract," and bolts, sheets, ribbons and, rarely, balls of lightning hit the ground.

There's not much you can do to ward off lightning except to avoid being in the wrong place at the wrong time. The summer months of June, July, August, and September have the highest number of lightning-related injuries and deaths. Usually light-

ning occurs during daylight hours, with the highest concentration between 3 P.M. and 4 P.M., when the afternoon storms peak. Lightning strikes usually occur either at the beginning or end of a storm, and can strike up to 10 miles away from the center of the storm.

Still, most people survive being struck. As long as the electrical surge is not to your brain, you are likely to be treatable. A lightning strike will often singe and burn a person's skin or clothes, but even when the electrical surge stops a victim's heart, emergency rooms have a high success rate of restarting the ticker.

Tips

• Stay vigilant and go inside as soon as clouds darken and thunderstorms develop.

• If the time between seeing the lightning flash and hearing the thunder is less than 30 seconds, take shelter.

• Stay away from the Gulf, pools, lakes, or other bodies of water.

• Avoid using a tree or other tall object as shelter. Lightning usually strikes the tallest object in a given area.

• Stay away from metal objects (bikes, golf carts, fencing are bad, but a car's rubber tires render the automobile's interior a safe retreat).

• The safest place to be during an electrical storm is inside and away from windows and electrical appliances.

Tampa

with free parking) or the sunset Thursday-night sailing races at the **Davis Island Yacht Club** (1315 Severn Ave., 813/251-1158, free to watch, even free to crew for the evening if you have experience and a skipper will take you on). Half the year the greyhound track is a slightly seedy place to see simulcasting and do a little wagering on thoroughbreds, trotters, jai-alai, and lots of stuff that capitalizes on the country's new mania for Texas Hold 'Em and other poker games. But July–December it's live greyhounds bounding after the little bunny. Not surprisingly, Tampa has an enormous and ferocious greyhound adoption program, finding homes for hundreds of retired race dogs. As for the sailing, in the winter the races take place at 2 P.M. on Sunday, but in the warm weather you can watch different classes of sailboats heading out into the bay on Thursday at 7 P.M., with the backdrop of Tampa's downtown bathed in a rosy sunset glow. It's beautiful to watch, especially when all the colorful, billowing spinnakers head out.

CANOEING

You want to see big gators? Great blue herons the size of the Wright brothers' first plane? River otters, turtles, families of wild pigs? Paddle down the gently flowing Hillsborough River in a 16,000-acre wildlife preserve called **Wilderness Park.** You can rent canoes or kayaks and head out on your own, choosing from a variety of trails: Sargeant Park to Morris Bridge Park (4.5 miles); Morris Bridge Park to Trout Creek Park (4 miles); the sunny Trout Creek Park to Rotary Park (5 miles); and others—a trip can be as short as two hours or as long as all day. Or you can take a 3.5-hour interpreted guided tour with **Canoe Escape** (9335 E. Fowler Ave., 0.5 mile east of I-75, 813/986-2067, self-guided tandem canoe or kayak rentals $19.50–27.50, which includes shuttle fee, paddles, and life vests; guided tours $40–90). Whether you go on a guided tour or on your own, call ahead, then drive to their building. Staff will equip you, give you maps and paddling pointers, then take you over to your debarkation point and establish a pickup time.

GOLFING

Tampa has a couple of dozen public and semi-private courses for the visitor to try. Many of them are open to the public but located in Tampa's swankier northeast residential developments. Here are a handful of the area's top public courses:

COURTESY OF TAMPA BAY CONVENTION & VISITOR'S BUREAU

canoeing on the Hillsborough River

Babe Zaharias Golf Club (11412 Forest Hills Dr., 813/932-8932, 18 holes, 6,142 yards, par 70, course rating 68.9, slope 121, greens fee $20–25)

University of South Florida Golf Course (4202 E. Fowler Ave., 813/632-6893, 18 holes, 6,809 yards, par 71, course rating 73.1, slope 131, greens fee $24–38)

Rocky Point Golf Course (4151 Dana Shores Dr., 813/673-4316, 18 holes, 6,444 yards, par 71, course rating 71.7, slope 122, greens fee $25)

Rogers Park Golf Course (7910 N. 30th St., 813/673-4396, 18 holes, 6,593 yards, par 72, course rating 72.3, slope 125, greens fee $24)

Heritage Isles Golf & Country Club (10630 Plantation Bay Dr., 813/907-7447, 18 holes, 6,976 yards, par 72, course rating 73.2, slope 132)

Westchase Golf Course (10307 Radcliffe Dr., 813/854-2331, 18 holes, par 72, 6,710 yards, course rating 71.8, slope 130, greens fee $37–45)

Persimmon Hill Golf Club (5409 E. Chelsea St., 813/620-3557, 9 holes, 1,772 yards, par 29, course rating 29.3, slope 96, greens fee $12)

If you are thinking about picking up the sport, the **Arnold Palmer Golf Academy** at the Saddlebrook Resort (5700 Saddlebrook Way, Wesley Chapel, 800/729-8383) teaches golfers of all skill levels. Classes combine classroom and practice time with course play. The New Player Academy and all their other packages include accommodations, 18 holes of golf a day, instruction, meals, and use of resort facilities. There are two 18-hole Palmer-designed championship courses on the property, as well as 45 tennis courts in the four Grand Slam surfaces (the resort is also home to the **Hopman Tennis Program**).

Just west of Orlando and about 25 miles from Tampa, the **Ben Sutton Golf School** (809 N. Pebble Beach Blvd., Sun City Center, 800/237-8200) was the first American school devoted to golf instruction. There are three-, five-, and seven-day courses.

Sights

MUSEUMS

The current **Tampa Museum of Art** (600 N. Ashley Dr., 813/274-8130, 10 A.M.–5 P.M. Tues.–Sat., 11 A.M.–5 P.M. Sun., until 8 P.M. the third Thurs. of the month, $7 adults, $6 seniors, $3 students and children over 6, children under 6 free) is an attractive waterside center right downtown. The permanent collection comprises 20th-century (there's a tremendous oil by American photorealist Ralph Goings) and contemporary art and a fairly nice assembly of Greek and Roman antiquities. Special exhibitions are usually pretty dynamic yet accessible (wildly hued African-American quilts, lithographic prints and posters of Toulouse-Lautrec), and the museum offers a near-constant array of classes, lectures, seminars, and children's activities. Ground will be broken for a new museum nearby on Ashley Drive in 2005, its completion date uncertain.

Looking regal yet totally out of place with its minarets, keyhole arches, and ornate Moorish revival architecture, the **Henry B. Plant Museum** (401 W. Kennedy Blvd., 813/254-1891, 10 A.M.–4 P.M. Tues.–Sat., noon–4 P.M. Sun., $5 adults, $2 children under 12) is housed in the dramatic hotel railroad baron Henry B. Plant built in 1891 at a cost of $2.5 million, with an additional $500,000 for furnishings. Its 511 rooms were the first in Florida to be outfitted with electricity. It operated as a hotel until 1930 and now houses the University of Tampa. The museum consists of opulent restored rooms with original furnishings that provide a window on America's Gilded Age, Tampa's history, and the life and work of Henry Plant. The best time to see it is at Christmastime, when the rooms are bedecked for the season with elaborately trimmed trees, lush greenery, antique toys, and Victorian-era ornaments.

University of South Florida is an enormous institution, casting its imposing shadow on the cultural scene of Tampa. The visitor, however, may have little reason to walk around the less-

Tampa

than-picturesque campus. A visit to the **University of South Florida Contemporary Art Museum** (4202 E. Fowler Ave., 813/974-2849, 10 A.M.–5 P.M. Mon.–Fri., 1–4 P.M. Sat., free admission) is a good excuse to drive around the university before parking at the small gallery containing a permanent collection of sculpture multiples by artists such as Roy Lichtenstein, Robert Rauschenberg, and James Rosenquist, plus impressive collections of contemporary photography, graphics, and African art. The museum also hosts USF student art shows and oversees sight-specific public art projects on campus.

☒ A WALK ALONG BAYSHORE BOULEVARD

Bayshore Boulevard may or may not be the world's longest continuous sidewalk, but it borders Tampa Bay for nearly five miles without a break in the gorgeousness. Joggers, walkers,

Claimed as the world's longest continuous sidewalk, Bayshore Boulevard borders Tampa Bay for 4.5 miles without a break.

skaters, and bikers dot its length, which goes from downtown through Hyde Park. Home to the fanciest homes in Tampa, the boulevard was named one of AAA's "Top Roads" for its panoramic views. Even if you don't feel like walking it, it's Tampa's most signature drive. (Also, Tampa Preservation has an excellent driving tour of Hyde Park and a walking tour of part of the neighborhood geared for younger readers; for copies call 813/248-5437.)

That's strictly an urban walking experience—for something out in nature, head to **Lettuce Lake Park** (6920 E. Fletcher Ave., near the I-75 exit, 813/987-6204). It contains a 3,500-foot-long boardwalk and a tower on the Hillsborough River, a perfect place from which to spy on tall wading birds and gators lurking in the cypress swamp. You can rent canoes, hike the trails (no dogs on the boardwalks), and bring a picnic. There's a kids' playground as well as barbecue facilities.

BIG CAT RESCUE

The world's largest accredited sanctuary for big cats, Big Cat Rescue provides a permanent retirement home to over 200 animals (12802 Easy St., across from Citrus Park Town Center down a dirt road next to McDonald's, 813/920-4130, www.BigCatRescue.org, regular tours 9 A.M. and 3 P.M. Mon.–Fri., 9:30 A.M., 11:30 A.M., and 1:30 P.M. Sat.; children's tour 9 A.M. Sat.; Wild Eyes at Night tour 8 P.M. the last Fri. of each month; regular tour $20 (for ages 10 and over), children's tour $10, feeding tour $25, Big Cat Expedition $100, cabin rental $100). For the visitor, the center offers tours, outreach presentations, animal interaction, and the opportunity to spend the night in the heart of the sanctuary. On the last Friday of each month, register for the Wild Eyes at Night tour, in which guests roam the grounds equipped with flashlights that illuminate the hundreds of shining eyes in the cat enclosures. Or be a zookeeper for a day with the all-day Big Cat Expedition. You'll get an education in animal husbandry, care, and feeding, and if you plan it for the last Friday of the month you can combine it with the exciting nighttime tour.

BALLOONING

Big Red Balloon Sightseeing Adventures (mailing address 7223 Creekwood Ct., Tampa, FL 33615; meeting place First Watch, 11610 Dale Mabry, 813/969-1518, www.bigredballoon.com, 6–10 A.M. daily, year-round by reservation only, weather permitting, $175 adults, $160 children). Up, up, and away in a beautiful hot-air balloon, and all you have to bring is a camera and your loved ones. Meet before dawn at a restaurant on the commerce strip of Dale Mabry, whereupon you are whisked into the Red Balloon van and taken to your agreed-upon launch site (there are more than 30 in the greater Tampa area from which to choose). Once inflated, the solid red balloon, the largest in the southeastern U.S., is 8.5 stories tall and contains 210,000 cubic feet of air. The balloon, which comfortably accommodates eight passengers, takes a one-hour sunrise flight at up to 1,000 feet, drifting over New Tampa, southeast Pasco County, Lutz, and Land O' Lakes. A champagne toast followed by a hearty breakfast back at First Watch is included in the price.

After landing, there is a champagne toast in the field where the pilot recites a traditional balloonist prayer, "The winds have welcomed you

PASCO COUNTY

Naked bowling. That got your attention. The sleepy, landlocked, mostly residential county to Tampa's north, Pasco County, has at least a day's worth of kooky fun, definitely worth a side trip, a couple of meals, and maybe even an overnight at one of the area's most luscious spa/golf/tennis resorts.

But back to the bowling in the buff. Lake Como Family Nudist Resort in the town of Land O' Lakes is the area's original nudist community, started in 1947. Since then, Pasco County has become a hotbed of naturist activity, with a number of all-ages nudist communities and recreational activities. The question is, if you're wearing rented bowling shoes, are you really nude? You can find out once a month at **Royal Lanes** (1927 Brinson Rd., Land O' Lakes, but call 813/962-8459 to get the nudist dates). Unless you're too chicken.

Another Pasco original requiring a little bit of chutzpah is **Skydive City** (4241 Skydive Ln., off Chancey Rd., 813/783-9399, $175, plus $80 if you want the video documenting your whole experience) in Zephyrhills. The town has been a world-famous "drop zone" since the 1960s, with a world meet (in the trade, it's called a "boogie") in 1972. Why here? According to owner T. K. Hayes, "It's in the middle of nowhere, with not a single picturesque thing about it. It's really about the people—Zephyrhills is the largest skydiving place in the world." Tandem jumping (where a rookie jumps physically harnessed to an instructor) has opened skydiving up to people who never would have had the opportunity—the elderly, the disabled, anyone can do it.

If the bowling flummoxed you, but jumping out of an airplane sounds doable: It takes about an hour to prepare, with a 20 minute briefing. The whole experience is a three- to four-hour adventure, with freefall at 120 mph for about a minute from 13,500 feet, followed by up to six minutes of steering with the parachute open. Hayes says he's never had a student fatality or serious injury (solo students have a higher rate of injury, especially on the landing), very few students lose their lunch, and, he says, "No one comes down and says they wish they'd never done that."

After that, take it down a notch and enjoy a walking tour of downtown **Dade City**. In the rolling hills of eastern Pasco County, the town has more than 50 antiques stores, gift shops, and boutiques. Stop into the historic 1909 Pasco County Courthouse and look at the sweet collection of artifacts from the turn of the 20th century. And then have a slice of history with a slice of pie at **Lunch on Limoges** (14139 7th St., 352/567-5685, $12–16). It's a darling throwback to a former era of refined and leisurely lunching, with a daily-changing menu served on Limoges china by nice old waitresses in nurses' uniforms with sensible orthopedic shoes. Excellent chocolate cake, but I don't like that they have a fairly steep "minimum order" to dine here.

(continued on next page)

Tampa

PASCO COUNTY (cont'd)

Not far from downtown and worth maybe an hour, **The Pioneer Florida Museum** (15602 Pioneer Museum Rd., 352/567-0262, www.pioneerfloridamuseum.org, 1–5 P.M. Tues.–Fri. and Sun., 10 A.M.–5 P.M. Sat., $5 adults, $4 seniors) consists of nine period buildings dating back to 1878. There's the John Overstreet House, the Lacoochee School, and the Enterprise Methodist Church, all displaying period furniture, clothing, toys, tools. There's also a spooky collection of miniature big-eyed dolls of Florida's first ladies. The museum has good raw material, but it should spend a chunk of volunteer hours redoing some of their signage, which looks a little tired. There often isn't quite enough explanation of what we're looking at—in a historical museum, signs so often tell the story.

After your visit in Dade City, climb aboard a converted, camouflaged former school bus called a "range buggy" at **J.B. Starkey's Flatwoods Adventures** (12959 Hwy. 54, nine miles west of U.S. 41, Odessa, 813/926-1133, www.flatwoodsadventures.com, $15.75 adults, $14.75 seniors, $8.75 children). You bump across pine flatwoods and pasture land while a guide (ours was Carol, the Audubon Society president in Pasco County) reveals a wealth of cool facts about the area's flora, fauna, and history. You'll see Cracker cows, gators, and lots of other animals (a Cuban tree frog jumped on my daughter's leg and scared the pants off her) on the 90-minute tour while learning about the area's Native Americans and early settlers like the cattle-ranching Starkey family. Bring bug spray.

If there's time, take a tour around **New Port Richey's Main Street** (www.newportricheymainstreet.com, tours 9 A.M.–noon) and then board a boat and ride the **Pithlachascottee River** to see historic homes once owned by Gloria Swanson, Thomas Meighan, and Babe Ruth. Then walk around **Centennial Cultural Park,** which contains the Pasco Fine Arts Council, the Centennial Library, and the 1882 Baker House, one of the oldest structures in Pasco County. If you're hungry, stop in at waterside **Catches** (7811 Bayview St., 727/849-2121).

If you're thinking about bedtime now, **Saddlebrook Resort & Spa** (5700 Saddlebrook Way, 800/729-8383, $300–600) is really Tampa's nicest four-star resort hotel, only it's in the sleepy Pasco town of Wesley Chapel. It has 800 guest rooms, all gorgeous, pools, tennis, the Palmer and the Saddlebrook golf courses (and the Arnold Palmer Golf Academy), and a variety of dining options (if you eat on the patio of the Cypress Restaurant you can see nesting wood storks). If this is too rich for your blood, **Azalea House** (37719 Meridian Ave., 352/523-1773, $65–79) is a sweet bed-and-breakfast with just a few rooms in Dade City.

For more information about Pasco County, visit www.visitpasco.net.

---

with softness, the sun has left you with warm hands, you have flown so high, and so well, that God has joined you in your laughter, and set you gently back again into the loving arms of Mother Earth." Feel free to join in.

N YBOR CITY

Cigars died out along with the men who looked most at home with a stogie—Winston Churchill, W. C. Fields, etc. But Demi Moore brought them back. Or maybe it was Linda Evangelista. Really it was when Marvin Shanken, of *Wine Spectator* fame, trotted out *Cigar Aficionado* in the early 1990s that cigar smoking had a new renaissance, and supermodels and movie stars started puffing with reckless abandon.

It was too late for Ybor City (pronounced "EEE-bore"). Cigarmakers Vicente Martinez-Ybor and Ignacio Haya moved their cigar factories from Key West to Tampa in 1886, essentially settling 40 acres of uninviting scrubland northeast of the city. A railroad, a port, and a climate that acted as a natural humidor for the product—Tampa had all the ingredients for cigar success. Soon other cigar factories joined suit until there were 140 cigar factories in the area producing 250 million cigars a year. The new

COURTESY OF VISIT FLORIDA

Ybor City is one of only three National Historic Landmark Districts located in Florida, but that doesn't make anyone overly reverential. It's still a party place.

"Cigar Capital of the World" became home to Cuban, Spanish, and Italian immigrants who worked the factories. These workers would hand-roll several kinds of tobacco into the signature shapes and sizes while listening to "lectors" read aloud great works of literature and the day's news. (For a window into this world, read Nilo Cruz's Pulitzer Prize–winning drama, *Anna in the Tropics*, which depicts a Cuban-American family of cigar makers in Ybor City in 1930.)

The area flourished until the early 1960s, when embargos against Cuban tobacco and declining cigar consumption caused the market to dry up. Today Ybor City is one of only three National Historic Landmark Districts in Florida, with red brick streets, wrought-iron balconies, and old-timey globe streetlamps.

During the day visitors can still see cigars being hand-rolled and munch a Cuban sandwich, while at night Ybor is the city's nightlife district, drawing 40,000 visitors on weekends to dine at sidewalk cafés and drink and dance at nightclubs. Whether you explore during the day or at night, park your car in one of the many parking lots or garages (metered parking is strictly enforced 24

hours) and walk around or take the Ybor City trolley. You can still see little cigar shops and Latin social clubs mixed in with tattoo parlors and restaurants along La Setima (7th Ave.).

The **Ybor City Museum State Park** (1818 E. 9th Ave., 813/247-6323, www.floridastateparks.org, 9 A.M.–5 P.M. daily, $3 adults, children under 6 free) contains photographs, cigar boxes, and other artifacts of the neighborhood's rich history. The museum also offers walking tours on Saturday mornings at 10:30 A.M. ($6, including museum admission) and cigar-rolling demonstrations. Another book, *The Immigrant World of Ybor City: Italians and Their Latin Neighbors in Tampa, 1885–1985* (Florida Sand Dollar Book), by Gary Mormino and George E. Pozzetta, University Press of Florida, September 1, 1998, $17.95, is a wealth of information. Oh, and there's another good one called *Urban Vigilantes in the New South: Tampa, Florida 1886–1936,* (Florida Sand Dollar Book) by Robert P. Ingalls, University Press of Florida, reprint edition, August 1, 1993, $24.95.

But still, you may get a more three-dimensional look at Ybor just by walking around: Walk by La Union Marti-Maceo mural (226 7th Ave.), pick up a copy of *La Gaceta* (the neighborhood's Spanish-language weekly for the past 75 years), and walk by the restored former cigar workers casitas on your way to buy a cigar at **Metropolitan Cigars** (2014 E. 7th Ave., 813/248-3304), a 1,700-square-foot walk-in humidor, or to get a Cubano sandwich.

The Cubano

In Tampa, the Cuban is the king of sandwiches, or should I say the earl of sandwiches. It starts with the bread. If you've eaten anywhere in Ybor City, you've probably eaten Cuban bread. But why not go to the source? Rumor has it **La Segunda Central Bakery** (2512 N. 15th St., 813/248-1531) churns out 6,000 Cuban loaves daily.

You only need one loaf, in the form of the archetypal Cubano sandwich. The loaves themselves are about 36 inches long, with a zipper-like seam down the top. The third-generation owners of La Segunda have reason to be proud of their thin, flaky crust and their soft, pillowy interior, even more so when

Tampa

CIGAR BASICS

Want to try a cigar but don't know the first thing? Tampa's a good place to begin. Even before you light up, a cigar's visual specifications can give clues to its character. The outer wrapper's color indicates a great deal about a cigar's flavor. A "maduro" wrapper is a rich, deep brown, imparting a cigar with deep, unctuous flavors. A "claro" wrapper, on the other hand, is a light tan and lends little additional flavor to a cigar. There are essentially six color grades. Roughly from lightest to darkest, these are: candela (pale green), claro, natural (light brown), colorado (reddish brown), maduro, and oscuro (almost black).

Shape is another central factor in cigar selection. Among "parejos" or straight-sided cigars, there are three basic categories. A corona is classically six inches long, with an open foot (the end that is lighted) and a closed head (the end that is smoked). Within this category, Churchills are a bit longer and thicker, robustos are shorter and much thicker, and a double corona is significantly longer. Panetelas, the second category, are longer and much thinner than coronas, and the third category, lonsdales, are thicker than panetelas and thinner and longer than coronas.

"Figurados" comprise the other class of cigar, which spans all of the irregularly shaped types. This includes torpedo shapes, braided "culebras," and pyramid shapes that have a closed, pointed head and an open foot.

A cigar band is generally wrapped around the closed head of a cigar. Its original function was to minimize finger staining, not to identify brands. Nonetheless, on the band you will find the name a manufacturer has designated for a particular line of cigars—names like Partagas, Macanudo, Punch, and Montecristo. Keep in mind that after 1959, many cigar manufacturers fled Cuba to open shop elsewhere, taking their brand names with them. Thus, a brand name does not always betray a cigar's country of origin.

For neophytes lighting up for the first time, a milder cigar may ease you in. The Macanudo Hyde Park is a mild smoke, as is the Don Diego Playboy Robusto or Lonsdale. For a fuller-bodied cigar, the Punch Diademas and the Partagas Number 10 are both popular. If you're looking for a robust, ultra full-bodied taste, you might try the Hoyo de Monterrey Double Corona. The best way to discover your own personal tastes is to stop into a fine tobacconist or cigar-friendly restaurant and have a chat.

---

piled high with roast pork and Genoa salami (a strictly Tampa twist), Swiss cheese (some say Emanthaler), sour pickles, and spicy mustard—the whole thing warmed and flattened in a special hot-press. Outside crisp, inside warm and a little gooey. It's perfection.

Arts and Entertainment

PERFORMING ARTS

Just about the only game in town for performing arts is the **Tampa Bay Performing Arts Center** (1010 N. W.C. MacInnes Pl., one block off Ashley St., 813/229-7827 or 800/955-1045, www.tbpac.org, times and ticket prices vary). It's a huge arts complex housing four distinct theaters, in which audiences can see Opera Tampa (the resident company), the Florida Orchestra, comedies, dramas, cabaret, dance, music, alternative theater, children's theater, and an annual Broadway series. Most local arts series and events find a home at the performing arts center—Arte 2005, Tampa Bay's Festival of Latin American art, Patel Conservatory's Tampa Bay Youth Orchestra Spring Concert—you name it, the curtain goes up here.

Maybe it's not the only game in town after all. In 2004 Tampa welcomed the brand-new **Ford Amphitheatre** (4802 U.S. 301 N, 813/740-2446, times and ticket prices vary), a state-of-the-art venue for 30–40 big-league music concerts a year. At an expense of $23 million, the outdoor open-air theater was constructed with huge video screens, a 7,200-square-foot stage, 9,900 reserved seats and room for 10,500 more on the lawn. It's gorgeous, like a huge circus tent mated with the Millennium Falcon. There are enough bathrooms and lots of fairly tasty food options.

But I'm leading up to a big gripe, and it's not really the amphitheater's fault. The idea was that it would host the myriad big-ticket acts that travel around the U.S. each year—Dave Matthews, Tim McGraw, or all those endless tours of Chicago or Earth, Wind and Fire. That's all fine and good, but the problem is that all those big acts gear up to do outdoor stadium and amphitheater shows in *the summer*. You do not want to go to an all-day Oz Fest show in Tampa in the middle of July. You could hurt something. The venue literature sports all this talk about how the plastic cover on top shields the amphitheater from the sun and keeps it cool. No dice. Get 10,000 sweaty bodies grooving to Jimmy Buffet in 90° heat at 90 percent humidity, and someone's going to pass out.

 TAMPA THEATRE

Tampa has its share of multiplexes, but eschew the 20-screeners in favor of two hours in the dark at the Tampa Theatre (711 Franklin St., 813/274-8981, www.tampatheatre.org, times vary, $8). Built in 1926, it's a beloved downtown landmark with an acclaimed film series, concerts (Elvis Costello, Steve Vai, Bright Eyes, it's a wide range), special events, and backstage tours. They say the grand motion picture palace's decor is something called Florida Mediterranean, but to me it's vintage creepy rococo, with statues and gargoyles and intricately carved doors. Speaking of creepiness, many believe that the theater is haunted by the ghost of Foster Finley, who spent 20 years as the theater's projectionist. So if you feel a hand in your popcorn, it may not be your seatmate's. Sometimes the films shown are classics, complete with Wurlitzer, other times it's more indie; look online at the schedule. Theater concessions include excellent popcorn, sophis-

ticated candies, and beer and wine. Interesting fact: It was the first public building in Tampa to be equipped with air-conditioning.

FESTIVALS

The biggest party in Tampa comes at the beginning of February with the **Gasparilla Pirate Fest,** a kooky celebration over 100 years old in honor of legendary pirate Jose Gaspar, "last of the Buccaneers," who terrorized the coastal waters of West Florida during the late 18th and early 19th centuries. The weekend festivities get underway when 1,000 ersatz pirates sail into downtown on a fully rigged pirate ship, a replica of an 18th-century craft that is 165 feet long by 35 feet across the beam, with three masts standing 100 feet tall. The ship is met by a flotilla of hundreds of pleasure crafts intent on "defending the city." The upshot is that pirates take over Tampa for a while, like Mardi Gras, only with more "argh, me matey" and eye patches accompanying the beads and buried treasure. The length of Bayshore Boulevard is lined with bleachers for the occasion, musical acts sprout on stages all over town, and there's general merriment and carousing.

Hundreds of thousands of parade-goers line Bayshore Boulevard and downtown for the annual Gasparilla Pirate Fest, the 102nd in 2006.

CRUISING

The Port of Tampa is said to be the fastest-growing cruise port in North America, with a passenger count going from 200,000 in 1998 to more than a million in the past couple of years. Cruise lines evidently beget cruise lines, with newer and larger vessels steaming into the downtown Channelside port all the time. It started with Carnival and Holland America cruise lines back in 1994, but these days a number of lines head out of Tampa on 4-, 5-, 7-, 10-, 11-, and 14-day itineraries.

It's **Carnival Cruise Lines'** busiest port, with the 2,600-passenger *Sensation,* the tallest ship to ever sail from the Port of Tampa; the smaller *Jubilee;* the newer *Inspiration,* which takes "Fun Ship" cruises to the Western Caribbean and New Orleans; and the *Miracle,* which goes on 7-day Caribbean cruises to Grand Cayman, Costa Maya, Cozumel, and Belize.

Holland America has been sailing seasonally from Tampa for more than 20 years, with the 1,600-passenger *Veendam,* which sails seasonally from Tampa to Key West, Jamaica, and Mexico. **Celebrity Cruises** has the *Zenith,* with 7-day cruises to Key West, Grand Cayman, Cozumel, Costa Maya, and Georgetown, and the *Horizon,* with seasonal 7-day cruises to Key West and the Western Caribbean. **Royal Caribbean International,** the parent company of Celebrity Cruises, recently began sailing 7-night cruises to the Western Caribbean from Tampa on the 1,800-passenger *Nordic Empress.* And most recently the *Radisson Seven Seas Navigator* joined the fleet.

Parking at the cruise terminal is $10 per day. The parking area is patrolled and no reservations are needed. For directions to cruise terminals call 813/272-0558.

Later in the month of February there's the more county fair–like **Plant City Strawberry Festival,** with a huge midway and lots of strawberry cookoffs. Plant City is known as the "Winter Strawberry Capital of the World," and these sweet babies are delicious.

The second biggest party is not unlike Gasparilla for its focus on wild costumes and wilder revelry. **Guavaween** is the city's Cuban-style Halloween celebration, held October 30. Riffing on the fact that Tampa was nicknamed "The Big Guava," the celebration features the Mama Guava, who has sworn to take the "bore" out of Ybor (EE-bore) City. Really, after the parade is over, it's a big excuse to drink too much and wander the streets of Ybor City in preposterous attire.

FOR KIDS

Of all the Gulf Coast cities, Tampa has the most lavish smorgasbord of kid-friendly attractions. This probably reflects the demographics of Tampa in recent years—it's a family town, wherein weekends are devoted, after Little League/soccer games/getting the car washed, to multigenerational outings to Busch Gardens, Adventure Island, the zoo, the aquarium, or the area's many sporting events.

Busch Gardens

Rides for Little Kids: Some people swear by the Myers-Briggs Type Indicator. Psychologists use the 16 PF to determine personality type. I think it all comes down to this: There are two personality types—those who ride the rides, and those who stay on the ground and hold the cotton candy for those who ride the rides. Using Skinnerian methods, I am trying to ensure that my child is the first type.

Busch Gardens is right there with me. The amusement park has a huge section of the park geared to children 2–7 years old (in a Dragon-centric part of the park to the far left when you're looking at the map, near **Stanleyville,** as well as in sections near the **Congo** and in **Timbuktu**). This is one of the biggest parks I've seen where there are those vexing height limitations that preclude you from riding if you're *taller* than the marker.

And therein lies a slight conceptual flaw. Hyping it fiendishly for days, parents bring their toddlers for their first taste of the intoxicating chills and thrills of the midway—mini tilt-a-whirls, little roller coasters, real training-wheels rides. The children are strapped in by the flat-lining teens who work Busch Gardens, and then the terror sets in. Some scream, others go dead white with their lips flattened in a grim look of determination. Parents stand on the ground, waving furiously and shouting encouragements while the children persevere, around and around. Is it torture? You be the judge.

I have advice. Drawing on the microscopic amount I know about developmental psychology, I say use modeling, to show *your* enthusiasm for the rides in order to sway them. Show them how to squeal on the vertical-lift rides, how to make catcalls to the folks down below you on the boring rides, and let them in on the unbridled joy of screaming really loudly while waving your arms in the air. They can hold the cotton candy while they watch you ride the big kid rides.

Rides for Big Kids: Major coasters are the biggest draw for those over 48 inches tall (for Montu and Kumba it's 54 inches) and with no serious health problems. The rides at Busch Gardens are either little-kiddie or pee-your-pants huge. The roller coasters, in descending order of excellence: The **Montu** at the far right of the park is one of the tallest and longest inverted roller coasters in the world. You are strapped in from above, so your feet dangle while you travel at 60 mph through 60-foot vertical loops and stuff. **Kumba** is second-best, with a full three seconds of weightlessness, an initial 135-foot drop, some cool 360-degree spirals. Good speed, long ride, one of the world's largest vertical loops. The **Python** has a double spiraling corkscrew and gut-lurching 70-foot plunge, but it's too short a ride, over in seconds. The **Scorpion** has some good 360s, fast speeds, but again too short. And the **Gwazi** is for purists—an old double wooden coaster, it's got that tooth-rattling charm as it barrels over the boards in 7,000 feet of track. By the time this is published, the park will have opened **SheiKra,** the nation's first dive coaster, which looks killer, with a 138-foot drop through

an underground tunnel, a water feature, and hurtling toward the ground at 70 mph at a 90-degree angle. Can't wait.

Beyond the coasters, the **Tidal Wave, Stanley Falls,** and **Congo River Rapids** boat ride are guaranteed to fully saturate you with water—so time them for the hottest part of the day and not right before you go see the modestly amusing 3-D movie called *R.L. Stine's Haunted Lighthouse.*

Animal Attractions: Busch Gardens contains something like 2,700 animals. Colorful lorikeets will land on your shoulder or flirt shamelessly with you in the aviary called **Lory Landing,** there's a **Birds of Prey** show, but the best animal attraction is the **Serengeti Plain,** which really takes up the whole right half of the park—you see it all by getting on the Serengeti Express Railway (or the Skyride or a Serengeti Safari). Ostriches may race the train, there are big cats and huffing rhinos. It's thrilling *and* a wonderful opportunity to sit down a spell and regroup. (The lamest attraction at the park, though, is **Rhino Rally.** Don't bother.)

The Details: Busch Gardens is expensive ($55.95 adults for the day, $45.95 children 3–9, children 2 and under free), so is it worth it? Definitely. It is a wonderful full-day extravaganza for people of any age (if you don't like rides, go to "Beer School," where you listen to some guy talk for a while about hops before you get free samples). Busch Gardens can entertain you for a full two days, but if you do just one day everyone will be clamoring for more. A 14-day 5 Park Orlando FlexTicket ($224.95 adults, $189.95 kids) is a fairly good deal if you have the stamina to hit SeaWorld Orlando, Universal Studios Florida, Universal Studios Islands of Adventure, and Wet'n Wild along with Busch Gardens.

Hours change seasonally: In the winter it's generally open 9:30 A.M.–6 P.M. daily; in the summer 9 A.M.–10 P.M. daily. If you visit in the summer, count on heavy rains in the afternoon. Bathrooms are plentiful and clean, there are scads of strollers to rent, the food is much better than it needs to be (a new Zambia Smokehouse serves good ribs and chicken), and there's even have a dog kennel to watch your pet while you enjoy the park. The park (888/800-5447,

Tampa

www.buschgardens.com/buschgardens/fla/) is at the corner of Busch Boulevard and 40th Street, eight miles northeast of downtown Tampa. Parking is an irksome additional $7, with a free shuttle that takes you from the 5,000-spot parking lot to the park's entrance.

Florida Aquarium

They've tried to gussy up this aquarium recently with outdoor water play areas and such, but the Florida Aquarium (701 Channelside Dr., 813/273-4000; www.flaquarium.org, 9:30 A.M.– 5 P.M. daily, $15.95 adults, $13.95 seniors, $10.95 children under 12) doesn't want for anything, in my opinion. Opened in 1995, the 152,000-square-foot aquarium is smart, focusing on the waters of Florida. It doesn't contain an exhaustive catalog of the world's aquatic creatures, but it tells a very compelling story about Florida's relationship to the Gulf, estuaries, rivers, and other waterways. There are some exotic exhibits (the otherworldly sea dragons, like seahorses mated with philodendrons), but the best parts are the open freshwater tanks of otters, spoonbills, gators, Florida softshell turtles, and snakes. The aquarium manages to have a very strong environmental message in its natives-versus-exotics exhibits, but it's all fun, never seeming pious or heavy-handed. There's also a wonderful big shark tank, a colorful coral grotto, and a sea-urchin touch tank. It's a small enough aquarium that three hours is plenty of time, and not so crowded that kids can't do a little wandering on their own. Regularly scheduled shows involve native Florida birds and small mammals, as well as shark feeding (in fact, the aquarium offers "swim with the fishes" wetsuit dives into the shark tank for the stalwart).

After perusing the marinelife within the eye-catching shell-shaped building, you can take your newfound knowledge out on the bay with one of the aquarium-run **Dolphin Quest Eco-Tours** ($18.95 adults, $17.95 seniors, $13.95 children under 12). Tickets are available at the aquarium box office the day of the tour only, when you'll head out in a 64-foot, 49-passenger Caribbean catamaran, watching all the while for dolphins, manatees, and a huge number of migratory birds.

MOSI

You spent a day riding the rides at Busch Gardens, then a day with the fishes at the aquarium,

The Florida Aquarium was essentially designed "from the inside out," with the interior's experience informing the architectural shell.

next what? The third day is Tampa's **Museum of Science & Industry** (4801 E. Fowler Ave., 813/987-6300, 9 A.M.–5 P.M. Mon.–Fri., 9 A.M.–7 P.M. Sat. and Sun., $19.95 adults, $18.95 seniors, $17.95 children 2–12), a wonderful resource for local schools, family vacationers, or local parents when they're just out of bullets (not literally). It's a sprawling modern structure that contains 450 hands-on activities grouped into learning areas. There's some goofy stuff (the "Gulf Coast Hurricane Chamber," which really just blows a bunch of loud air), but ignore that and head to the High Wire Bicycle, the longest high-wire bike in a museum, which allows visitors to pedal while balanced on a one-inch steel cable suspended 30 feet above ground. The exhibit "The Amazing You" teaches all about the human body. The museum has an IMAX dome and hosts traveling exhibits as well. The center hosted a compelling Titanic exhibit recently that actually mirrored the experience of riding the ship (you assume the identity of a passenger and then find out if you lived or died), and currently has a huge exhibit called **SPACE: A Journey to our Future** that's nearly as good. If you time your visit to allow some cooler temperatures, the free-flying butterfly garden is a treat, with microscope viewing, magnifying glasses, and chemistry stations.

Lowry Park Zoo

I almost hesitate to voice my preference for mid-size zoos like this, lest animal rights zealots hunt me down like an unspayed pooch. The San Diego and San Francisco zoos are fine, with their wide-open spaces and generously configured habitats. But sometimes going to them is like going to a Rolling Stones concert: That speck in the distance may be a hamadryas baboon or it may be Mick Jagger, there's no telling. Little kids don't know from habitats, they just want to see the animals up close and personal. With lots of space at their disposal at zoos like that, the big cats can pull a no-show with other animals coyly revealing only a tail or an ear in the deep grass.

At the Lowry Park Zoo (1101 W. Sligh Ave., 813/932-0245, www.lowryparkzoo.com, 9:30 A.M.– 5 P.M. daily, $14.95 adults, $13.95

seniors, $10.50 children 3–11), habitats are naturalistic and nicely landscaped, but they are still designed for maximum viewing. All told there are around 1,500 native and exotic animals, organized into sensible housing developments (Wallaroo Station, African Veldt). Lots of shade provided by big lush tropicals seems to keep all species fat and sassy, even in the fairly substantial summer heat. One of the zoo's highlights is its Manatee and Aquatic Center, one of only three hospitals and rehabilitation facilities in the state of Florida for lugubrious sick sea cows.

Adventure Island

Adjacent to Busch Gardens but only open March–October is Adventure Island (4500 Bougainvillea Ave., 813/987-5660, hours and days vary, $32.95, $30.95 children 3–9, children 2 and under free; if you buy a ticket to Busch Gardens, you can combine it with a ticket here for a discount). This park will wet your whistle, and pretty much everything else. It's a 30-acre water park, with slides, corkscrews, waterfalls, a monstrous 17,000-square-foot wave pool, and a child's play area. There are 50 lifeguards on duty, but it's still only appropriate for the truly water-safe. There's also a championship white-sand volleyball complex.

Malibu Grand Prix

If they've been really, really good, take them to Malibu Grand Prix (14320 N. Nebraska Ave., 813/977-6272, 11 A.M.–10 P.M. daily, $5–12, depending on the activity). It's got killer mini golf with lots of windmills, pagodas, and water play, Grand Prix-style go-cart racing, batting cages, and a frenetic game room that features that interactive dance video game on which even good dancers look spastic (a fun spectator sport).

Kid City

Very young children will be more suited to an afternoon at Kid City (7550 North Blvd., 813/935-8441, 9 A.M.–2 P.M. Mon., 9 A.M.– 5 P.M. Tues.–Fri., 10 A.M.–5 P.M. Sat., noon– 5 P.M. Sun., $5). In kind of a miniature outdoor city, it has 16 exhibit buildings with hands-on exhibits about different kinds of work (a

Tampa

firehouse, a bank, a grocery store, etc.) and their necessary skills. Find out what you should be when you grow up.

Dinosaur World

If your progeny are dinosaur-obsessed, it is your duty to get in the car and drive about a half hour east of Tampa to an otherwise agricultural town called Plant City. It is the strawberry capital of the state, but among the strawberry fields lurks Dinosaur World (5145 Harvey Tew Rd., Plant City, 813/717-9865, 9 A.M.–6 P.M. daily, $9.75 adults, $8.95 seniors, $7.75 children

3–12, children 2 and under free). There are 160 huge models of prehistoric beasts arrayed in a huge subtropical garden. Having recently spent time in the dinosaur exhibit at the Museum of Natural History in New York, I have a sneaking suspicion that Dinosaur World isn't preoccupied with strict accuracy (for instance, we don't really know about dinosaur coloring, but these ones are all the mottled greeny-brown made popular in movies). In addition to the dinos, there are spooky fake caves to explore and an archaeological dig/sandbox area. This is best for kids under 7.

Accommodations

Tampa's hotel scene is stymied by one thing: Tampa has no beaches. Although it's on the water—with the active Port of Tampa and waterside residential communities like Davis and Harbour Islands—there is no possibility for a luxury resort hotel or charming bed-and-breakfast just steps from the waters of Hillsborough Bay. For that kind of experience you must head over the bay to St. Pete or Clearwater.

Still, Tampa has a preponderance of pleasant, fairly priced accommodations, spread around the greater Bay Area, from the Latin Quarter of Ybor City to the Westshore business district or the Tampa Convention Center, to near Busch Gardens and the University of South Florida.

UNDER $50

For when you're looking for a wild experience at a tame price, **Gram's Place** (3109 N. Ola Ave., 813/221-0596, www.grams-inn-tampa.com, hostel rates $19–23, room rates $55–95) in Ybor City will surely fit the bill. It's eccentric, with a different music theme (jazz, blues, rock) in each of the private suites and youth hostel-style bunks. All rooms come with a "music menu" of CDs. The hostel part looks like a railroad car fashioned around a 100-year-old train depot. The rooms are set in two circa 1945 cottages and share an oversized in-ground Jacuzzi, a BYOB bar in the courtyard, and a 16 multitrack record-

ing studio. Lest you are imagining some cool old Grandma jamming in the recording studio with a bunch of longhairs, the "Gram" in question is Gram Parsons, once member of the Byrds and the Flying Burrito Brothers, the deceased musician responsible for that heartbreakingly beautiful song, "Grievous Angel" that Emmylou Harris made famous.

$50–150

For a different kind of experience in Ybor City, head to the historic **M Don Vicente de Ybor Historic Inn** (1915 Republica de Cuba, 813/241-4545, $129–159), constructed in 1895 by Cuban patriot Vicente Martinez Ybor. The boutique hotel's 16 guest rooms contain genteel flourishes like four-poster beds but also offer broadband, voicemail, and in-room desks. Even if you don't stay here, the opulent grand salon is worth peeking at.

If you want to stay near USF or Busch Gardens and MOSI, there are a handful of reasonably priced chains. **Days Inn** (2904 Melbourne Blvd., 813/623-3591, $50–70, $129–155 for suites) is adjacent to Busch Gardens' entrance, with 130 nicely appointed rooms with roomy bathrooms, good lighting, large desks, and computer-friendly dataport telephones. There's also a good-sized pool. The USF hotel of choice is **Embasssy Suites** (3705 Spectrum Blvd.,

813/977-7066, $129–209) across the road. It's a tall, suites-only hotel with a soaring atrium. Rooms are pretty, with spacious living rooms and private bedrooms with either a king or two double beds. There are two TVs in every room, a weird superabundance, but nice if the kids want to watch something execrable in the next room. Although the rooms are a little more, included in the price is a very nice daily cooked-to-order breakfast buffet and the manager's reception, where you get a free cocktail and some chips in the early evening.

If you prefer independently owned hotels, the **Tahitian Inn** (601 S. Dale Mabry Hwy., 813/877-6721, $99–209) is a lovely two-story family-run motel that had a huge remodel in 2003, yielding 60 Tahitian-theme (dark wood, tropical accessories) moderately priced rooms and 20 executive suites, a lovely pool with tiki huts and hammocks, and the Serenity Spa with massage and Tahitian hot stone treatments. There's also a lovely little on-site café with patio seating near a koi pond. The location is close to I-275 and lots of commerce.

Numerous hotels cluster along Rocky Point Drive and Cypress Street, just a couple of minutes from the airport, Westshore business district, and Tampa Convention Center. These hotels have lots of business amenities and often offer significantly cheaper rates on the weekend. Of the chains, there's **DoubleTree Hotel Tampa Airport Westshore** (4500 W. Cypress St., 813/879-4800, www.tampadoubletree.com, $109–199 weekdays, $99–139 weekends), **Courtyard by Marriott Tampa Westshore** (3805 W. Cypress St., 813/874-0555, $139–199), the **Holiday Inn Express and Suites Rocky Point** (3025 N. Rocky Point Dr., 813/287-8585 $100–130), among many others, all with water views of the bay and with pools and other allures.

For a more independent approach in the same location, try **Sailport Waterfront Suites** (2506 N. Rocky Point Dr., 813/281-9599), a four-story, all-suites hotel (all rooms have a queen sleeper sofa in the living room, convenient for families) with full-sized kitchens, barbecue grills, outdoor heated pool, lighted tennis court, and fishing pier.

OVER $150

A little pricier, the **Grand Hyatt** (2900 Bayport Dr., 813/874-1234, www.grandtampabay .hyatt.com, $225–320) is another big hotel near the airport that caters mainly to the corporate traveler. There are 445 deluxe guest rooms and suites, including 38 Spanish-style casita rooms and 7 casita suites in a secluded area at the south end of the property, which is set in a 35-acre wildlife preserve on the shores of Tampa Bay. The Hyatt contains two of the best restaurants in town, Armani's and Oystercatchers.

The Weirdest Hotel in Tampa Award goes to **Seminole Hard Rock Hotel And Casino** (5223 Orient Rd., www.hardrockhotel-casinotampa.com, $169–250). This huge luminous purple tower rises up in the middle of nowhere off of I-75 (well, it's not totally in the middle of nowhere, as the Ford Amphitheatre just opened across the highway from it) like a mirage. With an illuminated 12-story tower that shifts colors, the signature huge guitar at the entrance, a 90,000-square-foot casino, and a see-and-be-seen restaurant/bar called Floyd's, it's like a little piece of Vegas right here in Tampa. The complex opened in March 2004, and it's been swamped with casino and overnight guests. The 250 guest rooms and suites have a hipster art deco design, with unique extras like Tivoli stereo and CD systems and ultraluxury beds. The most luxurious part is the pool area, with cascading fountains and cool private cabanas with televisions and refrigerators.

Tampa's newest luxury hotel is the **Renaissance Tampa Hotel International Plaza** (4200 Jim Walter Blvd., 813/877-9200, $259–334) near the Westshore business district at the International Plaza mall. The lush decor is reminiscent of a Mediterranean villa, an illusion bolstered by things like the complimentary olive bar and the jewel-toned, high-style Pelagia Trattoria at its center. The hotel's not small—with 293 guest rooms on eight floors—but the service is personal and attentive, and it seems especially geared to the repeat-business, high-end business traveler.

Food

Maybe it's Tampa residents' deep streak of loyalty, maybe their plodding constancy, but marketing geniuses have determined that Tampa is the perfect test market for new chain restaurant concepts. They are trotted out here, and if they fly, launched upon the rest of the country. For this reason, Tampa is the home base of numerous national and regional chains—Hooters, Durango Steakhouse, Beef O' Brady's, Checkers, Hops Restaurant Bar and Brewery, Shells' Seafood Restaurant, Carrabba's, and Outback Steakhouse. (Outback is also the diabolical mastermind behind newish chains Lee Roy Selmon's, Fleming's Prime Steakhouse, Bonefish Grill, and Roy's.)

You will find more Chili's, Macaroni Grills, T.G.I. Friday's, and Bennigans restaurants than you could possibly patronize. For this reason, only the unique, discrete, more-or-less independently owned restaurants that are the exception to the rule in Tampa are covered here.

HYDE PARK

This is the glamorous, old-money part of town, the part of town where everyone knows the correct pronunciation of bruschetta (it's "bru-SKEH-tah," just so you can blend) and can tell lima beans from edamame at 10 paces. If there are foodies in Tampa, they are in Hyde Park. It's a historical residential district, serviced by the Old Hyde Park Village of upscale shops and the long stretch of South Howard Avenue, or SoHo, where the good restaurants are:

Asian

Picking out just a handful along "Restaurant Row" is difficult. For casual dining, **Ⓜ Water, Unique Sushi** (1015 1/2 S. Howard Ave., 813/251-8406, $8–9) was one of the most celebrated openings of 2004, a savvy Japanese-inspired seafood joint showcasing the work of young Culinary Institute of America graduate Erin Van Zandt. A late-night hangout for the neighborhood's beautiful people, Water specializes in rice-paper rolled sushi (no nori) paired with punchy sauces and dynamic side dishes. A minimalist design aesthetic and a no-reservations policy cannot douse the enthusiasm for vibrant combos like unagi, banana, and avocado. Its sister restaurant next door, **Ciccio & Tony's,** is also a favorite around here for thin-crust pizzas and California-style wraps.

TC Choy Asian Bistro (301 S. Howard Ave., 813/251-1191, 11:30 A.M.–2:30 P.M. and 5:30–10 P.M. Mon.–Thurs., until 11 P.M. Fri., 11 A.M.–3 P.M. and 5:30–11 P.M. Sat. and Sun., $6–15) serves fairly authentic Cantonese cuisine and noonday dim sum (and a competent assortment of other pan-Asian dishes) in a chic, airy space with big tables perfect for large parties.

Spanish

If you're in the mood for Spanish tapas, Hyde Park has two laudable purveyors. **Sangria's Spanish Tapas Bar & Restaurant** (315 S. Howard Ave., 813/258-0393, 5 P.M.–midnight Mon.–Thurs., until 2 A.M. Fri. and Sat., $6–25) is a sweet little place with pitchers of decent sangria, a good Spanish tortilla, and lots of messy shrimp in garlic. Not on the row, but off on more posh waterside Bayshore, the suave late-night **Ceviche Tapas Bar & Restaurant** (2109 Bayshore Blvd., 813/250-0203, 5–11 P.M. Tues.–Thurs., until 3 A.M. Fri. and Sat., $12–26) serves its namesake citrus-cured fish, sea scallops with manchego, and an array of little dishes with addictive olives and almonds, all in a sleek nightclub atmosphere.

Casual

Cappy's Pizzeria (309 S. Howard Ave., 813/254-4948, 5–9:30 P.M. daily, no credit cards) is Tampa's top place for pies, whether you're in the deep-dish camp or the New York–style group. Sign up on the long waitlist for a booth, then grab a seat and choose a pie from the menu (on the back of old LP covers, camp yet nostalgic). The meaty combo is the best, and the Greek salad makes a good foil.

Perhaps the biggest scene in Tampa is the lunchtime crowd at **Ⓜ Pane Rustica** (3225 S.

MacDill Ave., 813/902-8828, 8 A.M.–6 P.M. Tues.–Fri., 8 A.M.–5 P.M. Sat., 8 A.M.–3 P.M. Sun., $6–9). It had to move to a bigger location not long ago because too many enthusiasts were crowding in for the stunning thin-crust pizzas, sophisticated panini, and glorious breads and cookies. Service is at the counter, and then you have to hang, plate in hand, until a table reveals itself.

Fine Dining

For fine dining, one of the hippest is **N** **St. Bart's Island House** (1502 S. Howard Ave., 813/251-0367, 5:30–10 P.M. Tues.–Thurs. and Sun., until 11 P.M. Fri. and Sat., $14–32, with less expensive small plates), a bastion of nuevo Latino and seafood (lump crab and avocado tower with crispy plantains and cilantro vinaigrette; grilled Caribbean lobster tail with spicy aioli—it may sound contrived, but it all works elegantly), with a great rum bar and nightclub attached.

Then there's the biggest gorilla of them all on the Tampa dining scene, the restaurant known around the world. It's on what is now a slightly seedy stretch of South Howard, but **Bern's Steak House** (1208 S. Howard Ave., 813/251-2421, 5–11 P.M. daily, reservations recommended, $17–59) fans are undeterred. It's a more than 50-year-old landmark, with a wine list that could break a toe and a menu that reaches new levels of hyperbole. Waiters go through a grueling years-long apprenticeship, resulting in a staff that could, and does, quote verbatim from the offerings. Steaks are so lovingly described that it wouldn't be surprising to hear the eye color, hat size, or hobbies of the cows in question. It's prime beef, aged and nurtured in Bern's own meat lockers, and you, the customer, dictate the size, cut, cooking temperature, and way too many other details. Just bring me a nice steak. Still, you gotta go to Bern's, if only to revel in the bordello-like decor of gilded plaster columns, red wallpaper, Tiffany lamps, and murals of French vineyards. After dinner take the tour of the kitchen and wine cellar.

Then head upstairs to **N** **The Harry Waugh Dessert Room at Bern's Steak House.** Nothing prepares you for it. Not even the rococo excess of Bern's downstairs. People tell you, "You dine in individual hollowed-out wine casks." Someone says, "There are individual wall-mounted radio thingies to set the mood at your table." You hear a rumor about an accordionist, maybe something about flambéing waiters. The romantic date-night possibilities of this dessert-only upstairs of Bern's (named after a wine-writing crony of Bern himself) get the heart racing. If that's not enough, there's Chocolate-Chocolate-Chocolate. That's actually the name of the demure chocolate-shellacked cylinder packing chocolate cheese pie, chocolate mousse, and chocolate cheesecake into one deadly package.

If Bern's doesn't sound like your cup of tea, try the more contemporary approach at the affiliated **SideBern's** (2208 W. Morrison Ave., 813/258-2233, 5–10 P.M. Tues.–Thurs. and Sun., until 11 P.M. Fri. and Sat., $18–28). Chef/partner Jeanie Pierola turns out gorgeous dim sum and world-beat small plates. The daily-changing selection of breads is absolutely knockout (curry sesame flatbread, kalamata and fig loaf).

Not among the 35 or so restaurants along South Howard, but still considered in Hyde Park, **Mise en Place** (442 W. Kennedy Blvd., 813/254-5373, 11:30 A.M.–2:30 P.M. and 5:30–10 P.M. Tues.–Thurs., until 11 P.M. Fri., only 5–11 P.M. Sat., $15–29, tasting menu $48) is a romantic, intimate spot near the University of Tampa. It's hard to characterize the sensibility in the kitchen when the weekly-changing menu ranges from pizza with chorizo, roast corn, chilies, and manchego to mole spice–rubbed seared tuna with purple potatoes, vanilla bean pineapple salad, and a prickly pear habanero vinaigrette. They also take great care to accommodate Atkins and South Beach practitioners.

DAVIS ISLAND

Nestled in the cute street-that-time-forgot business district of Davis Island, **220 East** (220 E. Davis Blvd., 813/259-1220, 11:30 A.M.–3 P.M. and 5–10 P.M. Mon.–Thurs., 11 A.M.–3 P.M. and 4–11 P.M. Fri., 11 A.M.–11 P.M. Sat., $13–18) beckons with a cheery turquoise-and-grape awning. Opinions are divided about the best tables—out front at one of the handful on the patio, or inside at one of the deep green booths. Either way, most tables are full of islanders and pilgrims from elsewhere in the Bay Area eager for a friendly face and a fairly priced, unfussy meal that ranges affably through American, Asian, or even Cajun dishes.

Across the street and equally beloved, **Estela's** (209 E. Davis Blvd., 813/251-0558, 11 A.M.–10 P.M. weekdays, until 11 P.M. weekends, $5–9) is known for exemplary carne asado (a rib-eye with lots of thinly sliced onions and a limey piquancy, served with a cheese enchilada and refried beans) and chocolate tacos.

YBOR CITY

Party central in Tampa, the century-old cigar-rolling center of town exhibits little of its Cuban heritage these days. The main drag is 7th Avenue, closed off to cars on weekend evenings so that the throngs of moderately impaired revelers are less likely to be roadkill on their way to see the next band or get the next tattoo. During the week, the area is more sedate—a better time to try out one or more of the many restaurants that range all over the gastronomic map.

Start your adventure at **Centro Ybor** (1600 E. 8th Ave.), a shopping, dining, and entertainment complex right at the pulsing heart of the neighborhood. None of the restaurants here will stir you to poetic excess, but **Big City Tavern** (813/247-3000, 5–10 P.M. Sun.–Tues., 5–11 P.M. Wed.–Sat., $15–28) is a large, attractive, all-American brasserie in a renovated ballroom. The best part is the wrought-iron balcony overlooking 7th Avenue. **Samurai Blue Sushi and Sake Bar** (813/242-6688, 11:30 A.M.–midnight Mon.–Fri., 5 P.M.–1 A.M. Sat., 5–11 P.M. Sun., $7–25) is another big, loud joint, but this one serves sake bombers, "spontaneous combustion rolls," and other kooky spins on Japanese bar staples. At **dish** (813/241-8300, 11:30 A.M.–10 P.M. Mon.–Thurs., until 11:30 P.M. Fri.–Sun., $11–25) you end up doing the cooking yourself, throwing your selection of meats, fish, and vegetables onto the barbie. How good it is depends on how good *you* are.

Named for a cantankerous (and poisonous) gila monster, **Adobe Gilas** (813/241-8588, 11 A.M.–2:30 A.M. Mon.–Sat., noon–2:30 A.M. Sun., $4–8) is more a drinking establishment, a fun place in which to pick your poison and let it

Florida's oldest restaurant, the Columbia Restaurant, offers an evening flamenco show.

rip. Think you can handle a 64-ounce margarita? Feel free to attempt it amongst these consummate 'rita professionals. Food runs to dips and chips, so the draw is the rustic indoor-outdoor space and abounding good cheer. After this, regroup at the Centro Ybor movie theater across the plaza.

Beyond Centro Ybor, the neighborhood's restaurants are spread along many blocks on 7th Avenue. Nearly at the end of the strip of commerce you'll find the **Columbia Restaurant** (2117 E. 7th Ave., 813/248-4961, 11 A.M.–10 P.M. Mon.–Thurs., until 11 P.M. Fri. and Sat., noon–9 P.M. Sun., $21–30), which bears the distinction of being the oldest restaurant in Florida (started in 1905) and the nation's largest Spanish/Cuban restaurant (13 rooms extending one city block). Frankly, the food's not spectacular these days, but the experience is worth picking through a ho-hum paella or sipping a pedestrian sangria. Some of these waiters have been here a lifetime, the many rooms manage to stay packed, and there are stirring flamenco shows Monday–Saturday nights.

People-watching is a robust pastime in Ybor City, with occasional catcalling and trash-talking adding a fillip of drama. For the best sidewalk seat in town, pull up a chair at **M** **Bernini** (1702 E. 7th Ave., 813/248-0099, 11:30 A.M.–10 P.M. Mon.–Thurs., until 11 P.M. Fri., 4–11 P.M. Sat., 4–9 P.M. Sun., $10–24). It's set in the historic Bank of Ybor City building and serves fairly sophisticated Cal-Ital cuisine—salmon carpaccio and filet mignon sparked with a perfume of white truffle. It attracts a more mature crowd than the bars and clubs all around it.

For something more casual, head back down the street to **Moses White BBQ** (1815 E. 7th Ave., 813/247-7544, 11 A.M.–6 P.M. Mon.–Fri., 11 A.M.–3 P.M. Sat., $8)—deeply smoky, kinda sweet, and a whole lotta heat make their juicy ribs a tongue-twirling fandango, the way they've been since 1932.

CHANNELSIDE

This is going to sound snide, but Channelside is what an entrepreneurial Martian would produce after seeing satellite photos of Baltimore's Inner Harbor. It's *almost* right, *almost* a tourist draw, and *almost* fun. Located dockside at the Port of Tampa where all the cruise ships come in, the shopping/dining/entertainment complex has a big movie theater with IMAX, a fun upscale bowling alley, little boutiques, and about a dozen restaurants.

Head first to the bowling alley-restaurant **Splitsville** (615 Channelside Dr., 813/514-2695, 4 P.M.–1 A.M. weekdays, 11 A.M.–3 A.M. Sat., 11 A.M.–1 A.M. Sun., $5–10). Spares, strikes, whatever: It's good food, a whimsical environment, and the coolest bowling shoes ever. Bowlers aren't known for their looks, so Splitsville lacks verisimilitude with its hottie waiters and equally glam clientele. The decor sets you straight with oversized "bowling pin" columns, red velvet ropes, and 12 pristine lanes, and the food is excellent upscale bar snacks. There's a pricier sit-down restaurant next door called Sally's Alley, mostly steaks and chops.

The best food in the complex is at **Tinatapa's** (615 Channelside Dr., 813/514-8462, 4–11 P.M. Mon.–Thurs., 11 A.M.–2 A.M. Fri., noon–2 P.M. Sat., noon–10 P.M. Sun., $12–18). Barcelona mosaics and logs for rafters give the spare, round room a decidedly Euro feel. There isn't total authenticity with some of the Spanish small plates—baked goat cheese with tomato sauce and salmon with a horseradish glaze might perturb the average barfly in Madrid. Still, flavors are bright and assertive, prices are low, and sharing makes it an adventure.

Grille 29 (615 Channelside Dr., 813/221-2929, 1–10 P.M. Sun.–Thurs., 5–11 P.M. Fri. and Sat., $11–26) draws a chic see-and-be-seen throng every night. The burble of gentle crowd noise from the bar does little to dampen the aura of romance in the moody dining room. The menu's "something for everyone" steakhouse approach pays off, with solid prime rib, rib-eye, filet mignon with all the fixings (rich creamed spinach, lush béarnaise). Ask for a table outside or along the windows. During the day the industrial Port of Tampa provides a neat gritty backdrop, and at night the lights from nearby Harbour Island add shimmering glamour.

While its parent restaurant, perched atop Chicago's John Hancock Center, aims high, Tampa's **The Signature Room** (615 Channelside Dr., 813/319-8888, 11 A.M.–2:30 P.M. Mon.–Sat., 5–10 P.M. Sun.–Thurs., until 11 P.M. Fri. and Sat., 10 A.M.–2 P.M. Sun. brunch, $21–44) doesn't quite live up. Still, you'll probably spot Buccaneers and their hangers on, many wearing outfits you usually see only on the cast of *The Surreal Life*. Steaks and chops are the mainstay here, but the kitchen clearly spends a great deal of time on accouterments (nice bread basket) and seasonal veggies.

Stump's Supper Club is fun for live music and **Howl at the Moon** has a dueling piano bar. The food at **Margarita Mama's** and **Banana Joe's** is to be avoided.

INTERNATIONAL PLAZA

Tampa's fanciest mall (how can this town support a Louis Vuitton store, a Gucci store, and a Furla store all in one place?) is also home to good restaurants. There are chains (**Cheescake Factory, California Pizza Kitchen,** and L.A.'s fabled **Fat Burger**). The mall's Bay Street is a vaguely Caribbean-themed pedestrian promenade lined with several respectable restaurants. **Blue Martini** is the most fun on Bay Street (2223 N. West Shore Blvd., 813/873-2583, 4 P.M.–3 A.M. Mon.–Fri., weekends opens at 1 P.M., $8–15), really a bar for full-fledged adults. There's an elevated stage behind the bar on which to see live rock nightly. The menu leans to attractive and contemporary small plates (seared tuna, hummus and pita chips).

A few steps away, funky artwork and a hard-to-resist soundtrack of '80s hits form the backdrop for a lineup of bar-food staples at **Bar Louie** (2223 N. West Shore Blvd., 813/874-1919, 11 A.M.–2 A.M. daily, $7–10). An urban industrial vibe makes you feel far from the ritzy shopping of International Plaza mall, and the encyclopedic array of beers can make you feel just about zippo in no time. It's a huge and echoey space, at its best when the after-work professionals swarm in for a casual nosh and a fancy brew or two.

The plaza's finest dining is to be had at the end of Bay Street in the new Renaissance Tampa International Plaza's restaurant, **M Pelagia Trattoria** (4200 Jim Walter Blvd., 813/313-3235, 6:30 A.M.–10:30 A.M., 11 A.M.–5 P.M., and 5:30–10 P.M. daily, $24–30). Opened in August 2004, this swanky hotel eatery has turned a lot of heads. The bold Mediterranean palette in the dining room is echoed in Chef Fabrizio Schenardi's lush cuisine. At breakfast, this means lemon soufflé pancakes; at lunch, crunchy fried olives stuffed with three meats or sultry pinot grigio-braised mussels; and for dinner, the stylish crowd enthuses about the cinnamon-juniper berry marinated quail and pistachio-crusted rack of lamb with fig-merlot sauce.

NEW TAMPA

Everyone's favorite restaurant in New Tampa—the mostly residential area northeast of downtown—is **Ciccio & Tony's** (16019 Tampa Palms Blvd., 813/975-1222, 11:30 A.M.–2:30 P.M. and 5–9:30 P.M. Mon.–Thurs., 11:30 A.M.–2:30 P.M. and 5–10:30 P.M. Fri., noon–3 P.M. and 5–10:30 P.M. Sat., 5–9:30 P.M. Sun., $7–15). Most nights it teems with families devoted to this health-conscious neighborhood favorite. C&T hits everything right: A super-friendly staff scoots efficiently around the pleasantly hip pale-blue interior ministering to the animated throngs of regulars. Thin, crunchy New York–style pizzas come topped with caramelized eggplant and goat cheese, while a turkey club "chop chop" pairs turkey breast with high-protein soy bacon bits, ripe tomato, crisp lettuce, and savory yellow rice.

New Tampa, as the name indicates, is all new. The upside is that things are clean, pristine, hygienic; the downside is that there's no sense of history, no gritty, time-worn ambience. If you are jonesing for something that seems older than a decade or so, **M Skipper's Smokehouse** has the ambience of a place 10 times its age. It's Tampa's best live music venue (blues, alt rock, Tuvan throat singers, the gamut), with concerts held outdoors under the canopy of a huge, moss-festooned live oak. It has a lively 30s-and-up bar scene (Pedro is a bartender par excellence; ask him to make a mojito), and a ramshackle restaurant serves a wonderful blackened grouper sandwich, gator nuggets, and black beans.

OTHER

When you want to get a sense of Tampa's scale, distance, and scope, you have to dig deep into your wallet and head to **Armani's** (6200 Courtney Campbell Causeway, 813/207-6800, 6–10 P.M. Mon.–Thurs., until 11 P.M. Fri. and Sat., $24–38) atop the Hyatt Regency Westshore. It's the undisputed top special-occasion and god-I-need-to-clinch-this-deal restaurant in town, partly for the view, partly for the solicitous service, and partly for the scaloppine Armani (thin-pounded veal sautéed with wild mushrooms and cognac in a creamy truffle sauce) or the grilled duck breast stuffed with liver pâté and dried cherries in a subtle vanilla sauce. The wine list shows depth and breadth, with an emphasis on important California/French wines. **Oystercatchers** is the hotel's No. 2 restaurant, a lovely seafood joint with water views.

One of the innovative Hawaiian-fusion restaurants founded by acclaimed chef Roy Yamaguchi, **Roy's** (4342 W. Boy Scout Blvd., 813/873-7697, 5:30–10 P.M. Sun.–Thurs., until 10:30 P.M. Fri. and Sat., $19–30) is another expense-account favorite in Tampa. An exceptionally good deal can be had with the three-course prix-fixe dinner for $30. It may start with a "Hawaiian fusion" sampler of Asian wontons and tiny Sichuan ribs, then segue to roasted macadamia mahi (by itself, a charge of $24), finishing up with Roy's signature melting hot chocolate soufflé.

In what is called the Westshore neighborhood, **Donatello** (232 N. Dale Mabry Hwy., 813/875-6660, 11:30 A.M.–2:30 P.M. Mon.–Fri., 6–11 P.M. daily, $18–28) draws crowds for its fancy Northern Italian cuisine served in a rarefied dark wood-and-tuxedoed-waiters kind of atmosphere. The menu reads like a greatest-hits list, but the carpaccio, tortellini in double cream sauce, and scaloppini dishes are nothing to sniff at.

In the sophisticated neighborhood of Carrollwood, Andrea and Michael Reilly's little **Michael's Grill** (11720 N. Dale Mabry, 813/964-8334, 11 A.M.–9 P.M. Mon.–Thurs., until 10 P.M. Fri. and Sat., $15–27) has become an institution, as much for the warm greeting and neighborly service as it is for the convivial patio and spare, brasserie-style dining room. You can eat your French onion soup or penne Bolognese at the bar and take in all the drama of the bustling open kitchen, but through the French doors and out onto the leafy patio the well-heeled crowd always seems to be having more fun. Borders Books next door makes a nice after-dinner browse.

Classic steakhouses seem to draw people no matter where they're located. A few of the area's best are far-flung: **The Palm** (205 Westshore Plaza, 813/849-7256, 11:30 A.M.–11 P.M. Mon.–Fri., 5–11 P.M. Sat., 5–10 P.M. Sun., $21–37), one of 25 in the chain, features prime Angus steaks and caricatures of Bay Area politicos and luminaries on the wall. **Shula's** (Wyndham Westshore Hotel, 4860 W. Kennedy Blvd., 813/286-4366, 11:30 A.M.–2 P.M. Mon.–Fri., 5:30–10 P.M. Mon.–Thurs., until 10:30 P.M. Fri. and Sat., until 9:30 P.M. Sun., $20–35), not surprisingly given coach Don Shula's hand in it, features decor that is all in tribute to the Miami Dolphins. It's the kind of steakhouse where they parade the meat in front of you before you select your slab (48-ounce porterhouse?!). And **Charley's Steakhouse** (4444 W. Cypress St., 813/353-9706) has more fat, grilled steaks and sturdy California cabs, served in a warren of formal, but a little tired looking, rooms.

Nightlife

YBOR CITY

They say that people are attracted to other people who look like themselves. I'm not sure I believe that, but an evening in Ybor City certainly raises a few questions along these lines. On weekend nights, packs of women promenade, four or five abreast, along the main drag of 7th Avenue. Some are in their early 20s, some 30s, some 40s. The curious thing is that within each pack, the women are wearing nearly identical outfits topped by indistinguishable hairdos. The question is, did these women become friends *because* they dress/look alike, or do they dress alike *because* they are friends? The same can be said of the men who troll Ybor City in small bunches, but it's less glaring because the universal uniform seems to be jeans, ball cap, T-shirt.

Ybor City is where people step out. During the week there are few bars with throbbing music oozing out onto the street—it's more about se-date dining weekdays. Forget date night on the weekend; then it's a place you rove with buddies, scaring up trouble.

Fairly young people head to the all-disco DJ **Platforms** (1625 N. 7th Ave., 813/241-6603, 9 P.M.–3 A.M. Wed.–Sat., cover usually $5) or **Masquerade** (1503 E. 7th Ave., 813/247-3319, 8 P.M.–2 A.M. Wed.–Sun., tickets and cover vary), a three-ring dance club circus at the site of the historic Ritz Theater movie house. Some nights it's a DJ, and some nights it's fairly big live music acts (OK, they also have professional wrestling and drunken dodgeball sometimes). Some nights it's where goth singles step out wearing their best come-hither black eyeliner.

Also drawing a young crowd, **Club Skye** (1509 E. 8th Ave., 813/247-6606, 1 P.M.–3 A.M. Mon.–Sat., cover varies, no cover before 11 P.M. on Sat.) is what's on the horizon for Tampa's party nights. Silky white curtains part to reveal the night's drama as it unfolds. What's it gonna be? Whether you're here for College Ladies'

Centro Ybor has an appealing mix of shops, restaurants, and entertainment.

Tampa

Night, International Night, Friday Night Bomb with Wild 98.7 FM broadcasting live, or Saturdays with DJ Trauma, Skye is the party to beat in Ybor. Although only certain nights are technically Naughty School Girl Nights, every night has a preponderance of slinky, sexy post-collegiate girls, especially notable when the club runs costume nights or competitions.

Coyote Ugly (1722 E. 7th Ave., 813/228-8459, 5 P.M.–3 A.M. Tues.–Sat.) aims older, not more mature, and is often just about the biggest party in Ybor City, presided over by the most audacious bartenders to ever wield a shot glass. If you have to ask what a body shot is, you're ripe for a hard life lesson from one of Coyote's devilish (and usually gorgeous) bartenders. Just like in the movie (which in turn was based on a bar in NYC), all-female bartenders drag the unsuspecting up on the bar for some raunchy drinking, dancing, and whatever. The bare-bones room is festooned with discarded brassieres from exuberant all-ages patrons.

M Twilight (1507 E. 7th Ave., 813/247-4225, info line 813/247-6234, www.twilightnightclub.com, ticket prices and times vary) is a wonderful small theater/club in which to see a show. It tends to book acts that a 30-something crowd will appreciate, most acts no longer at the top of their game (The Fixx, Yo La Tengo, even Third Eye Blind). Still, it's great to see real acts in an intimate space with a good sound system and a largely sober crowd.

If music and drinking aren't your objective, stop into the **Tampa Improv** (1600 E. 8th Ave., 813/864-4000, hours vary, $20) for an evening of live stand-up. Mostly local/regional acts.

The Rare Olive (1601 E. 7th Ave., 813/248-2333, $3) is a good place to end a night on an adult note, maybe with a martini, a cigar, and a little live jazz.

HYDE PARK

Lots of good nightlife to be had in this sophisticated South Tampa neighborhood. **M Whiskey Park** (720 S. Howard Ave., 813/259-9669, 5 P.M.–2 A.M. daily) is my favorite. It's got a hip vibe with a broad range of ages, ethnicities, etc.

The food is good, the drinks are better, and the pool tables aren't too hard to snag.

And then there's **The Rack** (1809 W. Platt St., 813/250-1595, 4 P.M.–3 A.M. Mon.–Fri., noon–3 A.M. Sat. and Sun., $6–10) for eightball and tekka maki—a combo made in yuppie heaven. You don't see the kind of serious players who bring their own spiffy Schon or Predator cues, but there's respectable play at most of the tables in the hip, low-light, leather-couched space. The crowd is young but not too young, cool but not too cool.

There's a lot of Irish zeal on and around Azeele. If you like your music—or your flirting—with a heavy brogue, head to everyone's favorite quaint Irish bar, **Dubliner Pub** (2307 W. Azeele St. 813/258-2257). **Four Green Fields** (205 W. Platt St., 813/254-4444) is another legendary Irish pub, with lots of regulars and lively conversation. The french fry basket is a bargain and could feed a small nation. **MacDinton's Irish Pub & Restaurant** (405 S. Howard Ave., 813/251-8999, 11:30 A.M.–3 A.M. Mon.–Sat., 5 P.M.–3 A.M. Sun., $7–10) is another Irish entry, with a killer black and tan, a warming Irish coffee, and a fair representation of Irish staples, from rib-sticking, mashed-potatoey shepherd's pie to respectable corned beef and cabbage. It's different, though, because there's a schedule: Some nights it's three-minute dating, others it's karaoke, then there's live music, free-pool-and-darts night, etc.

ELSEWHERE

M Skipper's Smokehouse (910 Skipper Rd., 813/971-0666, 11 A.M.–11 P.M. Tues.–Fri., opens at noon on Sat. and 1 P.M. on Sun., $8–14) and **Bahama Breeze** (3045 N. Rocky Point Dr. E, 813/289-7922, roughly 4 P.M.–2 A.M. daily, $8–22) could not be more different, but both are worthy of the drive time. The former, in northern New Tampa, is the city's beloved indoor-outdoor live blues venue, part Cracker and part islandy-Key West. The latter is a froufrou tropical-drink singles hangout with a huge waterside deck on which you will occasionally see Devil Rays, Buccaneers, and large men who could have been contenders.

Shopping

OLD HYDE PARK VILLAGE

Tampa's downtown doesn't really have a retail center. For that, you need to visit Hyde Park. It's not vast, but the outdoor shopping area along Hyde Park's West Swann Avenue, South Dakota Avenue, and Snow Avenue is the most appealing shopping destination in town, especially when the weather's nice. There's a large covered parking lot, free to shoppers, and a lovely landscaped plaza at the center. Pottery Barn and Williams-Sonoma are among the bigger stores, with Ann Taylor, Brooks Brothers, Anthropologie, Talbots, Tommy Bahama, and the more fashion-forward BCBG Max Azria. Top restaurants include the Cal-Ital Wine Exchange, a recent glamorous addition called Timpano Italian Chophouse, and another newcomer in 2005, a slick pan-Asian bistro called Restaurant BT. In the summer, **Old Hyde Park Village** (813/251-3500, store hours vary) hosts a free evening movie series, the classic films projected outside on a huge screen. The rest of the year, take in an indie or mainstream flick at Sunrise Cinemas.

INDOOR MALLS

With anchor stores Neiman Marcus and Nordstrom, **International Plaza** (2223 N. West Shore Blvd., 813/342-3790, 10 A.M.–9 P.M. Mon.–Sat., noon–6 P.M. Sun.), opened in 2001, gets the nod for fanciest shopping. A handful of usual mall stores (J. Crew, Banana Republic, Ann Taylor) are spiffed up by their proximity to 200 other specialty shops like Tiffany & Co., Christian Dior, Louis Vuitton, Gucci, and Furla. Really, it's the poshest assembly of stores in any shopping center on the Gulf Coast, served by an open-air village of restaurants called Bay Street, all in a location minutes from the airport and downtown. The Christmas decorations in the Neiman Marcus store alone are worth the drive.

About a minute from International Plaza, **Westshore Plaza** (250 Westshore Plaza, 813/286-0790) features more than 100 similarly fancy specialty shops and 4 major department stores, including a lovely Saks Fifth Avenue. It contains a 14-screen AMC Theater and restaurants like Maggiano's Little Italy, PF Chang's, and The Palm.

Located across the street from USF, **University Mall** (2200 E. Fowler Ave., 813/971-3465) is a garden-variety indoor shopping center, not very well maintained, with sullen teenagers talking on cell phones, mostly familiar mall stores, a 16-screen movie theater, and a fairly decent food court.

Fairly far from where most visitors stay, **Westfield Shopping Town, Brandon** (459 Brandon Town Center Dr., 813/661-5100) and **Westfield Shopping Town, Citrus Park** (8021 Citrus Park Town Center, 813/926-4644) are both pleasant malls with the full gamut of small shops and anchors, mostly serving the local community. Citrus Park is a little nicer, with a 20-screen Regal Cinema.

And if you want to roll up your sleeves and get serious about retail, you need to drive south on I-75 for 40 minutes until you reach the **Prime Outlets** in Ellenton (5461 Factory Shops Blvd., Ellenton, 941/723-1150). There, you'll find Bose, Ann Taylor, Nine West, Samsonite, DKNY, Black & Decker, Donna Karan, Villeroy & Boch, Nike, Sak's Off Fifth, Wilson Leather, Polo Ralph Lauren, Versace, and Waterford/Wedgewood—all offering deep, deep discounts.

OTHER

Channelside (615 Channelside Dr.), the recent-vintage entertainment center on Tampa's downtown waterfront adjacent to the Florida Aquarium and the cruise terminal, has just a few stores worth investigating—a wine shop, Antonio's Cigars, Bob the Fish sportswear, and a couple of galleries. And shopping along **7th Avenue in Ybor City,** Tampa's Latin quarter, will yield some interesting finds. It's a little grittier, with a few vintage clothing shops, a fair amount of racy lingerie, GBX Fashion Shoes, and a funky Urban Outfitters.

Information and Services

AREA INFORMATION

All telephone listings are within the 813 area code unless otherwise indicated. If you're trying to call the other side of the bay (Clearwater, Dunedin, St. Petersburg), the area code is 727, but you don't need to dial a 1 before it. Tampa is on eastern time.

Tourist Information

The Tampa Bay Convention and Visitors Bureau's **Visitor Information Center** is in the waterfront Channelside entertainment complex (615 Channelside Dr., Ste. 108A, 813/223-2752, www.visittampabay.com, 9 A.M.–5:30 P.M. Mon.–Sat., 11 A.M.–5 P.M. Sun.) at the Port of Tampa. It provides lots of brochures and information on attractions, events, and accommodations.

Tampa's daily newspaper is the *Tampa Tribune*, with kiosks most places. The *St. Petersburg Times* also covers the greater Bay Area. The *Weekly Planet* (813/739-4800, www.weeklyplanet.com), the city's free alternative weekly, has great entertainment schedules, restaurant reviews, and a view into local politics. For quick and easy info on events, attractions, and restaurants, visit www.tampabay.citysearch.com. There are also numerous magazines: *Tampa Bay Magazine* is a little stodgy, *New Tampa Style* covers the northern burbs of the city, and there are many glossy freebies in Hyde Park (many of them are here today, gone tomorrow, so I won't list them).

Police and Emergencies

In any emergency, dial 911 for immediate assistance. If you need police assistance in a non-emergency, visit or call the **Tampa Police Department** (411 N. Franklin St., 813/276-3200). The police department operates three districts that serve the greater Tampa Bay area—they

will assign your problem to the proper district. Tampa has several hospitals equipped with emergency rooms: If you have a medical emergency in the Hyde Park area, go to **Memorial Hospital of Tampa** (2901 Swann Ave., 800/341-7729). In Carrollwood, visit the **University Community Hospital Carrollwood** (7171 N. Dale Mabry Hwy., 813/558-8068). In the Westshore area, go to **University Community Hospital** (2223 N. West Shore Blvd., 813/615-7272). In the downtown area, make your way to **Tampa General Hospital** (2 Columbia Dr., 813/844-7000) near the causeway to Davis Island.

Radio and Television

Of the local radio stations, my favorite is **WMNF 88.5 FM,** which has a huge following for its independent and quirky programming—tune in and you'll hear salsa, or maybe Hawaiian slack-key guitar, or maybe a little alt-country. It has a snuggly relationship with Skipper's Smokehouse, and together they sponsor many of the city's best concerts. For a nonthreatening mix of light rock, turn to **WMTX 100.7 FM. WARM 94.9 FM** is "today's favorites with less talk," **WCOF 107.3 FM** is hits of the '70s, and for sports talk turn to **WDAE 1250 AM.**

On the television, if you're looking for the FOX affiliate, turn to **Channel 13,** for NBC turn to **WFLA Channel 8,** for ABC turn to **WFTS Channel 28,** and for CBS turn to **WTSP Channel 10.**

Laundry Services

If you find yourself in need of coin-op laundry, head to **B & W Coin Laundry** (4810 E. Busch Blvd., 813/987-9847) or **Bay To Bay Coin Laundry** (3331 Bay To Bay Blvd., 813/837-1002). Most big hotel chains offer laundry services.

Tampa

Getting There and Around

DRIVING

Both I-75 and I-275 travel north–south, but I-75 skirts the edge of Tampa while I-275 travels through the city and over the bay. Both connect to I-4, which travels east–west, connecting Tampa Bay to Orlando and the east coast of Florida.

Once in town, from north to south, Bearrs, Fletcher, Fowler, and Busch Boulevards are the big east–west roads. Dale Mabry and Bruce B. Downs are the biggest north–south roads. This all sounds fairly simple, but once you get downtown in Tampa you really need a map to find your way out. There are lots of one-way streets, and the highway on-ramps are a bit difficult to find. The Busch Gardens area and USF lie between I-75 and I-275 northeast of downtown. The airport is just southwest of downtown.

FLYING

Tampa International Airport (5503 W. Spruce St., 813/870-8700) is an excellent midsized airport—clean, easily traversed, with good signage and efficient staff. It's ranked Florida's third busiest airport, located just seven miles southwest of downtown Tampa. Domestically, it's serviced by AirTran Airlines, America West Airlines, American Airlines, Continental Airlines, Delta Airlines, Delta Express, Frontier Airlines, JetBlue Airways, Midwest Express Airlines, Northwest Airlines, Song Airways, Southwest Airlines, Spirit Airlines, Ted, United Airlines, and US Airways. International carriers include AirCanada, British Airways, Cayman Airways, and American Eagle.

Located on the airport premises, **Avis** (800/831-2847), **Budget** (800/527-0700), **Dollar** (800/800-4000 domestic, 800/800-6000 international), **Enterprise** (800/736-8222), **Hertz** (800/654-3131), and **Thrifty** (800/847-4389) provide rental-car service. Tampa has unbelievably good deals on rental cars from the airport—celebrate by upgrading to something stylin' (a Jaguar X-Type, or at least a Lincoln Town Car).

PUBLIC TRANSPORTATION

Taxi service from the airport to downtown is about $18. Tampa is a call destination, not a flag destination. Most hotels offer shuttle service to the airport and major attractions.

Amtrak (800/872-7245) and **Greyhound** (800/229-9424) both service Tampa, with stations downtown. Amtrak operates out of historic Tampa Union Station, offering north–south connections as well as links to nationwide rail travel.

Within the city, **Hillsborough Area Regional Transit Authority (HARTline)** provides intercity bus service, with 207 buses on 26 routes, nine trolleys, and eight electric streetcars. The "In Town Trolley" runs north and south through downtown and connects to the "TECO Line Streetcar System," which runs from downtown to the Channel District/Port and Ybor City. Still, Tampa is so spread out that it's not a city in which to be without a car.

Pinellas County

In some ways, Henry Ford's affordable $400 Model T foreshadowed the real estate boom in St. Petersburg in the early 1920s. It was the beginning of road tripping, folks hopping in the car in search of sun, sand, and a little fun. They found the peninsula that hangs down Florida's west side like a thumb, the east side of it nestled against the placid Old Tampa Bay, its west side flanked by sandy beaches and the Gulf of Mexico. People liked what they saw. They bought up land, building big resort hotels, affordable motels, and homes.

Before the hordes of sun worshippers came, what is now Pinellas County had a diverse set of visitors-turned-residents. As was so common along the Gulf Coast, the original pre-Columbian Native American settlers were killed and run off upon the arrival of Hernando de Soto and other

Spanish conquistadores in the 1500s. Long after that, there came an intrepid Frenchman, Odet Philippe, who established a large orange grove near Safety Harbor in 1842; and just after that the Scottish merchants who settled Dunedin; the Russian immigrants who worked the Orange Belt Railroad and named St. Petersburg after their Russian hometown; and finally the Greeks who came to harvest the area's rich sponge beds around 1900.

Today, **St. Petersburg** is Florida's fourth-largest city, the anchor of Pinellas County. Combined with neighboring Tampa, it's the largest market in the state. It's had another boom period in recent years, an influx of high-tech businesses drawing younger families and driving down the median age (the area until the 1990s was more of a retirement community). The city's downtown—on

Must-Sees

Look for **M** to find the sights and activities you can't miss and **M** for the best dining and lodging.

Caladesi Island, 20 minutes by ferry from Honeymoon Island, annually is voted one of Florida's best beaches in a number of publications.

COURTESY OF VISIT FLORIDA

M Honeymoon Island and Caladesi Island Beaches: There are some wonderful choices for sun and sand, so why settle for just one when you can opt for the double-whammy of Honeymoon and Caladesi, a pair of white-sand barrier islands flanking Dunedin north of Clearwater. Caladesi is accessible only by ferry from Honeymoon Island (page 179).

M Friendship Trail Bridge: The Tampa-to-St. Petersburg Old Gandy Bridge has been reinvented as the Friendship Trail Bridge, a 2.6-mile overwater trail for all types of nonmotorized recreational activities, especially suited to a leisurely walk or bike ride (page 181).

M Sunken Gardens: It puttered along as a kitschy "Old Florida" attraction for years, until the City of St. Petersburg restored the four-acre tropical gardens to their former glory (page 182).

M Sunshine Skyway Fishing Piers: Another local bridge has been repurposed. Sunshine Skyway Fishing Piers is the world's longest fishing pier, with a tremendous concentration of sportfish lurking in the deep waters below. You can rent fishing gear on the pier (page 184).

M Salvador Dalí Museum: The famous mustachioed Spanish surrealist is honored in a sleek museum of his work and the work of those inspired by him (page 187).

PINELLAS COUNTY

Honeymoon Island Beach
Clearwater
Caladesi Island Beach
Tampa
St Petersburg
Friendship Trail Bridge
Sunken Gardens
Tampa Bay
Salvador Dalí Museum
Gulf of Mexico
Sunshine Skyway Fishing Piers
0   5 mi
0   5 km
Bradenton

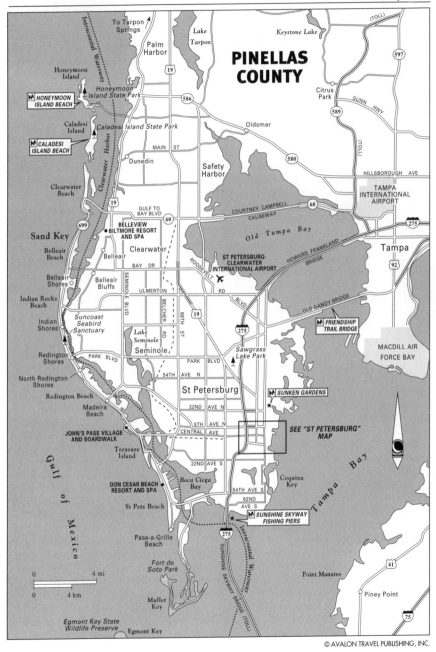

PINELLAS COUNTY

To Tarpon Springs

Lake Tarpon

Keystone Lake

Palm Harbor

(TOLL) 597

Honeymoon Island

Honeymoon Island State Park

Intracoastal Waterway

HONEYMOON ISLAND BEACH

Citrus Park

GUNN HWY

589

19

586

Oldsmar

Caladesi Island

Caladesi Island State Park

CALADESI ISLAND BEACH

Clearwater Harbor

MAIN ST

Dunedin

Safety Harbor

580

HILLSBOROUGH AVE

Clearwater Beach

GULF TO BAY BLVD

60

COURTNEY CAMPBELL CAUSEWAY

60

TAMPA INTERNATIONAL AIRPORT

275

92

Tampa

699

Sand Key

BELLEVIEW BILTMORE RESORT AND SPA

Clearwater

Old Tampa Bay

Belleair Beach

Belleair

BAY DR

ST PETERSBURG-CLEARWATER INTERNATIONAL AIRPORT

HOWARD FRANKLAND BRIDGE

ROOSEVELT

Belleair Shores

Belleair Bluffs

ULMERTON

SEMINOLE BLVD

BELCHER

RD

19

BLVD

OLD GANDY BRIDGE

FRIENDSHIP TRAIL BRIDGE

Indian Rocks Beach

Indian Shores

Suncoast Seabird Sanctuary

Lake Seminole

68TH ST

275

MACDILL AIR FORCE BAY

Redington Shores

PARK BLVD

Seminole

RD

PARK BLVD

Sawgrass Lake Park

North Redington Shores

54TH

AVE N

Redington Beach

Madeira Beach

St Petersburg

22ND AVE N

SUNKEN GARDENS

JOHN'S PASS VILLAGE AND BOARDWALK

5TH AVE N

CENTRAL AVE

SEE "ST PETERSBURG" MAP

Treasure Island

22ND AVE S

DON CESAR BEACH RESORT AND SPA

Boca Ciega Bay

54TH AVE S

Coquina Key

Tampa Bay

St Pete Beach

62ND AVE S

SUNSHINE SKYWAY FISHING PIERS

Gulf of Mexico

Pass-a-Grille Beach

275

SUNSHINE SKYWAY BRIDGE (TOLL)

Intracoastal Waterway

Point Manatee

41

Fort de Soto Park

Piney Point

0   4 mi

0   4 km

Mullet Key

75

Egmont Key State Wildlife Preserve

Egmont Key

the bayside, mind you, not the Gulf side) has seen lots of new growth, from pricey condos to the $40 million BayWalk shopping complex.

Here's a tricky fact you must assimilate quickly around here: St. Pete Beach is not just the shortened name for St. Petersburg Beach. St. Petersburg is the big city adjacent to Old Tampa Bay, which looks out across at the big city of Tampa. **St. Pete Beach,** on the other hand, is an autonomous barrier-island town to the south and west of St. Petersburg. St. Pete Beach is really on Long Key, although you'll seldom hear that used. It stretches seven miles from Pass-A-Grille on the south to Blind Pass on the north, before Treasure Island. Also, the city of **Clearwater** is on the mainland, but **Clearwater Beach** is on a barrier island connected by Memorial Causeway.

The Gulf beaches are 20 minutes from downtown St. Petersburg across the peninsula. More than 20 little towns dot the coastline in Pinellas County, St. Pete and Clearwater Beaches being perhaps the favorites for family vacations. Clearwater Beach offers a wide, inviting shore, serious beach volleyball, and lots of nightlife and casual seafood restaurants. The Jolley Trolley whisks visitors from their hotel, through town, and right to the beachside Pier 60, something of the center of town.

Clearwater and St. Pete Beaches aren't the only strands that draw accolades—**Caladesi Island State Park,** accessible only by boat to the north of Clearwater Beach, is often rated one of the top 10 beaches in the country, as is **Honeymoon Island.**

PLANNING YOUR TIME

Pinellas County is a peninsula, with Tampa Bay to the east and the Gulf of Mexico to the west. Its location, adjacent to Tampa, but with the benefit of long and wonderful beaches, makes it an ideal home base for a lengthy Gulf Coast stay, especially for families. Even Disney World is a fairly convenient 90 minutes to the east. The sights and attractions are more compelling on the Tampa side of the bay (Busch Gardens, lots of professional sports), but these are easily accessed by either the Howard Frankland Bridge

(I-275) or the Courtney Campbell Causeway (Hwy. 60). In high-season traffic, the drive can be 45 minutes.

Where you stay depends on your priorities: The city of St. Petersburg lies on the bay side of the peninsula. It has more history, more of a sense of place and sophistication than the beach towns along the Gulf side. There are romantic bed-and-breakfasts, fine restaurants, cultural attractions. Clearwater Beach and St. Pete Beach on the Gulf side have the densest concentrations of beachside accommodations—in Clearwater this often means tall resort hotels and condos right on the beach; in St. Pete Beach it's low-rise motels that date back a few decades. The communities in between these two—Belleair and Belleair Beach; Indian Rocks Beach and Indian Shores; Redington Shores, North Redington Beach, and Redington Beach; Madeira Beach; and Treasure Island—are fairly residential, but with pockets of beachside hotels/motels/rentals. The whole Gulf side is really composed of a series of tiny barrier islands connected to the mainland by causeways—it may not be totally clear to you when driving, but spend a little time with the map so you know when you're looking at boats bobbing on the Intracoastal Waterway, Boca Ciega Bay, Clearwater Harbor, or the Gulf.

The peak season typically runs November–May. It's a little more spread out than elsewhere among the Gulf Coast's beach spots, partly because American families on spring break come in March and April, and lots of European travelers fill in the time around that. In the summer the waters here are so warm as to be slightly off-putting. September and October are great times to visit. In October, added enticements include the beloved annual **Clearwater Jazz Holiday** (727/461-5200) during the third week of the month, with four days of free world-class jazz in Coachman Park. There's also the local **Stone Crab Festival** during that same time. Add to that the hugely popular **Florida Birding Festival** (www.pcef.org) and the month seems all the more alluring. In September, on the other hand, the **Taste of Clearwater** (www.clearwater-florida.org) is a big bash catered by all the best local restaurants.

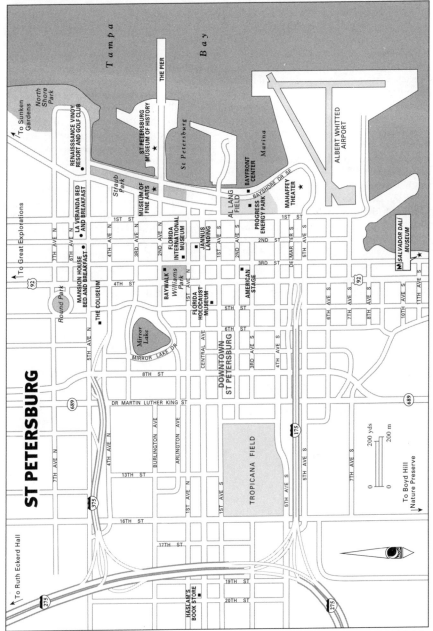

ST PETERSBURG

Tampa Bay

THE PIER

To Sunken Gardens
North Shore Park

RENAISSANCE VINOY RESORT AND GOLF CLUB

ST PETERSBURG MUSEUM OF HISTORY ★

St Petersburg

Marina

ALBERT WHITTED AIRPORT

To Great Explorations

LA VERANDA BED AND BREAKFAST ●

Straub Park

MUSEUM OF FINE ARTS ■

BAYFRONT CENTER ■

BAYSHORE DR SE

PROGRESS ENERGY PARK

MAHAFFEY THEATER ★

AL LANG FIELD ■

MANSION HOUSE BED AND BREAKFAST ●

THE COLISEUM ■

Round Park

FLORIDA INTERNATIONAL MUSEUM ■

JANNUS LANDING ■

SALVADOR DALÍ MUSEUM ★

BAYWALK ■
Williams Park

AMERICAN STAGE ■

FLORIDA HOLOCAUST MUSEUM ■

Mirror Lake

MIRROR LAKE DR

DOWNTOWN ST PETERSBURG

To Ruth Eckerd Hall

DR MARTIN LUTHER KING ST

BURLINGTON AVE

ARLINGTON AVE

TROPICANA FIELD

To Boyd Hill Nature Preserve

0   200 yds
0   200 m

HASLAM'S BOOK STORE

N
Pinellas County

© AVALON TRAVEL PUBLISHING, INC.

Sports and Recreation

BEACHES

When you conjure in your mind a Florida Gulf Coast beach, it's Clearwater and St. Pete you're imagining. These are textbook stretches of white sand and clear, warm Gulf water, with lots of comfy beachside hotels and waterside amenities for families. The area is home to a couple of world-class beach destinations, the kinds of places that often make Dr. Stephen Leatherman's ("Dr. Beach" has been ranking America's beaches for ten years) annual top-ten list.

First, a fairly urban city beach,  **Clearwater Beach** (west on Hwy. 60), the only Pinellas County beach with year-round lifeguards (9:30 A.M.–4:30 P.M. daily) is a long, wide stretch offering showers, restrooms, concessions, cabanas, umbrella rentals, volleyball, and metered parking. **Pier 60,** where the beach meets the causeway, is the locus of lots of local revelry and activity—during the day it's a heavily trafficked fishing pier, while at night the focus is "Sunsets at Pier 60," a festival that runs Thursday through Monday evenings two hours before sunset to two hours past sunset, with crafts, magicians, and musicians all vying for your attention with the ostentatious sunset display over the Gulf of Mexico. Pier 60 also contains a covered playground for the little ones, who will also like catching the bright red Jolley Trolley ($1 to ride) from Clearwater Beach and heading back to your hotel, downtown, or to Sand Key.

Clearwater Beach has a few rules to follow: No alcohol on the beach. Swim within the "safe bathing limit" area, extending 300 feet west of the high water line and clearly marked by buoys or pilings. Jet Skis and boats are not allowed within this line.

Clearwater Beach is just the warmup, just to get your feet wet, so to speak. The area's other best beaches require more of a commitment and are more of a full-day adventure.

South of St. Petersburg, **Fort de Soto Park** (3500 Pinellas Bayway S, Tierra Verde, 727/582-2267, www.fortdesoto.com, open daylight hours, free) is an embarrassment of riches, with 1,136

Often ranked the #1 beach in the continental United States, Fort de Soto Park offers 900 unspoiled acres and seven miles of beaches.

COURTESY OF VISIT FLORIDA

Pinellas County

unspoiled acres, seven miles of beaches, two fishing piers, picnic and camping areas, a small history museum, and a 2,000-foot barrier-free nature trail for guests with disabilities, set on five little, interconnected islands. The fort itself is in the southwest corner of Mullet Key, and there's a toll ($.85) on the bridges leading into the park. The islands were once inhabited by the Tocobaga and visited by Spanish explorers. It was surveyed by Robert E. Lee before the Civil War, and during the war Union troops had a detachment on both Egmont and Mullet Keys. The fort was built in 1898 to protect Tampa Bay during the Spanish-American War and is listed on the National Register of Historic Places. And during World War II, the island was used for bombing practice by the pilot who dropped the bomb on Hiroshima. But you thought we were talking about beaches, right?

Well, exploring the old fort is part of what makes this experience special, drawing more than 2.7 million visitors annually. After fondling the four 12-inch seacoast rifled mortars (the only ones of their kind in the U.S.), head on to one of the two swim centers, the better of which is the North Beach Swim Center (it has concessions). At the beach, you're likely to see laughing gulls, ibis, and ospreys, as well as beach sunflowers and beach morning glories peeking out from the sea oats. Fishing enthusiasts can choose between the 500-foot-long pier on the Tampa Bay side or the 1,000-foot-long pier on the Gulf side. Each has a food and bait concession.

Once in the park, take a right at the stop sign, go one mile, and on the right look for **Canoe Outpost** (3500 Pinellas Bayway S, Tierra Verde, 727/864-1991, www.canoeoutpost.com/fd-home.htm, 9 A.M.–5 P.M. daily, last rental at 3:30 P.M., single kayaks $15/hour, $35 a day; canoes $17/hour, $40 a day; bikes $6/hour, $20 a day, cash only). It rents bikes for exploring the paved bike and skate trails, and canoes and kayaks as well. Numbered signs along the shore mark a 2.25-mile kayak trail through Mullet Key Bayou.

Fort de Soto Park has the best camping in the area, with campsites directly on the Gulf. Camping is $27.75 per night, but here's the rub for visitors. Most of the 235 campsites require reser-

vations, which must be made *in person* far in advance. I figure it's a way to give locals the benefit of first dibs. If you're visiting from Peoria, how are you going to nab a campsite for next month if you can't do it online or over the phone? There are a handful of walk-in campsites available, but they are hot commodities. All sites have water and electrical hookups, and there are modern restrooms, dump stations, a camp store, washers/dryers, and grills.

Ⓜ Honeymoon Island and Caladesi Island Beaches

Honeymoon Island and Caladesi Island are more of a double-whammy, perfectly suited to visiting back to back. In fact, the two islands were once part of a single larger barrier island split in half during a savage hurricane in 1921. Together, they offer nearly 1,000 acres of mostly undeveloped land, not too changed from how it looked when Spanish explorers surveyed the coast in the mid-1500s.

The Tocobaga were the first known residents of Honeymoon Island, with ventures in more recent centuries having been quashed by deadly hurricanes. First known as Sand Island, then more inelegantly as Hog Island, it got its current name in the 1940s when marketing people tried to pitch it as a retreat for newlyweds, with little palm-thatched bungalows and cottages. It didn't quite take, stymied also by World War II, and the island went through several changes of hands before becoming a state park.

Honeymoon Island (1 Causeway Blvd., at the extreme west end of Hwy. 586, Dunedin, 727/469-5942, 8 A.M.–sunset daily, admission $5 for up to eight people per car, single driver $3, pedestrians and bicyclists $1) offers visitors all kinds of fun activities, but especially good is the fishing—you're likely to catch flounder, snook, trout, redfish, snapper, whiting, sheepshead, and, occasionally, tarpon. The island is home to 208 species of plants and a wealth of shore and wading birds, including a few endangered bird species. As per the beaches, my favorite part is the pet beach. It is where I learned that my dog sinks like a stone when immersed. If you subscribe to the hypothesis that people look like

COURTESY OF VISIT FLORIDA

Caladesi has remained largely uninhabited. Florida purchased it for a state park at a cost of $2.9 million in 1968.

their pets, this is prime observation opportunity, as both pets and owners are scantily clad as they cavort in the warm water.

Caladesi (directly to the south of Honeymoon, it is accessible only by boat, hourly ferry service available from Honeymoon, 727/469-5918, 8 A.M.–sunset daily, $4 for up to eight people per private boat, $1 kayakers) is the wilder of the two islands. There's the state park marina and swim beach right near where the ferry lets you off, but the rest of the island remains undeveloped. The Gulf side of the island has three miles of white-sand beach (this is the part that always makes the top rankings of beaches), and the bay side has a mangrove shoreline and seagrass flats. So, Gulf side for swimming and beach lolling, the bay side for birding and wildlife watching. You'll see lots of beautiful creatures, but the most entertaining are the armadillos, which are so myopic as to walk right over your shoe if you're very still. Like a bunch of befuddled, yet armored, Mr. Magoos.

If you're a strong kayaker or sailor, there are kayak and sailboat rentals on the causeway near Honeymoon Island. Once on Caladesi, there's a 3.5-mile canoe trail starting and ending at the

south end of the marina that leads paddlers through mangrove canals and tunnels and along seagrass flats on the bay side of the island.

Two cautions about Caladesi: Don't miss the last ferry or you'll be in a real pickle. And if you have brought a dog over to the dog beach at Honeymoon, it's a shame but Caladesi doesn't allow pets.

Other Beaches

Oh, I could go on about beaches. **St. Pete Beach** has a lot of low-rise pastel motels and an easy, laidback lack of civic planning. Sprawling and unfussy, its only organizing principle is "the beach is over there." For some reason you'll run into a lot of European travelers here—thus, by implication, those disconcertingly smaller bathing suits on men—especially the British. It's a livelier vibe than many Gulf Coast beaches, but not quite a "spring break" magnitude of sybaritic indulgers. The hammered and the "Girls Gone Wild" bunch go elsewhere, although my friend and I were asked by young baseball-capped men to show our breasts. We declined in a huff, but secretly I was flattered. Don't tell my friend.

The beach itself is long and renourished, sandwise. There are concessions, picnic tables, lots of parking, showers, and restrooms. In all, a very nice day at the beach.

There are a bunch of good beaches along **Sand Key,** which contains eight communities between John's Pass and Clearwater Pass. **John's Pass Beach** at the southern end of Sand Key and north for a couple of miles in **Madeira Beach** is beautiful sand and good fishing. Going north, the beaches in **Redington Beach** have limited public access but are pretty. Still farther north, **Indian Rocks Beach** has good public access and a party vibe (lively bars in town). Bypass the beaches in **Belleair,** as access and amenities are very limited, in favor of an afternoon at **Sand Key County Park** (north end of Gulf Blvd. at Clearwater Pass, 727/595-7677), which has lifeguards, playgrounds, cabana rentals, and lots of wide, white-sand beach.

SPECTATOR SPORTS
Baseball
Tropicana Field (1 Tropicana Dr., St. Petersburg, 888/326-7297, game days vary, times usually 2:15 or 7:15 P.M., tickets $5–32), home of the Tampa Bay Devil Rays, closed its doors in October 1996 for a 17-month, $85 million facelift. The Devil Rays played their first season here in 1998, and since then it has been named the second most fan-friendly stadium in the major leagues, according to a fan survey by Sports Travel Inc. As a concession to summer temperatures and humidity in these parts, the ballpark has a dome roof (which is lit orange when the Devil Rays win at home) and artificial turf. Out of season, Tropicana Field hosts other athletic events, conventions, trade shows, concerts, and other entertainment, with a seating capacity of 60,000.

For spring training, though, the Devil Rays play at **Progress Energy Park, Home of Al Lang Field** (180 2nd Ave. SE, St. Petersburg, 888/326-7297, $7–19). Spring training games are all month in March, and tickets usually go on sale January 15. The **Philadelphia Phillies** (Bright House Networks Field, 601 Old Coachman Rd., Clearwater, 727/442-8496, game days vary, times

usually 1:05 or 7:05 P.M., tickets $9–25) have been training in Clearwater since 1948. It's a great venue, with a tiki-hut pavilion in left field, a kids' play area, group picnic areas, party suites, and club seats. The **Toronto Blue Jays** also have spring training in the area, playing at Knology Park, formerly Dunedin Stadium (311 Douglas Ave., Dunedin, 727/733-0429, game days vary, times usually 1:05 P.M., tickets $13–18). Built in 1990, it's a serviceable little ballpark in a fairly residential area (you end up paying almost as much for parking as for your ticket). There are upper and lower sections, the upper section having a slight overhang, which can be cooling during warm day games.

BIKING AND RUNNING
Ⓜ Friendship Trail Bridge
The best way to get oriented in the greater Tampa Bay area is to take a bike ride: The Old Gandy Bridge, which spans the bay to the south of I-275, recently underwent a $7 million transformation into an all-recreation park called the Friendship Trail Bridge. The 2.6-mile trail is open for all types of nonmotorized activities including biking, walking, running, rollerblading, and fishing. Saved from the wrecking ball, it's the world's largest over-the-water recreational trail, open dawn to dusk daily and free of charge (the cool fishing catwalks that flank the bridge are open 24 hours). From I-275 in St. Petersburg, take "old" Exit 15 to Gandy Boulevard (U.S. 92) and go east to Gandy Bridge. See a small brown "Friendship Trail Bridge" sign prior to going onto the bridge, directing you to turn left or north to a short approach to the parking lot at the west end of the bridge.

Now you just need to rent a bike. **Northeast Cycles** (1062 4th St., St. Petersburg, 727/898-2453, $15/day, nice road bikes $25/day) will rent you bikes, and a rack for an additional $10 so you can load them up and take them over to the bridge parking lot, as will **Chainwheel Drive,** with two locations (1770 Drew St., Clearwater, 727/441-2444; and 32796 U.S. 19 N, in Palm Lake Plaza, Palm Harbor, 727/786-3883, 10 A.M.–7 P.M. Mon.–Fri., 10 A.M.–5 P.M. Sat., $20/four hours for hybrid, $26/four hours for road bike).

Pinellas County

Other Biking and Running Trails

Now that you've got the bikes, you may want to avail yourself of one of the other local beauties, the 34-mile-long **Pinellas Trail** (ranger 727/549-6099), one of the longest linear parks in the southeastern U.S., running essentially from St. Petersburg up to the sponge docks of Tarpon Springs. A rails-to-trails kind of deal, the original rail track was home to the first Orange Belt Railroad train in 1888, and is now a well-maintained 15-foot-wide trail through parks and coastal areas for bikers, rollerbladers, joggers, etc. There is a free guide to the Pinellas Trail, available at the trail office, area libraries, and the Pinellas County Courthouse Information Desk (it can also be downloaded at www.pinellascounty.org/trailgd /default.htm). It lists rest stops, service stations, restaurants, pay phones, bike shops, and park areas along the trail.

GARDENS AND PARKS

M Sunken Gardens

Sunken Gardens (1825 4th St. N, St. Petersburg, 727/551-3100, www.stpete.org/sunken .htm, 10 A.M.–4:30 P.M. Mon.–Sat., $8 adults, $6 seniors, $4 children 2–11) was snatched from the jaws of death in 1999, nursed back to health under the careful ministrations of the City of St. Petersburg. Nothing a little nurturing and $3 mill couldn't fix. It's a four-acre plot of land, much of it 100 years old and counting. There are 50,000 tropical plants and flowers, demonstration gardens, a 200-year-old oak tree, cascading waterfalls, flamingos, etc.

It's more than a garden, though—it's St. Petersburg's most beloved "Old Florida" attraction. In 1903, a plumber named George Turner Sr. bought the property, which contained a large sinkhole and a shallow lake. By dint of effort and a huge maze of clay tile, he drained the lake and prepared the soil for gardening. He sold tropical fruit that he grew here at a roadside stand, but folks liked walking through the tranquil greenery so much that he started charging admission. By 1935 the garden was officially opened as Turner's Sunken Gardens (because of the former lake and sinkhole, the whole thing sits down low in a

basin), attracting approximately 300,000 visitors per year. It was followed by some other attractions of dubious taste: the World's Largest Gift Shop and the King of Kings Wax Museum. It was one of those places that had loud, modestly literate billboards on the southbound highway up through a couple of states.

But, as is common for these kinds of Florida attractions, its business fell off as more glitz was mandated by ever more sophisticated patrons. It drizzled along until the city felt compelled to help, also restoring the gift shop/wax museum space to its former Mediterranean Revival glory (it's where **Great Explorations, the Children's Museum** is housed; see the *For Kids* section). I know I'm painting a picture of hard times and empty pockets, but Sunken Gardens is beautiful, ever so slightly campy, and a definite slice of local history. A must if you can tear yourself away from the beach.

Other Gardens and Parks

For a much more rough-and-ready nature experience, drive up to **Brooker Creek Preserve** (1001 Lora Ln., Tarpon Springs, 727/943-4000, www.friendsofbrookercreekpreserve.org, trail open sunrise–sunset daily). It's an 8,500-acre wilderness in the northern section of the county near Tarpon Springs. Currently, the preserve offers a 1.5-mile looped self-guided hiking trail at the southern end of Lora Lane off of Keystone Road, about one-half mile east of East Lake Road. The preserve also offers guided hikes every Saturday (reservation required, 727/453-6910), and it hosts the annual **Run in the Woods** in April, the area's only walk/run that is completely cross-country through beautiful backwood pinelands and prairies.

Extending along the west side of Tampa Bay in Pinellas County, **Weedon Island Preserve Cultural and Natural History Center** (1800 Weedon Island Dr., St. Petersburg, 727/453-6500, www.weedonislandcenter.org, preserve open sunrise–sunset daily, cultural center open 10 A.M.–4 P.M. Wed.–Sun., free) is an odd bird, an attraction hard to classify exactly. Weedon Island Preserve is a group of low-lying islands in north St. Petersburg that as long as 10,000 years or so ago was home to Timucuans and Manasotas. The largest estuarine preserve in the county, it is also home to a large shell midden and burial mound complex. Visitors to the cultural center can see artifacts excavated from the site by the Smithsonian in the 1920s in exhibits designed collaboratively by anthropologists, historians, and Native Americans.

But you can't spend all your time at the cultural center watching videos about the art and history of the early peoples of Weedon Island—the park has a four-mile canoe trail, a boardwalk and observation tower, four gentle miles of hiking trails, a fishing pier (snook, redfish, spotted trout), and waterfront picnic facilities. Weedon Island Preserve Center offers guided nature hikes every Saturday and regularly scheduled guided canoe excursions (registration 727/453-6506).

Accessible only by ferry or private boat, **Egmont Key State Wildlife Preserve** (at the mouth of Tampa Bay, southwest of Fort de Soto Beach, St. Petersburg, 727/893-2627, www.floridastateparks.org/egmontkey, 8 A.M.–sundown daily, free) makes a great day trip. There aren't a lot of facilities on the island, which is wild except for the ruins of historic Fort Dade and brick paths that remain from when it was an active community with 300 residents. You'll see the 150-year-old working lighthouse (constructed in 1858 to "withstand any storm" after a first one was savaged up by two hurricanes in 1848 and 1852), gun batteries built in 1898, a pretty stretch of beach, and lots of gopher tortoises and hummingbirds. There is no camping on Egmont Key.

Owned by the State of Florida and maintained by the Manatee County Conservation Lands Management team, **Snead Island** (take Business 41 into Palmetto, turn right on 10th St. W. and follow signs to island, 941/776-2295, 8 A.M.–sundown daily, free) is just east of Egmont Key, and another good excuse to tramp around in nature—15 miles of it bordering shoreline along the Gulf and the lovely Manatee River. The park is favored by hikers because of its variety of trails and loops, with occasional boardwalks hugging the waterways.

Snead Island is home to **Emerson Point Preserve** (west end of Snead Island, at the end of 17th Street, Palmetto, 941/776-2295, 8 A.M.–sundown daily, free), worth tacking on to your adventure—the park's 195 acres of salt marshes, beaches, mangrove swamp, lagoons, grass flats, hardwood hammocks, and semi-upland wooded areas are viewable from a well-maintained 8-foot-wide shell path as well as more rustic walking and biking paths. Manatee County has poured money into this park in recent years such that master gardeners convene here regularly for guided walking tours of the varied plant and animal life. Call 941/722-4524 to find out the tour schedule.

Of special note to Native American historians, Emerson Point Preserve is home to the **Portavant Temple Mound** (east end of 17th Street W., Snead Island), an impressive mound complex. Walkways and boardwalks take you over and around a huge 150-foot flat-top temple mound and several horseshoe-shaped shell middens. Interpretive markers explicate the site.

Anclote Key Preserve State Park (1 Causeway Blvd., Dunedin, 727/469-5942, 8 A.M.–sundown daily, free) is a similar island preserve accessible by boat, only this one offers primitive camping and is pet-friendly (keep pets on the southeast end, as protected nesting birds have taken up residence in the north).

NATIVE AMERICAN SITES

Pinellas County's rich Native American heritage is just faintly perceptible—but there are a couple of sites that command quite a bit of enthusiasm among historical travelers. Called both the **Safety Harbor Mound** and the **Philippe Park Temple Mound** this platform mound is set in a lovely county park (2525 Philippe Pkwy, Safety Harbor, 727/669-1947, 7 A.M.–sunset daily, free). The mound is located behind shelter number two and is explicated with interpretive markers. The large mound complex is believed to be the village of Tocobaga, for which the Tocobaga are named. It is said that in 1567 Pedro Menedez de Aviles, the founder of St. Augustine, visited this Tocobaga village. (For a little more insight, two miles south of Philippe Park is the **Safety Harbor**

Museum of Regional History (329 S. Bayshore Dr., 727/726-1668, 10 A.M.–4 P.M. Tues.–Fri., 1–4 P.M. Sat. and Sun., free), which contains artifacts from the Weeden Island, Safety Harbor, and Mississippian periods.

Seeing more Tocobaga handiwork requires only a short drive to the **Pinellas Point Temple Mound** (east on 62nd Ave. S., turn south onto 20th St. and it ends at the mound, 7 A.M.–sunset daily, free). The large flat mound, topped by a comfy bench, is all that remains of a sizeable village. It, too, sports illuminating historical markers, but much of their information is a bit speculative-de Soto and Narvaez's interactions with Native tribes in the area have been claimed by many towns around here.

BIRDING

Every October Pinellas County hosts the annual Florida Birding Festival & Nature Expo, to which 3,000 avid birders flock. They come to hear a dynamic array of speakers and attend seminars, but mostly they come to tramp around on field trips to some of the region's top birding and wildlife areas. They come to look for some of the state's rarer bird species, like the reddish egret, little burrowing owls, and the Florida scrub jay, the only bird species unique to Florida.

If you're an avid birder or would like to learn more about birds, here's what you do: go to the **Great Florida Birding Trail** website (florida-birdingtrail.com/guide.htm) and print out the "West Section" guide to the birding trail, which is divided into 17 smaller sections. Many important birding sites are in Pinellas County.

Brooker Creek Preserve (see *Other Gardens and Parks*) and **East Beach** at Fort de Soto Park (see *Beaches*) are both wonderful for birding. Beyond these, **Shell Key** (shuttle and charter boat access only, located at the southern end of Pass-A-Grille channel, just west of Tierre Verde), an undeveloped 180-acre barrier island in the area, is an important place for wintering and nesting seabirds and shore birds, with more than 100 species sighted. **Boyd Hill Nature Preserve** (1101 Country Club Way S, St. Petersburg, 727/893-7326, 9 A.M.–8 P.M. Tues.–Thurs., 9 A.M.–6 P.M.

Fri. and Sat., 11 A.M.–6 P.M. Sun., $2 adults, $1 kids) is 245 acres of pristine Florida wilderness, with five distinct ecosystems—hardwood hammocks, sand pine scrub, pine flatwoods, willow marsh, and the Lake Maggiore shoreline. This may be my favorite, as it is incredibly convenient, just minutes from downtown, but it nonetheless feels far from the madding crowds. Precious green space in an urban landscape, it is an important stopover on the Atlantic Flyway—165 bird species have been observed here. You can camp at Boyd and there's a small educational center with exhibits on the five ecosystems.

Another spot on the Great Florida Birding Trail, also lauded by the National Audubon Society, is **Sawgrass Lake Park** (7400 25th St. N, immediately west of I-275 in Pinellas Park, St. Petersburg, 727/217-7256, environmental center 727/526-3020, 7 A.M.–sunset daily, free). Thousands of birds migrate through the park during the fall and spring. A one-mile elevated boardwalk winds through a maple swamp and oak hammock. There's an observation tower with views of the park's swamps, canals, and lake, where you're likely to see wood storks, herons, egrets, and ibis in addition to gators and turtles. The park has naturalist-led nature tours and field trips, and its Anderson Environmental Center contains a large freshwater aquarium and exhibits on the area. My only caution is that during the wet months it can get a bit flooded in this park.

If you find an injured bird in your wandering, call **Suncoast Seabird Sanctuary** (18328 Gulf Blvd., Indian Shores, 727/391-6211), one of the country's largest nonprofit wild bird hospitals. With a brand-new hospital facility, the sanctuary rescues and releases hundreds of birds each year into the wild. The sanctuary also offers a free tour every Wednesday and the second, third, and fourth Sunday of every month at 2 P.M., meeting at the beachfront deck.

FISHING
Sunshine Skyway Fishing Piers

It must have been a sight to see. In 1990, Hardaway Constructors of Tampa and a demolition team from Baltimore joined forces to perform

COURTESY OF VISIT FLORIDA

Completed in 1987, the Sunshine Skyway is the world's longest cable-stayed concrete bridge, bridging the mouth of Tampa Bay between Pinellas and Manatee counties.

the largest bridge demolition in Florida history. They were doing away with the old Sunshine Skyway Bridge opened in 1954, a 15-mile crossing from St. Petersburg to Bradenton. From a long causeway on both sides, the steel bridge had a steep cantilever truss, 750 feet wide and with 150 feet of clearance above the water.

It wasn't enough clearance.

There had been some indication of this—at least five freighters or barges were roughed up by this bridge, most of them with minor damage (the Coast Guard cutter *USS Blackthorn* met with disaster, but it was just west of the bridge and it was weather related).

But it was during a violent storm on May 9, 1980, at 7:38 A.M., when Captain John Lerro's visibility was nil, that empty phosphate freighter *Summit Venture* slammed into the No.

2 south pier of the southbound span. It knocked 1,261 feet out of the center span, the cantilever, and part of the roadway into Tampa Bay. Thirty-five people on the bridge at the time perished, most of them in a Greyhound bus headed for Miami. The only victim who survived had his truck fortuitously land on the deck of the *Summit Venture*.

One of the worst bridge disasters in history, it prompted the design, funding, and building of the new Sunshine Skyway Bridge. At a cost of $245 million, it's the world's longest cable-stayed bridge, with a main span of 1,200 feet and a vertical clearance of 193 feet. The four-mile bridge opened for business in April 1987, equipped with a bridge protection system involving 36 large concrete bumpers (oddly, called "dolphins") built to withstand an impact from rogue freighters and tankers up to 87,000 tons traveling at 10 knots.

So, you probably think I'm leading up to saying, "It's a gorgeous bridge, a real local landmark, you gotta drive over this thing." It's all true, but it's only a part of the story. After the construction of the new bridge, the old bridge spans were demolished like I said, by Hardaway Constructors and that demo team from Baltimore, except they preserved portions of it as fishing piers, piling the rubble alongside to form fish-friendly artificial reefs.

Since the original bridge span was built, fisherfolk have been bragging about the variety of game they catch: shark, tarpon, goliath grouper, kingfish, Spanish mackerel, grouper, sea bass. It's anomalous, because usually you have to be in a boat in order to have water deep enough for many of these species. Anglers have caught 1,000-pound tiger sharks from the bridge, traffic honking behind them. And now, with the artificial reefs adding extra enticement to the fish, the Sunshine Skyway Fishing Piers are killer fishing spots.

There's a .75-mile-long North Pier and a 1.5-mile-long South Pier—together said to be the world's longest fishing pier. You can drive your car onto the pier and park it right next to your fishing spot, parallel parking on the left lane, with room for cars to drive and walkways on either

Pinellas County

SMOKIN'

Here's a tricky scenario. You're on a great Gulf Coast vacation, the weather's perfect, you're feeling relaxed, so you decide to do a little charter fishing. You're out on the boat, you feel a yank, and there's a 40-pound greater amberjack on your line. You work a while and haul in a couple more of those and a whole mess of 20-inch Spanish mackerel. What a great day. My question: Now what? Are you going to take that fish cooler back to the Radisson and have them stink up the joint?

Here's what to do. You go to **Ted Peters Famous Smoked Fish** (1350 Pasadena Ave., South Pasadena, 727/381-7931, 11:30 A.M.–7:30 P.M. Wed.–Mon., $10–20, no credit cards) and they'll smoke them for you for $1.50/pound. They can even make kingfish taste good, and that's saying something. They fillet them, throw them over a smoldering red oak fire in the smokehouse, then package them up for you to take. (The smoked fish keeps for 4–5 days in the fridge.)

And if you don't have fish to smoke, still go to Ted Peters. It's been an institution for more than 50 years in Pinellas County, prized for its laidback style and inviting picnic tables. The main attraction is obviously the smoked fish—the smoked fish spread with saltines is good, the salmon is excellent, the mullet is an intensely fishy acquired taste— but Ted Peters also produces some fabled cheeseburgers and German potato salad that is balanced precariously between the zing of vinegar and the smoke of bacon. Perfect, a good thing because you can't have fries with your burger—no fryolator. This is a beer-drinking establishment, it gets fairly busy, and it closes early.

---

side of the span. There are restrooms on both piers, and bait shops sell live and frozen bait, tackle, drinks, and snacks. They also rent rods. The North Pier has a large picnic area next to the bait shop.

To get there, head south on I-275 toward Bradenton. The North Pier (727/865-0668) is about a mile past the toll ($1). To reach the South Pier (941/729-0117), continue over the bridge and follow the signs. There is a $3 per vehicle charge, plus $2 general admission, $1.50 seniors, $1 kids 6–11, children under 6 free. *You don't need a fishing license to fish off the piers.*

So, yeah, drive over the new bridge but, more importantly, wet a line on the remnants of the old one.

Sights

ART MUSEUMS

Maybe a little quiet currently, but definitely worthy of a couple of hours, the **Museum of Fine Arts** (255 Beach Dr. NE, St. Petersburg, 727/896-2667, www.fine-arts.org, 10 A.M.–5 P.M. Tues.–Thurs. and Sat., until 8 P.M. Fri., 11 A.M.–5 P.M. Sun., $12 adults, $10 seniors and students, $5 kids 7–18, 6 and under free) is right on the waterfront adjacent to Straub Park, with the full gamut of art from antiquity to the present day. The collection of 4,000 objects includes significant works by Cézanne, Monet, Gauguin, Renoir, Rodin, Henri, Bellows, and O'Keeffe. Its permanent collection's strength is 17th- and 18th-century European art, and the museum has a lovely garden as well.

If you have the stamina for more art, a couple of small community venues are located around Pinellas County. The **Gulf Coast Museum of Art** (12211 Walsingham Rd., Largo, 727/518-6833, 10 A.M.–4 P.M. Tues.–Sat., noon–4 P.M. Sun., $5 adults, $4 seniors, $3 students, free for children under 12) is in the Pinewood Cultural Park and features contemporary art by Floridian artists from 1960 on. The center also offers classes and workshops for children and adults in ceramics, metalsmithing, painting, sculpture, photography, and drawing. **The Arts Center** (719 Central Ave., St. Petersburg, 727/822-7872, 10 A.M.–5 P.M.

Mon.–Sat., noon–5 P.M. Sun.) exhibits contemporary art and local student exhibits, but also hosts visiting exhibits such as "Grandma's Hands: 100 Years of African-American Quilts."

 Salvador Dalí Museum

Perhaps the most lauded art museum in Pinellas County is the Salvador Dalí Museum (1000 3rd St. S, St. Petersburg, 727/823-3767, 9:30 A.M.–5:30 P.M. Mon.–Sat., noon–5:30 P.M. Sun., $14 general, $12 seniors, $9 students, $3.50 children 5–9, children 4 and under free), the world's most comprehensive collection of permanent works by the famous Spanish surrealist master, with other exhibits relating to Dalí.

He himself is as recognizable as his "paranoiac-critical" paintings. Maybe only Van Gogh in his post-ear-incident self-portrait is more reliably identified than Salvador Dalí. The long, waxed mustache, the arched eyebrows, the shock of black hair. Upon moving to the United States in the 1940s, Dalí made himself the lovable eccentric who introduced the average American to surrealism. The crazy part is, the average American seemed to like it, to be less intimidated by it than by art movements such as cubism or abstract expressionism. And what's not to love? Melting clocks, elephants with spiders' legs—I'll say one thing for him, no one's ever stood in front of his work and said, "Man, I coulda done that one."

The Salvador Dalí Museum is a dense concentration of his surrealist works, what he described as a "spontaneous method of irrational knowledge based on the critical and systematic objectivation of delirious associations and interpretations." Although he's identified strongly with the movement, in 1934 Dalí was formally expelled from the surrealist Group of Paris with a mock trial (some of the reason for his expulsion had to do with an unsavory enthusiasm for Adolf Hitler). But after he came to the U.S. (a trip paid for by Picasso), he embarked on his classical period, characterized by what he called "Nuclear Mysticism."

Son of a notary public in Figueres, Spain, Dalí started drawing and painting at a young age, studying art in Madrid. He became great friends with the poet Federico García Lorca and the filmmaker Luis Buñuel (with whom he did that

The Salvador Dalí Museum in St. Petersburg features six of Dalí's 18 "Masterworks." Pictured here is *The Hallucinogenic Toreador* from the museum's collection.

COURTESY OF THE ST. PETE/CLEARWATER AREA CVB

surrealist movie called *Un Chien Andalou* that every cinema student still has to see, the movie with the slit eyeball). After his studies, Dalí left for Paris and joined the surrealist group of painters and sculptors. *The Persistence of Memory, The Great Masturbator,* and *The Spectre of Sex Appeal* all date from this time.

During the Second World War, Dalí settled in the U.S. and enjoyed serious celebrity as he dabbled in cinema, theater, opera, and ballet. But in the 1950s and 1960s he did some of his most famous work, much of it focused on themes of religion, history, perception, and science commingling in a big stew—*Christ of St. John of the Cross, The Discovery of America by Christopher Columbus,* and *The Last Supper.* One thing the museum does well in a new exhibit called "Dalí Revealed" is to explore and illustrate these themes with a selection of works from its permanent collection.

The museum is wonderful—a great space, the work elegantly annotated and curated. But I have to admit it, I'm not a fan of the artist. He was indeed prolific, and a popularizer of sorts,

Pinellas County

something I admire. The thing I object to is the vast number of prints and lithographs he allowed made of his work, cheapening art ownership and preying on the unsophisticated, people who aren't savvy about pencil signing and numbering, who don't know bubkes about demanding authentication on graphic work.

HISTORY MUSEUMS

The **Florida Holocaust Museum** (55 5th St. S, St. Petersburg, 727/820-0100, www.flholocaustmuseum.org, 10 A.M.–5 P.M. Mon.–Fri., noon–5 P.M. Sat. and Sun., $8 adults, $7 seniors and college students, $3 children under 18) is the fourth largest of its kind in the United States. Some of the museum is devoted to the memory of millions of innocent people who suffered, struggled, and died in the Shoah. But it also showcases only loosely linked exhibits such as the lush, life-affirming work of Czech artist Charles Pachner (who lost his whole family during the war) in his show "Imagined Landscapes," a collection of luminous watercolors, big colorful paintings, some pen and ink work, and moody black-and-white canvasses and collage.

St. Petersburg Museum of History (335 2nd Ave. NE, St. Petersburg, 727/894-1052, www.stpetemuseumofhistory.org, noon–7 P.M. Mon., 10 A.M.–5 P.M. Tues.–Sat., noon–5 P.M. Sun., $7 general, $5 seniors and students, $3 children 7–17) is one of the oldest historical museums in the state, with family-friendly displays and exhibits depicting St. Petersburg's past. It had a recent remodel and enlargement, with a local history exhibit that contains a Native American dugout canoe, a cannon ball fired by Union sailors at the home of a Confederate resident, an exact replica of the world's first scheduled commercial airliner (it flew out of St. Petersburg), and lots of other cool stuff. If it's still there, the temporary exhibit about the grand hotels of the 1920s is neat, especially if you happen to be staying in one of these historic beachside babies.

Beyond these, the history buff can visit the restored homes and buildings of the **Heritage Village** (11909 125th St. N, Largo, 727/582-2123, www.pinellascounty.org/Heritage, 10 A.M.–

4 P.M. Tues.–Sat., 1–4 P.M. Sun., free admission). It's a living history kind of thing with people roaming around purposefully in period costume, spinning, weaving, and whatnot. Most of the 28 structures date back to the late 19th century. If you go to Heritage Village, make a day of it and visit the work-in-progress **Florida Botanical Gardens at Pinewood Cultural Park** (12175 125th St. N, Largo, 727/582-2200, 7 A.M.–7 P.M. daily, free admission to gardens), where you can take a tour through recently completed gardens led by a local master gardener. You walk 1.5 miles, it takes 1.5 hours, and you learn all about Florida gardening. The approaches can be vastly different—there's a rose garden, a beach garden, a tropical courtyard, a poodly topiary garden, a bromeliad garden (now that's what I like—these colorful, leathery epiphytes have no real roots but tanks inside them collect water), and more. On a nice day, it's a glorious spot.

FLORIDA INTERNATIONAL MUSEUM

This is an exciting time to stop in for a visit at the Florida International Museum (100 2nd St. N, St. Petersburg, 727/822-3693, 9 A.M.–6 P.M. Mon.–Thurs. and Sat., until 9 P.M. Fri., noon–6 P.M. Sun., tickets for Diana $19.50 adults, $15.50 seniors and students, $9 children 7–12, 6 and under free). Launched in February 2005, "Diana" is going great guns. The visiting exhibition presents the life and humanitarian work of Princess Di with 150 objects including her famous 1981 wedding gown, with 28 other designer dresses and gowns, family heirlooms, personal mementos, paintings, and home movies and photos. The show has been a huge hit, with crowds eager to glimpse the public and private life of this humanitarian and icon of fashion and style.

The museum has a permanent exhibition called "The Cuban Missile Crisis," which explores the 13 most frightening days of the Cold War when the world teetered precariously close to all-out nuclear conflict. It includes a fully stocked fallout shelter and a circa 1960s living room from which you can see President Kennedy's October 1962 speech on an old RCA set. Beyond this, there's a wonderful exhibit of jewelry from the Levine Jewelry Collection, with beautiful 18th- and 19th-century necklaces, cameos, bracelets, and earrings. Some big rocks, too.

Opened especially for the launch of "Diana," the museum has a lovely café for sitting a spell after all the art.

AQUARIUMS

Just over the bay in Tampa, the Florida Aquarium usually gets the bulk of the kudos. **Clearwater Marine Aquarium** (249 Windward Passage, Clearwater, 727/441-1790, 9 A.M.–5 P.M. Mon.– Fri., 9 A.M.–4 P.M. Sat., 11 A.M.–4 P.M. Sun., $9

adults, $6.50 children·3–12) is a smaller, more modest facility with, in some ways, loftier aims. It's a working research facility and home to rescued and recuperating marine mammals (dolphins, whales, otters, etc.). For the visitor, the thrust is on education, with hourly animal care and training presentations and exhibits on animal rescue, rehabilitation, and release—and how the public can help to protect and conserve endangered marinelife. It's like the ACLU for fish. The aquarium offers on-site feeding and care programs for interested guests and operates a daily two-hour-long **Sea Life Safari** (25 Causeway Blvd., Slip #58, Clearwater Beach, 727/462-2628) that takes visitors around

SOAK IT ALL UP

There are more than 10,000 species of fresh- and saltwater sponges, simple multicellular animals that sit quietly feeding on plankton and warding off enemies with little toxin-tipped spikes. They are not, as recent cartoons may indicate, loud and obnoxious with a weakness for physical comedy. Still, for some reason, since before the birth of Christ we have been hauling them out of the deep and using their skeletons to clean behind our ears or wipe up a mess.

These days **Tarpon Springs,** a coastal town 15 miles due north of Clearwater, is more about the *idea* of sponges than actual sponges. Since the 1950s and the advent of synthetic sponges, the Greek sponge divers who populated this town have been largely reemployed as fisherfolk, restaurateurs, tour boat captains, etc.

Sponge diving had been a family business in Greece at the end of the 19th century, with naturally adept swimmers assisted by rubber suits and heavy copper helmets to which air was pumped via hose. John Corcoris brought the apparatus to north of Tampa around 1900 and persuaded friends and family, sponge divers all, to relocate from Hydra and Aegena, Greece, to this little Florida backwater. Greeks begot more Greeks and a booming town of Greek restaurants, Greek Orthodox churches, and Greek festivals centered around the sponge industry. Tarpon Springs was the largest U.S. sponge-diving port in the 1930s, but a

sponge blight and new synthetic sponge technology caused business to dry up.

The town is still more than a third Greek, with a sweet, kitschy, "Old Florida" tourist attraction charm and several fine restaurants. Sponges are everywhere, most of them imported from more sponge-rich far-flung lands (although someone told me there was another flurry of sponge-diving here in the 1980s when another bed was found).

It's well worth an afternoon of your time—see the museum and the sponge docks, shop a little, and have dinner.

First stop, **Spongeorama** (510 Dodecanese Blvd., 727/938-5366, 10:30 A.M.–6 P.M. Mon.– Sat., 11:30 A.M.–6 P.M. Sun., free). God I love that name; the building itself is also called the Sponge Factory, but let's stick with Spongeorama. A little down at the heels, the attraction has mannequins dressed as sponge divers and shows an old crackly movie called *Men and the Sea,* which you view before wandering around the little sponge museum with dioramas of sponge-diving history (one gory diorama depicts a diver dying of the bends—kids hang out for a long time in front of this one). Afterwards, you buy a couple of specimens (the "wool" ones are highly prized) at the gift shop. Several people have told me that Spongeorama is haunted; maybe it's that diver with the bends.

If you're still angling for more sponge action, **St. Nicholas Boat Line** (693 Dodecanese Blvd.,

(continued on next page)

Pinellas County

SOAK IT ALL UP (cont'd)

727/942-6425, $5 adults, $2 children 6–12, free for kids under 6) offers a fun 30-minute narrated boat cruise through the sponge docks, with its own sponge-diving demonstration.

Out on the main drag, Dodecanese Boulevard, there are seven blocks of shops and restaurants. Before you settle on a place to eat, stop into nearby **St. Nicholas Church** (18 Hibiscus St., 727/937-3540), made of 60 tons of Greek marble once on display at the Greek exhibit at the first New York World's Fair. The church is a copy of the Byzantine Revival St. Sophia in Constantinople, with beautiful Czech chandeliers and stained glass. If you happen to be here in January, time a visit for Epiphany on the 6th—this church is the center of the biggest Epiphany celebration in the country. Festivities move from the church to nearby Spring Bayou, where young Greek men dive for a cross that has been blessed and thrown into the water.

If the weather's nice, you may want to stroll along one of the well-maintained paths in nearby **Anclote River Park** (1119 Baileys Bluff Rd., Holiday, 727/938-2598, open dawn–dusk daily, free admission). The park boasts an easy two-mile roundtrip trail, as well as fishing access, a boat ramp, playground for the kids, a swimming beach, and picnic facilities. It's also a notable destination for birders—beloved for its resident reddish egrets, black-bellied plovers, and osprey nests. Actually, it's part of a cluster of parks on the Great Florida Birding Trail, along with the nearby **Key Vista Nature Park** (2700 Baileys Bluff Rd., Holiday, 727/938-2598, open dawn–dusk daily, free admission), which has even more diverse natural habitats, from fresh- and saltwater marshes to pine uplands and tidal flats, all the better for observing species like loons, buffleheads, eagles, and migratory warblers.

So now you're hungry. Everyone has a different favorite Greek restaurant here. Mine is **Hellas** (785 Dodecanese Blvd., 727/943-2400, 11 A.M.–10 P.M. daily, $10–20), a lively spot with a full bar and a wonderful Greek bakery attached to it. The best entrée is slowly braised tomatoey lamb shanks, served somewhat mysteriously atop spaghetti. There are addictive garlic shrimp, nice gyros in warm Greek pita, and a delicious Greek salad that comes with a scoop of potato salad hidden in its midst. Others swear by **Mykonos** (628 Dodecanese Blvd., 727/934-4306, 11 A.M.–10 P.M. daily, $10–17) for the lamb chops, Greek meatloaf, and slightly more refined atmosphere. Still, **Mama's** (735 Dodecanese Blvd., 727/944-2888, 11 A.M.–10 P.M. daily, $7–14) often gets the nod for casual, family-friendly booths and delicious but messy chicken souvlaki sandwiches. If you're visiting on a Saturday night, head over after dinner to the bouzouki club called **Zorba** (508 W. Athens, 727/934-8803), for some zesty belly-dancing and an ouzo.

For more information about Tarpon Springs, contact the **Tarpon Springs Cultural Center** (727/942-5605) or the **chamber of commerce** (11 E. Orange St., 727/937-6109, www.tarponsprings.com).

As seen at Spongeorama, the sponge industry was prosperous in the 1930s, bringing millions of dollars annually to Tarpon Springs.

the Clearwater estuary and Intracoastal Waterway, with commentary by a marine biologist.

Smaller, more like a really big pet store, the **Konger Tarpon Springs Aquarium** (850 Dodecanese Blvd., Tarpon Springs, 727/938-5378, 10 A.M.–5 P.M. Mon.–Sat., noon–5 P.M. Sun., $5 adults, $3 kids, 3 and under free) has a 120,000-gallon main tank aquarium with more than 30 species of fish, including nurse sharks, bonnet head sharks, snook, tarpon, and protected Jewfish (these huge guys have recently been renamed something slightly less anti-Semitic—they're "Goliath grouper" now, but it hasn't totally taken off). The best time to visit is for shark or alligator feeding times: alligators at 12:30 P.M., sharks at 1 P.M. and 4 P.M.

FOR KIDS

The No. 1 kids' draw is the beach, hands down. All the beaches of Pinellas County are enormously kid-centric, with amenities, snacks, bathrooms, and all the necessities for a day of seaside bliss. For when you need a break—from beachcombing, sandcastle building, and the chief teen activity of moving his or her towel far enough away to pretend he or she is not in your party—the area has lots of other allures.

Money Up Front Michele, Plundering Pete, Gangplank Gary, and the other pirates will greet you with an "argh, me matey" on the deck of **Captain Memo's Original Pirate Cruise** (25 Causeway Blvd., Dock 3, Clearwater Beach, 727/446-2587, 10 A.M. and 2 P.M., $30 adults, $25 seniors, $20 children), a two-hour pirate cruise on a fancy bright red pirate ship. In a similar vein, **John's Pass Village & Boardwalk** (12901 Gulf Blvd. E, on Gulf Blvd. just between Madeira Beach and Treasure Island, 727/423-7824, www.thepirateshipatjohnspass.com, 11 A.M., 2 P.M., and sunset daily, $28 adults, $18 for children 2–20, children under 2 free) offers a **Pirates at the Pass** cruise on a fully kitted out pirate ship. You'll engage in water pistol battles and treasure hunts and listen to pirate stories.

John's Pass Village is home to a large commercial and charter fishing fleet, as well as art galleries, restaurants, and boutiques along a waterfront boardwalk. Families also seem to enjoy the dolphin tours out of John's Pass and into scenic Boca Ciega Bay. A couple of companies offer these—**Hubbard's Sea Adventures** (departs from John's Pass boardwalk, 727/393-1947, www.hubbardsmarina.com, 1 P.M., 3 P.M., and 6 P.M. daily, $11.95 adults, $6 children 11 and under) brings you face to face with the bay's breadth of wildlife.

Farther south, **Dolphin Landings** (4737 Gulf Blvd., behind the Dolphin Village Shopping Center, St. Pete Beach, 727/367-4488, www.charterboatescape.com, sailing times vary, $25–35) conducts two-hour dolphin-watch cruises and longer three- to four-hour trips to Shell Key, an undeveloped barrier island. The scheduled trips and private charters are conducted on one of 40 locally owned sailboats, pontoon boats, and deep-sea fishing yachts.

After spending time at Sunken Gardens (see *Gardens and Parks*), give the kids their due next door at **Great Explorations** (1925 4th St. N, St. Petersburg, 727/821-8992, www.greatexplorations.org, 10 A.M.–4:30 P.M. Mon.–Sat., noon–4:30 P.M. Sun., $9 general admission, $8 seniors, children 1 and under free). The hands-on science center had a much-needed cash infusion in 2003, with lots of slick educational exhibits on things like the hydrologic cycle or ecosystem of the estuary. Many of the exhibits are best appreciated by late elementary-aged kids (let's say kids up to about 11), but exhibits such as "Gears" and the "Laser Harp" have appeal even to little kids. If your family enjoys hands-on science museums, head over to Tampa's MOSI for a bigger dose. This makes a fun afternoon, though, especially when capped by an ice cream at Coldstone Creamery, craftily located on the premises.

The artistically inclined kid might enjoy visiting Dunedin Fine Art Center, which contains the **David L. Mason Children's Art Museum** (1143 Michigan Blvd., Dunedin, 727/298-3322, 10 A.M.–5 P.M. Mon.–Fri., 10 A.M.–2 P.M. Sat., 1–4 P.M. Sun.), a gallery space for children. This smaller part of the museum provides hands-on activities that assist families in understanding and appreciating the work of

Florida artists exhibited in the galleries. Recent exhibits in the art center have included "The Comic Book Hero," which in the kids' museum gets deconstructed with projects and stories about classic superheroes. There are frequent "family-time" workshops for parents and children to learn about art together, and summer art camps for kids. Even if you spend your time in the art center and not the children's museum, the scale is such that it's not intimidating or boring for kids (and they had a cool miniatures show in the beginning of 2005).

Sound too effete for your brood? **Celebration Station** (24546 U.S. 19 N, Clearwater, 727/791-1799, www.celebrationstation.com, noon–9 P.M. Sun.–Thurs., noon–midnight Fri., 10 A.M.–midnight Sat., tokens $10/roll, different prices for activities) brings you go-karts, bumper boats, games, miniature golf, batting cages, laser tag, and pizza.

Arts and Entertainment

MUSIC

A couple of big venues host a range of performances. **Ruth Eckerd Hall** (1111 McMullen Booth Rd. N, Clearwater, 727/791-7000, www.rutheckerdhall.com, times and prices vary) is the locus for much of the area's lively arts activity. The 2,200-seat space was designed by the Frank Lloyd Wright Foundation more than 20 years ago and the space still looks fresh, the sound still full and lush (acoustically, it had a fairly recent overhaul). It's home to the **Florida Orchestra** (mailing address 101 S. Hoover Blvd., #100, Tampa, FL 33609, 727/286-1170), which is the top regional orchestra, performing more than 150 concerts annually here, at the Mahaffey Theater, and elsewhere. Beyond symphonic music, Ruth Eckerd hosts pop acts, visiting theater, and other performing arts. (Its new educational wing, the Marcia P. Hoffman Performing Arts Institute, features a 182-seat Murray Studio Theatre, three studio classrooms, four private teaching studios, a dance studio and rehearsal space, and an arts resource library.)

The **Mahaffey Theater** (400 1st St. S, St. Petersburg, 727/892-5767, www.mahaffeytheater.com, times and prices vary), in the Bayfront Center, is a similarly sized venue, with a seating capacity of 2,000 and cool European-style boxes. A lovely theater, it hosts the *St. Petersburg Times'* Broadway by the Bay Series, many performances of the Florida Orchestra, jazz, ballet, opera, the circus, and contemporary performers as well. The Mahaffey is directly on the waterfront,

within walking distance of shopping, some of the area's finest restaurants, and many of the downtown's museums. It is undergoing a huge renovation and may be closed.

A smaller venue for rock and contemporary acts, **Jannus Landing** (220 1st Ave. N, 727/896-1244, www.jannuslanding.net, times and prices vary) is supposedly the oldest outdoor concert venue in Florida. From jam bands like Medeski, Martin, and Wood, to Snoop Dogg, to Lucinda Williams—it all sounds fabu from a spot in the outdoor courtyard. It's bigger than a nightclub, with bigger acts, but there's still a cool club vibe and usually a 30s-and-up crowd.

The historic **Coliseum** (535 4th Ave. N, 727/892-5202, parking area on the left $4, times and prices vary) was built in 1924 and purchased by the City of St. Petersburg in 1989. They've gussied up the gorgeous space and reopened it as a multi-use facility, hosting a range of things from Florida Orchestra pops concerts to the Toronto All Star Big Band to an exotic bird show.

THEATER

At the top of the dramatic arts heap in Pinellas County, **American Stage** (211 3rd St. S, St. Petersburg, 727/823-7529, curtain usually 7:30 P.M. Wed. and Thurs., 8 P.M. Fri. and Sat., weekend matinees 3 P.M., tickets $22–32) is Tampa Bay's oldest professional theater, with a five-play mainstage season, children's theater, educational outreach, and the annual Shakespeare in the Park festival. The mainstage season shows breadth, reaching from musicals such as *Tapestry: The Music of Carole King* to the Tampa Bay premiere of the riveting *The Exonerated* about wrongly accused Death Row inmates. The Family Series is a good deal, with single tickets $7. Many American Stage productions are performed at the midsize, 800-seat **Palladium Theater** (253 5th Ave. N, St. Petersburg, 727/822-3590).

For local community theater, several companies are worth checking out, all with reasonable ticket prices. Throughout its 80 years as Florida's oldest continuously operating community theater, **St. Petersburg Little Theatre** (4025 31st St. S, St. Petersburg, 727/866-1973, curtain 8 P.M. and 2 P.M. matinees, musicals $18, nonmusicals $15) has presented up to six community productions per season, split fairly evenly between

musicals, comedies, and dramas. It's usually crowd-pleasers like *Noises Off* or Neil Simon's *Brighton Beach Memoirs*. **Francis Wilson Playhouse** (302 Seminole St., Clearwater, 727/446-1360, curtain 8 P.M. and 2 P.M. matinees, musicals $18, nonmusicals $14) is another venerable community playhouse, having opened in 1930. The intimate, 182-seat theater showcases eight comedies and musicals (*La Cage Aux Folles, Auntie Mame*) per season and a family-oriented program in December.

In the little town of Gulfport on Boca Ciega Bay, the fairly new **Catherine Hickman Theater** (5501 27th Ave. S, Gulfport, 727/893-1070) hosts Gulfport Community Players community theater productions and Pinellas Park Civic Orchestra concerts.

Accommodations

$100–150

For Romance Seekers

La Veranda Bed and Breakfast (111 5th Ave. N, St. Petersburg, 727/824-9997, $99–299) is wonderful for couples as it's right near the heart of downtown St. Petersburg, but still quiet and romantic. It's set in a 1910 mansion girdled by wide wraparound porches and sweet tropical gardens, its suites decorated with canopy beds, antiques, and Oriental rugs. Each suite opens directly onto the large veranda, ergo the name. Just up the block is a similar inn called **Mansion House Bed and Breakfast** (105 5th Ave. NE, St. Petersburg, 727/821-9391, www.mansionbandb.com, $99–220). There are 12 pretty rooms set in two Craftsman-style houses, one of which is thought to have been built in between 1901 and 1904 by St. Petersburg's first mayor, David Mofett. A courtyard in between the houses is perfect for a little reading or down time.

A little smaller and more intimate, even, is **Bayboro House Bed and Breakfast** (1719 Beach Dr. SE, St. Petersburg, $149–249), which is said to be the oldest B&B in St. Petersburg. It's the only waterside bed-and-breakfast in town, located on a quiet cul de sac in a busy shopping

area. Guests often seem content to sit in the swing or wicker furniture on the wide veranda and gaze off at Old Tampa Bay, but the inn also provides complimentary bikes to visitors for exploring the city. Eight rooms are kitted out with hand-carved mahogany canopy beds and early 1900s antiques.

For Families

It's not cheap, but the **TradeWinds Island Resorts** (5500 Gulf Blvd., St. Pete Beach, 727/367-6461, www.tradewindsresort.com) offers families a bunch of accommodation choices with nary a clinker among them. The resort, supposedly the largest on the Gulf Coast, comprises the TradeWinds Island Grand ($168–457) and the Sandpiper Hotel and Suites ($121–226), and whichever one you choose includes playtime privileges at the other. The Island Grand is the fancier, a four-diamond property with soaring palms, a grand lobby, and really lovely rooms. Sandpiper would be my choice with little ones. The whole complex offers multiple pools, something like a dozen places to eat and drink, mutiple fitness centers, tennis courts everywhere, a paddleboat canal meandering through the grounds, and a wide, private expanse of beach.

Right out the back of the properties you can rent equipment for snorkeling or fishing, and try your hand at parasailing, water skiing, and water scooters. The kids' program (KONK, Kids Only, No Kidding!) is tremendous, with seasonal programs like the "Swashbucklin' By the Sea" pirate package in which you get to meet Redbeard and walk the plank.

N Sirata Beach Resort (5300 Gulf Blvd. St. Pete Beach, 727/363-5100, $127–370) used to be connected to the TradeWinds but is now an independent, family-run midsize hotel, with a range of kids' programs and activities. It's the kind of place that locals in Tampa take their brood for a weekend of R&R, as is the very nearby **N Alden Beach Resort** (5900 Gulf Blvd., St. Pete Beach, 727/360-7081, $115–269), which is an attentively staffed, family-owned beach resort of 149 suites, especially beloved by kids. It has tennis, volleyball, two pools (a little far from the beach, so the walk back and forth takes time for little ones), and a video game room. Rooms on the pool side are significantly cheaper than on the Gulf side.

For Golfers

Westin Innisbrook Golf Resort (36750 U.S. 19 N, Palm Harbor, 800/456-2000, www.westin-innisbrook.com, $139–479) is a 900-acre property just north of Clearwater. It has four top-ranked golf courses, 11 tennis courts, six swimming pool (including the super kids-oriented Loch Ness Monster Pool), a children's recreation center, several restaurants, and 60 acres with a series of jogging and cycling trails. Rooms are all suites, with nice working kitchens. Its Copperhead Golf Course stretches more than 7,300 yards long and is home to the PGA Tour's Chrysler Championship.

OVER $150

Some of this area's greatest landmarks are grand old hotels. In order to feel comfortable with the splurge, tell yourself it's like the price of the hotel plus the admission to a local historical attraction. A historical attraction with room service.

Built in 1897 by railroad magnate and west-central Florida pioneer Henry Plant, the 292-room **Belleview Biltmore Resort & Spa** (25 Belleview Blvd., Clearwater, 727/442-6171, www.belleviewbiltmore.com, $140–800) is reputed to be the largest continuously occupied wooden structure in the world (its roof is 2.5 acres). On the National Register of Historic Places (there are tours daily, even if you're not staying here), it's a historical retreat from the beach bustle of Clearwater, situated high on a coastal bluff, where it's easy to unwind and indulge in a little golf or the gamut of spa treatments. There's been some recent scuttlebutt that high roller developers are thinking about buying the property, knocking it down, and putting up condos. So, go quick.

The huge, Pepto Bismol-pink **Don CeSar Beach Resort & Spa** (400 Gulf Blvd., St. Pete Beach, 727/363-1881, www.doncesar.com, $194–559) is a landmark in St. Pete and a long-time point of reference on maritime navigation charts. Named after a character in the opera *Maritana,* the Don CeSar has hosted F. Scott Fitzgerald and wife Zelda, Clarence Darrow, Al Capone, Lou Gehrig, and countless other celebrities. Originally opened in 1928, the property was commandeered by the military during World War II and eventually abandoned. These days, it's a Loews hotel, with 340 lovely rooms, fishing, golfing, tennis, and the soothing Beach Club & Spa. Again, if it's too rich for your blood, take the tour and stop in for ice cream at its old-fashioned ice cream parlor (get the coffee flavor).

The hits just keep on coming. The **N Renaissance Vinoy Resort & Golf Club** (501 5th Ave. NE, 727/894-1000, www.renaissancehotels.com, $199–600) was built by Pennsylvania oilman Aymer Vinoy Laughner in 1925. At $3.5 million, the Mediterranean Revival-style hotel was the largest construction project in Florida's history. Exquisitely restored in 1992 at a cost of $93 million, the resort exudes the kind of rarefied glamour that helps put life's quotidian woes behind you. There are 360 guest rooms and 15 suites, many with views of the marina. The hotel also has a spa, a lovely pool with a waterfall, five restaurants, tennis courts, an 18-hole golf course designed by Ron Garl, and its own marina.

Again, it's the kind of hotel that was frequented by people like Calvin Coolidge, Babe Ruth, and Herbert Hoover, and is listed on the National Register of Historic Places.

Another piece of history, but I'm not sure if I'm buying this one, is claimed by **Safety Harbor Resort and Spa** (105 N. Bayshore Dr., Safety Harbor, 888/237-8772, www.safetyharborspa.com, $99–311). About a zillion places along the Gulf Coast profess to be what Spanish explorer Hernando de Soto identified as the "Fountain of Youth." Is it the mineral pools here at this 50,000-square-foot spa and tennis academy? Got to give you a dunno on that one. The waters are mighty nice either way, filling three pools and used in the spa treatments. The resort is also home to the Oscar Parks Golf Academy and the Phil Green Tennis Academy, with a sophisticated restaurant called 105 North and a fancy-pants salon. The 189 guest rooms and four suites are spacious and offer nice views of Tampa Bay.

Food

Pinellas County is awash in restaurants, most of them fun and casual, many of them worthy of recommendation. Because the area is densely populated and traffic can get fairly impacted during high season, you're more likely to grab a bite near where you're staying or near the beach from which you're departing. For this reason, I'm listing the restaurants in the Clearwater-St. Petersburg area geographically, from north to south. There are, on the other hand, those restaurants that are worth a drive in traffic, what restaurateurs call "destination restaurants." You may just call them "expensive restaurants." I'll list these first.

EXPENSIVE RESTAURANTS

In keeping with the glamour of the historic Vinoy, its restaurant, **Marchand's Grill** (Renaissance Vinoy Resort, 501 5th Ave. NE, St. Petersburg, 727/894-1000, 11:30 A.M.–2:30 P.M. and 5:30–10 P.M. daily, $18–35) sparkles with opulent appointments and an equally opulent clientele. What's your mood? One side of the restaurant features sleek Mediterranean fare and the other side traffics in American contemporary dishes. Where to look, that's the problem—is it up at the frescoes dating from when it was the dazzling Pompeii Room, is it out to the view of Tampa Bay and the gently bobbing boats, or is it at the well-heeled and elegant patrons that surrounds you? If you want to pull out all the gastronomic stops at the Vinoy, **Fred's** is even more

of a splurge. But not so fast—you have to be a member or a resort guest to enjoy it.

Eric's New World Bistro (1026 Florida Ave., Palm Harbor, 727/787-7734, 4–10 P.M. daily, $15–29) is downtown Palm Harbor's most sophisticated special-occasion dining, set in an old bank building (the Teller's Cage Lounge, where the bank teller counter used to be, serves one of the finest martinis around). The menu is the height of contemporary, blending vital Floribbean flavors with Mediterranean lushness and California chic. An elegant date-night crowd sips something from the stellar wine list while choosing between blue cornmeal-dusted shrimp (sautéed with tequila-lime-garlic-tomato butter) and black sesame tuna with cucumber wasabi sauce.

N Cafe Ponte (off Ulmerton Rd. in the Icot Center, 13505 Icot Blvd., Clearwater, 727/538-5768, www.cafeponte.com, 11:30 A.M.–2 P.M. Mon.–Fri., 5:30–10 P.M. Tues.–Thurs., until 11 P.M. Fri. and Sat., $18–36) is a newcomer in the area, but it was deemed the "best restaurant of 2004" by the *St. Petersburg Times.* Chef Christopher Ponte trained at Taillevent in Paris and turns out ultra-luxe mushroom soup with a dollop of truffle cream; crispy whole snapper with mango, mint, and macadamia nuts over a ginger-vanilla rum sauce; and a supremely comforting yet vaguely exotic braised short rib tagine.

Redwoods in downtown St. Petersburg (247 Central Ave., 727/896-5118, www.redwoodsrestaurant.com, 5:30–10 P.M. Tues.–Thurs., until

11 P.M. Fri. and Sat., $23–50) also generated a huge buzz since its recent opening. Its original concept to me was just slightly whack—Pacific Rim cuisine that married elements God nor Julia Child ever intended (venison with green papaya salsa). Now it's New American cuisine, only this time with a Latin twist, so you'll find Argentine beef tenderloin and chicken stuffed with queso fresco and herbs. Still, it's got buzz, the energy and dynamism of a hit place, with a sleek interior and fine service.

Salt Rock Grill (19325 Gulf Blvd., Indian Shores, 727/593-7625, www.saltrockgrill.com, 4–10 P.M. Sun.–Thurs., until 11 P.M. Fri. and Sat., $15–37) is another relative newcomer that's fairly mobbed every night. No worries if you have to wait, though, as a cocktail on the front deck is glorious on a warm night. The menu has enticing seafood—pan-seared scallops, salmon Oscar—but the steaks emerge from the kitchen with the most expert handling, aged in-house and grilled over a super hot natural oak and citrus wood pit fire. It's more formal than most beachside spots around here, and the glamorous clientele seems thrilled.

Maritana Grille at the Don CeSar (3400 Gulf Blvd., St. Pete Beach, 727/360-1881, www.doncesar.com, 5:30–10 P.M. Sun.–Thurs., until 11 P.M. Fri. and Sat., $18–37.50) has "special occasion" written all over it. There's a great chef's table for groups up to eight, at which executive chef Eric Neri is put through his Floribbean-cuisine paces, from marmalade-roasted Gulf red snapper served with pea vines or grilled filet mignon with truffled mashed potatoes and candied shallots. The restaurant's interior is lovely, the patrons surrounded by 1,500 gallons of saltwater aquariums and indigenous Florida fish.

DUNEDIN AND OLDSMAR

The best place to start casually dining in Pinellas County is **Bon Appetit** (148 Marina Plaza, Dunedin, 727/733-2151, 11:30 A.M.–9 P.M. Mon.–Thurs., until 10 P.M. Fri. and Sat., 11 A.M.–8:30 P.M. Sun., $12–35). It's in the Best Western Yacht Harbor Inn and Suites, so there's a certain amount of that holdover "Continen-

tal" cuisine fanciness one associates with hotel restaurants. Owners Peter Kreuziger and Karl Heinz Riedl manage to add a definite panache to the seafood-heavy menu, whether it's a passel of garlic-heady mussels steamed in herbaceous sauvignon blanc or the season's freshest stone crabs adorned with only a squeeze of lemon and a pool of clarified butter. The kitchen gets jiggier with dishes like intensely smoky sea scallops heaped on crisp, pizza-like flat bread spread with goat cheese and tangy red-onion marmalade and an anomalous-seeming but tasty yellow beef curry dolled up with chutney, cucumber raita, and toasted coconut. The thing is, you don't have to get all uppity and pay the big prices—guests can watch the dolphins play as the sun sets out on the water and not spend a bushel if they dine at the Marine Café adjacent to the restaurant. It's a different menu than the fancier sibling, but a single sheet of "signature dishes" from the main restaurant is available outside.

Downtown Dunedin has been charmingly reinvigorated with restaurants and cafés in recent years. For casual Mexican, go to **Casa Tina** (369 Main St., 727/734-9226, 11 A.M.–10 P.M. Sun.–Thurs., until 11 P.M. Fri. and Sat., $7–15). It's lively, with an eye-catching color scheme and engaging clientele. It's a little less heavy than many local cheese-centric Mexican joints—that said, try the wild mushroom quesadilla. About as family friendly, **Kelly's Restaurant** (319 Main St., Dunedin, 727/736-5284, 8 A.M.–10 P.M. Sun.–Thurs., until 11 P.M. Fri. and Sat., $8–18) has the kind of far-reaching comfort food menu that leaves no stone unturned, from eggplant-portobello-tomato Napoleons to butternut squash ravioli. It's a kids' kind of joint, very friendly and accommodating.

All right, maybe it's a little bit of a splurge, but **The Black Pearl** (315 Main St., 727/734-3463, 5–9:30 P.M. daily, $18–30) next door is good enough to undermine my categorization this early in the game. Try the cedar-planked salmon or the crab imperial. It's one of those rarefied places that embody the outré word "nouvelle," meaning fairly steep prices and aesthetic aspirations, fairly low quantity on each plate. It works for me, you be the judge.

CLEARWATER

Clearwater has a fairly dense concentration of good restaurants, nothing too cutting-edge, mind you, but good. But really, you owe it to yourself and owl fans everywhere to go to the original **Hooters** (2800 Gulf-To-Bay Blvd., 727/797-4008, 11 A.M.–11 P.M. Sun.–Thurs., until midnight Fri. and Sat., $7–16). More than 20 years old, the original pleasant, ramshackle sports-oriented joint has spawned an international empire and airline (if you join the Hooters Mile High Club do you get extra bragging rights?). I've eaten here with gusto, and I was even a women's studies major. It's a family restaurant, really, with good chicken wings (order them not breaded, with the really hot sauce, but a little dry so they don't come all goopy). Only, it's a family restaurant in which all waitresses are wildly pneumatic and wearing those flesh-colored pantyhose from the 1970s under orange nylon short-shorts.

By the way, a cooter is a red-bellied turtle that was historically serious eats for the Florida Cracker. That's why **Cooters Raw Bar and Restaurant** (423 Poinsettia Ave., 727/462-2668, www.cooters.com, 11 A.M.–11 P.M. Sun.–Thurs., until midnight Fri. and Sat., $9–20) is called that, not to rhyme with Hooters. A fun but gastronomically challenged place, the steamed crab legs and the grouper cheeks aren't bad.

My Clearwater favorite is **ℕ Carmelita's** (5042 E. Bay Dr., 727/524-8226, 11 A.M.–9:30 P.M. Sun.–Thurs., until 10 P.M. Fri. and Sat., $7–14; but also worthy is 5211 Park St. N, St. Petersburg, 727/545-2956). Each of the three legendary locations serves up the same luscious, zingy-spicy green enchiladas to dispatch with a potent margarita.

Lenny's Restaurant (21220 U.S. 19 N, 727/799-0402, 6 A.M.–3 P.M. daily, $5–12) is the hands-down winner for breakfast, but for the Jewish staples of blintzes, knishes, latkes. You can get an omelet here, too, if you want to look like a goy.

I'm not including a nightlife section in this chapter, partially because evening revelry is to be found all around, in tiki huts and outdoor decks along the Gulf beaches. One bar, though, merits mention. **ℕ O'Keefe's Tavern and Restaurant** (1219 S. Fort Harrison Ave., Clearwater, 727/442-9034, 11 A.M.–2 A.M. daily, $7–14) is the bar to beat for St. Patrick's Day. A good-times, pint-or-three shambling Irish pub, its history goes back to the 1960s when it was O'Keefe's Tap Room, a history still visible despite the many additions and remodelings. A white brick exterior gives way to a comfortable series of rooms festooned with lots of green accents and Irishobilia. The brogue-required bartenders are fast and furious with the beers (more than 100 offerings) and the all-ages crowd is unified by their affection for the place. Once known for its "seven-course Irish dinner" (that's six beers and a potato), O'Keefe's fare is pretty good.

INDIAN ROCKS BEACH AND REDINGTON SHORES

Crabby Bill's (401 Gulf Blvd., Indian Rocks Beach, 727/595-4825; www.crabbybills.com, 11:30 A.M.–11 P.M. daily, $8–22) is a family-owned regional chain that has made a name for itself with family-style seating, group singing, fast-and-loose seafood cookery, and flowing beverages.

An institution since 1978, the **Lobster Pot** (17814 Gulf Blvd., Redington Shores, 727/391-8592, 4:30–10 P.M. Mon.–Thurs., until 11 P.M. Fri. and Sat., 4–10 P.M. Sun., $13–28) is a comfortable seafood place with hokey lobster traps on the wall. Seafood is straightforward but fresh; it's the place to try local grouper or stone crab in season.

ST. PETERSBURG

Remember, downtown St. Petersburg's on the east side of the peninsula, not on the Gulf, but on Old Tampa Bay. There are several wonderful picks here—definitely the densest concentration of sophisticated dining in Pinellas. First, **Mattison's American Bistro** (111 2nd Ave. NE, 727/895-2200, www.mattisons.com, 11 A.M.–2 P.M. Mon., 11 A.M.–9 P.M. Tues.–Thurs., until 10 P.M. Fri. and Sat., $17–32) is a slick, New American restaurant with ace servers and a lovely interior. The menu adopts a sturdy middle-of-the-road approach, which pays dividends with the rack of New Zealand lamb or pesto-crusted Idaho trout. The restaurant is situated just across from St. Petersburg's trendy Bay Walk.

If you feel like a little Asian fusion, on the other hand, there's that, too. **Pacific Wave Restaurant** (211 2nd St. S, 727/822-5235, 5–10 P.M. Mon.–Thurs., until 11 P.M. Fri. and Sat., $21–31) has a cool late-night crowd that comes for Hawaiian fish with chipotle grits or Laotian springrolls sparked by Thai basil.

For a simple burger, go to **El Cap** (3500 4th St. N, 727/521-1314, 11 A.M.–11 P.M. Mon.–Sat., until 10 P.M. Sun.), and for classical French, the place is **Chateau France** (136 4th Ave. NE, 727/894-7163, 5–11 P.M. Mon.–Sat., $17–28), set in an elegantly renovated St. Petersburg mansion.

ST. PETE BEACH

I'm running out of room. If you can go to just one place in St. Pete Beach, it's to get the blackened grouper sandwich at **Ⓜ The Hurricane** (really on Pass-A-Grille Beach, 807 Gulf Way, 727/360-9558, 11 A.M.–9:30 P.M. Sun.–Thurs., until 10 P.M. Fri. and Sat., $8–24). I don't care if the place seems a little touristy; give me that sweet white fish, amped with red and black pepper and lots of salt, add in some tomato, lettuce, and a big swath of mayo, all on a pretty soft roll. It's as good as it gets in Pinellas County. There's a nice bar adjacent to the restaurant and a rooftop sundeck up top for sunset scrutiny.

On the other hand, if you go only to Hurricane's, then you'll miss out on the orange-pecan French toast or the creamed chipped beef on toast for breakfast at **Skyway Jack's Restaurant** (2795 34th St. S, 727/867-1907, 5 A.M.–3 P.M. daily, $5–10). It's a kitschy classic around here, moved once because it was on the approach to the Skyway Bridge and got pushed out to make room for more lanes. It still sells stuff like scrambled pork brains served with eggs, potatoes, and grits—who buys this stuff? Stick with regular breakfast food, or the smoked mullet if you're feeling bold.

Shopping

THE PIER

The Pier (800 2nd Ave. NE, St. Petersburg, 727/821-6443) is really the heart and soul of visitor activity in St. Petersburg, looking like an inverted pyramid, or the good guys' home base in a sci-fi movie. You can rent bikes, grab a rental rod and reel and fish off the end, depart from the Pier on a sightseeing boat charter, see a flick at the 20-screen movie theater, visit the little aquarium, dine in the family-friendly food court, or browse the complex's many shops. It's not high-end stuff, more touristy—there's a pet accouterment store, a entertainment-celebrity collectibles shop, candle store, T-shirt stores, that kind of thing.

BAYWALK

Baywalk (125 2nd Ave. N, St. Petersburg, 727/895-9277, www.baywalkstpete.com) is the much more upscale shopping destination in St. Petersburg, not far away. It's right downtown, with an indoor-outdoor array of shops (some independents, some like Ann Taylor and Chico's), fairly fancy restaurants with a number of cuisines represented, and outdoor entertainment on the "Mainstage." It also has a 20-screen movie theater—stop in before or after at Dan Marino's restaurant for heavenly martinis.

HASLAM'S BOOK STORE

Florida's largest new and used bookstore merits a couple of hours of browsing, especially if the weather is inclement (a rarity). Haslam's Book Store (2025 Central Ave., St. Petersburg, 727/822-8616, www.haslams.com, 10 A.M.–6:30 P.M. Mon.–Sat.) is now owned by the third generation of the same family, with more than 300,000 volumes. In a world populated increasingly by Borders and Barnes & Noble (hey, I'm a frequenter of both), it's refreshing sometimes to hang out in an independently owned bookstore. Haslam's has a large number of rare books, and they seem to be really into science fiction.

Information and Services

AREA INFORMATION

Clearwater and St. Petersburg are on eastern time. The telephone area code is 727, but here's the annoying thing: Right over the causeway in Tampa the area code is 813. So, you need to dial it as if it's long distance, but you don't precede the phone number by dialing 1. It's long distance, but not long-long distance, evidently.

Tourist Information

St. Petersburg/Clearwater Area Convention & Visitors Bureau (14450 46th St., Ste. #108, Clearwater, 727/464-7200) is not wildly convenient, but its website is tremendous (www.floridasbeach.com). St. Petersburg Area Chamber of Commerce (100 2nd Ave. N, Ste. 150, 727/821-4069, www.stpete.org, 9 A.M.–5 P.M. Mon.–Fri., 10 A.M.–4 P.M. Sat., noon–4 P.M. Sun.) has a decent walk-in site with brochures and maps.

The area is awash in great websites. The various chambers of commerce have their own sites: Tarpon Springs (www.tarponsprings.com), Clearwater (www.clearwaterflorida.org) and Clearwater Beach (www.beachchamber.com), Dunedin (www.dunedin-fl.com), among others. For outdoors information, there's **Clearwater Parks** (www.clearwater-fl.com/City_Departments/parksrec/index.asp), **Florida Parks** (www.floridaparks.com), **Pinellas County Parks** (www.pinellascounty.org/parkdpt.htm), and **St. Petersburg Parks** (www.stpete.org/parkrec.htm).

St. Petersburg is blessed with the very best newspaper on the Gulf Coast. The ***St. Petersburg Times*** (490 1st Ave. S, St. Petersburg, 727/893-8111, with a useful website for locals and visitors, www.sptimes.com) is a serious metro daily with hard-hitting investigative journalists, award-winning columnists, and great arts coverage. You'll see kiosks everywhere.

COURTESY OF VISIT FLORIDA

Pinellas County

Sailing in protected Tampa Bay is a regular pastime.

Police and Emergencies

In an emergency, dial 911. If you need medical assistance, the area has several large hospitals with good emergency care: **St. Petersburg General Hospital** (6500 38th Ave. N, St. Petersburg, 727/341-4870) and **St. Anthony's Hospital** (1200 7th Ave. N, St. Petersburg, 727/825-1100) in the south of the county, and **Suncoast Hospital** (2025 Indian Rocks Rd., Largo, 727/581-9474) in northern Pinellas County. For a nonemergency police need, contact the **St. Petersburg Police Department** (1300 1st Ave. N, St. Petersburg, 727/893-7780).

Radio and Television

Because it's a big metropolitan area, Tampa and St. Pete have an enormous number of radio stations between them. There's independent radio at **WMNF 88.5 FM,** light rock at **WMTX 100.7 FM,** '70s hits at **WCOF 107.3 FM,** and NPR and classical at **WUSF 89.7 FM.**

For local television programming, **Bay News 9** is Bright House Networks' 24-hour local news station, **WFLA Channel 8** is the local NBC affiliate, **WTSP Channel 10** is the CBS affiliate, **WTVT Channel 13** is the FOX affiliate, and **WFTS Channel 28** is the local ABC affiliate.

Laundry Services

Many of the larger hotels offer laundry service, as do most marinas in the area. For coin-operated laundry in St. Petersburg, try one of two **Soapy** locations (1202 28th St. S, 727/323-5480, or 3435 15th Ave. S, 727/322-1652). To the north in Clearwater, there's 24-hour laundry at **Thompson's Dry Cleaners and Laundry** (1713 Drew St., 727/461-2589).

Getting There and Around

DRIVING

Pinellas County is easily accessible from major interstates along the Midwest (I-75) and Northeast (I-95) corridors, as well as Orlando (I-4). I-275 serves the western portions of the Tampa–St. Petersburg area, including downtown Tampa, St. Petersburg, and Bradenton. It starts in the south at I-75 in Bradenton and extends up through St. Petersburg and Tampa, connected by two major bridges (Sunshine Skyway in the south and Howard Frankland Bridge to the north) before reuniting with I-75 at Lutz. I-75, by contrast, skirts both cities and acts as a bypass to southwest Florida and the Gulf Coast.

Once in Pinellas, Clearwater is in the north along the Gulf, St. Petersburg is in the south along the bay. To reach St. Petersburg from Clearwater, head south on U.S. 19A, a slow, densely trafficked mess. Farther east, the regular U.S. 19 cuts down through the center of the peninsula to St. Petersburg.

In St. Petersburg, streets are set up in a grid pattern, with avenues running east–west and streets running north–south. Central Avenue divides north and south St. Petersburg, with the numbered avenues on either side—it's tricky, though, as to the left of Central there's 1st Avenue North, to the right it's 1st Avenue South. There are some sections of town that are all one-way streets, so you may make a lot of little squares while driving.

From St. Pete Beach all the way up through Clearwater, all you need to know is that Gulf Boulevard (Hwy. 699) runs right up the coast and through each little town. The city of Clearwater is on the mainland, but Clearwater Beach is on a barrier island connected by Memorial Causeway.

FLYING

The area is served by two midsize, easily traversed airports. **Tampa International Airport** (5503 W. Spruce St., 813/870-8700) was recently ranked by *Condé Nast* as the seventh best airport worldwide, located just over the bridge and causeway from St. Petersburg and Clearwater and about 30–45 minutes from beachfront accommodations. Domestically, it is serviced by AirTran Airlines, America West Airlines, American Airlines, Continental Airlines, Delta Airlines, Delta Express, Frontier Airlines, JetBlue Airways, Midwest Express Airlines, Northwest Airlines, Song Airways, Southwest Airlines, Spirit Airlines, Ted, United Airlines, and US Airways. International carriers include AirCanada, British Airways, Cayman Airways, and American Eagle.

You'll probably fly in and out of Tampa, unless you're coming from Canada. But there's also **St. Petersburg-Clearwater International Airport** (14501 Roosevelt Blvd., Clearwater, 727/531-1451), which has a newly enlarged terminal and is served by American Trans Air and USA 3000 Airlines; Canadian airlines CanJet, Air Transat, Sunwing, and Jetsgo Airlines; and Seacoast Airlines to Key West.

Alamo (800/327-9633), **Avis** (800/831-2847), **Budget** (800/527-0700), **Dollar** (800/800-4000 domestic, 800/800-6000 international), and **National** (800/227-7368) provide rental cars from both airports.

PUBLIC TRANSPORTATION

Amtrak (800/USA-RAIL, www.amtrak.com) offers service into nearby Tampa and other surrounding areas. Some services even allow you to bring your car with you. Also, Greyhound Bus Line (800/229-9424, www.greyhound.com) provides regular service into St. Petersburg (180 9th St. N, 727/898-1496). If you stay in Clearwater, it's easy to ditch your rental car and use the **Jolley Trolley** 727/445-1200) or the **Suncoast Beach Trolley** (727/530-9911) to get around. **Pinellas Suncoast Transit Authority** (727/530-9911) also has a fairly extensive busing system around the city.

Pinellas County

The Nature Coast

The Nature Coast is the rebuttal to Orlando's Disney slickness. Civic-minded boosters have tried to sell this area as "Mother Nature's theme park," but that moniker doesn't quite work. Nothing here is marketed, packaged, or sanitized by crackerjack public relations specialists. It's rural, with the majority of the area set aside as parkland, preserves, reserves, and animal refuges.

In the weathered fishing villages along the coast and the quaint little inland towns, you're likely to see a spiffy fishing boat in every driveway, but you're just as apt to see a dead pickup truck up on blocks in the yard. Residents stay for the affordable living, for the area's easy live-and-let-live tolerance, for the unhurried pace, and—for many, the most important reason—the fish. And that's pretty much why visitors come, too. People drive here to see manatees, black bears, and wading birds; to catch fish; and to dive, to kayak, or to simply contemplate the area's wealth of waterways. There are no white-sand beaches crowded with bikini-clad college kids, no swanky nightclubs

COURTESY OF PURE WATER WILDERNESS/STACEY BROWN

Must-Sees

Look for **M** to find the sights and activities you can't miss and **M** for the best dining and lodging.

M **Nature Coast Canoe and Kayak Trail:** Imagine how the Native Americans or early Spanish explorers saw this area, from the seat of a canoe or kayak along the backwaters of this 17-mile paddling trail. Hernando de Soto, on his quest for gold, was said to have paddled waters in the this area in the summer of 1539 (page 208).

M **Homosassa Springs State Wildlife Park:** Find out why Rodale's Scuba Diving awards the area the "Best Place to See Large Animals." The manatee is the goliath in question, and you can see it up close in the underwater "fishbowl" at this wildlife park (page 209).

M **Cedar Key Scrub State Reserve:** Walk this rare ecosystem to catch a glimpse of threatened Florida scrub jay and endangered burrowing owls (page 215).

COURTESY OF PURE WATER WILDERNESS/STACEY BROWN

Much of Cedar Key's waterways and little islands have been designated a National Wildlife Refuge.

M **Dock Street:** Stroll around Dock Street any time of day and enjoy the shops, galleries, and restaurants along the wooden boardwalk. Join the anglers and pelicans on the pier and watch the sunset (page 220).

M **Offshore Fishing with Big Bend Charters:** Roughly 62 miles of Gulf Coast, 106 miles of rivers, and 19,111 acres of lakes, and that's just in Citrus County alone. This is fishing country. There are lots of trophy fish in these waters—tarpon, redfish, bass—so you and your fish smile for the camera before you release it gently back into the water. Thanks to bag limits, closed seasons, and catch-and-release indoctrination, there seem to be more fish than ever, enlivening a day of offshore fishing in Steinhatchee (page 223).

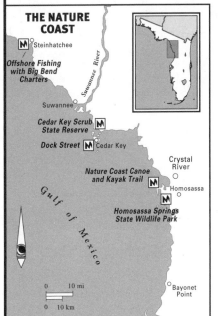

THE NATURE COAST

Steinhatchee

Offshore Fishing with Big Bend Charters

Suwannee River

Suwannee

Cedar Key Scrub State Reserve

Dock Street Cedar Key

Crystal River

Nature Coast Canoe and Kayak Trail

Homosassa

Gulf of Mexico

Homosassa Springs State Wildlife Park

Bayonet Point

0   10 mi
0   10 km

THE NATURE COAST

To Tallahassee

Madison

Perry

Keaton Beach

Mayo

Gulf of Mexico

Steinhatchee

Horseshoe Beach

Shired Island

Suwannee

0   10 mi

0   10 km

M CEDAR KEY SCRUB STATE RESERVE

Bronson

M DOCK STREET

Cedar Key

Trenton

Suwannee

Waccasassa Bay

Yankeetown

Lake Rousseau

Crystal River

M NATURE COAST CANOE AND KAYAK TRAIL

M HOMOSASSA SPRINGS STATE WILDLIFE PARK

Homosassa

Inverness

Weeki Wachee

Hudson

Brooksville

To Tampa

with throbbing VIP rooms. From north of Clearwater all the way to the "Big Bend" (where the Florida peninsula tucks west into the Panhandle), there are precious few multiplexes, museums, or high-fallutin' cultural attractions. All that would get in the way of enjoying one of the least developed stretches of Florida's Gulf Coast.

PLANNING YOUR TIME

With more than 700 square miles of scenic driving along the Nature Coast, here's the rub: The main drag, U.S. 19, is just not charming. From south of Spring Hill, the long strip festers with transmission shops, minimarts, and desperate auto dealers. North of Crystal River, 19 gets rural, with only the occasional mailbox and long driveway leading back to some misanthrope's private world. Along the way you'll see swallowtail kites swoop overhead and patient, yellow-headed cattle egrets stalking grasshoppers along the side of the road. But still, there's no getting around the ugliness of this inland highway.

Weeki Wachee Springs, Homosassa, and **Crystal River** are located directly along U.S. 19. To get to any of the little towns perched along the Gulf's edge—**Yankeetown, Cedar Key, Suwannee,** and **Steinhatchee,** from south to north—you have to drive west on rural two-lane roads. None of these can be reached one from the other, except by boat or by driving back east, rejoining U.S. 19, and then more driving.

Weeki Wachee Springs, a juicy slice of Florida history, is well worth a day trip, especially for families, either as an add-on to seeing Tarpon Springs farther south, or an addition to a trip to elsewhere on the Nature Coast. Since manatee viewing is best early in the morning, and fishing trips usually head out fairly early as well, it makes sense to stay over a night in Crystal River or Homosassa. Cedar Key and Steinhatchee, partly because they're harder to get to and partly because they're so charming, are each worth a couple of days of exploration.

Weeki Wachee to Crystal River

Florida is home to 700 freshwater springs, 33 of them first-magnitude, meaning they discharge at least 100 cubic feet of water per second. Several of these first-magnitude springs are along the Nature Coast, a huge draw for swimmers and divers. It wasn't always such an easy sell, though. Weeki Wachee Springs, dutifully pumping 170 million gallons of crystal-clear water a day, languished as a tourist attraction until 1947, when a local entrepreneur figured out a way to lure the crowds: mermaids. Its underwater mermaid show is the kind of "Old Florida" attraction that makes people misty-eyed about the good old days. The town of Spring Hill owes its existence to the spring and its water park—not surprisingly, allies have rallied in the past few years as the park's commercial success has waned and the mermaids have beseeched Spring Hill to, "Save our tails."

Farther north, the manatee is the 800-pound gorilla. But even bigger. Local cynics refer to these gentle mammals as "cash cows," and in-deed the sea cows bring in a sizable revenue stream to the little towns of Homosassa and Crystal River. Upwards of 400 West Indian manatees make this their winter home, drawn by the warm waters of the seven spring-driven rivers that meet here at the Gulf of Mexico. Were it not for the manatees, both towns would still be on the map as fishing destinations. The area's anglers and manatee advocates make uneasy bed-fellows, however: Many fisherfolk feel that overzealous "save the manatee" legislation has put unnecessary strictures on boating here.

Older than Crystal River by a good bit, Ho-mosassa has more charm and the greater reputa-tion as a fishing draw. The Calusa and the Seminole tribes were the first to inhabit the area, but after the Civil War, independent-minded families escaping the conflict and its aftermath settled many of the smaller islands, carving out a hard-scrabble life of subsistence farming and fishing (often the little keys were named for the

COURTESY OF VISIT FLORIDA

The West Indian manatee has a large, seal-like body that tapers to a powerful, flat, paddle-shaped tail.

The Nature Coast

HOMOSASSA–
CRYSTAL RIVER

To Eco
Walk Trail

19
98

495

Crystal River State
Archaeological Site

MUSEUM
POINT

FORT ISLAND TRAIL

Fort Island
Trail Park

CRACKER'S BAR
AND GRILL

Crystal River

Crystal River

To Hernando and Ted
Williams Museum

US FISH AND
WILDLIFE OFFICE

Kings Bay

44

Crystal
Bay

NATURE COAST
CANOE AND KAYAK TRAIL

PLANTATION INN
AND GOLF COURSE

SUNCOAST BLVD

494

490

Homosassa
Springs

W GROVER CLEVELAND BLVD

W HALLS
RIVER RD

HOMOSASSA SPRINGS
STATE WILDLIFE PARK

Homosassa

FISHBOWL DR

490

KC CRUMP ON
THE RIVER

Yulee Sugar Mill Ruins
State Historical Site

Homosassa River

OLDE MILL HOUSE GALLERY
AND PRINTING MUSEUM

MACRAE'S OF
HOMOSASSA

RIVERSIDE CRABHOUSE/
YARDARM LOUNGE

SUNCOAST
BLVD

19
98

Gulf   of

Mason Bay

MOON

Mexico

To Withlacoochee
State Forest

480

96

Chassahowitzka
National Wildlife Refuge

Chassahowitzka River

Chassahowitzka Bay

To Weeki Wachee Springs,
Buccaneer Bay, Spring Hill, and
Lower Suwanee National
Wildlife Refuge

0   0.5 mi

0   0.5 km

© AVALON TRAVEL PUBLISHING, INC.

THE SILVER KING

Homosassa is the place. Any fly-fisher will tell you, this little "Old Florida" town is where the big tarpon congregate, for no reason anyone can fathom. The current world record—202.8 pounds—was caught right here. But you won't find annual tarpon tournaments broadcast from here on ESPN2. It's a respectful, almost reverent endeavor, with patience often yielding nothing but sunburn. On any given day, you'll see the river dotted with 25 or 30 flats boats navigated with push poles in a hushed silence of profound concentration, everyone waiting to see one roll along the surface in water depths of 5–25 feet. People come from all over the world to the Nature Coast to sight fish, spin casting or fly-fishing for these behemoths before releasing them gently into the warm, clear waters. Tarpon begin to run the last weeks of April and fade out in July. What many consider the "Super Bowl of fishing," tarpon fishing requires a special $50 tag to keep one, and some serious knowhow. If you catch one—using live crabs, baitfish, or hand-tied flies—the initial jumps and runs of that angry hooked fish will take your breath away.

If you want to try your hand at chasing giant tarpon on the Gulf or, even better, fly-fishing with light tackle in the backwaters from Homosassa to Cedar Key, try **Capt. Rick LeFiles** (Osprey Guide Services, 6115 Riverside Dr., Yankeetown, 352/447-0829, $350 for a day of reds and trout, $450 for tarpon) or fourth-generation Homosassa **Capt. William Toney** (352/621-9284, www.homosassainshorefishing.com, half day $300, full day $350 for 1–2 people, $50 each additional person).

families who lived there). As real communities developed, commercial fishing became the mainstay, with the local catch transported north to Cedar Key by sailing sloop and, later, by railroad.

By the end of the 19th century, this rural backwater had developed a mighty reputation among affluent sportspeople, and in 1886 a group of New England financiers, aiming to cash in on this, bought up much of the swampy riverfront

property on the Homosassa River. Extensive land filling, highway projects, and a major marketing blitz in the 1920s failed to drum up a serious incursion of prospective investors and residents. And it remains pretty much that way today: a few thousand people drawn by beautiful rivers, unmanicured wilderness, and fish.

SPORTS AND RECREATION

Buccaneer Bay

After you've been entranced by the undulating, lip-synching mermaids of Weeki Wachee, you'll be inspired to try some of your own aquatic tricks at the adjacent Buccaneer Bay water park (6131 Commercial Way, Spring Hill, 352/596-2062, 10 A.M.–4 P.M. daily, $18.95 adults, $14.95 children 3–10). Pure, cold spring water laps against a tiny white-sand beach while families zoom down the flume rides and water slides or hang out on the floating dock. It's a safe place to let kids roam free (lots of strict, eagle-eyed lifeguards), and when they're exhausted you can trot off to the riverboat cruise, petting zoo, and sweet animal show. (Weeki Wachee Springs also hosts two-day mermaid camps, in which kids are taught the finer points of mermaid-hood, $175, 352/596-2062, ext. 30.)

When you're ready to get away from the crowds, head for the rear of the water park parking lot and follow the arrows for **canoe rental** (352/597-0360, $24 single-seat kayak, $33 two-seat canoe). It takes about three hours to paddle this serene stretch of the Weeki Wachee River, and when you've finished they'll pick you up and bring you back upstream by van. Bring lunch or a beverage: There are spots along the river where you can hop out on a sandy beach, swim, and relax.

Golfing

Golfers will be sorely tempted to sneak away while their families visit Weeki Wachee Springs. The big kahuna of courses in these parts is the famous Tom Fazio–built **World Woods** (352/796-5500, www.worldwoods.com, greens fees $40–120), just minutes away in Brooksville. It's a 45-hole complex with challenges for every golfer. Begin the day warming up on one of the hugest driving ranges you've ever laid eyes on (23 acres). From there, you can bone up on the 9-hole short course featuring seven par 3s and two par 4s, and then attempt either the 18-hole Pine Barrens, modeled after the great Pine Valley, or the stately and refined Rolling Oaks parkland course, an homage to Augusta National.

Swimming with the Manatees

The West Indian manatee is still listed as an endangered species, but the population has rebounded tremendously in the past few years in this area. Manatee "season" is October 15 to March 31, but you'll spot them all year long. Kings Bay in Crystal River has the densest concentration, but the Blue Waters area of the Homosassa River is a little less trafficked by boats, thus a bit quieter. Either way, you can commune with these lumbering mammals from the distance that suits you (up close their size is unsettling—just remember they are herbivores, with blunt teeth so far back in their heads that you could, were it legal, hand feed them with no worries). **Manatee Tour & Dive** (888/732-2692, www.manateetouranddive.com, $25 for tour, $20 for gear) offers two-hour manatee swim and snorkeling trips suitable for the whole family in the waters of Crystal River, and scuba trips in Crystal Springs and Kings Spring, an underwater cavern praised for its excellent visibility, size, and potential for underwater photography (thousands of saltwater fish congregate at the cavern's two exits).

Sunshine River Tours (352/628-3450, www.sunshinerivertours.com, $25–50, depending on tour) has a similar range of guided ecotourism escapades in Homosassa. If a manatee swim and snorkel tour doesn't sound like a good way to take the waters, you can try your hand at scalloping or just a boat ride to follow the river out to the Gulf of Mexico.

Canoeing, Kayaking, and Boating

During the warm months when manatees are a little scarce elsewhere in Crystal River and Homosassa, head to **N** **Chassahowitzka National Wildlife Refuge** (accessible from Rd. 480 off

U.S. 19, south of Homosassa, 352/563-2088, 8 A.M.–sundown daily, no fee), where they seem to congregate. And during the colder months you're likely to spot endangered whooping cranes that make this their winter home. There are no walking trails at the refuge, but there is a small visitors center that will quickly connect you with a commercial boat tour or rental. The 30,500 acres of saltwater bays, estuaries, and brackish marshes are home to nearly 250 species of birds, 50 species of reptiles and amphibians, and at least 25 species of mammals. You can't camp here, but several miles east of the refuge you'll find **Chassahowitzka River Campground** (352/382-2200), which has a nice canoe and boat launch of its own.

N Nature Coast Canoe and Kayak Trail

This trail is 17 miles long, beginning in the north on the Salt River off Crystal River (near the Marine Science Station on Hwy. 44). Follow the markers on the Salt River south to the Homosassa River. From here, the trail goes east on the Homosassa River a few hundred feet to a little stretch of water called Battle Creek, and then it jags to the south through Seven Cabbage Cut to the mouth of the Chassahowitzka River. The calm, protected waters of this estuarine ecosystem, soon to be part of the Great Florida Birding Trail, is home to ospreys, cormorants, wood storks, and loads of other wading birds.

To rent kayaks and canoes, go to **Aardvark's Florida Kayak Company** (452-B N. Citrus Ave., Crystal River, 352/795-5650, $30 singles, $40 for tandem, closed Mon. and Tues., but will open by prior arrangement). But if paddling out on your own sounds daunting, **Riversport Kayaks** (2300 S. Suncoast Blvd. Homosassa, 352/621-4972) leads tours along this trail, as well as lovely paddling along the Halls River.

Birding

The area's salt marshes, hammocks, uplands, forest and prairie, freshwater marshes, swamps, lakes, and rivers provide a variety of habitats, which in turn draw a variety of birds. Hundreds of bird species call this area home, and birders can observe them via boating along waterways, driving trails, and walking trails all over Citrus County. Roseate spoonbills, great blue herons, ibis, and other wading birds; ospreys, bald eagles, and other birds of prey; shore birds, wetland birds, and beach birds are all on view. March–May is a good time to see colorful mating plumage. One of the largest undeveloped river delta-estuarine systems in the United States, the **Lower Suwannee National Wildlife Refuge** (from U.S. 19, go west on County Road 347 for 16 miles, 352/493-0238) was established in 1979 in an effort to protect and maintain a rare ecosystem. The park is bisected by the Suwannee River, its tributary creeks fringed with majestic cypress (this part is best seen from the one-mile River Trail). Be sure to visit the upland area dotted with scrub oak and pine, and then explore some of the 26-mile stretch of tidal marshes along the Gulf.

Birders also gravitate to the **Withlacoochee Bay Trail** (from U.S. 19, turn east on the Sunset Parkway Rd., 352/447-1720), a five-mile walking trail from Felburn Park Trailhead to the Gulf; the child-friendly, two-mile looped **Eco Walk Trail** (north of Crystal River off U.S. 19, one block south of Seven Rivers Hospital at Curtis Tool Rd.); and **Fort Island Trail** (from U.S. 19, turn west onto Fort Island Trail and drive five miles), a flat, paved, nine-mile trail that ends at Fort Island Trail Beach. All of these parks are open 8 A.M.–sunset, and admission is free.

Motorcycling
And when you're tired of all that sissy nature stuff, you can hop on a hog and play "Easy Rider" at the **Harley-Davidson Shop of Crystal River** (1803 S.E. U.S. 19, 352/563-9900). Touring, Dyna, Softail, and Sportster models are for rent by the day for those over 21 with a valid driver's license.

SIGHTS
ⓜ Homosassa Springs State Wildlife Park
How could even the most myopic and woman-starved ancient mariner have mistaken these slow and lugubrious sea cows for mermaids? Manatees, so famous in these parts, can weigh up to 2,000 pounds and look like submerged, limbless elephants, often festooned with algae and barnacles. You'll catch sight of them most often during cooler months, December–March, in the Suwannee River or at Manatee or Fanning Springs State Parks. From boat or shore, look for swirly "footprints" on the water's surface or torpedo-like shapes ambling across the shallow bottom. If you want a guaranteed viewing, stop into Homosassa Springs State Wildlife Park (4150 S. Suncoast Blvd., Homosassa, 352/628-5343, 9 A.M.–5:30 P.M. daily; adults $9, children $5), where you can see these marine mammals several ways. Visitors are loaded onto pontoon boats and shuttled through the canopied headwaters of the Homosassa River to a refuge for injured manatees and other animals. Alternatively, at 11:30 A.M., 1:30 P.M., and 3:30 P.M., a manatee program allows you to watch docents wade out to feed stubby carrots to a slow-moving swarm of these creatures, many etched with outboard motor scars from run-ins with boats, after which you can walk down to the glass-fronted Fishbowl Underwater Observatory and see eye-to-eye with the gentle giants and the park's other indigenous aquatic creatures. (Mysteriously, the park hosts a hippo named Lucifer—a washed-up animal actor—that former governor Lawton Chiles declared an "honorary" Florida native.)

Yulee Sugar Mill Ruins
David Levy Yulee, the man responsible for bringing his Atlantic and Gulf Railroad to Cedar Key in 1860—and thus putting Cedar Key on the map—enjoyed a number of other successful and not-so-successful ventures. When Florida became a state in 1845 he was the state's first U.S. senator, and he had another sweet business on the side: By 1851, his mill on the Homosassa River employed more than 1,000 people, producing sugar, syrup, and molasses. Siding with the Confederacy during the Civil War (while the rest of this area sided with the North), Yulee paid dearly with a brief imprisonment and the permanent closure of the mill. Now the **Yulee Sugar Mill Ruins State Historical Site** (2.5 miles west of U.S. 19 on County Rd. 490, Homosassa, 352/795-3817, 8 A.M.–sundown daily, no fee)

A concrete path and interpretive plaques lead visitors through the Yulee Sugar Mill Ruins, one of Florida's most significant historical sights.

is hardly more than a huge stone chimney and the bones of a partially restored 40-foot-long structure that houses steam boilers, crushing machinery, and large cooking kettles. Visitors walk on a short path through the six-acre site tagged with interpretive plaques, and there is a small nearby picnic area with grills.

If the Yulee Sugar Mill doesn't sound like quite enough to make you detour from U.S. 19, right down the block is a cute museum/café called the **Olde Mill House Gallery & Printing Museum** (10466 W. Yulee Dr., 352/628-1081, 10 A.M.–3 P.M. Tues.–Sat., free admission, tours by appointment). Presided over by Jim Anderson, the little museum explores the history of printing, focusing on the letterpress era. The café sells fairly exemplary Cuban sandwiches and black beans and rice. And if you want to get even more return on your mileage investment, continue west on County Road 490 just a bit until you reach **Historic Old Homosassa,** a collection of craft and gift shops, restaurants, and one of the oldest residential communities on Florida's Gulf Coast.

Howard's Flea Market

Inveterate shoppers will be a little flummoxed by the Nature Coast's meager retail options. There is a serviceable mall in Crystal River (1801 N.W. U.S. 19, 352/795-2585) with ubiquitous stores such as Sears, Waldenbooks, and Foot Locker, and Cedar Key's Dock Street is host to the kinds of shell-themed giftware and handicrafts stores found in many little seaside towns. For a real local frisson of excitement, sift through the 300 or so booths at Howard's Flea Market (6373 S. Suncoast Blvd., Homosassa Springs, 352/628-3532, 7 A.M.–2 P.M. Fri., 7 A.M.–3 P.M. Sat.–Sun.). To safeguard against rain and muggy weather, the market is enclosed, with vendors hawking Nascar merchandise, leather goods, tools, even puppies. A bird aviary and food vendors (good barbecue, excellent old-fashioned root beer) make it fun for the whole family.

Crystal River State Archaeological Site

In 200 B.C., this was a happening spot. Florida's Native Americans came from all over to bury their dead and to participate in ceremonies and trade activities. People estimate that, for 1,600 years, roughly 7,500 Indians visited these 14 acres every year. Today, Crystal River State Archaeological Site (3400 N. Museum Point, Crystal River, 352/795-3817, park open 8 A.M.–sundown daily, visitors center 9 A.M.–5 P.M. daily; admission $2 per vehicle) is still hosting a fair number of visitors to the banks of the Crystal River. They come to see the six mounds built by what are now referred to somewhat prosaically as the pre-Columbian mound builders. After viewing an eight-minute interpretive video and seeing the small museum's exhibit chronicling the archaeological excavations begun in 1903, you'll be better equipped to walk a paved, half-mile loop and marvel at the mounds, studded with shells, bones, jewelry, and pottery from early civilizations. Recently, the park has added a dugout canoe exhibit and a "Sifting for Technology" interactive exhibit. With the latter, there are biweekly programs for the general public in which participants use sifting screens and other archaeological tools to recover artifacts from the spoils of a dredged boat slip.

TAIL SPIN

The job requirements are tough: A winning smile, powerful athleticism, and a great body. Now add to that the ability to hold one's breath for 2.5 minutes. Florida is home to a variety of rare aquatic creatures, but perhaps none are so singular as the 19 mermaids who swim through their daily choreographed show at **Weeki Wachee Springs** (6131 Commercial Way, Spring Hill, 352/596-2062, 10 A.M.–4 P.M. daily, $18.95 adults, $14.95 children 3–10, which includes admission to Buccaneer Bay).

In 1947, former U.S. Navy frogman Newton Perry thought of a way to bring added draw to one of the United States' most prolific freshwater springs. More than 170 million gallons of 72°F water pour dramatically into the Weeki Wachee River daily. Perry's notion was to gussy up the headwater with a bevy of beautiful mermaids—to this end, he taught a group of powerful swimmers to breathe through submerged air hoses supplied by an air compressor, the upshot being a remarkable 30- to 45-minute, entirely underwater extravaganza.

Conceived in the heyday of MGM's trademark aquatic musical spectaculars starring Esther Williams, the show at Weeki Wachee Springs is nonetheless a family affair. There are plenty of ogling opportunities, but these bathing beauties are put through their paces in a show that usually draws from past Disney movies (recent shows have included, unsurprisingly, *The Little Mermaid* and *Pocahontas*).

The audience sits in a small underground amphitheatre in front of a 4-inch-thick plate-glass window, behind which the blue waters of the springs teem with fish, turtles, eels, and women in oversized, shimmering tails who twirl, undulate, and lip synch on cue. Many of the mermaids have been with the show for decades, a fact that can be ascertained with a quick look through photos and memorabilia in the small Mermaid Museum (a wall of fame includes early sea nymphs cavorting with Elvis and Don Knotts), opened to commemorate the show's 50th anniversary in 1997.

After getting your picture taken with a mermaid, it's off to the rest of the 200-acre family entertainment park, Florida's only natural spring water park. This includes a flume ride at Buccaneer Bay, a low-key Birds of Prey show, petting zoo, and jungle river cruise.

Ted Williams Museum

Southwest Florida lures baseball enthusiasts with spring training, but the Nature Coast has got the **Ted Williams Museum and Hitters Hall of Fame** (2455 N. Citrus Hills Blvd., Hernando, 352/527-6566, www.twmuseum.com, 10 A.M.–4 P.M. Tues.–Sun., $5 adults, $1 children). The creepy controversy about cryogenically freezing his body upon his death in 2002 may have marred the memory of Williams, but a quick spin around the "bases" (the museum is laid out in a diamond) of the tidy museum, just about the only reason to head east to Hernando, will remind you of the beauty of his swing and all the other reasons he was Boston's version of Joe DiMaggio. It's worth an hour or two, even if you're not a Williams devotee (your personal hero may be among the "20 greatest hitters of all time" honored in the Hall of Fame part of the museum). But before you go waxing rhapsodic about "Smoky" Joe Wood, remember that Williams remains the last player to hit .400 without benefit of the sacrifice fly rule.

ARTS AND ENTERTAINMENT

Festivals

The average year-round temperature along the Nature Coast is 70°F, with an average of 294 days of sunshine. That means it's pretty all year, but you might want to schedule a visit to correspond to one of the local festivals.

In January, Crystal River hosts the three-day **Florida Manatee Festival** with free manatee-sightseeing boat tours, crafts, food, and entertainment. The **Cedar Key Arts and Crafts Festival** in April used to be known as a hot place to find new talent. These days it's just a big crafts show, but it's fun. The Homosassa River is home to a number of fishing tournaments worth watching: The annual **Cobia Tournament** is in mid-June and the famous **Southern Redfish Tour** comes a few weeks later in July. Cedar Key has recently begun a Fourth of July **Clam America Festival** with live music, clam hunts, clam-shucking demonstrations, clam bag races, and so forth. And the third weekend in October, the **Cedar Key Seafood Festival** draws 30,000 people for two days of seafood gluttony (book a room far in advance for this one). In 2004, the whole Nature Coast launched an annual celebration at the end of October called the **Nature Coast Wildlife Experience**, with birding field trips, paddle and water tours, photography events, seminars, and other outdoor activities. And the second weekend in November, the **Homosassa Arts, Crafts, and Seafood Festival** whips up chowders and soft-shell crabs for the masses.

ACCOMMODATIONS

People are drawn to the Nature Coast for a raw, unmediated view into the natural world. They come with rods and reels, without hair dryers or sometimes even a decent change of shirt. Thus, this swath of Florida is replete with RV parks, campgrounds, and "fish camps" that run from rough wooden cabins to no-frills motels. In nearly all the small towns that dot U.S. 19 or the little roads west to the Gulf, you can bet on finding a clean room in a mom-and-pop venture where the decor is uninspired and the amenities limited.

But in addition to these or the more upscale lodgings listed here, the area provides opportunities to indulge a lot of people's moony-eyed fantasy of endless, tranquil mobility: house boating. You can go "way down upon the Suwannee River" with a 44-foot houseboat rented from **Miller's Marine & Suwannee Houseboats** (County Rd. 349, Suwannee, 800/458-2628, $640 Friday afternoon to Sunday afternoon). The crafts rent by the day, weekend, or week, sleep up to eight, and are equipped with showers, bathroom facilities, linens, full kitchens, and cookware. The owners take renters on a warm-up cruise to teach them the basics, then you're on your own with 70 miles of river, countless springs, and an up-close view of the area's wildlife.

Under $50

For RV travelers, there are 398 picturesque sites at **Rock Crusher Canyon RV Park** (275 S. Rock Crusher Rd., Crystal River, 352/795-3870, sites $35), which also contains a 7,000-seat outdoor amphitheater that has welcomed Willie Nelson and Three Dog Night, as well as Joan Jett and some humungous RV rallies. Also in Crystal River, with lakeside ($30) and canal-side spots ($37) that include your own boat dock space, **Encore Crystal River** (11419 W. Fort Island Trail, Crystal River, 352/795-3774) is a 30-acre RV resort not far from the Fort Island Trail Beach. For inexpensive and pleasant waterside accommodations in Cedar Key, try **Sunset Isle RV Park/Motel** (11850 Hwy. 24, 800/810-1103, RV campsites start at $16, motel rooms start at $45).

In Crystal River you'll find many of the inexpensive chains, such as **Best Western Crystal River Resort** (614 N.W. U.S. 19, Crystal River, 352/795-3171; with its own marina and excellent fish/dive shop); **Comfort Inn** (4486 N.Suncoast Blvd., Crystal River, 352/563-1500); **Days Inn** (2380 N.W. U.S. 19, Crystal River, 352/795-2111); and **Econo Lodge** (2575 N.W. U.S. 19, Crystal River, 352/795-9447). Most cater to visiting anglers and ring in somewhere around $50, many without a lot of bells and whistles beyond a computer in the lobby to check email, etc. But for a more authentic experience, head for one of the independently owned places listed below for just a bit more.

$50–150

If for some reason you want to be right near Weeki Wachee Springs (you may need to rethink this, as the area's unapologetic suburban sprawl doesn't even whisper "vacation spot"), **Best Western Weeki Wachee Resort** (6172 Commercial Way, Spring Hill, 800/359-4827, $71–75) is your best bet. It's right across the street from the spring and its water park, with 122 rooms in a pleasant enough two-story building.

Homosassa Riverside Resort (5297 S. Cherokee Way, Homosassa, 352/628-2474, $75–100), recently remodeled, is the oldest resort along the Homosassa River. Many rooms have full kitchens, so you have dining flexibility, but the on-site restaurant and lounge are definitely worth a visit. From the hotel you can arrange a manatee-awareness tour, kayak and canoe rentals, airboat rides, and other adventures.

Presided over by Gator MacRae, **MacRae's of Homosassa** (5300 S. Cherokee Way, Homosassa, 352/628-2602, $75) is the rustic fisherman's pick, with a series of log cabin-like squatty structures and old-fashioned rockers on the front porches. The 12 rooms and 10 efficiencies are equipped with kitchens, and there are laundry facilities on the premises. Its riverside marina offers boat rentals, a bait shop, and fishing charters.

Also in the "something different" category, **Nature's Resort Campground and Marina** (10359 W. Halls River Rd., Homosassa Springs, 352/628-9544, www.naturesresortfla.com, $90 for the cabins, $28 for an RV site, $21 per campsite) has cabins; several hundred RV campsites; tent camping; canoe, kayak, and pontoon boat rentals; a marina; a country store; hiking trails; a pool; restaurant; tiki bar; and more on 97 lush acres along the Halls River. Oh, and there's a band shell that hosts country and gospel acts when the weather accommodates.

The Nature Coast doesn't offer the glut of golfing opportunities of elsewhere in Florida. If you're jonesing to tee off, the **Plantation Inn and Golf Resort** (9301 W. Fort Island Trail, Crystal River, 352/795-4211, www.plantationinn.com) boasts a par-72 18-hole championship course and a 9-hole executive course for training and practice, in addition to manatee snorkeling tours, guided scuba diving, and 126 guest rooms (with 12 golf villas and 5 condos). Given all the amenities and glitz, room rates are a fairly reasonable $72–309 (which includes greens fees).

The **Izaak Walton Lodge** (1 63rd St., Yankeetown, 352/447-2311) is one of the few reasons to get off U.S. 19 and amble down County Road 40 to Yankeetown. Named for the English biographer and author of the 1653 book, *The Compleat Angler,* the small inn has a serene setting on the banks of the Withlacoochee River. Room rates are $89 for queen, $99 for king. Out in back of the rustic building—a replica of the original lodge, lost in a fire a few years ago— Yankeetown old-timer **N** **Captain Bill O'Bry**

(352/447-5400) takes guests on fishing charters, scenic river tours, and photo excursions where visitors marvel at the ancient, shaggy cypress and catch a glimpse of a bald eagle or the splash of a rolling gar.

FOOD

Weeki Wachee

The town of Spring Hill, where Weeki Wachee Springs resides, has a couple of fun family-friendly places in which to refuel after a grueling day at the water park. **B.J. Gators** (4054 Shoal Line Blvd., Spring Hill, 352/596-7160, 11 A.M.–3 P.M. Mon.–Thurs., until 11 P.M. Fri. and Sat., until 9 P.M. Sun., $8–15) is a crowd pleaser, purveying familiar American pub staples (with the addition of prime rib on the weekend) in a pleasant dining room or out on the deck. It also has a spirited bar, open until 2 A.M. daily, with live music some nights. And **Nellie's Restaurant** (6234 Commercial Way, Spring Hill, 352/596-8321, 6 A.M.–8 P.M. daily, $6–12) is an old favorite for lunches of cottage pie or chicken-fried steak, and dinners of pot roast and meatloaf.

Homosassa

The north shore of the Homosassa River, accessible from Halls River Road, is host to two memorable places. **N** **K.C. Crump on the River** (11219 W. Halls River Rd., Homosassa, 352/628-1500; dockside casual dining, 11:30 A.M.–10 P.M. Tues.–Sun.; fine dining 3–10 P.M. Tues.–Sat. and noon–10 P.M. Sun.; $15 dockside, $25 inside) is Homosassa's premier restaurant, even more beloved since new ownership has updated the 19th-century clapboard home, retaining the nautical antiques, wildlife paintings, driftwood tables, and fireplaces that give it its charm. The single-malt scotch selection is quite a distraction, but eat something first: There's prime rib, grouper "Oscar," and scallops worthy of some attention. A 57-slip boat dock allows the river crowd to drift in, and the new owners operate a shuttle boat to take customers across the Homosassa River to wander the shops and resorts on the south shore.

Dinner at **Riverside Crabhouse** (5297 S. Cherokee Way, Homosassa, 352/621-5080, 11 A.M.–9 P.M. weeknights, until 10 P.M.weekends, $10–20) is another thing entirely. A relaxed and casual joint, it specializes in two-foot platters (OK, so they're garbage-can lids) heaped with sweet corn, hush puppies, scallops, soft shell crab, steamed blue crab, clams, catfish, and a little gator tail to make the visitors squirm. (Believe me, it doesn't taste just like chicken. More like swordfish morphed with frogs' legs.) Thursday night is all-you-can-eat crab night, $16.95 for the delicious garlic version. The attached Yardarm Lounge is a great place from which to spy on the four mostly tame monkeys who live on a tiny island a stone's throw away. After a few drinks, it's easier to advance some inspired theories as to *why* there are monkeys on Monkey Island (for my money, I'm betting they were extras from Tarzan films made in Homosassa in the 1960s).

Dan's Clam Stand (7364 W. Grover Cleveland Blvd., Homosassa, 352/628-9588, 11 A.M.–8 P.M. daily, $8–15) is no-frills, but makes a mean clam chowder, a serviceable lobster roll, and a fine fried grouper sandwich. If you don't love seafood, the Buffalo wings are zingy. And **The Yulee Café** (10605 W. Yulee Dr., Homosassa, 352/628-7177, 6 A.M.–2 P.M. Mon.–Fri., until noon Sat. and Sun., cash only, $8) is the place to try the local breakfast: fried cornmeal-crusted mullet with cheese grits.

For nightlife in Homosassa, locals go to the new comedy club called **Giggles** (Park Inn, 4076 S. Suncoast Blvd., Homosassa, 800/359-4827), they attempt a little karaoke at the **Old Mill Tavern** (10465 W. Yulee Dr., Homosassa, 352/628-2669), or they have a leisurely riverside beer at **The Shed at MacRae's** (5300 S. Cherokee Way, Homosassa, 352/628-2602).

Crystal River

In Crystal River, people tend to send visitors to **Charlie's Fish House Restaurant** (244 N.W. U.S. 19, Crystal River, 352/795-3949, 11 A.M.–9 P.M. daily, $9–14) for the views of the river and the simply prepared local fish as well as oysters and stone crab claws (you eat only the claws because fisherfolk haul 'em up, yank off one claw, and throw them back to grow another). The restaurant has a substantial boat dock for waterborne diners.

Cracker's Bar and Grill (502 N.W. 6th St., Crystal River, 352/795-3999, 11 A.M.–11 P.M. Mon.–Thurs., until midnight Fri. and Sat., until 10 P.M. Sun., $6–13), just up the block, is a locals' hangout with a commitment to big portions and providing something for everyone. The menu is vast, with burgers, nachos, and such alongside sautéed scallops and shrimp. Live entertainment has things hopping in the tiki bar and deck on the weekend, and karaoke provides wince-worthy off-notes just often enough to be funny. Tie your boat up to one of the restaurant's 14 slips, or hop on the restaurant's water taxi and see some of Kings Bay.

The young folks gather at **Gabby's** (Crystal River Mall, 1801 N.W. U.S. 19, 352/563-5666) for nightlife, while the older, classic-rock crowd patronizes **Gypsy's Den** (155 S.E. U.S. 19, Crystal River, 352/564-9595).

Cedar Key

When you hear the same joke a couple of times in a town, it becomes more of a credo than a garden-variety yuck. Here it is: They say in Cedar Key it takes two hours to watch *60 Minutes*. There's only one road in and out of town, there's no movie theater, no Starbucks, and no fast food. In fact, there's no fast anything.

But it wasn't always that way. Back in the 1880s, Cedar Key was the busiest port in Florida, with a population of around 5,000. It was founded in 1842 by Judge Augustus Steele as a seaside resort colony for prosperous plantation owners, but a wealth of local cedar trees quickly transformed the town into the foremost producer of pencils (Eberhard-Faber, Eagle, and others) in the country, and a relatively deep harbor made Cedar Key the natural choice as the first Gulf port and the terminus for David Yulee's cross-state Atlantic and Gulf Railroad in 1860.

A flattening 10-foot tidal surge from a hurricane in 1896, followed by other bad luck (fire, poor civic planning, reckless consumption of natural resources) crippled the little town, and when Henry Plant finished his own competing railroad, linking more cosmopolitan Tampa to Florida's east coast, it was the nail in Cedar Key's cedar coffin.

Today, the constellation of tiny islands that juts three miles out into the Gulf of Mexico is inhabited by fewer than 900 year-round residents. Years of over-fishing led to Florida's 1995 net ban law, which ended the bustle of commercial fishing fleets. What that leaves are all the charms Judge Steele saw back in 1842: an abundance of birds, fish, and other wildlife; beautiful sunsets; and a profusion of dappled creeks and rivers that flow into the warm Gulf. Town boosters have made a lot of noise recently about the resident artist community, trying to refashion Cedar Key as a sophisticated seaside artist's colony. But don't be fooled. It is precisely the unrefined, rough-edged enjoyment of nature that makes Cedar Key an easygoing pleasure. The only locals who seem impatient are the pelicans on the Dock Street pier, lurking like so many pea-brained pterodactyls hoping for some fisherman runoff.

SPORTS AND RECREATION
Fishing
It's more sporting than shooting fish in a barrel, but Cedar Key has lots of ways to make you feel "reel" talented. Freshwater anglers can wet a line in the 3,657-acre **Lake Rousseau/Withlacoochee River** area to bag bluegill, redear sunfish, catfish, black crappie, or largemouth bass. For saltwater fishing, the waters of **Cedar Keys National Wildlife Refuge** and the **Lower Suwannee National Wildlife Refuge** teem with spotted sea trout, redfish, and sheepshead. And **Waccasassa Bay Preserve State Park** provides both freshwater and saltwater fishing ops.

If you want your kids to acquire some rod and reel skills, the Florida Fish and Wildlife Conservation Commission's Cedar Key Lab has a free program called **1-2-3 Fish!** in which small groups of kids are taught basic angling skills (along with some gentle proselytizing about fish habitats and the effects of pollution on ecosystems) on a private stretch of beach in Cedar Key. All equipment is provided, and at the end of the day kids get to take home lures they've made and their own Shakespeare rod and reel combo. Many days are booked by scouting groups, so to reserve a spot for your kids, call 352/543-9200.

Cedar Key Scrub State Reserve
See some scrub before it vanishes. Okay, so scrub doesn't sound too sexy, but a scrub is an austere local plant community characterized by the dominance of shrubs (whereas forests are dominated by trees, prairies by grasses), and it is one of the fastest disappearing habitats in Florida. In the wet months, rainwater and wind rush through, cutting channels in the loose soil; when it's dry, fires sweep in and burn the scrub to the ground. And then those scrappy little shrubs grow again.

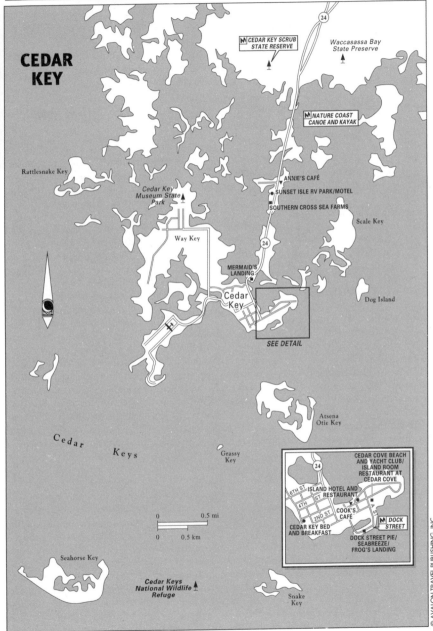

CEDAR
KEY

CEDAR KEY SCRUB
STATE RESERVE

Waccasassa Bay
State Preserve

NATURE COAST
CANOE AND KAYAK

Rattlesnake Key

ANNIE'S CAFÉ

SUNSET ISLE RV PARK/MOTEL

SOUTHERN CROSS SEA FARMS

Cedar Key
Museum State
Park

Scale Key

Way Key

Dog Island

MERMAID'S
LANDING

Cedar
Key

SEE DETAIL

Atsena
Otie Key

Cedar   Keys

Grassy
Key

CEDAR COVE BEACH
AND YACHT CLUB/
ISLAND ROOM
RESTAURANT AT
CEDAR COVE

ISLAND HOTEL AND
RESTAURANT

6TH ST

4TH

3RD ST

2ND ST

COOK'S
CAFÉ

DOCK
STREET

CEDAR KEY BED
AND BREAKFAST

DOCK STREET PIE/
SEABREEZE/
FROG'S LANDING

0   0.5 mi

0   0.5 km

Seahorse Key

Cedar Keys
National Wildlife
Refuge

Snake
Key

© AVALON TRAVEL PUBLISHING, INC.

COURTESY OF PURE WATER WILDERNESS/STACEY BROWN

Little Atsena Otie Key was once a thriving village, as evidenced by its 1890's cemetery.

Extremely hot in summer, the arid, sandy terrain is home to the Florida scrub jay and a bunch of other tough nuts of the animal world. Cedar Key Scrub State Reserve (six miles northeast of Cedar Key on Hwy. 24, 352/543-5567, 8 A.M.–sundown daily, no fee) consists of 12 miles of marked walking trails good for serene contemplation. It's dramatic in a very quiet way; kids may balk.

Canoeing, Kayaking, and Boating

Designated a refuge by President Hoover way back in 1929, the **Cedar Keys National Wildlife Refuge** (352/493-0238) encompasses approximately 800 acres and is composed of 13 barrier islands in the Gulf of Mexico. The refuge is home to as many as 200,000 birds, making it a hot spot for bird-watchers. To protect the area's wildlife and fragile ecosystems, the refuge is accessible only by boat (time your trip for high tide, otherwise the shallow mud and grass flats can slow your progress), and all of the islands' interiors are closed to the public, except Atsena Otie Key, the easiest island to access. You can paddle out from Cedar Key and collect shells, identify birds, picnic, and take pictures all year-round (Seahorse Key is closed entirely

March–June to accommodate nesting birds). The rest of the year, Seahorse Key, the outermost island, is worth the effort of getting there— egrets, white ibis, cormorants, herons, pelicans, and anhingas make it a veritable avian convention out there. Formed as a giant kidney-shaped sand dune, Seahorse Key rises to a height of 52 feet, the highest point on the state's west coast. It was a military hospital and detention center for captured Indians during the Seminole Wars, and its decommissioned lighthouse, built in 1855, is now used as a center for marine research by the University of Florida. Visitors are asked to pack out anything they take onto the islands, and to refrain from taking any island animals, vegetables, or minerals out. If you don't think you can get there under your own power, there are slightly hokey "Island Hopper" cruises (352/543-5904; adults $14, kids $7) run out of the city marina, where you can also rent pontoon boats, kayaks, and canoes (for kayaks and canoes call 352/949-0200). You can also rent canoes and kayaks from **Nature Coast Canoe & Kayak** (Hwy. 24 at Mermaid's Landing, Cedar Key, 352/543-6463, $18 for single kayak for half day, up to $44 for tandem for full day).

Adjacent to Cedar Key Scrub State Reserve, the **Waccasassa Bay State Preserve** (352/543-5567, 8 A.M.–sundown daily, no fee) is also accessible only by boat. (Boats can be launched from C40 in Yankeetown, C326 in Gulf Hammock, and Cedar Key.) This 32,777-acre coastal wilderness area consists of salt marsh scattered with wooded islands, themselves striated with more than 100 tidal creeks that flow into the estuary. Once here, visitors enjoy fresh- and saltwater fishing, canoeing, primitive camping (you know, where no one combs his hair and you have to dig your own latrine), and checking out the local population of bald eagles, black bears, and manatees.

Biking

At the turn of the 20th century, steamships won out over the railroad as preferred freight and passenger carriers in this area. As in so many parts of the country, this left miles of abandoned track, which have slowly been "repurposed" to meet

CATCH OF THE DAY

No matter the time of year, there's something fishy along the Nature Coast. But just what are you likely to catch, when, how many of 'em can you keep, and why should you go to the effort?

Fish: Amberjack, Greater
When: Caught year-round, this Atlantic species is often caught way offshore
Limit: 1 fish per person, minimum size requirement of 28 inches to the fork of the tail
What's fun about them? They're a big, strong fish, offering a wonderful pull and feisty runs to the bottom.

Fish: Cobia
When: They have a spring run and a late-fall run, but are generally caught in spring.
Limit: 1 fish per person, 33-inch minimum
What's fun about them? Exceptional pullers, they will readily bite (they're not real bright). They prefer to hang out near structures like pilings or channel markers.

Fish: Flounder
When: Caught year-round
Limit: 10 fish per person, 12-inch minimum
What's fun about them? A smaller species than the Atlantic version (often under 10 inches), they are excellent table fare, but cleaning them is tricky.

Fish: Grouper
When: Caught year-round, but they swim way out in the summer. They move inshore fall and winter, in as little as 6 feet of water.
Limit: 5 fish per person, 22-inch minimum
What's fun about them? People love their fight and flavor so much that the big ones are mostly fished out. You'll find lots under 22 inches.

Fish: Jack Crevalle
When: Caught year-round, they school in the summer months.
Limit: No limits
What's fun about them? The thuggish brute that hangs out in the dark alley, it's the toughest fighting fish in the Gulf. No good to eat.

Fish: Kingfish
When: Caught year-round, but better in late winter
Limit: 2 fish per person, 24-inch minimum
What's fun about them? With lots of fight, they are a beautiful, long, silvery fish that tastes terrible. They tend to hunt in schools.

Fish: Mangrove Snapper (also called gray or mango snapper)
When: Caught year-round
Limit: 5 fish per person, 10-inch minimum
What's fun about them? One of the smaller snappers, it rarely exceeds 5 pounds. Find them around docks and piers. Watch out—they bite.

Fish: Mullet
When: Caught year-round
Limit: 50 per person, no size limit
What's fun about them? This is a weird fish that jumps out of the water for no reason. You cast net for them because they are basically vegetarian and won't eat your bait fish, or you can use cane poles and dough ball of white bread.

Fish: Redfish (also called red drum)
When: Caught year-round
Limit: 1 fish per person, 18-inch minimum, 27-inch maximum
What's fun about them? The bread-and-butter fish in this area, they are delicious table fare and good fighters, especially from 22 to 35 inches in size. They have become the new inshore/shallow water tournament fish of choice.

Fish: Seabass, Black
When: Caught year-round
Limit: 10 fish per person, 10-inch minimum
What's fun about them? Extremely small in this area, they are generally too small to keep. More of an offshore and Atlantic species.

Fish: Sheepshead
When: Caught year-round, but easier to get in winter
Limit: 15 fish per person, 12-inch minimum
What's fun about them? With jailhouse stripes, it's not surprising they're bait thieves. They hang out near barnacle-crusted structures. Good table fare but a little on the bony side.

Fish: Spanish Mackerel
When: Caught spring through fall
Limit: 15 per person, 12-inch minimum
What's fun about them? Caught on very light tackle, they are generally under 5 pounds, travel in large schools, and are easy to catch. Most locals smoke them.

Fish: Spotted Sea Trout
When: Caught year-round
Limit: 5 fish per person, 15-inch minimum, 20-inch maximum (and you can keep one over 20 inches per day)
What's fun about them? One of the most abundant fish in the area, they like the grass flats. The commercial netting ban has increased their numbers recently.

Fish: Tarpon
When: Caught April, May, and June
Limit: 2 fish per person
What's fun about them? A protected species, they require a $50 tag to keep one, and the only reason to keep one is to set an IGFA world record, which happens a lot around here. People fly fish for tarpon, the most explosive of inshore species.

the needs of outdoor enthusiasts. The 32-mile paved **Nature Coast Trail State Park** (U.S. 19 just south of downtown Chiefland, 352/493-6072, 8 A.M.–sundown daily, no fee) links several wildlife and recreation areas together, including **Fanning Springs State Park** and **Andrews Wildlife Management Area.** The various trails wind along the Suwannee River, ranging in lengths from 4.3 miles up to 10 miles, with trailheads in the downtowns of five communities, including Cross City (near County Rd.); Old Town (adjacent to the Old Town Fire Station); Fanning Springs (near the Agricultural Inspection Station); Trenton (two blocks off Main St. at the railroad depot); and Chiefland (near the railroad depot two blocks beyond downtown). This makes it easy to enjoy a ride and finish up with lunch or dinner in one of these sweet inland towns.

Bikes can be rented at **Suncoast Bicycles** (322 N. Pine Ave., Inverness, 352/637-5757, $7.50 per hour, $15 for the day). Or, right downtown in Cedar Key, the **Golf Kart Company** (A St. at 1st, across from City Park, 352/543-5300) rents bikes ($10 per day/$2.50 per hour) as well as golf carts that seat three, four, or eight people ($50 per day, $30 for four hours—a really fun way to wander around the island).

SIGHTS

"Clamelot"

Cedar Key is a clamming town. It's a backbreaking, difficult business that requires the salty seadog's perseverance and grit combined with a huge amount of scientific knowledge. All you need to know is that the town is the U.S.'s No. 1 producer of farm-raised littlenecks, available for your delectation year-round. But if you want to learn more, sweet-talk your way into **Southern Cross Sea Farms** (12170 Hwy. 24, Cedar Key, 352/543-5980, www.clambiz.com). They don't give official tours, but if you show an interest, they'll walk you through the process, from the saltwater larvae tanks thick with silt (which, under a microscope, is millions of perfect clams, each 60 microns in size) to the clam nursery and out to the clam bags sunk in the Gulf, where the bivalves spend 18 months maturing. Interesting clam tidbit: All are born male. It is at maturity that 50 percent become female. There's a male-bashing joke in there somewhere.

Dock Street

Glance down the page and you'll see that Cedar Key is a little lean on attractions, and that's part of the attraction. Cedar Key is made up of a series of little squiggly barrier islands, but the commercial and residential parts of town are clustered on Way Key. And on Way Key, the place to be is Dock Street.

The fishing pier is the center of the action, where anglers, pelicans, and onlookers peaceably watch the sun set over the wide wooden boardwalk. On the weekends a little live music wafts out from Seabreeze or Frog's Landing, along with the aromas of just-caught seafood getting its culinary due. The couple of blocks of Dock Street that fan out on either side of the pier are crowded with gift shops, galleries, restaurants, and bars—a rewarding stroll at any time of the day.

Cedar Key Museums

St. Clair Whitman invented tools and gizmos for the Standard Manufacturing Company in the early 1900s, but more importantly, he was an incorrigible collector of stuff. He accumulated antique glassware, old bottles, photographs of Cedar Key, and an impressive number of seashells. The **Cedar Key Museum State Park** (12231 S.W. 166 Ct., Cedar Key, 352/543-5350, 9 A.M.–5 P.M. Thurs.–Mon., admission $1), in Whitman's house restored to its 1920s heyday, proudly displays all his collections. But it's more than just a sweet little museum in which to see his treasures. Exhibits provide insight into the Timucuans who once inhabited this stretch of coast, as well as Cedar Key's 19th-century history as a center for pencil manufacturing and fiber broom and brush manufacturing. Docent-led tours are offered 1–4 P.M. Save this for an afternoon when the weather is gloomy or the fish aren't biting.

If your interest in Cedar Key history is piqued, there are more opportunities for investigation at the **Cedar Key Historical Museum** (609 2nd St., Cedar Key, 352/543-5549, 11 A.M.–4 P.M.

COURTESY OF VISIT FLORIDA

Cedar Key draws 30,000 revelers every fall for its two-day Seafood Festival.

Mon.–Sat., 1–4 P.M. Sun., admission $1, children 50 cents) right downtown. Housed in one room of a former private residence circa 1871, the museum tells the story of Cedar Key through historic photos and a somewhat idiosyncratic assortment of memorabilia, as well as displays of Native American artifacts, minerals, and woodworking tools. It's worth an hour of your time, especially if one of the more zesty docents is willing to talk about the glory days of the local pencil, lumber, and fishing industries. Although it's a little pricey ($4.50), the brochure for a self-guided historical walking tour of downtown is a great short course on the area. Also, across the street from the museum is a quirky bookstore called **Curmudgeonalia** (2nd St. and D St., 352/543-6789, 9 A.M.–5 P.M. daily) that proffers a discerning collection of birding, naturalist, and offbeat Florida history books.

ACCOMMODATIONS
$50–150
Cedar Cove Beach and Yacht Club (192 2nd St., 352/543-5332, www.cedarcove-florida.com, $109–185) has a fair number of luxurious amenities, which somehow seem out of place in this sweet town-that-time-forgot. All rooms are fully equipped efficiencies with private balconies and access to a heated pool and a fancy fitness facility.

Cedar Key Bed and Breakfast (3rd St. and F St., 352/543-5050, www.cedarkeybandb.com, $95–175) feels a little more at home here. A stop on the town's historical district walking tour, the bed-and-breakfast was built in 1880 as a home for Eagle Pencil Company employees. Today, it's a comfortable, not overly antique-addled six-room inn with a nice breakfast.

FOOD
Cedar Key isn't exactly a gastronomic mecca, but there are a handful of respectable places. **Annie's Café** (just over the causeway on Hwy. 24, 352/543-6141) may look like a tenuous pile of scrap sheet metal, but it's a local favorite for bird-watching over breakfasts of mullet, grits, sliced tomato, and a flaky biscuit. Another breakfast joint, **Cook's Café** (434 2nd St., 352/543-5548, 6:30 A.M.–2 P.M. daily, $8–10), is right downtown and accommodates pets on the patio if they're polite. Built in 1859,

the **Island Hotel and Restaurant** (2nd St. and B St., 352/543-5111, 6–9 P.M. Tues.–Sun., $15–24) is purportedly haunted by 13 ghosts, particularly during grisly weather. Even if you don't believe the story of the restless spirit of a murdered former owner, you'll enjoy the hearts of palm salad (supposedly invented here by the hotel's original owners), the crab bisque, or just a drink in the chummy bar.

For elegant waterside dining, head to the **Island Room Restaurant at Cedar Cove** (10 E. 2nd. St., 352/543-6520, 5–10 P.M. Mon.–Fri., 2–10 P.M. Sat., 10 A.M.–9 P.M. Sun., $14–24) for Chef Peter Stefani's house-grown veggies and greens or his less pious velvety bread pudding with bourbon sauce. After dinner, if you're not quite ready to turn in, head over to Dock Street and drink with the locals at **Frog's Landing** (420 Dock St., 352/543-9243) or **Seabreeze** (520 Dock St., 352/543-5738). (And when you're feeling fortified and emboldened, order the single weirdest dish the island has to offer— Seabreeze's signature salad is a mélange of lettuce, hearts of palm, peach, pineapple, and dates, "dressed" with a slowly melting scoop of peanut butter ice cream.)

COURTESY OF VISIT FLORIDA

Head to Cedar Key's downtown Dock Street as the sun goes down and your hunger rises.

Steinhatchee

If you're the kind of outdoorsperson who likes nature 100 percent natural, and even something like Cedar Key's handful of gift boutiques and art galleries starts you grumbling about "gentrification," you can get purer still in Steinhatchee (pronounced STEEN-hachee), pop. 1,500. It's 33 miles north of Cedar Key on U.S. 19 and about a dozen miles west on Highway 51. To call it a sleepy little town is a misnomer. A glut of trout, redfish, and wild game has kept things jumping around here since the mid-1800s. The mouth of the Steinhatchee River, called Deadman's Bay, was home to thousands of Native Americans who came for the easy eats and the spectacular scenery. Hunters and fishers have been following suit ever since. In recent years Steinhatchee's appeal has broadened, thanks in large measure to a Georgian entrepreneur named Dean Fowler.

Fowler's place, Steinhatchee Landing Resort, has drawn accolades from an array of travel magazines in recent years, and the town has been beset by the affluent and famous wishing to commune with nature (former president Jimmy Carter has come twice). This hasn't picked up the pace around here—in fact, at his place the posted speed limit is 9 mph. Why, you ask? "If it was 10, no one would pay it any mind," says Fowler. It's that kind of folksy, down-home sensibility that makes Steinhatchee such a joy to explore.

The Steinhatchee River—along with the Suwannee, Wacissa, Econfina, Fenholloway, and St. Marks Rivers—has emptied its rich contents here into the Apalachee Bay of the Gulf of Mexico for centuries. The shallow bay's gentle, gradual slope and fertile grass flats have made it a world-class fishing destination and a summer scalloping hot spot. It's a place where everyone has a big fish story and the time to tell it right, a place where "live bait and cold beer" sound like two of the central ingredients in happiness.

SPORTS AND RECREATION
Fishing and Scalloping

Beginning July 1 and ending September 10, the scalloping season brings thousands of visitors to the little town of Steinhatchee. You need a recreational saltwater fishing license (888/347-4356, www.wildlifelicense.com, $6.50 for a three-day license) before you can wade out into the grassy shallows to scoop up the sweet bay bivalves. Each harvester is limited to two gallons of whole scallops or one pint of shucked meat per day. Pack a snorkel, swim shoes, and a mesh bag for your catch.

 Offshore Fishing with Big Bend Charters

The rest of the year, folks spend their time on half-day or full-day charters out into the Gulf in search of amberjack, kingfish (the most terrible-tasting of the fiercely beautiful sportfish), redfish, cobia, and grouper. Black grouper limits are five per person, per day, and they must be at least 22 inches long. Big Bend Charters (352/498-3703, www.bigbendcharters.com) takes groups far out on offshore ($650), nearshore ($500), and inshore ($350) trips. Keep the grouper you catch, and pawn the rest of it off on someone else. Fresh-caught local grouper is a revelation.

Farther in, spotted sea trout, catfish, and redfish can be coaxed out of the grass flats of Deadman's Bay or the slow-moving Steinhatchee River. Kingfish travel through Steinhatchee spring and fall to stay in the perfect water temperature (72 degrees or so), and the town is a legendary trout and redfish fishery in the wintertime when the fish move up into the river. Freshwater fishing can be accomplished dockside or from a rented canoe, but it's more fun in a shallow-draft boat with a motor: A 20-foot Carolina Skiff with a 75-horsepower motor will run you $125 per day plus fuel at the **Ideal Marina & Motel** (114 Riverside

Steinhatchee is an old fishing village located in the pristine Big Bend region, a fishing retreat of the cognoscenti.

Dr. SE, Steinhatchee, 352/498-3877). First-timers should hire a guide (it's an eminent place to learn saltwater fly-fishing techniques), but if you're striking out on your own, head to one of the local marinas (Sea Hag, River Haven, or Ideal) and listen carefully to suss out the latest hot spots and irresistible baits. (Tip: Wear sunglasses with polarized lenses so you can see into the water more effectively.)

Diving
Rodale's Scuba Diving magazine is always heaping kudos on the Nature Coast, and scuba devotees come from all over to try cave and freshwater diving in the crystal-clear waters. Many of the draws are north and east of Steinhatchee and Cedar Key.

Ginnie Springs (from U.S. 19, head northeast on Hwy. 47; it's along the Santa Fe River in High Springs, 386/454-7188) may be one of the most popular freshwater dive sites in the world, a place Jacques Cousteau once characterized as "visibility forever." Certified cave divers will also have heard of its Devil's Eye/Ear cave system. If you're diving for the first time, Ginnie Springs is perfect—no waves or breaking surf, no boats to contend with. There's a noncertification guided Discover Scuba Diving program (386/454-7188, $99 per student).

There are also two first-magnitude springs, **Manatee Springs State Park** (on Hwy. 320 west of Chiefland, 352/493-6072) and **Fanning Springs State Park** (U.S. 19, Fanning Springs, 352/463-3420), 10 minutes from each other and 30 minutes northeast from Cedar Key. Situated in a 2,075-acre park, Manatee Springs produces 117 million gallons of clear blue water daily, a haven for manatees, fish, wading birds, scuba divers, and swimmers alike. There are two spots for excellent cavern and cave diving, **Manatee Spring** itself and **Catfish Hotel Sink.** You can camp, fish, boat, and hike in the park as well, but for a quick day trip the boardwalk through cypress swamp to the Suwannee River is a must-see. At Fanning Springs, which releases about 50 million gallons of water a day, swimmers and snorkelers explore the 20-foot-deep spring basin fed by two springs, Big Fanning and Little Fanning. Fanning Springs also has a cool boardwalk to the river, a nature trail, volleyball, and picnic facilities.

And a little farther away on Highway 3 in the town of Williston, there are two diving draws: Visitors to **Devil's Den Resort & Springs** (5390 N.E. 180th Ave., 352/528-3344) descend wooden steps through a rock tunnel to a floating dock, and then the dive begins about 40 feet down with swim-throughs, nooks, and crannies to explore. One of the safest cavern dives in the state is the nearby **Blue Grotto** (3852 N.E. 172nd Ct., 352/528-5770), a limestone sink with heavy-duty guidelines and platforms down to the 100-foot depths.

Farther south, if you want to get a sense for the history of the Suwannee River steam-boating era, you can dive to see the **City of Hawkinsville Underwater Archaeological Preserve** (western bank of the Suwannee River, Old Town, accessible only by boat, 850/245-6444). Built in 1896 for the Hawkinsville Deep Water Boat Lines, the steamboat was used on the Suwan-

COURTESY OF VISIT FLORIDA

Scuba divers come from all over to try cave and freshwater diving in the crystal clear waters of Ginnie Springs, Manatee Springs, Fanning Springs, and Devil's Den.

nee River for the booming lumber industry before it ceased operation in 1922. Today, divers can explore the intact 141-foot hull of the sunken steamer, swimming along the long deck of the vessel to the stern paddlewheel alongside the area's more intrepid fish.

For diving equipment and services, options are plentiful. **American Pro Diving Center** (Crystal River, 352/563-0041), **Bird's Underwater** (Crystal River, 352/563-2763), and **Steve's Scuba & Snorkeling** (Crystal River, 352/795-1551) all have good reputations in the area.

SIGHTS
Beaches
Of all the hundreds of miles of Florida's Gulf Coast, the Nature Coast offers the most limited beach access, much of it unsuitable for swimming. Tiny barrier islands and shallow grassy flats protect the coast from getting buffeted by

Gulf winds and surf, but also preclude the soft, white-sand beaches of elsewhere on the Gulf Coast. If you want to make a day of it, your best bet is **Keaton Beach,** a neat little beach town 17 miles north of Steinhatchee. Families and fisherfolk are drawn to the wide natural public beach, the 700-foot fishing pier, and the capacious boat ramp. The trick is getting there: Follow U.S. 19 north through Cross City, go approximately 11 miles, turn left onto Highway 358. At the flashing light, stay to the right and once you go through Jena, turn right. Go over the bridge, turn left at the stop sign, and at next stop sign turn right. Go another 17 miles and turn left at the stop sign.

Beyond that, Cedar Key has a fair amount of private beach, but public access is limited to the downtown **city park** adjacent to a new kids' play structure on 2nd Street. The bay here is very shallow and muddy, due to the outflow of numerous creeks and rivers, and the sand is rocky and hard on bare feet. A better bet is to head out to **Fort Island Trail Beach** (from U.S. 19, turn west on Fort Island Trail and drive 10 miles). This Gulf-side beach is about 1,000 feet long, with a new fishing pier, concessions, and picnic facilities. A lifeguard is on duty Memorial Day through Labor Day, and the beach is open daylight to 9:30 P.M.

ACCOMMODATIONS

M Steinhatchee Landing Resort (228 N.E. Hwy. 51, Steinhatchee, 800/584-1709, www .steinhatcheelanding.com, $160–476) is as swanky as it gets along the Nature Coast. The brainchild of patrician Georgian gentleman Dean Fowler, its 35 acres are dotted with dozens of individual one-, two-, and three-bedroom Victorian and Florida Cracker cottages, most equipped with French country furniture, oversized spa tubs, and wildly luxurious appointments for such a down-home fishing village.

If that's too rich for your blood, the same folks own the nearby 17-room budget-friendly **Steinhatchee River Inn** (1111 Riverside Dr., Steinhatchee, 352/498-4049), where the rates range seasonally $60–85.

FOOD

The dining scene is dominated by **Fiddler's Restaurant** (1306 Riverside Dr., 352/498-7427, 4–10 P.M. Mon.–Thurs., 11 A.M.–10 P.M. Fri.–Sun., $10–20), a sprawling, lively spot populated by men swapping big fish stories and tucking into fried grouper (you can bring your own cleaned catch and have them cook it up). **Roy's** (corner of Hwy. 51 and County Rd. 351, 352/498-5000, 11 A.M.–9 P.M. daily, $13–16), a local favorite for 35 years, doesn't serve any booze but has an exhaustive salad bar, fried seafood, and fat burgers that keep people happy. **Lamb's BBQ** (Hwy. 51, 352/498-7773, 6 A.M.–2 P.M. Tues. and Wed., 6 A.M.–9 P.M. Thurs.–Sat., $10–14) offers up evangelical fire and brimstone on its menu along with some fairly good Texas-style barbecue. And for breakfast, head to the north end of the bridge to the open-air **Bridge End Café** (310 10th St., 352/498-2002, 6 A.M.–9 P.M. Mon.–Sat., until 2 P.M. Sun., $7–15), which serves a lavish buffet brunch on the weekend.

Downtown Cedar Key features a little urban beach with this nearby playground.

Information and Services

AREA INFORMATION

The Nature Coast is on eastern time. The telephone area code is 352.

Tourist Information

Citrus County Chamber of Commerce has three offices (208 W. Main St., Inverness, 352/726-2801; 28 N.W. U.S. 19, Crystal River, 352/795-3149; and 3495 S. Suncoast Blvd., Homosassa, 352/628-2666), each of which stocks racks of local brochures and pamphlets (8:30 A.M.–4:30 P.M. Mon.–Fri., until 1 P.M. Sat.). For more information about local events, pick up the *Citrus County Chronicle* (25 cents), the largest daily in the county. There's also an easy-to-use online version at www.chronicleonline.com.

Cedar Key Chamber of Commerce (525 2nd St., 352/543-5600, 10 A.M.–1 P.M. Mon., Wed., and Fri.), stuffed in the same building as the City Hall and library, has limited hours and limited offerings. You're better off waiting for each Thursday's *Cedar Key Beacon* (50 cents), the little island newspaper that directs you to events and activities.

For other tourist information and maps of the area, call **Florida's Pure Water Wilderness** (352/486-5470, or visit www.purewaterwilderness.com). Birders will want to check out the award-winning www.citrusbirdingtrail.com, which catalogs birding opportunities on virtually every trail in the area.

Police and Emergencies

The **Crystal River Police Department,** the largest along the Nature Coast, is in back of City Hall (123 N.W. U.S. 19, 352/795-4241).

In the event of a medical emergency, **Seven Rivers Regional Medical Center** (6201 N. Suncoast Blvd., Crystal River, 352/795-6560) has emergency services, as does **Nature Coast Regional Hospital** (125 S.W. 7th St., Williston, 352/528-2801). For anything major, you may want to head to **North Florida Regional Medical Center** in Gainesville.

Radio and Television

WXCV "Citrus" FM 95.3 broadcasts popular music and information about the Nature Coast; for news, tune in to **WFSU FM 88.9** out of Tallahassee; **WKTK FM 98.5** out of Gainesville pumps out easy '70s and '80s rock (and is the station to turn to for info on suspected flooding); **WJUF FM 90** sends out classical, jazz, and folk; and **WRGO FM 102.7** gives you oldies from Cedar Key.

On the television, **WCJB CH 20** is the ABC affiliate out of Gainesville and Ocala. Also out of Gainesville and Ocala, **WOGX CH 51** is the FOX affiliate; and **WGFL CH 53** is the WB affiliate out of nearby High Springs.

Laundry Services

Catering to fisherfolk, who can frankly get a little dirty in pursuit of fish, many of the Nature Coast's motels, hotels, fish camps, and campgrounds offer laundry facilities. But if you have need of a launderette, try **Crystal Center Laundromat** (648 S.E. U.S. 19, Crystal River, 352/795-0979) or **Sundance Wash 'n' Go Laundromat** (12291 Hwy. 24, Cedar Key, no phone).

Fishing Licenses

If you haven't planned ahead, fishing licenses can be purchased on the fly at the Kmart in Crystal River or the Wal-Mart in Homosassa.

Getting There and Around

Florida's Nature Coast is west of I-75 and is accessible by the north–south corridor of U.S. 19. If you happen to be piloting your own small plane, Cedar Key has a single 2,300-foot hard-surfaced runway, but this is uncontrolled airspace. The closest commercial airports are **Gainesville Regional Airport** (approximately one hour away, with service provided by Delta and US Airways, 352/373-0249) and **Tallahassee Regional Airport** (also one hour away, seven miles north of Tallahassee, with service provided by Delta, 904/891-7800). **Orlando International Airport** (407/825-2001) and **Tampa International Airport** (813/870-8700) are both approximately an hour and a half away by car, both offering many more commercial flights.

Alamo (800/327-9633), **Avis** (800/831-2847), **Budget** (800/527-0700), **Dollar** (800/800-4000 domestic, 800/800-6000 international), and **National** (800/227-7368) all provide rental cars from these airports.

Most of the Nature Coast is accessible by car or boat only. There is no public transportation to speak of (OK, there are two southbound and two northbound Greyhound buses that stop daily in Crystal River and Chiefland—but then once you've arrived, you still need a car to see anything). From south to north, Spring Hill (the town in which Weeki Wachee Springs lies), Homosassa, and Crystal River are lined up adjacent to each other right along U.S. 19. To get to Cedar Key, head north on U.S. 19 and then 23 miles southwest on Highway 24, the only road in and out of town (much of which is a quite rural two-lane highway until you cross the causeway into town). Steinhatchee is 33 miles north of Cedar Key on U.S. 19 and then 12 miles west on Highway 51.

Driving in Florida during the summer months can be especially challenging, with periods of heat and humidity punctuated by tremendous thunderstorms. It pays to have your car equipped with the following: first-aid kit, jumper cables, flashlight with new batteries, a jack, and cellular phone (although cell phone service can be sketchy in the more rural communities).

Tallahassee

During the late summer of 2004, when hurricanes Charley, Frances, Jeanne, and Ivan swirled ominously off the Gulf Coast of Florida, television viewers everywhere got an earful of Governor Jeb Bush and an eyeful of Florida's capital city of Tallahassee. Prior to that, the city was the punchline to jokes about Secretary of State Katherine Harris, the state's inability to deal with wayward hanging and pregnant chads, and more generally the circus that was the 2000 presidential election.

Tallahassee deserves better. Some say the word means "beautiful land" or "natural beauty," while others say it's a Apalachee word meaning "old town." Let's split the difference and say it's a beautiful old town. A Florida anomaly in many ways, it has none of the manic fun-in-the-sun energy of beach towns on the peninsula or even out the state's Panhandle.

It's a rooted place with a sense of history, more genteel and dignified than any of the state's other urban centers, and infinitely more southern. It's counterintuitive, but farther south on the Florida peninsula (Tampa, Sarasota, Naples) it hardly smacks of the American South at all. But here in Tallahassee, a scant 20 miles from the Georgia border, you'll encounter thick drawls, tall glasses

Must-Sees

Look for **M** to find the sights and activities you can't miss and **M** for the best dining and lodging.

M **Big Bend Saltwater Paddling Trail:** Extending 60 miles along the Gulf Coast, the Big Bend Wildlife Management Area is home to hundreds of bird and animal species as well as a meandering 105-mile mapped kayak and canoe trail (page 232).

M **Wakulla Springs State Park:** What do *Airport '77* and *Tarzan's Secret Treasure* have in common? They were both filmed in the lush wilderness surrounding these crystal-clear springs, which pump 600,000 gallons of water per minute (page 234).

M **Canopy Roads:** Five official canopy roads radiate out from downtown Tallahassee, the gnarled live oak tunnels festooned with lacy Spanish moss. They make a wonderful driving tour, culminating in a visit to Bradley's Country Store out on Centerville Road (page 236).

COURTESY OF VISIT FLORIDA

The beautifully restored 1845 Old Capitol and the modern, businesslike New Capitol dominate the skyline of Tallahassee with a dramatic synergism.

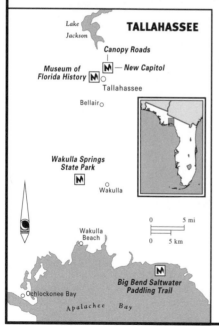

M **New Capitol:** The sleek edifice sticks out like a glamorous modern thumb against the low-rise Tallahassee skyline. To orient yourself, head to the 22nd-floor observatory level before taking the guided tour of this center of state government (page 236).

M **Museum of Florida History:** The Old Capitol, now home to the Florida Center for Political History and Governance, is one of the five sites that this downtown historical museum comprises, a good place to get your bearings in Florida's capital (page 238).

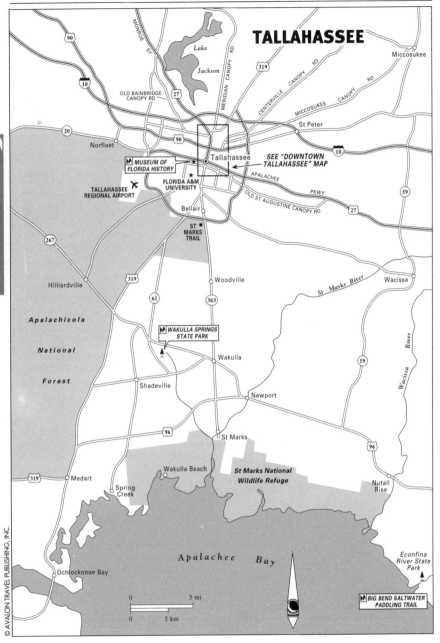

Tallahassee

of sweet iced tea, and rocking chairs on the porches of old plantation houses. And the people sitting in those rocking chairs, drinking their iced teas, and speaking with those drawls, they are the state legislators and civil servants, university professors, and the other sophisticated professionals who make up the citizenry of Tallahassee. Even the area's landscape is different from the rest of Florida, with rolling hills, oak-canopied roads, red clay, and an arresting riot of dogwood, magnolia, oleander, and confederate jasmine blossoms.

Tucked in the foothills of the Appalachian Mountains, at the juncture of Florida's Panhandle and peninsula (an area called the Big Bend), Tallahassee hasn't always been the capital. It was a compromise. When the east and west Florida territories combined in 1822, officials shuttled between the western capital of Pensacola and the eastern capital of St. Augustine. All that travel time and no frequent flyer miles to show for it—state officials balked and it was decided to relocate the capital at a hilly backwoods spot between the two cities. Tallahassee was chosen in 1824.

Hardly a stylish urban center at that time, the capital began as a dangerous and lawless place, prompting Ralph Waldo Emerson to call Tallahassee "a grotesque place . . . rapidly settled by public officers, land speculators, and desperados." Those desperados were tamed by the land itself, land that proved rich enough to support crops like cotton, corn, and sweet potatoes. It was a plantation town, with more than 9,000 slaves in 1860.

After the Civil War, many of Tallahassee's large plantations were repurposed as hunting lodges for wealthy winter residents from the North. Growth was slow but steady right through the Depression, the wars, and until today. Some of the population is accounted for by the presence of Florida State University, Florida A&M (Agricultural and Mechanical), and Tallahassee Community College. FSU has a total enrollment of 33,971, Florida A&M has 12,126 students, the community college boasts another 11,966—that's a lot of youthful exuberance in a city of roughly 150,000 people.

As with any college town, the attendant acad-

COURTESY OF VISIT FLORIDA

Tallahassee

Florida's historic past can be found in the charming museum set in the turn-of-the-19th-century Old Capitol building.

emic and cultural amenities permeate the area. Add to that the heady power of state government, the genteel good manners of the South, and abounding natural beauty and it's a recipe for a lovely, restful vacation. Kids may be less than enthralled with tours of painstakingly restored 19th-century plantation homes and picturesque canopied roads, but there are enough outdoor activities and natural enticements to provide fun for all ages.

PLANNING YOUR TIME

The city makes a wonderful weekend getaway, or a several-day add-on to another Gulf Coast destination. Timing a trip to Tallahassee is fraught with difficult choices. It's a city with four distinct seasons, unlike much of Florida where there seem only to be two. All year-round it's pleasantly moderate: In December the average high temperature is about 65 degrees, with five inches or so of rain. In the summertime, the temperature hovers in the low 90s and it can rain nearly nine inches a month. There are numerous local events and festivals worth considering, not to mention the mayhem that is Seminoles' home games.

Sports and Recreation

COLLEGE FOOTBALL

Doak Campbell Stadium (bordered by Stadium Dr., Pensacola St., and Gaines St., 850-64-Go-FSU, seminoles.collegesports.com/tickets, $27 tickets, which sell out far in advance) is the site of an unseemly amount of school spirit. The **Florida State University Seminoles** play here, and game days transform dignified Tallahassee into a big beery-smelling slavering idiot. The occasional champions are a source of much jubilation and celebration for their diehard fans. The most difficult tickets to get are those against their long-time rival, Virginia Tech. Call for a schedule of games, dates, and times.

BEACHES AND PARKS

Tallahassee isn't on the coast exactly, thus making it a bit of a ringer in a book about the Gulf Coast. But all you have to do is hop in the car and drive less than an hour to hit a bunch of wonderful beaches and parks along the wild Big Bend area, an area sparsely populated by humans and dense with subtropical flora and fauna.

St. Marks National Wildlife Refuge

St. Marks National Wildlife Refuge (1255 Lighthouse Rd., St. Marks, 850/925-6121, sunrise–sunset daily, no fee) is one of the oldest refuges in the National Wildlife Refuge System (established in 1931), with 68,000 acres of protected coastal land. The coastal marshes, islands, tidal creeks, and estuaries of seven north Florida rivers can be explored by boat or by foot. Stop in first at the visitors center (8 A.M.–4 P.M. Mon.–Fri., 10 A.M.–5 P.M. Sat. and Sun.) to get an overview of what there is to do and see in the park.

The refuge has 75 miles of trails, including a 35-mile segment of the Florida National Scenic Trail, but there are wonderful short walking trails as well: the Plum Orchard Pond Trail (.33 mile), Headquarters Pond Trail (.25 mile), and Lighthouse Levee Trail (.25 mile—the St. Marks Light-

house is still in use today), and the Mounds Interpretive Trail (1 mile), which offers a diversity of habitats for bird- and wildlife-viewing. Hiking here is less pleasant in the summer months, when you might opt to explore with a driving tour with the air-conditioning on.

The park is a magnet for birders, who come for the myriad wading birds as well as the ospreys, red-cockaded woodpeckers, kestrels, red-shouldered hawks, and bald eagles. The refuge is open to fishing year-round and hunting in season. There are restrooms at the Refuge Visitor Center, Mounds Trail, and Otter Lake Recreation Area, and picnic facilities are next to Mounds Trail and at Otter Lake.

Big Bend Saltwater Paddling Trail

Birders also enthuse about the **Big Bend Wildlife Management Area's** Hickory Mound Impoundment (from Tallahassee, take U.S. 98 east, turn right on Cow Creek Grade and go six miles to the check station, 850/838-1306). The list of birds that hang out here includes wading birds, ospreys, swallow-tailed and Mississippi kites, bald eagles, and a whole lot of birds I've never even heard of (buffleheads, gadwalls, American wigeons—who comes up with these names?). This area is just one of the five areas, along with Spring Creek, Tide Swamp, Jena, and Snipe Island, that make up the Big Bend Wildlife Management Area. It extends about 60 miles along the Gulf Coast, with Tallahassee approximately 40 miles north of the northernmost part, all of it a gorgeous wilderness explored by bike, horseback, foot, or—the best way—by kayak. The 105-mile Big Bend Saltwater Paddling Trail is open September–June. To order the $15, 40-page paddling guide for the trail, call 850/488-5520 or go online at myfwc.com/recreation/big_bend/paddling_guide.asp.

Canoes and kayaks can be rented in Tallahassee at **The Wilderness Way** (4901 Woodville Hwy., 850/877-7200, www.thewildernessway.net, single kayaks $25 per day, $100 per week; ca-

PANACEA AND SOPCHOPPY

It's a competition for the two best names in Florida. These little colorful towns are both in Wakulla County south of Tallahassee between Carrabelle and Crawfordville, along U.S. 98 near Apalachee Bay and the Gulf of Mexico, and tucked between Apalachicola National Forest and the St. Marks Wildlife Refuge. Neither one is the kind of place you'd spend a whole vacation, but each has its charms.

Panacea is good for whatever ails you. (That should be the town bumper sticker, don't you think?) It was developed as a tourist resort more than 100 years ago by people overly optimistic about the allures of a couple of local springs. These days it's a sweet town of 850 or so people, with a few good seafood shops along the main drag.

You can also visit Anne and Jack Rudloe's **Gulf Specimen Marine Laboratory** (222 Clark Dr., 850/984-5297, 9 A.M.–5 P.M. Mon.–Fri., 10 A.M.–4 P.M. Sat., noon–4 P.M. Sun., $5 adults, $3 children 3–11). The Rudloes are both marine biologists and authors of well-known books on Florida natural history and marine life. The independent nonprofit environmental center and aquarium has recently opened to the public, enabling visitors to get a peek at green shrimp, scarlet sponges, comb jellyfish, and other local marinelife in a seagrass meadow or on a limestone outcrop in a collection of seawater tanks and aquariums. It's a "small is beautiful" approach to aquatic creatures.

There's a tiny airport in Panacea, really just a grassy landing strip, out of which a few enterprising pilots take small charters. Pilots like **John Haberson** (850/984-5832, $50–100) will take you up and around the area and even drop you on Dog Island for the day.

The first weekend in May draws more than 20,000 people to Panacea for the **Blue Crab Festival.** At night in the summer, the thing to do in these parts is to go swimming in the Gulf when the water's **bioluminescence** lends an eerie shimmer to the dark water. Totally safe (after all, it's just the chemical-based light produced by a whole bunch of marine organisms), the gleam seems to echo the zillions of stars visible in the Panacea or Sopchoppy night sky.

For dinner in Panacea, the obvious choice used to be Posey's for topless oysters or smoked mullet; these days, you'll have to enjoy the restorative comforts at either the **Coastal Restaurant** (1305 Coastal Hwy., 850/984-2933) or **Harbor House** (107 Mississippi Ave., 850/984-2758) before bunking down for the night at the **Panacea Motel** (1545 Coastal Hwy., 850/984-5421).

And here's what you need to know about Sopchoppy: Its biggest industry is raising worms. Worm "grunters" pierce loose soil with a wooden stake called a "stob." Once the stob is driven into the soil it gets rubbed with a flat piece of metal called the "bat." The vibrations in the ground drive the big earthworms up, where they are scooped, packaged, and sold for bait. This is such a compelling calling that the town of about 500 holds a well-attended **Worm Gruntin' Festival** each April. The second-biggest festival comes in June with the **June Jam** of mostly local musicians working a musical synergy stew in the square.

George the Potter is a beloved local attraction, with a studio down a dirt road south off of U.S. 319 just east of Sopchoppy. Look for his sign. He makes lovely bowls and mugs, and has a savvy self-promoting bumper sticker that says "Been to Sopchoppy met the Potter."

Then think of camping in Sopchoppy at the **Myron B. Hodge City Park** (Sheldon St. and Park Ave., 850/962-4611).

Sopchoppy is the nearest town to Alligator Point, and between those two towns there's a strange preponderance of **white squirrels.** There are many lyrical myths about how and why these creatures got here, and the same can be said of the **monarch butterflies** that appear here in September and October in their migration south to Mexico. During the fall the beaches can be dotted with fluttering orange majesty.

noes $20 per day, $80 per week), which also leads nature-based canoe and kayak tours around the Panhandle; **The Canoe Shop** (1115 W. Orange Ave., 850/576-5335); and **Blue Water Scuba and Travel Center** (2320 Apalachee Pkwy., 850/656-7665).

COURTESY OF VISIT FLORIDA

An "Old South" charm and grace permeates Maclay State Gardens in Tallahassee.

Maclay State Gardens

New York financier Alfred Maclay wanted to design a garden where both native and exotic plants of Florida could grow together in peace and harmony. He did so on the grounds of his Tallahassee winter home. Maclay State Gardens (3540 Thomasville Rd., 850/487-4556, park open 8 A.M.–sunset daily, gardens 9 A.M.–5 P.M. daily, overstreet trails open 8 A.M.–6 P.M. daily, Maclay House 9 A.M.–5 P.M. daily Jan.–Apr., parking $4) has stunning formal gardens, designed to be at their height of gorgeousness during the winter and early spring (when Maclay and his family would have been in residence). Visitors can walk the gardens ($4 adults, $2 children) or enjoy the park's nature trails, boating, swimming, fishing, and picnicking.

WAKULLA SPRINGS STATE PARK

Johnny Weismuller and Ricou Browning probably froze their tuchases off. The former appeared as Tarzan in numerous films between 1932 and 1942. The latter portrayed the aquatic version of the *Creature from the Black Lagoon* (a guy named Ben Chapman played the creature in the out-of-water scenes). Both of these actors were filmed cavorting in Wakulla Springs, said to be the world's largest and deepest freshwater springs, in which the water temperature remains a fairly constant 70°F. The springs have been the site of lots of Hollywood filming because of their wild, untouched jungle feel, just 15 miles south of Tallahassee.

But it was a tourist attraction long before Weismuller slipped into his loin cloth or Browning donned the rubber suit. In fact, as a teenager Browning was a lifeguard at Wakulla Springs and put on underwater shows for the glass-bottomed boat tours (he helped develop the underwater hose-breathing that has made the mermaid show at Weeki Watchee Springs a hit for so long).

That same glass-bottomed boat tour is a must today at Wakulla Springs State Park (550 Wakulla Park Dr., Wakulla Springs, 850/224-5950, 8 A.M.–sundown daily, $4 per vehicle entrance to the park, $6 for the tour). The 30-minute tours offer a glimpse into the clear 125-foot depths, but more than that they offer a window into north Florida's past. It's a dying tradition, but the people who lead the tours part-rap, part-soliloquize the mysteries and history of this magical place. Oh, and there's a high-jumping fish named Henry involved. The park offers a 40-minute riverboat tour that takes a different route, but I'd opt for the former.

The park also contains a wonderful six-mile nature trail, picnic facilities, swimming (only in designated areas, as it's gator country), and the stately **Wakulla Lodge** (850/224-5950, $85–105) for overnight guests. The lodge was built in 1937, with 27 rooms, each individually decorated with antiques and period furniture. The lodge has a pleasant restaurant called the Ball Room Restaurant—order the navy bean soup or the fried chicken.

Flowing from Wakulla Springs nine miles to the St. Marks River are the crystal-clear waters of the **Wakulla River.** Along the Spanish moss–trimmed cypress lining the river's banks you'll see abundant wildlife, from manatees, otters, and eagles to numerous waterfowl. Several boat ramps provide access to the river, a perfect day's paddle by kayak or canoe. **TNT Hideaway** (6527 Coastal Hwy., Crawfordville, 850/925-6412) is a small, family-owned business with 20 canoes and 20 kayaks, offering guided tours on the Wakulla River (and also off-the-beaten-path tours to St. Marks Lighthouse and Wildlife Refuge, Spring Creek, Aucilla River, Sopchoppy River, and Ochlockonee River). If your aim is to spot a manatee, the weekly *Wakulla News* carries a manatee-watch section that gives all the specifics of recent sightings.

After a day at the springs or along the river, you can bunk down at the **Sweet Magnolia Bed & Breakfast** (803 Port Leon Dr., St. Marks, 850/925-7670, $75–145) or at one of the area's campgrounds: **Ochlockonee River State Park** (four miles south of Sopchoppy on U.S. 319, 850/962-2771, $15), **Holiday Campground** (14 Coastal Hwy., Panacea, 850/984-5757, $22–31), or **Alligator Point Campground** (1320 Alligator Dr., Alligator Point, 850/349-2525, $26 for camping, $51–61 for these cute little cabins with hot tubs).

GOLF

Just for comparison's sake, Naples and Tallahassee are roughly similar in size. In Naples, there are 50 or so public, resort, and semiprivate golf courses within a 30-minute drive of each other. In Tallahassee, cut that number down, way down. There are fewer than 10 courses in the capital city, the public ones models of utility and no-nonsense egalitarianism. This isn't a luxury golf retreat with acres of perfect rolling greens. There are no resort-level courses that draw golfers here, but that doesn't mean you can't play, mostly for a very fair price.

The city of Tallahassee's Park & Recreation Department manages two city-owned golf courses. **Hilaman Park Municipal Golf Course** (2737 Blair Stone Rd., 850/891-3935, greens fee with cart $20–30). It's a par-72, 18-hole course purchased by the city in 1981 and refurbished. The park also offers a swimming pool, tennis courts, racquetball and squash courts, driving range, and golf pro shop. The second one is **Jake Gaither Municipal Golf Course** (801 Tanner Dr., 850/891-3942, greens fee $6.45–13.98, cart additional) a par-36, 9-hole course. Tee times are offered on the weekend, with open play during the week.

The **Seminole Golf Course** (2550 Pottsdamer St., 850/644-2582, greens fee $10–32) has had a recent $7 million upgrade, improving the quality of play on this 1962-vintage course. But the area's newest semiprivate course, completed at the end of 2002, **SouthWood Golf Club** (3750 Grove Park Dr., 850/942-4653, www.southwood-florida.com) is what has golfers exercised. They cite the course's variety of holes, through gorgeous secluded woods and open fields, and they mention that *Golf Magazine* named it among the top 35 courses to open nationwide in 2002.

And for a relaxed day of golf outside the city, head west to the little town of Quincy. The **Golf Club of Quincy** (2291 Soloman Dairy Rd., Quincy, 850/627-9631) is a quiet course of rolling hills and tree-lined fairways.

Tallahassee

Tallahassee

Sights

CANOPY ROADS

Five "official" canopy roads radiate out from downtown Tallahassee—Old St. Augustine, Miccosukee, Meridian, Centerville, and Old Bainbridge. It is mandatory that visitors steer their vehicles through at least one of these moss-draped live-oak tunnels. Narrow, curvy and with an eerie ubiquitous gloaming feeling because of all that leafy greenness, these 60 miles of road were the work of plantation owners. The roads follow earlier trails forged in the 16th century by Spanish missionaries, but their antebellum purpose was to provide shade for the plantations' mules on their long journeys to the Gulf of Mexico. All local maps indicate the canopy roads. If you choose Old St. Augustine Road, look for the **stump-carving work** of chainsaw artist John Birch. And if you head out on Centerville, stop in and pick up sausages at old-time **Bradley's Country Store** (10655 Centerville Rd., 850/893-1647).

NEW CAPITOL

The New Capitol building (Apalachee Pkwy. and Monroe St., 850/488-6167, 9 A.M.–5 P.M. Mon.–Fri., free admission) is hard to miss downtown, a sleek modern edifice providing a visual and metaphoric counterpoint to the classic domed Old Capitol next door. At the top of the New Capitol, on the 22nd floor, there's an observatory level from which one can see all the way to Georgia, 20 miles away. The new building was completed in 1977 and became the center of state government business. Guided tours are available on the hour. The **Governor's Mansion** (700 N. Adams St.) also provides tours three days a week during the legislative sessions.

Around the new and old capitol complex there's a 10-block historical district worthy of a long stroll, with gracious old Victorian homes and manicured antebellum dignity.

COURTESY OF VISIT FLORIDA

Forget the palm trees, Tallahassee is all about hills, grass, and millions of live oaks draped with Spanish moss (which is neither Spanish, nor a moss).

DOWNTOWN TALLAHASSEE

Lake Ella

W 10TH AVE

GIBBS DR

PROCTOR ST

JACKSON ST

MILTON ST

MONROE ST

MERIDIAN ST

COLONIAL ST

W 7TH AVE

OLD BAINBRIDGE RD

MARTIN LUTHER KING JR ST

BRONOUGH ST

DUVALL ST

ADAMS ST

W 6TH AVE

THOMASVILLE RD

▼ CHEZ PIERRE

INGELSIDE ST

MARTIN ST

PINE ST

W 4TH AVE

MACOMB ST

W 3RD AVE

▼ CAFÉ CABERNET

McDANIEL ST

GOVERNOR'S MANSION ★

BREVARD ST

GEORGIA ST

CALHOUN ST

GADSDEN ST

MICCOSUKEE RD

CAROLINA ST

VIRGINIA ST

DUVALL ST

ADAMS ST

TENNESSEE ST

FLOYD'S MUSIC STORE/ ■ BULLWINKLE'S SALOON

CALL ST

MONROE ST

MERIDIAN ST

FRANKLIN BLVD

▼ CYPRESS RESTAURANT

Ponce de Leon Park

PARK AVE

PARK AVE

PARK AVE

FLORIDA STATE UNIVERSTY

MACOMB ST

DOWNTOWN MARKETPLACE

PARADIGM ▼

★ KNOTT HOUSE

ANDREW'S CAPITAL GRILL AND BAR ▼

▼ JASMINE

FSU RUBY DIAMOND ■ AUDITORIUM

MLK JR ST

● GOVERNORS INN

RILEY CENTER MUSEUM ★

JEFFERSON ST

PENSACOLA ST

CITY HALL ■

Ⓜ NEW CAPITOL

APALACHEE PWY

LAFAYETTE ST

ST AUGUSTINE ST

LEON COUNTY CIVIC CENTER

DUVALL ST

★ ★ ★ OLD CAPITOL

CALHOUN ST

■ UNION BANK

MADISON ST

Ⓜ MUSEUM OF FLORIDA HISTORY

WAHNISH WAY

GAINES ST

BRONOUGH ST

MooN

0 ⊢—⊣ 250 yds

0 ⊢—⊣ 250 m

COURTESY OF VISIT FLORIDA

The New Capitol, the most recognizable landmark on the Tallahassee skyline, is the seat of Florida's state government.

MUSEUMS AND HISTORIC HOMES

Because the area is fairly historically rich, a number of small museums lovingly examine certain periods and elements of Tally's past.

Museum of Florida History

Start with the Museum of Florida History (500 S. Bronough St., 850/488-1484, 9 A.M.–4:30 P.M. Mon.–Fri., opening at 10 A.M. on Sat. and noon on Sun., free admission). It actually has five different sites: the Main Gallery, the Old Capitol, the Union Bank, Mission San Luis de Apalachee, and the Knott House, which each highlight a different period of Florida history. It's a weird assortment of stuff, nearly 44,000 items, but if you're patient, and you read the signage and literature, there's a wealth of cool stuff to learn. Movie posters, quilts, furniture, cigar box labels, citrus labels, governor portraits, Civil War flags,

Seminole basketry—it's all arrayed and annotated to give you a slice of the area's cultural history. The main gallery's setting is a little bland, but the material is rich.

Head to the museum's **Old Capitol** site (400 S. Monroe St. at Apalachee Pkwy., 850/487-1902), in a stunning original 1845 building with red candy-striped awnings and a stained-glass dome, and housing exhibits on the state's political history, constitutions, and the history of the building. The building has pretty much been restored to its 1902 appearance and now houses the Florida Center for Political History and Governance. It's a good way to get a duckies-and-horsies multimedia instruction on the state's history, and visitors get to hang out in the Governor's Suite, State Supreme Court, and Senate and House chambers.

The **Knott House** (301 E. Park Ave., 850/922-2459, 1–4 P.M. Wed.–Fri., 10 A.M.–4 P.M. Sat.) is freaky, if you pay attention. Its construction dates to 1843, but it's the Knott family who lived there from 1928 on that gave it its flavor. It's a typical gorgeous Victorian manse, with all original furnishings. But here's the thing: Luella Knott, the matron of the house, wrote rhyming verse about items of furniture all over the house. Her poems, many of them with strong temperance themes, hang from these items of furniture today.

Mission San Luis (2020 W. Mission Rd., 850/487-3711, 10 A.M.–4 P.M. Tues.–Sun., free admission) is a living history museum at the site of a Franciscan mission to the Apalachee Indians circa 1656. While many people know about the missions of California and the Southwest, the Florida missions were earlier and there were more than 100 of them. Mission San Luis has a visitors center and an orientation exhibit that presents text and an audio tour in both English and Spanish.

The **Union Bank** (Apalachee Pkwy. at Gadsden St., 850/561-2603) part of the museum is less compelling. As an extension of the Florida A&M University Black Archives, it houses artifacts and documents reflecting black history.

Other Museums

For a richer look into the area's African-American history, stop into the **Riley Center Museum** (419 E. Jefferson St., 850/681-7881, 10 A.M.–4 P.M. Mon.–Fri., tours $2 adults, $1 children). Set in the historic 1890 John G. Riley House, the center has an oral history program and a multicultural outreach program that includes workshops, lectures, a speaker's bureau, walking tours, special exhibits, and cultural events. Small permanent exhibits tell the story of the Tallahassee African-American community, but recent traveling exhibits have covered things like the art of the Harlem Renaissance. It also serves as a resource center for those doing African-American genealogical work.

Spanish explorer Panfilo de Narvaez liked it here. So much so that he hyped the place after his 1528 visit, prompting Hernando de Soto and his 600 men to come back to this area at the confluence of the Wakulla and St. Marks Rivers in 1539. By 1679, the Spanish Governor of

Florida constructed a fort here (destroyed almost immediately by pirates). Only modestly deterred, the Spanish built a second wooden fort here in 1718, then a third fort made out of stone in 1739—after which, occupation of the fort seesawed back and forth between the Spanish and British, ending in 1821 when Florida was ceded to the United States. Eventually a federal marine hospital was constructed at the site, using stones from the Spanish-built fort, providing care for victims of yellow fever (once a serious epidemic in this swampy, mosquito-ridden wilderness). In the Civil War, the Confederates took control of the fort, renaming it Fort Ward. Built on the foundation of the old marine hospital, **San Marcos de Apalache State Historic Site** (1022 Desoto Blvd., 850/922-6007, 9 A.M.–5 P.M. Thurs.–Mon., $1 admission) has a little visitors center and museum containing exhibits and artifacts of Gulf Coast history, while a walking trail meanders through the ruins of the historic fortification.

For an extremely kid-friendly look at Florida history, the **Tallahassee Museum of History and Natural Science** (3945 Museum Dr., 850/576-1636, www.tallahasseemuseum.org, 9 A.M.–5 P.M. Mon.–Sat., 12:30–5 P.M. Sun., $8 adults, $7.50 seniors, $5 children) has a range of entertaining exhibits that are seldom seen under one roof. It's one roof metaphorically, as the 52-acre museum features a natural-habitat zoo for indigenous wildlife (Florida panthers, red wolves, river otters, black bears), an African-American church and schoolhouse dating to the 1850s, an environmental science center, an 1840s plantation house, an 1880s farmstead, and 20 acres of walking trails. It's not an elegantly or tidily curated museum, but it's fun to wander through the birds of prey aviary and the hands-on Discovery Center. The museum is in heavy rotation with school groups and hosts many outreach events throughout the year.

For more insight into Tallahassee's plantation era, **Goodwood Museum & Gardens** (1600 Miccosukee Rd., 850/877-4202, 9 A.M.–5 P.M. Mon.–Fri., free admission to gardens, $5 for museum) is a restored plantation house with 13 outbuildings set on 19 acres of lawns, heirloom gardens, and gargantuan, moss-draped live oaks. The main house, built around 1840, has been restored to its 1920s look (check out the beautiful frescoed ceiling), surrounded by a skating rink, a reflecting pool, water tower, carriage house with stables, etc. Like the Tallahassee Museum of History and Natural Science, it's the kind of indoor-outdoor museum you stroll your way through. Tours, scheduled 10 A.M.–3:30 P.M. Monday–Friday, are a good way to get a snapshot of antebellum life in these parts.

Arts and Entertainment

MUSIC AND THEATER

The presence of Florida State University lends a certain cultural liveliness to town. The university usually has a visiting artist series every year, along with special events and three theaters to serve the well-regarded FSU theater program. Check with the student newspaper *FSView & Florida Flambeau* (or visit www.fsunews.com) or the *Tallahassee Democrat* for performances at the Mainstage, The Lab, and the Studio Theatre on campus. The university's Music School also hosts more than 400 performances a year, including the "Artist Series" and the "Kaleidoscope" faculty chamber music series (check www.music.fsu.edu for concert schedules).

The **Leon County Civic Center** (505 W. Pensacola St., box office 850/222-0400, times and prices vary) sees lots of entertainment over the year, from Florida State Seminoles basketball to six traveling Broadway musicals each year and concerts that range from Ted Nugent to Boston Pops.

The **Tallahassee Symphony Orchestra** (FSU Ruby Diamond Auditorium, Westcott Building, corner of College Ave. and Copeland St., 850/224-0461, www.tsolive.org) is a professional company including music faculty from Florida State University, music graduate students, and professional musicians from the community. The orchestra puts on an annual "Masterworks Series" in addition to holiday concerts and young people's concerts. Less professional but a lot of fun (and all concerts are free), the **Big Bend Community Orchestra** is an all-volunteer community orchestra that performs mostly at Lee Hall Auditorium on the Florida A&M University campus.

Tallahassee Ballet Company (218 E. 3rd Ave., 850/222-1287, www.tallaballet.com) stages three productions a year, drawn mostly from local amateur dance talent with the occasional guest professional making an appearance. At Christmastime, this usually means *The Nutcracker,* with a couple of other family-friendly ballet classics to round out the season.

There is no professional theater company in Tallahassee, but one of the area's oldest community theaters, **Tallahassee Little Theatre** (1861 Thomasville Rd., 850/224-4597, performances 8 P.M. Thurs.–Sat., 2 P.M. Sun., $14, $12 for student and seniors) stages mainstream dramas and musicals *(A Funny Thing Happened on the Way to the Forum, Damn Yankees)* with a second, more experimental coffeehouse series. The **Quincy Music Theatre** (Leaf Theatre,118 E. Washington St., Quincy, 850/875-9444), about 15 minutes west of Tallahassee, is in its 23rd year of production. Its mainstay is family-friendly musicals *(Gypsy, Jesus Christ Superstar, Babes in Toyland),* with a seasoned community cast and a pretty 400-seat theater.

MOVIES

For mainstream movies, a clean, bright **AMC 20** at the Tallahassee Mall (2415 N. Monroe St., 850/386-4330) has lots of family-friendly first-run films; **Movies @ Governor's Square** (1501 Governor's Square Blvd, 850/878-7211) offers mainstream movies with a minimum of teen junk; **Miracle 5** (1815 Thomasville Rd., 850/224-2617) balances the offerings with five screens of foreign, artsy, and indie flicks (it's also home to the Tallahassee Film Club); and **Movies 8** (2810 Sharer Rd., 850/422-0051) is the cheapskate pick with second-run movies for $2 most days and 50 cents on Tuesdays.

So you could go spend a lot of time at Tallahassee's multiplexes, but then you'd miss out on a local institution, the **Student Life Cinema** (in the Student Life Building on the FSU campus, 113 S. Wildwood Dr., 850/644-4455, www.fsu.edu). Parking won't be easy, but it's fun to sit with a bunch of rowdy undergraduates (they get in for free; you have to pay $4) and watch *High Noon* or *Casablanca* or maybe even *Team America: World Police.*

FESTIVALS

The middle of February has become increasingly busy during Tallahassee's **Seven Days of Opening Nights** (850/644-6500, www.sevendaysfestival.org) annual fine- and performing-arts festival, which draws big national stars as well as local luminaries. Equally well attended is April's **Springtime Tallahassee** (850/224-5012, www.springtimetallahassee.com), a city festival with parades and a giant arts and crafts jubilee, and December's **Market Days Tallahassee,** a downtown fine arts sale and festival.

Foodies can time a trip for the **Blue Crab Festival** in Panacea in May or the **Florida Seafood Festival** in November in Apalachicola, while music lovers can choose between the **Havana Music Fest** in April or the bluegrass **Swamp Stomp** at the Tallahassee Museum of History and Natural Science in July.

Accommodations

Tallahassee has lots of inexpensive, no-frills hotels and motels to accommodate the regular influx of college parents and government workers in session. What it doesn't have are resort hotels, golf-and-spa destinations, or fabulous boutique inns.

UNDER $50

Hotel and motel rates start right around $50 in Tallahassee. If you want to chisel a few dollars off your room rate and don't much care about amenities, drive down Apalachee Parkway or North Monroe Street and check out the signs for the numerous small chains along both sides. You'll see Quality Inn, Howard Johnson, Hampton Inn, and other familiar entries.

$50–150

Best Western has two properties locally, the **Best Western Pride Inn & Suites** (2016 Apalachee Pkwy., Tallahassee, 850/656-6312, $65–75) and the **Best Western Seminole Inn** (6737 Mahan Dr., Tallahassee, 850/656-2938, $49–60). Both are geared to the business traveler, with pleasant rooms and executive suites and a complimentary continental breakfast. The former is closer to town, Florida State University, and the capitol. The latter is directly off I-10 at Exit 209A.

La Quinta also has two properties in Tallahassee, **La Quinta Inn, Tallahassee South** (2850 Apalachee Pkwy., Tallahassee, 850/878-5099, $65–99) and **La Quinta Inn, Tallahassee North** (2905 N. Monroe St., Tallahassee, 850/385-7172, $70–94). The south property is within walking distance of several decent restaurants, the IMAX theater, Governor Square Mall, and AMC 20 theater, and it's five miles from Florida State University. The north property is closer to the capitol and downtown.

The **Radisson Hotel Tallahassee** (415 N. Monroe St., Tallahassee, 850/224-6000, $100–200) is a little more upscale, with greater amenities, and it's in the historic downtown district. The hotel features 116 guest rooms, an exercise room, sauna, business center, and six meeting/banquet rooms, with a complimentary airport shuttle.

OVER $150

The undisputed finest accommodations to be had in Tallahassee are to be found at the **Governors Inn** (209 S. Adams St., Tallahassee,

850/681-6855, $139–229). It's half a block from the capitol building right downtown, with complimentary continental breakfast, cocktails, turndown service, and valet parking. Each of the 40 rooms and suites is named for a past Florida governor. It has an antebellum grace and dignity, with creaky stairs and wood-burning fireplaces. The coolest rooms are the loft suites with these circular staircases up to the bedroom.

Food

BREAKFAST AND LUNCH

The problem with starting a visit to Tallahassee at **Another Broken Egg** (3500 Kinhega Dr. 850/907-3447, www.anotherbrokenegg.com, 7 A.M.–2 P.M. Tues.–Sun., $6–10) is that your expectations for the remainder of the trip may be unreasonably high. It's a small regional chain, but they do things right, with beignets, excellent cinnamon rolls, crab-filled omelets, blackberry grits, and lots of coffee served in these pretty earthenware mugs. **Torrey's Neighborhood Grille** (1415 Timberlane Rd., Market Square, 850/893-0326, breakfast Tues.–Sun., lunch Tues.–Fri., $5–10) is another local breakfast favorite, with rib-sticking biscuits and gravy.

For a quick lunch on the fly (either eat-in or takeout), **Crispers** (1241 Apalachee Pkwy., 850/656-4222, 10:30 A.M.–10 P.M. Mon.–Sat., 11 A.M.–8 P.M. Sun., $6–8) has good soups, gumbos, and chowders, as well as fairly nice salads. In a similar vein, **Manna** (3507 Thomasville Rd., 850/668-1966, 11 A.M.–10 P.M. Tues.–Fri., 8 A.M.–10 P.M. Sat., 8 A.M.–2:30 P.M. Sun., $7–14) features a wonderful cheese selection, and soups and salads to go. **Hopkins' Eatery** (1700 N. Monroe St., 850/386-4258 and 1415 Market St., 850/668-0311, 11 A.M.–9 P.M. Mon.–Fri., 11 A.M.–5 P.M. Sat., $7–12) has a pleasant patio on which to enjoy fat specialty sandwiches.

CASUAL AMERICAN

Andrew's Capital Grill & Bar (228 S. Adams St., 850/222-3444, 11:30 A.M.–10 P.M. Mon.–Sat., $8–30, valet parking) has been a Tally downtown landmark for 29 years, with a sandwich "express line" weekdays for government types (some of these local luminaries have been immortalized with sandwiches named after them). At night, the terrace is the place to be, where upon you can dig into retro meatloaf with brown mushroom sauce or something a little zingier like a cumin-crusted pork loin. Downstairs is **Andrew's 228,** the more upscale counterpart, with an architecturally stunning bilevel dining room. Prices are steeper, and the menu includes a variety of Italianate items: butternut squash and walnut ravioli, seafood fra diavolo, risottos. Andrew's also boasts a fairly mobbed after-work happy hour scene and an expertly prepared classic martini.

By day an excellent gourmet goodies shop, **Clusters & Hops** (707 N. Monroe St., 850/222-2669, 5–11:30 P.M. Tues.–Sat., $9–21) becomes a stylish small restaurant in the evenings, serving the likes of Madeira-marinated mushrooms served with red pepper and goat cheese polenta between layers of puff pastry, or an elegant warm apple pie with caramel sauce. **Food Glorious Food** (Betton Place, 1950 Thomasville Rd., 850/224-9974, 11 A.M.–3:30 P.M. and 5:30–10:30 P.M. daily, $14–18) has always had glorious, if eclectic, food (apricot-balsamic glazed chicken with honey mashed sweet potato and green beans, chilled Thai coconut soup with tempura shrimp and sake, Cuban roast pork with black beans), and a recent remodel has made it much more glorious visually. Opt for a seat in the twinkle-lit courtyard.

There are a couple of good restaurants in Tallahassee hotels—**Marie Livingston's Steakhouse** (Holiday Inn, 2714 Graves Rd., 850/562-2525, 7–10 A.M. Mon.–Fri., 8–11 A.M. Sat. and Sun., 11 A.M.–2 P.M. Mon.–Fri., 5–10 P.M. Sun.–

Thurs., until 11 P.M. Fri. and Sat., $15–21) for standard steak, chops, and pretty good baby-back ribs, and the **Monroe Street Grill** (Ramada Inn, 2900 N. Monroe St., 850/386-1027, 6:30–10:30 P.M. and 11:30 A.M.–2 P.M. daily, 5–10 P.M. Mon.–Sat., until 9 P.M. Sun., lunches under $8, most dinners under $15) for prime rib and a huge salad bar.

UPSCALE

Where locals go to impress out-of-town guests, **Café Cabernet** (1019 N. Monroe St., 850/224-0322, 5 P.M.–2 A.M. Mon.–Sat., small plates $8–9, entrées $16–22) has lived a long and impressive life. With a 500-label cellar and 30 pours by the glass, wine is a focus here. It's a fairly raucous meeting place, where you'll see local luminaries tucking into a grilled tuna steak paired with peanut rice and napped with sweet Asian glaze, or pecan-crusted chicken glazed with a brandy blueberry sauce.

Capital Steak House (Holiday Inn Select, 316 W. Tennessee St., 850/222-9555, 6 A.M.–11 P.M. daily, $15–33) is more of a straight steakhouse idiom, with normal-sized steaks up to a goofy 26-ounce porterhouse. The best part about it is the gallery of photos that tell the story of Florida State and Florida A&M universities' histories. Nice martinis, too.

When Tallahassee has something to celebrate—anniversaries, new jobs—**Chez Pierre** (1215 Thomasville Rd., 850/222-0936, 11 A.M.–10 P.M. Mon.–Sat., 11 A.M.–2:30 P.M. brunch and 6–9 P.M. Sun., $20–30) gets the business. It's usually the top winner in annual "best of" magazine articles, with French/continental cuisine that has many admirers. But in addition to a lovely pinenut and sun-dried tomato–crusted rack of New Zealand lamb with mint au jus, or a cedar-planked salmon, Chez Pierre serves a great hamburger. Another perennial local award winner is **Georgio's** (3425 Thomasville Rd. 850/893-4161, 5–10 P.M. Mon.–Sat., $18–25). An elegant, rather staid place, it proffers rich American/continental dishes like Charleston she-crab soup and blue-crab-stuffed Gulf red snapper.

N Cypress Restaurant (320 E. Tennessee St., 850/513-1100, 11 A.M.–2 P.M. Tues.–Fri., 5:30–10:30 P.M. Tues.–Sat., about $8 for little dishes, $18–27 for big dishes) is more my speed, with imaginative takes on Southern regional cooking. Chef-proprietor David Gwynn has a sense of humor and panache, exhibited by his super-luxurious version of shrimp and grits. The wine list is thoughtful (largely American boutique wineries), and the decor casually elegant.

BOILED P-NUTS

Sometimes "boiled" is spelled wrong, too. There are stands that dot all the back roads of the rural Florida Panhandle. They each have tortuously hand-lettered signs that tout the glories of the green peanut. The outskirts of Tallahassee are P-nut Central, so you owe it to yourself to stop (also, the stands' proprietors tend to look like folks who could really use the cash, often hunkered over burners at the back of their rattletrap trucks in the hot sun).

Technically, boiled p-nuts are supposed to be the fresh, green nuts, so look for them in the fall. They're hawked all year-round, but these are garden-variety peanuts, sold to the unsuspecting. There are four species of peanuts—Valencia, Spanish, Virginia, and runners. Northern Florida peanuts tend to be "southern runners," with a medium-sized nut, two to a pod.

The raw peanuts are boiled in the shell for several hours, then a huge amount of salt is added to the water and the whole mess is boiled some more. Then the peanuts sit in the brine until a customer pulls up. They are then drained and sold to enthusiasts by the quart at the road's shoulder. Soft, and salty, and a little damp, they are the perfect foil for cheap lite beer. There's a southern tradition of floating shelled peanuts in a bottle of Coke, but this is not to be undertaken with boiled p-nuts. These you must eat warm, right away, as you pull away from the p-nut stand, the shells forming a huge detritus pile in the front seat as you start thinking about where you're going to stop for that beer.

ITALIAN

Ask around for Italian, and everyone will steer you to **Anthony's** (Betton Place, 1950 Thomasville Rd., 850/224-1447, 11 A.M.–2 P.M. Mon.–Fri., 5–9:30 P.M. Mon.–Thurs., until 10 P.M. Fri. and Sat., until 9 P.M. Sun., $17–25). It's not a conspiracy, exactly, but a local habit. The decor is comfortable but not all that notable. The menu covers utterly trammeled ground (veal marsala). Still, it has the warmth and charm of an old favorite.

OTHER ETHNIC FOODS

If you're looking for purity and gastronomic verisimilitude, you won't like **Jasmine** (109 E. College Ave., 850/681-6868, 11:30 A.M.– 9:45 P.M. Mon.–Fri., 6–9:45 P.M. Sat., 5:30–9:30 P.M. Sun., $7–15). But everyone else in Tallahassee seems to. It's got sushi, and a little bit of Italian food, and froufrou things like a chicken and brie sandwich on a toasted baguette. Then the peanut butter pie for dessert. Most people swear by the sushi, in familiar combinations and offered in a twin-roll option. Jasmine is popular with downtown professionals for lunch, does a fairly brisk happy-hour business, and then appeals to College Avenue revelers in the evening. A more coherently Japanese dining experience can be found at **Osaka** (1690 Raymond Diehl Rd., 850/531-0222, 5–10 P.M. Sun.–Thurs., until 11 P.M. Fri. and Sat., $17–26). It's a Japanese steakhouse with all the shrimp-flipping shenanigans, but the hibachi chefs make very good food.

Tallahassee has more than its share of inexpensive Mexican restaurants, the best of which is **El Tapatio** (1002 N. Monroe St., 850/224-0351, 11 A.M.–10 P.M. Mon.–Thurs., until 11 P.M. Fri. and Sat., until 9 P.M. Sun., $7–10). Burritos, tacos, enchiladas.

SEAFOOD

There are lots of little mom-and-pop fish joints in Tallahassee, many lean on ambience but rich when it comes to Southern fried fish. For a more pleasant sit-down experience, **Crystal River Seafood** (2721 N. Monroe St., 850/383-1530, and 1968 W. Tennessee St., 850/575-4418, 11 A.M.–9 P.M. daily, $8–15) is a homey family restaurant with fried fish, hushpuppies, and sweet tea. **Barnacle Bill's** (1830 N. Monroe St., 850/385-8734, 11 A.M.–11 P.M. daily, $12–22) is more the place to go for steamed seafood, topless oysters, and cold beers. I hesitate to recommend it because it's a chain, and a sister restaurant to Outback Steakhouse and Carrabba's Grill, but locals really like their **Bonefish Grill** (3491-7 Thomasville Rd., 850/297-0460, 11:30 A.M.– 10 P.M. daily, $14–25). The spins on simple grilled fish are stylish and contemporary, the restaurant interior sleek and inviting.

Nightlife

By day, Tallahassee seems like all sedate antebellum charm. Maybe it's just the influence of a large university in its midst, but at night, Tallahassee tears it up. For live music, **M Floyd's Music Store** (666-1 W. Tennessee St., 850/222-3506, hours usually 8 P.M.– 2 A.M., cover $6–12) is where to go when you need to swing your arms and look mean in the mosh pit. When you're more interested in listening to the blues, head to **Bradfordville Blues Club** (7152 Moses Ln., off Bradfordville Rd., 850/906-0766, 8 P.M.–2 A.M. Fri. and Sat.). Just ease your car down the tiki torch–lined dirt road and you'll hear the one-room cinderblock juke joint before you see it. Blues greats have played in this little rural club, called the BBC, nestled in an old oak grove. Then there's **The Moon** (1105 E. Lafayette St., 850/878-6900), a club with multiple-personality disorder, in a good way. Fridays it's called "Stetson's On The Moon" and is a country-western bar with line dancing, mechanical bulls, etc. Saturdays you'll find a pretty standard dance club, with a slightly older crowd (no T-shirts, sneakers, or ball caps allowed); Wednesday night is college night when the age drops precipitously. There's karaoke in the Silver Moon Lounge, whether that's a threat or a promise is up to you.

Established in 1979, **Bullwinkle's Saloon** (620 W. Tennessee St., 850/224-0651) has been a Florida State institution for most of that time. It's another rowdy college bar with DJs some nights, live bands on others. Things get ugly on nights when it's $5 for all you can drink 9 P.M.–1 A.M. with a student ID (usually Wednesday).

The trendier and possibly more mature crowd will appreciate **Club Deep** (1660-15 N. Monroe St., 850/224-4144) a fairly new, upscale Miami-style dance club. Saturdays it's a young professional crowd and Thursdays it seems more college-age. And for when you're tired of all that dancing and just want a bit of convivial conversation over a glass of wine, try **Paradigm** (115 W. College Ave., 850/224-9980), a trendy bar that attracts legislators during session and more mature FSU students throughout the year.

SPORTS BARS

College towns are, ipso facto, sports bar towns. One of the best in Tallahassee is **Tallahassee Ale House & Sports Bar** (Holiday Inn Capital, 1355 Apalachee Pkwy., 850/878-4399), an upscale example of the species with a fairly nice raw bar. **AJ's** (1800 W. Tennessee St., 850/681-0731, 11 A.M.–2 A.M. daily) is a college-student hangout, especially on Tuesday nights. There are coin-op pool tables and gigantic beers called "big daddies." **4th Quarter Bar & Grill** (2033 N. Monroe St., 850/385-0017, 11 A.M.–2 A.M. daily) has a cacophonous 17 televisions tuned to different games, and lots of regulars talking trash about the teams, their players, their players' mothers, etc. And **Sports Deli** (1912 Sunset Ln., 850/577-0711) has a fun outdoor deck and horseshoes, darts, so you don't have to be just a spectator.

There are a few worthy pool halls in Tallahassee, too: The most fun is **Snookers** (1861 W. Tennessee St., 850/224-8644), with good drink specials, nicely maintained pool tables, and a huge fish in a tank (mascot? bouncer?). There's also **Halligans** (1700 Halstead Blvd., 850/668-7665) and **Pockets** (2810 Sharer Rd., 850/385-7665).

Shopping

Governor's Square Mall (1500 Apalachee Pkwy., 850/219-9996) has the kind of serviceable stores in which you can handily buy a new washer/dryer or a three-pack of sweat socks. JCPenney, Sears, Burdines, and Dillard's are the big anchors, with ubiquitous mall stores like Auntie Anne's Pretzels and Limited Too filling the space in between. The **Tallahassee Mall** (2415 N. Monroe St., 850/385-7145) isn't much fancier, but it has 15 or so restaurants, along with the Gap, Barnes & Noble, and a 20-screen AMC 20 movie theater.

The weekly **Downtown Marketplace** (Ponce de Leon Park, Monroe St. at Park Ave., 850/297-3945, 8 A.M.–2 P.M. Sat., March–Nov., free admission) is framed as a farmers market, but for the visitor, the live music, chef demos,

children's storytelling, and author appearances steal the show.

Some of the area's most delicious shopping requires a drive to the northern town of **Havana,** which, true to its name, was once a locus of cigar manufacturing. When that business dried up, Havana was not much of anything. It was when trailblazing Tallahassee antiques shop owners Henderson and Lee Hotchkiss bought up a block of downtown in 1983 that the town's luck started to change. The pair began selling and leasing store spaces to other antiques dealers, with the idea that if there were a certain critical mass, the sleepy little town would become an antiques shopping destination. Their calculation seems to have worked, as now the town has nearly 100 dealers of antiques, fine arts, crafts, and tchotchkes. The center seems to be at **The Cannery** (115 E. 8th Ave., 850/539-3800), with lots of shops tucked into a renovated, historic canning plant. Also worth checking out are the **Florida Art Center & Gallery, Wanderings,** and **Nicholson Farmhouse & Shops** (three miles west of town), **First Street Gallery, Planters Exchange,** and **Main Street Market.**

If you time your visit correctly, visit Havana during April when they hold MusicFest, a fairly elaborate lineup of acts, food, and crafts. Havana also hosts a Bead and Jewelry Fest and a Pumpkin Fest, both in October.

Information and Services

AREA INFORMATION

All telephone listings are within the 850 area code unless otherwise indicated. Tallahassee and environs are on eastern time.

Tourist Information

For information or trip-planning assistance and rates before you arrive, call the **Tallahassee Area Convention and Visitors Bureau** (850/413-9200 or 800/628-2866). Once here, your first stop for information should be the **visitors' center** (Apalachee Pkwy. and Monroe St., 850/413-9200) on the first floor of the West Plaza entrance of the New Capitol building. The gentleman who runs the center, Don Hardy, is a wealth of local lore and history. He'll equip you with maps and a plan and send you on your way.

Tallahassee has its own daily newspaper, the *Tallahassee Democrat.* You will find kiosks all over the downtown area, for a price of 50 cents. It's a Knight Ridder paper, printed mornings, with a super weekend entertainment section. There's also an African-American weekly called the *Capital Outlook* published every Thursday, and the *FSView,* the twice-weekly student newspaper covering Florida State University.

Police and Emergencies

In any emergency, dial 911 for immediate assistance. If you need the police in a nonemergency, visit or call the **Police Department** (234 E. 7th Ave., 850/891-4200). Tallahassee has two hospitals equipped to care for patients in need of emergency medical care: **Capital Regional Medical Center** (2626 Capital Medical Blvd., 850/325-5000) and **Tallahassee Memorial Hospital** (1300 Miccosukee Rd., 850/431-1155).

Radio and Television

Spinning the dial on your car radio, you'll encounter public radio at **89.1 FM WFSM,** classical at **91.5 FM WFSQ,** classic rock at **99.9 FM WWFO,** and country at **103.1 FM WAIB.** If you really want to listen like a local, turn to the cool college stew of genres that is played on **89.7 FM WVFS,** the Florida State independent station.

Leon County's television offerings include **WCTV Channel 6,** the CBS affiliate; **WFSU Channel 11,** the PBS affiliate; and **WTXL Channel 27,** the ABC affiliate.

Laundry Services

Undergraduates and coin laundries go together like peanut butter and jelly—there's the **Northwood Coin Laundry** (1940 N. Monroe St., 850/385-9121) and the **Plaza Laundromat** (1911 N. Monroe St., 850/422-0262) for starters.

Getting There and Around

DRIVING

The main access road in and out of town from the east or west is I-10. From Gainesville, it's about 120 miles west, the easiest route I-75 north to I-10 west. From Pensacola at the westernmost edge of the state, it's four hours east to Tallahassee. To reach the Gulf of Mexico and the little coastal towns along the Panhandle, take U.S. 319 south to U.S. 98.

Once in town, you need to know that the main north–south road is Monroe Street, which is also the east–west dividing line for addresses. The downtown is bounded by Tennessee Street to the north, Van Buren Street to the south, the FSU campus to the west, and Magnolia Drive to the east. FSU is about three-quarters of a mile west of Monroe Street, and Doak Campbell Stadium (where the Seminoles play football) is on the southwestern part of campus. Florida Agricultural & Mechanical University (FAMU, pronounced "fam-you") is just south of downtown, bordered by Canal Street on the north and Perry Street on the south.

FLYING

Tallahassee Regional Airport (3300 Capital Circle SW, 850/891-7800) is 10 miles southwest of downtown and is serviced by six national/regional airlines including Delta and USAir. Check out the airport's "Artport Gallery," a nice touch. There's also a small air charter service called **Flightline Group, Inc.** (3256 Capital Circle SW 850/574-4444), which has its own aviation support center, charter/rental aircrafts, flight school, and fueling and repair.

Alamo (800/327-9633), **Avis** (800/831-2847), **Budget** (800/527-0700), **Dollar** (800/800-4000 domestic, 800/800-6000 international), **Enterprise** (800/736-8222), **Hertz** (800/654-3131), and **National** (800/227-7368) provide rental cars from the airport.

PUBLIC TRANSPORTATION

Amtrak (Downtown, Railroad Ave., 850/224-2779 or 800/872-7245) offers east–west service three times a week aboard the transcontinental Sunset Limited with limited stops in L.A., New Orleans, Jacksonville, Orlando, and Miami.

Within the city, **TalTran City Bus** (C.K. Steele Plaza, 111 W. Tennessee St., 850/891-5200, $1) is a pretty extensive public transit system with 31 routes, university shuttles, and Dial-A-Ride services for the elderly and disabled. **Yellow Cab** (850/580-8080) provides 24-hour passenger or package transportation, with wheelchair accessibility and charter van service. From the airport to downtown is about a $15 cab.

Tallahassee

The Forgotten Coast

In the early 1990s, the area between Panama City and St. Marks was a marketing nightmare. As far as tourists knew, there was no *there* there. And so someone came up with the catchy phrase, "The Forgotten Coast." But who forgot it, and when, and does its increasing popularity mean that we now collectively remember? It was probably Hurricane Opal in 1995 that got tourists recollecting. Damage to other popular tourist destinations on the Panhandle prompted peo-

ple to cast about for where to vacation. Hmm. Franklin and Gulf Counties, 60 percent national or state park, top-rated yet under-populated beaches, good seafood, low prices? Yep, it got people thinking.

But it probably wasn't until the paper mill in Port St. Joe went silent a few years after that—its smokestacks no longer belching out foul-smelling smoke, its waterways no longer tainted with the mill's noxious effluvium—that the area took on

Must-Sees

Look for **M** to find the sights and activities you can't miss and **M** for the best dining and lodging.

The Porter House, one of over 200 antebellum homes in town.

M **Apalachicola Estuary Tour:** Take a guided boat trip through the Apalachicola National Estuarine Research Reserve to see some of the 308 species of birds, 186 species of fish, and 57 species of mammals who call this fertile estuary home (page 253).

M **St. Joseph Peninsula State Park:** Dr. Beach knows a few things. Scientifically considering sand, surf, shells, and such, Dr. Stephen Leatherman has taken it upon himself to bestow annual kudos on the country's best beaches. A funny-shaped barrier peninsula near Cape San Blas, St. Joseph Penin-

sula State Park rightfully makes it to the top of his rankings (page 254).

M **Self-Guided Historic Walking Tour:** Go back in time to an era of antebellum grace and charm with a leisurely stroll in downtown Apalachicola. More than 200 of the buildings and homes downtown made the National Register of Historic Places, and many of them are open for tours (page 257).

M **Florida Seafood Festival:** You'll gain a robust appreciation for Apalachicola's beloved eastern oysters in November at the annual Florida Seafood Festival held in Battery Park (page 259).

M **St. George Island State Park:** The Forgotten Coast has another top beach contender, this one taking up the eastern nine miles of St. George Island. A nighttime beach walk on St. George reveals one of the darkest night skies in the United States (telescope optional) and the mystery of baby loggerhead turtles flapping their way back out to sea under a luminous moon (page 266).

M **Biking St. George Island:** If you're staying on the Plantation (western) side of the island, stop in town halfway for a sustaining ice cream cone and continue along the roadside path until you reach the state park at the island's eastern end (page 268).

The Forgotten Coast

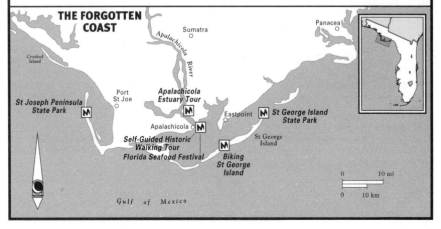

the gleaming patina of a bona fide, quaint tourist destination. These days, Port St. Joe, the county seat, is known instead for its sweet scallops. Even the famous seem to be remembering the Forgotten Coast recently: Peter Fonda, Josh Brolin, Minnie Driver, Lauren Hutton, even members of Pearl Jam are purported to have vacationed in these parts.

But before it was "forgotten," it was an area with a plan. Established in the early 1800s, **Apalachicola** initially provided the South's cotton plantations an accessible port. Extending 300 miles up to Columbus, Georgia, the Apalachicola River made Apalachicola an ideal place in which to collect cotton for transport to mills in New England and overseas to mills and lace-manufacturing centers in Western Europe. Cotton warehouses were quickly erected to house and bale the Old South's most successful crop—at one point the town boasted 43 warehouses, making it the third-largest cotton port on the Gulf Coast (behind Mobile and New Orleans).

Then during the Civil War, the shipping industry foundered (a blockade sealed off the harbor; railroads became ubiquitous). Retooling, residents responded by looking to the fertile Gulf waters for new revenue sources. From the 1870s until the early 20th century, Apalachicola's sponge-diving industry ranked third in the state. Greek émigrés began harvesting sponges in Apalachicola, eventually relocating their industry south to Carrabelle, Cedar Key, and finally settling in Tarpon Springs.

Timber and turpentining proved lucrative land-based endeavors around the same time—the Apalachicola River floodplain was fairly rapidly stripped of cypress. And if you look carefully, you can still spot turpentining scars on St. George Island's larger slash pines. Historians say the demand for turpentine in the early 1900s was comparable to our reliance on petroleum today. It was a nearly universal ingredient in manufacturing—to meet demand the area's trees were milked of their sap like so many root-bound cows, the sticky mess then distilled.

That fell off as the call for turpentine abated, and during World War II the area was used as a training camp. After this, Apalachicola and environs were blissfully without a master plan. It was independent-minded fisherfolk coaxing what they might from the generous Apalachicola Bay and River. Apalachicola still leads the state in the production of oysters, serving too as a principal supplier of crabs, shrimp, and fish. The area is also the gateway to some of the country's most gorgeous beaches, barrier islands, and national wildlife preserves.

As with other rural spots along the Gulf, the Forgotten Coast does not offer everything to everyone: There are no multiplexes or amusement parks, few malls, even fewer fast-food restaurants. In planning a trip here, adopt a bring-it-if-you-need-it attitude. Pack the car to the gills with fishing gear, beach toys, bikes, skates, juicy paperbacks, and all the other ingredients for leisure bliss.

Where you set up your base camp is a matter of preference—the historic port of Apalachicola, founded by 19th-century cotton and lumber barons, is chockablock with restored Georgian and Victorian homes and repurposed cotton warehouses containing antiques shops and darling seafood restaurants. **St. George Island,** on the other hand, is an unparalleled barrier island retreat, with hundreds of beachfront rentals ranging from modest to fantastically sumptuous. And **Eastpoint,** on the mainland, is where to go if you're here to fish, watch others fish, or generally have a down-home good time.

PLANNING YOUR TIME

The Forgotten Coast, roughly speaking, is bounded on the west by Mexico Beach and on the east by St. Marks. From west to east, it includes the communities of St. Joe Beach and Port St. Joe, Simmons Bayou, Cape San Blas, Indian Pass, Apalachicola, St. George Island, Eastpoint, Carrabelle, Ochlockonee Bay, and Panacea. The best way to explore is by car, and the communities worthy of most of your attention are Apalachicola and St. George Island. (Apalachicola will hold your interest for a minimum of a weekend, and St. George Island rentals, at least during high season, are mostly by

THE FORGOTTEN COAST

the full week.) Beyond that, Eastpoint and Carrabelle deserve a half day or so, the latter if only to see "the world's smallest police station." It's a telephone booth, no lie.

The area is served by U.S. 98, a poky and picturesque roadway that stretches 300 miles along the northwest Florida Panhandle coast. Driving south from Alabama and Georgia, you can make time along east–west I-10, but it's about 65 miles to the north. Sooner or later you've got to hook up with 98 and slow down.

Which suits the area. The beaches of St. George Island, Cape San Blas, St. Vincent's Island, and St. Joe State Park often make people's lists of top beaches in the United States. There are faded, leaning lighthouses, tall dunes, miles of white sand dotted with perfect sand dollars, and hardly another person in sight.

High season here is very different from that in the rest of coastal Florida. It stays cooler here than elsewhere on the Gulf, making it a little nippy in the winter and more than tolerable in the summer. Summer is the peak, with rental prices jumping substantially on beach houses on St. George and hotel rooms in Apalachicola. Many beach houses book as far as a year in advance during the summer months. If you are more impulsive, try "off peak" times to get a room on the fly. Spring is just gorgeous on this stretch of the coast (but watch out, Easter week tends to be a difficult reservation), and the early fall is even better.

Apalachicola

Say it with me: apple-LATCH-chee-CO-la. The locals, some of them parsimonious with words, even syllables, shorten it to "Apalach." More so than most places along the Gulf Coast of Florida, Apalach has the stately elegance and mellifluous accents that are the strict purview of the Old South. Georgian and Victorian manses, some the worse for wear, are settled in along wide avenues shaded by aged, moss-slung live oaks.

Here is a true yet illustrative Apalachicola story: We idled at the corner of 5th and Avenue F, watching as a slow, grizzled dog stepped out into the intersection. She stopped, swinging her head first one way, then the other. Now, I'm no Dr. Dolittle, but I know a lost dog when I see one. She was off course and clearly flummoxed about it. Behind us, a man got out of a shiny new pickup.

"Sadie's lost again (names have been changed to protect innocent canines)," he noted.

"Does she live around here?" I asked out my window.

"About five blocks. I'll have to follow her home. She doesn't like to ride in cars."

Getting back in his pickup, he yelled, "Go home, Sadie."

She set off, looking balefully back at the pickup. The pickup followed behind, its driver occasionally shouting a gentle encouragement at the old girl.

This story indicates two things. First, Apalachicola is the kind of town in which neighbors are so neighborly that they know each other's pets at 30 paces. And second, they not only recognize the pets, they are familiar with, and accommodating of, said pets' idiosyncrasies. But before you start talking about Mayberry and whistling the *Andy Griffith Show* theme song, Apalachicola is more than just a small town straight out of yesteryear. Population roughly 3,000, Apalachicola is imbued with the sophistication and dignity of a much larger city.

Perhaps it's the tall shadows cast by the area's long history that give its residents such civic pride. Apalach could have been a contender were it not for the blockade of Apalachicola Bay by Union forces during the Civil War. It was a huge port city in the 1830s and '40s, with all the attendant sophistication and erudition of a cultural center. The end of steamboat travel at the end of the war in some ways froze the city—it never grew much bigger or more populous, its houses and accomplishments achieving their acme during those antebellum years. For the visitor today, this means

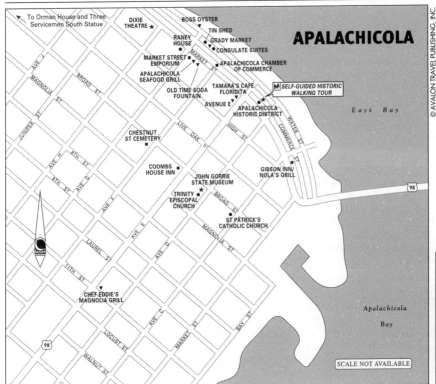

© AVALON TRAVEL PUBLISHING, INC.

beautiful houses on wide, tree-lined avenues, fine restaurants, and a pace that harkens back to the 1840s or so.

SPORTS AND RECREATION
M Apalachicola Estuary Tour
Apalachicola Bay is one of the most productive estuarine systems in the Northern Hemisphere (an estuary is where a river meets the sea). You might get a sense for this while touring the **Apalachicola National Estuarine Research Reserve** (907 20th St., just beyond the Scipio Creek Marina, 850/653-8063, 8 A.M.–5 P.M. Mon.–Fri., free admission) and its affiliated **Nature Center.** The reserve is said to house 1,162 subspecies of plants, 308 species of birds, 186 species of fish, and 57 species of mammals.

Much of it is inaccessible unless you have a boat, and stomping around in some parts is discouraged except for those conducting long-term research, education, and stewardship programs. The Nature Center, though, is an excellent outing for the whole family, with educational exhibits and information, aquariums of local fish and turtles, a bird-viewing area, and a nature trail that goes out to a boardwalk overlooking Scipio Creek and the Apalachicola River. You're likely to see horseshoe crabs, turtles, snakes, salamanders, largemouth bass, and lots of other fish.

A fabulous way to explore the estuary is by taking an Apalachicola Estuary Tour. Captain Gibby offers two-hour tours ($25) and charters ($75/hour), both with fascinating commentary as you wander upriver, through the marsh, and into the swamps.

St. Joseph Peninsula State Park

Dr. Beach, really a guy named Stephen Leatherman, has appointed himself the arbiter of all things beachy in this country. He conducts an annual ranking of American beaches, rating them by things like water temperature, number of sunny days, color of sand, algae, smell, pests, and about 40 other criteria. No horsing around, this is serious. And one beach that keeps cropping up on his top 10 list is St. Joseph Peninsula State Park (8899 Cape San Blas Rd., Port St. Joe, 850/227-1327)—it was clear up at No. 1 in 2002. Projecting out into the Gulf at a jaunty angle, this little barrier peninsula is reachable from the mainland across Apalachicola Bay and via Cape San Blas. Sand blows up across the beach and lodges in the spindly but tenacious sea oats to produce some seriously tall dunes (30–40 feet), the water is a sparkling aquamarine and hovers around 84° in summer, the surf is gentle, and the 2,500-acre beach park is never crowded.

And here's what Dr. Beach has to say about the local sand:

The sand is nearly pure quartz crystal. While most noncarbonated (noncoral) beaches are composed of 15 to 20 different types of sand, the Panhandle beaches are like a bar of Ivory soap—99.44 percent pure. The remarkable purity of the Florida Panhandle sand is related to its geologic history. Like most all beaches along the East and Gulf Coasts, the Panhandle sands came from the wearing down of the Appalachian Mountains, which brought an array of different minerals to the shore. But unlike other coastal areas, the rivers stopped bringing any new sand for tens of thousands of years. During this long period of time, wave action has ground the particles down to size. Quartz, being the most resistant mineral commonly available on the face of the earth, is the only type of sand grain left as the other minerals were ground down to dust. . . . What we find on the Panhandle beaches today is quartz sand crystal at its terminal size, meaning that all the grains are nearly the same size (well sorted in geologic terms).

It's not all beach, though. The park includes a huge expanse of heavy pine forest that is home to bobcats, deer, raccoons, and rattlesnakes as well as bald eagles, ospreys, and endangered peregrine falcons. In the fall hawks and monarch butterflies perch for a while on their migration along the "Yucatan Express" to Mexico. And in July and August you'll find visitors hunkered down along the bayside looking for sweet scallops.

There are no hotels in the park, although there are eight loft-style, furnished cabins on the bay side of the park (they accommodate 5–7 people, $80/night) and 119 campsites with water and electric available in two areas: Gulf Breeze sites are more open (better for RVs and big cars), and Shady Pines area is more secluded and shaded ($21.90 per night in either spot). You may also do more primitive camping ($4/person/night, reservations a must).

Ever have that fantasy of riding a horse on an empty beach, the salty sea air tossing his mane, a whinny of joy echoing the gulls' exultation? You're in luck. **Broke-A-Toe** (9852 County Rd. C-30A, Port St. Joe, 850/229-9283) will have you galloping, or at least trotting, in no time. Owned by Tom Brocato, thus the name, the business traffics in beach rides, full-moon rides, forest trail rides, and riding lessons for the equine-challenged.

And on your way to the park you might want to stop off to visit **Cape San Blas's lighthouse.** On the site of two former brick lighthouses (beach erosion is tough on these kinds of structures), the current iteration is a picturesque iron tower.

Barrier Islands

The Forgotten Coast's barrier islands serve to separate Apalachicola Bay from the Gulf of Mexico, acting as "shock absorbers" to protect the mainland from howling winds, vicious storms, and rogue waves. In addition to that, these little islands make for fabulous and varied exploration.

Birding, shelling, surf fishing, beach contemplation—these are the offerings on **Dog Island** to the east of St. George Island, accessible by water taxi from Carrabelle. It's also known as a refuge for loggerhead and leatherback turtles. A handful of people really do live on the island, and there's

COURTESY APALACHICOLA BAY CHAMBER

St. Vincent National Wildlife Refuge on St. Vincent's Island is more than 12,000 acres of windswept dunes and dense woods, home to numerous indigenous and exotic animal species.

The Forgotten Coast

a single funky hotel called the **Pelican Inn** (800/451-5294, $300 for two nights; $375 for three; $475 for four; $775 for seven; pets welcome for an additional $10/day) with eight studio units that each sleep up to four people. But be advised—there are no stores, no restaurants, really no other amenities on the island.

It used to be that St. George Island was 28 miles long. In 1954, the island had a little nip and tuck courtesy of the Army Corps of Engineers, with a manmade channel carved out to create two separate barrier islands (this was primarily to make it easier for the shrimpers to get out to the Gulf). The larger is still St. George Island, and the smaller, boomerang-shaped island is known locally as **Little St. George Island** and more formally as **Cape St. George State Reserve.**

Little St. George can be reached only by private boat—a very worthwhile excursion. The nine-mile-long island was purchased by the state of Florida in 1977 under the Environmentally Endangered Lands program as part of the Apalachicola National Estuarine Research Reserve to protect it from development and to contribute to the protection of Apalachicola Bay. It's

remote, and wild, and populated only by an idiosyncratic assortment of creatures.

Originally established for waterfowl, the reserve's aim has been broadened to protect a range of endangered species: You'll see bald eagle nests in pines along the island's freshwater marshes; loggerhead sea turtles nest on the white-sand beaches; wood storks and peregrine falcons are frequent visitors; and indigo snakes burrow in the dunes.

But that's not all. In 1990, the island became a haven and breeding ground for endangered red wolves. These solitary animals once roamed the Southeast, but habitat loss reduced their numbers such that there were a mere 100 confined to a small area of coastal Louisiana and Texas. The wolves (bigger than a coyote, smaller than a gray wolf) now populate Little St. George, and when pups are weaned they are taken to reintroduction facilities around the country.

The 72-foot **Cape St. George Lighthouse** is another of the island's attractions. It's the third lighthouse to occupy the island, the others falling prey to hurricanes. This one is currently leaning a little precariously, beach erosion doing its part to topple humans' most obvious presence on the island. In recent years, the *Apalachicola Times* spearheaded a campaign to save the lighthouse, raising more than $250,000 to have the base of the tower secured. Its location at water's edge is still precarious, and concerned citizens are talking about having the lighthouse moved to St. George Island in the state park.

Little St. George is open to the public for swimming, fishing, birding, and hiking. Primitive camping is permitted at designated sites at West Pass and Sike's Cut (at either end of the island; call 850/653-8063 to give them your dates and number of people). Fires are permitted at the campsites, but no live wood can be cut. A public dock has recently been repaired after serious hurricane damage in 2004, so you won't have to wade ashore.

You have to book your own shuttle to get over to **St. Vincent Island,** to the west of Little St. George. **Captain Joey Romanelli** (850/229-1065) will take you out on his 24-foot pontoon boat, departing from the end of Indian Pass Road. The whole island constitutes the **St. Vincent National Wildlife Refuge,** with 12,358 acres of dunes and woods.

Before becoming a refuge, the island was used as a private hunting and fishing preserve. Previous exotic-minded owners introduced Southeast Asian elk called sambar deer (big guys, they weigh up to 600 pounds, as opposed to the native white-tailed deer that weigh in at a modest 100 or so pounds) to the island, and they can be spotted to this day. There are native white-tails here too, and a fair number of other species (lots of rattlers, so beware) on what is one of the 500 refuges in the national system. You can bring a bike with you on the shuttle or just hike the trails and beaches of the island.

Fishing

Apalachicola Bay, Apalachicola River, and the Gulf of Mexico each provide stellar fishing experiences for the rookie or serious angler. There are dozens of charter providers in the area, but a handful of names come up time and again when you ask for locals' recommendations: **Captain Charlie's Charters** (850/653-9008, $250–450)

leads offshore fishing groups, sightseeing and shelling expeditions, oystering adventures, and, in season, tarpon trips; **Backwater Guide Service** (850/653-2820, $200 half day/$300 full day) will take people bass or fly fishing on the river on a 17-foot homemade wood boat; marine biologist Chip Bailey takes anglers out on a 23-foot SE Parker open-fisherman with his **Peregrine Charters** (850/653-2204, $250 half day/$350 full day); and the **Robinson Brothers Guide Service** (850/653-8896, $400) gets the nod for both "skinny water" fishing (that's shallow water, where anglers stand on the bow of a flats boat with their fly rod or spinning rod—usually all catch-and-release) as well as bay fishing with live bait in a little bigger boat in deeper water. Tommy and Chris Robinson's knowledge of the area is impressive.

If finfish and oysters leave you cold, you may want to experience shrimping. **Irish Town Shrimping Charter** (Scipio Creek Commercial Marina, Market St., Apalachicola, 850/653-8164) takes you out with third-generation shrimper Kevin Martina to harvest these crustaceans firsthand on a trawler in Apalachicola Bay.

The more independent-minded fisherman may want to rent a boat on his or her own. **The Entrance** (8048 Cape San Blas Rd., Port St. Joe, 850/227-7529) rents boats for you to take out on St. Joseph Bay, from pontoon boats holding ten people ($169/half day) to center consoles for four ($150/half day) and kayaks and canoes for one, two, or three ($25–45).

Diving

Scuba enthusiasts have a few excellent options in the area (including some nice artificial reef diving and clam-covered rock ledges in St. Joe), but the most celebrated wreck dive can be found 105 feet down, 20 miles south of Cape San Blas. Undulating with packs of curious amberjack, barracuda, snapper, and rays, the ***Empire Mica*** lies in disarray on the floor of the Gulf. A British oil tanker built in 1941, the ship was en route from Houston to England on June 29, 1942, when two German submarine torpedoes ignited the 12,000 tons of oil she was carrying. The ship went down in a series of fiery explosions, killing

33 men on board. Today, the bow section of the 479-foot-long ship is intact, as are 60–80 feet of deck, the metal getting lacey and thin. **Killfish Custom Charters** (Port St. Joe, 850/227-7480, $150 per person with three air tanks) provides wonderful all-day trips to the *Empire Mica* as well as trips to the *Exxon Template,* another favorite local dive 32 miles off of Apalachicola. **Capital City Dive Charters** (850/528-1926) also does full- and half-day dive charters, and **Seahorse Water Safaris** (850/227-1099), after rebuilding its dive boat in the wake of 2004's hurricane season, is again running dive tours.

Forests

Here's how the story goes: A guy named Cebe Tate once entered a vast swamp in search of a Florida panther that was killing his livestock. Gone for seven days and nights, when Tate emerged with his trusty hunting dog, shaken and thirsty, he announced, "My name is Cebe Tate, and I just came from Hell!" That's how **Tate's Hell State Forest** (access the forest from U.S. 98, County Rd. 67, or Hwy. 65, 850/697-3734) got its inauspicious name. It's 185,000 acres between the Apalachicola and Ochlockonee Rivers, much of it suitable for hiking and biking. There's an observation tower at the **Ralph G. Kendrick Boardwalk** from which visitors can look out over a dense stand of rare "dwarf" or "hatrack" cypress, many of them 150 years old and only 15 feet tall. A number of endangered or threatened species call Hell home, including the bald eagle, red-cockaded woodpecker, gopher tortoise, and Florida black bear.

The forest contains 35 miles of rivers, streams, and creeks available for canoeing, boating, fishing (boat launch at Cash Creek and other sites), and primitive camping. The **High Bluff Coastal** trail is a wonderful hiking path that's part of the Florida Division of Forestry's Trailwalker Program, its trailhead located on U.S. 98, four miles west of Carrabelle.

To the north, abutting Tate's Hell State Forest, is **Apalachicola National Forest** (850/643-2282), the largest national forest in Florida. The area was largely destroyed at the turn of the 20th century by the timber and turpentine industries,

but since 1936 it's been allowed to percolate unharassed and now has the largest red-cockaded woodpecker population in the world. Much of the forest is difficult to get to, but there are a few nice day hikes easily accessible: the 4.5-mile-long **Wright Lake Trail,** the 6-mile-long **Trail of Lakes,** and the 5.4-mile-long **Leon Sinks Geological Area Trail.** Mountain bikers will head to the **Munson Hills Off-Road Bicycle Trail,** in the eastern part of the forest, and the 16-mile paved **St. Marks Trail,** which is part of a rails-to-trails program that passes through the forest and terminates in the town of St. Marks. For serious backpackers and more remote hiking, there's also a 68.7-mile section of the **Florida Trail** running through the forest that's designated part of the Florida Statewide Greenways and Trails System. For a trail map and more information, visit www.florida-trail.org.

SIGHTS

Self-Guided Historic Walking Tour

Stop in at the **Apalachicola Chamber of Commerce** (122 Market St., Apalachicola, 850/653-9419) for a copy of the self-guided historic walking tour map. More than 200 of the regal antebellum homes in Apalachicola are listed on the National Register of Historic Places. Not all of them are in mint condition, but an hour or two of walking, gawking, and reading the brochure is a lovely way to get to know the downtown.

There is a handful of exquisite little historic churches: **Trinity Episcopal Church** (79 6th St., 850/653-9550) dates all the way back to when Andrew Jackson was president and Florida was still a territory. It was actually built of white pine in New York and shipped down to Apalachicola—the little white Greek Revival church is the sixth-oldest church in the State of Florida, the second-oldest church still holding services. Not far away, there's the **First Baptist Church** (46 9th St., 850/653-9540), originally built on the corner of 6th Street and Avenue H, and the Romanesque **St. Patrick's Catholic Church** (27 6th St., 850/653-9453), built in 1929 (although the congregation goes back to

COURTESY OF APALACHICOLA BAY CHAMBER

One of the many sites along Apalachicola's historic walking tour, the Willis House was built in 1873 by John and Henry Grady.

1845, the first structure was destroyed in a big fire that consumed 70 downtown buildings in 1846).

The historic homes are even more compelling, several of them tourable inside and out. As part of a Florida state park, the **Orman House** (177 5th St., 850/653-1209, 9 A.M.–5 P.M. Thurs.–Mon., $2), the original 1838 home of cotton merchant Thomas Orman, is open to the public. There is an hour-long narrated tour of the Federal and Greek Revival two-story house, the wood for which was cut and measured near Syracuse, New York, and shipped to Apalachicola by sailboat around the Florida Keys. The majestic, columned **Raney House** (46 Ave. F, 850/653-9851, 1–4 P.M. Sat.) dates to the same year, the home of David Greenway Raney and family. The interior is now a little museum run by the Apalachicola Area Historical Society.

Chestnut Street Cemetery

And after you've seen how folks in Apalach lived, check out how they died. Opened for business in 1831, **Chestnut Street Cemetery** (U.S. 98 between 6th St. and 8th St.) contains loads of Confederate veterans and the broad range of surnames that speaks to the town's early diversity (Spanish and French settlers, shipwreck victims, etc.). To some spooky, to others just peaceful, the little urban cemetery contains beautifully carved funerary art tucked in the dappled shadows cast by gnarled old live oaks shrouded with Spanish moss.

Dixie Theatre

If you're looking to determine whether Apalachicola's on the wax or wane, the Dixie Theatre (21 Ave. E, 850/653-3200, performances usually 8 P.M. Fri. and Sat., 3 P.M. Sun.) is a pretty optimistic sign. Built in 1912, it was the locus of cultural activity—stage performances, then silent pictures, then the "talkies"—in the county for decades. It foundered in the late 1960s, but recent boosters have gotten it back up and running. The original building's decrepitude led to some ingenious restoration and re-creation. In 1998 the building was completed, with a facade that looks much like it did in 1912 and the original

ICE, ICE, BABY

Ice cube museum. Hmm. Are you imagining a very cold room containing, maybe, a piece of the berg that sank the Titanic, a cube from Dean Martin's final cocktail, or the original "fly-in-the-ice cube" novelty gag? Buzz, thanks for playing, and we have some very nice consolation prizes for you today.

Apalachicola luminary John Gorrie is known in the history books as the father of air-conditioning and ice manufacturing, recipient of the first patent for mechanical refrigeration in 1851. A tiny, charming museum in a little historic house tells the Gorrie story.

By the time the young doctor arrived in town in 1833, Apalachicola was bustling as the third-largest port on the Gulf, shipping cotton to Europe and New England. During his time in town, Gorrie served as mayor, postmaster, city council member, bank director, and founder of Trinity Church. But all that civic-mindedness pales when compared to his medical work. Yellow fever was a menace in those years, no one linking the terrifying sickness to those swarms of pesky mosquitoes that plagued these swampy, humid, low-lying floodplains. In addition to chills, headache, muscle aches, vomiting, and backache, the onset of the illness was marked by high fever. Gorrie posited that bringing the fever down was essential to prevent the shock, bleeding, and kidney and liver failure that often led to death.

As cold temperatures were hard to come by in these parts, he set about making some. His idea is one used in today's refrigeration: Cooling can be achieved through the rapid expansion of gases. He built a machine with two pumps that condensed and then rarefied air. He cooled the air all right, but the machine kept clogging with ice cubes. There's no evidence that his invention saved any lives, and Gorrie died unable to market his apparatus.

The little **John Gorrie State Museum** (46 6th St., Apalachicola, 850/653-9347, 9 A.M.–5 P.M. Thurs.–Mon., $1) contains a replica of Gorrie's ice machine, built from his specs. Truth be told, this isn't even the most interesting part of the museum. There are wonderful exhibits on the history of the area, from its days as a cotton port to sponge diving and oyster harvesting. The docents are a real wealth of knowledge (especially Mr. Moody, if he's there) and are willing to expound at length on Apalachicola lore.

ticket booth lovingly restored. There's now a summer repertory season June–September, and it shows movies most of the year, along with the occasional ragtime piano show or big town gala.

Three Servicemen Statue

Brand-new in 2005, Apalachicola City Commission's *Three Servicemen South* statue has been unveiled in front of the historic Orman House and adjacent to the Chapman Botanical Gardens, which is currently closed to the public. It's a seven-foot replica of the one at the Vietnam Veterans Memorial in Washington, D.C., designed by the late Frederick Hart, which depicts three Vietnam-era soldiers in battle regalia. The first such replica in the country, the bronze honors veterans of all American wars, and cost $500,000 raised over several years by individual donors in Apalachicola.

ARTS AND ENTERTAINMENT

Florida Seafood Festival

Apalach and surrounding towns are the undisputed eastern oyster capital of the world. The oyster industry began in the later part of the 19th century, and by 1896 there were three oyster-canning factories shipping something like 50,000 cans of oysters daily (the first time canning was attempted in Florida). In 2000, approximately $3.5 million worth of oysters were harvested in Apalachicola. This is the foundation for the area's biggest annual party. The Florida Seafood Festival (850/653-9319) is actually the oldest maritime festival in the state, drawing thousands each year during the first weekend in November. There are oyster shucking contests, parades, arts & crafts, musical entertainment, and a running race—but clearly the big draw is pot upon pot of just-caught seafood in chowders, steamed, etc.

The other big annual draw is the **Big Bend Saltwater Classic** (850/216-2272) fishing tournament in Carrabelle in June, an opportunity to see serious anglers competing for big prizes in a weekend event that benefits the Organization for Artificial Reefs.

ACCOMMODATIONS

$50–150

Pretty much nothing in Apalachicola runs under $50, but the **Best Western Apalach Inn** (249 U.S. 98 W, 850/653-9131) and the **Rancho Inn** (240 U.S. 98 W, 850/653-9435) both ring in around $60–80, right next to each other in a convenient location. The former offers complimentary continental breakfast and an outdoor pool, and children 17 and under stay free. The latter accepts pets for a mere $6 fee.

The Gibson Inn (57 Ave. C, 850/653-2191, $95–140), on the National Register of Historic Places, had some major cosmetic surgery in the mid-1980s, but it still has the antebellum dignity that comes of wide wraparound porches, four-poster beds, antiques, and slowly revolving ceiling fans. This gracious tin-roofed Victorian right downtown (built in 1907 as a hotel, never a private residence) contains 30 rooms, all different. More for romance-seekers or history buffs than for family travelers, The Gibson Inn does allow pets.

In a similarly Victorian vein, but even more spruce, is the sunny yellow **Coombs House Inn** (80 6th St., 850/653-9199, $79–225), built in 1905 by a lumber magnate. The three-story mansion has high ceilings, an ornate and creaky oak staircase, nine wide fireplaces that perennially exude the homey smell of recent wood smoke, and a slew of historical photos. Guests in the 19 antique-bedecked rooms enjoy a pleasant breakfast, weekend evening wine receptions, and use of the inn's bikes, umbrellas, and beach chairs. If the quiet and rarefied chintz-and-doilies bed-and-breakfast experience isn't your idea of fun, you can still tour the Coombs House after checking out the Chestnut Street Cemetery across the street as part of a whirlwind local history lesson.

COURTESY OF APALACHICOLA BAY CHAMBER

The Gibson Inn was built in 1907 and originally owned by the Gibson sisters. It's a sprawling cypress and pine Victorian inn with a picturesque cupola.

The Forgotten Coast

If you're looking for a little more privacy, the **Raney Guest Cottage** (46 Ave. F, 850/653-9749, $125/night, $750/week) is a quaint house that dates back to around 1835, one of the oldest buildings in Apalachicola. Sit on a rocker on the wraparound porch and pretend that Andrew Jackson's still president, or walk the block into town (two to the river). It's not fancy, but the historic house is all yours, with two cozy bedrooms, one bath, dining room, kitchen, screened back porch, washer/dryer, and gas grill.

Over $150

Then again, you could stay at the **Consulate Suites** (76 Water St., 850/653-1515, $175–290) and pretend you're visiting dignitaries. Prior to the Civil War, when Apalachicola had its commercial heyday, the French Consulate was located in the second story of the bustling Grady Building, a ships' chandlery. The Grady Building was renovated several years back and transformed into a breezy shopping attraction of galleries and gift boutiques. Above it are four apartment-sized luxury suites with 11-foot tin ceilings and lots of exposed brick. Three of the four suites overlook the river, and all have balconies and sleep four people (not a bad deal when compared to two rooms in an inn or hotel).

FOOD

Oyster Bars

▟ Boss Oyster (125 Water St., 850/653-9364, lunch and dinner daily, $10–23) seems to be the oyster palace to beat. Topped with things sensible (a squeeze of lime, a splash of tequila, and a dash of Tabasco) and things nearly obscene (envision a broiled oyster "reuben" complete with sauerkraut and corned beef), the local oysters are briny bliss. A lively family-oriented crowd, decent nightly drink specials, and a casual Apalachicola River-side setting keep it full. Some of the presentations lack, well, presentation—the heads-on shrimp come in a metal tray that looks unnervingly like a bedpan. Roll up your sleeves and don't be fussy. And if you advocate gussying an oyster with something out of the ordinary, tell them and they just might name a dish after you.

Those in the other camp are staunch adherents of the slippery bivalves at **Papa Joe's Oyster Bar and Grill** (301 B Market St., at Scipio Creek Marina, 850/653-1189, 11:30 A.M.–10 P.M. Thurs.–Tues.). It's another waterside seafood-and-steak joint with a serious emphasis on local oysters, raw or broiled.

About 17 miles west of Apalachicola, the absolute must-eat destination is the **▟ Indian Pass Raw Bar** (8391 County Rd. C-30A, Indian Pass, 850/227-1670). It is always a party in this faded roadside shack, every vinyl stool filled with someone vigilantly watching as the oyster shucker works his magic at the end of the bar. Raw on the halfshell is best, but the garlic butter and parmesan baked version is a delicious spin on these briny beauties. Grab your own drink from the cooler and be sure to order the key lime pie (and kids, this place serves a killer corn dog).

Lunch

Apalachicola Seafood Grill (100 Market St., 850/653-9510, 11:30 A.M.–8 P.M. Mon.–Sat., $8–15) seems mighty proud of its fried fish sandwich—"largest in the world," although that may be a little gastronomic hyperbole—which may explain why the restaurant under the town's only traffic light has kept 'em coming since 1903.

Another longtime lunch favorite is **The Owl Café** (15 Ave. D, 850/653-9888, Mon.–Sat., $18–24). It's gone a little more upscale recently, with gorgeous black-and-white photos by local photographer Richard Bickel on the walls (if you like his work, local shops carry his latest book, *Apalachicola: Florida's Last Great Bay*), pretty wood floors, and about a dozen tables. The high-ceilinged clapboard building is a replica of the original, lost to fire in 1911. Again, seafood is the strong suit, from the black grouper with garlic, capers, and artichokes to seafood pastas. The chicken Caesar salad is also not to be missed, and the wine list merits some perusal.

And the **Old Time Soda Fountain** (93 Market St., 850/653-2606, 10 A.M.–5 P.M. Mon.–Sat., $4–9) will satisfy your hankering for malts, floats, ice-cream sodas, and diner-style sandwiches. It's a 1950s-style, stools-at-the-counter relic that was once the town's drugstore.

EASTERN OYSTERS

"Twas a brave man indeed that 'et the first oyster."

Jonathan Swift wasn't whistling Dixie when he wrote that. In late 2004 the local oyster economy took a serious hit (35 percent off in sales) when two oyster-related deaths were reported in Florida. The culprit: *vibrio vulnificus,* a bacterium naturally present in marine environments that is especially dangerous to those with compromised immune systems. Bad news for Franklin County, which historically harvests 90 percent of the state's oysters and 10 percent of the nation's. More than 1,000 people in the county make their living in the oyster business. To give you a sense of quantity, in recent years the U.S. oyster haul has been roughly 30 million pounds of meat—about 75 percent of that eastern oysters, or *Crassostrea virginica,* the species that is shown off to finest effect right here in Apalachicola.

Found all around the Gulf of Mexico and up the eastern seaboard all the way to Canada, eastern oysters really seem to flourish in the bay, which encompasses the waters of St. George Sound and St. Vincent Sound and is renewed constantly by the nutrient-rich freshwater of Apalachicola River. It's this balance of fresh- and saltwater that seems to act as some kind of magic growth serum. Oysters grow fast and sweet here, reaching marketable size in under two years (in colder climates it can take as long as six years). The 210-square-mile estuary is shallow, between six and nine feet deep at low tide, with oysterers skimming along in small boats to scoop up their harvest from the bottom with long-handled tongs.

Despite the occasional oyster scare in the news (and California and other states' banning of them), local oysters are carefully monitored and husbanded. The Department of Health Services, the EPA, and other agencies test for water purity and natural threats such as red tide. In addition, the Department of Agriculture and Consumer Services has sponsored extensive efforts to restock oyster shell in the bay to create new oyster bars, and even to "plant" more than 100,000 bushels of adult and juvenile oysters on public oyster reefs in the bay. These transplanted oysters are taken from waters where harvesting is not allowed or where growth is poor and relocated to approved waters where conditions are more favorable for oysters to healthfully grow to market size. The ultimate aim: enhancing oyster production and ensuring oyster quality.

You know that expression, "If it doesn't kill you it makes you stronger"? A few bad oysters have given these bivalve mollusks a bum rap, but really oysters are fairly good for you. A dozen rings in at approximately 110 calories, rich in iron, copper, and iodine and high in calcium and vitamin A. Around here they are sold by the dozen, half bushel, peck, or bushel, graded according to size: The largest marketed are "selects" and the average are "standards." Look for oysters that close tightly when handled. They'll live in a cold fridge for more than a week (cover them loosely with a damp cloth, never in an airtight container). If you buy them already shucked, use them right away and don't freeze them.

In an introduction to *Aromas and Flavours* by Alice B. Toklas, Poppy Cannon writes, "I began to comprehend a little the French resentment against change without reason. It began to dawn upon me that certain dishes like sonnets or odes cannot be brought into being without obeisance to classic rules and restrictions." This is all by way of saying, "Don't muck around with a good thing." While you're in Apalachicola, throw caution to the wind: A dozen raw eastern oysters, shucked right in front of you, doused with lemon or a splash of Tabasco, and slid right down your gullet, one at a time—that's paradise on the Forgotten Coast. Still, if you aren't in the mood to challenge fate by eating them raw, they are a treat eaten fried, baked, steamed, broiled, or, shudder, microwaved.

The nine square blocks that make up downtown Apalachicola are packed with casual restaurants and cafés.

COURTESY OF APALACHICOLA BAY CHAMBER

Fine Dining

Boss Oyster's sister restaurant, **Caroline's Dining on the River** (123 Water St., 850/653-8139, breakfast, lunch, and dinner daily) adopts more of a fine-dining mindset, but the same straightforward, fish-centric American food sense. Presided over by Caroline Maddren, it's in the Apalachicola River Inn and is the place to luxuriate in a lengthy Sunday brunch (opt for the oystercakes or zingy shrimp Creole heaped over buttermilk biscuits). As with most places around here, the oysters and fresh finfish get the nod—you can watch the shrimp and fish boats tooling by outside with the day's catch.

Another historic inn nearby houses **Nola's Grill at the Gibson Inn** (51 Ave. C, 850/653-2191, 7:30–11 A.M. daily, 11 A.M.–4 P.M. Fri.–Sun., 5–9:30 P.M. Wed.–Sun.), right at the foot of the Gorrie Bridge in a long, narrow dining room from an era past. Dinners can get fairly fancy with oysters en brochette drizzled with lemon butter or stuffed grouper Florentine, but then you'd miss out on the fried grouper sandwich on a Kaiser roll. Nola's also does a laudable breakfast for inn guests and visitors, ranging from eggs Benedict to rib-sticking biscuits and sausage gravy.

Ethnic/Eclectic

While seafood—oysters in particular—dominates this area, a few restaurants give their marine creatures a little twist.

 **Tamara's Cafe Floridita** (17 Ave. E, 850/653-4111, 10:30 A.M.–10 P.M. daily, $12–20) is the brainchild of Tamara Suarez, a former TV producer in Caracas, Venezuela. Here local seafood gets Caribbean and South American inflections, such as paella or a pecan-crusted grouper with a creamy jalapeño sauce, everything served with black beans and rice. Wednesday nights are the best times to take a group—it's tapas night, with classics like shrimp sautéed with lots of garlic and a Spanish tortilla, all the little dishes very affordable.

At **Chef Eddie's Magnolia Grill** (99 11th St., 850/653-8000, dinner only, $16–24) you'll find seafood like down on the bayou. In a sweet 1880s bungalow, Eddie Cass sends out sophisticated oak-grilled rib-eye steaks, a New Orleans-style seafood gumbo redolent of all the succulent local catches, and a no-holds-barred death by chocolate cake. There is a very fairly priced wine selection drawn mostly from Napa, Sonoma, and Burgundy.

Cocktails

The locals are still grumbling a bit about having a "wine bar" open up in town, especially a breezy, loft-like one with a sophisticated copper bar. Fear of things hoity-toity hasn't thrown people off too much, as **Veranda's Bistro** (76 Market St. and Ave. D, 850/653-3210, 11 A.M.–10 P.M. daily) is a resounding success. The lovely view seems to be a bigger draw than the short menu or even the nice selection of wines by the glass. On the second story, it's a good place to end a day or take in a sunset.

SHOPPING

The nine square blocks that make up downtown Apalachicola are fruitful for idle window-shopping or serious retail therapy. Shops are spread

The Forgotten Coast

amongst repurposed brick and tin cotton warehouses and cute early-1900s cottages. Located across from the docks, the **Grady Market** (76 Water St., 850/653-4099) seems to be the locals' pride and joy, a 19th-century ship's chandlery made over to house about a dozen boutiques and galleries (including that of black-and-white photographer Richard Bickel). A block from there is a more quirky spot called the  **Tin Shed** (170 Water St., 850/653-3635), specializing in antique nautical items like Japanese fishing floats, captains' telescopes, compasses, ships' bells, and hammered tin gewgaws of unknown origin.

Avenue E (15 Ave. E, 850/653-1411) is my absolute favorite. Very fairly priced antiques and reproduction pieces; an adorable, yet small, assortment of children's clothing and gifts; lamps; folk art; and marine-themed interior accessories have all been chosen with a refined aesthetic that never loses sight of whimsy and utility. (I bought a rough-hewn folk art halibut, an antique Chinese rice bin, and a pair of insane, flower-bedecked flip-flops—all fabulous.)

Women tend to lose themselves in the lotions and potions, crystal jewelry, flouncy gowns, wraps, and accessories at **Riverlily** (79 Commerce St.; 850/653-2600). Nearby, there's **Oystercatcher** (118 Commerce St., 850/653-1616), a rather funky gallery (featuring the owner's assertive oils) and gift shop. Also a nice spot for gift buying, **Betsy's Sunflower** (14 Ave. D; 850/653-9144) has a sensible small collection of garden gear and fancy housewares such as Cornell linens and Vietri tableware.

Forgotten Coast Outfitters (94 Market St., 850/653-9669), an authorized Orvis dealer, is where fly-fishers—or those who just want to look like fly-fishers—get their gear and clothing. While they're engrossed there, the rest of you can head up a couple of doors to **Chez Funk** (88 Market St., 850/653-3885) to browse the antiques and painted furniture.

Sweet Success

She's as sweet as tupelo honey
She's an angel of the first degree

Apalachicola's upscale boutiques make for a day of fruitful retail therapy.

She's as sweet as tupelo honey
Just like honey from the bee.

Just what was Van Morrison singing about, anyway? He was comparing his sweetie to a rare honey, thought by connoisseurs of such things to be among the world's finest. Prized for its flavor and for the fact that it never granulates, **tupelo honey** is produced by bees that cavort in the tupelo gum trees that grow with gusto along Apalachicola River. Harvested for two short weeks in late April, tupelo honey was featured in the Peter Fonda vehicle *Yulee's Gold*, a film about a reclusive beekeeper with a dysfunctional family, directed by Victor Nunez.

The locus of tupelo production is in Wewahitchka, the only place in the world the honey is produced commercially. The process starts when bees are placed on elevated platforms along the river's edge. The bees then swarm the tupelo-blossom-laden swamps and return with their treasure. The resulting honey is a pale amber color with a slight greenish cast, its flavor delicate and distinctive. Because it costs more to produce, tupelo is more expensive that many other honeys. But listen to Van the Man—this is the good stuff.

Every spring at Lake Alice Park in Wewahitchka, folks gather to celebrate the apian masterpiece. For years the **Tupelo Festival** took place the third week in April during the tupelo pollinating time, but in recent years it's been moved to the third weekend in May to coincide with when the keepers scoop the honey from the hives. There's entertainment, arts and crafts, kids' activities, and a whole lot of things containing tupelo honey, from lotions to snacks.

If you're looking for some honey to take back home with you, many shops in the area stock it, but you can also call **L.L. Lanier & Son's Tupelo Honey** (they were the ones who tutored Peter Fonda on beekeeping for the film, 850/639-2371) or **Smiley Apiaries** (850/639-5672).

St. George Island

On Friday, February 27, 2004, the new St. George Island Bridge in Franklin County was officially opened and dedicated. It is 4.1 miles long, cost $71 million, and took three years to construct. The largest Design-Build effort ever undertaken by the Florida Department of Transportation, it's the third-largest bridge in Florida.

So what, you say? The old bridge certainly did the job of shuttling vacationers and residents from the mainland fishing village of Eastpoint to the narrow, wooded barrier island of St. George Island. The new bridge, though, is a rock-solid testament to the island's recent growth, burgeoning affluence, and rampant optimism. East of St. Vincent Island, St. George shelters Apalachicola Bay and St. George Sound, both productive bodies of water for commercial and sport fishing. The whole eastern end of the island is taken up with the 1,900-acre St. George Island State Park, which contains some of the most pristine and underpopulated, white-sand beaches in Florida. First-class fishing and fabulous beaches, but what really accounts for St. George's boom is more of a feeling. It has the same constellation of easy, beachy pleasures that make people misty-eyed when describing the Nantucket or Cape Cod of a generation ago. But St. George has got it all *right now*, and only a blissful few seem to know about it.

For much of its 5,000-year tenure, the island has been inhabited mostly by the avian, the reptilian, with a few small mammals thrown in for interest. Humans swooped in in the early 1900s to harvest the sap from the island's slash pines (used to make turpentine). The island's dunes were used for training exercises during World War II, but it's been mercifully underutilized since then.

In 1970, a Tallahassee real estate developer named John R. Stocks bought up much of the island, then sold Little St. George and the east end, now the state park, to the state of Florida. His company, Leisure Properties, then started selling five- and eight-acre tracts like hotcakes.

COURTESY OF APALACHICOLA BAY CHAMBER

St. George Island is a world-class destination for birders, anglers, and naturalists.

Growth was quick in what is now the Plantation area, but strict environmental rules keep the sight lines low and the water views spectacular. There are still only around 700 year-round residents, but thousands flock to the island for luxurious beachfront house and condo rentals during the summer months.

SPORTS AND RECREATION

M St. George Island State Park

It's officially called the Dr. Julian G. Bruce St. George Island State Park (1900 E. Gulf Beach Dr., 850/927-2111, open dawn to dusk), but most people around here just call it the state park. And what a state park it is. The land was acquired for the park in 1963, the completed park facilities opened to the public in 1980. Imagine 1,900 acres of windswept, sea-oat-fringed dunes, gorgeous enough and under-populated enough to make most aficionados' lists of best beaches in the United States. The whole east end of the island is taken up with the state park, so officially it's the longest beach of any beachfront state park in Florida—nine miles of white sand.

The water is warm, shallow, and calm enough for hours of swimming (sorry, surfers),

the beaches seem to be stocked with perfect shells by some beneficent chamber of commerce types, and the fish are often biting with gusto. Along the beach you'll see starfish and sand dollars, alien-but-beautiful big purple jellyfish, loggerhead sea turtle nests during the summer, and hardly another person. For when you get tired of all that perfect sand, there are nature trails through the pine flatwood forest and live oak hammocks.

The park has no lifeguards or concessions, so bring your own picnic provisions and toys. There are, however, two sets of rustic wood-beamed pavilions with sheltered picnic tables, water fountains, outside showers, and bathrooms. It is illegal to walk through the sea oats along the high sand dunes—walk from the parking area out to the beach only along the weathered wooden boardwalks. Be on the lookout for the burrowing ghost crab, its translucent carapace and huge goggly eyes making it a wild sight (they can also run up to 10 mph, quick little buggers), and in the woods you might glimpse raccoons and a fair number of snakes and diamondback terrapins.

Anglers most often catch whiting, but you'll see them reeling in flounder, redfish, pompano, sea trout, and Spanish mackerel as well. (A saltwater fishing license is required.) Birders, on the other hand, train their sights on osprey, snowy plover, least tern, black skimmer, and willet.

RV and tent camping is permitted in the 60 pine-shaded campsites in the forests on the bay side set behind the dunes. The campground features a dump station, flush toilets, and nature trails. No pets, maximum 14-night stay. There are also primitive campsites at Gap Point for those who wish to hike in along the 2.5-mile trail, which meanders from the bay through the pine flatwood forest to the campground. Boat ramps are located at the Youth Camp Area and East Slough.

At Loggerheads

St. George Island is said to have one of the darkest night skies in the continental U.S., making it a dreamy place for stargazing. While a lot of this is merely a byproduct of low population

COURTESY APALACHICOLA BAY CHAMBER

St. George Island State Park has nine miles of undeveloped beaches and dunes. It's the longest beachfront park in Florida.

density, some of it is by design. Franklin County adopted the Lighting Ordinance for Marine Turtle Protection in 1998, which restricts house lights, streetlights, and even flashlight use on the island.

Florida beaches are home to 90 percent of the loggerhead sea turtle nests in the southeastern United States, the largest population in the Western Hemisphere and one of the two largest in the world. And St. George Island gets more than its share, with some green and leatherback turtles thrown in for good measure. Every year, starting around May 1, would-be mother loggerheads travel tremendous distances to come ashore here to nest (scientists think they return to the beach on which they were born). It's been shown that lights on and around beach homes can distract the mothers from their task and disorient the hatchlings enough to make them crawl inland instead of toward the sea, easy snacks for their many predators.

At this point, loggerheads are merely "threatened," but there's worry that they may slip into that endangered zone if more isn't done on their behalf. What can you as a visitor do? At the very least, if you've rented a beach house, keep outdoor houselights off as much as possible, and pull your shades at night to minimize window light pollution on the beaches. Beyond that, you can call Apalachicola Bay and River Riverkeepers (ABARK, 850/670-5470) or the Florida Fish and Wildlife Conservation Commission (888/404-FWCC) to report disoriented hatchlings or injured or stranded turtles.

If your visit to St. George Island coincides with nesting season (May–Oct.), you can take a night beach walk in the hopes of glimpsing mother loggerheads crawling ashore—they leave a distinctive, filigreed track in the sand—or the hatchlings inelegantly flapping their way back out to sea. A single female builds as many as three or four nests in a single season, laying about a hundred eggs in each one—it's quite a sight to see the little guys struggling to meet the sea, but try to minimize the impulse to take flash photography. And if you're compelled to help, you can volunteer with St. George Island Volunteer Turtlers to find, mark, and protect turtle nests incubating in the warm sand. Call the Estuarine Reserve (850/670-4783) to ask about volunteer efforts.

M Biking St. George Island

It's hard to say, but perhaps the single nicest thing about St. George Island is its bike-accessibility and its nearly ubiquitous paved bike paths. All the way from the Plantation side (west end) to the state park at the east end, there are straight, flat roadside paths for bicyclists, and miles of off-roading possibilities as well. Bikes can be rented from **Island Adventures** (105 E. Gulf Beach Dr., 850/927-3655, $5/day) or **Tropical Trader** (137 E. Pine St., 850/927-2300, $8/day). If you're vehemently opposed to physical exertion, you used to be able to rent a zippy scooter to tool around, but it seems the island scooter shop is in the process of closing down.

Birding

The shores and inland areas of St. George Island and the sheltered harbor of Eastpoint are rife with birding possibilities. In the latter, loons, gulls, and waterfowl play host to a number of vagrant bird species in the fall.

If you're attentive, from the new bridge linking Eastpoint with St. George Island you'll see the nests of large colonies of least terns and black skimmers April–July. As its name implies, the least tern is the smallest of the terns, weighing about one ounce (don't confuse them with the medium-sized gull-billed terns with their heavy black bills and short forked tails that also occasionally hang out here).

Florida birders also boast of the area's preponderance of sprague's pipit (although these little guys are hard to see, usually choosing to hang out in fields of short grass) in the late fall, and in the winter it's not uncommon to see the common goldeneye in nearby water.

Walking the shores of St. George Island, you'll view American oystercatchers, spotted sandpipers, ruddy turnstones, willets, sanderlings, several kinds of plovers, and loads of other shorebirds. And driving down the island's many wooded dirt roads yields a wealth of sightings in the spring and fall—bald eagles nest here, and in the fall you're apt to see sharp-shinned hawks, peregrine falcons, northern harriers, and American kestrels.

In the early spring, the youth campsite's oak hammock at St. George Island State Park is a

COURTESY OF APALACHICOLA BAY CHAMBER

Paddling trips with Journeys of St. George often pass by Goose Island (pictured).

good place to spot newly arrived migrant birds, maybe even something as rare as a Connecticut warbler. Continuing to the end of the park's paved road and walking out to the beach, you may be treated to the sight of plucky little snowy plovers. In the winter, northern gannets are sometimes seen in the park or in offshore waters.

If you want to view many of the area's 200 species of birds—or even if you have your heart set on seeing one specific feathered treasure—you may want to arrange a bird-focused kayak trip with guides at **Journeys of St. George Island** (850/927-3259). They really specialize in family ecotours, including dolphin watches, nighttime crab-catching (and -releasing) adventures, and marine-biology day camps, but they will craft kayak tours to accommodate your interests.

BEACH HOUSES

On St. George, hotel or inn accommodations are only sensible if you are staying very briefly or are traveling alone or as a couple. Families tend to rent one of 700 beach cottages or houses on the island, most offered by the week (and, off season, by the weekend). Some of these houses are absolutely enormous, a super opportunity to convene several generations of your family, or even a way to get several families together under one roof. Pets are often allowed, many homes have private pools, game rooms, and tremendous kitchens for preparing the daily catch.

M Prudential Realty handles many of the upscale rental houses (800/332-5196, www.stgeorgeisland.com), with wonderfully detailed descriptions and photos of properties on their website. They deal with properties all over the island but seem to have a special lock on the gorgeous, big houses in the Plantation, the private community on the western end of the island. Other realtors that traffic in properties all over the island include Anchor Realty (800/525-4793, www.florida-beach.com), Collins Vacation Rentals (800/853-9015, www.sgirentals.com), and Suncoast Realty (800/341-2021, www.uncommonflorida.com). Beyond picking your price range (they go from $1,000/week up to more than $5,000 for some of the more luxurious ones), there are lots of other factors to consider, such as Gulf side versus bayside, how close to town you want to be, and the kind of neighborhood with which you feel most comfortable.

St. George Plantation

This is a gated community stretching from Gulf side to bayside on the island's west end, with slow, winding roads and lots of speed bumps to keep the pace leisurely. Homes are all distinctive in terms of architecture, amenities (many with spa or pool), and decor, but the general vibe is "luxury." It's mostly large, three-story homes that sleep eight or more. The gate attendant and security folks are supposed to make you feel secure, but they really serve to add to this community's aura of poshness. Remember, the farther west you settle toward the end of the island, the longer the car ride it is to get a gallon of milk back in town.

Within the Plantation is an even more exclusive and secluded area called The Bluffs. It's two quiet cul-de-sacs of luxury homes, each with spectacular views of the Gulf and Apalachicola Bay beyond towering 25-foot dunes.

Gulf Beaches and East End

The four miles in the center of the island are called the "Gulf Beaches" area. In this, the first populated area on the island, the architectural styles are all over the map, from little Cracker cottages to huge windswept wooden structures on stilts, kitted out with widow walks and zany decorative fillips. Not as fancy as those at the Plantation, the homes have the benefit of being a quick bike ride into town for ice cream or a video rental. Going east, the two miles before you get to the state park are called, not surprisingly, "East End." This is less densely populated, with comfortable-looking houses widely spaced, mostly up on high stilts with great beach access. In the East End area, there are also townhouses in a community called 300 Ocean Mile. Very close to the state park, the look is utilitarian and slightly barracks-like for my taste, but the rentals are fairly affordable.

Sunset Beach

To me much less appealing than the west end of the island or even in town, this is a gated community of Spanish terracotta tile-and-stucco villas, densely packed. It looks like a condo village, with big parking lots that take away from the beachside location. The beaches in this area also seem less picturesque, and with less vegetation than elsewhere on the island. It has easy access to the state park, though, which is nice.

OTHER ACCOMMODATIONS

Under $50

St. George Island State Park (1900 E. Gulf Beach Dr., 850/927-2111, $19 per day) offers 60 campsites with electric and water hookups for RV and tent camping. Reserve far in advance with Reserve America (800/326-3521, www.reserveamerica.com). Primitive campsites are also to be had at Gap Point, a 2.5-mile backpacking hike in, and there is tents-only youth-group camping for organized groups of up to 25 or a minimum of 6 campers.

$50–150

Very affordable and geared toward families, the **Buccaneer Inn** (160 W. Gorrie Dr., 850/927-2585, $50–130) is a 1960s-style low-rise beachfront motel. Rooms are clean and no-nonsense, with a lot of wicker furniture and serviceable kitchenettes, and there's a courtyard swimming pool and a Gulf-side tiki hut.

A little fancier, the **St. George Inn** (135 Franklin Blvd., 800/824-0416, $119–189) is two blocks from the beach, with clean, modest rooms (the pink-and-aqua bedspreads may set your teeth on edge if you're persnickety about such things). The sprawling white house, with wraparound porches affording Gulf and bay views, has been recently remodeled to include a few two-room suites and a little conference room.

In the gated community of the Plantation, the **Inn at Resort Village** (1488 Leisure Ln., 850/927-4000, $95–245) gives you the opportunity to enjoy the west side of the island without having to rent a whole house or cottage. The midrise resort complex seems to host lots of meetings and corporate retreats, with a breezy, contemporary look and a range of attractive beachfront, pool-view, and island-view rooms.

FOOD

We walk into Banana Starfish Café one morning. The locals pause, en masse, to scrutinize our puny band of interlopers. The host/chef, Capt. Ahab-meets-Jimmy Buffet, asks, "What'll you have, folks?" No menus are proffered. We can't work under these conditions—we choke. He urges us: "It's just breakfast. What do you like?" My daughter, frequently wrong but never in doubt, gets the ball rolling. "Pancakes." We make ourselves comfortable and conversations resume. The next customer, clearly a regular, is a gigantic hound, jowly and well endowed. He has his customary order, dishearteningly identical to my own, except he eats his scrambled eggs and bacon on the floor adjacent to our table.

That's all by way of saying that St. George adopts a very casual attitude to dining out. The majority of the island is given over to beach houses, many with opulent kitchens overlooking the bay or Gulf. Thus, vacationers come prepared to dine in with some regularity. There's a **Piggly Wiggly** (130 U.S. 98, 850/653-8768) and an **IGA** (425 U.S. 98, 850/653-9526) in Apalachicola, the former a little nicer than the latter, and the island has a pleasant little market called the **Market Place** (148 E. Pine St., 850/927-2808) with decent meat, deli, and groceries. Beyond that, you definitely need to patronize some of the local seafood retailers. On the island, look for the guy who parks his trailer at one of a couple intersections in town—he's got exemplary shrimp, scallops, oysters, and grouper. Or head back over the bridge to Eastpoint, where in the 300 to 500 blocks of U.S. 98 there are about a dozen seafood vendors from which to choose: **Sharon's Place** (420 U.S. 98, 850/670 8646), **Roberts Seafood** (446 U.S. 98, 850/670 8350), and **Island View Seafood** (326 Patton Dr., 850/670 8555) each have vocal devotees.

Casual Seafood

Restaurants on the island are a little less sophisticated than those in Apalach, but that's fitting. On the "beach side" (the Gulf side, as opposed to the bay side of this long strip of an island), people gravitate toward the **Blue Parrot Oceanfront Café** (68 W. Gorrie Dr., 850/927-2987), to relax on the wide deck or sidle up to the tiki bar, enjoying a froufrou cocktail over an excellent po-boy sandwich or burger. Opt for the local seafood (grouper and oysters) over the imports (conch fritters and Alaskan crab, for crying out loud) and you'll navigate the menu just fine.

As an aside, often in the month of June the Blue Parrot holds the annual **mullet toss.** They build a mullet-tossing range and you pay a small fee to try your hand at flinging these slippery raw fish as far as you can. Underhanded, overhanded, football-style—there are several divisions that compete: men, women, children, and "free form" (in which you build a mechanical device to catapult your fish to victory).

On the bay side, **Finni's Grill & Bar** (200 Gunn St., 850/927-2600, 5–9:30 P.M. Wed., Thurs., and Sun., until 10:30 P.M. Fri. and Sat.), in a new location—an eye-popping blue, inside and out—has a convivial, sports bar atmosphere, with 12 small TVs and one big whopper vying for diners' attention. Again, it's fried oysters, notable crabcakes, grilled grouper, a small sushi selection, and the ubiquitous key lime pie. A lot of Tallahassee party bands take a turn at Finni's on the weekends.

The Friday night seafood buffet at **Han's by the Sea** (63 W. Gorrie Dr., 850/927-3969, breakfast, lunch, and dinner daily) is a fun time for young and old. There's also a "country-cooking" lunch buffet that is somewhat less appealing, but Han's weekend brunch menu of omelets and other egg-centric dishes is commendable.

And if you want to catch a sunset over simple seafood, **Oyster Cove** (210 E. Pine St., 850/927-2600, 5–9 P.M. Tues.–Sun.), with its huge picture window in the second-floor restaurant, is the place to do it. The menus are fairly similar at most of these places—shrimp or grouper, broiled, blackened, or fried; and oysters, naked or dressed up.

Other

On St. George, if you aren't seafood-bound, "other" is limited to sandwiches, pizza, an ice cream cone, or maybe a cup of coffee. At **St. George Island Gourmet** (235 W. Gulf Beach Dr., 850/927-4888, 7:30 A.M.–6 P.M. Mon.–Thurs., until 9 P.M. Fri.–Sun.) you can pick up competent paninis and salads to go. **BJ's Pizza & Subs** (105 W. Gulf Beach Dr., 850/927-2805) tosses decent pizzas (also offered by the slice) and has a raucous game room in which to rapidly lose a pocketful of quarters. We were told that **Aunt Ebby's Island Deli & Ice Cream** (147 E. Gulf Beach Dr., 850/927-3229) was the place to stop for a cooling frozen confection, but the ice cream was ho-hum and rumor has it the place is changing hands. A better bet is one of the frozen fruit smoothies at the shockingly purple **Juice and Java** (49 W. Pine St., 850/927-3925, 7 A.M.–6 P.M. daily), which also has a fairly refined selection of coffee drinks and baked goods.

A big sign out front enumerates what the aforementioned **Banana Starfish Café** (139 E. Gorrie Dr., 850/927-4222) doesn't sell (no nuclear devices) along with what it does (but you're in luck if you're looking for ice cream or T-shirts). Beyond that, it's a quirky, colorful spot for a cozy (and sometimes interspecies) breakfast or lunch.

Cocktails

Harry A's (28 W. Bayshore Dr., 850/927-9810, Mon.–Sat.) is just about the oldest building on the island, with the kind of wide, inviting front porch that's more and more difficult to forsake after each successive beer. The tavern where locals meet visitors over a pint and some hot wings, Harry's A's brings in musical entertainment most nights (beware the comedy night on Tuesday).

SHOPPING

Not known for its shopping, St. George boasts a couple of gas stations, a handful of bikini and boogie board shops, and a preponderance of ice cream scoop stands (most of these with prices that reflect a little "isolation inflation"). If you have the urge to shop and don't feel like heading back over the bridge to Apalach, meander over to

Island Outfitters (235 E. Gulf Beach Dr., 850/927-2604), where you can peruse "resort wear" along with the latest in saltwater fishing tackle, rods, reels, and accessories. Island Outfitters is also the place to charter a boat or rent a 19-foot Carolina skiff or catamaran so you can explore the barrier islands and the Apalachicola River system. **Sometimes It's Hotter Seasoning Company** (37 E. Pine Ave., 850/927-5039) is a unique local institution and a nice place to pick out a gift basket of dried herbs and herb blends for the folks back home. Not far from there, **Island Emporium** (160 E. Pine St., 850/927-2622) is a two-story souvenir shop of collectibles, beachwear, and sandcastle-building supplies.

If you arrived on-island without your outdoor-fun essentials, the nearby **Tropical Trader** (137 E. Pine St., 850/927-2300) rents beach umbrellas ($6 per day), bicycles (a pretty good deal by the week, $30 for adult bikes, $20 for kids), kayaks ($30 per day for a two-seater), boogie boards ($5), and other necessities. It also rents bigger boats and offers charter fishing trips on the bay side or the Gulf side as well as lighthouse tours and sightseeing trips.

Eastpoint

Not long ago one out of every ten residents in Franklin County had an oyster permit. There were oyster beds out in Apalachicola Bay that people swore by, magical spots with names like Cabbage Top, Catpoint, North Spur, and West Lump. With worn wooden poles, oysterermen would tap along, waiting for the thud to sharpen as the pole hit shell. Then the tongers, men with ropy arm muscles and profound tans, heave their tongs over the side of their small wooden flats boats and get to work. Like two metal rakes hinged together scissor-style, the long-handled tongs rake the bivalves off the shallow bottoms. Pulled aboard, the oysters are sorted with practiced eye on a culling board, only those three inches long kept as the morning's catch.

Things are changing, though. Franklin County's gorgeous setting has drawn luxury condos and other, more lucrative, beachy development that have inched out some of the career oysterers. In addition, the population growth of greater Atlanta to the north—more than four million people and growing fast—has tapped more and more water from Georgia's Chattahoochee River, a river that as it heads into Florida becomes the Apalachicola River.

The one place in Franklin County that remains seemingly unchanged is Eastpoint. It has a gruff, fishing-village beauty that is amplified by its own unselfconsciousness. Stop along the roadside waterfront to watch "housemen" at the wholesale seafood houses manhandle oysters, shrimp, and finfish, brusquely sorting and packing the catch into boxes or bags. It's a year-round venture, with the oyster harvest rotated seasonally from 10,000 acres of oyster beds in St. George Sound and environs. Virtually the whole length of Eastpoint's commercial district is perfumed with the briny waft of seafood docks and the sounds of WOYS-FM, "Oyster Radio" out of Apalachicola competing with the boisterous calls of fourth-generation oystermen getting off work for the day.

For the visitor, Eastpoint doesn't have the kind of bells and whistles that would make it a big tourist draw, just a few restaurants, a couple of rustic bars, and more oysters than you could shake a tong at.

SPORTS AND RECREATION
Tee Time
Putt-n-Fuss Fun Park (236 U.S. 98, 850/670-1211, 10 A.M.–10 P.M. Mon.–Sat., noon–7 P.M. Sun., golf $6 adult, $5 child) is Eastpoint's rebuttal to Disney World. The lighted 18-hole miniature golf course is a hoot for all ages—then add in the bumper boats, arcade, and snack bar with 16 flavors of ice cream, and you've got a wild evening on the town.

ACCOMMODATIONS

Pretty much the only game in town is **Sportsman's Lodge Motel & Marina** (99 N. Bayshore Dr., 850/670-8423, $49–59), a rustic, fishcamp-style motel, marina, and RV park overlooking the East Bay. It's wooded, quiet, very family friendly with kitchenettes, a nice boat dock, ramp, and easy access to fishing guides and charters. Eastpoint's only other motel of note was Aaron's on the Bay Motel, which closed in 2004—even if you aim to explore the oyster-fishing charms of Eastpoint, you have a much greater range of hotel options in nearby Apalachicola.

FOOD

Former PGA money winner Mike Keller owns **That Place on 98** (500 U.S. 98, 850/670-9898, 11:30 A.M.–9 P.M. Mon., Tues., and Thurs.–Sat., open at noon on Sun.), a comfortable, casual oyster joint with a couple of wide decks overlooking the Apalachicola Bay. Keller himself changes the number from time to time on the sign out front that takes a stab at how many dozen oysters have been proudly served. And as the most popular oyster joint in Eastpoint, That Place has served enough on the half shell, in a velvety stew, etc., to rack up serious digits. They're gonna need a bigger sign.

Just at the turnoff from Eastpoint before you cross the bridge to St. George Island, **Eastpoint Oysterhouse/Lighthouse** (346 Patton Dr., 850/670-1448) is another oldtimey raw bar with especially good smoked mullet (although for many, that's oxymoronic). It also has satisfyingly sweet steamed shrimp and oysters, and well-behaved dogs are allowed to hang out at the waterfront picnic tables.

MORE OF SOMETHING FISHY

"**R**ustic," "quaint," even "crusty"—words like this were invented to describe places like **Carrabelle.** East of Eastpoint, it's still an active fishing town with shrimpers and fin fishers unloading their daily catch with thin-lipped, taciturn resolve. For just this reason, it's been the filming location for a couple of Victor Nunez movies, including *Ulee's Gold* starring Peter Fonda and the more recent *Coastlines,* with Josh Brolin. There are still fewer than 1,200 residents, and the downtown has never been gentrified or prettied up for the tourists.

It's got the world's smallest **police station** (a phone booth), the State Forestry Division's **Carrabelle Fire Tower** on the east side of town with great views of the area, and the little **Camp Gordon Johnston WWII Museum,** which pays tribute to the amphibious soldiers who trained here and served in WWII, Korea, and Vietnam. Camp Gordon Johnston actually covered 165,000 acres along the Big Bend, with 36 miles along the shores of the Gulf of Mexico. The area was left in its natural state for training purposes, where thousands of soldiers learned to land the crafts that would be used on the beaches of Normandy on D-Day.

Carrabelle also boasts the **Crooked River Lighthouse,** a rickety decommissioned lighthouse. The 103-foot iron tower was built in 1985, and plans are afoot amongst Carrabelle Lighthouse Association members to restore it to its former glory. **Carrabelle Beach,** just west of town, is a popular spot for picnickers and beachcombers. And the town is the debarkation point for the **Dog Island water taxi,** which is the only link for residents and visitors out to the more remote island and its **Pelican Inn.** (Captain **Ron Treutel,** 850/697-8984, will also take you out to Dog Island for the day.)

What's left to do in Carrabelle? Bumper stickers describe the town as a "small drinking village with a fishing problem." You can drink and/or eat at some of the more convivial establishments around. For straight drinking, head to **Harry's Bar & Package** (306 Marine St., 850/697-9982), have sandwiches and coffee at **Carrabelle Junction** (88 Tallahassee St., 850/697-9550), barbecue at **Hog Wild BBQ** (1593 U.S. 98, 850/697-8394), and a whole lot of fun at **Wicked Willie's** and its sister restaurant **Riverview Restaurant** (both at 600 Marine St., 850/697-8488).

Continue east to Carrabelle and you'll find **Harry's in Carrabelle** (306 Marine St., 850/697-9982, 6 A.M.–9 P.M. Mon.–Sat.) just behind the Georgian Motel, which opens bright and early to serve the fisherfolk heading into the Gulf. It's mostly a drinking establishment, as is the later-night spot around the corner, **Wicked Willie's** (600 Marine St., 850/697-8488). Nurse a beer and eavesdrop on the boisterous banter of the career anglers and the weekenders.

Even farther east, in Panacea, **Angelo's** (5 Mashers Sand Rd., 850/984-5168) is a long-standing and justifiably famous purveyor of the local blue crabmeat (try the seafood cakes). There are waterside tables, a wide wraparound porch, and friendly locals.

Information and Services

AREA INFORMATION

The Forgotten Coast is on eastern time. The telephone area code is 850.

Tourist Information

Chuck Spicer's *Forgotten Coastline* is a crusty, cantankerous locals-only paper you'll see being read all over. It gives you the inside track on the area's issues, gripes, and secret treasures. There's also an online version called http://forgotten-coastline.com.

Beyond that, you'll find lots of useful information on the area by visiting www.apalachicolabay.org or www.visitgulf.com. Anita Grove at the **Apalachicola Chamber of Commerce** (122 Market St., Apalachicola, 850/653-9419) is also a tremendous resource. Be sure to pick up the historic walking tour brochure while you're there.

Police and Emergencies

For any real emergency, dial 911. For nonemergencies, there's the **Apalachicola Police Department** (1 Ave. E, 850/653-9432), the **Franklin County Sheriff's Department** (850/670-8500), and the **Carrabelle Police Department** (smallest in the U.S., it's the phone booth in town, 850/697-3691).

If you find yourself in need of a doctor during your visit, you may choose between **Franklin Family Medicine** (just for nonemergencies, 35 Island Dr., Eastpoint, 850/670-8585, 9 A.M.–5 P.M. Mon.–Fri.) or **George E. Weems Memorial Hospital** (1 Washington Square and Ave. D, Apalachicola, 850/653-8853). For your pharmacy needs, try **Lanier Pharmacy** (45 Ave. D, Apalachicola, 850/653-8825) or **Eckerd** (139 Ave. E, Apalachicola, 850/653-8350). Pet emergencies are best handled at **Apalachicola Bay Animal Clinic** (187 U.S. 98, Eastpoint, 850/670-8306).

Radio and Television

When you're feeling musically nostalgic, tune in to **The Coast,** WFCT FM 105.5 out of St. Joe, with a mix of "favorites from yesterday and today." To seem like a real local, twist the dial to **Oyster Radio** at WOYS 100.5 FM out of Apalachicola, with daily local news, national news, and hourly weather reports. There are no local television stations, but out of Tallahassee, WFSU Channel 11 is the PBS affiliate, WTXL Channel 27 is the ABC affiliate, and WTLH Channel 49 is the FOX affiliate.

Laundry Services

Most rental houses on St. George Island have laundry facilities. If you're without access where you're staying (at an inn in Apalachicola, for instance), many of the marinas have self-serve laundries. There's also a nice little laundry in Eastpoint, **Pearl Linen** (91 U.S. 98, behind the car wash, 850/670-8703).

Fishing Licenses

Fishing licenses are sold in the County Tax Collector's Office and in many local bait and tackle shops, or by calling 888/347-4356. Saltwater and freshwater year-long licenses are each $13.50; a nonresident three-day pass is $6.50.

Getting There and Around

The Forgotten Coast is just west of the Big Bend (where the Florida peninsula attaches to the Panhandle), 80 miles southwest of Tallahassee, accessible by the east–west corridor of U.S. 98. If you're piloting your own small plane, St. George Island Plantation Airport (850/927-2362) has 3,800-foot by 65-foot runway (no lights, no fuel), and Apalachicola Airport (850/653-2222) has a 5,400-foot by 150-foot concrete runway (fuel available). The closest commercial airports are **Tallahassee Regional Airport** (service provided by Delta, United, and Northwest, 904/891-7800) and Panama City (served by Delta, Northwest, and US Airways, 850/763-6751), 60 miles to the west.

Alamo (800/327-9633), **Avis** (800/831-2847), **Budget** (800/527-0700), **Dollar** (800/800-4000 domestic, 800/800-6000 international), and **National** (800/227-7368) provide rental cars from these airports. There is no real public transportation (no buses or trains) to speak of along this stretch of coast, so you need a car.

To reach the Forgotten Coast by car, there are several routes worth considering. From the north, if your aim is to minimize back roads, take I-75 south to Tifton, then U.S. 319 to Tallahassee, then U.S. 98 to the St. George Bridge at Eastpoint, or continue west to Apalachicola. If you're coming west from, say, Orlando, find your way to I-75 heading north; exit on U.S. 441 west at Alachua, just before Lake City, quickly changing to U.S. 27, which intersects with U.S. 98 near Perry.

By boat, on the Gulf Intracoastal Waterway from Florida's west coast, enter at St. George Sound through East Pass, between Dog Island and St. George Island, or through Bob Sikes Cut. From the west, take the ICW through East Bay from Panama City, then on past White City. Continue east through Wimico to the Jackson River, which leads to the Apalachicola River. Follow markers past the Railroad Bridge to Apalachicola.

The Forgotten Coast

The Emerald Coast

Like something from the set of the Wizard of Oz, the water here is an unearthly emerald green. Some cynics will say that the bright color is the result of a pernicious blue-green algae. Not true. It's just very clear water, shown against super-reflective white sand in the shallows that produces the green color—the deeper the water, the bluer it gets.

Unified by this eye-catching water color, the beaches of northwest Florida, from Pensacola Beach to the long stretch of the Beaches of South Walton and beyond to the east in Panama City Beach, offer miles of unspoiled natural beauty and a range of options for vacation fun. But they're really different options—I've chosen to break this chapter into three sections because there seem to be three discrete draws, each with its own dramatically different character.

First, the **Destin** and **Fort Walton Beach** area in the westernmost part, closest to Pensacola

Must-Sees

M **Fishing in Destin Harbor:** Offshore, inshore, cobia, sailfish, wahoo—Destin is a serious fishing destination. Arrange a fishing charter to suit your interests and what's biting, and find out why Destin is often called the "World's Luckiest Fishing Village" (page 282).

M **Crab Island:** Rent a boat or watercraft of some kind and attend the biggest daily impromptu lunch party in Destin on a partially submerged island north of the Destin Bridge (page 285).

M **Big Kahuna's Water and Adventure Park:** If the beach isn't enough to fully occupy the family, take them to Big Kahuna's Water and Adventure Park in Destin, with 25 acres of slides, flumes, tubing, lagoons, wave pools, and more (page 287).

M **Seaside:** Spend a day exploring the picturesque pastel beach town of Seaside, featured in the Jim Carrey movie, *The Truman Show* (page 292).

M **Biking Along Scenic Route 30A:** Explore the Beaches of South Walton slowly and under your own power, with a bike ride along the 19-mile paved path that follows Scenic 30A at the coast (page 296).

COURTESY OF VISIT FLORIDA

Seaside is a pedestrian-oriented planned community designed in a New Urbanist Neo-Vernacular style.

M **St. Andrews State Recreation Area:** With its luminous green water and fine white sand, the Emerald Coast has numerous beaches to recommend. This one in Panama City, named "the world's best beach" not long ago by *Travel Magazine,* offers miles of Gulf-side beach as well as a broad, inviting Grand Lagoon and a 700-acre offshore barrier strip called Shell Island (page 300).

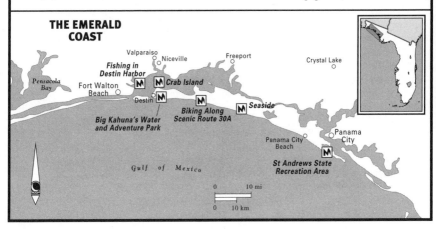

THE EMERALD COAST

Valparaiso
Niceville
Freeport
Crystal Lake
Pensacola Bay
Fort Walton Beach
Fishing in Destin Harbor **M**
M Crab Island
Destin **M**
Big Kahuna's Water and Adventure Park
Biking Along Scenic Route 30A **M**
M Seaside
Panama City Beach
Panama City
St Andrews State Recreation Area **M**
Gulf of Mexico

0   10 mi
0   10 km

The Emerald Coast

Beach, is the best-known destination (or Destin-ation, as so many websites feebly pun). Incorporated as recently as 1984, the fishing village of Destin has seen enormous growth as tourism has taken off, with lots of new construction, visitor attractions, restaurants, etc., to lure ever more people. It's getting built up, but most of the beachfront is still low-rise (condos cometh, though). You visit Destin, Fort Walton Beach, and Okaloosa Island to do some fishing, splash in the emerald-green water, have a good time with the kids.

The **Beaches of South Walton** region, on the other hand, constitutes a 26-mile stretch of shoreline to the east of Destin, containing 13 beach communities. Pristine and environmentally sound, these beaches offer pure, clear, emerald-green water, fine sugar-white sand, and meandering coastal dune lakes, which create a unique and varied landscape. It's the only place in the country to receive "Blue Wave" Environmental Certification from the Clean Beaches Council for all 26 miles of its coastline. Mostly it's private residences in newish, forward-thinking, and eco-friendly planned communities. You won't find a lot of go-cart tracks, minimarts, or ticky-tacky T-shirt shops. Remember that oh-so-perfect town in *The Truman Show?* It was shot here in Seaside—nearly all of the area's towns have this old-fashioned-beach-retreat-through-rose-colored-glasses nostalgia. None of this comes cheap, though. It's pricey to stay in the Beaches of South Walton, but the understated elegance and back-to-basics innocence are memorable.

The third section is **Panama City Beach,** about 20 miles farther east. It bears the distinction of being the only draw along the Gulf Coast of Florida for high school and college-age spring breakers. It is perhaps the only part of the Panhandle in which residents and visitors freely use the word "party" as a recurrent verb. If the Beaches of South Walton sounded good, this is not for you—and vice versa. It's all about mini golf, video game arcades, hubbub, souvenir shops, hordes of people enjoying themselves on the beach. It's bustling with Wave Runners and para-sailers, girls in bikinis, restaurants heavily reliant on fry-o-lators, and car windows down. Gosh,

this is all sounding like lyrics from a Don Henley song or something ("your brown skin shinin' in the sun, you got that top pulled down and that radio on, baby"), but you get the picture?

HURRICANES

This is maybe an indelicate thing to say, in light of Pensacola's protracted Hurricane Ivan cleanup, but the Emerald Coast in some ways benefited from the whole disaster. In the Okaloosa area, which in fact did incur damage, beachside restrooms have been reconstructed and the beach itself has been widened significantly, due to an Army Corps of Engineers emergency dredge project. Hurricane Ivan created shoaling in the Intracoastal Waterway through Choctawhatchee Bay, a safety hazard for commercial navigation. Thus, 30,000 cubic yards of beach-quality sand were dragged up onto Okaloosa area beaches. The Beaches of South Walton, the 13 beach communities stretching along the Panhandle from Seascape east to Inlet, certainly suffered during the hurricane season but many public beach accesses were reopened by spring 2005. Many area resorts took this fallow period to expand or remodel, and a couple of brand-new luxury resorts will open concurrently. Panama City Beach also had a huge beach nourishment effort in the works ($25 million), and Hurricane Ivan served to streamline the rejuvenation project, forcing hotels to close and refurbish in tandem, some of them a little earlier than scheduled.

There was indeed enormous property damage in this area, but most accommodations, restaurants, and attractions were back up to speed to welcome spring breakers in 2005. Eventually there will be few reminders of the vicious storm, outside of a paucity of densely canopied full-grown trees.

PLANNING YOUR TIME

High season along the Panhandle is summer, with rates dropping precipitously in the fall and winter. Spring break is a brief flurry around here in March and April, at its densest in Panama City Beach. But where to stay? Anglers: Go to

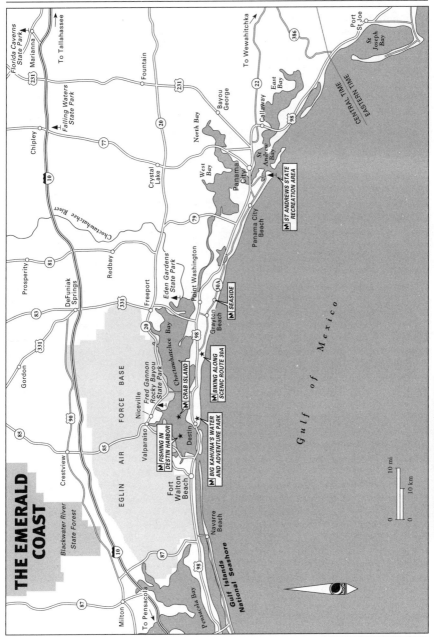

THE EMERALD COAST

Gulf of Mexico

© AVALON TRAVEL PUBLISHING, INC.

Destin or Fort Walton Beach. You monied leisure seekers who aim to commune with your inner eyelids at least as much as the coastal beauty all around: Visit the Beaches of South Walton. Spring breakers: Get thee to Panama City Beach, and remember to have a designated driver (that's not the one who *seems* the most sober). The latter is worth two days of intensive revelry, three if you have a long attention span. Many of the rentals along the 13 communities of the Beaches of South Walton have a minimum stay, some as much as a week during high season. The area could certainly occupy you for that long, with a day trip to Pensacola, another one to visit the amusements in Panama City Beach, and a third to one of the wonderful state parks here.

Fort Walton Beach and Destin

Spanish explorer Panfilo de Narvaez landed along the Emerald Coast in 1628 to find himself a drink of water. The Creeks chased him and his men back to the boat, thirst unslaked. It wasn't that the inhospitable natives left a centuries' long curse on the place. There's no telling, really, why up until about 50 years ago a wide swath of the Emerald Coast, from Destin to Panama City, was unsettled sand dunes and quiet green waters. Most of the growth here dates back only a couple of decades.

Not so of Destin and Fort Walton Beach. Okaloosa County has got roots. In 1830, New England seafarer Leonard Destin fell for the place, the first white man to settle in the area among several local Native American tribes. He lured other New England fishermen with big fish stories, and by 1845 there were 100 white residents, all employed in the fishing business. And Fort Walton Beach was a Civil War campsite, its location chosen because of its protection from the Gulf by the Santa Rosa Sound and Okaloosa Island.

During Prohibition the joint was jumping. "Entrepreneurs" like Al Capone came down to the area to hide out. Mobsters being mobsters, the area was soon dotted with hopping casinos filled with shady characters evading the law up North.

The casinos and mobsters are gone, but what's left is a beloved fishing destination, one that boasts five saltwater world records. It looks the part: Destin and Fort Walton Beach were the shooting location for *Jaws II,* both towns admirably portraying charming Southern fishing villages. It was serious method acting—only the great white was a little unconvincing.

SPORTS AND RECREATION

Beaches

There are 24 miles of beach—the sand a shockingly fine, white quartz that somehow made its way here down 130 miles of the Appalachian River, the water a brilliant jewel green. Nearly 60 percent of the beach around here is preserved in perpetuity, or at least for a long, long time. There are five beachfront parks and twelve beach access ways along the Destin, Fort Walton Beach, and Okaloosa Island shoreline.

One of the best is the 208-acre **Henderson Beach State Park** (17000 Emerald Coast Pkwy., east of the city of Destin on U.S. 98, for camping call 800/326-3521 or visit www.reserveamerica.com, 8 A.M.–sundown daily, $3/vehicle with single occupant, $4/vehicle with up to eight passengers, $1 pedestrian or cyclist, $21 camping), which has 6,000 feet of shoreline. There's urban sprawl off to the west in Destin; in fact, the beach's entrance is just across the street from a Super Wal-Mart. Once out on the coastal dunes you'd never know it—sea oats anchor the soft sand in the dunes, while the ocean's salt spray and wind cause the rosemary, magnolias, and scrub oak to grow low and horizontal, their limbs bent shoreward. During the fall the beach is dotted with colorful wildflowers, blanket flower and beach morning glory festooning the clean sand.

At Henderson you can swim, surf fish, picnic, bike, walk the three-quarter-mile nature trail, or camp (the campground recently doubled in size, from 30 to 60 full-facility campsites for tents or RVs). Colored flags indicate the wave and swimming conditions—red means no swimming.

BEACH BASICS

So that your day at the beach can be an, um, day at the beach, keep a few things in mind.

Beach Husbandry

Bare coastal dunes are vulnerable to destruction by the same forces that form them: wind and waves. Dunes are built when sand blows up through beachside plantlife and is trapped, creating ever-taller mounds. These mounds in turn protect the shore during storms by washing back out to sea and decreasing the energy of the storm waves. For these reasons, do not trample, pick, spindle, or mutilate any beachside plantlife (like the sea oats). In fact, along public beach accesses, always use the **boardwalks and raised walkways** rather than tramping through the sand.

Sea turtles nest on the gulf beaches of Okaloosa County April–November. The 2004 hurricane season wrought havoc on these already threatened and endangered species. Again, no spindling (it's illegal to disturb a nest or harm a turtle in any way), or even taunting. Never crowd around a turtle nest, don't impede a turtle's progress toward the water, and don't shine lights on the beaches at night if possible.

This area's beaches are all **clothing-required.** Navarre Beach used to have a lot of nude sunbathers, but federal agents have cracked down on the depravity and lawlessness that comes of lying nude on a beach towel. Be advised. Also, beaches in this area **prohibit pets,** and that goes double for nude pets. If you see animals on the beach, they probably belong to residents who have gotten special beach pet permits, available only to locals.

Beach Safety

Jellyfish are common to Gulf beaches. Not the big terrifying man-o-war types, but the local species' sting can still be pretty fierce. Shuffle your feet in the water to alert nearby jellyfish to your presence. In the event that you do get stung, the experts say ammonia poured on the sting relieves the pain, as does meat tenderizer and toothpaste. (Who figures these things out—is someone getting stung and then applying poultices of household products just in the name of science?—"Preparation H, yes. Mr. Clean, no.")

Rip currents occur in any type of weather. If caught in a rip current, swim parallel to the shore until the current weakens and you can swim in.

And although shark attacks in these waters are very infrequent, there are ways to further minimize your chances of a **shark encounter.** You're more vulnerable if you're swimming alone, and if you swim far from shore. Sharks are most active at dusk, when they have a competitive sensory advantage. They tend to hang out in areas between sandbars or steep drop offs—use caution when swimming in these areas. As you know, sharks smell blood—if you have a wound, if you are menstruating, or if nearby fishermen are cleaning fish or throwing out bait, think about postponing a swim. And remove shiny jewelry before you go in—its reflective glinting looks like the sheen of fish scales to a hungry predator.

Sunscreen, and lots of it. Experts say that an average-sized person should use about two tablespoons per application.

James Lee County Park (3510 Scenic U.S. 98, Destin, 8 A.M.–sundown daily, free parking) is another good beach, right at the Walton/Okaloosa county line. This park has three pavilions, 41 picnic tables, nine dune walkovers, a playground, restrooms with changing rooms, and 166 parking spaces. It's a popular beach for families as the water is shallow and clear. The Crab Trap restaurant is in the middle of this beach's parking lot.

Okaloosa Island has a series of beaches, really contiguous—first, the **John Beasley Wayside Park** (U.S. 98, Okaloosa Island, 1.2 miles east of Fort Walton Beach, 850/651-7131) is on the bay side of the barrier island just yards from the Okaloosa Boardwalk (an entertainment complex with clubs and restaurants). John Beasley has restrooms, picnic tables, showers, changing rooms, vending machines, and lifeguards. It has a fair amount of fishing for trout and reds, snorkeling activity, and even a little surfing. The same can be said of the adjacent **Brackin Wayside**

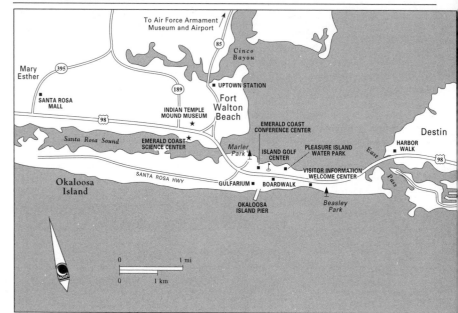

Park and Boardwalk (U.S. 98, Okaloosa Island, one mile east of Fort Walton Beach, 850/651-7131), which also has lots of volleyball during the warmer months.

Fishing in Destin Harbor

About 30 miles offshore (only 10 miles from Destin's East Pass), the Gulf of Mexico turns from emerald green to deep blue. It's at this point, called the 100-Fathom Curve, where you're in deep, deep water all of a sudden. This deep-water curve is closer to Destin than to any other spot in Florida, meaning it's quicker out to deep water on a fishing charter than most fishing towns on the Gulf. Lucky thing, because these waters are churning with fish. In the spring there's the migration of mighty cobia (you can sight fish for these), and in May come the kingfish (inshore troll). People bottom fish for grouper, red snapper, triggerfish, and amberjack year-round. Then in summer when the waters warm up it's serious marlin and sailfish (offshore troll), and wahoo and tuna (inshore troll). Destin bills itself, so to speak, as the Bill-fish Capital of the World. The best I can figure, based on conversation with sometimes-taciturn fishermen types, "billfish" is a category of tuna-like fish species like marlin, sailfish, and spearfish—those fish with the big, swordlike bill. Destin is also known by some as the "World's Luckiest Fishing Village," because its waters harbor four times more types of fresh fish per season than any other Florida destination except for Key West. Supposedly, during any given season there are 20 edible species of gamefish to be found in local waters.

So you have to come here and fish. Offshore, bottom, inshore, or even surf-casting—there are lots of people around here with enormous experience willing to take you out on a saltwater charter or just hook you up with gear. Oh, and the area's rivers offer decent freshwater fishing for catfish, bass, and bream. And many restaurants in the area are amenable to cooking up your fresh catch.

The price of a private charter averages $120–140 per hour, for up to six people. Many boats only accommodate six people, so make clear how many people are in your party. You can also sign up for a group charter, pooling

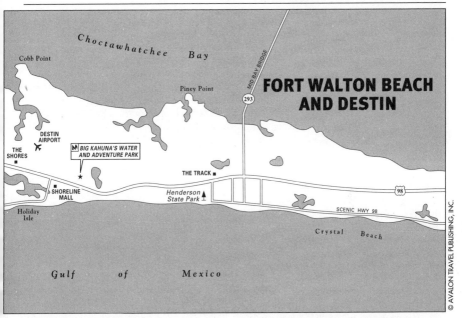

Choctawhatchee Bay

Cobb Point

Piney Point

MID BAY BRIDGE

**FORT WALTON BEACH
AND DESTIN**

293

DESTIN
AIRPORT

THE
SHORES

M BIG KAHUNA'S WATER
AND ADVENTURE PARK

THE TRACK

SHORELINE
MALL

Henderson
State Park

98

Holiday
Isle

SCENIC HWY 98

Crystal Beach

Gulf   of   Mexico

© AVALON TRAVEL PUBLISHING, INC.

M The Emerald Coast

with other people who are looking to go out (the prices are the same, you just split it between all the people on the boat). Obviously, you have to find others who are simpatico, in terms of what they're fishing for and how long they want to be out.

Fleet Charter Service (Fisherman's Wharf, Destin, 850/837-1995) is one-stop shopping, with access to 40 of Destin's best charter boats (there are more than 140 vessels for hire around here). These boats offer year-round fishing trips for individuals or groups, from four-hour trips to overnight, either on the Gulf or on the bay side. **Harborwalk Fishing Charters** (next to Lucky Snapper off U.S. 98, 850/837-2343, four hours $480, six hours $720—it's customary to tip 15 percent) is another well-regarded local charter company. They will clean, fillet, and bag your catch at trip's end. Captain **John Holley** (797 Pine St., Destin, 850/837-4946, cobia $1,000 full day, $600 half; trolling and live bait fishing for marlin, tuna, wahoo, mahimahi, and king mackerel $150/hour, bottom fishing for amberjack and grouper $150/hour) specializes in big fish. He has a

number of marlin, cobia, and kingfish tournament wins to his credit and has been involved in many of the local billfish tournaments (they're tag and release). He's been Destin Rodeo Sportfishing Captain of the Year for nine consecutive years.

If you just feel like finding your own boat and giving it a go, **Gilligan's Water Sports** (Destin Harbor, 850/650-9000) rents pontoon boats for reasonable prices ($125 half day, $225 full day), good for snorkeling, fishing, or just tooling around. You can also head out into the Blackwater, Shoal, or Yellow River in search of bass, bream, and catfish.

No boat required, from the water's edge, the **Okaloosa Island Fishing Pier** is open 24 hours a day. The cost for fishing is $6.50 for adults and $3.50 for children 6–12, no license necessary. It's a 1,261-foot pier, lighted at night, with rod holders and benches built into it. You'll catch all kinds of things (big mahimahi, etc.). You can also cast from the area's finger jetties, sandy shores, and the 3,000-foot **Destin Bridge Catwalk** to hook speckled trout, white snapper, and redfish. And there are stocked

EAST PASS

Originally, the Gulf of Mexico and the Destin Harbor did not connect to the Choctawhatchee Bay in this area, which posed some navigational challenges to the local fishing fleet and some flooding danger to the settlements as well. In 1926, three local, stalwart families took it upon themselves to change that. The Destins, the Marlers, and the Melvins grabbed a bunch of shovels and started digging by hand, making a two-foot-wide ditch across Okaloosa Island. Within two hours, supposedly, the trench was over 100 yards wide. A torrent of water rushed in, creating what is now East Pass. In 1935, the East Pass Bridge was built. To this day, the Army Corps of Engineers keeps close tabs on the pass, dredging it every two years or so (more in hurricane years) to ensure the water's deep enough for boats to move safely through it.

The East Pass is the only waterway connecting the Choctawhatchee Bay to the Gulf of Mexico for 60 miles in either direction (Pensacola to the west and Panama City to the east each have waterways that connect the bay with the Gulf). The East Pass is the lifeblood of the Destin fishing fleet—without it, the town would surely not be the angler's paradise that draws fisherfolk from around the world. All because of a few shovels.

ponds in the area, such as the 350-acre **Hurricane Lake** in Blackwater River State Park, filled with channel catfish, large-mouth bass, bluegill, and shellcracker.

Eyes rolling back in your head from all of my lists of fish? Here's what you do—visit www.gulfcoastangling.com and find out what is biting, and where, then plan your fishing accordingly.

Shelling and Diving

The beaches are uniformly fine white sand, very few shells in sight. So how can the Emerald Coast be ranked as a top shelling destination? They're offshore; you have to dive for them. Giant sandbars about a mile from shore and a natural coral-encrusted limestone outcropping (the pre-Ice Age shoreline) three miles out act as natural shov-

els to collect perfectly formed shells—pastel lion's paws, true tulips, huge queen helmets, and Florida's signature shell, the horse conchs, are there for the picking.

The center of much of this shelling mania is **Sand Dollar City,** a fairly new artificial reef complex the county has put together about a mile out. It's got six patch reefs placed in a hexagonal pattern around a single center point, the sunken 1941 tugboat called the *Mohawk Chief.* The whole area is a fish and shellfish haven, and by extension, a shelling bonanza. **Timber Hole** is another hot spot of shelling and intriguing marine life (sea squirts, four-foot basket sponges, aqua and purple sea whips) observation, a natural limestone reef 6–18 feet high and 110 feet deep and also the site of sunken planes, ships, and a railroad car. There are also loads of natural reefs in this area, for shelling, diving, and fishing. **Amberjack Rocks** is one of the area's largest reef systems, within three miles of Destin Pass. About 80 feet deep, it is known for shelling as well as spearfishing for black snapper and amberjack. **Long Reef** features staircase ledges and is known for lobsters and shells. The area also has intriguing wrecks to explore—an air force barge, a Liberty Ship, Butler's Barge, and the rubble of the Destin Bridge. Divers here often enjoy 40–100 feet of visibility.

For safety reasons, all divers must display a free-flying, 12-by-12-inch flag with a white diagonal stripe on a red background—the divers-down flag—in the area in which the dive occurs. Divers should try to stay within 100 feet of the divers-down flag, and the flag and diver should never be in areas that might constitute a navigational hazard.

Sand Dollar Charters (2961 Sholtz Ave., Crestview, 850/902-1492, snorkeling $25, scuba $65–85, equipment extra) offers scuba charters through many of these areas, and **Emerald Coast Scuba** (110 Melvin St., Destin, 850/837-0955) provides scuba instruction and charters. Many other dive shops offer theme excursions like spearfishing, deep sea, shell, and lobster, with certification classes.

They will also take you out snorkeling from their boats. If you just want to snorkel on your

Destin has been touted as having the top beaches in the South by readers of *Southern Living* for the past four years—with brilliant green water and white sand, it's 24 miles of beautiful beachfront.

own, you can do so from the beach at **Destin jetties** or from the **Old Crystal Beach Pier.**

Crab Island

You've got an appointment you've got to keep. To get there, you need something that floats, preferably a boat. Maybe a pontoon boat, or a glass-bottom boat, or a fishing boat, or even a Wave Runner. You can shop at **Boogies Watersports** (U.S. 98 at the foot of the Destin Bridge, Destin, 850/654-4497) or **Destin Water Toys** (302C U.S. 98 E, Destin, 850/837-7755) to pick up a rental that suits your budget, skill level, and personal sense of style. But you're in a hurry. It's a lunch date.

You're going to need directions, but you can ask any local: "How do I get to Crab Island?" North of the Destin Bridge, it used to be two islands in the middle of nowhere, made of sand dredged by the Army Corps of Engineers from East Pass. It used to even be a real island with sea grass, shrubs, and seabirds. But now it's submerged a few feet and only surfaces at low tide. But it's where people congregate for a lunchtime bash. Boats all pile up out there and people jump

off into the three-foot shallows, eating, chatting, drinking. Sometimes there's even live music on the back of a boat. There are often even floating vendors serving food and drinks to all the folks gathered there.

Golf

Emerald-green waters mirrored by emerald-green golf courses. There are 1,080 holes of golf in these parts, many of the courses designed by some of the world's best architects: Robert Cupp of Jack Nicklaus fame, or Finger, or Dye, or Fazio. Many of these courses utilize the area's lush natural beauty and surrounding waterways, with contrasts of woods and wetlands, for challenging and memorably beautiful play.

The 18-hole **Regatta Bay Golf Club** (465 Regatta Bay Blvd., Destin, 850/650-7800, $59–119, par 72, 6,864 yards, course rating 73.8, slope 148) is fairly new, designed by Robert Walker, winding along the shore of Choctawhatchee Bay and carved through wetlands and protected nature preserves. Another new one, the creation of Fred Couples and Gene Bates, **Kelly Plantation Golf Club** (307 Kelly

The Emerald Coast

Plantation Dr., Destin, 850/650-7600, $65–123, par 72, 7,099 yards, course rating 74.2, slope 146) utilizes the Choctawhatchee Bay as well, nestled along its southern edge with undulating greens and lush fairways.

Acclaimed by *Golfweek* as one of the "50 Most Distinctive Development Courses in the Southeast," **Emerald Bay** (40001 Emerald Coast Pkwy., Destin, 850/837-5197, $50–84, par 72, 6,802 yards, course rating 73.1, slope 135) was designed by nationally recognized architect Robert Cupp. He said of the course, "There is no signature hole, it is—instead—a signature golf course."

At **Indian Bayou Golf and Country Club** (1 Country Club Dr. E, Destin, 850/837-6191, $45–70, par 72, 7,000 yards, course rating 74, slope 132–142) there's an assortment of Earl Stone–designed nines, the Choctaw, Seminole, and Creek, which can be played in any 18-hole combination. The Creek course, the newest, has lots of water that comes into play; the Choctaw is heavily wooded; and the Seminole has wide fairways and large greens.

Also situated on the banks of Choctawhatchee Bay, **Shalimar Pointe Golf and Country Club** (302 Country Club Rd., Shalimar, 850/651-1416, $29–49, par 72, 6,765 yards, course rating 72.9, slope 125) is a Finger/Dye-designed course that *Links* magazine accused of having "Two of the Hardest Holes on the Emerald Coast," the 11th and 17th. It is bordered by rolling white dunes and dense hammocks of pine, oak, and magnolia. Shalimar Pointe has been host to The Emerald Coast Tour.

Beyond these, there's **Shoal River Country Club, Fort Walton Beach Municipal Course,** the two courses at **Eglin Air Force Base** (available only with government I.D.), and the world-class courses at Sandestin.

SIGHTS

Museums

Located near Eglin Air Force Base's main gate, the **Air Force Armament Museum** (Hwy. 85 and Hwy. 189, seven miles north of Fort Walton Beach, 850/882-4062, 9 A.M.–4:30 P.M. daily, admission free) is the only facility in the U.S. dedicated to the display of air force armament. You'll see thousands of weapons, an educational film called *Arming the Air Force,* and photography exhibits in addition to 25 cool reconnaissance, fighter, and bomber planes. There's a B-17 Flying Fortress, an F-4 Phantom II jet, and an SR-71 Blackbird Spy Plane. The museum spans four wars in its scope—WWII, Korea, Vietnam, and Persian Gulf. Kids love the fighter cockpit simulator.

The Fort Walton Beach community has a rich Native American past, settled by a number of prehistoric tribes as far back as 12,000 B.C. The **Indian Temple Mound Museum and Park** (139 Miracle Strip Pkwy. SE, Fort Walton Beach, 850/833-9595, 9 A.M.–4:30 P.M. Mon.–Sat., 12:30–4:30 P.M. Sun., closes at 4 P.M. all week in winter, $3 adults, $1 children 3–17, 3 and under free) provides a peek into the area's Native American history, with a thoughtfully assembled collection of Southeastern Indian ceramic artifacts and an Indian Mound Temple that dates to A.D. 1400 and originally served as a religious and civic center.

It was the first schoolhouse constructed for the children of Camp Walton, later to be known as Fort Walton Beach. **Camp Walton Schoolhouse Museum** (107 1st St., Fort Walton Beach, 850/833-9595, 10 A.M.–3 P.M. Tues. and Thurs. in June, July, and Aug., $1) was built of native pine and oak, and when it opened in 1912 there were 15 students and one teacher. It was restored in the early 1970s and opened as an educational museum in 1976. These days, it's mostly for the benefit of local school groups, but it still makes a sweet nostalgic look at a past most of us never knew.

ARTS AND ENTERTAINMENT

If you're coming to the Emerald Coast for the arts, you've been sorely misled or are suffering from sunburn-induced dementia. That's not what it's all about. The attractions are mostly outdoors, where the sun, sand, and fish are. Still, if you're looking for a little cultural solace, the Emerald Coast doesn't disappoint.

The **Northwest Florida Ballet** (101 Chicago Ave., Fort Walton Beach, 850/664-7787) is the longest-running arts organization in northwest Florida, producing full-length semiprofessional ballets in a number of local venues, including summer ballet in the park and the requisite holiday *Nutcracker*. **Stage Crafters Community Theatre** (Fort Walton Beach Civic Auditorium, 107 Miracle Strip Pkwy., Fort Walton Beach, 850/243-1101, 7:30 P.M. and 2 P.M. matinees) is a small community troupe that puts on the familiar *(Forever Plaid)* and the unfamiliar *(Meshuggah-Nuns)*. The **Okaloosa-Walton College Arts Center Proscenium Playhouse and Music Theater** (100 College Blvd., Niceville, 850/729-5382) stages plays in its large 1,600-seat main theater but also hosts dance, opera, the Northwest Florida Symphony Orchestra, and other arts events.

In visual arts, the **Fort Walton Beach Art Museum** (38 S.W. Robinwood Dr., Fort Walton Beach, 850/244-5319, 1–5 P.M. Sun.) a while back bought half interest in the Okaloosa Symphony building and showcases a nice permanent collection of American paintings, sculptures, pottery, and Chinese relics. (It also sponsors the Fort Walton Seafood Festival in the spring.) The **Arts & Design Society** (17 1st St. SE, Fort Walton Beach, 850/244-1271), founded in 1956 by a group of local artists, is more of a community art outreach, with classes, lectures, and kids' programs, but it also hosts monthly exhibits of local, regional, and national exhibits that are quite nice (like the recent quilt exhibit).

Festivals

In the Destin area, there are annual events like the Spring Splash, the Billy Bowlegs Festival, and the Christmas Boat Parade—but the biggest of them all is the month-long **Destin Fishing Rodeo** in October. There are 30 different categories of prizes, with all saltwater gamefish eligible—so you'll see people fishing all over the place with a vengeance. There's a more focused, single-species event in March and April with the annual Cobia Tournaments.

FOR KIDS

I feel like in every chapter I'm writing about a fairly compelling science museum for kids. What's the deal, every town has one of these now? **Emerald Coast Science Center** (139 Brooks St., Fort Walton Beach, 850/664-1261, 9 A.M.–4 P.M. weekdays, 11 A.M.–4 P.M. weekends, $5 adults, $4 seniors, $3.50 children 4–17) is a good example of the species, with a section devoted to color and light (laser harp, same as the one in St. Petersburg—think the state of Florida bought in bulk?). You can fly and land a model airplane in a mini-air tunnel, noodle with a laser spirograph or a Van de Graff generator (you know, that orb that makes your hair stand on end). There's also a nature part to the museum, with tarantulas and giant millipedes, and a human body section with stuff about the digestive system, the five senses, and the skeleton.

Opened in 1955, **Gulfarium** (1010 Miracle Strip Pkwy., Fort Walton Beach, 850/244-5169, 9 A.M.–8 P.M. daily, last ticket sold at 6 P.M., earlier in the winter, $17.25 adults, $15.25 seniors, $10.25 children 4–11, 3 and under free) was one of the country's original marine parks. Like a mini Sea World, it hosts Atlantic bottlenose dolphins, California sea lions, Peruvian penguins, Ridley turtles, with lots of Gulf-focused educational marine exhibits. Due to hurricane damage, the Gulfarium was closed for six months, reopening at the end of March 2005. Let's hope Delilah the dolphin diva is back with her high jumps and soccer games with her buddies Princess and Panama. The Gulfarium also sponsors the Dolphin Project, which focuses on interaction between dolphins and children with disabilities (like autism).

◼ Big Kahuna's Water and Adventure Park

Even adults get a little wide-eyed when they begin describing Big Kahuna's Water and Adventure Park (1007 U.S. 98 E, Destin, 850/837-8319, www.bigkahunas.com, 10 A.M.–6 P.M. all summer, water park closed in the winter and adventure park with weekend hours only, $33 adults, $29 children and seniors, under 2 free), with more than 40 water attractions and an adventure park spread over 25 acres. Clad in your bathing suit and a smile, you can wind through caves and waterfalls (the Tiagra Falls pumps 30,000 gallons of water per minute over 250 feet of mountain granite rock). There are three rivers, speed slides, body flumes, white-water tubing, leisurely lagoons, two wave pools, four children's areas with kid-sized slides and variable-depth pools, and other exciting wet and wild attractions for kids of all ages. Then once you dry off, there are the attached Adventure Park attractions (be aware, it's a separate ticket price, and a steep one—it's cheaper if you get the combined all-day pass for, gulp, $43.25). There are 54 holes of mini golf, a go-cart raceway, a bunch of other rides, and an arcade.

ACCOMMODATIONS

If you want to rent a beach cottage or luxurious condominium, **Newman-Dailey Resort Properties** (12815 U.S. 98 W, Ste. 100, Destin, 850/837-1071 or 800/225-7652, www.Destin-Vacation.com) is a well-regarded property management and vacation rental company, in the area for the past 20 years. The website offers virtual tours of properties.

$50–150

Because of spring break maniacs, most of the hotels around here don't rent to people under 25 (unless they're with an "adult"—how insulting, we send 24-year-olds off to war, but they need mommy to rent a hotel room). One of the good and bad things about the Destin area is that there aren't too many big hotels right on the beach. Most things are just a bit of a drive. If you are looking for a quiet, independently owned place right at water's edge, try **Sea Oats Motel** (3420 Old U.S. 98 E, Destin, 850/837-6655, $111–133), which is a long, low-slung motel right on the sand, offering condo rentals as well.

If you're willing to hop in the car or on a bike, there's the **Beachside Inn** (2931 Scenic U.S. 98, Destin, 850/650-6300, $80–100) with brightly colored rooms in a modest-sized low-rise hotel. The **Best Western Summerplace Inn** (14047 Emerald Coast Pkwy., Destin, 850/650-8003, $107–139) is in the heart of Destin, a quick drive to public beach access. There's a decent complimentary continental breakfast, indoor and outdoor pools with a big Jacuzzi, and free high-speed Internet access. **Comfort Inn Destin** (19001 Emerald Coast Pkwy., Destin, 850/654-8611, $89–179) is new and pretty deluxe for a Comfort Inn, no offense. It's got 100 rooms, nicely appointed, and two pools (one indoors).

Over $150

If you want to stay in a tall condo right on the beach, there are some, many only renting by the week in high season. The **Pelican Beach Resort and Conference Center** (1002 U.S. 98 E, Destin, 888/735-4226, $150–206) is a big, imposing cube. **Hidden Dunes Beach and Tennis Resort** (9815 U.S. 98 W, Destin, 888/837-3521, $130–600) has several ways to go, from a unit in a 20-story tower at water's edge, to luxurious three- and four-bedroom villas overlooking the private Hidden Dunes' lake, to Carolina-style cottages with private screened porches, nestled in a wooded landscape. Farther east, into the Beaches of South Walton town of Seascape, the **Majestic Sun** (1160 Old U.S. 98, Destin, 850/837-8264, $153–221) was brand-new in 2001, with beautiful pools, tennis, and golf, all just across the street from the beach. **Sandpiper Cove** (775 Gulfshore Dr., Destin, 850/837-9121, $150–300) is pretty much a Destin landmark, with a 43-acre landscaped property that has its own 1,100 feet of beach. It's individually owned condo units, so look at the pictures before deciding what's right for you. The property has five swimming pools and three outdoor hot tubs.

FOOD

The restaurants of Destin, Fort Walton Beach, and Okaloosa Island focus, unsurprisingly, on fish, with lots of casual oyster bars and fish shacks per capita. There are fancier spots around, too, but the best places are the vaguely Southern-inflected casual seafood joints.

Breakfast

Start your day, and your visit, at the **Donut Hole** (635 U.S. 98 E, Destin, 850/837-8824, open 24 hours, $4–8). It's breakfast all day, with sturdy baked goods and nice people. (Ivan tore the roof off the place, but it's opening back up in spring 2005.)

Casual

The ⓜ **Back Porch** (1740 Old U.S. 98 E, Destin, 850/837-2022, 11 A.M.–10 P.M. Sun.–Thurs., until 11 P.M. Fri. and Sat., $11–23) is a fun cedar-shingled seafood shack, an ideal place to try your first chargrilled amberjack (not always the most gastronomically accessible sportfish). The view is great—you won't mind waiting because you can hang out right on the beach while they ready a table. Also, it's a notable surf spot, so you can watch surfers paddling out hopefully to the break.

The tiki-topped **AJ's Seafood and Oyster Bar** (a quarter mile east of the Destin Bridge, Destin, 850/837-1913, 11 A.M.–midnight daily, until 9:30 P.M. in the off season, $9–21, no reservations) is another longtime beachside visitor favorite. Overlooking Destin Harbor, AJ's Club Bimini is the place to see the sunset over a plate of "Oysters AJ" (oysters baked with jalapenos, Monterey jack, and bacon). AJ's charter fleet offers daily trips into shallow or deep waters to hunt for grouper, amberjack, and wahoo—the kitchen will cook your catch straight off the line. Try the fried fish sandwiches or the shrimp po boy. Another locals' fave is **Lucky Snapper** (76 E. U.S. 98, Harborwalk Marina, Destin, 850/654-0900, 11 A.M.–10 P.M. daily, $10–20). Easy, fun seafood, a kids' menu, and you can watch the Destin fleet unload the catch of the day right outside. There's also live music.

Don't like fish? Even though it sounds vaguely pornographic, **Fudpucker's Beachside Bar & Grill** (20001 Emerald Coast Pkwy., Destin, 850/654-4200, and Okaloosa Island, Fort Walton Beach, 850/243-3833, 10:30 A.M.–10 P.M. weekdays, late night menu on weekends until 2 A.M., $8–20) is the place for burgers, drinks on the deck, and some of the best bands on the beach.

In Fort Walton Beach, **The Crab Trap** (1450 Miracle Strip Pkwy., Okaloosa Island Boardwalk, Fort Walton Beach, 850/301-0959, 11 A.M.–10 P.M. daily, $7–25), nestled in the beautiful James Lee County Park and overlooking the water, graciously accommodates the sand between your toes and your unmistakable whiff of suntan oil. Grouper, tuna, and amberjack are the freshest catches, with lots of fried seafood and all-you-can-eat snow-crab legs (they're not from around here, though). It's casual, but not as casual as the nearby **Angler's Beachside Grill and Sports Bar** (1030 Miracle Strip Pkwy., Okaloosa Island, Fort Walton Beach, 850/796-0260, 11 A.M.–midnight Mon.–Thurs., until 1 A.M. Fri. and Sat., Sun. brunch 10 A.M.–2 P.M., $7–16). You can eat right on the boardwalk or inside with the game of the moment on the big TVs.

Fine Dining

No question, the best food in the area is to be had at the hands of Chef Tim Creehan at the ⓜ **Beach Walk Café** (1st Fl., The Inn at Crystal Beach, 2996 U.S. 98 E, Destin, 850/650-7100, www.BeachWalkCafe.com, 11 A.M.–2:30 P.M. and 5:30–10 P.M. Sun.–Fri., 4:30–10 P.M. Sat., Sun. brunch, $26–54). He has won nearly all the awards and plaudits that are possible to win (DiRoNA Award, *Wine Spectator* award, high praise from *Bon Appetit*), and no wonder. The guiding culinary aesthetic is all about luxury, without ever getting heavy and ponderously Continental. There is seared Hudson Valley foie gras with roasted peaches and a plum wine reduction; jumbo sea scallops, delicately fried and paired with grilled orange; and tempura-fried softshell crab with sticky rice, stir-fried napa cabbage, and a tangy pineapple gastrique. It's a splurge restaurant, but this kind of art requires the blank canvas that only big cash can provide.

Louisiana Lagniappe (775 Gulf Shore Dr., Holiday Isle, Destin, 850/837-0881, no reservations, 11 A.M.–9:30 P.M. daily Mar.–Oct., $15–26) overlooks Old Pass Lagoon and is a locally beloved bastion of upscale Louisiana-style seafood, like pannéed fillet of grouper topped with lobster medallions and napped with garlic beurre blanc. It also traffics in live Maine lobsters and has a lovely outdoor deck.

Marina Cafe (Destin Yacht Club, 850/837-7960, 5–10 P.M. nightly, $17–28) is another special-occasion destination. It's owned by Harbor Restaurant Group, which also owns Destin Chops (a good steak and chop house not far away) and Tratorria Borago in Grayton Beach. There's an outdoor dining deck overlooking the Destin Harbor, but inside seating is just as gorgeous, with a jeweled mosaic archway and lovely dining room lighting and appointments. The menu is all over the map, with Cajun/Creole dishes, a sushi bar, and Latin-inspired dishes like citrus/adobo-rubbed yellowfin tuna with black bean lime sauce, saffron basmati rice, pickled onions, and charred tomato salsa.

Nightlife

Destin and Fort Walton Beach can get lively, then it's quiet again to the east in the Beaches of South Walton area, then farther east in Panama City Beach it gets hopping again. Here, head dockside to **AJ's Club Bimini** (on the Destin Harbor, a quarter mile east of the Destin Bridge, 850/837-1913, 11 A.M.–4 A.M. nightly) for a Bimini Bash, a powerful concoction of cranberry, orange, and pineapple juices with a five-rum roundhouse punch. Then try out one of the theme nights at the sprawling **Nightown** (140 Palmetto St., 850/837-6448) and groove to DJ Boom or DJ Kruzh (I have to think about what my DJ name would be—clearly it has to be one syllable and kind of onomatopoetic). Or there's **Nico's** (757 U.S. 98 E, Destin, 850/650-5253,

until 4 A.M. daily), in front of the Destin Cinemas and featuring happy hour twice daily, the second time between midnight and 2 A.M. (could that *possibly* be a good idea?). Get crazy on the dance floor at **Harry T's** (320 U.S. 98 E, Destin, 850/654-4800). Opened by a big top trapeze artist, Harry T's is adorned with a peculiar assortment of circus-obilia, including a stuffed giraffe, and treasures from the sunken luxury liner *Thracia*. It's a hoot, with Wednesday's ladies night the best night to stop in. Then warm up with a few scales, because crowd participation is required at the dueling piano bar of **Howl at the Moon** (The Boardwalk, Okaloosa Island, 850/301-0111).

SHOPPING

Silver Sands Factory Stores (10562 Emerald Coast Pkwy. W, on U.S. 98, eight miles east of Destin, near Sandestin Golf & Beach Resort Destin, 850/654-9771, www.silversandsoutlet.com, 10 A.M.–9 P.M. Mon.–Sat., 10 A.M.–6 P.M. Sun.) is supposedly the nation's largest designer outlet center. And they keep growing, adding a new Off Saks Fifth Avenue and Ann Taylor to its fashion court area (which already is crowded with Polo Ralph Lauren, Dooney & Bourke, Tommy Hilfiger, Ellen Tracy, Adrienne Vittadini, Banana Republic, Liz Claiborne, etc.). If shoes are your thing, it's deadly: Nine West Outlet, Famous Footwear, Liz Claiborne Shoes, Kenneth Cole, and Cole-Haan. There are more than 100 designer outlet stores within 450,000 square feet of retail space, drawing something like six million shoppers annually.

Beaches of South Walton

The Beaches of South Walton are fairly new. Obviously, the long expanses of white-sand beach have been here all along, but it's in the past 20 years that developers have set their sights on this area. Residents have kept a tight handle on growth—not out of a fear of change as much as a clear vision of how they'd like these communities to meld and enhance their natural settings. Some of it you may find contrived, like Disney for adults, but the idea of "New Urbanism" has really taken hold with the creation and restoration of compact, walkable, mixed-use towns. Visitors have most of what they need within walking distance of where they're staying, and the Gulf of Mexico and Choctawhatchee Bay are soothing backdrops for a deeply restful vacation.

Some of these 13 communities actually developed organically, while others were master-minded by architects and savvy developers. From west to east:

Seascape is the closest to Destin, with lakefront and golf villas in a luxurious setting. **Miramar Beach** begins at the Gulf along Scenic Gulf Drive and then curves around to join Emerald Coast Parkway. It's mostly condos and private homes, and is very close to the Silver Sands Factory Stores. Next up, **Sandestin,** probably the most famous of these little communities, nearly overrun with enormous luxury golf/beach resorts, but all very tasteful. The new **Village of Baytowne Wharf** is here, very lovely, in the style of a rustic Southern fishing village, only cuter.

Dune Allen Beach is a quaint and quiet beach community two miles long with mostly classic wood-sided beach houses, homes on a lake, and smaller-sized condo developments. This is where the area's eight-foot-wide, off-road bike path begins, winding all the way to Inlet Beach. Fairly developed, **Santa Rosa Beach** has a number of shops and commercial bits, with some golf and beachside amenities. There's a newish outdoor mall here with boutiques, bike rentals, medical offices, antiques stores, a seafood market, and a big handful of restaurants. Then there's **Blue Mountain Beach,** the highest point along the Gulf of Mexico, with wonderful views and beautiful sand. It seems to be attractive as an artists' retreat.

Grayton Beach is the oldest town between Pensacola and Apalachicola. Settled in the early 1900s, it is a tree-lined beach community of old cypress cottages and small narrow streets. There is a preponderance of home interior stores and a great bar called the Red Bar, also many fine restaurants.

With Seaside to its east fully built out, builders turned not long ago to neighboring **WaterColor,** which is primarily a residential community. Many of the new stylized Cracker-style buildings are available for rent, and the town has a fun hostelry, the 60-room WaterColor Inn.

The next town over is **Seaside** an upscale, planned beach community of pastel Victorian-Post Modern homes and cottages organized

Each of the 13 communities along the Beaches of South Walton has its own personality and easy, family-friendly feel.

COURTESY OF VISIT FLORIDA

The Emerald Coast

around a town square with an outdoor amphitheater, galleries, restaurants, and boutiques. You either love it, using words like "charming" and "picturesque," or you hate it and sling around words like "contrived" and grumble about it looking like a stage set (which, I suppose, it technically was, as the shooting location for *The Truman Show*).

Seagrove Beach is next door to the newer and more fancy Seaside. This peaceful beach town is tucked between the coast's natural sand dunes and pine trees. Visitors can choose from rambling beach houses, cottages, or condos. Then there's **Seacrest Beach,** a new beach community made up of cottages and condominiums hidden behind natural dunes.

One of my more favorite communities, very new, is **Rosemary Beach.** Like Seaside, it's completely planned in a very narrow architectural idiom, but this time it's all natural earth tones in Caribbean-inspired homes connected to the shore by boardwalks and footpaths. It's kind of all loosely Dutch and West Indies style, including the town square and the "eternity pool."

And finally, **Inlet Beach** is just west of Panama City Beach (over the bridge) and next to Rosemary Beach. Named for the large lagoon on its eastern shore, Phillips Inlet, the peaceful community is known for its secluded natural areas and minimal development.

Ⓝ SEASIDE

Remember the improbably perfect town in the Jim Carrey vehicle *The Truman Show*? Each flawless waterfront cottage in synch with its neighbors, the common green space meticulous, the downtown some utopian experiment in mutual respect and civic conviviality? It's a real place, not a back lot in Hollywood.

It used to be that Americans retreated during the summers to simple beachside cottages for months at a time. Every day, after you got your sunburned hide up off the porch, you biked or walked into the little town center to take in a movie or get the local gossip and an ice cream. In 1946, J. S. Smolian bought 80 acres near Seagrove Beach on Florida's Panhandle with this vi-

sion floating in his mind—a utopian summer camp for his employees. His grandson, Robert Davis, was smitten by the same vision, growing up to become a fancy developer in Miami in the 1970s. Still, the sweet multigenerational seaside summer village eluded him. He infected Miami architects Andres Duany and Elizabeth Plater-Zyberk with his gentle dream, and they built in their minds a fantasy town based on the northwest Florida architectural idiom of wood-frame cottages with peaked roofs, deep overhangs, big windows for cross-ventilation. They traveled through Florida with sketchpads and eyes wide open: broad straw hats on sun-lazy vacationers, white picket fences, screened porches, and shiny metal soup pots steaming with fresh crab and just-harvested clams.

Then they made it real in the early 1980s. They built a small town nestled against an idyllic curve along the Gulf Coast shoreline, against a wide swath of beach and mild emerald waters. There are 200 or so homes now, in a paradigm called "New Urbanism" situated around a town square with an amphitheater, restaurants, elegant boutiques, a repertory theater, and the beach off at the edge of it all. There's a much-lauded charter school (paid for with location fees for *The Truman Show*), a chapel, a medical arts building. It's a living laboratory, an experiment in harmonious beachside community life. If you still aren't visualizing this place, pick up a copy of Andres Duany, Elizabeth Plater-Zyberk, and Jeff Speck's great book entitled *Suburban Nation: The Rise of Sprawl and the Decline of the American Dream.*

The kicker is that you can go to Seaside and visit. If you vacation here, you pull your car in, turn off the ignition, and that's the last you need of it for the duration. Everything is walking distance in what *Time* called "the most astounding design achievement of its era." Panama City is 40 miles to the east, Destin is 20 miles to the west—but Seaside seems miles and miles from anywhere.

Sports and Recreation
Seaside Swim & Tennis Club (850/231-2214) is at the center of lots of the town's activities. It offers private tennis lessons and clinics for kids

ArtQuest is South Walton's annual week-long celebration at the beginning of May, sponsored by the Cultural Arts Association.

and adults, shuffleboard and horseshoes (the rubber kind), bike rentals (including trikes), and three beautiful croquet courts. There are three pools—the West Side Pool is the largest, with an adult pool at the north end of Seaside Avenue and a family pool at the northeast corner of Seaside. **Camp Seaside** is a special program for kids 5–12, with half-day or full-day crafts, sports, swimming, etc. It also offers a kids' night out with dinner and a movie, and regularly scheduled free story time in the amphitheater.

Beyond that, Seaside has nearby golf, a long biking/walking path, deep-sea fishing, hiking, kayaking, and swimming in the Gulf to keep people occupied.

Accommodations

To rent a cottage at Seaside, you need only to call 888/732-7433. The tricky part comes in figuring out what you want—people have built their dream homes in Seaside, and the prices and level of formality and sophistication are all over the map. The website (www.lfoa.com/seaside) gives a list of accommodations with photos, virtual tours, descriptions of amenities, reserved dates, and prices. If you don't want to rent a whole place, **Josephine's French Country Inn** (P.O. Box 4767, Seaside, 850/231-1940, $200–240) offers nine elegantly furnished rooms and suites with private baths in a Georgian plantation–style house.

Food

Seaside's restaurants work as a team to satisfy most of your needs and gastronomic idiosyncrasies. There is a large handful of restaurants within the village, with **Bud & Alley's** (2236 E. Hwy. 30A, 850/231-5900) the most upscale, purveyor of Mediterranean-Coastal South cuisine. **Fermentations Wine Bar & Café** (25 Central Square, 850/231-0167) is a more casual place for a glass of wine and a few shared tapas; **Cafe Spiazzia** (2236 Hwy. 30A, 850/231-1297) gives you accessible Italian; **Hurricane Oyster Bar** (2236 Hwy. 30A, 850/534-0376) covers the casual seafood niche, and there are a few others for family dining or romantic assignations.

Shopping

Ruskin Place, named after John Ruskin, the famous supporter of 19th-century Victorian art, is the town's center for galleries, with a fine coffee shop and a few other diversions. There are plenty of boutiques worth a bit of exploration in Seaside, but definitely check out the elegant vessels, chandeliers, sinks, and other Dale Chihuly-like blown-glass art of **Suzanne Guttman Glass** (63 Central Square, 850/231-5405, www.SuzanneGuttmanGlass.com).

SPORTS AND RECREATION

Beaches

Of the numerous beaches along the stretch, many have public beach access, with additional beach accesses located within the 13 beach communities if you're staying there. From west to east, most with access right along scenic Highway 30A, the beaches are: Miramar Beach, Legion Park, Cessna Park (on the Choctawhatchee Bay side), Dune Allen Beach, Ed Walline, Gulfview Heights, Blue Mountain Beach, Grayton Dunes, Van Ness Butler Jr., Santa Clara, Inlet Beach, and Pier and

Boat Ramp 331 (bay side). Which is the nicest is hard to say; most are sparsely populated, many have no-fee small parking lots, and several have restrooms and showers. My favorite is probably Santa Clara, with a pretty stretch of sand and picnic facilities, but the windswept dunes of Grayton Dunes make a mighty nice afternoon of exploration, too.

Nature

There's a surfeit of outdoor activities, so bring your most comfortable hiking shoes. At the top of the heap is **Grayton Beach State Park** (357 Main Park Rd., south of U.S. 98 halfway between Panama City Beach, near the intersection of Hwy. 30A and County Rd. 283, 850/231-4210, 8 A.M.–sundown daily, $4/vehicle, $1/pedestrian or biker, $19 camping, $110 cabin rental), with sugar-white sand, emerald-green water, little development, and huge sea oat-covered sand dunes. Foot traffic is prohibited in the dunes and in bird nesting areas. Despite its natural setting, there are great restaurants and accommodations in nearby Grayton Beach or Seaside. Camping is popular, with 37 campsites

In the last five years, the South Walton Tourist Development Council has spent nearly $12 million developing and maintaining 33 public beach accesses.

The Emerald Coast

EGLIN AIR FORCE BASE

Eglin Air Force Reservation in Fort Walton Beach is the largest air force base in the free world. It's the size of Rhode Island, covering 724 square miles of reservation and 97,963 square miles of water in the Gulf of Mexico. Eglin employs approximately 10,000 military and approximately 10,000 civilians.

Unless you're in the military, much of it is off limits to you. For instance, Eglin has two 18-hole championship golf courses (850/882-2949) open year-round. The Eglin Golf Course, host of a 2000 U.S. Open qualifier, has a hill on the seventh hole so steep that the course provides a towrope to golfers. Here's an ironic tidbit: Al Capone funded the layout of this course originally. In fact, Capone's private beach hideout/manse is now the officers' club at Eglin.

Much of Eglin you wouldn't want to have access to if you could: Recently the Mother of all Bombs (MOAB), the most powerful nonnuclear bomb ever created, was tested at Eglin. And for years Eglin Air Force Base has been testing depleted uranium, with an estimated 220,000 pounds of DU penetrators expended there since 1973. In light of the mysterious illnesses befalling soldiers working with DU in Iraq, I wouldn't want to be waltzing around the Eglin testing range.

But I digress. The Air Force Armament Museum (see *Sights*) is definitely a wonderful public part of Eglin, but it is just one of many opportunities for the visitor. The reservation covers 464,000 acres in Santa Rosa, Okaloosa, and Walton Counties. If you go to the **Jackson Guard** office (107 Hwy. 85 N, Niceville, 850/882-4164) you can get an outdoor recreation permit, a comprehensive map, and a list of regulations. This allows you to avail yourself of the area's many activities—hunting, fishing, primitive camping, canoeing, and hiking part of the **Florida National Scenic Trail** (www.florida-trail.org).

Hunting (which accounts for 4,200 of the 12,000 recreation permits granted annually) is for deer, turkey, wild hogs, and small game, seasonally. There's a huge managed quail area, another for "planted" doves, and two duck management units totaling 78,000 acres. There's even an annual hunt open to the mobility-impaired. Fishing in the reservation is on any of 17 stocked ponds (two of them handicapped accessible).

Birders will enjoy the old-growth longleaf pine swath of Eglin reservation that is a designated part of the **Great Florida Birding Trail** (www.floridabirdingtrail.com). You may see the endangered Okaloosa darter, found in only six creek systems in the central portion of the air force base. It's also the fourth-largest red-cockaded woodpecker population in the country. The area is home to more than 93 rare or listed plant and animal species.

Within the reservation there are seven miles of barrier island for swimming and canoeing, with lots of other creeks; **kayakers** enjoy open-water kayaking in the Choctawhatchee Bay, Santa Rosa Sound, or the Gulf.

The **Anderson Pond Recreation Area** (off Hwy. 85, three miles north of Niceville) is open to the public year-round, with an elevated boardwalk, a picnic shelter, a pier, and camping area. All the facilities are handicapped accessible.

The Emerald Coast

and 30 cabins. Make reservations early. Due to the number of endangered plants and animals found within the park (like the rare Choctawhatchee beach mouse), pets are not allowed. If you visit in the fall, you may catch the thousands of monarch butterflies resting beachside during their southward migration to Mexico.

Identified as the most pristine piece of coastal property in the state, **Topsail Hill State Preserve** (7525 W. Hwy. 30A, in Santa Rosa Beach 10 miles east of Destin, 850/267-0299, 8 A.M.–sundown daily, honor $2/vehicle, $1 pedestrian or bicyclist, $38 camping, $575/week for the bungalow) owes its existence to turpentine. More than a century ago workers turpentined old-growth longleaf pine trees here for caulking the seams of wooden ships, a key mode of transport. Today, it's 1,600 acres of stunning Gulf-front pine forest, nature trails over mountainous sand dunes, and two freshwater dune lakes. It is one of only two remaining natural populations of the nocturnal, endangered Choctawhatchee beach mice. The park features a 140-acre RV resort as well as tent camping and bungalows.

In the southernmost portion of Walton County, the 15,000-acre **Point Washington State Forest** (5865 E. U.S. 98, Santa Rosa Beach, 850/231-5800, 8 A.M.–sundown daily, $1/person, $10 reserved picnic space, $5–13 camping) is home to more than 19 miles of trails and boasts 10 different habitats with rare plant and wildlife species, from gopher tortoises to red-cockaded woodpeckers. For an easy day hike, the Eastern Lake Trail System was the first trail established in this forest. It consists of three double-track loop trails. The hiker or bicyclist can travel the 3.5-, 5-, or 10-mile loops. Access to the trail system is at the parking lot and trailhead on County Road 395.

Nearby, and worth a stop off to see, **Eden State Gardens** (off U.S. 98 on County Rd. 395, just north of Seagrove Beach, 850/231-4214, 8 A.M.–sundown daily, honor $3/vehicle, guided tour $3 adults, $1 children), in historic Point Washington on the shore of Tucker Bayou, is a beautiful 1895 Greek revival estate surrounded by resplendent gardens of azaleas, camellias, and gargantuan, gnarled, moss-draped live oak. This 12-acre sprawling park was once the home of lumber baron William Henry Wesley and his family. Find yourself a picnic spot on the wide, manicured lawn.

Just east of Seagrove Beach, **Deer Lake State Park** (357 Main Park Rd., off Hwy. 30A, Santa Rosa Beach, 850/231-0337, 8 A.M.–sundown daily, no fee) is the newest park in these parts. It has a fine beach with a new dune walkover/boardwalk, from which there are great views of this dynamic dune ecosystem. North of here are acres of rough hiking trails.

If you're interested in enjoying all this nature within the context of an eco-tour or guided adventure, there are plenty of guides in the area. **Wetland Wilderness Adventures** (537 Wicker Ave., Santa Rosa Beach, 850/534-0107) offers Choctawhatchee and Intracoastal interpretive tours, fishing, and floundering trips. **Choctawhatchee Delta Tours** (710 Black Creek Rd., Freeport, 850/585-0445) also offers tours of

this area, departing from the 331 Bridge. **Island Winds Sailing** (801 Kell-Aire Dr., Destin, 850/259-8982) has catamarans for sailing, offering eco-tours, lessons, sunset/moonlight cruises, and sand dollar excursions. And **Big Daddy's Bike and Beach** (2217 Hwy. 30A, Santa Rosa Beach, 850/622-1165) offers eco-bike tours along Highway 30A and through state forest area.

Biking Along Scenic Route 30A

A cyclist's bonanza, with a 19-mile paved path along Scenic 30A alone, winding among the area's coastal dune lakes and villages and better suited to road or touring bikes. For the mountain biker, there is also a 10-mile loop in the Point Washington State Forest called the **Eastern Lake Bike/Hike Trail**, which winds through natural vegetation and wildlife habitat. They've recently added a stretch of trail to Seagrove. Or go in the opposite direction for a scenic ride from Seaside to Blue Mountain Beach.

Depending on where you're staying, there are several convenient bike rental shops. From west to east: **Island Sports Shop** (Santa Rosa Beach, 850/622-2032, $25–35/week), **Seaside Bike Shop** (87 Central Square, Seaside, 850/231-2314, $15/day, $60/week), **Butterfly Bike & Beach Rentals** (3657 E. Hwy. 30A, Seagrove Beach, 850/231-2826), and **Bamboo Beach & Bicycle Company** (Rosemary Beach, 850/231-0770, $15/day, $55/week, children's bikes less).

Fishing

Baytowne Marina at Sandestin is a good place to start. **Baytowne Bait and Tackle Store** (850/267-7777) provides basic boating necessities, and it's a good place to hook up with a fishing guide. If you'd like to fish along the Choctawhatchee Bay and the four rivers running into it, try **Fishing with Bob** (850/231-2441). Trips start at Eden State Gardens on Tucker Bayou at the end of County Road 395. For deep-sea sportfishing or fly fishing on the bay, **Lucky Star Charters** (850/650-1036) in Sandestin has a good reputation for custom trips in the Gulf and Choctawhatchee Bay, as well as overnight tuna and billfishing expeditions. And

Yellow Fin Ocean Sports (850/231-1717) in Grayton will take you fishing for redfish or trout in coastal bays or head out into the Gulf for grouper, snapper, dolphin, or marlin.

ACCOMMODATIONS

Under $50

The way to slide in under $50 is by camping around here—it's warm much of the year, with nice evening breezes, lots of beach, plenty of fresh air, and not so rural that you can't scrap the whole Grizzly Adams plan and go out to dinner. In Sandestin, you can camp on the Gulf at **Camping on the Gulf** (10005 W. Emerald Coast Pkwy., Destin, 850/837-6334, $40–91), with an activity center, fishing, cable TV, and full hookups. Then in Miramar Beach, the **Ciboney RV Resort** (2078 Scenic Gulf Dr., 850/654-2882) is one block from the beach. **Destin RV Beach Resort** (362 Miramar Beach Dr., Destin, 850/837-3529) is a "luxury RV resort," right across from the beach, with a swimming pool and a free deep-sea fishing trip for a paid stay. You can also camp at **Grayton Beach State Park,** at **Topsail Hill State Park Preserve** (at Topsail Hill RV Resort), and on **Santa Rosa Beach** (at Willows Campground).

$50–150

The **Hilton Sandestin Beach Golf Resort & Spa** (4000 Sandestin Blvd. S, Destin, 850/267-9500, www.sandestinbeachhilton.com, $109–209) recently completed a major renovation project and spa expansion. The hotel's newly named Emerald Tower features the addition of granite countertops in bathrooms and tasteful new interior design elements. The pool deck has been redone, as has the lobby. In all, it's a gorgeous golf-and-spa resort of 600 rooms, the largest beachfront resort hotel in the northwest Florida region. There are 190 executive rooms, 22 parlor suites, two presidential suites, and 385 junior suites (many with a bunk bed area for kids). The hotel has an award-winning program for kids, with accessible on-site dining at Sandcastles Restaurant & Lounge (there's a fancier restaurant called Seagar's Prime Steaks & Seafood).

The Sandestin is the grand dame of accommodations along the Emerald Coast.

COURTESY OF THE BEACHES OF SOUTH WALTON, WALTON COUNTY TDC

Over $150

So many of the nicer accommodations around here are private homes or condos. There are numerous property management companies—try **Coastal Properties** (866/232-6278, www.coastal-properties.ws) or **Emerald Sun Properties** (800/403-5271, www.emeraldsun.com) to begin your search.

Then there's the **Sandestin Golf & Beach Resort** (9300 Emerald Coast Pkwy. W, Sandestin, 850/267-8150, $166–420), really the premier resort in this area, set on 2,400 beach- and bay-front acres. There are four championship golf courses, 15 world-class tennis courts, a full-service marina, water sports, charter sailing and fishing, fine and casual dining, a fancy fitness center, a professional salon and day spa, and fun children's programs. It's got 1,350 different rooms and accommodations, with a range of options— it's kind of like a little city unto itself, with leisure as the town's central preoccupation.

Rosemary Beach (on Hwy. 30A, in between Seacrest and Inlet Beach, 850/278-2100, www.rosemarybeach.com, roughly $150–400) is something else entirely, with one- to five-bedroom Gulf-front and midtown cottages for vacation rentals. All designed in a loose Caribbean style,

The Emerald Coast

there are family cottages, carriage houses, flats, and contemporary lofts, all connected to the shore by boardwalks and footpaths. It's a good location for families, because it's close to the hubbub of Panama City Beach but still out of the fray.

In a similar vein, the **Village of Baytowne Wharf** (9300 Emerald Coast Pkwy. W, Sandestin, 850/267-8100, $166–600) is a sweeping pedestrian village of recent advent, right on the beach. There are different choices on where to stay: The **Grand Sandestin** is a 168-unit Southern plantation-style estate featuring a sweeping two-story veranda with views of the bay and lush formal gardens. Then there's the **Lasata** private area within the village, **Le Jardin** gated townhome community, the **Market Street Inn** located centrally in the village along Tupelo Courtyard, and units in **Observation Point** and **Pilot House.**

FOOD

Each of the little communities of South Walton has its own cluster of restaurants, in a range of price points and culinary traditions. The ones worth going out of your way for include **Criolla's** (170 E. Hwy. 30A, Grayton Beach, 850/267-1267, 5:30–9:30 P.M. Mon.–Sat. Mar.–Oct., closed Mon. Nov.–Feb., $26–35), where executive chef and owner Johnny Earles sends out something called "contemporary Creole-Caribbean," which translates as sautéed Creole-spiced redfish fillet served with a velvety oyster charlotte, finished with tomato cream and a side of rock shrimp cole slaw; or plantain-wrapped grouper with lobster polenta–stuffed poblano; or maybe Aunt Irma's banana and pecan beignets. It's pricey, but there's usually a three-course prix-fixe menu for about $44. **Ṇ Bud and Alley's Restaurant** (2236 E. Hwy. 30A, Seaside, 850/231-5900, 11:30 A.M.–3 P.M. and 5:30–9 P.M. daily, until 9:30 P.M. weekends, closed Tues. in off season, rooftop bar 11:30 A.M.– 2 A.M., $20–28) was opened in Seaside in 1986 and named after a dog and a cat. It's a casual and unpretentious place, but the menu is all understated sophistication, with a cooking style that nods to the coastal Mediterranean, Basque country, Tuscany, and the American Deep South. Oysters Seaside are baked Apalachicola beauties with shrimp, scallops, calamari, cilantro, garlic, and lime in a piquant mélange, and there are tempura-fried softshell crabs with rémoulade, or heads-on shrimp amped up with garlic and shallots. The wine list is also notable, and the bar is a suave spot for erudite conversation, or your best facsimile thereof.

Cafe Thirty-A (3899 E. Hwy. 30A, Seagrove, 850/231-2166, 6–10 P.M. nightly, $12–34) is more casual, with a far-reaching wine list, many offerings by the glass. The menu has broad appeal, with fancy stuff like confit of suckling pig with truffled mashed potatoes. I'm pretty content to just tuck into one of the wood-fired pizzas (the grilled chicken with goat cheese) paired with a glass of Rutz Cellars pinot noir. (I'll have you know, I was drinking and enthusing about pinot noir long before that nebbish in *Sideways* got all hot and bothered about the "heartbreak grape" on the big screen. Paul Giamatti should have been nominated for an Oscar and all, but he still did pinot drinkers everywhere a grave disservice.)

Hmm, next there's **Basmati's Asian Cuisine** (W. Hwy. 30A, Blue Mountain Beach, 850/267-3028, 5:30–9:30 nightly, $9–16) with a full sushi bar and accessible mostly Japanese-fusiony dishes served in a pretty dining room. Or **The Lake Place** (5960 Hwy. 30A, Dune Allen, 850/267-2871, 5:30–10 P.M. Mon.–Sat., $16–27) for prime rib and fancy seafood in a sweet little A-frame with two cozy dining rooms.

SHOPPING

Shopping is clustered in a handful of tasteful centers along the Beaches of South Walton. The **Market Shops at Sandestin** (9375 U.S. 98 W. at Sandestin Gold & Beach Resort, 850/267-8092) complex has 30 shops, split between kitchen widget boutiques, skin care, chocolates, housewares, etc. The **Shops at Grayton** (26 Logan Ln., Grayton Beach) are less fancy, but you'll find jewelry, clothing, and antiques. In Seaside you'll find **Ruskin Place Artist Colony** near the new Seaside Chapel and the rest of the 40 or so **Merchants of Seaside** (63 Central Sq., 850/231-5424) for cafés, galleries, clothing, books, and gifts.

Panama City Beach

Panama City Beach gets billed as the No. 1 spring break beach in the country, attracting more than 300,000 people per annually. I don't know if I'm buying that. What you don't realize after you've become an adult who doesn't road trip a thousand miles, sustained by 7-Eleven burritos, to a sunny stretch of beach each March, is that the hottest spring break places change. In the 1980s it was places like Palm Springs or Fort Lauderdale, for a while after that people seemed more focused on Cancún, Mazatlán, or Cabo San Lucas. Most recently, according to my sources and *Girls Gone Wild* videos, South Padre Island in Texas and Lake Havasu in Arizona are neck and neck for spring break mania.

Anyway, let's just say Panama City Beach attracts a huge crowd of rowdy young people, and, ergo, has attractions that rowdy young people are attracted to. The city even publishes a little booklet that's roughly *Spring Break for Dummies*. With the same green water and white-sand beaches of elsewhere on the Emerald Coast, the beaches are more action-oriented, with volleyball, Frisbee, skim boarding, Jet Skiing, parasailing, etc. Although the beach is wide and with a lengthy expanse of shallows, there are hundreds of natural and artificial reefs offshore—Panama City Beach ranks with Key Largo in providing some of the best diving in the country. The fishing is also fairly good, with mackerel, flounder, redfish, and other gamefish careening through the clear waters.

At the east end of the city, St. Andrews State Park is fabulous, one of the most popular outdoor recreation spots in Florida. It contains verdant woods, sea oat–fringed sand dunes, fresh- and saltwater marshes, a lagoon swimming area, fishing jetties, hiking trails, 2.5 miles of beach, and two campgrounds. From here, you can also take a pedestrian ferry to Shell Island, an undisturbed 700-acre barrier island just across from the mainland for sunning, shelling, birding, or watching the sunset.

Outside of the beaches, the area is known for its goofy, oh-so-American attractions like mini golf, water slide parks, go-cart tracks, and a marine park. The Miracle Strip, which lent Panama City Beach its name as a nickname, was a beloved amusement park—one of the area's biggest draws—but it closed in 2004.

So, we know it's packed in March and April, and tourists from Georgia and Alabama flock to PCB during the summer. But it's in the early fall or during May, between the hordes, when Panama City Beach makes for an entertaining beachside playground, with loads of modestly priced accommodations. It's at these times that you can understand why the area has been a popular beach vacation spot for more than 40 years.

SPORTS AND RECREATION
Diving and Snorkeling
Panama City Beach was dubbed the "Wreck Capital of the South" by *Skin Diver* magazine. If you're now worried about side air bags and other passive restraint systems, rest assured, I mean

COURTESY OF VISIT FLORIDA

Recent dredge and fill projects in Panama City have resulted in new expanses of clean, fine sand.

The Emerald Coast

shipwrecks. As such, this part of the warm Gulf of Mexico is an excellent home and breeding ground for all types of sea life. You'll see sea turtles, manta rays, puffer fish, sand dollars, blue marlin, horseshoe crabs, small coral, colorful sponges, and lots of other marine life.

Of the "natural" wrecks in this area, you can investigate a 441-foot **World War II liberty ship,** a 220-foot tug called *The Chippewa,* a 160-foot coastal freighter called the **S.S.** *Tarpon,* the 100-foot tug *Chickasaw,* another tug called *The Grey Ghost,* and the Gulf's most famous wreck, the 465-foot *Empire Mica.* A bunch of other artificial reef projects have sunk bridge spans, barges, and the City of Atlantis (a different one). Many of these dive sites are of depths of 80–100 feet and are just a few miles offshore, and the best time for diving is April–September.

Experts say that the top five dives are the **USS** *Strength,* a naval mine sweeper; the *Blackbart,* a supply vessel; another supply vessel called the *B.J. Putnam;* the *Accokeek,* a 295-foot navy tug boat; and a huge aluminum **hovercraft** in 100 feet of water. If you want to rent diving equipment, **Hydrospace Dive Shop** (Hathaway Marina, 6422 W. U.S. 98, 850/234-3063), **Diver's Den** (3120 Thomas Dr., 850/234-8717), **Panama City Dive Center** (4823 Thomas Dr., 850/235-3390), and the **Scuba Shack** (7510 Thomas Dr., Ste. L, 850/249-7946) will help you out.

Snorkelers will have a better time around the **St. Andrews Jetties,** an area with no boat traffic. Nineteen feet under the surface here is an old tar barge ideal for underwater exploration. If you want to snorkel with a guide, **Island Time** (Treasure Island Marina, 3605 Thomas Dr., 850/234-7377) offers 3.5-hour catamaran excursions, wetsuits available, and **Capt. Ashley Gorman Shell Island Cruises** (5701 U.S. 98, east end of Hathaway Bridge, 850/785-4878) does swim and snorkeling tours for the whole family.

St. Andrews State Recreation Area

As I said before, St. Andrews State Recreation Area (4607 State Park Ln., Panama City, 850/233-5140, 8 A.M.–sundown daily, $5/vehicle, $1/pedestrians or cyclists, $24 camping) is a doozie of a state park, with rolling, white-sand dunes separated by low swales of either pinewoods or marshes. There are 2.5 miles of beach, with two different parking lots with access. You can rent bicycles during the summer at the park and explore the trails, there's a double-sided concrete boat launch for water crafts (if you're boat-poor, you can take a boat tour out to Shell Island in the spring and summer, tickets at the park concession), and they rent canoes at the boat ramp (paddle around Grand Lagoon or across the boat channel to Shell Island). If you want to fish, there are two fishing piers and jetties, from which you're likely to catch Spanish mackerel, redfish, flounder, sea trout, bonito, cobia, dolphin, and bluefish. The concession stores in the park sell bait and fishing licenses, among with other beachside necessities. For hikers, there's Heron Pond Trail (starting at a reconstructed Cracker turpentine still) and Gator Lake Trail (yep, you'll see gators), both easy and well marked. And if it's all too fabulous to leave, there are 176 campsites in the park or on the barrier Shell Island.

Go fishing at Panama City Beach: One day cast for redfish in St. Andrews Bay and the next go out into the Gulf and try for huge marlin.

Other Nature Areas

All the other parks around here get overshadowed by St. Andrews, which is a shame. **Pine Log State Forest** (5583-A Longleaf Rd., Ebro, 850/535-2888) is a favorite locals' spot for picnicking, hiking, off-road bicycling, horseback riding, fishing, and hunting. There are 23 miles of hiking trails winding through the forest. Nearby **Point Washington State Forest** (5865 U.S. 98 E, Santa Rosa Beach, 850/231-5800) is less developed but has 19 miles of trails for mountain biking, birding, and hunting.

SIGHTS

The biggest local thrills around here were the coasters and big rides at the historic **Miracle Strip Amusement Park,** which closed in September 2004. Let us observe a moment of silence.

Now, the second-best family attraction is to be had at **Gulf World** (15412 Front Beach Rd., Panama City Beach, 850/234-5271, opens 9 A.M. daily, last ticket sold at 2 P.M., $20.44 adults, $14.40 children 5–11, 4 and under free), which got pumped up seriously in 2000, with a $6.5 million expansion that netted it a state-of-the-art dolphin habitat, a new bird theater, and enclosed tropical gardens. It needed it. The marine mammal park opened in 1969 with animal shows and displays, but it also has a facility to rehabilitate stranded or injured marine animals from all over the Panhandle.

Coconut Creek Mini Golf and Gran Maze (9807 Front Beach Rd., Panama City Beach, 850/234-2625, www.coconutcreekfun.com, 9 A.M.–6 P.M. daily, $15 one price, $8.50 just for mini golf, $8.50 for gran maze—why there's no "d" on that is a mystery) has two mini golf courses in a kind of African safari/jungle motif. The maze is the better part, built in 1987 and completely rebuilt recently. It's a huge human-sized maze the size of a football field in which you will find disoriented children weeping at intervals. You will also find lots of military personnel using their professional navigational skills to find the four checkpoints (for some reason, they are Fiji, Tahiti, Samoa, and Bali) essential to successfully navigating the maze.

There's no shame in crawling under to get the heck out of here. Well, maybe a little shame.

Shipwreck Island Water Park (12201 Middle Beach Rd., Panama City Beach, 850/234-3333, www.shipwreckisland.com, 10:30 A.M.–5:30 P.M. daily during the summer, 50 inches and above $27, 35–49 inches $22, under 35 inches free, seniors $17) is the kind of water park with long slides and flumes, a wave pool, kiddie pools—in other words, what to do if the beach isn't holding kids' interest for another warm summer day. There is a 48-inch height restriction on two of the more exciting rides (the Rapid River Run and Tree Top Drop), and you're not allowed to bring food in from outside, or flotation devices, goggles, or masks. Little ones are required to wear those waterproof swim diapers.

ACCOMMODATIONS

Under $50

The **Sandpiper Beacon** (17403 Front Beach Rd., 850/234-2154, $39–100) is a comfortable family-friendly place with lots of on-site amenities for the price. It has 1,000 feet of beachfront, with parasailing, Wave Runners, and the "Big Banana Ride" right out the back door. There are three pools (one indoor), a lazy river ride, and twin turbo water slides, a game room, restaurant, children's playground, gift shop, and tiki bar. There are family units, with some suites sleeping up to 10 people.

Super 8 Panama City Beach (11004 Front Beach Rd., 850/747-4788, $29–80) is another no-frills but totally acceptable beachside home base. Clean rooms, very basic amenities, but get this: During March and April a deposit of $200 is required, and you have to wear *wristbands* to prove you're actually staying here and aren't just crashing the joint. Yeesh.

$50–150

Chateau Motel (12525 Front Beach Rd., 888/84-BEACH, $119–189) is a favorite among young people, with 150 Gulf-view rooms 500 feet from the sand. It's right at the center of all the "Miracle Strip" hullabaloo, with restaurants, attractions, shopping, and nightlife within walking

The Emerald Coast

distance. If you're under 25, they make you pay an extra $100 deposit until they inspect the room.

Days Inn Beach Hotel (12818 Front Beach Rd., 850/233-3333, $161–179) is hopping, with 188 Gulf-front rooms and suites with private balconies. Room decor is tropical and breezy, but you'll spend most of your time outside at the seven-story volcano mountain waterfall. It's in the huge pool situated between the Days Inn and Ramada Limited. It's a scene out there, with athletic young people sipping tropical drinks and flirting shamelessly in the whirlpool.

Over $150

Edgewater Beach Resort (11212 Front Beach Rd., 800/874-8686 $123–516) is worth the splurge, really Panama City Beach's premier resort, very family friendly. It had a recent $21 million restoration project, which brought new luster to the 110-acre property. It's a great location on the beach, right across the street from Cinema 10 Theaters, Rock-It Lanes, and Shoppes at Edgewater. On-site there are two restaurants, two bars, 11 heated outdoor pools, an executive 9-hole golf course, and the 27-hole Hombre Golf Club championship course just minutes away. The rooms themselves are spread throughout a vast property, from the Gulf Front Towers, to the Golf and Tennis Villas, to the Winward & Leeward Suites.

Another excellent place, a little bit removed from the fray, is the relatively new **Marriott's Legends Edge at Bay Point** (4000 Marriott Dr., 850/236-6000, $280–419). Each villa has a fully equipped kitchen, spacious living and dining areas, and well-appointed bedrooms. It's adjacent to the Marriott Bay Point Resort Village and situated in the midst of the Club Meadows and Lagoons Legends golf courses (designed by Bob Vonhagge and Bruce Devlin in 1985, and a notoriously challenging course). The Gulf of Mexico is 10 minutes away and the Grand Lagoon of St. Andrews Bay is within walking distance.

FOOD

You'll hear people speaking encouragingly about the progress of the restaurant scene in PCB. But it's more like the culinary Special Olympics.

Mostly you get competent fried seafood, wings, pizza, burgers. When they try to get all fancypants, it's unlikely and inane combos, garniture that has no bearing on the dish (with lots of non sequitur chopped herbs around plate rims or huge bushes of rosemary looming off the plate), and sauces I would have gotten slapped for in culinary school. The best bet is to keep it simple. For an honest cheeseburger, go to **Flamingo Joe's** (2304 Thomas Dr., Panama City Beach, 850/233-0600, 11 A.M.–10 P.M. daily, $8–21). It also has an addictive salsa, served warm. **Sharky's Seafood** (15201 Front Beach Rd., 850/235-2420, 11 A.M.–10 P.M. daily, $15–27) is a longstanding favorite for a good sunset, fine live entertainment in the world's largest tiki hut, and perfectly acceptable seafood-centric food (it's the kind of place where jalapeño poppers constitute a green vegetable, so we're not talking health food).

The Boat Yard (5325 N. Lagoon Dr., 850/249-9273, 11 A.M.–11 P.M. daily, later on the weekend if things are hopping, $10–26) has a similar open-air feel on the docks of Grand Lagoon, with gigantic margaritas, conch fritters with hot pepper jelly and wasabi mayo, or crispy fried lobster sandwiches, and a notable dessert invention of creamy key lime pie dipped in dark chocolate and frozen on a stick. **J' Michaels** (3901 Thomas Dr., 850/233-2055, 11:30 A.M.–9:30 P.M. daily, $8–15) is dockside of Grand Lagoon and is the place to go for comfort food like slow-burn red beans and rice.

You want to take it a little more upscale? **Angelo's Steak Pit** (9527 Front Beach Rd., 850/234-2913, 5–10 P.M. daily, $14–26) always gets the nod for fat steaks grilled over aromatic hickory. It's been here since 1958, which might explain their menu's word choice of "ladies top sirloin" (what could that mean? a female cow? a demure feminine portion?), and the resident "Big Gus" 20,000-pound steer is practically a local celebrity. It closes in the winter. **Captain Anderson's Restaurant** (5551 N. Lagoon Dr., 850/234-2225, 4:30–10 P.M. Mon.–Fri., open at 4 P.M. Sat., $11–35) is another serious locals' establishment, heavy on the seafood. It's a waterfront fave that's been here for years—go for the heads-on shrimp or the slightly more sophisticated Greek-style open-hearth whole fish presentations.

And then, for when you really want to do something zany, maybe with the kids, maybe just because, take your appetite to **The Treasure Ship** (3605 Thomas Dr., 850/234-8881, main dining room 4–10 P.M. daily, $15–28), a full-scale replica of Sir Francis Drake's Golden Hind, permanently docked. Now who said this trip wasn't going to be educational? You can eat seafood, book a charter fishing boat, or quietly mock the people in pirate costumes.

SHOPPING

There are little pockets of shops all over, mostly of the sunglasses-and-suntan lotion variety. You may need to stock up on bathing suits at **Beach Scene Superstore** (10059 Middle Beach Rd., 850/233-1662), which has something like 25,000 suits to try on (that sounds like my own personal ninth circle of hell). If you feel the need for more broad and fruitful browsing, the **Shoppes at Edgewater** (4412 Delwood Lane, Panama City Beach, 850/234-6112) complex has a number of nice boutiques. Also, the Edgewater Movie Theater and Rock-It Lanes Family Entertainment Center are adjacent to the shopping center. **Panama City Mall** (at the intersection of U.S. 231, Hwy. 77, and 23rd St., 850/785-9587) is a standard enclosed mall anchored by Dillard's, JCPenney, and Sears, with stores like American Eagle Outfitters, Victoria's Secret, Kirkland's, Bath & Body Works, The Gap, and Express.

Information and Services

AREA INFORMATION

The Emerald Coast area is in the central time zone. Its area code is 850.

Tourist Information

The Panama City *News Herald* is the daily around here, but its parent company, Florida Freedom Newspapers, also operates the *Northwest Florida Daily News, The Destin Log, The Walton Sun,* and www.emeraldcoast.com.

To get tourist information, there are several different locations, depending on where your home base is. For Destin and Fort Walton Beach information, visit the **Emerald Coast Convention and Visitors Bureau** (1540 E. U.S. 98, Fort Walton Beach, 850/651-7131, www.destin-fwb.com). There's also the **South Walton Tourist Development Center** (25771 U.S. 331 at U.S. 98, on Santa Rosa Beach, 850/267-3511, 8 A.M.–4:30 P.M. daily) and the **Destin Area Chamber of Commerce** (4484 Legendary Dr. at U.S. 98, 850/837-6241, 9 A.M.–5 P.M. Mon.–Fri.).

For more information about the Beaches of South Walton, write or call for information about the area (Beaches of South Walton, P.O. Box 1248, Santa Rosa Beach, FL 32459, 800/822-6877) or visit the heartbreakingly beautiful website www.beachesofsouthwalton.com.

In Panama City Beach, visit the **Panama City Beach Convention & Visitors Bureau** (17001 Panama City Beach Pkwy., 850/233-5070, 8 A.M.–5 P.M. daily) for brochures, maps, and information about attractions and accommodations.

Police and Emergencies

As always, if you find yourself in a real emergency, pick up a phone and dial 911. For a non-emergency police need, call or visit the **Fort Walton Beach Police Department** (7 Hollywood Blvd., Fort Walton Beach, 850/833-9533) or the **Panama City Beach Police Department** (17110 Firenzo Ave., Panama City Beach, 850/233-5000).

In the event of a medical emergency, you may stop into **Sacred Heart Hospital Office** (7800 U.S. 98 W, Destin, 850/857-1700) in the western part of the Emerald Coast, or in the eastern part, go to **Bay Medical Center** (615 N. Bonita Ave., Panama City, 850/769-1511).

Radio and Television

There's lots of music radio in this area, heavy on the rock and pop for all those spring breakers. **Hot 107.9 FM** is pop, **Beach 99.9 FM** is oldies, **Pirate Radio 94.5 FM** is rock, for country go to **92.5 FM**, **Sunny 98.5 FM** is more soft rock, and **93.5 FM** is more alt rock.

And on the television, there are two local ABC affiliates, **WMBB Channel 13** out of Panama City and **WEAR Channel 3** out of Pensacola. The CBS affiliate is **WCTV Channel 6** out of Tallahassee, the PBS affiliate is **WFSG Channel 56** out of Panama City, and the NBC affiliate is **WJHG Channel 7** out of Panama City.

Laundry Services

Laundry options are at their best in Panama City Beach. There's **Beachside Laundry and Dry Cleaning** (21902 Front Beach Rd., 850/234-1601) or **Express Coin** (275 S. Arnold Rd., 850/233-6491).

Getting There and Around

DRIVING

Ground travel is easy around the Emerald Coast, along several primary feeders: U.S. 98, U.S. 331, Highway 85, and I-10. Fort Walton Beach, the hometown of Eglin Air Force Base, is 60 miles west of Panama City and 35 miles east of Pensacola. U.S. 98 travels east–west along the Emerald Coast, edging the Gulf through Destin and Fort Walton Beach. The beach of Fort Walton Beach is actually on Okaloosa Island, a barrier island at the southern end of Choctawhatchee Bay. Destin is about five miles east on U.S. 98 (sometimes called the Miracle Strip Pkwy.). To get to this area from the north, take U.S. 331 south, take Highway 85 south at the Alabama/Florida line, straight into Destin and Fort Walton Beach. From I-10, exit onto Highway 85 south at the Fort Walton Beach exit.

The Beaches of South Walton communities are about 35 miles west of Panama City Beach, along

COURTESY OF THE BEACHES OF SOUTH WALTON, WALTON COUNTY TDC

Adjacent to Eglin Air Force Base, the town of Milton is a must for railroad enthusiasts, with a museum housed in the old L&N Depot.

The Emerald Coast

Highway 30A (also called Scenic 30A and Scenic Gulf Coast D.). Highway 30A splits off from U.S. 98 just before Highway 393 in the west and right after Panama City Beach in the east.

Panama City Beach is on a barrier island. If you're visiting, Panama City Beach and Panama City are two separate cities and their names should not be used interchangeably. The Hathaway Bridge crosses St. Andrews Bay and connects the two of them. U.S. 98 splits at Panama City Beach and becomes U.S. 98 in the north (also called Panama City Beach Pkwy.) and U.S. 98A along the beach (also called Front Beach Rd.).

FLYING

The nearest airport to Destin and Fort Walton Beach is **Okaloosa Regional Airport** (1701 Hwy. 85 N, on Eglin Air Force Base, 850/651-7160), a small airport serviced by Northwest Airlines, US Air Express, Delta Airlines, and Atlantic Southeast Airlines. **Bay County International Airport** (3173 Airport Rd., Panama City, 850/763-6751) is convenient to Panama City Beach and about 60 miles east of Destin and Fort Walton Beach. It's also fairly small. A 50-minute drive to the west, the **Pensacola Regional Airport** (2430 Airport Blvd., Pensacola, 850/436-5000) is the biggest airport in northwest Florida. It's still not huge, serving a moderate number of flights from Air Trans, American Eagle, Continental, Delta, Northwest, and US Airways. Delta has the largest number of direct flights.

Car-rental agencies are inside the main terminal entrance at Pensacola Regional Airport across from baggage claim. **Alamo** (850/434-5676), **Avis** (850/433-5614), **Budget** (850/432-5499), **Dollar** (850/474-9000), **Hertz** (850/ 432-2345), and **National** (850/432-8338) are all on the premises. Enterprise and Thrifty are off-site.

PUBLIC TRANSPORTATION

Amtrak's (800/USA-RAIL) Sunset Limited stops near the Emerald Coast in Chipley, coming from Orlando in the east and all the way from Los Angeles in the west. You still need wheels to get around locally. **Greyhound** (800/229-9424) has a bus station in Panama City (917 Harrison Ave., 850/785-6111), but really, public transportation won't get you to most places along the Emerald Coast, unless you're just hanging out on the beach in Panama City Beach.

The Emerald Coast

Pensacola

The Spanish tried to colonize Pensacola in 1559, but the hurricane-addled settlers abandoned the place after two years. Thus, Pensacola missed out on its claim as North America's first European settlement. That honor goes to St. Augustine. So what does Pensacola boast about instead? It depends on to whom you speak. On the one hand, it's affectionately known by some locals as the Redneck Riviera, the kind of place where there are only two seasons of note: hunting and fishing. On the other hand, it's a culturally rich city that has seen five flags—Spain, France, England, United States, and the Confederacy—flown proudly at different historic moments in the past four centuries. And on the third hand (unsightly but often very practical), military enthusiasts extol the virtues of the area as the site of numerous important forts as well as Naval Air Station

Must-Sees

M **Pensacola Beach Fishing Pier:** The pier, longest on the Gulf of Mexico, is really at the heart of festive, action-packed Pensacola Beach. You don't need a fishing license to wet a line (page 312).

M **Gulf Islands National Seashore:** Hurricane Ivan did its darnedest to erase this 150-mile-long string of undeveloped barrier islands, but the windswept dunes still stand. Scheduled to reopen entirely during the summer of 2005, the protected area has miles of delicate beach habitat along Santa Rosa Island as well as Fort Pickens and other historic sights (page 313).

M **Historic Pensacola Village:** Stop off for sustenance at the Seville Quarter's Rosie O'Grady's

The Julee Cottage, home to a free "woman of color," was built in 1554. The cottage is part of Pensacola's Historic District, located in downtown Pensacola.

before heading on to the cluster of 18th- and 19th-century museums and homes that constitute the Historic Pensacola Village (page 314).

M **National Museum of Naval Aviation:** Find out why Pensacola is called the "Cradle of Aviation" at this vast and spectacular aviation museum on the grounds of the Naval Air Station Pensacola (page 316).

M **Sam's Fun City:** A new addition to Sam's Fun City is Surf City Water Park. There are enough water slides, wave pools, and water sprayers to keep the whole family cool in the steamy Pensacola heat (page 319).

PENSACOLA

Sam's Fun City **M**

Pensacola

Historic
Pensacola Village **M**

Pensacola Bay

National Museum
of Naval Aviation **M**

M **M**

Pensacola
Beach

Pensacola Beach
Fishing Pier **M**

Gulf Islands
National Seashore

Gulf of Mexico

| 0 | 10 mi |
| 0 | 10 km |

Pensacola, the launching point for the flight training of every American naval aviator, naval flight officer, and enlisted aircrewman. It is also home to the Blue Angels. And even after you've run out of hands, still others claim Pensacola as a picture-perfect beach retreat with deep turquoise waters and fine, white sand.

Pensacola has a long history. Native Americans left pottery shards and artifacts in the gentle coastal dunes here centuries before Tristan de Luna arrived with his fellow Spaniards in 1559. Even after this first exploratory settlement didn't take, Pensacola was settled by white Europeans very early on. It was one of a handful of Colonial period communities in the southeastern United States, its Seville Historic District one of the oldest and most intact in all of Florida. Within this small neighborhood is Old Christ Church, Florida's oldest church (1832), and St. Michael's Cemetery, deeded to Pensacola by the king of Spain in 1822. A walk through Historic Pensacola Village will give you insight into the area's history.

Pensacola has a strong military presence with Naval Air Station Pensacola and nearby Eglin Air Force Base, and is often called the "Cradle of Naval Aviation." The free National Museum of Naval Aviation showcases the history of aviation through indoor and outdoor exhibits.

And then there are the beaches. Some are developed, urban beaches such as Pensacola Beach. There's also the island beach community of Gulf Breeze, which may well be the UFO capital of the world, just about every resident able to spin tales of flying saucers, alien abductions, etc. (Of course, it could just be the military crafts from nearby NAS Pensacola and Eglin that people see.) For more uninhabited beaches, the Gulf Islands National Seashore cuts through this area, a 150-mile-long, discontinuous string of undeveloped barrier islands that begins at Santa Rosa Island and extends into Mississippi. Santa Rosa Island contains seven undeveloped miles of beach, with clear water, lots of fish and wildlife, and not as many people. Unfortunately, all of the area's beaches suffered during recent Hurricane Ivan.

HURRICANES

Pensacola's location on the Panhandle makes it particularly vulnerable to hurricanes. Many storms over the years have made landfall here—a number during years before storms were named, and then Hurricane Juan in 1985, the devastating Hurricane Opal in 1995, and Hurricane Ivan on September 16, 2004. It made landfall as a Category III hurricane, wreaking particular havoc around Perdido Bay and Pensacola Beach. The area's bridges and roads sustained major damage, and locals say 99 percent of the buildings in the area were damaged, with a staggering 40 percent utterly destroyed or catastrophically damaged by the 130-mph winds and 10- to 12-foot storm surge.

On the highways in the days after that storm one could see cherry pickers streaming in from all over the state, along with military vehicles and pickups loaded up with good Samaritans eager to help. Still, repairs and restoration are slow going. As is common to our species, the country's concerned citizens quickly turned their attentions from the devastation in Pensacola and Alabama to newer disasters and events in the news. Meanwhile, the locals began cleaning up, waiting for FEMA assistance, for insurance money, for roofers who weren't too busy.

Much of the area is still a construction zone, only portions open yet to tourists and the few functional hotels taken up with construction and FEMA workers. Some road restoration in natural areas is further complicated by the fact that it's a habitat for endangered species—all work must be approved by the Fish and Wildlife Service and other government bodies.

Although things in the area have improved since the hurricane, it will be years before all traces of Ivan have been covered over. Unfortunately, most websites have not been updated to reflect post-Ivan circumstances. Be very wary when booking online—call to ask specific questions about the state of the accommodations. Also, when choosing restaurants or attractions, don't be lured by billboards. Many storm-rippled billboards still stand, advertising restaurants and businesses destroyed by Ivan the Terrible.

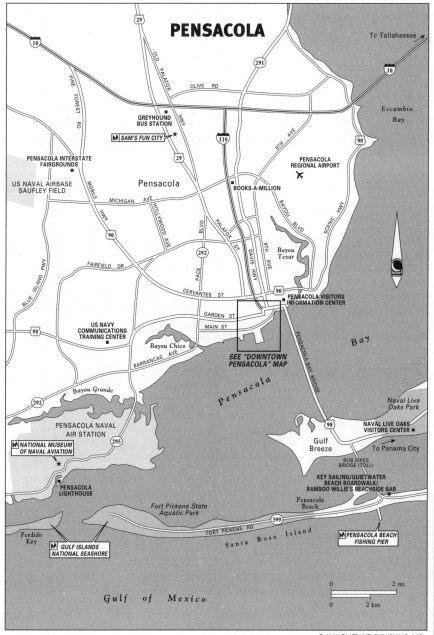

PENSACOLA

To Tallahassee

Escambia Bay

OLIVE RD

OLD PALAFOX HWY

GREYHOUND BUS STATION

SAM'S FUN CITY

PENSACOLA INTERSTATE FAIRGROUNDS

US NAVAL AIRBASE SAUFLEY FIELD

Pensacola

MICHIGAN AVE

PINE FOREST RD

MOBILE HWY

HOLLYWOOD AVE

PENSACOLA REGIONAL AIRPORT

BOOKS-A-MILLION

9TH AVE

BAYOU BLVD

SCENIC HWY

BLVD

PALAFOX ST

DAVIS HWY

9TH AVE

Bayou Texar

FAIRFIELD DR

PACE

CERVANTES ST

BLUE ISLAND PWY

US NAVY COMMUNICATIONS TRAINING CENTER

Bayou Chico

BARRANCAS AVE

GARDEN ST

MAIN ST

PENSACOLA VISITORS INFORMATION CENTER

SEE "DOWNTOWN PENSACOLA" MAP

Bayou Grande

PENSACOLA NAVAL AIR STATION

NATIONAL MUSEUM OF NAVAL AVIATION

PENSACOLA LIGHTHOUSE

Perdido Key

GULF ISLANDS NATIONAL SEASHORE

Fort Pickens State Aquatic Park

FORT PICKENS RD

Santa Rosa Island

Pensacola Bay

PENSACOLA BAY BRIDGE

Naval Live Oaks Park

NAVAL LIVE OAKS VISITORS CENTER

To Panama City

Gulf Breeze

BOB SIKES BRIDGE (TOLL)

KEY SAILING/QUIETWATER BEACH BOARDWALK/ BAMBOO WILLIE'S BEACHSIDE BAR

Pensacola Beach

PENSACOLA BEACH FISHING PIER

Gulf of Mexico

0   2 mi
0   2 km

MOON

Pensacola

© AVALON TRAVEL PUBLISHING, INC.

PLANNING YOUR TIME

As on most of the Panhandle, high season is April–August. The "value season" runs roughly August–March. Regardless of when you'd like to visit, make reservations in advance. The recent hurricane has cut the number of available rooms by more than half, many rooms taken up by longstanding aid and construction workers. Also, visitors at the naval base tend to fill the hotels nearest it. Assuming hurricane reconstruction proceeds apace, the greater Pensacola area can occupy you for a couple of days with its historical attractions, beaches, and nature parks. If you fly into Pensacola and rent a car, think about tacking on a couple of extra days to explore the Emerald Coast area just to the east.

Sports and Recreation

BEACHES

This is tricky—there are wonderful beaches here, all in varying states of disarray since Hurricane Ivan's departure. The long stretch of the **Gulf Islands National Seashore** and the **Naval Air Station Pensacola** and **Eglin Air Force Base** farther east have imposed restrictions on commercial growth. The communities in the area set quotas on density and height restrictions on new construction. Thus, the more urban beachfront areas around Pensacola aren't littered with high-rise condos and resort hotels, and there's another six miles of utterly preserved seashore in the park. Still, the area had been recovering from Hurricane Opal for nine years before it got walloped, in nearly identical ways, by Hurricane Ivan in 2004.

Perdido Key is the westernmost island in the long chain of barrier islands that line the Panhandle's edge, an island that Florida shares with the state of Alabama. The developed beach areas are called **Orange Beach** and **Johnson Beach** and the more natural part is **Perdido Key State Park** (12301 Gulf Beach Hwy., 15 miles southwest of Pensacola, off Hwy. 292, 850/492-1595, 8 A.M.–sundown daily, $2 honor system). The

Perdido Key bore the brunt of Hurricane Ivan's wrath. It will be a long time in recovery.

COURTESY OF VISIT FLORIDA

Pensacola

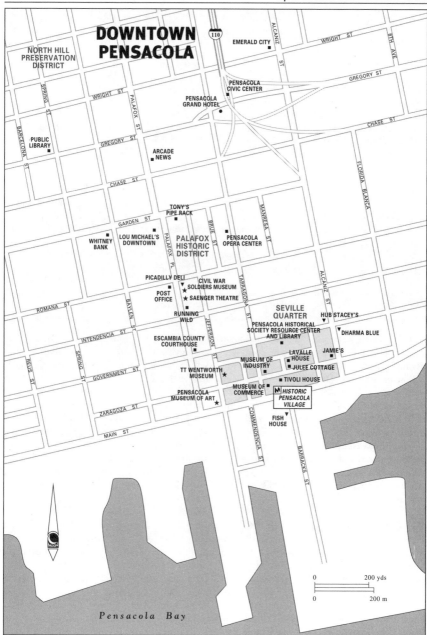

DOWNTOWN PENSACOLA

110

EMERALD CITY

WRIGHT ST

NORTH HILL PRESERVATION DISTRICT

GREGORY ST

PENSACOLA CIVIC CENTER

PENSACOLA GRAND HOTEL

CHASE ST

SPRING ST

WRIGHT ST

PALAFOX ST

BARCELONA ST

PUBLIC LIBRARY

GREGORY ST

ARCADE NEWS

FLORIDA BLANCA

CHASE ST

TONY'S PIPE RACK

MANRESA ST

GARDEN ST

WHITNEY BANK

LOU MICHAEL'S DOWNTOWN

PALAFOX HISTORIC DISTRICT

BRUE ST

PENSACOLA OPERA CENTER

PALAFOX PL

PICADILLY DELI

CIVIL WAR SOLDIERS MUSEUM

TARRAGONA ST

ALCANIZ ST

ROMANA ST

POST OFFICE

SAENGER THEATRE

SEVILLE QUARTER

HUB STACEY'S

BAYLEN ST

RUNNING WILD

PENSACOLA HISTORICAL SOCIETY RESOURCE CENTER AND LIBRARY

DHARMA BLUE

INTENDENCIA ST

ESCAMBIA COUNTY COURTHOUSE

JEFFERSON ST

LAVALLE HOUSE

JAMIE'S

SPRING ST

BEUS ST

GOVERNMENT ST

TT WENTWORTH MUSEUM

MUSEUM OF INDUSTRY

JULEE COTTAGE

TIVOLI HOUSE

PENSACOLA MUSEUM OF ART

MUSEUM OF COMMERCE

M HISTORIC PENSACOLA VILLAGE

ZARAGOZA ST

COMMENDENCIA ST

FISH HOUSE

MAIN ST

BARRACKS ST

MOON

0   200 yds
0   200 m

N

Pensacola

Pensacola Bay

© AVALON TRAVEL PUBLISHING, INC.

FAST TIMES

Addicted to speed? Pensacola has a couple of ways to scratch that itch. **Five Flags Speedway** (7451 Pine Forest Rd., on Hwy. 297 a mile south of Exit 2 on I-10, 850/944-0466, www.five-flagsspeedway.com, dates and times vary, $10–20) was built in 1956, one of the oldest established short track races still in existence. A high-banked asphalt oval, it is the fastest one-half mile track in the country and home to the annual Snowball Derby (usually the first few days of December). The Snowball Derby is widely recognized as the country's premier short track Super Late Model event. The rest of the season features racing of different kinds, from the fire-breathing, fuel-injected, winged sprint cars of the United Sprint Car Series, to the Bombers, Spectators, Super Stocks, Vintage, and Pro Late Models. The track attracts top drivers like Carl Yarborough and Rusty Wallace, and fans from all over.

Pensacola Greyhound Track (951 Dog Track Rd., off U.S. 98, 850/455-8595, www .pensaco-lagreyhoundpark.com, 7 P.M. Wed.– Sat., 1 P.M. Sat. and Sun., $2 admission but tourists are admitted free with a hotel/motel key, up to four admitted per key) offers the thrill of high-speed greyhound racing and the equally thrilling attendant betting. There's an air-conditioned restaurant/lounge called the Kennel Club from which you can watch the races, or there are railside seats. The facility also has live and instant replay televisions throughout the complex.

Greyhound rescuers may remember the track in the news a few years ago for illegally "disposing" of past-their-prime dogs. A couple of people did hard time for the serious animal-rights infraction—since then, Pensacola activists have worked diligently to find homes for hundreds of retired racing dogs, more evidence of what Margaret Mead once famously said: "Never doubt that a small group of concerned citizens can change the world. Indeed, it's the only thing that ever has."

---

latter is open to the public, but all the buildings, nature trails, beach crossovers, and roadbeds were destroyed. Authorities estimate that Perdido Key will be open to car traffic, including the main parking lot, by March 2005. Once fully restored, these beaches provide some of the best swimming in the state—warm, clear water, gentle surf, long stretches of shallows.

Santa Rosa Island, just to the east, is one of the longest barrier islands in the world, stretching 50 miles from Pensacola Bay on its western side to Choctawhatchee Bay to its east. The beaches here are all fine, white quartz sand.

Pensacola Beach Fishing Pier

Pensacola Beach (Pensacola Beach Visitor Information Center, 800/635-4803) itself covers much of the island, with restaurants, shops, and entertainment at their highest density near the Pensacola Beach Fishing Pier—at 1,471 feet long and 30 feet above the water, the longest on the Gulf of Mexico. Crossing the two bridges from Pensacola to Santa Rosa Island, you'll be on Pensacola Boulevard—it splits left and right, but directly in front of you is Pensacola Beach. The area is rich with water-sport possibilities: parasailing, sailboarding, deep-sea fishing, Jet Skiing, scuba. Pensacola Beach is open again to the public, accessible by car or by ECAT bus or trolley. The fishing pier is open to the public, except for the last 200 feet. The sand has been sifted and groomed along the main beach area, and is open. The pier costs $1 to walk on, $6.50 to fish.

At the corner of Pensacola Boulevard and Fort Pickens Road, which goes to the west, is **Casino Beach.** It is the heart of Pensacola Beach, named for an old beachside casino resort from 1933. The casino is long gone, but its "beach ball water tank" is still the beach's landmark. Casino Beach is home to the huge brick Gulfside Pavilion, site of numerous free concerts and events over the year. The beach has picnic tables, restrooms, restaurants, and souvenir shops. And just past the tollbooth onto the island, **Quietwater Beach,** on the Santa Rosa Sound side, is a gentle, shallow beach great for kids.

⚕ Gulf Islands National Seashore

The Gulf Islands National Seashore (800/365-2267, $8 for a seven-day pass) has numerous beaches along Santa Rosa Island. At its westernmost edge is **Fort Pickens Park,** maintained by the National Park Service. Because Fort Pickens Road was breached, this beach is available to the public only by boat at this point. The campgrounds have been restored. Historic buildings in the area have been shored up, but painstaking preservation work is just beginning. Fort Pickens Fishing Pier, at the western tip of the island, is still being repaired. Really within the Fort Pickens area is another beach called **Langdon Beach,** which has picnic tables, restrooms, and outdoor showers. The scenic bike path, going from Langdon Beach all the way to the fort, has not yet been restored, nor have the Dune Nature Trail and the Blackbird Marsh Nature Trail.

Also part of Gulf Islands National Seashore, **Opal Beach** is three miles east of Pensacola Beach. It is generally less populated than Pensacola Beach, with lots of picnic facilities, bathrooms, and parking lots. Opal Beach is, as of spring 2005, still accessible only by boat, with extensive damage to the picnic structures. The Florida Department of Transportation is repairing County Road 399, as six miles of road were washed out.

Navarre Beach

Navarre Beach is the easternmost beach on Santa Rosa Island, and despite its proximity to Eglin Air Force Base, this remote strand has historically been known as a nudist beach. The nudie stuff has been quashed in recent years, and it's more of a family-friendly beach, with bathrooms, picnic facilities, and a fishing pier. Again, the beach was hit hard—as of February 2005, work crews were still patching roofs, repairing roads, and hauling off debris, and visitor numbers are down 90 percent.

FISHING

The area's had some losses, but also some gains. The Three Mile Bridge over Pensacola Bay has in recent years carried traffic alongside the long-abandoned U.S. 98 bridge. The bridge, prior to Hurricane Ivan, was used by local anglers as their huge personal fishing pier. Now much of that pier lies on the bottom of Pensacola Bay. The fishing, however, is in for an upswing. Scheduled for after hurricane season in 2005, maybe in November, the decommissioned aircraft carrier **USS *Oriskany*** will be sunk as an artificial reef in the Gulf of Mexico 22.5 miles southeast of Pensacola Pass. The navy committed $2.8 million for its preparation and deployment as a reef, the first time a ship of this size has been sunk for this purpose. Stay tuned in the next few years for fisherfolk to flock in greater numbers to the greater Pensacola area. And if you're interested in seeing the sinking of the ship, call 850/595-4395 for more information.

Sights

Downtown Pensacola is awash in historical attractions, many of them clustered in one of several historic districts.

SEVILLE SQUARE

The survivors of an early, thwarted attempt to settle Santa Rosa Island hightailed it to more solid ground and established a permanent settlement in 1752. After the French and Indian War of 1763, the British took west Florida and occupied the area, laying out a tidy grid of houses. The Spanish, upon capturing Pensacola after that, said yes to the tidy grid in the old town square but no to the bland, Anglophone names. So about 20 blocks of historic 18th-century to 19th-century residential and business streets have kicky Spanish-language names. It's a beautiful area, with a strong sense of civic pride—a cross of Greek Revival architecture, Victorian, and French-influenced Gulf Coast Vernacular cottages (these are often 1.5-story houses with steeply pitched gabled roofs and a gallery porch on the main facade).

The Seville Historic District makes for a wonderful afternoon of walking. First, I encourage a stop-off at **Seville Quarter** (130 E. Government St., 850/434-6211, 11 A.M.–10 P.M., late night menus until 1 A.M., $10–25) for live music, some food, or fortifying libations. Within this historic complex, down an east alleyway, stop into **Rosie O'Grady's** for some Dixieland jazz, a Flaming Hurricane, and the historic setting—it was built in 1871 as the Pensacola Cigar and Tobacco Co. Directly across from Rosie O'Grady's is the entrance to **Lili Marlene's World War I Aviators Pub,** once the Pensacola Printing Co., which for a long time was the oldest print shop in continuous operation in the country, and the original home of the *Pensacola News Journal.* Beyond these, there are several other themed rooms in this entertainment and dining complex, outfitted with period antiques and decor. The complex also has two lovely courtyards and a gift shop.

Historic Pensacola Village

Also part of the Seville historic district, Historic Pensacola Village (850/595-5985, 10 A.M.–4 P.M. Mon.–Fri., admission $6 adults, $5 seniors and active military, $2.50 for children 4–16, 3 and under free) is bounded by Government, Taragona, Adams, and Alcanz Streets. It includes the Museum of Commerce, Museum of Industry, Julee Cottage, Lavalle House, Lear House, Dorr House, Old Christ Church, Weaver's Cottage, Tivoli House, and Colonial Archaeological trail. Do them all if you've got the stamina—the guided house tour is the way to go. House tours are included in admission price and leave from the Tivoli House at 11 A.M. and 1 P.M. Hurricane Ivan did about $1.5 million in damage to many of the delicate 19th-century structures, especially the T. T. Wentworth Jr. Museum, the Museum of Commerce, and Barkley House, but roof damage has been entirely repaired and cleanup is complete. Perhaps more discombobulating for the museum was the recent death of longtime museum director John P. Daniels in February 2005—call ahead to make sure the village is in full swing.

T. T. Wentworth Jr. Florida State Museum (Plaza Ferdinand) is an elaborate Renaissance Revival building that houses rotating exhibits on West Florida's history, architecture, and archaeology (kids will go more willingly if you tell them there's also a shrunken head on display).

The T. T. Wentworth Museum, located in the historic part of downtown Pensacola, is a must if you are a history buff, or a buff-in-training.

The **Museum of Commerce** (201 E. Zaragoza St.) is a brick turn-of-the-20th-century warehouse containing a reconstructed 1890s-era streetscape with a toy store and leather, hardware, music, and print shops, and horse-drawn buggies. The **Museum of Industry** (200 E. Zaragoza St.) houses an exhibit depicting several important 19th-century industries in West Florida: fishing, brick-making, railroad, and lumber industries.

The **Julee Cottage** (210 E. Zaragoza St.) is a museum classroom dedicated to the memory of Julee Panton, a legendary free African-American woman who owned the cottage. Then there's the **Weaver's Cottage** (207 E. Zaragoza St.), a historic little house containing a weaving exhibit.

Other historic homes in the village include the **Lavalle House** (205 E. Church St.), an example of French Creole colonial architecture; the **Dorr House** (311 S. Adams St.), Greek Revival architecture furnished with fine antiques; and the **Lear-Rocheblave House** (214 E. Zaragoza St.), which is a two-story Folk Victorian home with several furnished rooms. The **Barkley House** (410 S. Florida Blanca St.) is one of the oldest masonry houses in Florida, and the **Quina House** (204 S. Alcaniz St.) is owned and operated by the Pensacola Historic Preservation Society and exhibits household items and furnishings from West Florida's past. The **Tivoli House** (205 E. Zaragoza St.) is a reconstructed version of an 1805 boarding and gaming house, and now houses the Historic Pensacola Village gift shop and ticket office.

After touring the homes, pick up the brochure for the **Colonial Archaeological Trail,** which was produced by the Archaeology Institute at the University of West Florida and leads you through the ruins of the colonial commanding officer's house, the foundations of the officer-of-the-day's building, and the remains of what might have been a trader's home and warehouse just outside the western gate of the British fort built during the American Revolution.

Also, the **Pensacola Historical Museum** (115 E. Zaragosa St., 850/433-1559, 10 A.M.–4:30 P.M. Mon.–Sat., free) is in the midst of the historic village, operated by the Pensacola Historical Society.

It offers three changing exhibits a year on topics of local history. They also sponsor a deliciously eerie haunted house tour in October if you can time your visit right.

PALAFOX HISTORIC DISTRICT

Palafox Historic District is another historic area downtown, contiguous with Seville Square, only just to the west of it. It runs up Palafox Street from Pensacola Bay in the south to about Wright Street in the north. Again, it's an area of beautiful homes and historic buildings with wide brick sidewalks. It's really the commercial heart of Pensacola, and it houses a couple of the area's big cultural draws.

The **Pensacola Museum of Art** (407 S. Jefferson St., 850/432-6247, 10 A.M.–5 P.M. Tues.–Fri., noon–5 P.M. Sat. and Sun., $5 adults, $2 students and military) is right at its center, with a wonderful space and intriguingly diverse visiting exhibits. They range from aboriginal art from Balgo, to a muscular Rodin exhibit, to a whimsical Smithsonian Institution Traveling Exhibition called "Lunchbox Memories" (all lunchboxes, through October 2005). The permanent collection has minor works, most on paper, by

COURTESY OF VISIT FLORIDA

The Winston E. Arnow Courthouse is one of many pristine historic buildings in the Palafox Historic District.

Pensacola

some heavy hitters (largely 20th century) as well as lots of fine decorative glass. The museum is housed in what was the city jail from 1906 to 1954, so there are sturdy bars on the windows.

The **Civil War Soldiers Museum** (108 S. Palafox Place, 850/469-1900, 10 A.M.–4 P.M. Tues.–Sat., $6 adults, $5 military, $2.50 children 6–12, 6 and under free) is essentially the private collection of Dr. Norman Haines Jr., who began collecting Civil War-obilia as a boy near Antietam, site of the bloodiest day of the Civil War. It's an interesting assortment of stuff that could be annotated with better signage, but it has a neat Pensacola Room of local history, with information about Stephen R. Mallory, the renowned Confederate Secretary of Navy. It also contains the handmade First National Confederate flag captured during the Battle of Santa Rosa Island, October 9, 1861. The museum bookstore is a smorgasbord for Civil War buffs.

NORTH HILL PRESERVATION DISTRICT

Before you tire of all this history, another worthy walk is the North Hill Preservation District, which occupies 50 city blocks due north of the Palafox District, away from the water, bounded on the west by Reus and on the east by Palafox. On the National Register of Historic Places, the neighborhood is pretty much residential, with great examples of fully restored Queen Anne, neoclassical, Craftsman bungalow, Mediterranean Revival, and Art Moderne architecture. You can't go inside unless you make friends, but some of the current owners are descendants of the original builders—Spanish nobility, lumber barons, French Creoles, and Civil War soldiers.

NAVAL AIR STATION PENSACOLA

Pensacola is known as the "Cradle of Naval Aviation," a bold claim that can be authenticated through an exploration of one of the many sites open to the public at the Naval Air Station Pensacola and environs. To reach the historic mainland forts and the **National Museum of Naval Aviation** from the north, take Exit 7 of I-10 (Pine Forest Rd., Hwy. 297), go about 1.5 miles, and take a right onto Blue Angel Parkway. Then drive 12 miles to the west gate of the Naval Air Station. (Visitors without military stickers can *depart* only from the main entrance on Navy Boulevard.)

National Museum of Naval Aviation

If you're only going to devote time to one historic attraction in the greater Pensacola area, the National Museum of Naval Aviation (1750 Radford Blvd. N.A.S. Pensacola, 850/452-3604, 9 A.M.–5 P.M. daily, free admission) is it. It's one of the largest air and space museums in the world, with 140 restored aircrafts representing navy, marine corps, and coast guard aviation. There's a seven-story glass and steel

The National Museum of Naval Aviation is home to dozens of displays that trace the history of flight from wooden planes to the sky lab module.

atrium in which four A-4 Skyhawks are suspended in formation. You can stand on the flight deck of the USS *Cabot* and fly an F/A-18 mission in Desert Storm in a motion-based flight simulator. There's an IMAX theater (it costs $6.50) with a film called *The Magic of*

Flight, or, if you want to see real-life flying, watch the **Blue Angels,** based in Pensacola, practice in an area adjacent to the museum. Practices are held most Tuesday and Wednesday mornings at 8:30 A.M., weather permitting. Follow the signs to visitor viewing and parking.

BLUE ANGELS

Watching them reveals just how much slower sound waves are than light waves. You look up to see a tight diamond formation of blue streaking past in the sky, the combined engine noise trailing behind like a memory. The **Blue Angels** at their fastest fly about 700 mph in an air show, in a maneuver called a sneak pass. At their slowest, 120 mph for something called a Section High Alpha. They fly as high as 15,000 feet for vertical rolls, and as low as 50 feet from the ground during that sneak pass.

At the end of World War II, Chief of Naval Operations, Admiral Chester W. Nimitz, ordered the formation of a flight demonstration team to showcase the glories of Navy and Marine Corps aviation. The team was assembled and put to work, performing its first flight demonstration less than a year later. Since its inception, the team has flown for more than 393 million fans—more than 17 million spectators during the 2004 show season alone.

The Naval Air Station Pensacola is the proud home of the Blue Angels, providing training and winter practice space for the team of talented active-duty Navy or Marine Corps tactical jet pilots. Since the Blue Angels' inception, there have been a little over 200 demonstration pilots, each with a minimum of 1,350 flight hours under their belts at the outset, with another 120 training flights required during winter training in order to perform a public demonstration safely. In the beginning they flew Grumman F6F Hellcats, but have transitioned over the years through eight types of aircrafts—since 1986 it has been the Boeing F/A-18 Hornet (which can actually fly at speeds of about 1,400 mph, which is almost twice the speed of sound).

This type of high-speed, low-altitude flying in tight formation is not without risks—in December 2004 one of the F/A-18s crashed into the Gulf of Mexico in the shallows off Perdido Key. The mirac-

COURTESY OF PENSACOLA BAY AREA CVB

The Navy's Blue Angels call Pensacola home and stage a huge air show over the city every July.

ulous thing is the pilot ejected safely, a little bruised but not requiring even an overnight at the hospital.

As part of the Blue Angels' regular season, they perform several shows in the Pensacola area (usually July 2 and around November 11–12), but you are welcome to attend a practice demonstration for free behind the Naval Aviation Museum at NAS Pensacola, held Tuesday and Wednesday mornings at 8:30 A.M., weather permitting. Check with the museum (850/452-3604) to confirm dates. Arrive early to sit on the bleachers and watch the warmup acts—training jets taking off and landing. Then the main act rolls out onto the runway, the F/A-18 Hornets diving and spinning in delicate choreography for nearly an hour. At the end, some of the pilots may stop by to sign autographs and kibbitz with the fans. A heavenly morning in Pensacola with the Angels, indeed.

Pensacola

Pensacola Lighthouse

Also on the grounds of the naval air station, the Pensacola Lighthouse (Hwy. 292 S) follows on the heels of other lighthouses constructed in this area. The construction of the first Pensacola lighthouse, the Aurora Borealis, was completed in 1824, the first lighthouse on the Gulf Coast and the second lighthouse in Florida. It stood at the northern entrance of the bay near the present-day Lighthouse Point Restaurant. Unfortunately, trees on Santa Rosa Island obscured the light beam to ships. The construction of the present lighthouse was begun in 1856, and it was lit January 1, 1859. At night it still shines for sailors 27 miles out at sea, 171 feet tall and with a first-order Fresnel lens. In 1965, the lighthouse was automated, obviating the need for an on-site lighthouse keeper. The Keeper's Quarters now house the Navy's Command Display Center, with an exhibit on the lighthouse and the naval air station. The tower is open Sunday noon–4 P.M. and other times by appointment; the lighthouse grounds are open to the public.

The Forts

Accessed through Naval Air Station Pensacola, the historic forts in this area are actually part of the **Gulf Islands National Seashore** (mailing address 1801 Gulf Breeze Pkwy., Gulf Breeze, FL 32563, 850/934-2600). In recent years one of the top 10 most visited national parks in the country, it spans 160 miles from Cat Island, Mississippi, east to the Okaloosa Day Use Area near Fort Walton Beach. The seashore was devastated by Category III Hurricane Ivan on September 16, 2004. Recovery is slow going, so call ahead to see what is open to the public.

Fort Barrancas sits on a sandy bluff overlooking the entrance to Pensacola Bay. This site has seen three forts—first an earth-and-log Royal Navy Redoubt in 1763, then a Spanish two-part fort with Bateria de San Antonio at the foot of the bluff and Fort San Carlos de Barrancas above. The American brick-and-mortar Fort Barrancas was mostly completed in 1846, boasting 37 guns. During the Civil War, Confederate forces held Fort Barrancas until 1862. It was rearmed in 1890 and used as a training facility briefly during the Spanish-American War, after which it was disarmed again and used as an observation and communications post until 1930. Fort Barrancas was deactivated in 1947 and lay unused until it became part of the Gulf Islands National Seashore in 1971. It was entirely restored by 1980 at a cost of $1.2 million. Today, there's a visitors center with exhibits on the history of Pensacola under five flags 1559–1971, with displays of Civil War and coast artillery artifacts. Fully up and running since Hurricane Ivan, the visitors center shows a 12-minute video on the fort and offers guided tours daily.

The **Fort Barrancas–Advanced Redoubt,** 700 yards south, was built 1845–1859 to defend the Pensacola Navy Yard from overland infantry assault. It was only manned during the Civil War, at which point it was deemed obsolete. Tours are available on Saturday at 11 A.M.

The largest of the four forts built to defend Pensacola Bay, **Fort Pickens** on Santa Rosa Island sustained serious damage during Hurricane Ivan and is currently closed to the public. All buildings in the historic area were flooded to a depth of several feet, the island experienced major erosion on its south side, and the Florida Department of Transportation is in the process of rebuilding sections of Fort Pickens Road, inland and north of where it used to be.

It is worth calling (850/934-2635) to ask about the reopening date of the historic site. Construction of the fort was begun in 1829, completed in 1834, and then it was used until the 1940s. It is said to be the only Southern fort not captured by the Confederacy in the Civil War, and that Geronimo surrendered here in 1886, marking the end of the Apache Wars. When Fort Pickens is open, it has a visitors center (flooded in the storm), with a self-guided tour map of the fort. There are also regularly scheduled ranger tours and a little museum with regular interpretive programs. There is year-round camping (850/934-2621, for reservations 800/365-CAMP) in the area on the west end of Santa Rosa Island, as well as the Blackbird and Dune Nature Trails (both with much of their boardwalks destroyed by the storm) and a fully repaired fishing pier.

While Fort Pickens is on the western tip of Santa Rosa Island, **Fort McRee** is on a narrow bar of sand on the eastern tip of Perdido Key. Or maybe I should say it used to be here. Once used as the third point of the triangle (with Pickens and Barrancas) by the U.S. Army to defend Pensacola Bay, Fort McRee was built there 1834–1839. It was heavily damaged during the Civil War and then really leveled by hurricanes over the years. History buffs may want to wander through its piles of weathered bricks in the sand or the remnants of Battery 233.

FOR KIDS

There are only so many historic sites a kid can endure before reprehensible behavior sets in. Beyond the area's beaches, there are a couple of fun enticements for young ones. **The Zoo** (5701 Gulf Breeze Pkwy., 10 miles east of Gulf Breeze on U.S. 98, 850/932-2229, 9 A.M.–4 P.M. daily, $10.95 adults, $9.95 seniors, $7.95 children 3–11, under 3 free) is home to something like 900 animals, spread across a 30-acre wildlife preserve. You can view the free-roaming animals from the boardwalk or from the cute red Safari Line train. The train ride is narrated by a guide who points out African wild dogs (a new addition), giraffes, pygmy hippos, gorillas, and native wildlife. The zoo also has a tranquil Japanese garden, a gift shop, Jungle Cafe, and Whistlestop Snack Bar.

If you happen to be in town during October, the **Pensacola Interstate Fair** (U.S. 90 W, 850/944-4500) is vast, with 147 acres of rides and exhibits. Admission is a mere $8, and it usually takes place the last 11 days of the month.

⋈ Sam's Fun City

It's fairly small-scale compared to Disney or Busch Gardens, but Sam's Fun City (6709 Pensacola Blvd., just south of I-10 on U.S. 29, Pensacola, 850/505-0800, noon–8 P.M. Sun.–Thurs., until 11 P.M. Fri. and Sat., $10.95–29.95) is Pensacola's amusement park. There are a bunch of midway-style rides along with go-karts, bumper boats, and mini golf. It also has a 1,600-square-foot arena for laser tag and a huge game arcade. Sam's is adding **Surf City Water Park** with a wave pool, 15 water slides, a 1,200-foot-long "endless river," spray grounds, water play structures, and kiddie pools. The on-site Bullwinkle's Restaurant is a pleasant, something-for-everyone family restaurant.

Accommodations

The **Ashton Inn & Suites Pensacola** (4 New Warrington Rd., 850/454-0280, and 910 N. Navy Blvd., 850/455-4561, $70–100) serves the Naval Air Station Pensacola and NTTC Corry Station, convenient to the National Museum of Naval Aviation.

The **Crowne Plaza Pensacola Grand** (200 E. Gregory St., 850/433-3336, $99–150) will open at the end of April 2005 after an extensive renovation. It has a lovely gym on the second floor, an extensive library on the first floor, a heated pool, upscale dining in the 1912 Restaurant, and cocktails in the L&L lobby bar. The downtown location is convenient to the historic areas.

In summer 2005, a new, 85-room **Hampton Inn & Suites** (800/HAMPTON) will open near University Mall, north of downtown. Its features include a grand two-story lobby, exercise room, meeting space for 40, outdoor pool, continental breakfast with "on the go" breakfast bags, in-room padded lap desks, and raised beds.

On Pensacola Beach, only a few hotels have reopened since Hurricane Ivan. The first one to open was the **Comfort Inn** (40 Fort Pickens Rd., 850/934-5400, $85–180), directly on the water overlooking Little Sabine Bay in the heart of Pensacola Beach action. It's a modest but pleasant place, with complimentary continental breakfast and 100 rooms equipped with microwaves, refrigerators, coffemakers, and king or queen beds. The **Hilton Garden Inn, Pensacola Beach** (12 Via de Luna Dr., 850/916-2999, $128–209) is a large beachfront hotel within walking distance of water sports, shopping, dining, and nightlife. There are 181 guest rooms, many of them Gulf-front rooms and suites with private balconies. Its sushi bar in the Bonsai Lounge and new menu in its H2O Cajun Asian Grill are worth checking out.

Food

DOWNTOWN

Many people give top dining honors to **Jamie's Restaurant** (424 E. Zaragoza St., 850/434-2911, 11:30 A.M.–2:30 P.M. and 6–10 P.M. Mon.–Sat., $20–30), which is anticipated to reopen mid-March 2005. Set in an 1879 cottage in the historic district, the restaurant has a sophisticated Continental-by-way-of-California vibe and has won a *Wine Spectator* award of excellence since 1992. Look for the fat pan-seared veal chop garnished with lump crabmeat and shiitake mushrooms, all napped with a luxurious béarnaise sauce, or the chicken "Seville," a breast stuffed with goat cheese, sun-dried tomato, and basil.

A hipper scene, also set in a historic cottage, is **Dharma Blue** (300 S. Alcaniz St., 850/433-1275, 11 A.M.–4 P.M. Mon.–Sat., until 3 P.M. Sat., 5–10 P.M. Sun.–Thurs., until 11 P.M. Fri. and Sat., $15–21). It overlooks Seville Square with wonderful tables on the front porch and three dining rooms inside (one with a gas-log fireplace during the chillier months). At lunch, they make a wonderful portobello foccacia sandwich; at night there are grilled medallions of beef layered with caramelized onions and Maytag bleu cheese, or marinated Maple Leaf Farms duck breast grilled and drizzled with a sweet-tart marionberry sauce and paired with Yukon gold mashed potatoes. The crowd is young and professional, enthusiastic about the cocktails and Dharma Blue's broad sushi bar.

Right adjacent is **Tre Fratelli** (304 S. Alcaniz St., 850/438-3663, 5–9;30 P.M. Mon.–Sat., $9–18), a sweet Sicilian joint with candles and red linens, across from Seville Park. A newcomer to downtown, **eat!** (286 N. Palafox St., 850/433-6905, 11 A.M.–2 P.M. and 5–9 P.M. Tues.–Sat., Sun. brunch 10 A.M.–2 P.M., $7–14) has made waves with its ultracontemporary

The annual Shrimp Fest at Perdido Key is one of many festivals devoted to the local seafood bounty.

spins on Southern classics (fried green tomatoes with feta cheese, brown butter sage vinaigrette, a balsamic drizzle, and micro sprouts; or cane syrup barbecue-glazed salmon with black bean-corn salsa, tortilla "hay," and avocado cream). It's fine dining in a lovely setting, but the prices are fairly low. Also new to the scene, at one of those "disaster café" locations that have seen a lot of restaurants come and go, **The Global Grill** (27 Palafox Pl., 850/469-9966, 5–10 P.M. Tues.–Sat., $4–10) offers Pensacola some of its most sophisticated tapas (actually, some of its only tapas). It's a world-beat approach to little plates that includes spicy seared tuna with wasabi aioli and five-pepper jelly, or a crab West Indies and avocado martini.

EAST HILL

To the north a bit and east of North Hill Preservation District, East Hill has a couple of my favorite restaurants. **Jerry's Drive-In** (2815 E. Cervantes St., 850/433-9910, 11 A.M.–9 P.M. Mon.–Sat., $5–9) offers killer cheeseburgers, onion rings, and fried okra in a comfy diner setting. It's been here since the '40s, I'm told, and still has a line at lunch (but it's not really a drive-in, it's a walk-in). **Madison's** (1010 N. 12th Ave., 850/433-7074, 11 A.M.–2:30 P.M. and 5–10 P.M. Mon.–Sat., $9–20) is in what was once the city's first modern hospital, Pensacola Hospital, opened in 1915. These days it's an elegant outpost of Southern cuisine, with a wine room and a beautiful glassed-in dining space. Unfortunately, since the hurricane, in which they lost a couple of big refrigerators, the menu has been curtailed significantly.

And not far from there is the Pensacola restaurant everyone knows about, **M McGuire's Irish Pub** (600 E. Gregory St., 850/433-6789, $10–30). "Irishmen of all nationalities" sign dollar bills and staple them to the ceiling, beer is brewed on the premises, the gorgeous wine cellar has a capacity of 8,000 bottles, and you can spend an ungodly sum on a burger (accompanied by caviar and champagne—but why?). It's a hard place to describe, really, set in Pensacola's original 1927 Old Firehouse. The steaks are good, and expensive (but it's fitting because all the beef is U.S.D.A. Certified Prime, a rarity these days), but it still has a wild-and-wooly Irish pub feel to it. It's vast, with 400 seats and 200 employees, sprawling through a bunch of gewgaw-packed theme rooms. Just go, it'll be fun.

PENSACOLA BEACH

Best breakfast used to go to **Chan's** (16 Via de Luna, 850/932-8454), closed for renovations, but check back. Greatest oyster bar? **Peg Leg Pete's** (1010 Fort Pickens Rd., 850/932-4139), also still closed, but worth a call.

So, what *is* open now on Pensacola Beach? Only a handful of places in spring 2005.

Flounder's Chowder House (800 Quietwater

SOMETHING FISHY

It's technically four inches over the Alabama line into Florida's Perdido Key, which took a savage lashing by Hurricane Ivan. You can't keep the irrepressible **Flora-Bama Lounge** (17401 Perdido Key Dr., Perdido Key, 850/492-0611, www .florabama.com) down though, which has risen again after tremendous clean up, repair, and rebuilding (if you want to see some scary hurricane photos, visit the website). Why should you care? It's a beachside roadhouse where fun flows as unchecked as the booze. The bartenders are famous—and there are 10 bars, along with three stages for bands, volleyball courts, an oyster bar, package store, and sprawling beachside patio.

But that's just the beginning. When it started in 1961, it was a goofy little local bar. It's grown over the years into a huge goofy local bar—one that hosts the international spectacle, the annual **Interstate Mullet Toss,** whereby contestants grip deceased yet slippery fish and throw them as far as they can into the state of Alabama. It's a straight distance competition, but you definitely get style points. Football spiral, underhanded, shot put-style—practice at home with a trout or something to hone your craft.

Several hundred people compete, and nearly 30,000 people turn out to watch the third weekend in April. There's a Ms. Mullet contest, barbecue, crawfish, peel-and-eat shrimp, topless oysters, and a whole lot of cocktails to sweeten the deal. Post-Ivan reconstruction efforts were galvanized by the approach of the 2005 Mullet Toss, April 22–24. The Flora-Bama has a couple of other annual events of note, one of which is the **Polar Bear Dip** on the morning of January 1, an early morning bar-to-water mad scramble. After a bracing splash in the Gulf (many "bears" eschew clothing entirely), revelers go back to the Flora-Bama for some warming black-eyed peas, and if you find a dime in your peas, it's reputedly good luck for the whole year. Perdido Key could use some good luck this year.

Beach Rd., 850/932-2003, 11 A.M.–midnight daily, until 2 A.M. Fri. and Sat. in summer, $15–24) is a fun, family-oriented place with stained-glass windows from an old New York convent and confessional booths from a church in New Orleans. On the bay side, it fared better in the hurricane, and still serves lobster, grouper, and shrimp, as well as ribs from the smoker outside. Also on the bay side, **Hemingway's** (400 Quietwater Beach Rd., 850/934-4747, 11 A.M.–9 P.M. daily, $8–24) features an open kitchen and two levels of outdoor, deck seating.

The menu is island-inspired, with roasted corn and crab chowder, Key West ribs, and shrimp basted with dark rum sauce, and the cocktails tend toward the tropical fruity and exotic.

At **Crab's** (2 1/2 Via De Luna Dr., 850/932-0700, 11 A.M.–10 P.M. daily, $8–18) the view is fab and the food's not great, but there are 25-cent wings, 25-cent oysters, and drink specials Monday–Thursday and happy hour 11 A.M.–7 P.M. daily. **Sidelines** (2 Via De Luna Dr., 850/934-3660, 11 A.M.–11 P.M. daily, $7–15) is a fun-loving sports bar.

Information and Services

AREA INFORMATION

Here's the funny thing: Pensacola is in the central time zone. It's that far west. The telephone area code is 850.

Tourist Information
Begin a visit with a stop to the **Pensacola Bay Area Convention & Visitors Bureau information center** (1401 E. Gregory St., at the foot of the Pensacola Bay Bridge, 850/434-1234, www.visitpensacola.com, 8 A.M.–5 P.M. daily) to pick up maps, brochures, and a copy of the self-guided historic-district tours. There's also a convenient **Pensacola Beach Visitors Information Center** (735 Pensacola Beach Blvd., Gulf Breeze, 850/932-1500, 9 A.M.–5 P.M. daily).

There are two local newspapers, the weekly *Pensacola Gulf Herald* and the daily *Pensacola News Journal.* There's a free city magazine called *Pensacola Downtown Crowd* that has decent restaurants and arts coverage.

Police and Emergencies
In an emergency, dial 911. If you need medical assistance, **Baptist Hospital** (1000 W.

Moreno St., Pensacola, 850/434-4811) has full emergency services, as does **Gulf Breeze Hospital** (1110 Gulf Breeze Pkwy., Gulf Breeze, 850/934-2020).

Radio and Television
On the radio, turn to **WUWF 88.1 FM** for NPR, **WTKX 101.5 FM** for straight-ahead rock, **WTKX 101.5** for alt rock, and **WFTW 1260 AM** for local talk radio.

For local television programming, **WEAR Channel 3** is the local ABC affiliate, **WKRG Channel 5** is the CBS affiliate out of Mobile-Pensacola, **WALA Channel 10** is the FOX affiliate out of Mobile-Pensacola, **WPMI Channel 15** is the NBC affiliate out of Mobile-Pensacola, **WSRE Channel 23** is PBS, and **WBQP Channel 12** is a local independent.

Laundry Services
If you find yourself in need of coin-op laundry services, try **Dave's** (4124 Mobile Hwy., 850/455-6931), **Chateau Coin** (7010 Lillian Hwy., 850/453-6866), or **Modern Day** (3109 W. Michigan Ave., 850/944-5151).

Getting There and Around

DRIVING

The major east–west roads in this area are I-10, U.S. 90, and U.S. 98. Running north–south are U.S. 29 and I-110. To get to Pensacola from I-10, you can travel south on Highway 85 into Fort Walton Beach, then west on U.S. 98 to Navarre, then west over Navarre Toll Bridge and finally west on Highway 399 approximately 20 miles to Pensacola Beach. Or you can go south on I-110 (lots of chain motels along this) or Highway 281, then east on U.S. 98, follow signs to the beaches, and finally drive over Pensacola Beach Toll Bridge into Pensacola Beach. To get to Perdido Key from Pensacola, go west on Highway 292 to Perdido and finally over Perdido Key Bridge onto Perdido Key.

In town, Palafox is the major north–south artery, and Garden Street, which becomes Navy Boulevard on the way to the naval station, runs east–west. The historic district to the waterfront is walkable; for most of the rest of the area you'll need a car. Naval Air Station Pensacola is southwest of the city, and Pensacola Beach is southeast of the city on Santa Rosa Island. Pensacola is connected to Gulf Breeze by the Pensacola Bay Bridge (also called Three Mile Bridge), which in turn is connected to Pensacola Beach by the Bob Sikes Bridge.

FLYING

Located in Escambia County approximately three miles northeast of the central business district of Pensacola, **Pensacola Regional Airport** (2430 Airport Blvd., 850/436-5000) is the biggest airport in northwest Florida, but that's not saying too much. It's not huge, serving a moderate number of flights from Air Trans, American Eagle, Continental, Delta, Northwest, and US Airways. Delta has the largest number of direct flights.

Taxis (Yellow Cab Company, 850/433-3333; Fantasy Limo 850/941-2354) queue up outside the main terminal entrance at baggage claim. Car-rental agencies are inside the main terminal entrance across from baggage claim. **Alamo** (850/434-5676), **Avis** 850/433-5614, **Budget** (850/432-5499), **Dollar** (850/474-9000), **Hertz** (850/432-2345), and **National** (850/432-8338) are all on the premises. Enterprise and Thrifty are off-site.

PUBLIC TRANSPORTATION

Amtrak (980 E. Heinberg St., 850/433-4966 or 800/USA-RAIL) has a centrally located train station in Pensacola with lots of service, as does **Greyhound** (505 W. Burgess Rd., 850/476-4800 or 800/229-9424) with fairly extensive bus service. Such a large military presence usually ensures decent public transportation. There's even a local bus line run by **Escambia Area County Transit** (850/595-3228, www.goecat.com) that includes a University of West Florida (UWF) trolley service and a Pensacola Beach trolley. All in all, it is possible to get around here without a car, but difficult, with some of the more significant attractions inaccessible via public transportation.

Know the Florida Gulf Coast

The Land

GEOGRAPHY

Florida is bounded on the north by Alabama and Georgia, to the east by the Atlantic, to the south by the Straits of Florida, and to the west by the Gulf of Mexico. The east coast of the state is comparatively straight, extending in a rough line 470 miles long. The Gulf side, on the other hand, has a more sinuous and convoluted coastline, measuring roughly 675 miles. In all, Florida's 2,276-mile coastline is longer than that of any other state in the continental U.S.

It's nearly pancake flat, without notable change in elevation, and young by geological standards, having risen out of the ocean a scant 300 to 400 million years ago. The state of Florida has six major geographical regions, only several of which are represented along the Gulf Coast. First, the **coastal lowlands** encircle the state and extend along the shores inland 10–100 miles. The most recent to emerge from the ocean, the lowlands are covered with forests of saw palmetto and cypress. To the northwest, between the Perdido and Apalachicola Rivers, the **western highlands** are hilly uplands of pine forest. The highlands offer the highest elevation in Florida—345 feet above sea level in the northwestern part of Walton County. And further east, between the Apalachicola and Withlacoochee Rivers, the **Tallahassee Hills** is a hilly region dotted with live oak and pine forests. It gradually slopes eastward to a plain until it hits the Suwannee River.

The Gulf side of the state has numerous deep-water bays: Tampa Bay, Apalachicola Bay, Charlotte Harbor, Pensacola Bay. There is also an abundance of rivers (Caloosahatchee, Peace, Withlacoochee, Manatee, Suwannee, Ocilla, Ocklockonee, Apalachicola, Choctawhatchee, Yellow River, Escambia, Perdido, and others), harbors on the Gulf side, and a record-holding number of first-magnitude springs. Thus, the fishing, boating, and swimming along the Gulf Coast are legendary.

Starting in the south, the **Everglades** region consists mainly of submerged sawgrass plains.

Sanibel Lighthouse, known to locals as Point Ybel Lighthouse, is the island's most photographed spot.

The water, about knee-deep and with a slight southward current, provides habitat to hundreds of fish species, birds, and small mammals. Some of the Everglades' water is overflow from **Lake Okeechobee,** the second-largest freshwater lake with boundaries entirely in the U.S., 30 miles wide and 33 miles long.

North of the lake, extending through De Soto, Manatee, Osceola, and Brevard counties, is a vast tract of prairie land with large swamp areas. This is where much of the cattle is raised in the state. North of that, in Polk, Marion, Orange, Sumter, Lake, and Alachua Counties, there's a little rise along the central ridge (up to 300 feet above sea level), with large and small lakes dotting the fertile, gently rolling terrain. The **coastal plain** that runs along the length of the Gulf Coast is low-lying and sandy, skirted by a dense pine region and marshes in many parts.

Several geographical features and plant communities are common in Florida, such as barrier islands, mangrove islands, marshes, hardwood hammocks, pineland, and flatwoods.

Barrier Islands

Barrier islands are ridges of sand that usually run parallel to the main coast (Sanibel sticks out the other way), separated from the mainland by a bay or lagoon. They are sand deposits of recent geologic origin, in much of the Gulf Coast composed of almost pure milky quartz. Delivered to the Gulf by rivers, this sand is washed and well sorted, resulting in fine, even-grained sand along many Gulf beaches. Buffering the mainland from storms and heavy surf, they are constantly being contoured and molded by wave action and wind. **Sea oats** and other beachside plants provide a little structure and foundation for dunes to develop. They capture and hold the blowing sand—thus, they are to be preserved and nurtured (there's a steep fine for trampling or messing with the sea oats on Gulf Coast beaches). **Swales** are wetlands formed on these islands where the wind has scoured out the sand down to the water table or below, and often a **maritime forest** can be found on the back side of barrier islands behind the secondary dunes.

Mangrove Islands

Along Florida's south coast and halfway up the peninsula, mangrove swamps hug the shoreline. They create a fringing network around most islands, growing at the high-tide line and helping to stabilize the shore. In the maze of the **Ten Thousand Islands** in between Marco Island and the Everglades, you can see entire island ecosystems created by saltwater-tolerant mangroves. These trees send their roots into the shallows, filtering pollution and providing a crucial habitat for fish and wading birds.

Marshes

Marshes comprise a large area near the Gulf Coast—areas that are partially or periodically submerged land, where the water table is near the surface of the soil. Water flows into marshes and swamps from rivers, creeks, and bayous, bringing with it rich organic debris that settles and accumulates in the marshes, compacting into peat. Trees in marshes, or in the larger category of **wetlands,** get used to living in standing water. Cypress and tupelo buttress

One way to explore the barrier and mangrove islands flanking the Gulf Coast is by airboat.

their trunks by sending up "knees" for support (and for breathing air).

In **salt marshes** there is a clear line drawn between the wetland and upland, because the salt is detrimental to the growth of so many plant species. (From Apalachicola Bay south to Tampa Bay, salt marshes are the main coastal community.) In freshwater wetlands that line is more blurred, with the wetland plants shifting subtly into upland species. In the case of **tidal marshes,** affected by the ebb and flow of tides, the demarcation line is even more pronounced. Many tidal marshes along the Gulf Coast are dominated by stands of black needle rush and salt-marsh cordgrass.

Freshwater and saltwater marshes, as well as a similar community called a **seagrass meadow,** are enormously important to Florida's fish species, providing the shelter as a "nursery" for many species, a safe haven in which to mature among the marsh grasses before adult fish go out into the predator-dense Gulf.

Swamps, certainly a defining feature of Florida, are just forested wetlands. About 10 percent of Florida is covered by forested wetland bordering rivers or ponds, populated by plant species that tolerate periodic high water levels. For great examples of swamps, visit **Fakahatchee Strand State Preserve** or **Big Cypress National Park.**

Hardwood Hammocks

Hardwood hammocks may be the oldest natural community type in Florida, dating back more than 25 million years ago. There are **upland hardwoods** and **bottomland hardwoods,** the latter being the transition forest between a dryer upland area and a wet river flood plain. Either way, the largest mature trees in a hardwood forest (laurel oak, sweetgum, Southern magnolia, and others) tend to hog all the light. The understory, the next level of stratification (trees like dogwood, shrubs like Elliots blueberry or Florida anise), has to grab whatever light is left over. And then the forest floor (moss and ferns) lives in the low-light murk. Vines and epiphytes have to hoist themselves up on the canopy trees to gain access to light.

Pineland

Longleaf pineland used to cover 70 million acres in the south. Sadly, Florida pineland is an endangered plant community, a habitat that must

Suwannee River State Park was among the first parks to become part of the Florida state park system. A great example of a hardwood hammock is found along the river trail.

be burned regularly to thrive. The small remaining pinelands in Florida are generally so close to residential and commercial areas that regular burning programs often aren't feasible. As if that's not bad enough, invading species like the Brazilian pepper are choking other species in these delicate habitats.

Long Pine Key in Everglades National Park is a great example of a pineland, much of it old-growth forest. And along the northwest Panhandle, **Blackwater River State Forest,** along with Conecuh National Forest and Eglin Air Force Base, contains the largest holding of longleaf pine trees in the world. Longleaf pine is a long-lived tree, between 350 and 500 years. A mature longleaf pine forest has an open canopy that allows sunlight to flood the forest floor, resulting in a forest floor of lots of plant species and grasses.

Flatwoods

Pine flatwoods (also called pine flats or pine barrens), on the other hand, are ubiquitous in Florida, historically covering almost half of the natural land area in the state. They are characterized by low, flat land, an open canopy of slash pine, and an understory dominated by palmetto prairie. Slash pine have historically been used to produce all kinds of commercial goods, from paper products to turpentine and household goods. Additionally, pine flatwoods provide important habitat for many wildlife species.

A **scrub** is a similar plant community, same pine up above and shrubby stuff and palmetto underneath, but it's in upland areas that are generally much harsher and dryer, with no organic matter in the soil. It's an austere habitat, but home to **gopher tortoises** and the endangered Florida **scrub jay.**

GULF COAST CLIMATE
Heat and Humidity

Florida is closer to the equator than any other continental American state, located on the southeastern tip of North America with a humid subtropical climate and heavy rainfall April–November. Its humidity is attributed to the fact

that no point in the state is more than 60 miles from saltwater and no more than 345 feet above sea level. If this thick steamy breath on the back of your neck is new to you, humidity is a measure of the amount of water vapor in the air. Most often you'll hear the percentage described in "relative humidity," which is the amount of water vapor actually in the air divided by the amount of water vapor the air can hold. The warmer the air becomes, the more moisture it can hold.

When heat and humidity combine to slow evaporation of sweat from the body, outdoor activity becomes dangerous even for those in good physical shape. Drink plenty of water to avoid dehydration and slow down if you feel fatigued or notice a headache, a high pulse rate, or shallow breathing. Overheating can cause serious and even life-threatening conditions such as heatstroke. The elderly, small children, the overweight, and those on some medications are particularly vulnerable to heat stress.

During the summer months, expect temperatures to hover around 90°F and humidity to be somewhere near 100 percent. The most pleasant times of the year along the length of the Florida peninsula fall between December and April—not surprisingly, the busiest time for tourism. Along the Panhandle, however, where temperatures are more moderate in the summer and chillier in the winter, the summer sees more tourist action.

The common wisdom is that the hard freeze line in Florida bisects the state from Ocala to Jacksonville. North of that, freezing temperatures rarely last long, and south of that it's just an hour here or there under the freezing point (with serious damage to tropical plants in years when the temperature dips low). The best approach for packing in preparation for a visit to Florida is layering—with a sweater for over-air-conditioned interiors or chilly winds, and lots of loose, wicking material for the heat.

Rain

It rains nearly every day in the summer along the Gulf Coast. And not just a sprinkle. Due to the abundance of warm, moist air from the Gulf

GULF COAST TEMPERATURES

City	Avg. Low (°F)	Avg. High (°F)
Apalachicola	59	79
Cedar Key	61	83
Fort Myers	64	84
Naples	64	85
Panama City Beach	53	81
Pensacola	59	77
Sarasota	62	83
St. Petersburg	66	82
Tallahassee	56	79
Tampa	63	82

of Mexico and the hot tropical sun, conditions are perfect for the formation of thunderstorms. There are 80–90 thunderstorms each summer, generally less than 15 miles in diameter—but vertically they can grow up to 10 miles high in the atmosphere. These are huge, localized thunderstorms that can drop four or more inches of rain in an hour, while just a few miles away it stays dry. The bulk of these tropical afternoon thunderstorms each summer are electrical storms.

Lightning

With these sudden thunderstorms comes lightning, a serious threat along the Gulf Coast. About 50 people are struck by lightning each year in the state. Most of them are hospitalized and recover, but there are about 10 fatalities annually. Tampa is the "Lightning Capital" of the U.S., with around 25 cloud-to-ground lightning bolt blasts on each square mile annually. The temperature of a single bolt can reach 50,000 degrees Fahrenheit, about three times as hot as the sun's surface. There's not much you can do to ward off lightning except to avoid being in the wrong place at the wrong time. The summer

months of June, July, August, and September have the highest number of lightning-related injuries and deaths. Usually lightning occurs during daylight hours, with the highest concentration between 3 P.M. and 4 P.M., when the afternoon storms peak. Lightning strikes usually occur either at the beginning or end of a storm, and can strike up to 10 miles away from the center of the storm. Keep your eye on approaching storms and seek shelter when you see lightning.

HURRICANES

Hurricanes are violent tropical storms with sustained winds of at least 74 mph. Massive low-pressure systems, they blow counterclockwise around a relatively calm central area called the eye. They form over warm ocean waters, often starting as storms in the Caribbean or off the west coast of Africa. As they move westward, they are fueled by the warm waters of the tropics. Warm, moist air moves toward the center of the storm and spirals upward, releasing driving rains. Updrafts suck up more water vapor, which further strengthens the storm until it can be stopped only when contact is made with land or cooler water. In the average hurricane just one percent of the energy released could meet the energy needs of the U.S. for a full year.

In Florida, the hurricane season is July–November. These storms have been named since 1953. It used to be just female names ("Hell hath no fury like a woman scorned," or some such nonsense), but now there's gender parity in the naming. Really powerful hurricanes' names are retired, kind of like sports greats' jerseys.

Hurricane Safety

Monitor radio and TV broadcasts closely for directions. Gas up the car, and make sure you have batteries, water supply, candles, and food that can be eaten without the use of electricity. Get cash, have your prescriptions filled, and put all essential documents in a large resealable bag. In the event of an evacuation, find the closest shelter by listening to the radio or TV broadcasts (pets are not allowed in shelters).

HURRICANE LINGO

Hurricane Terms:

Severe Thunderstorm—a thunderstorm with winds 58 mph or faster or hailstones three-quarters of an inch or larger in diameter

Tropical Depression—an organized system of clouds and thunderstorms with a defined circulation and maximum sustained winds of 38 mph (33 knots) or less

Tropical Storm—an organized system of strong thunderstorms with a defined circulation and maximum sustained winds of 39–73 mph (34–63 knots)

Hurricane—a warm-core tropical cyclone with maximum sustained winds of 74 mph (64 knots) or greater

Eye—the "calm" center of a hurricane with light winds and partly cloudy to clear skies, usually around 20 miles in diameter (but the range is 5–60 miles)

Eye Wall—the location within a hurricane where the most damaging winds and intense rainfall are found

Tornadoes—violent rotating columns of air that touch the ground; they are spawned by large severe thunderstorms. They can have winds estimated 100–300 mph. A **tornado watch** means they're possible; a **tornado warning** means they're in your area.

Hurricane Warnings:

Tropical Storm Watch—issued when tropical storm conditions may threaten a particular coastal area within 36 hours, when the storm is not predicted to intensify to hurricane strength

Tropical Storm Warning—winds ranging of 39–73 mph can be expected to affect specific areas of a coastline within the next 24 hours

Hurricane Watch—a hurricane or hurricane conditions may threaten a specific coastal area within 36 hours

Hurricane Warning—a warning that sustained winds of 74 mph or higher associated with a hurricane are expected in a specified coastal area in 24 hours or less

Hurricane Scale:

Category I—winds 74–95 mph with a storm surge of 4–5 feet and minimal damage

Category II—winds 96–110 mph with a storm surge of 6–8 feet and moderate damage

Category III—winds 111–130 mph with a storm surge of 9–12 feet and major damage

Category IV—winds 131–155 mph with a storm surge of 13–18 feet and severe damage

Category V—winds 155+ mph with more than an 18-foot storm surge and catastrophic damage

2004 Hurricane Season

Hurricane Charley, a Category IV, came ashore on the southwest coast of Florida on Friday, August 13, 2004. The right eyewall (the most destructive quadrant of the storm) passed over North Captiva Island and divided the barrier island into two parts with a breach that was 450 feet wide. The hurricane made landfall at Cayo Costa, a barrier island just west of Cape Coral, at approximately 3:45 P.M., with winds estimated at 145 mph and a minimum central pressure of 941 millibars. An hour later, wind gusts of 111 mph were measured at the Punta Gorda Airport before equipment failed.

Charley continued its track northeast across De Soto, Hardee, Polk, and Osceola Counties, and at 9:15 P.M. that night, the eye of the storm was centered at Kissimmee, over northern Osceola County. Charley then moved over the Orlando area, with gusts reported to near 105 mph at the airport. The storm then tracked back across the state and emerged off the Volusia County coast and back into the Atlantic.

Charley took approximately nine hours to traverse the Florida peninsula, the strongest hurricane to make landfall in the state since Hurricane Andrew in 1992. A little more than a day prior to Charley's landfall, Tropical Storm Bonnie struck the Florida Panhandle near Apalachicola. At the time, meteorologists were talking about how it hadn't been since 1906 that two storms had struck the state of Florida so close together.

The state hadn't seen the half of it.

Next up, **Hurricane Frances.** A Category II storm, it came ashore on the central-east coast of Florida on September 5, 2004. The impacts of Frances were felt much more widely, from where it made landfall near Stuart to north of Daytona Beach. Compared to Charley's narrow and fierce zone of destruction, Frances had a broad impact zone, but there were fewer structures destroyed and more sporadic overwash than occurred during 2003's Category II Hurricane Isabel.

A Category III, **Hurricane Ivan** came ashore near Gulf Shores, Alabama, on September 16, 2004. With maximum sustained winds near 130 mph and storm surges over 8 feet, Ivan devastated coastal areas along the Florida Panhandle, most seriously in the greater Pensacola area. The storm continued to move toward the north-northeast, bringing devastating flooding to the Appalachians and as far as southern New England.

And finally, the eye of **Hurricane Jeanne,** a Category III, made landfall on the east coast of the state, near the southern end of Hutchinson Island, east of Stuart, on Saturday, September 25, 2004. With winds estimated at 120 mph, the greatest storm tide occurred over southern Brevard, Indian River, St. Lucie, and Martin Counties near and to the right of where Jeanne made landfall. Jeanne tracked northwestward, eventually clipping the northeast portion of Hillsborough County on Sunday as a tropical storm, moving on to hug the coast of the Big Bend. Jeanne was not nearly as devastating to the Gulf Coast as Ivan or Charley.

Ivan undid much of the beach restoration work completed earlier in 2004 near Pensacola, pushing sand back out to sea, into roadways, and into yards. The beaches lost about 50 feet of width, and are lower by 4–6 feet. Farther east on the Emerald Coast (including Destin, Fort Walton Beach, and the Beaches of South Walton), the beaches are reopened with only minimal dune work remaining. In southwest Florida where Hurricane Charley hit, most beaches are now cleaned and open, with a fair amount of restoration work still ahead. The biggest remaining problem in the aftermath of both Charley and Ivan is home repair—insurance companies have been slow to pay out or have paid amounts insufficient to fix the damage, roofers are hard to find, and even FEMA money has been slow to find its way to those in need. Parts of the Gulf Coast may be notable for their blue-tarp roofs for some time to come.

Flora and Fauna

The abundance of sunlight and rain and the near absence of four traditional seasons allow for the successful growth of nearly 4,000 plant species and nearly that many animals in Florida. The lower Gulf Coast's palms, the great cypress swamps, mangroves, and on the Panhandle one of the greatest forested regions in the East—Florida's plant life is richly diverse, providing a range of habitats. Even nonnative plants and animals flourish in these lush conditions, a fact that troubles Floridian scientists as more exotic species take hold. The trade in exotic pets and plants, as well as the movement of huge numbers of people and vehicles, can intentionally or unintentionally bring new species into Florida, devastating native species and invading natural areas.

FLORA

On March 27, 1513 (Easter Day), Ponce de Leon landed on the coast of Florida and pronounced it a "land of flowers." And it's true, mostly. Florida Gulf Coast plants—if you're from somewhere else, they can either creep you out or fill you with wonderment. The subtropi-cal climate is warm, moist, lush, with the kind of foliage in the summer for which you don't need a stop-action film in order to document growth. There are plants that grow like Audrey in *Little Shop of Horrors.* Fast, loose, and weird. The even greater thing is that many native and even flourishing exotic Florida plants have huge advocates and devotees.

There are avid clubs devoted to carnivorous plants, to orchids, to bromeliads, to palms (which are really not trees—despite the fact that the state "tree" is the cabbage palm). It's a gardener's state, but there's a certain humility gardeners bring to the table. It's not a state for regimented topiary or manicured rose gardens. Serendipity, chance, and Mother Nature's whim play a part in Florida gardening. So much is given, but, as the hurricane season in 2004 showed, so much can be taken away.

Trees
Palm trees are practically a Florida cliché. Also known as "cabbage palm" and "palmetto," it's from the **sabal palm** that hearts of palm are harvested. Sabal palm grows in all conditions in the

Just off Highway 41 in the heart of Florida's Ten Thousand Islands, Chokoloskee is tucked in a labyrinth of mangrove islands.

COURTESY OF VISIT FLORIDA

state—wet, dry, coastal, swampy—and it is from the fronds of the sabal that the Seminoles built watertight chickee roofs. In some parts of the Gulf Coast, you'll encounter **royal palm**, identified by its towering 80-foot pale gray trunk and bright, glossy crown shaft. Many of the other palm species usually associated with Florida are not native—the easily recognized **coconut palm**, the heavy-trunked **Canary Island date palm**, the slim, statuesque **red latan palm.** You'll see them all along the Gulf Coast, but it's what they're in contrast to that gives this subtropical landscaping its own flavor.

Mangroves are often called walking trees because they hover above the water, their arching prop roots resembling so many spindly legs. Seeds sprout on the parent tree and drop off, bobbing in the water until they lodge on an oyster bar or a snag in the shallows. There, the seed begins to grow to a tree, the foundation of a new, tiny island. Around its roots sediment and debris build up to create a thick layer of peat upon which other plant species begin to grow. This first tree drops more seed tubules, which get stuck in the mulch ground and create more trees. This is how islands are often created off the Gulf Coast.

There are three types of mangrove along the Gulf: The red mangrove forms a wide band of trees on the outermost part of each mangrove island, facing the open sea. The red mangrove encircles the black mangrove, which in turn encircles the white mangrove at the highest, driest part of each mangrove island. Mangroves are protected by federal, state, and local laws.

Cypress is another oh-so-Florida tree. Forested wetlands in the state are often dominated by cypress trees, located along stream banks and riverbanks or in ponds with slow-moving water. Bald cypresses (they aren't always bald, they just lose their leaves in winter) are the largest trees in North America east of the Rockies. They can live for hundreds of years, quietly ruminating with their roots in water, their "knees" protruding above the soil and waterline. The function of these knees, part of the root system that projects out of the water, isn't totally known, other than that they provide stability and more air for the

base of these flood-tolerant trees. The Gulf Coast offers several cypress swamps to explore.

Live oaks are certainly not the sole custody of Florida. In all of the South these huge semideciduous trees loom, gnarled and woebegone, draped with Spanish moss (which is neither Spanish, nor a moss). The Tallahassee area is especially dense with live oak, but you'll see them all over.

The **gumbo limbo,** one of only three native tree species in North America, is common down toward the Everglades. They call it the sunburn tree, as its smooth bark peels off in sheets to reveal a red trunk color beneath. I love these trees, and I love saying their name even more.

Sawgrass

Also a defining feature of the Everglades, sawgrass looks like smooth, soft hay. It dominates wide swaths of marshland in this area known as "The River of Grass," but sawgrass blades have little saw-like teeth along one side that make walking through it very painful.

Epiphytes

"Epi" means "on" and "phyte" means "plant." Thus, an epiphyte is a plant that grows on another plant. They're sometimes called airplants because they grow above ground, in the air, roots wiggling in the breeze. Host plants support them high off the ground, where they don't need to compete for light and rain water, and where they don't have to cope with floodwater and marauding animals. Epiphytes generally do no harm to the host plant and get their nutrients from their own photosynthesis and their own water from runoff on their host. Cardinal airplant, resurrection fern—these are all wonderful plants to explore.

Within this category, **orchids** are probably the best known, with more genera than any other plant. They are among the most exotic and delicate flowers in the world, holding a special fascination for collectors, photographers, and hobbyists. Orchids abound in the Everglades' hardwood hammocks, marshes, pineland, and prairies. To see thousands of orchid species, visit Marie Selby Botanical Gardens in Sarasota.

Bromeliads are another type of epiphyte, members of the pineapple family. They use shallow roots only to anchor themselves to a tree or the ground, and absorb through their leaves the water and nutrients they need from the air and from the rain. These leathery, brightly colored tropical plants often collect water in little "tanks" or between their leaves. Of Florida's 16 species of bromeliads, 13 are not found elsewhere in the United States.

Crops

The citrus fruit industry has been big business in the state since the 1890s when Chinese horticulturist Lue Gim Gong introduced a new variety of **orange** and a hardier **grapefruit.** Today, citrus is Florida's leading cash crop, producing 70 percent of the country's oranges. Some reports place the value at $1.6 billion—not surprisingly, the orange blossom is the state flower. The 2004 hurricane season, especially Hurricane Charley, cut orange and grapefruit harvests by 20 percent for the year and jeopardized some of the 89,000 jobs in the state involved in the citrus industry. Here's an interesting fact: 95 percent of the state's oranges are made into juice.

Beyond citrus, though, Florida is the "winter salad bowl," providing 80 percent of the fresh vegetables grown in the U.S. during January, February, and March. The Gulf Coast is responsible for lots of tomatoes, peppers, and strawberries—Plant City near Tampa is the state's strawberry capital.

There are also exotic tropical fruits and vegetables grown along the Gulf Coast, from smooth-skinned avocados the size of softballs to mangoes (Lee County), guavas, lychees, sapotes, cherimoyas, and others.

FAUNA

Fish

No other state in the U.S. and few other countries boast a more varied marine environment. Florida has hundreds of species of fish teeming in its waters. There's the Atlantic and the fertile Gulf of

The tarpon, a saltwater game fish often called the silver king, is among Florida's most celebrated fish.

Mexico with its hundreds of bays, sounds, inlets, and brackish marshes. But there are also freshwater rivers, lakes, estuaries, and a bazillion other marine environments.

The **Panhandle** has long stretches of white-sand beaches and ocean that quickly drops off to deep water—boaters in 70 feet of water can often see bathers on the beach. The area is also home to bountiful estuaries (where rivers meet the sea) tucked behind long, narrow barrier islands.

From **Apalachicola** to the **Big Bend,** estuaries are protected by oyster bars and rocky islands. Here the water depths drop off very gradually. Off the Suwannee River and St. Marks Light, ordinary outboard motorboats can run aground more than three miles from shore. This area has few beaches and is dominated by marshes with vast seagrass beds. Farther south along the Gulf, anglers enjoy a number of exciting species, from huge **tarpon** to tasty **grouper, cobia,** and the fabled **snook.**

In much of this area, freshwater fishing is most productive in the spring while sport fishing is good all year. But you need a license. An annual nonresident saltwater fishing license is $31.50; a seven-day license is $16.50. The same prices apply to the freshwater licenses. You need to figure out what you're fishing for before you purchase your license, but either way the revenue generated by the sale goes to the Florida Fish and Wildlife Conservation Commission.

There are also numerous shellfish species: **scallops** in Steinhatchee, **oysters** in Apalachicola, **stone crabs** in Everglades City, **clams** in Cedar Key, and **Florida blue crabs** all over.

Birds

With 500 bird species, both those native to the state and those that migrate here, the Gulf Coast is a bird lover's paradise in a range of habitats. Mangrove estuaries are home to many species of **egrets, herons,** and numerous other **wading birds. Waterbirds** occupy interior wetlands, and countless **shorebirds, terns,** and **gulls** populate the white-sand beaches. Unique to the state, the **Florida scrub jay** lives in a small patch of scrub-oak habitat; **ospreys** and **bald eagles** make their gargantuan nests all along the Gulf Coast. The woods are aflutter with **red-shouldered hawks** and endangered **red cockaded woodpeckers.** In backyard ponds you'll spy the long, sinuous neck of the **anhinga**—what Native tribes called "snakebirds"—they vogue in rakish poses as they dry their wings after a deep dive for fish. You'll spot **white pelicans,** the second-largest flying bird in North America, sailing low over the Gulf waters, while high above a **frigate** is barely a speck. You'll bristle at the shrewish nagging cry of a **little blue heron** and startle at the trilling bray of the enormous **sandhill cranes** that promenade gracefully in small family groups of three.

I could go on. It's serious birding country, with loads of expert birders to lead you through the prime birding spots. There are numerous birding festivals along the Gulf Coast, and the **Great Florida Birding Trail** (floridabirding-trail.com) for when you want to go it alone.

COURTESY OF VISIT FLORIDA

One of 30 cougar subspecies, the endangered Florida panther is tawny brown on its back and pale gray underneath, with white markings on the head, neck, and shoulders.

Big Mammals

After the alligator, the **West Indian manatee** is the Florida Gulf Coast's most famous animal. A manatee is a large, gray aquatic mammal with a body that tapers to a flat, paddle-shaped, beaver-like tail. Completely herbivorous, they are gentle and slow moving, found in shallow rivers, estuaries, saltwater bays, canals, and coastal areas. Manatees are migratory, meaning they move around and are concentrated in the warm Florida waterways in the winter. Most of their time is spent traveling, resting, and eating—they can consume 10–15 percent of their body weight daily in vegetation (and that's a lot, since adult males weigh 800–1,200 pounds). They have no known predators, but habitat destruction and collisions with watercraft propellers have made the species endangered. There are an estimated 3,000 West Indian manatees left in the United States, many of them convened along the Nature Coast in Homosassa and Crystal River in the winter. Manatees are protected under federal law, and the Florida Manatee Sanctuary Act of 1978 states: "It is unlawful for any person, at any time, intentionally or negligently, to annoy, molest, harass, or disturb any manatee." It's a steep fine and imprisonment, so look but don't touch these guys. In many waterways on the Gulf Coast there are reduced boat speed zones for manatee protection.

Another locally protected animal is the **Florida panther.** They're called the Florida panthers, but really they once roamed throughout the Southeast from east Texas to the Atlantic and north to parts of Tennessee. Overhunting, loss of habitat, and reduction of their primary prey reduced their population to just a handful living in southern Florida in pinelands and mixed swamp forests. Fewer than 100 remain in Florida, making them one of the rarest and most endangered mammals in the world. A subspecies of cougar that has adapted to the subtropical environment of Florida, they are still to be found occasionally in Fakahatchee Strand State Preserve and Big Cypress National Preserve, where there is a 26,400-acre **Florida Panther National Wildlife Refuge.** The Florida Fish and Wildlife Conservation Commission monitors panther activity using radio telemetry collars.

Cattle were first introduced to North America in 1521, when Ponce de Leon landed on the Gulf Coast. He brought a small herd of Andalusian cattle, the descendants of which might be the foundation stock of Florida's **piney-woods cattle.** Spanish missions had herds of cattle, and the Native Americans learned to raise cattle from the Spanish. British and Creek invasions of Spanish Florida in 1702 and 1704 destroyed the Spanish herds, but the Seminoles kept their own herds intact. During the English occupation of Florida, the British brought their own longhorn and shorthorn cattle, which eventually bred with the surviving Andalusians, resulting in a tough, compact cow weighing a scant 600 pounds. A

ALLIGATORS

In his excellent memoir, ***Totch, A Life in the Everglades,*** Totch Brown describes a gator's sounds:

"Gators make three different sounds. One is the "grunt" used by young gators in distress to call their mothers. When you pick up a baby gator it'll start grunting every time. The mother will come to this sound right away. (With practice, you can imitate this "grunt" and often fool a grown gator into coming to you.)

Then there's a blowing sound gators make when they're more or less hemmed up, or cornered and are good and mad.

The third sound is the gator bellow—a blood-curdling sound that can be heard for miles across the Everglades. When one gator bellows, usually another will answer. . . . When a 12-foot gator bellows, he raises his head up as high as possible, his mouth wide open, and with a full breath, lets out his air. It's a sight to be seen! The bellowing is generally in mating season, the late spring, when the rains

are about to start. The gators seem to be asking Mother Nature for a drink of water. "

I've seen a gator bellow, right at the edge of my backyard pond, his head tipped way back. To me he didn't seem like he was asking anybody for anything other than to buzz off. It's a monster noise, deeply unsettling, apt to have the kind of effect that everyone's first viewing of Jaws did back in 1975.

Alligators were first listed as an endangered species in 1967, their numbers threatened by hunting and habitat loss. Then the American alligator was removed from the endangered species list in 1987 after the U.S. Fish and Wildlife Service pronounced a complete recovery of the species. I'll say—conservative estimates put the population at around a million in Florida, Louisiana, Texas, and Georgia. Because they can tolerate brackish water as well as freshwater, they can be found in rivers, swamps, bogs, lakes, ponds, creeks, canals, swimming pools, and lots of Florida golf courses.

(continued on next page)

ALLIGATORS (cont'd)

The American alligator is the largest reptile in North America (distinguished from the American crocodile by its short, rounded snout and black color). They can live 35–50 years in the wild, 60–80 years in captivity. The average adult male is 13 feet in length (half of the length taken up by the tail), although they can grow up to 18 feet long. Bulls are generally larger than females, weighing 450–600 pounds.

They're everywhere in Florida, and they eat just about anything. Usually that means lizards, fish, snakes, turtles, even little gators, but they'll also enjoy bologna sandwiches and schnauzer.

Florida residents have heretofore learned to be blasé about gators. They're an everyday part of living in this subtropical climate. But things are changing. Sanibel Island may be leading the way for a new stance on gators in the state. In the past three years several people have died in alligator attacks in Sanibel. It's hard to be as sanguine about gator-human relations when women are getting chomped while pruning their gardens.

The problems are not just a function of large numbers—people feed the gators and thus the alligators have gotten chummy and less fearful of humans, and vice versa.

So now new policies are being put in place. In many spots along the Gulf Coast, if gators get large (over eight feet) they are taken away and "processed" (not a good euphemism). Smaller ones get relocated. The jury is out on this inter-species relationship.

Stay Safe

Alligators are cold-blooded (literally, maybe figuratively). It's a good survival tactic because they don't need to eat as much or as often as their warm-blooded counterparts. In fact, they can't eat unless their internal body temperature is 90 degrees. Thus, they don't eat all winter, and in the

COURTESY OF VISIT FLORIDA

Alligators have 80 teeth. They lose them in the course of capturing and crushing prey (they don't really chew), so they have a second row of little teeth behind the first ready to grow into position.

spring can be seen in the midmorning basking on the banks in a sunny spot. They're hungry and horny in April and May—a good time to steer especially clear. In the summer the females lay their eggs in a nest (up to 70 eggs) and cover them over, then the eggs incubate for 65 days. (As a cool aside, alligators lack sexual chromosomes, so that sex is determined by the temperature at which eggs incubate. Between 90 and 93 degrees they're all male, between 87 and 89 degrees they're female.) The mom stays close, carrying the freshly hatched babies to the water. Even after they're swimming around, mama is protective for up to the first two years (supposedly she can hear their cry for help up to a mile away). Still, it's said only one in 10 alligators lives through the first year.

So, to review:

• Don't feed the gators. And if you see others doing so, give them a hard time.

• Don't bother the babies or come between a mother and her young.

• Don't bug them during their cranky spring mating season.

• Closely supervise kids playing in or near fresh or brackish water. Never allow little kids to play by water unattended. The same goes for pets. In fact, just don't let your dog swim in fresh or brackish water in Florida, period.

• Alligators feed most actively at dusk and dawn, so schedule your lake or river swim for another time.

• They don't make good pets. They are not tamed in captivity, and it's illegal besides.

• If you are bitten, seek medical attention, even if it seems minor. Their mouths harbor very infectious bacteria.

• If you see a big one that seems inordinately interested in humans, call the local police nonemergency number.

• Don't throw your fish scraps and guts back into the water when fishing. This encourages gators to hang around boats and docks.

A Little Florida Gator Humor

An old codger in Florida owned a large farm with a big pond in the back. He had it fixed up pretty nicely, with a picnic table, a shady fruit orchard, a little fishing dock.

One evening the farmer decided to go down to the pond and have a look around. He grabbed an old five-gallon bucket to bring back some fruit.

As he neared the pond, he heard voices, with shouting and laughter. As he came closer he saw it was a bunch of young women skinny-dipping in his pond. He made the women aware of his presence and they all went to the deep end.

One of the women shouted to him, "Sir, we're not coming out until you leave!"

The old man frowned. "I didn't come down here to spy on you ladies swimming naked." Holding up the bucket, he said, "I'm here to feed the alligator."

Moral: Old men can still think fast.

Gator Reading

Bare, Colleen Stanley. *Never Kiss an Alligator.* New York: Puffin Books, 1994. (A children's book.)

Behler, John and Deborah Behler. *Alligators and Crocodiles.* Stillwater, MN: Voyageur Press, 1998.

Brown, Loren G. "Totch." *Totch: A Life in the Everglades.* Gainesville, FL: University Press of Florida, 1993.

Carmichael, Pete and Winston Williams. *Florida's Fabulous Reptiles & Amphibians.* 1st edition. Tampa, FL: World Publications, 1991.

Huffstodt James T. *Everglades Lawmen: True Stories of Game Wardens in the Glades.* Sarasota, FL: Pineapple Press, 2000.

Larson, Ron. *Swamp Song: A Natural History of Florida's Swamps.* Gainesville, FL: University Press of Florida, 1995.

Strawn, Martha A. *Alligators, Prehistoric Presence in the American Landscape.* Baltimore, MD: Johns Hopkins University Press, 1997.

Taylor, Dave. *The Alligator and the Everglades.* Crabtree Pub Co., 1990.

GREAT GUIDES TO FLORIDA WILDLIFE

Birds:

Tekiela, Stan. *Birds of Florida Field Guide*. Minnesota: Adventure Publications, 2001. It's a great small-sized book organized by bird color. This makes it easy to narrow things down when you've just spotted a flash of wing color in your binoculars.

Even better than this book, though, is a sand- and waterproof *Florida's Gulf Coast Birds* flip map illustrated by Ernest C. Simmons (email slewers@tiac.net if you can't find it in area bookstores). It puts birds into rough groups—wading birds, shore birds, wetland birds, birds of prey, etc.

Fish:

Arnov, Boris. *Fish Florida: Saltwater/Better than Luck-The Foolproof Guide to Florida Saltwater Fishing*. Gulf Publishing, 2002. This is a fairly good beginner book: it describes a kind of fish, let's say amberjack, then tells you how it fights (fiercely); appropriate tackle, whether you're spinning or plug casting or fly fishing; and technique for live bait or light tackle casting. It also gives catch and size limits and other regulations.

Dew, Gregory. *The Barefoot Fisherman's Guide to the Emerald Coast: From Gulf Shore, Alabama, to Apalachicola, Florida*. Crane Hill Publishers, 1999. Flip to Chapter 3, which enumerates 40 or so fabulous fishing spots on this gorgeous stretch of coast, and what you're likely to catch there.

Mammals:

Adams, Alto. *A Florida Cattle Ranch*. Sarasota, FL: Pineapple Press, 1998. You'll learn about Cracker cows, scrub, and the hardscrabble world of Florida ranching.

Maehr, David. *The Florida Panther: Life and Death of a Vanishing Carnivore*. Island Press, 1997. The author makes these endangered cougars spring to life in their last frontier in the Big Cypress National Preserve and around the Okaloacoochee Slough.

Butterflies:

Daniels, Jaret. *Butterflies of Florida Field Guide (Our Nature Field Guides)* Adventure Publications, 2003. It's a lovely field guide with great pictures and not-too-Latin text.

Shells:

Williams, Winston. *Florida's Fabulous Seashells: And Other Seashore Life*. Tampa: World Publications, 1988. It's light enough to pack in your beach bag, with good color photos and interesting text about the marine animals.

Where to find good Florida wildlife books: **Haslam's Book Store** (www.haslamcorp.com) is a St. Petersburg institution and one of the best bookstores in Florida, while in Tampa **Inkwood Books** has a broad Florida nature, wildlife, and gardening section.

Pineapple Press (www.pineapplepress.com) is the best local small press, producing a handful of books on Florida each year, all of high caliber and many with an environmental bent.

The **University Press of Florida** (www.upf.com/esse), the consolidated publishing efforts of all of the Florida state universities, groups Florida books by helpful categories (environment, people, arts, and artifacts).

Florida Plants Online Bookstore (www.floridaplants.com) indeed lists lots of excellent books on local flora, but its reach also extends to fauna, highbrow literature, and books for young readers.

For rare or out-of-print books, **Grove Antiquarian** (www.abebooks.com/home/GROVBOOK/home.htm) traffics in pre-owned books specializing in South Florida and the Caribbean.

The bookstore at **Everglades National Park** (www.nps.gov/ever/fnpma/fnpma4.htm) features a long reading list of Everglade-centric books. And way up in Cedar Key there's **Curmudgeonalia** that proffers a discerning collection of birding, naturalist, and offbeat Florida history books.

speckled brindle pattern, sharp horns, and a cranky disposition still define the Florida piney-woods cow. Cows used to roam the state free, branded or earmarked for owner identification. In order to round them up, Florida cattlemen would crack long whips to get them moving. Some people say it is this that caused rural Floridians to be called Crackers.

Reptiles and Amphibians

There are so many sexy, exciting wild animals in Florida, from alligators to roseate spoonbills, that the little everyday animals often get short shrift. The Gulf Coast is Lizard Central, with several species duking it out for dominance. The **Cuban knight anole** was introduced into Florida in the 1950s. These guys and the **brown anole** are hardy and aggressive (although not in any way harmful to humans), and they have displaced the native **green anole** along the Gulf Coast. The green anole is still the top lizard species in the state's interior.

Turtles are also plentiful in Florida, with 26 different species. Of the species that prefer dry land, there is the **Florida box turtle,** common to upland scrub and marshes. They can live up to 100 years but are now protected and fairly uncommon. The **gopher tortoise** you'll see in upland scrub areas. They are protected but occur throughout the state. **Florida snapping turtles** can get up to 70 pounds and are common throughout the state, whereas **alligator snapping turtles** are only to be found along the Panhandle. Both have powerful jaws and could snap a finger in half. Equally fractious is the **Florida soft shell turtle,** which has a rubbery shell to allow it to bury itself in the sand as well as swim very fast. The **Florida cooter** lives in large ponds, canals, slow-moving rivers, and lakes—it's historically a delicacy among Florida Crackers, and you'll still find it on menus on the Gulf Coast.

You'll also see frogs—from the exotic **giant marine toad** once imported to control cane beetles to the ubiquitous **Cuban tree frog,** which has displaced many local frog species and has a pretty noxious skin toxin—as well as a fair number of snakes. The **Florida cottonmouth** is the one that seems to worry everyone, almost always near water, reaching up to six feet, and highly venomous. You'll often encounter them sunning themselves on semi-submerged logs along southern Gulf Coast rivers, whereas Florida's **eastern diamondback,** the largest and most dangerous local snake, is more common in palmetto flatlands and pine woods. **Black racers** are much more common, most of them fairly small despite the fact that they can grow to six feet. They're the common, nonvenomous snakes in many Florida gardens.

Spiders and Insects

There are loads of big spiders in Florida, too. One of the coolest is the really large **golden silk spider** common to wooded areas or groves, but there are excellent brightly colored **jumping spiders** that don't build webs but instead hunt for their prey and pounce on the unsuspecting. The **black and yellow argiope spider** is another distinctive and fairly common Gulf Coast species—they build big webs with zipper-like zigzag bands of silk at the center.

There are two species of **fire ants** in Florida, the red imported fire ant and the tropical or native fire ant. Either way, their sting is a nasty shock. They form loose, sandy mounds on the ground, and when perturbed they swarm out of their house to bite you, leaving raised white or red welts that really hurt and itch for days. Be aware of where you're standing while visiting Florida, avoiding mounds of loose dirt at all costs.

History

SPANISH EXPLORATION

The southernmost state in the U.S., Florida was named by **Ponce de Leon** upon his visit in 1513, clearly taken with the lush tropical wilderness. This expedition, the first documented presence of Europeans on the mainland of the U.S., was ostensibly "to discover and people the island of Bimini." On the return voyage he rounded the Dry Tortugas to explore the Gulf of Mexico, entering Charlotte Harbor. He soon realized that Florida was more than a large island. Near Mound Key he encountered the fierce Calusa people, and while on Estero Island repairing his ship he narrowly escaped Calusa capture. Eight years later he returned and headed to the Calusa territory with 500 of his men, aiming to establish a permanent colony in Florida. In an ensuing battle with the Calusa, Ponce de Leon was pierced in the thigh by an arrow and carried back to his ship. He never returned again.

Many of the subsequent explorers' missions were less high-profile. In 1516 **Diego Miruelo** mapped Pensacola Bay. In 1517, **Alonso Alvarez de Pineda** went the length of the Florida shore to the Mississippi River, confirming Ponce de Leon's assertion that Florida was not an island. In 1520, **Vasquez de Ayollon** mapped the Carolina coast (which at the time Spain claimed in the vast region they called "Florida").

Panfilo de Narvaez was a veteran Caribbean soldier, hired by Spanish authorities in 1520 to overthrow Hernán Cortés's tyrannical rule. After a lengthy imprisonment by Cortés, Narvaez went back to Spain and obtained a grant to colonize the Gulf Coast from northern Mexico to Florida. Together with **Cabeza de Vaca,** an armada of five ships, and 400 soldiers, Narvaez landed north of the mouth of Tampa Bay in 1527. Spanish–Native American relations deteriorated quickly during this period; the Spaniards' ruthless hunt for gold and riches met with violence on the part of the Indians.

Narvaez ordered his ships back to Cuba, while a band of men headed northward to the Panhandle in search of gold. Empty-handed, Narvaez finally returned to the Gulf at St. Marks. Assuming Mexico to be only a few days' journey to the west, Narvaez had five long canoes constructed, which capsized in a storm off the coast of Texas. Narvaez drowned, and only Cabeza de Vaca and four others survived. This little band traveled 6,000 miles and in 1536 reached Mexico City to report on their ill-fated mission.

SPANISH, FRENCH, AND ENGLISH COLONIZATION

Then came **Hernando de Soto.** In the spring of 1539 he sailed for Tampa Bay with seven vessels, 600 soldiers, three Jesuit friars, and several dozen civilians with the intent of starting a settlement. Where he went exactly is a topic of much debate: Some say he landed in Manatee County, others believe it was in Charlotte Harbor. Like many of the conquistadores before him, de Soto was attracted to the stories of Indian riches to the north, so he sent his fleet back to Cuba, left only a rudimentary base camp on the Manatee River, and set off inland from the coast. He and his men never found what they sought, moving ever northward into Georgia, South Carolina, Tennessee, Alabama, Mississippi, and Arkansas, where he died of fever.

There were religious missions to the state during the same time—Dominican priest **Father Luis Cancer,** three additional missionaries, and a Christianized Indian maiden named Magdalene arrived on the beaches outside Tampa Bay in 1549. Given the Native Americans' experience with white men, it's probably no wonder that Father Cancer was quickly surrounded and clubbed to death. The survivors in his party hightailed it back to Mexico to put the skids on future missionary proposals for Florida.

In 1559, the viceroy of Mexico decided a settlement on the Gulf was essential in helping shipwrecked sailors and to discourage French trading visits. He hired **Tristan de Luna** to establish this colony. With 1,500 soldiers and 13 ships, de Luna landed at Pensacola Bay. De Luna's poor leadership led to the group becoming scattered, five ships being destroyed, and a period of near starvation for the settlers. They gave up and went home. (As an aside, in 1992 the Florida Bureau of Archaeological Research found the remains of a colonial Spanish ship in Pensacola Bay that might have been one of de Luna's sunken ships.) Following this, King Philip II of Spain announced that Spain was no longer interested in promoting colonial expeditions into Florida.

French Protestant Huguenots prepared to challenge Spain's sovereignty in Florida. Another failure, really. Jean Ribault, France's most lauded seaman of the time, set sail for Florida on April 30, 1562, establishing a colony at Port Royal, South Carolina, that year. It didn't work out, and somehow on his return to Europe England's Queen Elizabeth had him arrested for establishing a French colony in Spanish territory. Spaniard Pedro Menendez de Avilés, a much-celebrated naval commander, took up where Ribault left off, establishing what is thought of as the first European settlement, in St. Augustine, Florida, in 1565.

The history of Florida during the first Spanish administration (1565–1763) centers along the east coast of the state, specifically around St. Augustine. The English neighbors to the north periodically attempted to capture the Florida territory (Governor Moore of South Carolina made an unsuccessful attempt in 1702, Governor Oglethorpe of Georgia invaded Florida in 1740), and in 1763 Spain ceded Florida to England. They, in turn, did an equally incomplete job of populating the country and developing its resources, especially in light of the increasingly aggressive Native American tribes. The British controlled Florida 1763–1781, at which point the Spanish occupied again 1783–1821. But in 1821 the Spanish government ratified a treaty turning over Florida to the United States.

THE GULF COAST'S NATIVE AMERICANS

Twenty-five thousand years before the birth of Christ, small tribes of primitive hunters crossed the Bering Strait from Asia to the Americas. Generation after generation traveled southward until these hunters arrived in what is now Florida—perhaps one of the last places on continental North America to be inhabited by humans. Warm and mild of climate, the waters teeming with fish, Florida was a hospitable home for early nomadic Paleo-Indians (circa 12000 B.C. to 7500 B.C.). They built small huts of animal fur and lived off the land's bounty, fishing the bays and streams. In the time between 1000 B.C. and A.D. 1500, the tribes developed advanced tools and pottery-making skills. And by A.D. 1500 Florida's natives were divided into large groupings, most ethnologically and linguistically related to the Creek family. Each grouping was divided further into small independent villages. Conservative estimates put the total numbers of Native Americans in Florida at 100,000 at that time.

In northwest Florida the **Apalachee** of the Tallahassee Hills, in between the Suwannee and Apalachicola Rivers, and the **Timucuans,** their dominion ranging more in the center of the Florida peninsula, between the Aucilla River and the Atlantic and as far south as Tampa Bay, brought farming skills to the area. They cultivated squash, beans, and corn, hunting to supplement with meat. Highly organized and hierarchical tribes, they lived in great communal houses and had an absolute ruler (who was assisted by a shaman and a council of noblemen) and a very delineated pecking order. They also built elaborate burial and temple mounds, the ruins of which can still be seen.

Along the southwest Gulf Coast the **Calusa** dominated, feared because of their fierceness. They were tall, with long flowing hair and simple garb consisting only of breechclouts of tanned deerskin. They were not farmers, living instead off the bounty of the local waters and the wealth of the nearby woods. Forty Calusa villages spread along the Florida Gulf Coast, with Mound Key near the mouth of the Caloosahatchee River the largest village. They had only primitive tools, but the Calusa built huge mounds of shell and deep moats to protect their villages of raised, thatch-roofed huts. They practiced sacrificial worship and exhibited little interest in the Spaniards' missionary overtures.

Franciscan friars fared better in bringing Catholicism to the Timucuans and the Apalachee, just as the Spanish soldiers were granted permission to steal from the native peoples. The missionaries taught the natives to read and write, and they became more like Spaniards, leaving their villages to build houses in St. Augustine or carrying corn along the Camino Real connecting St. Augustine with the Tallahassee area.

Both tribes lost numbers to diseases brought by the Spaniards, and then more to the British who tried to raid the Spanish missions and gain control of Florida. The British brought the Yamasee Indians from South Carolina, and together they destroyed the mission buildings and took many of the natives as slaves. In 1763, when the Spanish ceded Florida to the British, the Spanish departed the fort at St. Augustine and took the remaining Indians to Cuba. While the Calusa were less amenable to coexisting peacefully with the Spanish, they met the same fate, dying out in the late 1700s. Enemy tribes from Georgia and South Carolina began raiding the Calusa territory, some Calusas were captured and sold as slaves, and the rest seem to have died of diseases such as smallpox and measles.

The **Seminoles** were originally of Creek stock, hailing from Georgia and Alabama. They moved into Florida during the mid-1700s, occupying the spaces indigenous Florida Indians had left behind. They, too, ended up being annihilated by disease and the Spanish, British, and American settlers. Their refusal to withdraw to reservations resulted in the Seminole Wars of 1835–1842. By the end of the war, 4,420 Seminoles had surrendered and been deported to the west. Another 300, however, defied every effort of the United States government, retreating to the backwoods of the Everglades to hide out.

Many of their descendants occupy the area to this day. According to a 1990 census, 36,000 Floridians claim Native American ancestry, from 48 different groups.

STATEHOOD, CIVIL WAR, AND RECONSTRUCTION

After the signing of the Adams-Onis treaty ceding Florida to the U.S. in 1821, Andrew Jackson was appointed military governor of the territory. Florida's present boundaries were established, with Tallahassee as the new capital and William P. Duval as its first territorial governor. It was a plantation economy, with settlers expanding ever southward and crowding out the Seminole Indians. Florida was admitted to the Union in 1845, the 27th state. After Abraham Lincoln's election to the presidency in 1860, Florida's proslavery stance led to it seceding from the Union in 1861 and joining the Confederacy. Florida furnished salt, cattle, and other goods to the Confederate army. Relative to population size, Florida furnished more troops than any other Confederate state, participating in the campaigns of Tennessee and Virginia. Florida was represented in the higher ranks of the Confederate service by major-generals Loring, Anderson, and Smith, and brigadier-generals Brevard, Bullock, Finegan, Miller, Davis, Finley, Perry, and Shoup. Florida was represented in the Confederate cabinet by Stephen H. Mallory, Secretary of the Navy. The most notable Civil War engagement fought in Florida was the battle of Olustee (February 20, 1864), a Confederate victory.

After the war, a new constitution was adopted, the Fourteenth Amendment ratified, and Florida was readmitted to the Union in 1868. It took a decade or so for the state to establish social, educational, and industrial health. The state's general level of poverty led to four million acres of land being sold to speculative real-estate promoters in 1881. The discovery of rich phosphate deposits in 1889 improved the state's economy, as did its increasing popularity as a winter resort destination.

FLORIDA'S FIRST BOOM

Along with the phosphate mining in the southwestern part of the state, agriculture (especially citrus) and cattle ranching brought wealth to Florida, as did residents from northern states who came to bask in the state's natural beauty and mild climate each winter. In the 1870s steamboat tours on Florida's winding rivers were a popular attraction. Sponge diving around Tarpon Springs, cigar-making around Tampa—industry was booming in the later part of the 19th century even along the less populated Gulf Coast.

The boom had its roots in the railroad and in road construction, industries that blossomed as a result of the state legislature's passage of the Internal Improvement Act in 1855. It offered cheap or free public land to investors, particularly those interested in transportation. On Florida's east coast, Henry Flagler was responsible for the Florida East Coast Railway, completed in 1912 and linking Key West all the way up the eastern coast of Florida. After making his money with Standard Oil, in retirement he realized that the key to developing the state of Florida was to establish an extensive transportation system. His biggest contribution might have been converting all of the small railroad lines he purchased to a standard gauge, allowing trains to travel the whole length without changing track.

On the Gulf Coast

Another Henry worked his magic on the other coast of Florida. **Henry B. Plant** was largely responsible for the first boom period along the Gulf, using his railroad to open vast but previously inaccessible parts of the state. Henry Plant's rails extended south from Jacksonville along the St. Johns River to Sanford then southwest through Orlando to Tampa. The Plant Investment Company bought up several small railroads with the aim of providing continuous service across the state, his holdings eventually including 2,100 miles of track, several steamship lines out of the port of Tampa, and a number of important hotels. The University of Tampa now occupies the lavish hotel Plant built at the terminus of his line. This new rail line not only provided passengers with easy access, but also gave citrus growers quick routes to get their produce to market.

Around the same time, in 1911, **Barron Gift Collier** visited Useppa Island off the Fort Myers coast and fell in love with the subtropical landscape. Over the next decade he bought up more than a million acres of southwest Florida, making himself the largest landowner in the state. His holdings stretched from the Ten Thousand Islands northward to Useppa Island and inland from Naples into the Everglades and Big Cypress. He invested millions of dollars to convert this vast wilderness into agricultural land and a vacation paradise (some would say a dubious gift to the state). His real gift, however, was his completion of the state's Tamiami Trail, a road that exists even today linking Tampa with Miami. In gratitude, the state created Collier County in his honor in 1923, with Everglades City as the county seat.

The Roaring '20s were good to Florida. With more Americans owning cars, it became de rigueur to visit the Sunshine State on vacation. Land speculators bought up everything, parcels being sold and resold for ever-increasing amounts of money. Great effort was expended to drain the Everglades and Florida swampland to create even more viable land for homes and agriculture. The land frenzy reached its peak after World War I in 1925, but a swift bust followed the next year due to a major hurricane, another one in 1928, and then the Great Depression.

CUBAN REVOLUTION

Located ninety miles south of Key West, Cuba has always been closely connected with the affairs of Florida, and vice versa. Under Spanish rule in the late 1800s, Cuban relations with Spain deteriorated, and in 1868 the two countries went to war, with 200,000 Cuban and Spanish casualties. In 1898, the Spanish-American War focused the country's attention on the Gulf Coast city of Tampa, the primary staging area for U.S. troops preparing for the war in Cuba.

During the war, many prominent Cubans fled to Key West, including Vicente Martinez Ybor, who opened a cigar factory, the El Principe de Gales, in Key West in 1869. (He eventually relocated the factory to a scrub area east of the Tampa in 1886, once Henry B. Plant had completed rail service to aid in shipping and importation. This first factory begat a huge cigar industry in Tampa, with 200 factories at its peak.)

The war lasted only a few months after American involvement. Cuba was relinquished to the U.S. in trust for its inhabitants by the signing of the Treaty of Paris on December 20, 1898. Spanish rule ended January 1, 1899, and U.S. military rule ended May 20, 1902.

Cuban history after that continued to be fractious: Thomas Estrada Palma was the first president of the new republic, but then he was ousted in 1906. Again, a provisional American government, which withdrew in 1909. There was a period of prosperity, another revolt, and then General Gerardo Machado was elected president in 1925 and reelected in 1928. During his second term he suspended the freedoms of speech, press, and assembly, and was forced to flee the country in 1933.

Colonel Fulgencio Batista y Zaldivar, who controlled the army, was elected president in 1940. During his term, Cuba entered World War II on the side of the Allies. Batista was defeated in 1944 by Grau San Martin, and then in 1948 Carlos Prio Socarras was elected president—but he was overthrown by Batista in 1952. Mayhem ensued, but Batista wasn't taking no for an answer. There continued to be strong anti-Batista resistance, and in 1959 Batista resigned and fled the country. Fidel Castro set up a provisional government with himself as premier. Political refugees from the Cuban revolution poured into Florida by the thousands.

Not long after came the Cuban Missile Crisis of October 1962, precipitated by the Soviets installing nuclear missiles in Cuba. Soviet field commanders in Cuba were authorized to use tactical nuclear weapons unless President John F. Kennedy and Premier Nikita Khrushchev could reach an understanding.

In 1980 more than 100,000 Cuban refugees came to this country, mostly through Florida, when Castro briefly opened the port of Mariel to a flotilla of privately chartered U.S. ships, and in the early 1990s Florida received refugees from the military coup in Haiti and another wave of refugees from Cuba in 1994. Many of the Cuban expatriates live in Miami and environs, less so on the Gulf Coast. Still, the Cuban influence is robustly felt in areas such as Tampa's Ybor City.

MODERN FLORIDA

While it was the first state to be settled by Europeans, Florida might be the last state to have entered fully into modernity. It remained more or less a frontier until the 20th century, with the first paved road not until 1920. It was really World War II that changed things in the state, prompting a period of sustained growth that lasted more than 50 years. Immigration to the state has been a real melting pot, with a dense concentration of Cuban émigrés in the greater Miami area.

Tourism has been responsible for much of the growth in modern times, with a serious assist from Walt Disney World, the biggest tourist destination on the planet. There are more hotel rooms in Orlando than in New York City, I kid you not. In spite of that, or because of that, recent history in Florida, now the country's fourth largest state, gets kooky, from Anita Bryant's anti-gay crusade to the Elián Gonzales soap opera in Miami, to Ted Bundy, to flight training of Islamic terrorists. It's the kind of state where religious icons shed tears (St. Nicholas in Tarpon Springs), where a six-year-old girl might bring $1,000 worth of crack to school (Orlando's Tangelo Park Elementary), and where there are near-constant UFO sightings and occassional reports of spontaneous human combustion (one in Miami, one in Tampa).

Facts are often stranger than fiction in Florida, and sometimes just plain embarrassing (House Speaker Tom Feeney hiring a degree-less, unqualified Hooters waitress as a fund-raiser for the state Republican Party, at a salary of $55,644). I suppose even more embarrassing is the 2000 presidential election, in which the state drew the nation's attention when George W. Bush and Al Gore found themselves separated by a microscopic margin in the contest for the state's electoral votes, which each needed to win the presidency. With the election undecided for weeks, the outcome was fought over in the state government, state and federal courts, and the media. Ultimately, the U.S. Supreme Court weighed in on Bush's side that December, but deficiencies that were exposed in the state's voting systems, recount methods, and even ballot design guaranteed that victory would be tarnished no matter the "victor."

Government and Economy

STATE GOVERNMENT

In 1968, Florida adopted a new state constitution. The governor is elected for a term of four years, and the legislature has a senate of 40 members and a house of representatives of 120 members. The state also elects 23 representatives and 2 senators to the U.S. Congress and has 25 electoral votes.

It's easy enough to say that the state is now solidly Republican. But it's more complicated than that. In a state that was historically Democrat, recent explosive population growth has brought with it many Republicans, leaving the state approximately evenly split between the two parties. Because of that, combined with its large number of electoral votes, Florida is considered by political analysts to be a key swing state in presidential elections.

North Florida and the length of the Panhandle voted like the Deep South over the past 12 years (where people seem to be ardent supporters of school prayer, guns, and the flag). Despite the fact that there are plenty of registered Democrats, Panhandle counties have trended Republican— the thought is that there are many old-style southern Democrats who, for whatever reason, have failed to change their registration. Leon County and the two counties on either side of it are dominated by socially conservative Democrats. The Midwestern retirees of Naples and southwest Florida are Republican but not *too* Republican, often electing pro-choice and anti-voucher candidates to state offices. Sarasota/Bradenton is where Katherine Harris, of the 2000 election debacle fame, is a Republican representative. And there are pockets of Democrats, largely in Broward and Palm Beach Counties on the east coast, who consistently vote for the most liberal candidate running, while the Cuban right-wing Republicans cancel out their votes. Tampa, once a hotbed of Democratic union support, is now much more heavily influenced by pro-business Republicans.

It's also the state that elected Democrat Bob Graham in five consecutive statewide elections, so go figure (maybe it's because he always wore ties with Floridiana on them and they distracted conservative voters). So, Florida went for Nixon in 1968 and 1972, but Carter in 1976, Reagan in 1980 and 1984, Bush in 1988, Bush, just barely, in 1992, Clinton in 1996, then depending on your take on the 2000 election, either Bush by a hair or Gore by a bigger hair, and Bush again by a little in 2004. I don't want to sound crotchety, but there are still some questions in my mind about the counties that used optical scanner machines to record votes in 2004, which showed a consistent pattern of far more votes for Bush and far fewer votes for Kerry than projected.

As for state government, Democrat Lawton Chiles, elected governor in 1990 and reelected in 1994, was succeeded by Republican John Ellis "Jeb" Bush, elected in 1998 and reelected in 2002. Term limits restrict him from running again, although his job-approval rating has been consistently high since the 2004 hurricane season.

FLORIDA INDUSTRY

Florida has historically been a poor state. It spent its early years luring any kind of industry here with big tax breaks and incentives, sometimes even free land. And there have been many waves of takers. The deep-water ports along the Gulf prompted ship-building booms as far back as the 1830s, with industries like cotton shipping utilizing the gentle open water and connecting rivers and Intracoastal Waterway.

Cheap labor, lax laws, rich natural resources, a general anti-union sentiment, and no state income tax—it's a recipe for get-rich-quick, environmentally damaging industries. And Florida has had them, from timber and turpentining to paper mills and chemical plants. It wasn't until the Clean Water Act in 1972—which regulates the discharge of pollutants into U.S. waters and makes it illegal for industry to discharge pollutants without a permit—that people in Florida started scratching their heads about all the dead fish washing up on the shores. It's gotten better, but the Gulf states (Florida, Texas, and Louisiana in particular) are still among the top offenders for allowing permit violations for high-hazard chemicals. The industries in question are varied, linked mainly by their propensity for toxic discharge and their political clout. State and federal agencies charged with monitoring are perennially hamstrung by Florida politicians.

Agriculture also plays a mighty role in the commercial well being of the state. The state produces approximately $5.8 billion in agricultural products annually, leading the nation in citrus fruits and second only to California in winter vegetables. Cattle ranches and dairy farms are dense in the middle of the state, and from Gulf waters commercial fishers haul millions of pounds of fish and shellfish, and sport fishers haul millions more. The lumber industry is still going strong in some parts of the state, while high-tech companies have flocked to the St. Petersburg/Tampa area recently, drawn by good weather and low housing costs.

All this is still beside the point in some ways. Tourism is the state's number one industry, plain and simple. From January 1 through December 31, 2004, more than 76.8 million people visited Florida, according to preliminary data released by Visit Florida, the state's marketing arm. It's an approximately $51.8 billion business, with 45,000 restaurants, 3,300 hotels and accommodations, and some of the world's top tourist attractions (Walt Disney World, Kennedy Space Center, did I mention Walt Disney World?).

Florida had a robust bounce back after the tourism falloff prompted by the events of September 11, 2001. Domestic travelers nervous about flying in the ensuing couple of years felt more comfortable hopping in the car and heading to the Sunshine State. More recently, the hurricane season of 2004 took a serious toll on state visitation. With six weeks of televised storms, much of the world was under the impression that the state of Florida had been either submerged or swept away in high winds. While there are parts of the state still discernibly compromised by the storms, the bulk of it is open for business. Governor Bush announced in February 2005 that despite the storm season in the third quarter, tourist spending was up just slightly for 2004 (but this number includes all the people who were part of the hurricane relief and reconstruction efforts). Still, 2005 and 2006 might be slightly quieter than usual during peak seasons, with better deals to be had on accommodations and attractions.

FLORIDA'S MILITARY

Governor Jeb Bush has worked diligently in the past couple of years to heighten the nation's awareness of Florida's military installations. At the end of 2005, President George W. Bush will make his recommendations for federal Base Realignment and Closures (BRAC), which could mean enormous job losses if any should fall in Florida. The $44 billion industry is the state's third top economic sector behind tourism and agriculture, employing more than 714,000 Floridians. There are 21 installations and three unified commands in the state, with military and defense activities in 52 of Florida's 67 counties.

Many of the bases and two of the unified commands are along the Gulf Coast. **U.S. Central Command** (CENTCOM) is at MacDill Air Force Base in Tampa and is responsible for U.S. security interests in 25 nations that stretch from the Horn of Africa, through the Gulf region, into Central Asia. The command was activated in January 1983 as the successor to the Rapid Deployment Joint Task Force. A few years after that, in 1987, **U.S. Special Operations Command** (USSOCOM) was established as a unified combatant command also at MacDill, composed of army, navy, and air force special operations forces. Its mission is to support the geographic commanders-in-chief, ambassadors, and their country teams and other government agencies by preparing special operations forces. Its annual budget is over $5 billion, 1.3 percent of the overall defense budget.

Of Florida's naval bases, **Corry Station** (Escambia County), **NAS Pensacola** (Escambia County), **NAS Whiting Field** (Santa Rosa County), **Naval Support Activity Panama City** (Bay County), and **Saufley Field** (Escambia County) are along the Gulf Coast. Of Florida's air force bases, **Eglin AFB** (Okaloosa County), **Hurlburt Field** (Okaloosa County), **MacDill AFB** (Hillsborough County), and **Tyndall AFB** (Bay County) are on the Gulf Coast.

But Florida's defense industry goes beyond its military installations; Florida ranks fourth in the largest dollar volume of Department of Defense prime contracts awards received by private-sector companies.

EDUCATION IN FLORIDA

In February 2005, Florida's Constitutional Accountability Commission released a report saying what any Floridian paying attention knows already: Florida's public education does not compete on a national level. The commission evaluated schools in 14 categories, finding the state above the national average in only three categories (third-grade reading is going okay, and the number of students returning for a second year at community colleges is commendable).

In areas such as scores on the ACT and SAT college-entrance exams, student-teacher ratios, high-school graduation rates, and reading and math scores on the National Assessment of Educational Progress exams administered to students across the country, Florida was deemed sub-par.

Money is part of the problem. The amount spent per student ranks 45th among 50 states. The state also lags in average teacher salary and funding of colleges (adjusted for cost of living, though, beginning teachers' salaries are slightly above average). Crowding is another problem. Class-size reductions have not kept up with those of other states, and the schools have seen a significant demographic bubble in elementary-age kids in the past few years.

But the problems are clearly just as much about ideology. Governor Jeb Bush's "A+ Plan" has rightfully come under sharp criticism for misusing the FCAT standardized tests. Like his brother's "No Child Left Behind" program, it uses standardized tests as a means of teacher accountability, withholding funds from schools whose students fail to meet the established standards. It ranks schools with a letter grade, the highest ranked schools getting the greatest funding, and then hands out state vouchers to students in the failing schools. The problem is, this ostensible "choice" is no choice at all when the best schools are often already at maximum capacity.

Governor Bush is also responsible for the "One Florida Plan" that did away with affirmative action in college admissions and state contracting. Its record has been mixed, but at places like the University of Florida, African-American enrollment has plummeted.

As Governor Bush's brother once so famously asked, "Is our children learning?" Got to give you a "dunno" on that one.

ENVIRONMENTAL ISSUES

In 1827, Ralph Waldo Emerson visited the Florida territory's new capital city and wrote in his diary that the place had been "rapidly settled by public officers, land speculators, and desperadoes." That seems to be still the case.

In reading the *New Yorker*'s review in 2004 of the biopic *Monster,* the story of Aileen Wuornos, I was struck by David Denby's assessment of the state in which the real-life Wuornos was executed in 2002:

"The scuzzy central-Florida setting gives [Charlize] Theron some acting ground to stand on. In such recent American movies as the Matt Dillon thriller Wild Things, *Larry Clark's* Bully, *John Sayles's* Sunshine State, *the Charlie Kaufman-Spike Jonze fantasia* Adaptation, *and Frederick Wiseman's documentary* Domestic Violence, *as well as Carl Hiaasen's novels, Florida has appeared as a kind of bedraggled kingdom of chaos. The swamps, the threadbare woods, the sagging, loose-hinged bungalows, the roadhouses with their grizzled and beer-bellied bikers, the long, droning freeways, cars tooling along to somewhere or other. . . . Florida is the place where life doesn't shape up . . . [where] there's no structure, nothing hard or dense enough to mold people into coherent human beings."*

Sounds pretty grim, huh? But still, I know what he means. There's a Wild West making-up-the-rules-as-they-suit-me frontier spirit in this state, a state in which environmentalism has been slow to catch on. For nearly two centuries land speculators have ridden roughshod over the wilderness, buying and selling it in ever-smaller parcels. Mismanaged growth has been the norm, with government officials routinely called to the carpet for cozying up to land developers.

Millions of acres have been bulldozed to make way for strip malls and condo developments—nothing new, really, it happens all over. It's the same story of insufficient infrastructure, deficient water supply, and oversubscribed highways that is told of most recently plundered natural settings. And with something like 1,000 new residents moving to Florida every day, something's gotta give.

It's not hopeless. There's been an enormous grassroots effort in the past decade in Florida, regular people who have balked at the shady characters and get-rich-quick schemes that have so wantonly reduced the state's resources and diminished natural habitats. If their efforts gain purchase, the state's natural treasures—which are truly so vast and so breathtaking—might be preserved and, in some cases, restored.

The People

DEMOGRAPHICS

Florida ranks fourth in the U.S. in population, behind California, Texas, and New York. In 2003, the population was estimated to be 17,019,068 (up from 9,746,961 in 1980). If you count Tampa/St. Petersburg/Clearwater as a single metropolitan area, it beats Miami for sheer numbers—2,396,000 versus 2,253,000. On the Gulf Coast, the other most populous areas are Sarasota/Bradenton (590,000), Fort Myers/Cape Coral (441,000), Pensacola (412,000), Tallahassee (285,000), and Naples (251,000). One thousand new people move to Florida each day, and despite a slight slowdown in the 1990s, Florida remains one of the fastest-growing states in the nation. Surprisingly, the fastest-growing part of the state is the central interior, particularly the corridor along I-4, which connects the Tampa Bay area through Orlando to Daytona Beach in the east.

Age

Florida's age distribution is in a state of flux: In 1990, there were 2,355,938 Floridians aged 65 and older (18.2 percent of the total population), whereas in 2000 the census counted 2,807,598 in this group (17.6 percent of the total). So the percentage of those over 65 has shrunk some, but the number of people over 85 has grown tremendously (maybe people just live longer in this climate). The Gulf Coast, especially the area around Tampa, has gotten younger in recent years. For

COURTESY OF LEEC CUNTY VISITOR AND CONVENTION BUREAU

The Grapefruit League's spring training takes place in Florida (the Boston Red Sox play at City of Palms Park in Fort Myers, pictured). Many of the players call Florida home.

instance, the youth population (those age 0–19) has shown increasing growth rates over the last 30 years, from 15.5 percent 1970–1980 to 25.2 percent 1990–2000.

The median age is at its lowest all along the northern border of the state, where it meets Georgia and Alabama all the way out the Panhandle. There's another dense concentration of youth around Miami and Tampa (sister city St. Petersburg, famously a retirement destination, has shifted younger, demographically). The oldest part of the state, age-wise, is in Sarasota, in Naples, and along the Nature Coast.

Race

The population of the Gulf Coast is primarily white and non-Hispanic (85–93 percent white at the last census), with the greatest ethnic diversity in the Tampa Bay area. Not surprisingly, the African-American population is twice that of the Latino population along the northern border of the state (along the Panhandle and the Alabama and Georgia borders), while in the southern part of the state, close to Miami, the correlation flip-flops. Tallahassee bears the distinction of being the only part of the Gulf Coast whose majority is African American (roughly 57 percent).

Religion

In modern times, the Gulf Coast is primarily Christian. Jewish retirees don't, for whatever reason, settle along the Gulf Coast, with the exception of Sarasota (3–6 percent Jewish, as compared to the east coast of the state from Coral Gables up through Palm Beach, which is roughly 13–15 percent Jewish). The southernmost part of the state is dominantly Catholic, as is the area just north of Tampa up through what is known as the Nature Coast. By and large, though, Floridians are Protestant, especially as you get closer to the Georgia and Alabama borders.

Much of the state's most intense conservative evangelical activity occurs along the Panhandle—something like the belt buckle of the Bible Belt. You'll see scads of Pentecostal churches, Bible factory outlets, and a series of "God Speaks" billboards along Florida highways. The campaign has won some marketing awards, but still the mastermind maintains his anonymity. Here are some of the best ones:

"Let's meet at my house Sunday before the game."–God

"We need to talk."–God

"Loved the wedding, invite me to the marriage."–God

"You think it's hot here?"–God

"Have you read my #1 best seller? There will be a test."–God

"Don't make me come down there."–God

SNOWBIRDS

First, what's a snowbird? It's a temporary resident in Florida, someone who comes from a colder, less hospitable winter climate to bask in the Sunshine State all winter. Snowbirds are usually of retirement age, or nearing it. But it gets more specific. New Yorkers account for 13.1 percent of Florida's temporary residents, followed by Michiganders at 7.4 percent, Ohioans at 6.7 percent, Pennsylvanians at 5.8 percent, and Canadians at 5.5 percent. The average length of stay is five months. If Florida has roughly 7 million households, there are an estimated 920,000 temporary residents during the peak winter months and another 170,000 during the late summer.

WHO YOU CALLING A FLORIDA CRACKER?

That's a good question, really. Many Florida historians are devoted to the theory that the term "Florida Cracker" originated with the area's cow hunters. As Jesse Otis Beall describes it in the book *Cracker* by Dana Ste. Claire:

"Well, people didn't know what cracker meant and they thought it was just a slang word, you know, for a person. But it was named after the whip, I think, the crackin' whip, as the cowhunters come in. There wasn't cowboys in those days, there was cowhunters, and they used those whips and

we'd say, 'Yep, here comes the Crackers.' That's where the word comes from. I'm always a callin' myself a Cracker."

Pretty convincing. This hypothesis goes back as early as 1810, with John Lambert's *Travels Through Lower Canada, and the United States of North America.* But a lot of historians aren't buying it, weighing in instead on the side of a different theory entirely. Even Florida cow hunter historian Joyce Peters believes that Florida Crackers were called such because of their diet—a poor, rural people, they had trouble rounding up enough calories. Cracked corn fit the bill, as it could be roughly stone ground and then made into a paste with water or fat, baked into a hard "cracker," and then either eaten as hard tack or reconstituted in a stew.

Still others say, yes, cracked corn is implicated, but in a more nefarious way. These Florida backwoodsmen were known to operate moonshine stills, stills that fermented cracked corn mash into a blisteringly alcoholic "white lightning."

Other theories that may or may not hold water: The people were named after the "crackerbox" shape of their simple log houses. Or, they were originally called *"cuaqueros,"* or Quakers, by the Spaniards who confused them for a colony of Quakers who settled early on in Florida. And the speculations go on like that.

The book *Cracker* wanders all over trying to figure out what one is exactly, but you have to wait until the glossary until it cuts to the chase: "Cracker—a self-reliant, independent, and tenacious settler of the Deep South, often of Celtic stock, who subsisted by farming or raising livestock and, as a general rule, valued personal independence and restraint-free life over material prosperity. Cracker settlers provided a spirited foundation for the peopling of the rural South and Florida."

These days Florida Cracker is something a Floridian can call him- or herself, and with pride, but it's not a moniker to go slinging around lightly. There are still Florida Crackers along the Gulf Coast, and you'll probably know one when you see one.

CIRCUS PERFORMERS AND CARNIES

Most people connect Sarasota and the circus. It was in 1927 when Sarasota became an official circus town, John Ringling bringing his Ringling Bros. and Barnum & Bailey Circus's winter quarters to Sarasota, thus giving the sedate Florida town an indelible whiff of spectacle. Many of the little people who starred in the circus retired in Sarasota (in specially built little houses in "Tiny Town"). Still, Sarasota doesn't get the moniker "Showtown USA." That high honor goes to another Gulf Coast town.

Gibsonton, or Gibtown as it's often affectionately called, was made famous as a wintering town for sideshow and circus performers as well as garden-variety carnies. Many of them retired permanently to Gibtown and have, in recent years, died off, but they leave the town with a colorful history. It's in Hillsborough County, south of Tampa on U.S. 41 near the town of Riverview.

It was home to Percilla "Monkey Girl" Bejano and her husband Emmitt "The Alligator Skin Man" Bejano (billed as the "World's Strangest Married Couple" on sideshow midways all over). There was Jeanie the Half Girl, Al the Giant, and Grady "Lobster Boy" Stiles, Jr. (from a long line of people with ectrodactyly, or "lobster claw" syndrome; Stiles committed murder but got off with probation because prison wasn't equipped to handle him, only to be murdered himself some years later). The conjoined twin Hilton sisters (different Hilton sisters) ran a fruit stand here. Melvin "Rubber Face" Burkhart was the most recent to die, in 2001. His most famous routine was to shove an icepick and five-inch nail into nose.

Gibtown has a post office counter that accommodates little people, and its zoning laws allow residents to keep elephants and circus animals in trailers on their front lawn. Still, it is home to the **International Independent Showmen's Association** (6915 Riverview Dr., 813/677-3590), a bar called **Showtown USA Lounge** (10902 U.S. 41 S, 813/677-5443) that has rollicking karaoke on the weekend, and a comfortable local eatery called **Giants Camp Restaurant** (9816 U.S. 41).

Even if you can't fit it into your trip, you can get a sense for Gibtown if you can get your hands on Episode 44 of the *X-Files,* in which Mulder and Scully travel to Gibsonton to investigate the death of Jerald Glazebrook, the Alligator Man. In the episode you'll meet Jim Jim, the Dog-Faced Boy, and the Enigma, who is covered in blue puzzle-piece tattoos and eats glass. Also, there is a 65-minute documentary called *Gibtown* that is hard to find, but worthwhile.

Gibsonton is also home to the largest tropical fish farm in the country, **Ekkwill Waterlife Resources** (www.ekkwill.com).

MOVIES SET ON THE GULF COAST

Florida has been a film location just about as long as there've been movies. The climate, the scenery, the dense and tropical foliage—it has all sparked the imagination of countless directors, cinematographers, and actors, standing in for far-flung lands on several continents. The earliest Florida films aren't anyone's flights of fancy, however, but the 1898 newsreels of U.S. troops in Tampa during the Spanish-American War.

The Museum of Florida History in Tallahassee has a collection of movie posters from films shot in the state. The following are some featured in this collection, and an idiosyncratic assortment of others, all shot along the Gulf Coast.

Hell Harbor (1930), the first full-length "talkie" to be made in the state, was shot in Tampa and depicts the story of the descendants of pirate Henry Morgan. *A Guy Named Joe* (1944), starring Spencer Tracy as a WWII pilot who dies and becomes the guardian angel of a young pilot in love with Tracy's girlfriend, was also shot in Tampa at Drew and MacDill air fields.

The Marx Brothers *The Cocoanuts* (1929) may well be set in Miami, it's not totally clear, but it revolves around Florida's first land boom. *The Yearling* (1946) is also educational and an absolute classic starring Gregory Peck, based on the Newbery award-winning book by Marjorie Kinnan

Know the Florida Gulf Coast

FAMOUS FLORIDIANS

It's an incomplete list, but these people, along with O. J. Simpson, Oprah Winfrey, Janet Reno, Clarence Thomas, and Rush Limbaugh, were born and raised in the Sunshine State or at least called it home for a long while.

Baseball players: Steve Carlton, Dwight Gooden, Barry Larkin, Sammy Sosa

Football players: Mike Ditka, Joe Namath

Tennis players: Jennifer Capriati, Martina Hingis, Anna Kournikova, Ivan Lendl, Martina Navratilova, Monica Seles, Andy Roddick, Serena and Venus Williams

Wrestlers: Hulk Hogan, Rick Flair, Dwayne Johnson "The Rock," Joannie Laurer "Chyna," Randy "Macho Man" Savage

Actors: Sidney Poitier, Butterfly McQueen, Burt Reynolds, Ben Vereen, Faye Dunaway, Buddy Ebsen, River Phoenix, Rosie O'Donnell, John Travolta

Writers: Marjorie Kinnan Rawlings, Zora Neale Hurston, Ernest Hemingway, Stephen King

Singers: Jim Morrison, Pat Boone, Frances Langford, Gloria Estefan, Enrique Iglesias, Lenny Kravitz, Tom Petty, Bo Diddley, Backstreet Boys *and* some of 'N Sync, the brothers Gibb, Beyoncé Knowles, Jennifer Lopez, Scott Stapp

Military figures: Joseph W. Sitwell (army general), Daniel James (air force general)

Famous Names in Florida History:

Pedro Menendez de Auiles: founder of St. Augustine

Osceola: Seminole Indian leader

William Pope Du Val: first territorial governor

David Levy Yulee: one of Florida's initial U.S. senators (first Jewish-American senator)

Henry Flagler: builder of the East Coast Railway, which connected the whole east coast of Florida

Henry B. Plant: famed Florida railroad baron of the late 19th century, on the Gulf Coast

Barron Collier: southwest Florida landowner and builder of Tamiami Trail

Hamilton Disston: bought four million acres in central Florida and created a canal system

A. Philip Randolph: labor leader

John Ringling: circus entrepreneur

Thomas Edison and Henry Ford: inventors (well, they both just lived here part time, but they left a big mark).

Rawlings and nominated for seven Oscars. Parts of the film were shot at Rawlings's homestead in Cross Creek.

Then we get into some real camp faves, from *Mr. Peabody and the Mermaid* (1948), a William Powell film shot at Weeki Wachee Springs with local mermaids, to *Beneath the 12 Mile Reef* (1953), the story of a Greek sponge diver from Tarpon Springs who falls in love with a girl from the rival Key West sponge divers. The king of Gulf Coast films, *Creature from the Black Lagoon* (1954) was filmed in Wakulla Springs and Tarpon Springs and was followed by two sequels.

Directed by Cecil B. DeMille and starring Betty Hutton, James Stewart, and Charlton Heston, *The Greatest Show on Earth* (1952) was filmed at the Barnum and Bailey headquarters in Sarasota and required all the actors to do their own stunts.

Elvis spent a little time on the Gulf Coast in Pasco County filming *Follow That Dream* (1962), not a great film. And Christopher Plummer, Gypsy Rose Lee, and Burl Ives got to hang out in the Everglades for the making of Nicholas Ray's *Wind Across the Everglades* (1958), a story about the hardscrabble life in the wilds of South Florida.

Vernon, Florida (1984) is actually on the other coast, but Earl Morris's documentary on small-town Florida is so quirky and delightful that I can't help but recommend it. When you get to the scene with the "double gobble," think of me.

Victor Nuñez has done a few excellent movies set along the Gulf Coast, from *A Flash of Green* (1988), based on novel by J. D. MacDonald about corruption in Sarasota, to *Ruby in Paradise* (1993), a small film about a young woman, played by Ashley Judd, set on the Panhandle. Then he did the Peter Fonda pic *Ulee's Gold* (1997), a Panhandle family drama about beekeepers.

More recently, Peter Weir's *The Truman Show* (1998), starring Jim Carrey, was set in the scary-perfect Panhandle town of Seaside; Volker Schlondorff's crime drama *Palmetto* (1998) is set in and around Sarasota; and Spike Jonze's *Adaptation* (2002), a loose interpretation of Susan Orlean's book *The Orchid Thief,* takes place in the oppressively lush mangrove swamps of the Everglades.

John Sayles's *Sunshine State* (2002) is set in a fictional town in Florida, which might be the east coast, but it so eloquently describes the conflicts of old-time Floridians and new developers that it's worth seeing.

Oh, and there's a movie that hasn't been released yet that I'm dying to see: *Man-Thing,* directed by Brett Leonard, tells the story of a real-estate tycoon who plans to drain parts of the Everglades and awakens a vindictive swamp monster made up of a mound of plantlife but whose skin exudes a flammable acid that is activated by fear. Environmentalists are going to love this one.

Getting There

BY PLANE

Tampa International Airport is the largest airport on the Gulf Coast, although the Southwest Florida International Airport in Fort Myers has experienced enormous expansion recently. Generally, the most direct routes and cheapest fares can be found through these airports, but it's worth pricing flights through Orlando, which is an hour east of Tampa. Gulf Coast airports are, from north and west to south:

Pensacola Regional Airport (three miles northeast of Pensacola, 850/435-1746)

Okaloosa County Air Terminal (one mile east of Destin, 850/651-7160)

Panama City Bay County International Airport (four miles northwest of Panama City 850/763-6751)

Hernando County Airport (forty miles north of Tampa, 352/799-7275)

St. Petersburg Clearwater International Airport (seven miles southeast of Clearwater, 813/531-1451)

Tampa International Airport (five miles west of downtown Tampa, 813/870-8700)

Sarasota Bradenton International Airport (three miles north of Sarasota, 941/359-5200)

Venice Municipal Airport (half a mile south of Venice, 941/485-9293)

Charlotte County Airport (three miles southeast of Punta Gorda, 941/639-1101)

Southwest Florida International Airport (ten miles southeast of Fort Myers, 941/768-1000)

Naples Municipal Airport (two miles northeast of Naples, 941/643-0733)

From Europe

The most international flights on the Gulf Coast arrive and depart out of Tampa or Southwest Florida International in Fort Myers. Additional international flights arrive in Miami, Orlando, and Key West. British Airways, KLM, and Lufthansa offer direct flights, as well as American carriers American, Delta, United, and Northwest. (From Canada, Air Canada has flights to Tampa and Fort Myers.)

Cheap Fares

All of the online travel resources (Orbitz, Travelocity, Expedia, etc.) offer last-minute specials and weekend deals on travel. The way to get a good fare in advance on air travel or hotel rooms is by traveling off peak season. That period is different for different parts of the Gulf Coast (each chapter gives the approximate peak season dates in its introduction). For instance, peak season on St. George Island is the middle of the summer, while in Naples the summer is the least desirable time to visit, thus the cheapest. Spring break in March and April seems to be the most expensive time to visit much of the Gulf Coast, but bear in mind that in the off season, hours for restaurants and attractions are sometimes more limited.

BY CAR

The main arteries into Florida include I-95, which crosses the Florida-Georgia border just north of Jacksonville and hugs the east coast of the state all the way down, and I-75, which runs south from Georgia through the state's middle, then works its way west to the coast just south of Tampa. I-4 extends southwest across the state from Daytona through Orlando and then connects to I-75 in Tampa. On the Panhandle, I-10 is the big east–west road, which can be accessed from the north by U.S. 29, U.S. 231, or U.S. 19.

BY BOAT

If you're traveling to Florida under your own sail power, in a yacht, or aboard another kind of boat, you probably have a host of chart maps and navigational tools at your disposal. A paragraph in this book is hardly going to keep you afloat. However, I do want to put in a plug for the **Gulf Intracoastal Waterway.** Most boaters are familiar with the 1,090-mile, toll-free, East Coast channel that is the Intracoastal Waterway (ICW), linking Norfolk, Virginia, to Miami, Florida, through gorgeous sheltered waters. Well, the Gulf has one too, extending about 1,300 miles from Carrabelle, Florida, to Brownsville, Texas. (And there's a noncontiguous section of the waterway connecting Tampa Bay with the Okeechobee Waterway.) The Gulf Intracoastal Waterway follows a course of sheltered bays, rivers, and canals along the Gulf of Mexico, perfect for recreational cruising. The sheltered Gulf waters aren't as punishing as the Atlantic Ocean, but still the Gulf Intracoastal Waterway makes for varied and scenic cruising.

Speaking of cruising, the **Port of Tampa** is a huge home port for a variety of cruise lines (Carnival, Royal Caribbean, Celebrity, Holland America, and Radisson Seven Seas Cruises). Nearly a million passengers pass through its cruise terminals each year on their way to days upon the wide open sea, shuffleboard, and cocktails on the Lido deck. (For the single funniest essay on cruise ships ever written, read the title essay in David Foster Wallace's *A Supposedly Fun Thing I'll Never Do Again.*) So, another vacation itinerary might be taking a cruise, followed or preceded by an exploration of Florida's Gulf Coast.

Getting Around

BY CAR

Florida's Gulf Coast is an ideal destination for those with a poor sense of direction. There are only a few major roads you have to master, and even the urban areas are mostly laid out in a grid (except Tampa, where driving visitors are known to browbeat the map-reading visitors in the passenger seat). On the Panhandle, I-10 runs inland east to west, while at the coast the major east–west road is U.S. 98. U.S. 98 curves all the way around the Big Bend of the Panhandle into the Florida peninsula, where it is also called U.S. 19. U.S. 19 extends along the coast all the way down to St. Pete. I-75 is the huge north–south artery on the Gulf Coast side of the Florida peninsula, stretching from where it enters the state at Valdosta, Georgia, all the way south to Naples, where it jogs across the state to the east along what is called Alligator Alley. One of the more famous north–south routes in Florida is U.S. 41, also known as the Tamiami Trail, which extends from Tampa down to Naples, where it, too, shoots east across the state (significantly south of I-75). The Tamiami Trail and I-75 run parallel, fairly close together—which you choose depends on your preference: I-75 has the speed, Tamiami Trail has the charm.

Car Rentals

Alamo (800/327-9633), **Avis** (800/831-2847), **Budget** (800/527-0700), **Dollar** (800/800-4000 domestic, 800/800-6000 international), **Enterprise** (800/736-8222), **Hertz** (800/654-3131), and **National** (800/227-7368) provide rental cars from most of the major airports on the Gulf Coast. You pay a small premium for the convenience of picking up and dropping off at the airport, and you pay an extra fee if you pick up a car in one city and drop off in another. Most rental car companies insist that the driver be at least 21 years old, some even older than that—be sure to have your driver's license and a major credit card (even if you aim to pay cash, they want a credit card for their own peace of mind) with you, or you're walking.

Whether to accept a rental agency's insurance coverage and waivers depends on your own car insurance—before leaving home, read your own car policy to determine if it covers you while renting a vehicle. Also, some credit cards cover damages to many basic types of rental cars, so it's worth checking into that as well. If you decline the insurance, rental car companies hold you totally responsible for your rental vehicle if damaged or stolen. The rental agency's insurance may add $12–25 per day to your bill.

Hitchhiking

Hitchhiking and Florida—together the two words conjure up scary images of Aileen "Lee" Wuornos (or at least scary images of Charlize Theron playing her in the movie *Monster*). She was the hitchhiking prostitute–serial killer who murdered seven men on Florida highways.

Florida is not a great hitchhiking state. The law reads: No person shall stand in a roadway for the purpose of soliciting a ride. Clearly, you can't stand *on the road* to thumb a ride, but there's nothing that says you can't stand on the shoulder. Still, the cops don't like it and most people won't pick you up. Need more reasons not to do it? Marilyn Manson is from Florida, mobster Al Capone lived here for a while, the Backstreet Boys *and* the Bee Gees are mostly from Florida, and PeeWee Herman was caught, um, red-handed in Florida. Florida has more than its share of the sinister, the down-and-out, and the truly bizarre. That's all fine and good when you're viewing it from a safe distance, but stuck in the cramped quarters of an automobile it might be plain-old creepy.

BY BUS

Greyhound (800/231-2222, www.greyhound .com) service has gotten spottier in recent years, but there are still regular routes that run from Naples up through Fort Myers, then up to Tampa and St. Petersburg, and all the way around the Big Bend of the Panhandle to Tallahassee, Panama City, and Pensacola. If traveling by Greyhound is new to you, here's some general information: There are no assigned seats (do not, under any circumstances, take the seats adjacent to the bathroom, it's olfactory suicide), no smoking, no pets, no meal service (but there are regular meal stops so you can jump out and buy something). There are no reservations, so you buy a ticket and show up. Stopovers at any point along the route are permitted if you've paid a regular fare. The driver gives you a notation on your ticket, or a coupon, and you can get back on whenever.

Who rides the bus these days? The elderly, the military, the poor, and people who just don't fly. Regular patrons include children who wish they were somewhere else, and their parents who also wish their children were somewhere else. There are better ways to see the state.

BY TRAIN

That way is not by train. **Amtrak** (800/872-7245, www.amtrak.com) offers service exclusively up the eastern side of the Florida peninsula, with the exception of the Gulf Coast city of Tampa. There is regular train service on the Panhandle, Tallahassee to Pensacola (to give some idea of price, the four-hour trip from Tallahassee to Pensacola is $20 one-way).

But here's the thing. You've heard the expression "wrong side of the tracks"? It's all wrong on both sides of Amtrak's tracks these days, with the least scenic stuff passing by your smudgy window.

Visas and Officialdom

FOREIGN VISITORS

Visas

Unless you're coming from Canada, you need a valid passport and a tourist visa (a Non-Immigrant Visitors Visa B1, for business, or B2, for recreation). Keep your passport in a safe place, and make a copy of the passport number and other critical information and keep it elsewhere.

Money

U.S. currency looks pretty fancy these days, with watermarks, lots of anticounterfeit devices, and huge heads (in the case of Ben Franklin, not a pretty turn of events), but working with dollars is fairly simple—there's the $1, the $5, the $10, the $20, and, less common, the $50. The $100 bill is very seldom used and very seldom accepted without a lot of scrutiny. (The old, small-head bills are still good, don't worry.) In coins, 1-cent pennies are practically only good for gumball machines and wishing wells, then there's the 5-cent nickel, the 10-cent dime, the 25-cent quarter, as well as the more rare 50-cent piece.

Money can be exchanged at a very limited number of airports (Tampa, Orlando, Fort Myers) on the Gulf Coast. Exchange money before you arrive, or work in U.S. travelers' checks. For the most part, if you have a Visa or MasterCard, put all of your accommodations, restaurant meals, and attractions expenditures on that—an easy way to keep track of how you spent your money on vacation.

Electricity

The U.S. uses 110 to 120 volts AC, as opposed to Europe's 220 to 240 volts. For the most part, Gulf Coast hotels will have hair dryers for your use, so leave yours at home. If you have other electrical devices for which you need a converter, bring one from home.

Telephone Basics

Each urban area along the Gulf Coast has its own area code of three numbers that must be dialed if calling from outside. For example, the area code in Tampa is 813, but you needn't dial it if you're calling within the area code. If you're dialing another area code, you must first dial 1, then the three-digit area code, then the seven-digit phone number. Since the telephone industry was deregulated, calling long distance from pay phones can be a total crapshoot, costing a different amount depending on the carrier. Public pay phone pricing is no longer regulated by the Florida Public Service Commission, but prices should be clearly marked, with local calls usually 35 cents. If you don't have a cell phone that works in Florida, you're better off getting a prepaid international calling card. Hotels also charge by the call, so making calling-card calls is often more cost-effective.

Tipping

Service-sector workers expect a tip, it's only in name a "gratuity," meaning an elective gift. It's how they make the bulk of their money. Fifteen percent is pretty much the minimum, whether it's at a restaurant, a hair salon, or in a taxi. Tip bellhops about $1 per bag; tip the valet parker $1–2 every time you get your car. Tip a good waiter or bartender 18–20 percent. But here's some tricky stuff: If the hairdresser or tour operator is the owner of the business, a tip can sometimes be seen as an insult. Crazy stuff. Keep lots of small bills at the ready for all these things, but don't ever tip at the movies, a retail shop, at the gas station, or at the theater, ballet, or opera.

Metric Conversions

The U.S. had a failed attempt at going metric in the 1970s. So, you need to know that 1 foot equals .305 meters; 1 mile equals 1.6 kilometers; and 1 pound equals .45 kilograms. Converting temperatures is a little trickier: To convert Fahrenheit to Celsius temperatures, subtract 32 and then multiply by .555. Got it?

Tips for Travelers

ACCESS FOR DISABLED TRAVELERS

The more developed and sophisticated parts of the Gulf Coast (Sarasota, Naples, Tampa) are very accessible to travelers with disabilities. As one would expect, the more remote areas that reflect a more "Old Florida" sensibility may not have ramps, handicapped-access bathrooms, and other amenities. You may want to consider buying a copy of *Wheelchairs on the Go: Accessible Fun in Florida* (727/573-0434, www.wheelchairsonthego.com, $19.95 plus $3 shipping), Florida's only access guide for visitors who use canes, walkers, or wheelchairs. The 424-page paperback covers wheelchair-accessible and barrier-free accommodations, tourist attractions, and activities across the state.

Society for Accessible Travel & Hospitality (561/361-0017, www.sath.org) provides recommendations and resources to help travelers with disabilities plan their vacations, and **Able Trust** (888/838-2253, www.abletrust.org) offers helpful links to disability resources throughout Florida.

Most major car-rental companies have hand-controlled cars in their fleets (give them 24- to 48-hours' notice to locate one), but if you want to rent a handicap-accessible van, call Accessible Vans of America (800/862-7475, www.accessiblevans.com/florida.htm). If you need to rent a scooter or wheelchair during your visit, **ScootAround** (888/441-7575, www.scootaround.com) is a mobility enhancement company with scooter and wheelchair rental service for older or disabled travelers in a number of Gulf Coast cities.

Diabetic travelers can call the **American Diabetes Association** (800/232-3472) to get a list of hospitals that provide services to diabetics, or log on to **Dialysis Finder** at www.dialysisfinder.com.

The **American Foundation for the Blind** (800/232-5463, www.afb.org) provides information on traveling with a seeing-eye dog.

TRAVELING WITH CHILDREN

It's a form of one-upmanship. One person says, "I got charged ten cents every time I asked, 'When are we gonna get there?'" Another counters, "I had to pee in a cup from Albany to Orlando." The indignities we suffered as children in the name of family road trips—we all have our war stories. As parents ourselves, we vow never to stoop to protracted games of "Who can be quiet the longest," or to resort to those age-old idle threats, "If you don't stop that, I'm going to turn this car around, young lady."

The Gulf Coast is the kind of destination suited to a rambling family car trip. But how to face the open road with a carful of antsy travelers? As with a NASA launch, it's all about careful planning and precision execution. Consider yourself lucky that this doesn't mean devising zero-gravity suits and dehydrating food—you just have to keep your astronauts comfortable, fed, and entertained. To that end, consider carrying a master list of all that you've packed. Although it sounds monstrously fastidious, it helps to see where your gaps are, it allows you to easily keep track of things from car to motel to final destination, and if you generate this list on the computer, it can be used as the basis for future trip lists.

The list should be divided into categories:

clothes and equipment (these are the things that go in the trunk, to be exhumed at your final destination) and the stuff that makes or breaks your travel time—food, entertainment, and car comfort. Older kids can each be put in charge of a category checklist as the car gets loaded.

For smaller kids, always take a change of underpants or diapers inside the car with you, rather than in the trunk with the luggage. For older kids, encourage a layered approach to dressing—when one child is chilly, donning another layer may be preferable to making everyone endure the car heater.

Think of packing foods that nature has already prepackaged—bananas, oranges, hard-boiled eggs. Avoid things with sauces or drip-potential, chips coated with the dreaded nacho cheese orange goo (deadly on seat covers), or things that crumb too easily (crumbs can turn itchy on small thighs on a long trip). And for drinks, carry a large, plastic, spill-proof cup for each child. This way, you can get juices at convenience stores but you won't be at the mercy of those wide-mouthed, splash-prone glass bottles in the car. Alternatively, bring a bevy of frozen juice boxes. You won't have to wait in line for sodas and the juice boxes will be nice and cold during the first leg of a trip.

The sight of the golden arches fills most kids with joy and most parents with dread. Fast food is the most common pitfall on long car trips, a wasteland of fat, salt, and sugar. To avoid the tortures of drive-through (it's everywhere, after all), you have to stand firm. Finding other food can be an adventure on long trips. On the Gulf Coast, this is easy: Get off the highway and hunt down an old-fashioned diner, one with counter stools, a good jukebox, and a short-order cook who makes the perfect, oozy grilled cheese. In preparation for your trip, research the indigenous foods of the areas you'll be passing through. Use the Internet to print out pictures and histories of each city's gastronomic highlights.

When traveling in the car with small children, allow more time to reach your destination. Count on stopping every hour to stretch your legs and run around. Churches are good stopping spots if rest areas aren't available, as they often have open, grassy areas and playgrounds. Traveling at night or during nap times is a good way to make up time. Put blankets, pillows, and any necessary stuffed animals in the back seat at the ready.

Your local party goods and dollar stores are perfect places to find inexpensive new forms of amusement. Wrap each new toy as a gift, to make the excitement last. Caveat: Do not buy travel games with small pieces sure to get lost immediately under the back seat. Maze books, magic-pen books, stickers, a magnetic puzzle of the U.S., even car bingo can keep everyone entertained. For long car trips, the book *Miles of Smiles* is filled with car games. Picture-puzzle books (like *I Spy* and *Where's Waldo*) can be made into games as well: One person names an object for the rest to find in the picture.

Even if you eschew the "plugged in" feel of video games or movies in the car, bringing a stereo headset for each child allows everyone to listen to their first choice, whether that's Hilary Duff or *Good Night Moon*. You can even make your own books on tape: Record your child's favorite stories on audiotape and then they can have the stories "read" to them in the car.

Bring lap desks and art supplies for projects. Dated spiral-bound drawing pads can be a nice way to chronicle a trip, with each child keeping the finished pad (parents can annotate as instructed). Encourage older kids to "journal" with a cool pad and a set of gel pens.

TRAVELING WITH PETS

More and more hotel chains are accepting people's canine companions (other pets, from pot-bellied pigs to naked mole rats, are a harder sell). Best Western, Motel 6, Holiday Inn, and even swishy chains such as Four Seasons often accept pet guests for an additional fee. To get good information, pick up a copy of *The Dog Lover's Companion to Florida,* by Sally Deneen and Robert McClure, or visit www.petswelcome.com.

Flying with your pet to and from Florida can be problematic, as most major airlines have an embargo against pets as checked baggage during the summer months (any day in which the outdoor temperature might reach 90 degrees), and even for small pets that fit under an airplane seat, the airlines only allow one pet per cabin. The ASPCA strongly discourages pets as checked baggage—I do, too, and here's why. A schitzy little dachshund in my family was checked at Tampa International Airport, whereupon he escaped his carrier, exited the belly of the plane unnoticed, and stopped air traffic as he barreled down the runway in abject terror, ears akimbo. This is a true story with a happy ending. The wiener dog was apprehended by authorities and returned to my uncle. Today, he lives a full and happy life, with occasional bouts of PTSD resulting in incontinence.

Dogs are prohibited on many walking trails in Florida, as well as many beaches. There are designated dog parks and dog beaches all over the Gulf Coast. Pensacola, Panama City, Tallahassee, Tampa, St. Petersburg, Sarasota, and Fort Myers all have designated dog beach parks with amenities such as fenced play areas, dog water fountains, and poop bags. Be aware that in much of the Gulf Coast's wilderness areas, poisonous snakes and alligators pose more of a threat to your dog than to you.

TRAVELING ALONE

Beach walking, fishing, kayaking, even the area's many cultural attractions—all the offerings of the Gulf Coast are blissfully suited to traveling alone. The only exception to that is backwoods camping in the Everglades or deep wilderness. Be extremely careful to give rangers your exact schedule and detailed whereabouts. Beyond that, I've traveled the length of the Gulf Coast by myself and experienced not a single troubling episode. As a slightly spindly 98-pound near-weakling, I wouldn't hesitate to recommend the

Gulf Coast as a spot for quiet, contemplative solo travel—except, perhaps, during colleges' spring breaks.

Spring Break Fever

Because school schedules vary across the country, spring breakers arrive in Florida at different times. Some come as early as late February, but March and April are the months most colleges and schools release for spring break. Students focus most of their attentions on certain key cities along the eastern coast of the state (Daytona Beach, Miami Beach), but along the Gulf Coast, Panama City Beach and down by Key West are the big draws.

GAY AND LESBIAN TRAVELERS

Miami's South Beach and Key West are clearly the locus of lots of gay travel merriment and enthusiasm. Nowhere on the Gulf Coast is the nightlife as chic and energizing, but that said, nothing on the Gulf Coast seems in any way homophobic or unsuitable for gay or lesbian travel. As with most places, the more rural the area, the more likely any discernible difference is likely to prompt unwanted notice. The Gulf Coast's wealth of outdoor activities seem suitable for any orientation, as do the restaurants and accommodations. It's a fairly nightlife-impoverished area regardless of your preference, so you may spend your evenings curled up with a good book.

To get oriented within your orientation, contact the **Gay, Lesbian & Bisexual Community Services of Central Florida** (407/425-4527, www.glbcc.org) for welcome packets and calendars of events, or the **International Gay & Lesbian Travel Association** (800/448-8550, www.iglta .org, to join is $150 annually) for a list of gay-friendly accommodations, tours, and attractions.

Information and Services

HEALTH AND SAFETY

Despite what it might look like in some of the more remote backwaters, Florida is a first-world kind of place, with good emergency services and medical care pretty much all over the Gulf Coast. Why, from Tampa to Sarasota you'll see more medical facilities, pharmacies, and billboards for MRI scanners (who goes by billboard ads on this kind of thing?) than nearly anywhere else, a remnant of the area's recent past as a mostly retirement-age ghetto (as the Bob Dylan song says, "it's younger than that now").

Still, you want to do what you can to stay healthy during a visit here. The sun is probably the biggest underestimated foe. **Sunburn** can be wicked, so be sure to slather with at least an SPF of 30, and because you'll be in and out of water, and sweating in the steamy humidity, opt for waterproof or water-resistant cream such as Banana Boat Sport Sunblock Lotion (waterproof/sweatproof, SPF 30). Even better, one of my favorite finds on the Gulf Coast, Avon now makes an SPF 30 Skin So Soft cream with a DEET-free pesticide in it to cope with the Gulf Coast's other big bully, the **mosquitoes.** DEET-based products are more effective in preventing mosquitoes from landing on you, but I hate to have that poison sitting on my skin all day. Lather up with the Avon product, then apply a DEET-based spray only if the mosquitoes are bad. Mosquitoes in Florida don't carry any diseases such as malaria, but their itching can certainly be preoccupying.

Another itchy subject is **fire ants.** If you see loose, sandy mounds on the ground, do not stand in them. These little devils get incensed at the foot in their house and swarm up your shoe and beyond to leave raised white or red welts that really hurt and itch for days. There is no known treatment for their bites, except several people have told me that if you douse the area within 90 seconds with Clorox bleach, it neutralizes the poison. Who are these people who whip a jug of bleach out of their handbags at a moment's notice?

The Gulf Coast's water is perfectly safe to drink, although it tastes a little funky in areas. A much bigger minefield is the food, mostly because it's so seafood-centric. I admit it, I am a chicken eater. I don't mean I'm a person with a marked propensity for poultry, but a person for whom eating is a test of endurance, strength, *cojones*—a game of chicken. A chicken eater is a person who wrestles with the hottest chile, braves all organ meats, unflinchingly consumes goose webs and sea urchins, who lip-smackingly sucks the green stuff from steamed crabs. This is the Sir Edmund Hillary of food. When asked, "Why did you eat that?" The answer is always a gravelly, "Because it was there." Thus, give me oysters, clams, whatever, raw on the half shell with a splash of Tabasco. For some, though, this is truly dangerous. Pregnant women, young children and the elderly, or anyone with an immune problem: Order all your seafood baked, broiled, steamed, fried. The bacteria *vibrio vulnificus* can, at the very least, ruin your vacation. For a list of safe (vis-à-vis mercury and so forth), sustainable, politically correct flat fish, California's Monterey Bay Aquarium's website (www.mbayaq.org) has a useful seafood watch section.

Many hysterical travel articles suggest getting **medical travel insurance.** If you have insurance, though, that's probably all the coverage you'll need. The best emergency rooms are listed in each chapter, and there's always dialing 911 or the Centers for Disease Control and Prevention (800/311-3435, www.cdc.gov) for information on health hazards by region.

COMMUNICATIONS AND MEDIA
Mail

Mail service within the U.S. generally takes 2–3 days, except during the Christmas holiday season when all bets are off. Within Florida post takes about two days to get anywhere (you speed things up if you use the full nine-digit zip code). There's some reason to think that by the time this book is published a first-class stamp will cost 41 cents (right now, it's 37 cents).

Telephone

If you are calling long distance, dial 1 + the three-digit area code + the seven-digit phone number. If calling from abroad, the international code for the U.S. is 1. Within the U.S., the 800, 888, 877, and 866 area codes are toll-free, meaning they cost you nothing to dial.

Fax

Most hotels and motels will send/receive a fax for a fee, and multipage documents can be sent at any Kinko's shop.

Internet Access

This is changing so fast on the Gulf Coast that it's probably fruitless to weigh in. Even budget hotels offer in-room dataports now, and many low-tech coffee shops and cafés sport the "Wi-Fi Hotspots" sticker in the window for wireless Internet connections. Even if you're not packing a laptop on your trip, you can check web-based email from almost any hotel or motel, often for no fee.

Newspapers and Magazines

Regional and city newspapers are listed at the end of each chapter. There are only a handful of daily papers of note. The best metro paper in the area is the *St. Petersburg Times,* a serious journalistic enterprise that is thought to be a feeder paper to the *New York Times* and a thoughtful, slightly left-of-center daily. The *Tampa Tribune* is hokier, with a more shucks-folks regional approach (and a more conservative political bent). Of the daily papers that don't have greater aspirations (reporters aren't fantasizing about Pulitzers as they chug their eighth Mountain Dew of the day), the *Naples Daily News* and the *Tallahassee Democrat* are probably the most lively, in terms of writing and coverage.

Sarasota wins a media prize for its sheer number of glossy monthly magazines (Naples comes in second), but Tampa has a super alternative newsprint tabloid weekly called the *Weekly Planet.*

Television

Nearly every hotel, motel, and inn on the Gulf Coast has cable TV now, providing scores of channels to click your way through. Local television stations are listed at the end of each chapter (along with their network affiliates).

MAPS AND TOURIST INFORMATION

Maps

Visit Florida (www.flausa.com) sends a great map of the whole state with its "Visit Florida" literature. (And, as always, AAA members should raid the free-map smorgasbord that is their divine right.) The state's tourism office also has several welcome stations near Florida's border (one north of Pensacola on I-10, one off U.S. 231, one in Tallahassee, one in Jennings off I-75, and one on the state's east coast on I-95) that give out good state and regional maps. Some cities (Apalachicola, Naples) can be navigated with only the Xeroxed map the desk clerk at the hotel hands out; just follow the yellow highlighter marks. Other cities (Tampa), you need a real map. And if you're traveling alone, don't be chintzy—buy the laminated flip map to the area; its ease of use in the car may keep your wheels on the road.

Tourist Offices

Tourist office addresses are listed at the end of each chapter. Most convention and visitors bureaus have extremely helpful websites at this point (see *Internet Resources*), and many will send you a vacation package of information, maps, and coupons free of charge.

Digital Cameras/Photo Development

With regular 35mm film, developing film along the way is a snap at one-hour photo places and most big drugstores. If you've gone digital, don't worry about photo development until you get home (uploading onto a website like Kodak Gallery is a cheap way to get prints made and to digitally share your trip with everyone). That said, you need to bring an adequate amount of

memory for the length of your trip. Digital memory cards are not affected by airport security X-rays, so bring extras. And don't forget extra batteries and your battery charger.

Suggested Reading

PARADISE COAST

Travel Guide

Molloy, Johnny. *A Paddler's Guide to Everglades National Park*. Gainesville: University Press of Florida, 2000. Paddling the Everglades is daunting, plain and simple. There are things in there that can kill you, others that can merely maim. This book describes in calm, clear prose, 53 designated paddling routes, camping spots, places to avoid, and wind and tide problems. Molloy is a fairly serious outdoorsman who has written a handful of well-regarded paddling and camping books for Florida and Colorado.

Memoir

Brown, Loren G. "Totch." *Totch: A Life in the Everglades*. Gainesville: University Press of Florida, 1993. It's my very favorite book about this area, told in glorious vernacular by the original Everglades renegade. An inveterate and unreconstructed tall-tale teller, Totch harkens back to his days in the Ten Thousand Islands, moonshining, selling gator hides, fishing, smuggling dope, and any other thing he thought might be fun, or lucrative, or both. It's memoirs like this that clinch Southwest Florida as this country's final frontier.

Nonfiction

Douglas, Marjory Stoneman. *The Everglades: River of Grass*. Sarasota, FL: Pineapple Press, 50th anniversary edition, 1997. Originally published in 1947, this was a book that actually changed the world. At the time the Everglades were a worthless swamp that developers were scheming about draining, damming, etc. The publication of this straightforward natural

history, heavy on the flora, fauna, and indigenous people, galvanized President Harry Truman to sign the controversial order protecting more than 2 million acres as Everglades National Park. Douglas has been called the "Queen of the Everglades," and her descriptions of the Native Americans, pirates, runaways, and ne'er-do-wells who populated the 'Glades is as compelling as it ever was.

Orlean, Susan. *The Orchid Thief: A True Story of Beauty and Obsession*. New York: Ballantine Books, 2000. This was the book that the film *Adaptation* was loosely based on, or, um, maybe just inspired by. *New Yorker* staffer Susan Orlean wrote an incredible piece on John Laroche, an orchid chaser who was arrested with three Seminole Indians in 1994 carrying contraband rare orchids and epiphytes from the Everglades. Orlean expanded upon the story, writing this book that reveals a whole world of weird and wonderful obsession. The "Wild West" feel of the Everglades and swampy environs is palpable, and the story is at times hilarious and touching. You also learn a lot about orchids.

Fiction

Matthiessen, Peter. *Killing Mister Watson*. New York: Vintage, reprint edition, 1991. It's a trilogy, along with *Lostman's River* and *Bone by Bone,* that paints a vivid picture of the early settlers living at the edge of civilization in the Ten Thousand Islands and the Everglades. Drawn from bits of historical fact, Matthiessen creates a fictionalized oral history set in Chokoloskee and other little mangrove islands. Edgar J. Watson, who is said to have gunned down the outlaw Belle Starr, came here to elude the law but instead faced the rough frontier justice of his fellow fugitives. It's an absolute must-read if you plan to spend any time in Everglades City.

LEE COUNTY
Nonfiction

Smoot, Tom. *The Edisons of Fort Myers*. Sarasota, FL: Pineapple Press, 2004. Lots of biographies cover Edison's public life as a world-famous inventor, but this one explores the big loves of his life: Mina Miller and Fort Myers, Florida. It's an especially fun read preceded or followed by a visit to the Edison estate.

Turner, Gregg. *Railroads of Southwest Florida*. Charleston, SC: Arcadia Publishing, 1999. Turner's written a ton about Florida railroads, so he's something of an expert on the rails. This book covers Henry Plant, the Florida Southern Railway, and all the other railway endeavors that prompted accelerated growth in this part of Florida. The writing isn't super exciting, but there's a lot of good information here.

Fiction

Hiaasen, Carl. Where do you even put Carl Hiaasen in a book about the Gulf Coast? He's everywhere in South Florida, bigger than a novelist, bigger than a *Miami Herald* columnist. He's like a rock star around here (good because he owns a Fender Strat that Dave Barry helped him pick out), with so many titles it's hard to really put forth a favorite with any kind of stalwart conviction. The most recent is *Skinny Dip*, New York: Knopf, 2004, before that *Basket Case, Sick Puppy, Lucky You, Stormy Weather, Strip Tease, Native Tongue, Skin Tight, Double Whammy, and Tourist Season*. What you, the reader, need to know, beyond the fact that he has a penchant for two-word titles, is that he loves the rich and iconoclastic zaniness that is South Florida, he has a real fondness for smart hookers with a heart of gold, finds tough-guy baldies especially amusing,

and is a bulldoggish environmentalist. In addition to his novels, Hiaasen has also published two collections of his newspaper columns, *Kick Ass* and *Paradise Screwed*, and an eviscerating anti-Disney book called *Team Rodent*. (Caveat emptor: Hiaasen keeps snakes as pets. They feature heavily in his books.)

Wayne White, Randy. *Sanibel Flats*. New York: St. Martin's Press, 1991. Randy Wayne White was a fishing guide at Tarpon Bay on Sanibel for 13 years. A prolific mystery novelist, he writes mostly about this part of southwest Florida, with numerous novels featuring super tough-guy Doc Ford solving various mysteries (*The Heat Islands, The Man Who Invented Florida, Captiva, North of Havana, The Mangrove Coast, Ten Thousand Islands, Shark River, Twelve Mile Limit, Everglades, Tampa Burn*, and *Dead of Night*). In all his books, Florida is one of the main characters, lovingly and lavishly described in all its loony glory. Wayne White is a columnist for *Outside Magazine* and *Men's Health* and he's written lots of other books of essays and such, including *Batfishing in the Rain Forest* and a just-published fish cookbook.

SARASOTA COUNTY
Photography

Evans, Walker. *Walker Evans: Florida*. Los Angeles: J. Paul Getty Trust Publications, 2000. Everyone knows Walker Evans' gutsy, gripping Depression-era photographs. But for six weeks in 1942, Evans focused his lens on Sarasota for *Mangrove Coast*, a book by Karl Bickel. These are some of the wonderful photos he took during that time of the circus's underbelly, old people, railroad cars, and decrepit Florida buildings. Text is by novelist Robert Plunket.

Nonfiction

Apps, Jerry. *Ringlingville USA: The Stupendous Story of Seven Siblings and Their Stunning Circus Success*. Madison: University of Wisconsin

Press, 2004. Apps writes pretty much exclusively about Wisconsin. But this story started there, in Baraboo, Wisconsin to be exact. A wonderful new history of the Ringling Circus and the seven brothers who made the "Greatest Show on Earth" from scratch. It's got great photos of early circus life.

TAMPA
Travel Guide
Murphy, Bill. *Fox 13 Tampa Bay One Tank Trips With Bill Murphy*. St. Petersburg: Seaside Publishing, 1999. An offshoot of a television segment Murphy does, the books showcase 52 Florida-based adventures that are all within a full tank of Tampa. It's lots of off-the-beaten path attractions, all worthy of your time, from Pioneer Florida Museum in Dade City to the excellent camping at Fort De Soto Park in Pinellas County. (The second book is called *More One Tank Trips*.)

Drama
Cruz, Nilo. *Anna in the Tropics*. Theatre Communications Group, 2003. This play won Cruz the Pulitzer Prize for drama in 2003. It is a romantic drama, loosely a retelling of Tolstoy's *Anna Karenina*, that depicts a Cuban-American family of cigar makers in Ybor City (Tampa) in 1930. It tells the story of the factory's new "lector," a person hired to read aloud great works of literature and the day's news to the cigar workers. A beautiful stage play—keep your eyes open for any performances of it during your visit to Florida.

CLEARWATER AND ST. PETERSBURG
Nonfiction
Klinkenberg, Jeff. *Seasons of Real Florida*. Gainesville: University Press of Florida, 2004. *St. Petersburg Times* writer Klinkenberg may have invented the term "Real Florida," which means the Old Florida, without Disney, fancy golf courses, or really anything glamorous.

This book is an assemblage of largely humorous essays he's written for the paper that tell great stories about the people, flora, and fauna in west central Florida. The one about the cigar-factory lector in Tampa is a three-hanky essay. Klinkenberg wrote another compelling book of essays entitled *Dispatches from the Land of Flowers: A Snake Man, a Sad Poet, a Lightning Stalker and Other Stories About Real Florida*. Gainesville: Down Home Press, 1996.

Fiction
MacDonald, John. *Condominium*. New York: Fawcett, reissue edition, 1985. For most of his life MacDonald was considered a pulp fiction writer, and prolific, who spent more than half his life in west central Florida, first in Clearwater, then in Sarasota and Siesta Key. This book still seems fresh, especially in light of 2004's hurricane season. The setting is Golden Sands, a Sunbelt condo in the path of Hurricane Ella. It's a multi-character disaster book, think *The Towering Inferno* or something like that. (*Cape Fear*, by the way, was based on a MacDonald book.)

NATURE COAST
Nonfiction
Warner, David T. *Vanishing Florida: A Personal Guide to Sights Rarely Seen*. Montgomery, AL: River City Publishing, 2001. I love this book, written by a guy who sounds like a dead ringer for Ernest Hemingway (Papa features occasionally in the book, so maybe Warner fancies a resemblance himself). Some of this book appeared as features in *Sarasota* magazine—mostly it's chapter-long ruminations and odes to small towns along the Gulf Coast (especially good chapters on Cedar Key and other parts of the Nature Coast), with lots of drinking and womanizing thrown into the mix.

Fiction
Cook, Ann. *Trace Their Shadows*. San Jose, New York, Lincoln, and Shanghai: Mystery and Suspense Press, 2001, and *Shadow Over Cedar*

Key. San Jose, New York, Lincoln, and Shanghai: Mystery and Suspense Press, 2003. To be honest, Ann Cook isn't exactly God's gift to mystery writing. As a baby the author was the model for the original Gerber baby (daughter of cartoonist Leslie Turner who drew the famous baby head in 1928), but as a now-retired adult she has turned to mystery writing. The cool thing about these books is the setting—they are easy, beachy reads with plucky reporter Brandy O'Bannon having exciting adventures all over charming Cedar Key.

TALLAHASSEE
Travel Guides

Robinson, Erik. *Tallahassee.* Charleston, SC: Arcadia Publishing, 2003. It's a slightly staid photo-and-benign-text history of the capital city, written by the man who has been the curator at the Museum of Florida History for twenty years. Good foundation information for the historical traveler.

FORGOTTEN COAST
Nonfiction

Cerulean, Susan, ed. *Between Two Rivers.* Tallahassee: Red Hills Writers Project, 2004. If you can find it—give it a serious college try—you'll be mesmerized with this new anthology of 29 writers telling stories about the rich cultural and environmental landscapes of the Red Hills and northern Gulf Coast. (The two rivers in question are the Aucilla to the east and the Apalachicola to the west.) The Red Hills Writers Project is a group of mostly Florida writers with a serious nature and ecological bent to their writing. Editors include Susan Cerulean (biologist, activist, and writer of *Book of the Everglades* and *Wild Heart of Florida*), Southern author Janisse Ray (*Ecology of a Cracker Childhood, Wild Card Quilt*), and Tallahassee poet Laura Newton (editor of the *Apalachee Review*).

Rudloe, Jack. *The Living Dock of Panacea.* New York: Alfred A. Knopf, 1977. Rudloe is one of the contributors to *Between Two Rivers*, listed above. He's a longtime Florida naturalist, director of Gulf Specimen Marine Laboratory, and author of nine or so books on the area. He's big into turtles, (*Time of the Turtle, Search For The Great Turtle Mother*), but this older book (recently reprinted with a new introduction and called just *The Living Dock*) is a lovely rumination on the Gulf Coast's marine life, told from the author's floating dock in the tiny fishing community of Panacea.

EMERALD COAST
Travel Guides

Hollis, Tim. *Florida's Miracle Strip: From Redneck Riviera to Emerald Coast.* Jackson, MS: University Press of Mississippi, 2004. This is a nostalgic look at the area that is now fairly glamorous Panama City Beach, Fort Walton Beach, Destin, and Pensacola Beach, with lots of fun descriptions of the campy "Old Florida" attractions that used to bring people here—like Castle Dracula and the Snake-A-Torium. It's got lots of cool vintage photos and postcards.

Fishing

Dew, Gregory. *The Barefoot Fisherman's Guide to the Emerald Coast: From Gulf Shore, Alabama, to Apalachicola, Florida.* Birmingham, AL: Crane Hill Publishers, 1999. It's a little techie, with lots of talk about tackle and rigs, so the beginning fisherman might just be interested Chapter 3, which enumerates 40 or so fabulous fishing spots on this gorgeous stretch of coast. Dew also gives great information on all of the species you're likely to catch here, and then what to do with them if you aim to eat 'em. In my opinion, the recipes are a little pedestrian.

PENSACOLA
Nonfiction

Pensacola Historical Society. *Pensacola in Vintage Postcards.* Charleston, SC: Arcadia Publishing, 2004. It's just a packet of postcards, but a riffle through and you'll get a sense for the way Pensacola used to be.

KIDS' LIT ABOUT THE GULF COAST

Travel Guides

DeWire, Elinor. *Florida Lighthouses for Kids*. Sarasota, FL: Pineapple Press. Great pictures and fun stories about Florida's 33 lighthouses (many on the Gulf Coast)—it gives kids something to read in the car and a way to participate in the process of planning a trip.

Fiction

DiCamillo, Kate. *Because of Winn Dixie*. Cambridge, MA: Candlewick Press, 2001. Now a major motion picture, this book about 10-year-old India Opal Buloni and her ugly dog Winn-Dixie (named for where she found him) has captured the attention of lots of families. It's a great story, set in a fictional town of Naomi, Florida (I like to think it's modeled on someplace down toward Port Charlotte). Opal's had kind of a hard life, so it might be too much for a really sensitive kid.

George, Jean Craighead. *Everglades*. New York: HarperTrophy, reprint edition, 1997. Geared toward littler kids (maybe 5–8), it tells the story of a man poling through the Everglades and teaching his five young passengers about the 'Glades' sawgrass, hundreds of species of animals, and delicate ecosystem. It's not as preachy as it sounds—the environmental message is gentle and Wendell Minor's illustrations are wonderful. Newbery medalist Jean Craighead George has written lots of wonderful kids' books with the Florida wilderness at their centers—older kids might like the eco-mystery *The Missing 'Gator of Gumbo Limbo*, New York: HarperTrophy, 1993.

Hiaasen, Carl. *Hoot*. New York: Knopf Books for Young Readers, 2002. Geared for readers 9-12, this Newberry-honor book by Florida great Carl Hiaasen does double duty. As with many of Hiaasen's novels there's a heavy environmental message (this one about protecting rare burrowing owls and their habitat), but it also tells an exciting and slightly iconoclastic tale of new kid Roy Eberhardt who moves to Coconut Grove and gets mixed up in crazy ecological adventure with Mullet Fingers and bully-beater Beatrice in a fight against Mother Paula's All-American Pancake House. A middle-school mystery, the language and plot are edgy.

Hogan, Linda. *Power*. New York: W.W. Norton & Company, 1999. In an area that was once populated exclusively by Native tribes, it's exciting to read about what life must have been like before all the white-man's development. This is a coming-of-age story about a 16-year-old Native American girl named Omishito, who witnesses the killing of a sacred animal, the Florida panther. It is based on a true story.

Konigsburg, E. L. *T-backs, T-shirts, Coat and Suit*. New York: Aladdin, 2003. A new-ish book from the author of the classic Newberry winner *From the Mixed-Up Files of Mrs. Basil E. Frankweiler*, this one tells the story of 12-year-old Chloe who spends the summer in Florida with her wild aunt Bernadette, who drives a commissary van and sells junk food at roadsides. For ages 9-12.

Rawlings, Marjorie Kinnan. *The Yearling*. New York: Simon Pulse, 50th edition, 1988. Rawlings wrote ten books while a resident in Cross Creek, Florida, the most popular of which was *The Yearling*, which won a Pulitzer Prize in fiction in 1939. It tells the story of scrappy young Jody Baxter and his pet fawn Flag, who together roam the Florida scrublands wrestling big swamp gators and cavorting with bear cubs. Rawlings second-best book is called simply, *Cross Creek* also with the same earthy Florida Cracker dialect.

Smith, Patrick D. *A Land Remembered*. Sarasota, FL: Pineapple Press, 1998. Beginning with Tobias MacIvey's arrival in Florida in 1858, this young-adult historical novel tells the story of three generations of Floridians carving out a hardscrabble life for themselves in the wilds of Central Florida. This sweeping story is rich in Florida history.

Internet Resources

GENERAL GULF COAST

Visit Florida
www.flausa.com
For a good introduction to the Gulf Coast, contact the state's official tourist information organization, Visit Florida (or call 888/7-FLA USA) for a copy of their excellent annual *Visit Florida* guide, the *Florida Events Calendar*, or *Florida Trails*. Visit Florida also has a 24-hour multi-lingual tourist assistance hotline at 800/656-8777.

Florida Secrets, The Insider's Guide to Unique Destinations
www.florida-secrets.com
The graphics have a cheese factor and it's heavy on the advertising, but the site is a treasure trove of little-known destinations in Florida, divided up on the Gulf Coast by southwest, west-central, eastern and western Panhandle.

FISHING

Fish We Catch in Florida
www.redfishhunter.com/fish
If you're looking for a no-nonsense description of what you're likely to catch, what they look like, how to nab them, and then whether they're worth eating, this is the site for you.

CAMPING

Florida Association of RV Parks & Campgrounds
www.floridacamping.com
It's an easy-to-use comprehensive database of Florida campgrounds, including amenities

information for each site. You can also go on their website and order a print version of the guide.

PARKS AND FORESTS

Florida State Parks Department
www.floridastateparks.org
Find a park, its affiliated camping and lodging, or get a bead on what events are coming up along the Gulf Coast. The site also has maps and directions to Florida's state parks, and it runs an amateur photo contest of state park photography.

Florida Trail Association
www.florida-trail.org
The Florida Trail Association is a nonprofit that builds, maintains, promotes, and protects hiking trails across the state of Florida, especially the 1,400-mile Florida Trail. From this site you can download all kinds of trail maps and park brochures.

SPORTS

Florida Sports Foundation
www.flasports.com
The foundation usually posts the "Grapefruit League" Florida spring-training baseball schedules on its website late in January. Another way to find out about spring training for your favorite team is by visiting the website of Major League Baseball (wwwmlb.com).

PARADISE COAST

Naples, Marco Island and Everglades Convention & Visitors Bureau

www.paradisecoast.com

A new website for the area, it features convenient charts for local accommodations, a round-up of attractions and recreation in the area, as well as well-written background on the area. The only thing that's missing here is detailed restaurant info.

Guide to Southwest Florida
www.florida-southwest.com

Naples and Marco Island enticements are laid out in categories, and the restaurant write-ups here are fairly reliable.

LEE COUNTY

Lee County Visitor and Convention Bureau
www.fortmyers-sanibel.com or **www.leeislandcoast.com**

One of the most professional-looking sites around from a convention bureau, its information is helpful, current, and entertainingly written. There are short essays on local attractions and a nice section called "itineraries" that may help organize your travel strategy.

Charlotte Harbor and the Gulf Islands
www.pureflorida.com

This area gets short shrift due to its proximity to more well-known vacation destinations. Still, as the website shows, Charlotte Harbor has loads to do and abundant natural beauty. It has an easily downloadable list of local accommodations.

SARASOTA COUNTY

Sarasota Convention & Visitors Bureau
www.sarasotafl.org

The convention and visitors bureau's newly designed site is about as user-friendly as they come, with easily sortable menus of restaurants, accommodations, outdoor attractions, and more. The excellent feature stories on the area's allures are written by local travel writers. The site is offered in English, Spanish, and German.

Anna Maria Island Chamber of Commerce
www.annamariaisland.info

Too far from Tampa in the north and too far from Sarasota to its south, Anna Maria Island doesn't really get covered in other, bigger regional websites. This one doesn't have as many bells and whistles as other sites, but it's got all the basics of where to stay, what to do, and where to eat.

TAMPA

Tampa Bay Citysearch
www.tampabay.citysearch.com

Probably the best local site for events and informative restaurant reviews (Okay, I wrote a lot of them), the site is owned by Ticketmaster and thus pushes its ticket sales fairly heavily. Still, it keeps you current on what's happening in Tampa.

Tampa Bay Convention and Visitors Bureau
www.visittampabay.com

This is a good site for background on the Bay Area as well as travel strategies and accommodations.

Weekly Planet
www.weeklyplanet.com

The local alternative weekly newspaper has a site that beats the *Tampa Tribune's*, hands down. The writing is provocative and witty, and the paper's arts critics have impeccable taste.

PINELLAS COUNTY

St. Petersburg/Clearwater Area Convention & Visitors Bureau
www.floridasbeach.com

Very similar to the Tampa convention & visitors bureau site, this one focuses, not surprisingly, on the beaches. It's easy to book a room from this site, and it features excellent downloadable maps.

St. Petersburg Times
www.sptimes.com

The Gulf Coast's best daily metro paper has an equally superlative website, the place to go if you want to be versed in local politics or find out the day's most exciting events. The paper's restaurant and movie critics are notably good.

NATURE COAST

Citrus County Tourist Development Council
www.visitcitrus.com

I've had lots of trouble loading this site, but when it works it's a wealth of information on Homosassa, Crystal River, and environs. It's a good site from which to choose a manatee snorkeling trip or fishing charter.

Cedar Key Chamber of Commerce
www.cedarkey.org

The chamber's site isn't going to win any award for high-tech graphics and bells and whistles, but it's a simple resource for information specifically about Cedar Key, especially good for local events.

Steinhatchee Landing Resort
www.steinhatcheelanding.com

Steinhatchee is one of the Gulf Coast's least-known destinations, and the web doesn't help much to illuminate. This is the best site about the area, a lovely, sophisticated site brought to you from the lovely, and most sophisticated, resort on the Nature Coast. The recreation section is most helpful in planning a trip.

TALLAHASSEE

Tallahassee Area Convention & Visitors Bureau
www.seetallahassee.com

It doesn't look super slick, but this site has all the info you might need to plan a great trip to the capital city, with easy downloadable pdfs of brochures and maps, and carefully written descriptions of restaurants, attractions, and accommodations. It has special sections devoted to people coming for the legislative session as well as those moving to Tallahassee.

Tallahassee Democrat
www.tallahassee.com

The local newspaper's website is the place to go for special-event information, including Florida State University sporting events.

APALACHICOLA

Forgotten Coast Line Online
www.apalachicolabay.com

My favorite resource for Forgotten Coast-obilia, it's the website for a paper of the same name edited by local curmudgeon Chuck Spicer. It's quirky and opinionated, like a good little local paper should be.

Apalachicola Bay Chamber of Commerce
www.apalachicolabay.org

It's a little blander and more no-nonsense than the Forgotten Coast Line site, but it has good background information on the area and a list of chamber members that actually provides guidance when you're choosing a fishing charter or beach house rental.

EMERALD COAST

Beaches of South Walton
www.beachesofsouthwalton.com

About as suave as a site like this can be, this resource eloquently describes the 13 little communities that make up the area, providing useful insight into where to eat, what to do, and where to stay. (Seaside has its own website, www.seasidefl.com, that is even more impressively swanky and stylish.)

Emerald Coast Convention & Visitors Bureau
www.destin-fwb.com

A fairly serviceable site that explores the areas of Destin, Fort Walton Beach, and Okaloosa Island. The best feature is the lodging locator in which you can sort by a long list of amenities.

Panama City Beach Convention & Visitors Bureau
www.thebeachloversbeach.com

For information specifically on Panama City Beach, this is the best resource. They offer lots of Spring Break-specific material during the months of March and April. From the site you can also order a 96-page vacation guide that provides helpful and accurate information about activities, entertainment, accommodations, and dining.

PENSACOLA

Pensacola Bay Area Convention & Visitors Bureau
www.visitpensacola.com

All there is to do in Pensacola, Pensacola Beach, and Perdido Key is outlined in an organized fashion, with a special emphasis on the historical and military attractions. The site was slightly tight-lipped about hurricane recovery, so be sure to call ahead if you choose accommodations or restaurants based on this site's information.

Index

Birding

general discussion: 336
Boyd Hill Nature Preserve: 184
Brooker Creek Preserve: 184
Caladesi Island State Park: 180
Corkscrew Swamp Sanctuary: 33, 36
East Beach: 184
Eglin Air Force Base: 295
Everglades National Park: 56–57
field guides: 340
Great Florida Birding Trail: 20–21, 184, 295, 336
itinerary tips: 20–21
J.N. "Ding" Darling National Wildlife Refuge: 8, 21, 66, 67, 85–86
Nature Coast: 208–209
Pelican Man's Bird Sanctuary: 119
Pinellas County: 184
Rookery Bay National Estuarine Research Reserve: 36
St. George Island: 268–269
St. Marks National Wildlife Refuge: 232
Sanibel Island: 81, 85
Sawgrass Lake Park: 184
Shell Key: 184
Suncoast Seabird Sanctuary: 184

Boating

general discussion: 356
Cedar Key: 217
Everglades National Park: 57–59
Naples: 37–38
Nature Coast: 208
pirate cruises: 191
Sarasota: 112

Big Cat Rescue: 150
Big Cypress Gallery: 59–60
Big Kahuna's Water and Adventure Park: 277, 287–288
Big Mound Key: 22
biking: Apalachicola 257; Cedar Key 217, 220; Pinellas County 181–182; St. George Island 249, 268; Sanibel Island 84–85; Sarasota 112; Scenic Route 30A 277, 296
bioluminescence phenomena: 233
Blackwater River State Forest: 329
Blue Angels: 317
Blue Grotto: 224
Blue Mountain Beach: 291, 294
Boca Grande: 97
boiled p-nuts: 243
Bokeelia: 99–100
bookstores: 136, 198, 221, 340
botanical gardens: Emerald Coast 296; Naples 37, 39–40; Pinellas County 182, 188; Sarasota 114–115, 116; Tallahassee 234, 239–240

bottomland hardwoods: 328
bowling: 151
Bowman's Beach: 82
Brackin Wayside Park and Boardwalk: 281–282
Briggs Nature Center: 36
Brohard Park: 110
bromeliads: 335
Buccaneer Bay: 207
budget tips: 5–6
Burroughs Home: 75
Busch Gardens: 142, 156–158
bus travel: general discussion 357; Emerald Coast 305; Lee County 103; Pensacola 323; Pinellas County 201; Sarasota County 140; Tallahassee 247; Tampa 172
butterflies: 116, 233, 340

C
Cabbage Key: 98–99
Cabeza de Vaca, Alvar Nuñez: 342
Cà d'Zan: 9, 115, 122
Caladesi Island State Park: 174, 176, 179–180
Calusa: 26, 50, 84, 100, 205, 343–344
Calusa Nature Center & Planetarium: 77
Calusa Shell Mounds: 27, 50
Camp Gordon Johnston WWII Museum: 273
camping/campgrounds: Everglades National Park 57; Internet resources 369; Nature Coast 208; Pinellas County 179; Sarasota 112
Camp Walton Schoolhouse Museum: 286
Canary Island date palm: 334
Cancer, Father Luis: 342
canoeing: Big Bend Saltwater Paddling Trail 232–233; Cedar Key 217; Everglades National Park 57–58; Naples 37; Nature Coast 207, 208; Pinellas County 179, 180; Sarasota 112; Tampa 148
canopy roads: 229, 236
Cape San Blas: 254

Fishing

Golfing

Parks, Reserves, and Preserves

Acknowledgments

This book is dedicated to Steve Blumenthal and Ann Memory,
for sharing with me their enthusiasms.

I'd like to thank the following people for their time, hospitality, and information during the researching of this book: Leon Corbett, Senior PR Representative, and Rachel Bray-Stiles, Public Relations Manager, both at VISIT FLORIDA; Paul Kayemba at VISIT FLORIDA for his assistance with photographs; JoNell Modys at the Greater Naples, Marco Island & Everglades City CVB; Michael Mancke, Director of Sales & Marketing at Radisson Suite Beach Resort on Marco Island; NACT-Everglades Rentals & Eco Adventures; Jane Watkins PR, Lemon Tree Inn of Naples; Lee Rose, Communications Coordinator, and Nancy Hamilton, Communications Director, both at Lee Island Coast Visitor & Convention Bureau; Jay Halcrow at West Wind Inn; Leslie Allen at Siesta Holidays; Dian Eddy at Island Inn Sanibel; the people at Palm Island Resort; Rebecca Allen of Charlotte County Visitor's Bureau; Virginia Haley, Executive Director, and several other people at the Sarasota Convention & Visitors Bureau; Peggy and Ashok Sawe of Palm Tree Villas; Mary Kay Ryan at The Resort at Longboat Key Club; Wit Tuttell and Zaneta Hubbard at the St. Petersburg/Clearwater Area Convention & Visitors Bureau; Offshore Sailing School; Kelly Prieto at Hayworth Creative; Kelly Earnest, Public Relations Representative of the Tampa Bay Convention & Visitors Bureau; Mary B. Craven, Tourism Development Manager at Citrus County Tourism Development Office; Marianne Graves; Stacey Brown, Marketing Director of Pure Water Wilderness; Dean Fowler at Steinhatchee Landing Resort; Nancy Petrucka and Dana Ingalls at Prudential Resort Realty; Anita Grove at the Apalachicola Bay Chamber of Commerce; Wade Berry, Publications Editor, and Loretta Shaffer, Director of Sales & Marketing, both of Beaches of South Walton; Jayna M. Leach, Director of Sales & Marketing at the Panama City Beach Convention & Visitors Bureau; and Stacy Garrett, Marketing/Communications Manager at the Pensacola Convention & Visitors Information Center.

At Avalon, I'd like to thank Rebecca Browning for believing in me, and my editor, Kevin McLain, for making her seem wise for having done so. I wish every writer had the opportunity to work with such smart and decent people. But then there'd be a lot more writers.

And although they say you can't choose your family, I have managed to surround myself with family and friends of catholic tastes and far-ranging knowledge. Thanks to Jon Rottenberg and Amy Hornstein for their unswerving devotion to arcana of all kinds; to Jim Harrington for assistance in the spheres of pop culture, rock 'n' roll, and *Girls Gone Wild;* to Nancy Reiley, Annette Kaufman-Horner, and Rana and Bob Rottenberg for being dedicated listeners and occasional editors; to Tim and Evan Reiley for a few of their best lines (you'll have to read carefully); and to Sophie Rottenberg for being my most favorite partner in crime.

U.S.~Metric Conversion

1 inch	=	2.54 centimeters (cm)
1 foot	=	.304 meters (m)
1 yard	=	0.914 meters
1 mile	=	1.6093 kilometers (km)
1 km	=	.6214 miles
1 fathom	=	1.8288 m
1 chain	=	20.1168 m
1 furlong	=	201.168 m
1 acre	=	.4047 hectares
1 sq km	=	100 hectares
1 sq mile	=	2.59 square km
1 ounce	=	28.35 grams
1 pound	=	.4536 kilograms
1 short ton	=	.90718 metric ton
1 short ton	=	2000 pounds
1 long ton	=	1.016 metric tons
1 long ton	=	2240 pounds
1 metric ton	=	1000 kilograms
1 quart	=	.94635 liters
1 US gallon	=	3.7854 liters
1 Imperial gallon	=	4.5459 liters
1 nautical mile	=	1.852 km

To compute Celsius temperatures, subtract 32 from Fahrenheit and divide by 1.8. To go the other way, multiply Celsius by 1.8 and add 32.

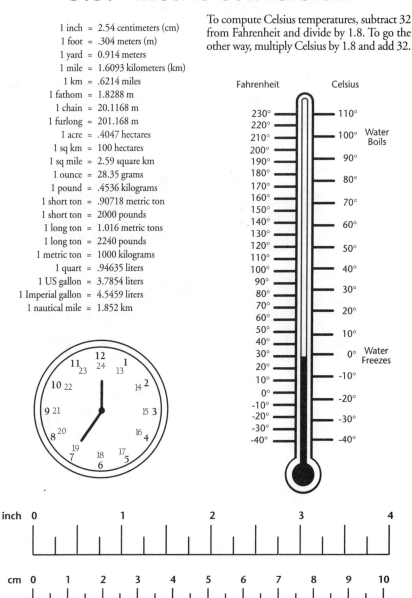

Keeping Current

Although we strive to produce the most up-to-date guidebook humanly possible, change is unavoidable. Between the time this book goes to print and the moment you read it, a handful of the businesses noted in these pages will undoubtedly change prices, move, or even close their doors forever. Other worthy attractions will open for the first time. If you have a favorite gem you'd like to see included in the next edition, or see anything that needs updating, clarification, or correction, please drop us a line. Send your comments via email to atpfeedback@avalonpub.com, or use the address below.

Moon Handbooks Florida Gulf Coast
Avalon Travel Publishing
1400 65th Street, Suite 250
Emeryville, CA 94608, USA
www.moon.com

Avalon Travel Publishing
is an Imprint of
Avalon Publishing Group, Inc.

Editors: Kevin McLain, Elizabeth McCue
Series Manager: Kevin McLain
Acquisitions Manager: Rebecca K. Browning
Copy Editor: Deana Shields
Graphics Coordinator: Stefano Boni
Production Coordinator: Domini Dragoone
Cover Designer: Kari Gim
Interior Designer: Amber Pirker
Map Editor: Kevin Anglin
Cartographer: Kat Kalamaras
Cartographic Manager: Mike Morgenfeld
Indexer: Judy Hunt

ISBN-10: 1-56691-571-6
ISBN-13: 978-1-56691-571-7
ISSN: 1556-0309

Printing History
1st Edition—November 2005
5 4 3 2 1

Text © 2005 by Laura Reiley.
Maps © 2005 by Avalon Travel Publishing, Inc.
All rights reserved.

Some photos and illustrations are used by permission and are the property of the original copyright owners.

Front cover photo: © Photosights

Printed in the USA by Malloy